PHILOSOPHY OF RELIGION
An Annotated Bibliography of Twentieth-Century Writings in English

William J. Wainwright

GARLAND PUBLISHING, INC. • NEW YORK & LONDON
1978

Library of Congress Cataloging in Publication Data

Wainwright, William J
  Philosophy of religion.
  (Garland reference library of the humanities; v. 111)
  Includes index.
  1. Religion—Philosophy—Bibliography. I. Title.
Z7821.W34 [BL51]   016.2'001   77-83374
ISBN 0-8240-9849-8

CONTENTS

Introduction   vii

Abbreviations   xi

I THE DIVINE ATTRIBUTES   I

General Discussions of God's
Attributes   I
God's Metaphysical Attributes   27
God's Necessity   52
Omnipotence   61
Omniscience and Foreknowledge   85
God's Relation to the World   117
God's Moral Attributes   130
The Divine Perfection   140

II ARGUMENTS FOR THE EXISTENCE
OF GOD   148

The Ontological Argument   148
The Cosmological Argument   196
The Argument from Design   224
Other Arguments for the Existence of
    God (The Moral Argument, The
    Argument from the World's Intel-
    ligibility, etc.)   244
The Nature of "God-Proofs"   262

v

III   THE PROBLEM OF EVIL   272

IV   MYSTICISM AND RELIGIOUS
     EXPERIENCE   367

 V   MIRACLES   438

VI   FAITH AND REVELATION   466

VII   RELIGIOUS LANGUAGE   528

     The Verification Controversy   528
     Explications of Religious Language
         in Recent Analytic Philosophy   560
     The Analogy Theory   617
     The Symbol Theory   641

VIII   THE JUSTIFICATION OF RELIGIOUS
       BELIEF   675

     Miscellaneous Studies   675
     Fideism   732
     Pascal's Wager and the Will to Believe   753

Index of Authors, Editors, and Reviewers   767

INTRODUCTION

This bibliography is addressed to professional philosophers and graduate students who work in the analytic tradition and who are primarily interested in the solution of philosophical problems rather than in the investigation of the systems of individual philosophers or the history of philosophical movements. Most philosophers in English-speaking countries and in Scandinavia fall into this category.

One tests and refines philosophical hypotheses by exposing them to the criticisms of others and by seeing how well they come off when compared with competing views. What the philosopher needs, therefore, is not a mere list of bibliographical items but a reference work which will lead him or her to the significant critical and creative work which has been done in his or her area. In practice, the views and criticisms to which a philosopher is exposed are determined by his or her teachers, colleagues and correspondents, and by the books and articles he or she happens to read. The nature of the critical material at his or her disposal is thus affected by accident, individual idiosyncrasy and philosophical fashion. Even first-rate philosophers are often surprisingly ignorant of the relevant philosophical literature. It is to be hoped that this bibliography will reduce the role which accident plays in the critical process.

Items have been included which either make a significant contribution to our understanding of the relevant problem or (irrespective of their merits) have proved to be influential. The majority of items have been drawn from the analytic tradition both because of the audience to which this bibliography is addressed and because of the dominance of the analytic tradition within English-speaking countries. The works of Process philosophers, Neo-Scholastics, Idealists, theologians, historians of religion, psychologists, and so on, have been cited, however, when in my judgment those works would (or should) interest analytic philosophers.

In each case, I have attempted to provide enough information for the reader to determine whether he or she will wish to examine that item. The length of the annotation is determined by the need to satisfy this requirement as well as by the item's importance. The annotations are critical as well as descriptive.

My critical observations have two purposes. The first is to indicate the strengths and weaknesses of individual items. Second, when read in its entirety, each section (e.g., the section on the Problem of Evil or the section on Fideism) is intended to provide an overview of the relevant problem, to indicate the nature of proposed solutions and the difficulties to which they are exposed, and to suggest promising lines for further inquiry. Each section, when taken as a whole, is thus in many respects similar to a bibliographical essay. These sections will, I hope, contribute to a solution of the problems to which they are devoted.

A selective and critical bibliography inevitably reflects the knowledge, interests and opinions of its author. I have undoubtedly included items which would not be included by others and omitted items which others would include. Nor am I so naive as to suppose that everyone will agree with my critical judgments. I do not believe, however, that this constitutes a serious problem. An examination of the items described in this bibliography will lead the reader to other works which I have decided not to include, and will allow the reader to form his or her own judgment as to the merits or demerits of the works which have been included. The use of this bibliography will, therefore, place the reader in a position to correct whatever deficiencies it may have.

One final observation. My bibliography is designed to provide easy access to the work which has been done on particular problems. Therefore, when a book contains interesting discussions of several topics, the sections which examine those topics have been described under the appropriate headings. Consequently, the reader should check all of the entries listed under an author's name if he or she wants a complete account of a particular book.

I would like to express my gratitude to the National Endowment for the Humanities, which supported this project during the summer of 1976, to the Graduate School of the University of Wisconsin-Milwaukee, which supported the project during the summer of 1977, and to the College of Letters and Science at the University of Wisconsin-Milwaukee, which provided me with clerical assistance. I would also like to thank my wife, Eleanor, whose help in preparing the manuscript was invaluable.

ABBREVIATIONS

Arch Gesh Phil	Archiv für Geschichte de Philosophie
Archiv Gen Psychiat	Archives of General Psychiatry
Amer Phil Quart	American Philosophical Quarterly
Amer Schol	The American Scholar
Austl J Phil	The Australasian Journal of Philosophy
Cambridge J	Cambridge Journal
Can J Phil	Canadian Journal of Philosophy
Can J Theol	Canadian Journal of Theology
Christian Schol	The Christian Scholar[1]
Downside Rev	Downside Review
East West	East and West
Harvard Theol Rev	The Harvard Theological Review
Heythrop J	The Heythrop Journal
Hibb J	The Hibbert Journal
Ideal Stud	Idealistic Studies
Int J Ethics	International Journal of Ethics[2]
Int J Parapsychology	International Journal of Parapsychology
Int J Phil Relig	International Journal for Philosophy of Religion
Int Phil Quart	International Philosophical Quarterly
JAAR	Journal of the American Academy of Religion[3]
J Bible Relig	Journal of Bible and Religion[3]
J Chin Phil	Journal of Chinese Philosophy
J Crit Anal	The Journal of Critical Analysis
J Hist Ideas	Journal of the History of Ideas

1. After the Winter 1967 issue, *The Christian Scholar* is issued under the title *Soundings*.
2. Issued under this title until April, 1938. Issued after that date as *Ethics*.
3. After 1968 the *Journal of Bible and Religion* becomes the *Journal of the American Academy of Religion*.

J Liberal Relig	Journal of Liberal Religion
J Phil	The Journal of Philosophy
J Relig	The Journal of Religion
J Relig Ethics	Journal of Religious Ethics
J Relig Health	Journal of Religion and Health
J Scien Stud Relig	Journal for the Scientific Study of Religion
J Sym Log	Journal of Symbolic Logic
J Theol Stud	Journal of Theological Studies
J Value Inq	The Journal of Value Inquiry
London Quart	London Quarterly and Holborn Review
Main Currents	Main Currents in Modern Thought
Man World	Man and World
Midwest Stud Phil	Midwest Studies in Philosophy
Mod Sch	The Modern Schoolman
Monist	The Monist
Month	The Month
New Scholas	The New Scholasticism
Notre Dame J Form Log	Notre Dame Journal of Formal Logic
Ohio J Relig Stud	Ohio Journal of Religious Studies
Personalist	The Personalist
Pac Phil Forum	Pacific Philosophical Forum
Phil East West	Philosophy East and West
Phil Forum	The Philosophical Forum
Phil Phenomenol Res	Philosophy and Phenomenological Research
Phil Quart	The Philosophical Quarterly
Phil Rev	The Philosophical Review
Phil Rhet	Philosophy and Rhetoric
Phil Stud	Philosophical Studies
Phil Today	Philosophy Today
Philosophia (Israel)	Philosophia: Philosophical Quarterly of Israel
Proc Amer Phil Ass	Proceedings of the American Philosophical Association

Proc Aris Soc	Proceedings of the Aristotelian Society
Proc Cath Phil Ass	Proceedings of the American Catholic Philosophical Association
Process Stud	Process Studies
Psychedelic Rev	Psychedelic Review
Relig Hum	Religious Humanism
Relig Life	Religion in Life
Relig Stud	Religious Studies
Rev Int Phil	Revue Internationale de Philosophie
Rev Metaph	The Review of Metaphysics
Rev Ottawa	Revue de l'Université d'Ottawa
Scot J Theol	Scottish Journal of Theology
S J Phil	The Southern Journal of Philosophy
Stud Leibniz	Studia Leibnitiana
SW J Phil	Southwestern Journal of Philosophy
Theol	Theology
Theol Stud	Theological Studies
Theol Today	Theology Today
Thomist	The Thomist

Note: The titles of journals which do not appear on this list are given in full.

I   THE DIVINE ATTRIBUTES

General Discussions of God's Attributes

(See also #s 546 and 952)

1 Barth, Karl. The Doctrine of God. Vol. 1. Translated
   by T. H. L. Parker (and others). Edinburgh: T. & T.
   Clark,]957. Pp. 257-677.

The second part of the first volume of this translation of Die Kirchliche Dogmatik II is devoted to an
extensive discussion of God's nature and attributes.
Since God's being is His absolutely free and self-
moved activity, God alone is a person in the "strict
sense." This absolutely free and self-moved activity
which constitutes God as God is love. God is He who
communicates blessedness, who seeks and creates fellowship for its own sake. (This is to be understood
primarily in terms of God's inner triune life and
only secondarily in terms of his relation to creatures. The love through which He bestows being and
grace upon us is absolutely free and gratuitous.)
Barth attempts to reconcile the unity or simplicity
of God's being with the multiplicity of His attributes. This multiplicity is real in the sense that
God really has (or is) these attributes independently
of His relation to creatures and to our intellects.
On the other hand, God is one or simple in so far as
each of these attributes "is the characteristic being
of God Himself." God's perfections are expressions
of two central aspects of His being. Unity, omnipresence, constancy, omnipotence, eternity and glory
express the perfection of God as He is in Himself,
His freedom or aseity. Grace, holiness, mercy, righteousness, patience and wisdom express the perfection
of God's activity or love. Since, however, each of

1

these perfections expresses God's whole being, all of
these perfections are interrelated. Therefore, in
speaking of the perfections of God's freedom we must
speak of the perfections of His love, and vice versa.
Barth's discussion of each perfection is extensive,
often interesting, and frequently obscure. Among
Barth's more interesting claims are the following:
(1) God's free act of love is compatible with His
righteousness. It is compatible with His righteousness because, in bestowing grace, God acts in a way
which is worthy of Himself, because His grace trans-
ports the wretched and outcast "into an identity of
. . . will with His" thus establishing righteousness,
and because in His mercy He bears His own wrath in
the person of Christ, thereby executing His judgment
upon sin without destroying the sinner. (Barth is
attempting to preserve the freedom of God's grace
and to protect the claim that there are no standards
of righteousness which are independent of God's being, while at the same time defending God against
the charge of caprice or arbitrariness.) (2) The
faithfulness and truthfulness of God are the "real
meaning and basis of His simplicity" for if He were
dissolvable or divisible, He would not be trustworthy. This simplicity of God's being is reflected
in His providential activity. (3) God's omnipresence
is said to be internal and not merely external.
(Barth thinks that it is always misleading to distinguish between what God is in Himself and what He is
for us or in relation to us. God reveals Himself as
He is. Therefore, whatever God is in relation to us,
He is in Himself. [Barth appears to be mistakenly
assuming that relational attributes as such aren't
fully real.]) Not only is God present to the world,
the persons of the trinity are present to each other.
God is, thus, not absolutely non-spatial for "pre-

sence includes distance" and distance implies "one place and another place." God not only transcends the sort of spatiality which implies dispersal and separation, He also transcends the non-spatiality of abstractions, numbers, points, etc. (4) We can't grasp the nature of divine power by analyzing the concept of omnipotence considered in abstraction from the divine subject whose being is freedom and love. (A similar point is made about the other divine attributes, but is particularly crucial at this juncture.) Power considered in isolation is evil, but God's power is legitimate power. (God can do all those things which it is legitimate for Him to do and vice versa.) Although possibility must be defined in terms of God's omnipotence and not vice versa, God can only do that in the doing of which He remains faithful to Himself as God. (Hence, God can't make round squares, lie, sin, or commit suicide.) (5) God's knowing and willing are coextensive in the sense that He not only knows whatever He wills but wills whatever He knows, Himself necessarily and creatures freely. (This is taken to imply that our free actions are grounded in God's will and that God knows them because He wills them, and also that evil and non-being are objects of God's knowledge only because they are objects of His permissive and repudiating will.) (6) Barth accepts Boethius's definition of eternity as the total, complete and simultaneous possession of unlimited life (and not as mere a-temporality). This eternity "doesn't lack absolutely what we know as present, as before and after, and therefore as time. . . [for it includes "the order and succession" by which the Father eternally generates the Son, etc., and as life it has a direction from origin to goal] . . . eternity simply lacks the fleeting nature of the present, the separation

between before and after." Just as God's constancy
or immutability is not a static immobility but
includes movement so God's eternity embraces time.
Barth appears to mean by this that while God in Himself is eternal (and not merely everlasting), He is
not merely the ground of time but acts savingly in
time (e.g., at the incarnation God assumes time). It
must be admitted that Barth's remarks at this point
are more than usually obscure. (7) The concept of
God's glory is interpreted as the self-declaration or
manifestation of the sum of His perfections, and connected with the concept of divine beauty. (Barth was
apparently unaware that Jonathan Edwards had anticipated him on this point.)

2 Bertocci, Peter Anthony. Introduction to the Philo-
   sophy of Religion. (Prentice-Hall Philosophy
   Series.) Englewood Cliffs, New Jersey: Prentice-
   Hall, Inc., 1951. Pp. 442-68.

In chapter 18, Bertocci provides a "systematic presentation" of his concept of a limited deity. The
most valuable part of this chapter is that in which
the author (1) argues that love and impassibility are
incompatible, and (2) develops the notion of a God
who suffers -- both because of His sympathy with us
and because He is engaged in struggle with recalcitrant elements in His own nature ("The Given" of E.
S. Brightman) and in the world -- but cannot be over-
whelmed by His suffering.

3 _____. "The Person God Is," Talk of
   God. (Royal Institute of Philosophy Lectures, vol.
   2, 1967-1968.) London, Melbourne etc.: Macmillan;
   New York: St. Martin's Press, 1969. Pp. 185-206.

A defense of the claim that God is a person. "Personalist theism" best accounts for the world's unity

and intelligibility (for God is a "unity-in-conti-
nuity" related to all that is, and God is intelligence) and for the fact that love is what most
enhances human existence (for God is love). The
notion of creation ex nihilo is preferable to either
dualism or monism. It is preferable to dualism because dualism is unable to account for the fact that
its principles are complementary and able to interact
in such a way as to produce an ordered cosmos. It is
preferable to monism because monism is incompatible
with human freedom.

4 Carman, John Braisted. The Theology of Rāmānuja, An
Essay in Interreligious Understanding. New Haven
and London: Yale University Press, 1974. xii +
333 pp.

A valuable study of one of India's major theists. Of
particular interest are (1) the division of God's
attributes into two sets, the first of which points
to His supremacy and transcendence and the second of
which points to His accessibility and condescension,
and Rāmānuja's account of the nature of these attributes, (2) Rāmānuja's contention that the cosmos is
God's body and that He is its Inner Self (where the
soul-body relationship is characterized as a relation between support and thing supported, between
controller and what is controlled, and between a master or owner and his disposable property), (3) the
claim that God also has a transcendent and perfect
bodily form, an immaterial body of splendor, and
(4) the doctrine of God's love, mercy, and grace (on
this point compare Rudolf Otto's India's Religion of
Grace and Christianity Compared and Contrasted
[London: S.C.M. Press, 1930]). When philosophers of
religion turn their attention to traditions other
than the Judeo-Christian tradition they usually con-

5

centrate on non-theistic religions such as Advaita
Vedānta and Zen. Those philosophers who are primarily interested in theism might, however, derive more
benefit from an examination of the philosophical
theology of theists like Rāmānuja and al Ghazzali.

5 Christian, William Armistead, Jr. An Interpretation of
   Whitehead's Metaphysics. New Haven: Yale University
   Press, 1959. Pp. 283-413.

Part 3 provides an interesting and influential exposition and development of Whitehead's doctrine of
God. Whitehead's own remarks, while highly suggestive, are somewhat unsystematic and give rise to
numerous questions. For this reason, those interested in Process Theism are well advised to turn their
attention to the work of those followers of Whitehead
who have articulated the position more fully and
consistently and who have addressed themselves to the
problems which beset it. Christian's interpretation
is more faithful to Whitehead than the better known
interpretation of Hartshorne. (For example, Christian retains the notion that God is a single everlasting actual entity rather than a personally
ordered series of divine "occasions.") One consequence of this fact is that while much of what
Hartshorne has to say (in, e.g., The Divine Relativity, #13 below) is logically independent of
Whitehead's metaphysics, the version of Process
Theism which is presented by Christian is inextricably bound up with that metaphysics.

6 Cobb, John B., Jr. A Christian Natural Theology,
   Based on the Thought of Alfred North Whitehead.
   Philadelphia: The Westminster Press, 1965. 288 pp.

A very lucid and specifically Christian version of
one type Process Theology. (Cobb is heavily

6

influenced by Hartshorne.) There are good discussions of Whitehead's metaphysics and value theory, the nature of the soul, etc. Chapters lV and V are particularly significant. In chapter IV Cobb discusses Whitehead's doctrine of God. In chapter V, Cobb presents a modification of that doctrine specifically addressing himself to the question as to whether or not God is a single actual entity (he decides He is not), to the nature of God's relationship to space, time and eternity, and to the nature of God's creativity.

7 Daher, Adel. "The Coherence of God-Talk," Relig Stud, 12 (December, 1976), 445-65.

A reply to Penelhum (#21 below). Daher argues (1) that if Penelhum is to avoid problems of (re)identification, it is not enough that there in fact be only one disembodied agent (viz., God). It must also be necessarily true that any disembodied agent which exists is God. (If this were not necessarily true, then we could always ask whether the disembodied agent which confronts us is God or someone else, and there are no criteria in terms of which this issue could be settled.) (2) Telekinesis is a coherent concept but only because the mental states which directly cause physical occurrences can be independently identified and situated vis à vis those physical occurrences. Unfortunately for Penelhum, mental states can only be identified by connecting them with the bodies of the beings who are in those states, and in order for x to be situated vis à vis y, x must be spatially distinct from y. Both points are questionable, however. It is true that in order for "x causes y" to be intelligible, "x" and "y" must differ in meaning. It may also be true that it is only reasonable to believe that x causes y if

there is some evidence for "x causes y" other than
the mere occurrence of y. (In the case at hand, this
evidence might be provided by the occurrence of other
effects of the same sort, by our inability to provide
normal explanations of these effects, and by their
similarity to the sorts of effects normally produced
by embodied minds.) What is not clear is that it
must be possible to identify x independently of the
effects which x produces, or to provide some kind of
"direct" or "immediate" evidence for the existence or
occurrence of x. (Can we independently identify, or
provide direct evidence for, theoretical entities in
science? If not, then the demand for these things is
not always in order.) In arguing for his second
point, Daher maintains that an agent can only be distinguished from the object of his action if he is
spatially related to that object, and this is by no
means obviously correct. (When I conjure up an image
at command, I am distinct from the image which I
conjure up but I am not spatially related to it.
There are qualitative, causal [and frequently] temporal differences between agents and their objects,
and it is by no means clear that these differences
are not sufficient to distinguish the two.)
Penelhum's discussion and Daher's reply provide one
of the more complete and lucid examinations of an
issue often thought to lie at the very heart of the
question concerning the meaningfulness of "God."

8 Deutsch, Eliot. Advaita Vedānta: A Philosophical
   Reconstruction. Honolulu: East-West Center Press
   (The University of Hawaii), 1969. 119 pp.

   According to Advaita Vedānta, the Brahman alone is
   real. It follows that anything which is not identical with the Brahman (e.g., the empirical world)
   is unreal, and that anything which is real (e.g., the

Pure Self) is identical with the Brahman. The Brahman itself is pure blissful empty consciousness which can, in the last analysis, only be described negatively. Within Vedānta positions are supported by appealing to scripture. Reason plays a secondary role in the interpretation of scripture, the removal of difficulties, and as a weapon to be employed against competing views. Deutsch succeeds in abstracting Advaita from its traditional contexts and presenting it as a (more or less) coherent philosophical system. If one of the tests for a philosophical hypothesis is how well it fares when compared with competing hypotheses, then the philosopher of religion must not only compare theism with various forms of naturalism but should also compare theism with some of its non-theistic religious alternatives such as Advaita Vedānta, Zen and Theravāda Buddhism. Deutsch is more sensitive to philosophical issues than most of those who have attempted to present Advaita Vedānta to the West.

9 Ford, Lewis Stanley, ed. Two Process Philosophers, Hartshorne's Encounter with Whitehead. (AAR Studies in Religion, 5.) Tallahassee, Florida: American Academy of Religion, 1973. 106 pp.

This anthology includes the following essays: (1) "Hartshorne's Encounter with Whitehead: Introductory Remarks," and "Whitehead's Differences from Hartshorne," both by Lewis Ford, (2) "Hartshorne's Early Philosophy" by William Lad Sessions (which shows that Hartshorne had arrived at many of his characteristic positions before his encounter with Whitehead), (3) "Hartshorne's Differences from Whitehead" by David B. Griffin, (4) "Hartshorne's Interpretation of Whitehead's Methodology" by William M. O'Meara, (5) "Relativity Theory and Hartshorne's

9

Dipolar Theism" by Frederic F. Fost, and (6) "Ideas
and Theses of Process Philosophers" by Charles
Hartshorne.   On the whole these essays provide an
illuminating examination of the differences between
Whitehead and Hartshorne and of some of the difficulties involved in their positions.

10 Garrigou-Lagrange, Reginald Marie. God, His Existence
    and Nature: A Thomistic Solution of Certain
    Agnostic Antinomies. Vol. II. Translated from the
    fifth French edition by Dom Bede Rose. St. Louis
    and London: B. Herder Book Co., 1936. vi + 576 pp.

The first two editions appeared in 1915. Volume **II**
is devoted to a discussion of God's attributes.
Several sections are of special interest. (1) Section 49 and Appendix IV discuss God's foreknowledge.
(2) Sections 54 and 57 discuss God's simplicity.
(These important sections are described at some
length under the appropriate headings. See #s 117
and 37 below.)   (3) In sections 52c and 64, Garrigou-
Lagrange attempts to explain how God can be a universal cause who acts instrumentally through secondary causes (including frèe agents) in such a way
that effects both spring wholly from these secondary
subordinate causes and wholly from God as first
cause. It is argued that our freedom is preserved
because God does not merely determine us to act, but
determines us to act freely. Garrigou-Lagrange
would appear to give away his case when he concedes
that the manner in which God does this must remain
a mystery. (The author returns to this issue in
Appendix IV and the Epilogue but does not succeed in
shedding additional light on the problem.)   (4) In
section 62, Garrigou-Lagrange argues against the
Leibnizian contention that God is morally bound to
create the best possible world. No possible world
is absolutely best. Nevertheless, God's gratuitous

10

choices do not lack "sufficient reasons." Where
two things are equally effective means to a certain
end, that one must be chosen in order to secure that
end is a sufficient reason for arbitrarily choosing
one of them. Again, God's love (unlike our love)
precedes the goodness of its object. It is not
elicited by the goodness of its object but bestows
that object's goodness upon it. God's free and
sovereign love provides a reason for the gratuitous
bestowal of good. Finally, a gratuitous choice of
certain goods expresses God's "sovereign liberty
and independence" and, thus, best manifests His
glory.

11 Gilson, Etienne. God and Philosophy. (Powell Lec-
       tures on Philosophy at Indiana University.) London:
       H. Milford, Oxford University Press; New Haven:
       Yale University Press, 1941. xviii + 147 pp.

Gilson argues that an adequate object of religious
attitudes must be a living being ("a god"). Since
Greek philosophy construed its first principles as
"things," Greek thought was characterized by tension
between philosophy and religious attitudes. Christian philosophy made the object of religious attitudes its philosophical first principle, and turned
its attention from a consideration of essences, or
the nature of things, to the fact of their existence, grounding contingent being in an unlimited
and self-existent act of existence. According to
Gilson, this conception of God began to come apart
in Descartes. For Descartes God was primarily a
principle of philosophical explanation, the first
principle of philosophy. God (the "author of nature") was thus once more divorced from the object
of religious attitudes (the "God of Abraham, Isaac
and Jacob"). Philosophy and science again turned

11

their attention to essences and natures, asking how things are, but forgetting to ask why they are. Gilson is not always convincing but his examination of the history of the concept of God in western philosophy is suggestive and occasionally illuminating.

12 Grant, Robert McQueen. The Early Christian Doctrine of God. Charlottesville: University Press of Virginia, 1966. Pp. 1-36 and 111-4.

The book's first chapter ("God the Father") contains an interesting account of early (through Origen) Christian discussions of the nature and attributes of God. Grant stresses the use made by these theologians of contemporary philosophical ideas. The second appendix ("The Impassibility of God") is also of interest.

13 Hartshorne, Charles. The Divine Relativity, A Social Conception of God. (The Terry Lectures, Yale University.) New Haven: Yale University Press, 1948. xvi + 164 pp.

In this important book, Hartshorne argues that the God of classical theism is logically impossible and develops a neo-classical conception of deity which is apparently consistent. Difficulties are created by classical theism's insistence that God is in all respects necessary, independent, immutable and impassible. It is, for example, not easy to see how God can be necessary and independent in all respects and at the same time know contingent states of affairs. Nor is it easy to see how God can be compassionate if He is neither dependent upon nor affected by His creatures. Hartshorne proposes that we adopt a "dipolar" conception of deity according to which God is necessary, independent, and immutable in

certain respects but contingent, dependent, and
mutable in other respects. Thus, it is necessary
that God exist and know whatever happens to be
actual. But God's knowledge of any particular
contingent actuality is contingent, and dependent
upon what He knows. Again, God exists and is good
in all possible worlds, but the manner in which His
goodness actualizes itself depends upon the actions
and responses of those contingent beings which happen to exist. Hartshorne's book contains a number
of suggestive arguments. His criticism of classical
theism is important and plausible, if not always
fully convincing. Hartshorne's neo-classical conception of deity depeņds upon Process Philosophy in
some respects but many of Hartshorne's points do not
depend upon Whitehead's metaphysics for their plausibility. (One noteworthy exception is
Hartshorne's account of divine power. The concept
of God's persuasive power is inextricably bound up
with some of the peculiarities of Process Philosophy.) This book deserves the serious consideration of anyone interested in the philosophy of
religion.

14 James, Edwin Oliver. The Concept of Deity, A Compa-
    rative and Historical Study. (The Wilde Lectures in
    Natural and Comparative Religion in the University
    of Oxford.) London, New York [etc.]: Hutchinson's
    University Library, 1950. 200 pp.

Chapters are devoted to a number of topics including anthropomorphism, monolatry and monotheism,
dualism, and revelation. James's lectures are
richly illustrated with material drawn from ancient
near eastern and western traditions. Most philosophers will find themselves unfamiliar with at
least some of this material. James contends that
theism alone provides a fully "adequate basis of

13

religion." This thesis (which is never adequately
established) colors the manner in which James
treats his material.

15 Joyce, George Hayward. Principles of Natural Theo-
    logy. (Stonyhurst Philosophical Series.) London,
    New York [etc.]: Longmans Green and Co., 1923;
    New York: AMS Press, 1972. Pp. 276-478 and
    524-56.

Chapters IX through XIV and chapter XVI contain a
Neo-Scholastic (and essentially Thomistic) account
of the divine attributes which is both comprehensive and lucid. Among the subjects discussed are
the claim that God's essence is His existence, the
"metaphysical attributes" (simplicity, immutability,
etc.), God's intellect, will and beatitude, and the
nature of God's creative activity. (Joyce's examinations of divine omnipotence and of divine
omniscience are described at more length under the
appropriate headings. See #s 89 and 127 below.)

16 Macleod, Alistair M. Tillich, An Essay on the Role
    of Ontology in His Philosophical Theology. (Contem-
    porary Religious Thinkers Series.) London:
    George Allen and Unwin, Ltd., 1973. 157 pp.

Tillich's ontology is closely connected with his
doctrine of God and with his account of man's
religious quest. Macleod shows that Tillich's
ontology includes five different enterprises: (1)
an attempt to show why the religious quest is inevitable, (2) an investigation of the nature of the
object of that quest, (3) an investigation of the
conditions which make experience possible, (4) an
attempt to come to grips with the fact that being
is, and (5) an investigation of the "root meanings"
of such fundamental concepts as love,

existence, and power. These enterprises are not
clearly distinguished, and Macleod succeeds in
showing that their pursuit is marred by many confusions and obscurities. (For example, in Systematic Theology, Tillich asserts that revelation is
the only source of the doctrine of God, while in
other places, he speaks as if ontology has its own
doctrine of God. Again, Tillich sometimes assumes
that in order to determine the conditions under
which experience is possible, we must examine the
structure of the objects of experience, but at
other times he supposes that we must instead examine the subject-object structure of being.)
Macleod has not succeeded in showing that Tillich's
thought is essentially incoherent, but he has
exposed a number of difficulties. The value of
Macleod's investigation lies in its sympathetic,
patient, and careful attention to the details of
Tillich's system. His book (together with Rowe's
Religious Symbols and God, #24 below) demonstrates
that the insights of analytic philosophy can be
applied to the work of a major non-analytic philosopher and theologian without distorting that work.
See Rowe's review (# 23 below).

17 Mascall, Eric Lionel. Existence and Analogy, A
    Sequel to "He Who Is." London and New York:
    Longmans, Green and Co., Ltd., 1949; Hamden, Con-
    necticut: Archon Books, 1967. Pp. 122-57.

Chapter 6 contains fairly interesting discussions
of a number of related issues -- the apparent
inconsistency of "goodness necessarily diffuses
itself" and "God might not have created a world,"
the apparent conflict between God's undisturbed
beatitude and His compassion, the precise nature of
the relation which is said to obtain between God

15

and the world when one asserts that "God creates
the world," and Vladimir Lossky's description (The
Mystical Theology of the Eastern Church, London:
James Clark & Co. Ltd., 1957) of the Eastern
Orthodox distinction between the divine essence and
the divine energies.

18 Nielsen, Kai. Contemporary Critiques of Religion.
    (Philosophy of Religion Series.) London and
    Basingstoke: Macmillan; New York: Herder and
    Herder, 1971. Pp. 112-34.

Chapter 6 lucidly presents what have become two
standard objections to the coherence of the concept
of God. (1) Agents must be able to act and yet (so
it is said) one can only act if one has a body.
Since God has no body, it follows that He cannot be
an agent. (2) God is said to be an individual but
individuals can be identified and God cannot be
identified. Nielsen's case for (1) consists of
(a) simply asserting that it is a conceptual truth
that one cannot act if one lacks a body, (b) arguing that the fact that agents can be distinguished from their situations, and that things like
heart trouble and kleptomania are sometimes included in the description of an agent's situation,
is not sufficient to establish the possibility of
disembodied agents, and (c) denying that D. D.
Evans ("Commentary on Paul Edwards' Paper," The
Idea of God, edited by E. H. Madden, R. Handy and
M. Farber, Springfield, Illinois: Charles Thomas,
1968) has shown that poltergeist talk makes sense
where poltergeists are thought of as disembodied
agents. Nielsen has failed to provide anything
remotely resembling a demonstration or proof. He
is, in spite of his intentions, appealing to our
intuitions. This is unsatisfactory because, given
the fact that most people find talk of disembodied

agents intelligible, the burden of proof would appear to be upon those who maintain that it is nonsense. The second objection is a mare's nest. We must at least distinguish the following four questions: (1) How can we distinguish God from other things of the same kind? (cf. "How can we distinguish one man from another?"), (2) How can we distinguish God from other things?, (3) How can we recognize God?, and (4) How can we determine whether or not "God" applies to anything? (Nielsen concentrates on the second and fourth questions. Others concentrate on the first and third.) Critics sometimes assume that the inability to answer (1) shows that God is not an individual. But the inability to distinguish an individual from other individuals of the same kind may be due to the fact that the kind in question admits of at most one instance. One would assume that the second question could be rather easily answered by offering a standard description of God (as omnipotent, creator, necessary, perfect, etc.). (3) presupposes that nothing can be an individual which cannot in principle be experienced by us, and the truth of this proposition is not obvious. In any case, theism does have an answer to the question "What would an experience of God be like?" (See its description of numinous and mystical experience.) No one will be bothered by question (4) who believes that he has a good argument for or against God's existence, or who believes that the considerations appealed to by natural theologians and their critics are relevant to a determination of the question as to whether or not God exists. In spite of their disclaimers, the atheologians' refusal to accept these responses strongly suggests that their demand for identification procedures

conceals the presumption that individuals must be
sensibly discriminable spatio and/or temporal particulars, and an unwillingness to countenance any
criteria except the sorts of criteria which are
used to identify spatio-temporal particulars.

19 Owen, Huw Parri. Concepts of Deity. (Philosophy of
    Religion Series.) London: Macmillan; New York:
    Herder and Herder, 1971 xi + 174 pp.

In the first chapter, Owen describes and defends
the classical conception of God. Although this
chapter contains several interesting observations
(e.g., on divine impassibility), it is -- on the
whole -- neither novel nor especially interesting.
Those who are concerned with the classical conception of God will find the work of Joyce or Garrigou-Lagrange (#s 15 and 10 above) more profitable.
In the second chapter, Owen offers some sound
criticisms of the concept of a finite God. However, his attempts to show that pantheism and process theism are inconsistent are quite unconvincing. The third chapter contains good brief
critical accounts of the views of Pringle-Pattison,
Barth, Brunner, Radhakrishnan, Tillich and Macquarrie. Owen does make some telling and suggestive
points. The book's principal defect consists in
the fact that arguments and criticisms are often
developed in insufficient detail and are, therefore, neither clear nor convincing.

20 Pailin, David Arthur. "The Humanity of the Theolo-
    gian and the Personal Nature of God," Relig Stud,
    12 (June, 1976), 141-58.

Pailin argues that we must ascribe personality to
God if we are to do justice to the theistic strand
in religion, that the concept of personality which

we ascribe to God can only be drawn from our understanding of our own mode of existence, and that the attempt to combine personal and impersonal modes of being in a concept of supra-personality is incoherent. Since God is absolute or ultimate as well as personal, it must be shown that ultimacy is compatible with personality. Pailin argues that personality is compatible with necessary perfection, with eternity (in the sense of everlastingness) and with certain senses of "infinity" (all-embracing knowledge and "infinite" creative power). Pailin is strongly influenced by Hartshorne. While many of Pailin's points are familiar, the article is lucid and well-argued.

21 Penelhum, Terence. Religion and Rationality, An Introduction to the Philosophy of Religion. New York: Random House, Inc., 1971. Pp. 148-57 and 331-55.

Penelhum argues that the concept of God is the concept of a disembodied agent and that this concept is coherent if (a) God is unique and if (b) sense can be made of the notion of disembodied perception and of the notion that mental states directly (i.e., without "bodily mediation") cause physical effects. The first condition must be met for the following reason: Minds can be distinguished from one another because we can distinguish between the bodies with which those minds are connected. (We can identify minds and mental states because minds and mental states are the minds and mental states of embodied beings, and because we have criteria for identifying bodies.) Since there is no way of distinguishing one disembodied mind from another, a plurality of disembodied minds is impossible. However, if we were to assume

that God is the only disembodied mind there is,
problems of identification and reidentification
would not arise. The force of Penelhum's argument
rests upon a number of interrelated assumptions:
(1) That in order for the notion of a person to
be coherent there must be criteria of personal
identity which can be used to distinguish one
person from another and to determine whether a given
person is the same person as some other person.
(2) That (at least some of) these criteria (bodily
continuity, the continuity of memory, etc.) must
constitute personal identity. (3) That these
criteria are only adequate if they provide logically
necessary and sufficient conditions for personal
identity. While (1) is plausible, (2) and (3) are
less plausible. Two general observations are in
order. (1) If God is a disembodied agent, then the
philosophical literature which is concerned with
the problem of personal identity and with the
coherence of the notion of disembodied survival
has a direct bearing upon the question of the
coherence of the concept of God. Thus, Penelhum's
observations on the latter (pp.148-57) depend upon
his examination of the former (pp.331-55. [And cf.
his more detailed discussion of these issues in
Survival and Disembodied Existence, London: Routledge and Kegan Paul, New York: Humanities Press,
1970, xi + 114 pp.]) (2) Even those who insist that
God cannot literally be a disembodied mind would
(or should) admit that God is importantly similar
to disembodied minds. If disembodied minds are
to provide adequate images or analogues of God, it
is essential that the concept of a disembodied
mind be coherent. See Daher's reply (#7 above).

22 Prestige, George Leonard. God in Patristic Thought.
    London and Toronto: William Heinemann Ltd., 1936;
    London: S.P.C.K., 1952. Pp. 1-75.

The greatest part of this important and influential
book is devoted to an examination of the development of the doctrine of the Trinity. Chapter I
(and, to a lesser extent, chapters II and III) are
of more general interest. Among the significant
points which Prestige makes are the following:
God's incomprehensibility was thought to be a
consequence of reason's inability to encompass
infinity and the fact that God's power and wisdom
extend to an infinite number of things, rather
than a consequence of God's irrationality. Impassibility was primarily, or at least in large part,
construed as a moral perfection -- a freedom from
the flesh and passions which corrupt our moral
nature. The doctrine of God's simplicity was
a simple consequence of the belief that composite
objects are liable to decay and destruction. A
consideration of these points suggests that some
metaphysical attributes may have been ascribed to
God for bad reasons and/or that the religious motives which expressed themselves in the ascription
of these attributes to God might be expressed in
a more adequate manner.

23 Rowe, William Leonard. "Critical Notice of A. Mcleod
    [sic] Tillich," Canadian J Phil, V (December, 1975),
    615-26.

A sympathetic critique of Macleod's Tillich: An
Essay on the Role of Ontology in His Philosophical
Theology (# 16 above). Rowe argues that although
Macleod has uncovered a number of confusions, he
has not shown that there is a major incoherence at
the heart of Tillich's thought.

24 _____. Religious Symbols and God, a
Philosophical Study of Tillich's Theology. Chicago
and London: The University of Chicago Press, 1968.
Pp. 11-96.

The first three chapters provide a sympathetic but
critical examination of Tillich's doctrine of God.
Particularly noteworthy are: (1) Rowe's explanation of why Tillich identifies God and Being-itself.
(God is the object of ultimate concern. Ultimate
concern is directed towards that which is ultimate
but expresses itself through a concrete symbol.
The fact that Being-itself is unlimited and the
fact that beings participate in Being-itself are
used by Tillich to explain (respectively) the element of ultimacy and the element of concreteness
in the religious attitude and its object (viz.,
God). (2) Rowe's attempt to explicate Tillich's
concept of Being-itself by employing two models --
a universal such as humanity-itself, and the One of
Plotinus. (3) Rowe's discussion of Tillich's refusal to attribute existence to God (Being-itself).
Most secondary works on Tillich either summarize
Tillich's doctrine of God employing Tillich's own
vocabulary, or explain the obscure by the obscure.
Rowe's book provides a notable exception to this
generalization.

25 Tennant, Frederick Robert. Philosophical Theology.
Vol. II: The World, The Soul, and God. Cambridge:
Cambridge University Press, 1930. Pp. 121-79.

In chapters V and VI, Tennant develops a conception
of a finite deity by asking what properties a
world ground must have in order to account for design. There are a number of items of interest,
including (1) an attempt to show that a world designer must also be a world creator (essentially

22

because the nature of things can't be separated
from their being so that to determine the first,
one must determine the second), (2) a critique of
the claim that God is infinite, absolute, and
metaphysically perfect (i.e., fully actual, immutable, etc.) which includes a useful examination of
the various senses in which terms like "infinite"
can be taken, and (3) an interesting discussion of
whether the world ground can be regarded as social.

26 Tillich, Paul Johannes Oskar. Biblical Religion
    and the Search for Ultimate Reality. (The James
    W. Richard Lectures in the Christian Religion,
    University of Virginia, 1951-52.) Chicago: The
    University of Chicago Press, 1955. 84 pp.

Tillich explores the relation between biblical revelation and a philosophy concerned with the nature
of being. He contends that the God of revelation
is essentially identical with the God of philosophy. They appear to be different. (1) The God
of biblical religion is a person but Being-itself
appears to be impersonal. (2) The God of biblical
religion interacts with beings but, because it is
difficult to see how beings can act upon Being-itself, and because Being-itself transcends change,
interaction between beings and Being-itself seems
to be impossible. (3) God's relationship to persons is mediated through the Word He addresses to
them while awareness of Being-itself is immediate.
(4) The God of biblical religion transcends a world
which He creates out of nothing whereas beings
participate in Being-itself. Tillich argues that
(1) qua unconditional, the God of biblical religion
transcends personality while one can stand in a
relation to Being-itself which is analogous to the
relation which one adopts towards other persons.
(2) Tillich's discussion of the second

23

difficulty is less satisfactory although he correctly observes that traditional Christianity has
found it equally difficult to reconcile God's
sovereignty and independence and the claim that
God enters into reciprocal relations with His
creatures. (3) Elsewhere, Tillich speaks as if
there are two sorts of awareness of Being-itself
--an immediate awareness and an awareness which
is mediated through beings (symbols). Since these
are compatible, one can accept the first without
rejecting the mediated awareness of biblical
religion. This solution is not, however, clearly
stated in these lectures. (4) Finally, although
beings share in Being-itself, Being-itself transcends all beings. The "otherness" of the Unconditioned is, thus, preserved.

27 _____. Love, Power and Justice, Analyses
and Ethical Applications. (Given as Firth Lectures in Nottingham, England, and as Sprunt
Lectures in Richmond, Virginia.) New York:
Oxford University Press, 1954. 127 pp.

According to Tillich, the concepts of love, power
and justice point to the nature of being and, thus,
to the nature of God (Being-itself). Love is
construed as "the drive toward the unity of the
separated." "Power" points to the prevalence of
being over non-being, and power manifests itself
in the actualization of being. "Justice" expresses
"the form of being in its universal and unchanging
character." It "preserves what is to be united."
In the concluding chapter, Tillich argues that
"power," "justice," and "love" can be symbolically
applied to God who is the Power of being in everything which is, and the ground of structure and
the source of those powers which overcome estrange-
ment and effect reconciliation. This little

book is suggestive although (even) more obscure than some of Tillich's other works.

28 _____. Systematic Theology. Vol I. Chicago: The University of Chicago Press, 1951. Pp. 163-289.

According to Tillich, God is neither a being nor the totality of beings but Being-itself, the ground of being or power of being, which resists the threat of non-being. "God is Being-itself" is the only non-symbolic statement which can be made about God. (A few other statements -- "God is our Ultimate Concern," "God is the Holy" -- are treated in practice as if they were non-symbolic.) Symbolic statements about God are legitimate if they disclose Being-itself, and illegitimate if they conceal it. In addition to his explication of the notion that God is Being-itself, Tillich provides detailed accounts of the way in which divine attributes should be understood. (For example, he argues that in saying that God is omnipresent, we imply that God is the ground of space, that no place can separate us from God, that any place can be a place in which God is revealed, and that God is the answer to our anxiety over homelessness, i.e., God is the source of the courage which enables us to overcome that anxiety.) Three comments are in order. (1) It is difficult to overestimate the influence which Tillich has had on contemporary religious thought, particularly in the United States. (2) Tillich's concept of God is not as radical as it appears to be. Much of what he says should appear familiar to those acquainted with the Christian mystical tradition and most especially with such figures as Dionysius the Areopagite and Meister Eckhart. (3) In spite

of its imprecision, occasional confusion, and
frequent obscurity, Tillich's work is impressive
in scope and (often) suggestive in detail. It
deserves more sympathetic and careful attention
from analytic philosophers than it has usually
received.

29 Whitehead, Alfred North. Process and Reality, An
    Essay in Cosmology by Alfred North Whitehead . . .
    Gifford Lectures Delivered in the University of
    Edinburgh during the Session 1927-28. Cambridge
    [Eng.]: The University Press; New York: The
    Macmillan Co., 1929. Pp. 519-33.

The final chapter contains Whitehead's most important discussion of God. God combines a primordial
nature which is the locus of possibility and a
consequent nature which preserves, and is pro-
gressively enriched by, everything that occurs in
the course of cosmic history. God and the world
both transcend, and are immanent in, one another.
God is as dependent upon the world as the world
is dependent upon Him. He is "the great companion
-- the fellow sufferer who understands." These
interesting and suggestive ideas are not worked
out systematically. Someone interested in Process
Theism is, therefore, perhaps best advised to turn
to Whitehead's most able followers -- particularly
William Christian, Lewis Ford, Charles Hartshorne
and John Cobb, Jr.

30 _____. Religion in the Making.
    (Lowell Institute Lectures, 1926.) New York: The
    Macmillan Company, 1926. 160 pp.

In these lectures Whitehead investigates the nature
of religion and explores several concepts of God.
According to Whitehead, western religion has
stressed God's transcendence while neglecting His

immanence. It has also tended to revert to the notion of God as enemy. An adequate account of God must bring out the fact that God is necessarily dependent upon the world in certain respects although independent of it in others, and the notion of God as enemy must be replaced with the notion of God as companion. Particular attention is paid to the way in which God introduces order into the world by providing ideals to it.

God's Metaphysical Attributes

(See also #s 1, 2, 12, 13, 15, 17, 19, 20, 22, 25, 26, 29, 30, 124, 129, 130, 134, 150, 157, 178 and 220)

31 Bennett, Daniel Clark. "The Divine Simplicity," J Phil, LXVI (October, 1969), 628-37.

The assumption that states, episodes and activities are properties, together with the assumption that God is simple, leads to absurdities: (1) If God is simple He cannot have both necessary and contingent properties. Therefore, if He has any necessary properties, all His properties are necessary including, e.g., the property of electing Abraham. (2) Since God is identical with His properties, His properties are identical with each other. If, therefore, Justice and Mercy are different properties, God cannot have more than one of them. It also follows that God is a property. (3) If one of God's essential properties is unknown, then (since His properties are identical) all His properties are unknown. (This isn't clear. "x stands in an epistemic relation, R, to y and y=z" does not entail "xRz.") Bennett argues that states, episodes and activities are not themselves properties but instances of properties, and that one and the same state, episode or activity can be an instance of quite different properties. He suggests that the doctrine of divine simplicity is best understood as asserting that there is only one (divine) state, activity or episode which is an instance of both necessary and contingent properties, an instance of such diverse properties as Wisdom and Justice, and an instance of both known and unknown properties.

32 Blumenfeld, David. "Leibniz's Proof of the Uniqueness of God," Stud Leibniz, VI (1974), 262-71.

At one point Leibniz concludes that there can only be one necessary being since one necessary being is sufficient to explain the world. The most plausible interpretation of the argument is, perhaps, this: Because the world exists there must be at least one necessary being to account for it. There cannot be a sufficient reason for a plurality of such beings. (The existence of the world does not provide such a reason for one necessary being will account for its existence. A sufficient reason cannot be found in the external cause(s) of a plurality of necessary beings for necessary beings have no causes. An examination of the concept of a necessary being will not provide a sufficient reason, for the examination of a concept "can never establish how many instances of it actually exist.") Therefore, there is only one such being. Leibniz could have argued that because a necessary being possesses an unlimited potentiality for existence, its "quantity" of essence or perfection is unlimited. It follows that any necessary being is absolutely perfect and that, therefore (since all perfect beings have the same properties), there can only be one necessary being.

33 Clarke, W. Norris. "A New Look at the Immutability
    of God," God Knowable and Unknowable. Edited by
    Robert J. Roth. New York: Fordham University
    Press, 1973. Pp. 43-72.

God's immutability appears to preclude His entering
into authentic and reciprocal personal relations
with His creatures. Clarke attempts to solve
this problem by distinguishing between changes in
the intrinsic real being of an agent (which always
involve the acquisition or loss of an ontological
perfection [!]) and changes in the intentional object of its consciousness. Only the latter can be
ascribed to God. God's being, love and knowledge
are neither increased nor diminished, with respect
to their perfection, by the fact that He creates.
Nevertheless, the intentional objects of His love
and knowledge are different from what they would
have been if He had not created and, thus, God is
"truly other, different, in His consciousness
because of His relations with us." Furthermore,
God's knowledge of our free acts depends upon them
although it is not caused by them. (The essay
concludes with a rather opaque explanation of how
this can be the case.) God's "real natural being
as it exists in its own right" is necessary, immutable and non-successive. The objective content
of God's loving consciousness (i.e., the intentional being of things in God) is contingent, mutable
and successive. Clarke's argument is interesting
and suggestive (although sometimes obscure). It
is not clearly successful. Clarke correctly maintains that something can be a property of what
is loved or known without being a property of the
lover or knower. The materiality and multiplicity

of an object of knowledge does not clearly entail
a corresponding materiality and multiplicity in
either the knower or the knower's act of knowledge.
It is not, however, clear that we can admit that
the contents of God's knowledge appear successively
(and, thus, grow by addition) without introducing
temporality into God's real being. (Can an act
of knowledge be non-temporal and immutable if its
objects appear successively? Don't we "count"
acts of knowledge by referring to such things as
the temporal sequence of the contents of knowledge?) Nor is it clear that the intentional object of a necessary act of knowledge can be contingent for the reasons provided by Hartshorne and
others. ("A knows p" entails "p." Hence, if it
is necessary that A knows p, p is necessary as
well.) This article has considerable intrinsic
interest. It also attests to the seriousness with
which many contemporary Roman Catholic philosophers
regard the criticisms of the classical doctrine of
God's metaphysical attributes which have been made
by Process Philosophy and by Existentialism.

34 Donceel, Joseph. "Second Thoughts on the Nature of
    God," Thought, 46 (Autumn, 1971), 346-70.

This article is of interest because it reviews and
illustrates attempts which have recently been
made by Roman Catholic philosophers to reach an
accommodation between the God of Aristotelian-
Thomistic tradition (who as Pure Act is both simple
and immutable) and the God of panentheism (who is
really related to His creatures, shares their sor-
rows and joys, and undergoes real changes).
Donceel's own solution involves an appeal to Hegel
and the claim that apparent opposites (mutability
and immutability, multiplicity and simplicity,

etc.) can be dialectically held together in a
genuine synthesis. This rather desperate measure
suggests that accommodation may be difficult to
achieve.

35 Englebretsen, George. "Sommers' Theory and Natural
    Theology," Int J Phil Relig, VI (Summer, 1975),
    111-6.

    A reply to Sommers (# 54 below). Englebretsen
    attempts to show that Sommers' theological assump-
    tions (e.g., that all the divine attributes entail
    one another) and ontological assumptions (e.g.,
    that "is potentially P" is equivalent to "is P-or-
    P̄") entail very odd consequences. For example,
    they entail that actuality and potentiality are
    equivalent for all beings, and that nothing fails
    to be divine. Englebretsen also argues that
    Sommers' ontological argument is circular.

36 Ford, Lewis Stanley. "Boethius and Whitehead on Time
    and Eternity," Int Phil Quart, VIII (March, 1968),
    38-67.

    Ford attempts to describe a type of (divine) eter-
    nity which is distinct both from a-temporality and
    from mere everlastingness (a beginningless and end-
    less succession of moments). A clue to the solu-
    tion of the problem is provided by the notion of
    "inclusive simplicity" -- a unity which includes,
    but cannot be reduced to, a multiplicity of ele-
    ments (e.g., consciousness or the life of a cell).
    The divine life (God's eternal present) includes
    all moments of actualized time. What is included,
    however, is not a mere series of abstract instants
    ordered by relations of before and after, but
    concrete events, each with its own particular past
    and its own indeterminate future. The divine

31

present which incorporates and unifies these
events as they occur, and thus grows "with the
successive addition of temporally present moments,"
"never becomes past and never gives way to some
future coming after itself." Ford argues that
this conception of divine eternity can be found
in both Boethius and Whitehead, but that it was
rejected by Aquinas who preferred the view that
God is a-temporal. Ford's discussion is interesting and does not appear to crucially depend upon
Whitehead's metaphysics. It is not clear, however,
that Ford's account significantly differs from the
account provided by those who affirm that God's
life is merely everlasting. (There are some [ap-
parent] differences. According to the first
account, nothing recedes into the past where it
is only remembered, and change is excluded if
change is understood as the replacement of one
divine moment by another. According to the second
account, one moment of the divine life replaces
another which, therefore, recedes into the past.
Again, the first account includes the notion of
a radical unification of the temporal actualities
which are incorporated into the divine life.
While this notion is not incompatible with the
second account it does not appear to be included
in it.)

37 Garrigou-Lagrange, Reginald Marie. God, His Existence and Nature; A Thomistic Solution of Certain
Agnostic Antinomies. Vol. II. Translated from the
fifth French Edition by Dom Bede Rose. St. Louis
and London: B. Herder Book Co., 1936. Pp. 190-9
and 225-46.

Sections 54 and 57 discuss God's simplicity.
Garrigou-Lagrange argues that perfections in
their pure state include one another. Therefore,

the terms for pure perfections (perfections which
include no imperfection) can be applied to God
literally (but analogically), even though the
supereminent mode in which God enjoys these perfections is such that what these non-synonymous
terms refer to in God is identically the same thing.
Garrigou-Lagrange distinguishes between three classes of divine perfections. (1) The distinctions
which we make between certain perfections have no
basis in God's nature but merely in the imperfection of our intellect. If there were a real
distinction between God's essence and existence,
or between His being and His intelligence or will,
or between these powers and their operation, there
would be a real distinction between potentiality
and act in that which is Pure Act. (2) A conceptual distinction can be made between certain perfections on the basis of the diverse relations
in which God stands to creatures. Thus, a distinction can be made between God's knowledge of possibilia and God's knowledge of actualia because
of the diverse relations which God's act of intellection bears to possibilia and to actualia.
Since these relations are real in creatures but
not in God this (real) diversity is compatible
with God's simplicity. (3) Intellection and
volition present a different problem. These perfections are "formally distinct" (i.e., they are
not related as potentiality to act). Furthermore, there is a basis for the application of both
concepts to God "independently of all relation to
creatures." However, reason can establish the
identity of these perfections in God. If God's
intellection is identical with His essence and if
God's volition is identical with His essence -- and
this is regarded as already established -- then

God's intellection and volition are really identical. (The interfusion of love and knowledge in
mystical contemplation provides a faint image of
this identity.) In spite of its obscurities,
these sections provide as coherent an explanation
of the doctrine of divine simplicity as we are
likely to get.

38   Geach, Peter Thomas. "Aquinas," Three Philosophers
     by G.E.M. Anscombe and P.T. Geach. Oxford: Basil
     Blackwell, 1961. Pp. 121-4.

     Geach provides an interesting account of God's
     simplicity. He suggests that just as "the square
     of" and "the cube of" designate different functions
     although one, the square of one and the cube of
     one are identical, so God, the Wisdom of God and
     the Power of God may all be identical even though
     "the wisdom of" and "the power of" designate
     different attributes.

39   Hartshorne, Charles. "The Dipolar Conception of
     Deity," Rev Metaph, XXI (December, 1967), 273-89.

     A reply to Westphal (#61 below). (1) Hartshorne
     attempts to show that something is eternal if
     and only if it is necessary. It is argued that
     necessity is the only criterion of eternity, and
     that an eternal contingent choice is unintelli-
     gible since a choice presupposes an indeterminate
     antecedent situation "in which it is not yet
     decided which way the agent will take." (2)
     Hartshorne argues that x ontologically depends
     on y if and only if without y x cannot be. It
     follows that logical dependence involves ontolo-
     gical dependence and that, therefore, if God's
     knowledge and love logically depend upon the

object known and loved, they ontologically depend
upon that object as well. (Ontological dependence [so defined] does not entail causal dependence. "God causes s" entails "s" and without s,
God's causing s could not be, but it is absurd
to say that God's causing s is causally dependent
upon s. Hartshorne's reply is, therefore, beside
the point.) The article concludes with some
reflections upon Process Philosophy's solution to
the problem of evil.

40 Hügel, Frederich von, Baron. "Suffering and God,"
    Essays and Addresses on the Philosophy of Religion,
    2nd series by Baron F. von Hügel. London: J. M.
    Dent and Sons, 1926. Pp. 165-213.

    A measured defense of the doctrine of God's im-
    passibility. Among the more important points
    made by von Hügel are the following: (1) Suffering
    is intrinsically evil and is, therefore, excluded
    by God's perfection. (2) Sympathy must be attri-
    buted to God, but there is no reason to suppose
    that the sympathy of a "Bodiless Spirit of Spirits"
    entails suffering. (3) Religious consciousness
    itself (religious experience, piety, worship)
    forces us to construe the Absolute as Pure Joy
    untouched by sin or sorrow.

41 Kneale, Martha. "Eternity and Sempiternity," Proc
    Aris Soc, LXIX (New Series), (1968-69), 223-38.

    Kneale argues that if eternity is conceived as a
    "totum simul of time," then eternity is self-con-
    tradictory, for it would involve a simultanaeity
    of past, present, and future, i.e., a simultaneity
    of that which is not simultaneous. If a timeless
    object is defined as an object which is such
    that the sentences used to assert its existence

require neither date nor tense, but express a true
proposition whenever they are spoken, and if a
sempiternal object is an object which always
exists, then timelessness and sempiternity entail
one another. (Kneale appears to assume that if,
for any time, one can at that time truly say
that x exists, then even if "x exists" contains
neither date nor tense, it is true that x exists
at that time.) Necessity entails sempiternity
but not vice versa. (Epicurean atoms are sempiternal but not necessary.) Kneale concludes
with some interesting observations on Spinoza's
use of "eternity."

42 Kneale, William C. "Time and Eternity in Theology,"
    Proc Aris Soc, LXI (New Series), (1960-61), 87-108.

    An interesting examination of theological uses of
    "eternity" in Greek philosophy and medieval theo-
    logy. Kneale suggests that what attracted Chris-
    tian theologians to the Platonic conception of
    eternity as timelessness was the alleged (logical)
    connection between timelessness and necessity.

43 Kolb, David Alan. "Time and the Timeless in Greek
    Thought," Phil East West, XXIV (April, 1974),
    138-43.

    In this interesting article Kolb explores the
    notion of a "timeless happening," examining Plato's
    contention that the Forms are generated from the
    One and the Indefinite Dyad, Aristotle's claim
    that the first mover engages in "pure self-
    coincident activity, thought thinking thought,"
    and the emanation of the hypostases in Neopla-
    tonism.

44 Kretzmann, Norman. "Eternity." University Lecture:
   Cornell University, April 3, 1975.

   The ESL (for "earlier than," "simultaneous with,"
   and "later than") sequence is distinguished from
   the PNF (for "past," "now," and "future") sequence.
   Eternity is an enduring present existence which is
   beginningless, endless, pastless, and futureless.
   The eternity ascribed to God by classical Christian theology involves indivisibility as well as
   these features. It is argued that God's eternity
   is compatible with both His knowledge and His
   activity. A significant essay.

45 La Croix, Richard. "God Might Not Love Us,"
   Int J Phil Relig, V (Fall, 1974), 157-61.

   A criticism of Tomberlin's account of non-relational divine properties (#59 below). According
   to traditional theism, "loving everyone" is a
   property which God possesses essentially. (One
   must be careful here. God may essentially possess
   the property of loving everyone who exists if any
   person other than God does exist, but it is not
   clear that God essentially possesses the property
   of loving everyone simpliciter.) The property in
   question is, however, a relational property in
   Tomberlin's sense and, if it is relational, it is
   presumably a property which God might not have
   had. It is, therefore, not essential after all.

46 Lee, Jung Young. God Suffers for Us, A Systematic
   Inquiry into a Concept of Divine Passibility.
   The Hague: Martinus Nijhoff, 1974. xi + 112 pp.

   This defense of God's passibility is based upon
   the assumption that God loves, that love is necessarily empathic and that empathy involves a

capacity for suffering. God's capacity for suffering is actualized when His love is sinfully
rejected. In spite of a certain imprecision of
thought, Lee's second chapter is philosophically
interesting. Lee maintains that there are basi-
cally three grounds for the doctrine of divine
impassibility: (1) The belief that saying that
the Father suffers confuses the distinction between Father and Son, (2) the moral devaluation
of passion and feeling, and (3) the belief that
God's self-sufficiency and immutability entails
His impassibility. It has also been argued that
suffering cannot be attributed to God (4) because
suffering is intrinsically evil and God is wholly
good, (5) because suffering entails frustration
and limitation whereas God is infinite in power
and free from all limitations, and (6) because
suffering involves an entanglement in time while
God altogether transcends time. (Notice that
"God suffers" entails "God is passible" but not
vice versa. Lee and others frequently equate
the two claims.) Lee's responses to these objections are not as clear as one would like but appear
to be as follows: (1) The union between Christ's
divine and human nature entails that his divine
nature participates in the suffering of his human
nature. (2) The model for God's pathos is not to
be sought in our own imperfect passion and feeling
but in Christ's passion and feeling. (3) God's
empathic reaction does not entail any "passive
potentiality to be perfected." According to Lee,
finite suffering and sin are the occasion but not
the cause of God's suffering. Evil is not the
cause of God's suffering for God suffers only
because He has chosen to suffer. (This choice is
implicated in God's decision to create and care

for the world.) Classical theism is said to be
unduly static. God is in fact dynamically active
and dynamic activity is incompatible with impassibility (but cf. the Thomistic notion that God
as Pure Act is creatively active but not acted
upon). (4) Vicarious sacrifice and redemptive
suffering are not intrinsically evil. (In arguing
for this point, Lee mistakenly assumes that "x is
intrinsically evil" entails "there are no circumstances in which it would be better for x to
exist than not exist.") (5) God's suffering does
not presuppose a lack in His own nature but rather
a lack in creatures. Furthermore, any limitations
involved are self-limitations since they are
consequences of God's free decision to create.
(6) Although God submits Himself to the conditions
of time, He remains time's transcendent Lord. In
his third chapter, Lee attempts to show that the
Christian doctrines of creation, the incarnation,
the atonement, the Holy Spirit, and the Trinity
entail God's passibility and are incompatible
with God's impassibility. At best, Lee shows that
given a certain (not wholly implausible) interpretation, these doctrines entail God's passibility
and are incompatible with His impassibility. He
has not shown that these doctrines as interpreted
by classical Christianity entail God's passibility.
The concluding chapter discusses the relation
between human suffering and divine suffering and
the significance which the latter can bestow on
the former.

47 Mozley, John Kenneth. The Impassibility of God, A
    Survey of Christian Thought. Cambridge: Cambridge
    University Press, 1926. xii + 187 pp.

In the first half of his book, Mozley shows that a

39

firm belief in God's impassibility was one of the
factors governing the Christological controversies
which occurred during the first few centuries of
our era. Two facts clearly emerge. (1) The
doctrine of impassibility has several roots. (a)
Impassibility was believed to be a necessary condition of God's incorruptibility, and a consequence
of His simplicity and immateriality. (b) It was
associated with a desire to protect God's transcendence and independence, and with a dread of
anthropomorphism. (c) The value placed upon
impassibility was, at least in part, a reflection
of the value placed upon the (human) virtue of
"apathy" or passionlessness. (2) There is an apparent conflict between the doctrine of the incarnation and the doctrine of impassibility. The
Orthodox solution of this problem was that the
Logos suffers, grieves, fears, etc., in His human
nature but not in His divine nature. Hence, the
divine nature remains impassible. The difficulty
with this solution consists in the fact that if
a divine person suffers in any nature, it would
appear to follow that that divine person is not
impassible in all respects and that the doctrine
of God's impassibility is, therefore, not true
without qualification. (This was sometimes clearly
recognized -- e.g., by the 17th century Protestant
theologian John Gerhard.) Mozley provides a brief
but very good discussion of the ways in which
Augustine, Anselm, Aquinás, Scotus, Luther, Calvin,
etc., handled the problem of God's impassibility.
The general tendency was to attribute the behavior
appropriate to an emotion or feeling to God, but
not the emotion or feeling itself. The position of
Aquinas was, however, more subtle. Aquinas maintained that since God is Pure Act, He cannot be

40

acted upon by another so as to receive "the
impression of a quality foreign and diverse." God
can, however, be said to be literally joyful and
loving since joy and love can be purely active
"emotions," rooted in the will rather than in
one's "sensitive" or "animal" nature. (It is worth
observing that God's impassibility can be understood in two ways -- as the absence of feeling or
emotion, and as the impossibility of God's being
acted upon, or modified by, another. The two are
often confused but, as Aquinas recognizes, impassibility in the second sense entails impassibility
in the first sense only if all emotion or feeling
is passive, i.e., an external modification.)
Mozley concludes by describing the repudiation
of God's impassibility in (much) modern philosophy
and theology. This repudiation appears to be a
consequence of three things: (1) an emphasis upon
God's immanence in, and interaction with, the
world, (2) an insistence upon the reality of God's
love, and a conviction that love necessarily
involves compassion where compassion is understood
as a sympathetic participation in the sufferings
of others, and (3) a conviction that Christ's
self-sacrificing love is a true reflection of God's
own inner life, the passion of the cross providing
an image of a passion in the heart of God. This
is a very useful book.

48 Penelhum, Terence. Religion and Rationality, An
    Introduction to the Philosophy of Religion. New
    York: Random House, 1971. Pp. 65-75.

    Chapter seven examines the claim that God is a-
    temporal and immutable, the claim that He is
    simple, and the claim that there is no distinc-
    tion between God's essence and His existence.

Although Penelhum argues that some of these claims are logically incoherent, he does try to show how these doctrines express legitimate religious concerns (e.g., the desire to preserve God's independence). Penelhum's discussion of the metaphysical attributes is rather pedestrian but deserves some attention if only because these attributes are so seldom discussed by philosophers in the analytic tradition.

49 Pike, Nelson Craft. God and Timelessness. (Studies in Ethics and the Philosophy of Religion.) London: Routledge & Kegan Paul; New York: Schocken Books, 1970. xiv + 192 pp.

After introductory remarks on the predicate "timeless" and the logical status of "God is timeless," Pike explores the relations between "timeless," "immutable," "incorruptible," "ingenerable," and "immortal." ("Timeless" entails and [given the assumption that it is logically possible for a temporal being to change, to cease to exist, and to begin to exist] is entailed by "immutable," "incorruptible," and "ingenerable.") Pike, then, proceeds to argue that "x is timeless, i.e., has neither temporal extension nor temporal location" is logically incompatible with "x produces or sustains y," and that (because a timeless being cannot deliberate, anticipate or remember, and can neither act nor respond) timelessness is incompatible with personality. Pike's arguments are sophisticated, ably presented, and must be taken seriously. Pike has not, however, clearly shown that "x produces or sustains y" entails "x and y are temporally related." (Pike deploys examples but does not provide a demonstration, and there appear to be counter examples. Dickens

42

created Pickwick but although both Dickens and
his creative activity are temporal neither Dickens
nor his creative activity are temporally related
to Mr. Pickwick in any obvious way.) Nor is it
entirely clear that personality entails temporality. Pike admits that it is at least possible
that the notion of a timeless knower is coherent.
Furthermore, if Pike is mistaken in supposing
that only temporal beings can produce or sustain
something, then it simply isn't clear that "because x prizes y, x is the voluntary ground of y"
entails "x is a temporal being." (Willing need
not precede what is willed [e.g., a dance, or a
question]. Must willing be simultaneous with
what is willed if it does not precede it? All
that is clear is that willing cannot <u>follow</u> what
is willed. Nor is it clear that volitions
must change, or have a beginning or end. Is it,
then, clear that the introduction of volition
introduces temporality?) If, however, a-temporality is compatible with knowledge and voluntary
"behavior," it is surely compatible with personality. Pike's case is, then, plausible but not
conclusive. (On these points see Sturch, #55
below.) In the last two chapters Pike attempts
to determine whether there are any good reasons
for the doctrine of God's timelessness. He concludes that "x is timeless" cannot be derived
from "x is a being greater than which none can be
thought" (where the latter is construed as "x is
a being than which a being more worthy of worship
cannot be conceived"). He admits that if there
were logical connections between timelessness on
the one hand, and immutability, incorruptibility,
and ingenerability on the other, and if there
were, in addition, good reasons for attributing

43

the latter to God, then there would be good reasons for attributing timelessness to God. He argues, however, that there are good reasons for attributing the latter to God only if we take them in a material sense (if, e.g., God is immutable in the sense that His character is such that He cannot bring Himself to act badly, and nothing can cause Him to lose His wisdom and power) whereas logical connections between timelessness and the other three attributes can be made out only if we take those attributes in a logical sense (if, e.g., God is immutable in the sense that it is logically impossible for God to change in any respect). Pike concludes by attempting to show that the doctrine of God's timelessness has no biblical support and is absent in at least one major Church Father, viz., John of Damascus. The author's examination of God's omniscience and perfection are described elsewhere (#s 142 and 201 below). It should be added that in addition to its valuable discussions of timelessness, omniscience, and perfection, Pike's book contains incidental observations on a number of other topics which should interest the philosopher of religion (e.g., on whether "God" is a proper name or a description, on whether terms like "good" can be applied to God in the same sense in which they are applied to human beings, etc., etc.).

50 Plantinga, Alvin Carl. God and Other Minds, A Study
    of the Rational Justification of Belief in God.
    (Contemporary Philosophy.) Ithaca, New York:
    Cornell University Press, 1967. Pp. 173-80.

Discussing God's immutability, Plantinga suggests that God's non-relational properties (those properties which do not logically involve the

existence of some contingent being distinct from
God) are essential and, hence, unchanging. See
Tomberlin's reply (#60 below).

51 Pollard, T. Evan. "The Impassibility of God," Scot
    J Theol, VIII (December, 1955), 353-64.

    A lucid exposition of the view that the concept
    of divine impassibility is a Greek notion alien
    to the Christian tradition. Pollard argues that
    it is unbiblical and incompatible both with the
    doctrine of the incarnation and with the doctrine
    of the atonement. (According to Pollard, if the
    divine in Christ is impassible and does not
    participate in the emotional life of Jesus, then
    God is not really incarnate in Jesus and the
    passion of Christ is a merely human passion. The
    orthodox would reply that Pollard has ignored
    the distinction between the divine person or
    hypostasis and the divine nature. The latter is
    impassible but the former suffers in its human
    nature. This distinction may, of course, be
    specious.)

52 Robinson, Henry Wheeler. Suffering, Human and
    Divine. Introduction by Rufus M. Jones. (Great
    Issues of Life Series.) New York: The Macmillan
    Co., 1939. Pp. 139-200, esp. 139-62.

    Robinson argues that if the imagery of the Bible
    is taken seriously, if Jesus actually reveals
    God, and if the Holy Spirit indwells redeemed
    humanity, then suffering must be ascribed to God.
    There are three objections to doing so. Suffering
    would seem to imply (1) frustration or limitation
    and (2) an entanglement in the time process, and
    (3) to be incompatible with God's self-existence,
    independence and sovereignty. Robinson responds

to these objections in the following way: (1)
God's suffering is not the sort of suffering
which is rooted in a physical body or moral failure. Furthermore, it is voluntarily assumed. (God
need not have created a world.) (2) His answer
to the second objection is unclear but appears to
be that if God suffers we are forced to conclude
that time matters for God or that temporal processes are valued by God but not that God is in
time. (3) It may be necessary to compromise
God's absolute independence in order to protect
His love. However, the doctrine of God's passibility is compatible with the claim that everything
else derives its being from Him while He derives
His being from nothing. An assumption running
throughout Robinson's argument is that the best
sort of love is a love which is costly to the
lover, i.e., sacrificial love. The truth of this
assumption may not be obvious. It is also worth
noting that Robinson raises the issue of God's
passibility in the context of a discussion of the
Problem of Evil. If God suffers, human suffering
can be a sharing in, a fellowship with, and a
continuation in time of, God's suffering. Suffering thus acquires significance and the problem
of evil is thereby mitigated. (One suspects that
the belief that the doctrine of a suffering God
mitigates the Problem of Evil is one of the major
reasons for the attraction of that doctrine. If
this is the case, then it is important to determine whether the doctrine in question actually
does make the Problem of Evil easier to handle.)

53 Ross, James Francis. Philosophical Theology.
    Indianapolis and New York: The Bobbs-Merrill Co.,
    Inc., 1969. Pp. 51-63.

Chapter 2, section 2.B. contains a very interesting discussion of God's simplicity. Many statements of the form "God is F" are necessary. Since necessary statements entail one another, these statements will all be logically equivalent. At the same time, the predicates which appear in these statements (e.g., "is wise," "is alive," "is omniscient") are not equivalent since it is possible for something to have some of these predicates without having others. Ross suggests that the doctrine of divine simplicity should be understood as asserting that it is impossible for God to have one divine attribute in the way in which He has it, without also having all the other divine attributes. (The mode in which God has His properties is not itself a property of God, and can only be imperfectly grasped by contrasting it with "our mode of limited, finite existence.") Again, it is logically possible for the essential properties of creatures (e.g., rationality and animality) to have diverse causal conditions. God's independence and necessity, on the other hand, preclude the possibility that His attributes have diverse "entitative preconditions." Ross appears to be rather confusingly interweaving two related but distinct accounts of God's simplicity. According to the first, to say that God is simple is to say that it is impossible for anything to possess an essential divine attribute in the way in which God possesses that attribute without also possessing all the other essential divine attributes (although it is, e.g., possible to be omniscient in the way in which God is omniscient without possessing such contingent divine attributes as the attribute of creating James Ross). According to the second, no divine

47

attribute (regardless of whether it is a necessary
or contingent attribute) could have diverse entitative conditions, i.e., for any two divine attributes F and G, what accounts for the fact that
God has F also accounts for the fact that God
has G.

54 Sommers, Fred. "Why Is There Something and Not
    Nothing?" Analysis, 26 (New Series, 114), (June,
    1966), 177-81.

    Sommers argues that if all God's attributes entail
    one another, then (1) God possesses no attributes
    in common with non-divine beings (for if any non-
    divine being had one divine attribute it would
    have all divine attributes and, thus, be divine),
    (2) in God there is no distinction between potency
    and act (for, where P is a divine attribute, P
    entails P-or-P̄ and -- because the divine attributes
    entail one another -- P-or-P̄ entails P), (3) God
    is perfect (since He lacks nothing which He could
    possibly have), (4) God is unique (for no two
    distinct beings can have any divine attribute in
    common since if they have any divine attribute
    in common they have all divine attributes in
    common and are, therefore, not distinct), and
    (5) God necessarily exists. See Englebretsen's
    reply (#35 above). (For a discussion of Sommers'
    ontological argument see #295 below.)

55 Sturch, Richard Lyman. "The Problem of Divine
    Eternity," Relig Stud, 10 (December, 1974),
    487-93.

    A fairly plausible reply to Pike's claim (#49
    above) that if x produces or sustains y, then x
    is temporal and his claim that a-temporality is
    incompatible with personality. Sturch suggests,

e.g., that "x sustains y" could be interpreted as
"if x wills y, then y and x wills y" and that the
latter does not clearly entail either that x is
temporal or that x stands in temporal relations
to y. According to Sturch, the author/work of
fiction analogy can help us to understand how x
can produce y without being temporally related
to y. Sturch also argues that we can make sense
of the notion of the personality of a timeless
being because we can make sense of the idea that
such a being intends certain things and is affected by what transpires in the world. (The
latter does not entail mutability since "x affects
y" can be interpreted as "y would not be as it is
were not x doing what it does.")

56 Sweeney, Leo. "Bonaventure and Aquinas on the
Divine Being as Infinite," SW J Phil, 5 (Summer,
1974), 71-91.

An interesting historical account of Bonaventure,
Aquinas and their predecessors on the subject of
God's infinity. For Bonaventure "infinity. . .
describes the divine essence with reference to
creatures rather than directly in itself." God
is infinite in so far as He can cause, be present
in, and contain an infinite number of creatures.
Aquinas identifies infinity with the freedom
"from the limiting determination of matter and all
potency."

57 _____. "Infinity in Plotinus," Gregorianium,
38 (1957), 515-35 and 713-32.

It is argued that Plotinus uses "infinity" in two
senses. In its first sense, the term signifies
a lack of form, limit and determination, and is

applied both to that which is below being (evil
and sensible matter) and to that which is above
being (the One). In its second sense, the term
is applied to productive power when that power
extends to a numerically infinite number of effects. (The powers of the One, of Nous and of
Soul are all infinite in this sense.)

58 _____. "John Damascene and Divine Infinity,"
New Scholas, XXXV (Winter, 1961), 76-106.

An interesting examination of the senses in which
John of Damascus uses the expression "God's infinity." God is infinite in so far as He is so
great "as to exceed any term of comparison."
(Thus, His goodness is infinite in so far as it
exceeds any [other] actual and conceivable goodness.) God is infinite in the sense that He is
uncircumscribed by space, time or (finite) intellect. God is infinite in so far as "He can create,
conserve, provide for, govern an infinite number of
creatures" and, finally, God is infinite in so far
as He transcends "all created beings and determination" and is, in this sense, above being. In
addition to its intrinsic interest, this article
illustrates the fact that "infinity" has no single
meaning in theology.

59 Tomberlin, James Edward. "Omniscience and Necessity: Putting Humpty-Dumpty Together Again,"
Phil Forum, II (New Series), (Fall, 1970), 149-51.

Further discussion of an objection to Plantinga
first formulated in the author's "Plantinga's
Puzzles about God and Other Minds" (#60 below).
Tomberlin proposes a reformulation of the concept
of a relational property which he believes will

enable us to retain the notion that God possesses
all His non-relational properties essentially.
Tomberlin's solution is attacked by LaCroix (#45
above).

60 _____. "Plantinga's Puzzles About God and Other
    Minds," Phil Forum, I (New Series), (Spring, 1969),
    pp. 376-84.

This section of Tomberlin's paper contains a criticism of Plantinga's claim that God possesses
His non-relational properties essentially. (Cf.
Plantinga, #50 above.) It is pointed out that
"knows there are no unicorns" is a property which
God has if He is omniscient, which is not relational in Plantinga's sense (since it does not
entail the existence of a contingent being distinct
from God), and which is not essential (for there
might have been unicorns). Tomberlin criticizes
Plantinga's formulation of the distinction between
essential and accidental properties and proposes
a new formulation of the distinction. Plantinga
has a brief response to this on page 147 of his
"The Incompatibility of Freedom with Determinism:
A Reply" (The Philosophical Forum, II [N.S.],
Fall, 1970, 141-8). The author develops his objection further in "Omniscience and Necessity:
Putting Humpty-Dumpty Together Again" (#59 above).

61 Westphal, Merold. "Temporality and Finitism in
    Hartshorne's Theism," Rev Metaph, XIX (March,
    1966), 550-64.

Hartshorne has argued that if God knows, loves
or causes contingent states of affairs, then
God's knowing, loving or causing those states of
affairs must, itself, be contingent. Westphal
agrees, but argues that Hartshorne is mistaken

when he supposes that God's acts of knowing,
loving or causing are temporal, mutable, and
dependent. There is no absurdity in supposing
that God contingently but immutably and eternally
knows, loves and chooses this contingent, changing,
and temporal world. Again, while knowledge and
love may be logically dependent upon the object
known or loved, it does not follow that knowledge
and love are causally dependent upon the object
known or loved. Westphal concludes by attempting
to show that this view is the view of Thomas
Aquinas. See Hartshorne's reply (#39 above).

62 Woolcombe, Kenneth J. "The Pain of God," Scot J
    Theol, XX (June, 1967), 129-48.

    A critical but appreciative survey of twentieth
    century Christian theologians on the subject of
    divine passibility. While this article does not
    advance the argument, it does provide a useful
    summary of theological opinion.

                    God's Necessity

Note: Many discussions of the ontological and cosmolo-
       gical arguments contain useful observations on the
       concept of necessary being. See especially #s 218,
       244, 245, 250, 268, 304, 333 and 340.

63 Adams, Robert Merrihew. "Has It Been Proved That
    All Real Existence is Contingent?" Amer Phil
    Quart, 8 (July, 1971), 284-91.

    According to Adams, we cannot show that all real
    existence is contingent (1) by arguing that any-
    thing which can be conceived to exist can be con-
    ceived not to exist, (2) by arguing that necessary
    truths express conditions which must be met if

our concepts are to apply but never assert that
a concept does apply, or (3) by arguing that it is
not "possible to build bridges between mere
abstractions and concrete existence" (Findley).

64 Bennett, Daniel Clark. "Deity and Events," J Phil,
    LXIV (December 21, 1967), 815-24.

    This article contains an interesting, but some-
    what implausible attempt to explicate God's neces-
    sity in terms of omnitemporality. Thus, e.g.,
    "God is a necessary being" is explicated as "if
    anything is God, then for any time, it exists at
    that time," and "What is God is necessarily God"
    is explicated as "if anything is God, then, for any
    time, if it exists at that time it is God at
    that time."

65 Clarke, Bowman Lafayette. "Linguistic Analysis and
    the Philosophy of Religion," Monist, 47 (July,
    1963), 365-86.

    When it is said that necessary propositions "say
    nothing" this can (only) mean either that they do
    not state contingent facts or that they are unin-
    terpreted. The first is obvious and the second
    is false. When it is said that necessary proposi-
    tions "reflect the use of words," this can (only)
    mean either that their use discloses something
    about the use of language or that they assert
    something about language. The first is true of
    all propositions, and the second is false of
    many necessary propositions. Logically true
    propositions are propositions whose truth is
    determined by syntactical and semantical rules.
    God's existence is necessary if a concept of God
    can be formulated in an adequate scientific

language and if the proposition that God
exists is true, given the syntactical and seman-
tical rules of that language. In the language
of Aristotelian physics and metaphysics, God is
defined as First Mover. First Cause, etc., and
the Five Ways can be regarded as attempts to show
that, given the rules of this language, "God
exists" must be true. Unfortunately, the language
of Aristotelian physics and metaphysics can no
longer be regarded as scientifically accurate.

66 Findley, John Niemeyer. "Can God's Existence Be
    Disproved?" Mind, LVII (April, 1948), 176-83.
    (Reprinted in #278 below, pp. 111-22, and in
    #923 below, pp. 47-56.)

In this influential article, Findley maintains
that a logically contingent being, i.e., a being
which is caused to exist or merely happens to
exist, cannot be an adequate object of religious
attitudes. He then proceeds to offer the following
argument: (1) God is, by definition, an appropriate object of religious attitudes. (2) Any
being which is an appropriate object of religious
attitudes must be a logically necessary being.
(3) It is logically true that no existential
propositions are necessary (for necessary propositions merely reflect the conventions of our language). Therefore, (4) God cannot exist. Findley
has since abandoned the third premiss. (See,
e.g., his otherwise undistinguished "Some Reflections on Necessary Existence" in Process and Divinity, edited by William Reese and Eugene Freeman
[LaSalle, Illinois: Open Court Pub. Co., 1964]
in which he concedes that necessary existence can
be meaningfully attributed to a perfect being.)
See the replies of Hughes and Rainer (#s 71 and 75

below). Findley's notion that God is the appropriate object of religious attitudes is discussed at more length below (#193).

67 _____. "God's Non-Existence," Mind, LVIII (July, 1949), 352-4. (Reprinted in #923 below, pp. 71-5.)

This response to Hughes and Rainer (#s 71 and 75 below) does not advance the discussion of the major points at issue. At the end of his reply Findley asks whether there is a genuine difference between the "analogical theism" of his opponents and an atheism which makes non-existent ideals the focus of religious attitudes. (Findley's atheism appears to be logically incoherent. If his own argument is sound, then these non-existent ideals can only be appropriate objects of religious attitudes if they are [necessarily] existent.)

68 Franklin, Richard Langdon. "Necessary Being," Austl J Phil, XXXV (August, 1957), 97-110.

Franklin makes two major points. (1) "Necessary being" acquires its meaning in the context of the contingency argument (for necessary being provides the only possible answer to the question "Why does contingent being exist?"). (2) Logically necessary being should be distinguished from (what others have called) factually necessary being. A being is factually necessary provided that "if it exists, it makes no sense to ask why or where it came into existence, or why it is as it is; and further that if anything exists, it exists." Franklin believes that the notion of a factually necessary being is free from the difficulties which beset the notion of a logically necessary being.

69   Hick, John Harwood. "God as Necessary Being," J
       Phil, LVII (October 27 and November 10, 1960),
       725-34.

In this important essay, Hick distinguishes between
a logically necessary being and a factually necessary being. A logically necessary being is a
being whose non-existence is logically impossible.
A factually necessary being is an eternal, indestructible, incorruptible being which is not
causally dependent upon anything for its own
existence and which is itself the cause of everything else. The notion of a logically necessary
being is incoherent because existential propositions cannot be necessary. The notion of a factually necessary being is coherent and it is in
this sense that God has been said to be necessary
in the Christian tradition. Although many
philosophers find this position attractive, it is
subject to at least two difficulties. (1) Is
Findley mistaken when he says that an appropriate
object of religious attitudes cannot merely happen
to exist? Hick argues that one should not say
that God merely happens to exist both because this
implies that there is a genuine alternative to
logically contingent existence (viz., logically
necessary existence) and because it implies that
if circumstances had been different God would
not have existed (and that, therefore, God's
existence is dependent upon the non-occurrence
of those circumstances). Nevertheless, the fact
remains that (if Hick is correct) God's existence
is logically contingent and there is no explanation for His existence. God's existence is, therefore, simply a brute fact. (2) Can a being which
is not logically necessary be factually necessary?
Is it intelligible to suppose that a being cannot

56

have a cause if the existence of that being is not
logically necessary? It should be noted that much
of the plausibility of Hick's position depends
upon the truth of the assumption that logically
necessary existence is impossible, and the truth
of this assumption has recently come to seem
less obvious.

70 _____. "Necessary Being," Scot J Theol, 14
(December, 1961), 353-69.

An expansion of the argument which was first presented in the author's "God as Necessary Being"
(#69 above). There are no major new points, and
most of the earlier paper is incorporated in this
paper. Nevertheless, some of the new material is
of interest (e.g., the last section in which
Hick compares his view of God's aseity with the
[similar] views of Karl Barth).

71 Hughes, George E. "Has God's Existence Been Disproved?" Mind, LVIII (January, 1949), 67-74.
(Reprinted in #923 below, pp. 56-67.)

A reply to Findley (#66 above). Hughes argues
(1) that the most that has been established by
contemporary analytic philosophy is that logico-
mathematical propositions cannot be existential and
that empirical existential propositions cannot
be necessary, (2) that we must distinguish
between a proposition (a) being self-evident to
"anyone who thinks clearly and thoroughly understands the subject matter," (b) being self-evident
to human reason at its best, and (c) being self-
evident to some actual human being, and (3) that
God's necessity can be construed in the following
way: Let a. . . n be the complete list of God's

57

necessary characteristics and let p be the proposition that a being possessing characteristics a. . .
n exists. (p is not a tautology for existence is
not a characteristic and is, therefore, not included in a. . . n.) "A being which did not
exist necessarily would not be God" can be construed as "only if p is a necessary proposition
should we call a being possessing characteristics
a. . . n 'God'." This interpretation of God's
necessity is intelligible in spite of the fact
that (since we are unacquainted with many of the
characteristics which belong on the list, and do
not fully understand many of the characteristics
with which we are acquainted which appear on the
list) we do not see the necessity of p.

72 Kenny, Anthony John Patrick. "God and Necessity,"
    British Analytic Philosophy. Edited by Bernard
    Williams and Alan Montefiore. (International
    Library of Philosophy and Scientific Method.)
    London: Routledge & Kegan Paul; New York: The
    Humanities Press, 1966. Pp. 131-51.

Most of this essay is devoted to an exposition of
recent discussions of a set of interrelated issues
-- whether necessary propositions are informative, whether existential propositions can be
necessary, whether "God exists" is necessarily
true, etc. Kenny's exposition is useful and lucid.
Towards the end of his essay the author suggests
that the Leibnizian notion of a logically necessary being should be rejected, but points out
that "necessary being" has other senses. Following
Aristotle, necessary propositions may be defined
as propositions which cannot change in truth
value. Since God is (by definition) eternal and
since He possesses His attributes unchangingly,
"God exists" and (e.g.) "God is good" cannot

change in truth value. From this it follows that
these propositions are necessary in the "Aristotelian" sense. Kenny maintains that recent
discussions have not shown that this conception
of necessary being is incoherent.

73 _____. "Necessary Being," Sophia, I (October,
    1962), 1-8.

An interesting exploration of Aristotelian and
Thomistic interpretations of necessity. Kenny
suggests that a necessary proposition could be
construed as a proposition which can at no time
change its truth value. (Notice that not
all propositions which are necessary in this
sense are logically necessary.) A being could
be regarded as necessary "if it is, always will
be, and always was, and cannot, nor could not,
nor will be able not to be." (God and an everlasting Lucretian atom would both be necessary
beings in this sense.) On a Leibnizian view, God's
necessity depends upon the logical necessity of
the proposition that God exists. On the proposed
view, the necessity of the proposition that God
exists depends upon certain properties of God
(His everlastingness, and indestructibility).

74 Plantinga, Alvin Carl. "Necessary Being," Faith
   and Philosophy, Philosophical Studies in Religion
   and Ethics. Edited by Alvin Plantinga. Grand
   Rapids, Michigan: William B. Eerdmans Pub. Co.,
   1964. Pp. 97-108.

After disposing of an ontological argument,
Plantinga proceeds to define the notion of a
necessary being. We can ask why something exists,
be told that it exists because something else
exists, ask why this second thing exists and so on.

A necessary being may be defined as a being which provides a final answer, putting an end to this series of questions and answers. Such a being must be a being which (logically) cannot have a cause. It is a logically necessary truth that if the God of classical theism exists, everything else causally depends upon Him and He causally depends upon nothing. It follows that the God of classical theism is a necessary being in the defined sense. (Plantinga's discussion leaves a certain ambiguity unresolved. It would seem that if the God of classical theism is to provide a satisfactory "final answer" which puts an end to the series of questions and answers about existence, then it must not only be true that causal independence is analytically connected with divinity, it must also be true that the being who is God, e.g., Yahweh, [logically] cannot have a cause. If the latter is not true, then even though the being who is God in fact has no cause [and cannot both have a cause and be God] the being who is God could have had a cause, and if the being who is God could have had a cause, the question "Why does God exist?" is logically in order.)

75 Rainer, A. C. "Necessity and God," Mind, LVIII (January, 1949), 75-7. (Reprinted in #923 below, pp. 67-71.)

A reply to Findley (#66 above). Rainer's most significant contention is that the necessity of God's existence is not logical necessity but "God's complete actuality, indestructibility, aseitas or independence of limiting conditions."

(See also #s 1, 13, 443, 447,
548, 552, 553 and 559)

76 Bonifacio, Armando F. "On Capacity Limiting State-
    ments," Mind, LXXIV (January, 1965), 87-8.

Either "God can make things which He cannot control" or "God cannot make things which He cannot
control" would appear to entail that God is not
omnipotent. Bonifacio concedes that the paradox
can be resolved if the second statement is construed as "Everything which God can make God can
control." He argues, however, that it should
instead be construed as "There is at least one
thing which God cannot make and this is that which
He cannot control," i.e., as $(\exists y)(-Mgy \cdot -Cgy)$.
He then shows that, given this construction, the
second alternative does entail that God is not
omnipotent. (It isn't clear, however, that this
construction will do. If God can both make and
control any possible being, then God cannot make
things which He cannot control, but there is no
possible being which is such that it can neither
be made by Him nor controlled by Him.)

77 Cargile, James. "On Omnipotence," Nous, I (May,
    1967), 201-5.

Cargile argues that an insuperable problem is
created by any attempt to define God's omnipotence
as the power to create any state of affairs such
that "God creates s" is consistent. It is logically possible that God create a chicken which
has the property of having been created by a

being which never at any time has the power to
create a duck, and it is logically possible
that God create a duck which has the property of
having been created by a being which never at any
time has the power to create a chicken. (Both of
these statements may be questioned. It is, for
example, necessarily true that if God creates a
chicken which has the property of having been
created by a being which never has the power to
create a duck, then God never has the power to
create a duck. From this necessary truth and the
first statement, it follows that it is logically
possible that God never has the power to create a
duck. But is this possible? It appears to be
logically false that "God" could be appropriately
applied to a being which lacked the power to create
a duck.) If God's omnipotence is defined as the
power to do all that He can consistently do, it
follows that God both can and cannot create chickens and ducks. However, Cargile points out that
in order to create a man not created by God, the
only power which one needs is the power to create
a man. The rest automatically follows from the
fact that one is not God. Since God has the power
to create men, we ought not to say that He is less
powerful than some other being which can create
a man not created by God. Similarly, to create a
chicken which has the property of having been
created by someone who cannot create ducks, all
that is needed is the power to create chickens.
The rest follows from the fact that one cannot
create ducks. And so on. In the light of these
considerations Cargile proposes the following
definition: x is omnipotent =df. For every action
A, if it is logically possible that there should
be an agent y, such that y can do A, then there

is an action B such that for every agent z, if z
can do A, then z's doing B amounts to z's doing A,
and x can do B. (However, while it is logically
possible for someone to ride a bicycle, is there
any action -- consideration of the incarnation
aside -- which amounts to riding a bicycle and
which God can perform?)

78 Cowan, Joseph Lloyd. "The Paradox of Omnipotence,"
    Analysis, 25 (Supplement), (January, 1965),
    102-8.

It is argued that if omnipotence is defined as the
ability to perform all logically possible tasks,
then no being can be omnipotent, for the power to
perform some logically possible tasks is incompatible with the power to perform other logically
possible tasks. For a further development of this
argument see "The Paradox of Omnipotence Revisited," #79 below.

79 _____. "The Paradox of Omnipotence Revisited,"
    Can J Phil, III (March, 1974), 435-45.

Cowan points out that the strategy of the Stone
Paradox is to find two powers each of which is
logically possible when taken by itself but which
cannot both be consistently ascribed to the same
individual. If this strategy is successful we
are entitled to conclude that any being will lack
at least one power, from which it follows that
no being is omnipotent. An unlimited power to
lift stones and a power to make stones one cannot
lift are powers of the required sort. Cowan
argues that the second power (like the power to
build a boat which will carry its builder and
which its builder can carry, or the power to

control one's temper) is irreducibly reflexive.
It is a real power (most of us can make things we
cannot lift) which is not equivalent to the power
to make stones which others cannot lift (nor to
the power to make and lift stones of any weight,
size, shape or texture, nor to any other power),
and which is incompatible with the power to lift
any stone. Cowan's argument should be taken
seriously even though it seems paradoxical to say
that a lack of this power involves a weakness
or infirmity in those cases in which one's lack
of this power is a direct consequence of one's
unlimited stone lifting power.

80 Fitch, Frederic B. "A Logical Analysis of Some
    Value Concepts," J Sym Log, 28 (June, 1963),
    135-42.

    This article contains an interesting proof of the
    proposition that if a being is omnipotent in the
    sense that it is logically possible that it brings
    about every actual state of affairs, then it in
    fact brings about every actual state of affairs.
    See Walton's discussion of this proof and its
    implications (#107 below).

81 Frankfurt, Harry G. "The Logic of Omnipotence,"
    Phil Rev, LXXIII (April, 1964), 262-3.

    Frankfurt points out that the Stone Paradox is not
    a problem for those philosophers who (like Des-
    cartes) assume that omnipotence includes the
    ability to perform logically impossible tasks.
    If an omnipotent being can perform logically
    impossible tasks, it can both create and lift
    stones which it cannot lift.

82 Geach, Peter Thomas. "Can God Fail to Keep Prom-
    ises?" Philosophy, 52 (January, 1977), 93-5.

    A reply to Harrison (#87 below). Geach argues
    that God cannot break promises because (1) He is
    truth, and because (2) He cannot help having made
    a promise once He has made it and cannot help
    being the kind of being who keeps whatever prom-
    ises He makes. See Harrison's response (#88
    below).

83 _____. "Omnipotence," Philosophy, 43 (April,
    1973), 7-20.

    Geach considers and rejects four "theories of
    omnipotence" -- that God can do everything, that
    God can do everything which is logically possible,
    that God can do everything which it is logically
    possible for God to do, and that God can bring
    about any future possibility which it is logically
    possible for God to bring about. Counter examples
    suggest that God is not omnipotent in any of these
    ways. Geach concludes that the doctrine of divine
    omnipotence (the doctrine that God has the ability
    to do everything) is incoherent, but adds that it
    does not follow that the doctrine that God is
    almighty is incoherent, where that doctrine is
    understood to imply that God has power over all
    things, that (because all power derives from God)
    "no creature can compete with God in power," and
    that God does whatever He wills to do. Geach's
    discussions of the first two theories of omnipo-
    tence are of more than average interest. (His
    counter examples to the third and fourth theories
    are somewhat suspect. It is true that God cannot
    now bring it about that someone who has lost her
    virginity never loses it, and it is true that God

cannot break His promises. Nevertheless, the
description of these feats may conceal hidden
contradictions, e.g., that God [a being who,
necessarily, cannot break promises] breaks a promise. If these descriptions do conceal contradictions, then they are not descriptions of feats
which God cannot in fact perform but could perform
if the third or fourth theory of omnipotence were
correct.) See Gibbs' and Harrison's replies
(#s 86 and 87 below).

84 Gellman, Jerome. "Omnipotence and Impeccability,"
    New Scholas, LI (Winter, 1977), 21-37.

    A reply to Pike (#100 below). Gellman argues
    that the doctrine of divine omnipotence is a
    partial explication of the doctrine of divine
    perfection and must, therefore, be understood in
    the context of that doctrine. Omnipotence should
    be defined as the power to do everything which it
    is logically possible for an essentially perfect
    being to do. Since it is logically impossible
    for an essentially perfect being to perform morally
    wrong actions, the fact that it cannot do so is
    compatible with its omnipotence. (It is, of
    course, logically impossible for such a being to
    perform wrong acts. If, however, those actions
    which are in fact wrong [e.g., killing innocents]
    are only contingently wrong then [since it is
    logically possible that these actions are not
    wrong] it is logically possible for God to perform
    them. In order to block this move, Gellman needs
    an additional premiss, viz., that those actions
    which are morally wrong [e.g., killing innocents]
    are necessarily wrong.)

85 _____. "The Paradox of Omnipotence, and Perfection," Sophia, XIV (October, 1975), 31-9.

A paradox arises when we consider actions the performance of which would diminish God's power or ability to control things, for it would seem that God either can or cannot perform these actions and that in either case He is not omnipotent. This paradox can be resolved by distinguishing between an essentially omnipotent being and a materially omnipotent being. If God is essentially omnipotent, it is logically impossible for Him to perform an act which would diminish His power. Therefore, the fact that He cannot do so does not count against His omnipotence. If God is materially omnipotent, then the fact that He _can_ divest himself of power (and, thus, of His omnipotence) does not show that He is not _in_ _fact_ omnipotent and so, once again, no problem arises. This solution, however, creates a new paradox. If an essentially omnipotent being cannot do something which a materially omnipotent being _can_ do, it would appear to follow that the essentially omnipotent being is not genuinely omnipotent. Gellman argues that what is crucial to the concept of omnipotence is the notion of perfect (i.e., worshipful) power and proposes to define omnipotence as the power to do all those and only those logically possible things which do not entail any imperfection in the doer. If divesting oneself of power involves diminishing one's perfection, then we have a solution to both paradoxes. No being can be (either essentially _or_ _materially_) omnipotent in the defined sense and have the ability to divest itself of power. Hence, the second paradox will not arise. Again, since any act which divests God of power diminishes His

perfection, the ability to perform such acts is
not included within the scope of omnipotence as
defined and, therefore, the fact that God cannot
perform them will not count against His omnipotence. The first paradox is, thus, resolved as
well. (Gellman argues that we do not actually
need the assumption that divesting oneself of
power diminishes one's perfection but his discussion at this point is somewhat obscure.)

86 Gibbs, Benjamin. "Can God Do Evil?" Philosophy,
    50 (October, 1975), 466-9.

    A reply to Geach's "Omnipotence" (#83 above) in
    which (1) Gibbs argues that in order to act well
    God must be able to act badly, and (2) accuses
    Geach of confusing the ability to act badly (which
    God must have) with a tendency to act badly (which
    -- given God's omniscience, perfect rationality,
    etc. -- God cannot have).

87 Harrison, Jonathan. "Geach on God's Alleged Ability
    to do Evil," Philosophy, 51 (April, 1976),
    208-15.

    Harrison argues that Geach (#83 above) has failed
    to show that God is unable to do evil or to break
    His promises. (He concedes that if the being who
    is God were to do evil it would follow that He
    was not properly described as "God," and that
    because evil is foreign to God's nature [He is not
    disposed to do evil] we can be assured God will
    not do evil. Cf. Pike, #100 below.) See Geach's
    reply, #82 above.

88 _____. "Geach on Harrison on Geach on God,"
   <u>Philosophy</u>, 52 (April, 1977), 223-6.

A response to Geach (#82 above) which clarifies
some of the issues between them. Harrison argues
that "God is truth" does not entail "God can't
break promises," and that arguments of the form
"I can't help p, I can't help that (p implies q),
therefore I can't help q" are invalid. (His
counter example [which was first mentioned in
passing in #87 above] is "I could not help it
that the only thing I wanted to do was go to bed,
nor could I help it that if the only thing I wanted
to do was go to bed [and I was not prevented] I
would go to bed, but I could help going to bed
because if I had wanted to stay up badly enough
I could easily have overcome my desire to go to
bed." It is not clear that this will work. Let
us concede that I cannot help it that if going to
bed is the only thing I want to do I will do it.
What I want is, however, either within my control
or it is not. If it is within my control, then
I <u>can</u> help it that the only thing I want to do
is go to bed. If it is not within my control then
it is not clear that the fact that I would not
have gone to bed <u>if</u> my wants had been different
shows that I could help going to bed.)

89 Joyce, George Hayward. <u>Principles of Natural Theol-
   ogy</u>. (Stonyhurst Philosophical Series.) London,
   New York, etc.: Longmans, Green and Co., 1923;
   New York: AMS Press, 1972. Pp. 412-38.

In chapter VIII, one of the most able Neo-Scholastics discusses God's omnipotence. The section
on the scope of omnipotence is particularly interesting. Since the object of power is "being
which is causally produced," God's power does not

include the ability to produce things which
(since they are self-contradictory) lack any
sort of being or the ability to produce things
the existence of which is incompatible with their
having been produced. Nor can God do things "which
are inconsistent with infinite perfection, and
only possible to a finite agent," such as alter
His purposes or do evil.

90   Keene, G. B. "Capacity-Limiting Statements," Mind,
     LXX (April, 1961), 251-2.

     A rather plausible response to Mayo's "Mr. Keene
     on Omnipotence" (#99 below). The solution pro-
     posed by Keene in this response and in his earlier
     note (#91 below) is, perhaps, most clearly stated
     by C. Wade Savage in "The Paradox of the Stone"
     (#103 below).

91   _____. "A Simpler Solution to the Paradox of
     Omnipotence," Mind, LXIX (January, 1960), 74-5.

     A reply to Mackie's "Evil and Omnipotence" (#94
     below). "x can't make a being x can't control"
     is equivalent to "Everything x can make, x can
     control." Since the latter is compatible with
     the omnipotence of x, the former must be compat-
     ible with the omnipotence of x.

92   Kuntz, Paul Grimley. "The Sense and Nonsense of
     Omnipotence," Relig Stud, 3 (April, 1968),
     525-38.

     Kuntz weaves together material from such diverse
     sources as Laurence Sterne, Feuerbach, Freud,
     McTaggart, Santayana and Whitehead in order to
     construct a critique of the concept of unlimited

70

power. The article is eclectic and synthetic, and
characterized by long quotations. Nevertheless,
in spite of its comparative unoriginality, it does
perform a valuable service, for in drawing this
material together, Kuntz provides a critical
perspective on the doctrine of omnipotence which
is frequently ignored by those who are concerned
with the logical analysis of the concept of
omnipotence.

93 _____. "The Sense and Nonsense of Omnipotence:
   What does it mean to say 'with God all things are
   possible?'" The Seventh Inter-American Congress
   of Philosophy, under the auspices of the Canadian
   Philosophical Association, Proceedings of the
   Congress. Vol. 1. Québec: Les Presses de l'Uni-
   versité Laval, 1967. Pp. 122-31.

In the first part of his paper, Kuntz wonders
whether "omnipotent" is only a courteous title
or hyperbolic term which should not be taken literally, suggests that omnipotence is not a necessary
attribute of God, and calls our attention to the
fact that "omni"-terms vary with respect to logical type. The second part of this paper is devoted
to a rather unoriginal comparison of Hartshorne's
God and the God of classical theism. See
Wainwright's reply (#106 below).

94 Mackie, John Leslie. "Evil and Omnipotence," Mind,
   LXIV (April, 1955), pp. 210-2.

In the latter part of his article, Mackie argues
that there is a Paradox of Omnipotence which is
similar to the Paradox of Sovereignty. If a body
is fully sovereign it would seem that it can
abrogate its sovereignty but, of course, if it
were to do so, it would cease to be fully sovereign. Analogously, God either can or cannot

create beings which He cannot control. If He cannot do so, He is not omnipotent and yet if He can do so, then if He does do so, He ceases to be omnipotent. (It looks as if there is a serious lacuna in the argument. Mackie's argument would seem to require that God's ability to create beings which he cannot control be incompatible with His omnipotence and yet what appears to follow from His possession of this power is not that He is not omnipotent but that if He exercises this power, He is not omnipotent. Of course, one might maintain that if God can create beings which He cannot control, then it is possible that there be beings which He cannot control, and that this possibility is incompatible with divine omnipotence. This does not, however, appear to be what Mackie has in mind.) Mackie suggests that we distinguish orders of sovereignty and omnipotence. The first order involves an unlimited power to make laws governing the actions of individuals or an unlimited power to act upon individuals. The second order involves an unlimited power to make laws about laws or to determine what powers things will have. No continuing legislative body can always be sovereign in both senses (although it can always be fully sovereign in the first sense). Similarly, no being can always be omnipotent in both senses (although it can always be omnipotent in the first sense). (Mackie's argument will work only if we conflate "possessing the second order power" and "exercising the second order power.") See Plantinga's reply (#101 below) and Steur's reply (#548 below).

72

95 _____. "Omnipotence," <u>Sophia</u>, I (July, 1962), 13-25.

This very interesting essay deserves more attention. There is a decent discussion of the problems involved in defining "omnipotence." (God's
omnipotence is tentatively defined as the power to
make it be that x, where God's making it be that
x is neither paradoxical nor incompatible with
logically necessary aspects of His nature.)
Mackie argues that powers (necessarily?) presuppose the existence of laws and structural facts
which enable an agent to do certain things if he
chooses to do them, but that it is unclear what
laws (causal laws? necessary truths?) sustain
God's powers. He returns to the Paradox of Omnipotence. (See "Evil and Omnipotence," #94 above.)
Mackie admits that it may be possible to escape
the Paradox by arguing that because it is logically impossible for there to be beings which an
omnipotent being cannot control, the inability
to create such beings is compatible with omnipotence. He points out, however, that one might
(alternatively) argue that because it is logically impossible for an omnipotent being to control a being which an omnipotent being cannot
control, the fact that an omnipotent being cannot
control such beings if he creates them is compatible with his omnipotence. (In spite of the fact
that God's <u>not</u> <u>controlling</u> a being which cannot
be controlled would not count against His omnipotence, is it clear that the <u>existence</u> of such
beings would not do so?) Mackie further argues
that the distinction between bringing something
about and merely permitting it to happen rests
upon the exertion of effort involved in bringing
something about and the inadvertence or inattention

which is normally involved in letting something
happen and that, therefore, this distinction
cannot be applied to the behavior of an omnipotent being.

96   Macquarrie, John. "Divine Omnipotence," The Seventh
      Inter-American Congress of Philosophy, under the
      auspices of the Canadian Philosophical Association,
      Proceedings of the Congress. Vol. 1. Québec: Les
      Presses de l'Université Laval, 1967. Pp. 132-7.

Macquarrie suggests that we should explore the
religious roots of the concept of omnipotence,
and proceeds to discuss its biblical background.
Macquarrie argues that omnipotence "belongs to a
group of divine attributes which together try to
express the overwhelmingness of God." If "omnipotence" is construed literally, we will become
involved in paradoxes. Omnipotence should be
understood as a symbol for a creative loving
power which "lets things be" or "stand out from
nothing." To understand this "power of being"
we must begin with human power, but it is, nevertheless, "other than" human power and free from its
limitations. A decent presentation of a familiar
point of view. See Wainwright's reply (#106
below).

97   McTaggart, John McTaggart Ellis, Some Dogmas of
      Religion. London: Edward Arnold, 1906; New York:
      Kraus Reprint Co., 1969. Pp. 202-20 and 224-34.

McTaggart's discussion of omnipotence (Section
166 ff.) is of some interest in spite of the fact
that he assumes that omnipotence must include the
ability to do logically impossible things.
McTaggart raises three objections. (1) The concept
of omnipotence (so understood) is incoherent.

(2) Personality and self-consciousness appear to
presuppose consciousness of an Other. If that is
the case, an omnipotent person cannot choose not
to create and is not, therefore, truly omnipotent.
(This objection does not -- in any obvious way --
depend upon McTaggart's non-standard interpretation
of omnipotence.) (3) If a being is able to do
impossible as well as possible things and creates
a world which contains evil, then that being is
not good. In section 183 ff. McTaggart argues
that if a being which is limited only by its own
nature (and is, thus, closer to what is normally
meant by "an omnipotent being") creates a world
which contains evil, then that being is not good,
for the only way in which that being's nature
could prevent it from creating a world which is
wholly good is by preventing it from willing a
world which is wholly good. (For a further discussion of this point see the annotation to #503
below.)

98 Mavrodes, George Ion. "Some Puzzles Concerning
    Omnipotence," Phil Rev, LXXII (April, 1963),
    221-3.

An attempt to resolve the Stone Paradox. Mavrodes'
major point is that since God is (essentially?)
omnipotent, "a stone too heavy for God to lift"
does not describe a possible stone. It follows
that "creating a stone too heavy for God to lift"
does not describe a logically possible task.
Therefore the fact that God cannot perform this
task does not count against His omnipotence.

99 Mayo, Bernard. "Mr. Keene on Omnipotence," <u>Mind</u>,
    LXX (April, 1961), 249-50.

    A reply to Keene's "A Simpler Solution to the
    Paradox of Omnipotence" (#91 above). Though
    frequently cited, Mayo's objections to Keene's
    equation of "x can't make a being x can't control"
    and "Everything x can make, x can control" are
    not convincing. See Keene's response (#90 above).
    Mayo concludes by suggesting that because "things
    which an omnipotent being can't control" is
    self-contradictory, the fact that a being cannot
    make such things fails to count against its
    omnipotence.

100 Pike, Nelson Craft. "Omnipotence and God's Ability
     to Sin," <u>Amer</u> <u>Phil</u> <u>Quart</u>, 6 (July, 1969),
     208-16.

    There appears to be conflict between the fact
    that there are states of affairs which are con-
    sistent but which it would be sinful to bring
    about, the doctrine of God's omnipotence, and
    the claim that God is unable to sin. This article
    contains an excellent discussion of Aquinas's
    attempt to solve this problem and Pike's own
    solution. Pike argues that "God" is a title
    which contingently applies to whatever indivi-
    dual happens to be God. Since this title is
    analytically connected with sinlessness, it is
    impossible for an individual to both bear this
    title (to be God) and sin. Nevertheless, because
    the title applies contingently, the individual
    who bears it (e.g., Yahweh) may be <u>able</u> to sin
    (although if that being were to <u>exercise</u> that
    power it would not be God). Pike concludes
    that (1) God cannot sin, in the sense that "being

God" and "not sinning" are analytically connected, (2) that God can sin in the **sense** that the individual who bears the title "God" has the power to bring about states of affairs which it would be evil to bring about (if any being lacked that power it would not be omnipotent), and (3) that God cannot sin in the sense that His nature or character provides "material assurance that He will not act in that way." There may be another solution. In classical Christian theology, divinity is a logically essential feature of whatever individual is God and, hence, if "God" applies to an individual it necessarily applies to that individual. It follows that not only is it necessarily the case that all beings who are God do not sin, it is also necessarily the case that the individual who is God (e.g., Yahweh) does not sin. Now it is sometimes supposed that statements of the form "(possible) state of affairs s is good (bad)" or "bringing about state of affairs s is good (bad)" are necessarily, though perhaps not analytically, true. If this is the case, then -- since the individual who is God (e.g., Yahweh) is necessarily sinless -- it would appear to follow that it is logically impossible for that individual to bring about any state of affairs the bringing about of which would be morally reprehensible. Hence, (if God's omnipotence does not include the ability to bring about a state of affairs which it is logically impossible for Him to bring about) the fact that the individual in question cannot bring these states of affairs about does not count against its omnipotence. See Gellman's reply, #84 above.

77

101 Plantinga, Alvin Carl. God and Other Minds, A
     Study of the Rational Justification of Belief
     in God. (Contemporary Philosophy.) Ithaca,
     New York: Cornell University Press, 1967.
     Pp. 168-73.

     Chapter 7 contains a brief but valuable discus-
     sion of Mackie's Paradox of Omnipotence (see
     #94 above). After considering and rejecting
     several (superficially plausible) definitions
     of omnipotence, Plantinga proceeds to argue that
     "It is possible that (God is omnipotent and it
     is possible that God is not omnipotent)" is either
     true or false. If it is true, then God's ability
     to create beings which He cannot control is
     compatible with His omnipotence (for if that
     proposition is true, the possibility of there
     being things which God cannot control is compat-
     ible with God's being actually omnipotent). If
     it is false, then (since God is necessarily
     omnipotent) it is logically impossible for anyone
     to create a being which God (i.e., an omnipotent
     being) is unable to control and, hence, the fact
     that God cannot do so does not count against
     His omnipotence.

102 Ross, James Francis. Philosophical Theology.
     Indianapolis and New York: The Bobbs-Merrill
     Co., Inc., 1969. Pp. 195-221.

     Chapter 5 contains an excellent discussion of
     omnipotence. Ross points out that God's power
     has usually been understood in terms of what
     God can do and "omnipotence" has, therefore,
     been defined as the power to do everything which
     meets certain conditions, e.g., everything that
     is intrinsically consistent, or everything which
     is such that a perfect being can consistently

78

do it, etc.). Ross tries to show that definitions of this sort are invariably defective
(either because they are circular, or because
the definiens fails to exclude things which an
omnipotent being clearly cannot do, or because
the definiens excludes **things** which should
fall within the power of an omnipotent being,
etc.). It is suggested that God's power can
be more fruitfully understood in terms of His
choice of contingent states of affairs and that
"omnipotence" may be defined in the following
way: S is omnipotent if and only if for every
logically contingent state of affairs, p, p's
being the case (p's not being the case) is
logically equivalent to the effective choice,
by S, that p is the case (that not-p is the
case). Ross recognizes that this definition
implies that if an omnipotent being exists,
it effectively chooses those contingent states
of affairs which consist in our freely choosing
this or that but argues (in chapter 6, section 5)
that this involves no inconsistency. It is also
assumed that God necessarily exists, for if an
omnipotent being exists contingently, there are
contingent states of affairs which are not logically equivalent to its effective choice of
those states of affairs (viz., those states
of affairs which obtain in possible worlds in
which it does not exist) and from this it would
follow that it is not omnipotent in the defined
sense.

103 Savage, Clarence Wade. "The Paradox of the Stone,"
     Phil Rev, LXXVI (January, 1967), 74-9.

     A very plausible resolution of the Stone Paradox.
     In essence, Savage argues that "if x cannot

create a stone which x cannot lift, then there
is at least one task which x cannot perform
(and so x is not omnipotent)" is not necessarily
true. "x cannot create a stone which x cannot
lift" is equivalent to "if x can create a stone,
then x can lift it" and the later does not entail
that x is limited in power. God's inability
to create stones which He cannot lift is in
fact a logical consequence of His unlimited
power to make and lift stones. It is not, therefore, a real inability.

104 Swinburne, Richard G. "Duty and the Will of God,"
     Can J Phil, IV (December, 1974), 213-7.

Although this article is primarily concerned
with the Euthyphro dilemma, it contains some
valuable reflections upon omnipotence. Swinburne
argues that evil choices are either a consequence
of ignorance or of non-rational factors (sen-
sual desires, nervous impulses, etc.) which
are beyond the agent's control. Because God is
omniscient and unconstrained by these factors,
He is unable to choose evil. This limits God's
omnipotence but it does not make Him less worthy
of worship. Again, some moral truths (e.g.,
"in circumstance C, action A is obligatory") are
necessary. Others (e.g., "[Because circumstances
C obtain] doing A is obligatory") are contingent.
God cannot make A non-obligatory in circumstances
C, but since it is logically impossible for
Him to do so, the fact that He cannot do so is
compatible with His omnipotence. Whether or
not A is in fact obligatory depends upon whether
or not C obtains, and whether or not C obtains
depends (directly or indirectly) upon God's will.
Hence, what is in fact obligatory ultimately

depends upon God's will.

105 _____. "Omnipotence," Amer Phil Quart, 10 (July, 1973), 231-7.

In this interesting essay Swinburne calls our
attention to the weaknesses which beset several
plausible definitions of "omnipotence," and
proceeds to explore the Stone Paradox, criticizing the solutions offered by Mavrodes, Mayo
and Savage (#s 98, 99 and 103 above). (In criticizing Savage, Swinburne points out that the
fact that God can make [or lift] stones of any
poundage does not entail that His stone-making
[or stone-lifting] power is unlimited. For even
if God can make [or lift] a stone of any weight,
it does not follow that He can make [or lift]
a stone of any shape or of any size, etc. This
is true but not decisive, for Savage's point
can be reformulated to take account of this
observation: If x can create and lift stones
of any poundage, of any bulk, with any sort of
surface texture, etc., etc., then x cannot create
a stone which x cannot lift but it does not
therefore follow that x's stone-making power
is limited.) Swinburne proposes to define omnipotence at a time t as the power which s has at
time t to bring about any logically contingent
state of affairs which is subsequent to t and
which is such that its occurrence after t does
not entail that s did not bring it about at t.
Since "a stone exists at t_{n+1} which S is unable
to lift" is contingent and does not entail that
S did not bring it about at t, S can bring it
about at t if S is omnipotent at t. Swinburne
recognizes that a consequence of his definition
is that an omnipotent being can divest itself

81

of its omnipotence (by, e.g., creating a stone
which it cannot subsequently lift) and that,
therefore, while a being can in fact be omni-
temporally omnipotent, it cannot be a necessary
truth that it is omnipotent at all times.
Swinburne believes that classical theism would
object to his interpretation because it places
God in time. There is, however, another objection which classical theism would consider to be
at least equally important. According to classical theism, the being who is God (e.g., Yahweh)
exists necessarily and (since He is necessarily
divine) is necessarily omnipotent. It follows
that no being who is God can divest Himself of
His omnipotence.

106 Wainwright, William Judson. "Divine Omnipotence:
     A Reply to Professors Kuntz and Macquarrie,"
     The Seventh Inter-American Congress of Philosophy,
     under the auspices of the Canadian Philosophical
     Association, Proceedings of the Congress. Vol. 1.
     Québec: Les Presses de l'Université Laval,
     1967. Pp. 138-49.

     In reply to Kuntz (#93 above) Wainwright argues
     that there is no contradiction between the claim
     that omnipotence is a courteous title and the
     claim that God is literally omnipotent, that
     it is difficult to see how language which des-
     cribes or addresses a perfect being can be exag-
     gerated, and that there is some reason to believe
     that God is necessarily omnipotent. Macquarrie's
     account of omnipotence (#96 above) is criticized
     for its vagueness and imprecision. The response
     concludes with a critical examination of the
     claim that "omnipotence" is a symbol.
     (Wainwright argues that even if the concept of
     omnipotence can only be applied to God

symbolically it must, nonetheless, be consistent.)

107 Walton, Douglas Niel. "Some Theorems of Fitch on Omnipotence," Sophia, XV (March, 1976), 20-7.

A sympathetic discussion of Fitch's contention that an agent which can bring about every actual state of affairs is in fact a universal agent. (See #80 above.) Walton suggests that omnipotence should be construed as ranging over unactualized (future) states of affairs rather than over possible states of affairs.

108 Werner, Louis. "Some Omnipotent Beings," Critica, V (Mayo, 1971), 55-72.

The "natural" argument for the impossibility of two omnipotent beings goes roughly like this: (1) "If there were two omnipotent beings their wills might conflict (and if their wills did conflict then at least one of their wills would be frustrated)" and (2) "The will of an omnipotent being cannot be frustrated." Therefore, (3) "There aren't two omnipotent beings." Since (1) and (2) are necessary, (3) is also necessary. Werner responds to this argument in the following way: Suppose that one omnipotent being wills that everything be green all over and that another omnipotent being wills that everything be red all over. If both are omnipotent neither gets its way. However, even though both wills are frustrated, it does not follow that either being is not omnipotent. This is because willing that everything be green (red) when an omnipotent being has willed that everything be red (green)

involves willing what is logically impossible and
the fact that a being cannot effectually will
what is logically impossible does not count
against its omnipotence. Werner is, in effect,
denying that the second premiss of the "natural"
argument is necessary, and near the end of his
essay he provides reasons why the frustration
of x's will by another omnipotent being fails
to count against x's own omnipotence. These
reasons are not wholly convincing. Being prevented from doing what one can do in other circumstances (viz., in those circumstances in
which the [other] omnipotent being refrains from
willing something which conflicts with one's
own will) is not on a par with being unable to
do what is impossible for all agents in all
circumstances (e.g., making round squares) or
with inabilities which are not shared by all
agents but which are a consequence of one's own
perfection and power (e.g., the inability to sin
or [because one can both create and lift any
sort of stone] the inability to create a stone
one cannot lift).

109 Wolfe, Julian. "Omnipotence," Can J Phil, I
     (December, 1971), 245-7.

Capacities should be distinguished from powers.
Thus, God has the power to make things of any
weight, but because He also has the power to lift
things of any weight He lacks a capacity which
I possess, viz., the capacity to make something
which I cannot lift. Since the only power I
exercise in making something which I cannot lift
is the power to make something of a certain
weight (that I make something that I cannot lift
simply follows from the fact that what I make

84

is heavier than anything I can lift), it would
be a mistake to suppose that I possess a power
which God lacks. It is concluded that omnipotence should be "analyzed in terms of power
rather than capacity." This proposal should
be compared with Cargile's proposal (#77 above.)

110 Young, Robert. Freedom, Responsibility and God.
     (Library of Philosophy and Religion.) London
     & Basingstoke: The Macmillan Press Ltd., 1975.
     Pp. 186-200.

Chapter 13 contains a good discussion of the
diffulties involved in defining omnipotence
and of the so-called paradoxes of omnipotence.
It is concluded that in spite of the difficulties
involved in providing a satisfactory definition,
the paradoxes can be resolved. Special attention
is paid to the contributions of Ross, Savage
and Swinburne (#s 102, 103 and 105 above).

Omniscience and Foreknowledge

(See also #s 433 and 434)

111 Adams, Marilyn McCord. "Is the Existence of God
     a 'Hard' Fact?" Phil Rev, LXXVI (October, 1967),
     492-503.

A very interesting reply to Pike's "Divine Omniscience and Voluntary Action" (#141 below).
Adams argues that we should distinguish facts
about the past which do not include facts about
the future ("hard facts") from facts about the
past which do include facts about the future
("soft facts"). While we cannot alter hard
facts about the past we can alter at least some
soft facts about the past. The existence of God

85

(or an omniscient being) at a past time is a
soft fact about the past. Hence, it is not
prima facie absurd to suppose that (pace Pike)
we do have the power to bring it about that
God who did exist never existed. Being God or
being omniscient is not constitutive of the
identity of the being who is God (e.g., Yahweh).
Therefore, in saying that we have the power to
bring it about that "God" or "omniscient" never
applies to Yahweh, we do not imply that we have
the power to bring it about that the person,
Yahweh, who existed in the past did not exist
in the past. We do, however, imply that we
have a power to act in such a way that something
which was in fact the case (that Yahweh was --
and is -- God or omniscient) was never the case.

112 _____ and Norman Kretzmann. Predestination,
God's Foreknowledge, and Future Contingents by
William Ockham. Translated with an Introduction,
Notes and Appendices by Marilyn McCord Adams
and Norman Kretzmann. (Century Philosophy Source-
books.) New York: Appleton-Century-Crofts,
1969. Pp. 1-33 and 115-28 (bibliography).

Ockham recognized that one can escape fatalism
by denying that propositions about future contingents are determinately true, but insisted
that this solution endangers God's foreknowledge.
According Ockham, we should regard a proposition
as determinately true if its truth is settled
by something which is actual, was actual, or
will be actual. Propositions about future contingents can be determinately true because their
truth is settled by what will be actual. Since
they are determinately true, they can be (fore)
known to be true, but since their truth is settled by what will be the case and not by what

86

is or has been the case, human freedom is not
endangered. Ockham believed that God has an
"intuitive evident cognition" of future contingents which is similar to our intuitive cognition
of present things but he does not explain how
God's cognition of future contingents can be
indubitable. The introduction discusses these
and related issues. The book's useful bibliography lists material on Ockham and both medieval
and modern discussions of foreknowledge, predestination, future contingents, etc.

113 Cahn, Steven Mark. Fate, Logic and Time. New
     Haven: Yale University Press, 1967. Pp. 67-84.

"Theological Fatalism" is discussed in chapter 5.
Cahn presents a "proof" of the proposition that
divine omniscience and human freedom are incompatible. He then argues that the references to
God in this proof are not essential, and that
a similar proof can be constructed which eliminates any references to God. (Both proofs
hinge on the alleged impossibility of making
what was the case not the case.) Although this
chapter has been frequently cited, it is not
sufficiently subtle to be of much interest.
(For example, it is assumed that the only way
in which I can make it false that God knew that
I am now writing these words is by "making it
true that God knew what was false," and that if
someone says that God timelessly knows successive
events, he can only mean that God knows the
future as clearly as we know the present.)

114 Castañeda, Hector-Neri. "Omniscience and Indexical
Reference," J Phil, LXIV (April 13, 1967),
203-10.

A reply to Kretzmann's "Omniscience and Immutability" (#130 below). It is difficult to adequately formulate one of Kretzmann's principle
points. Kretzmann wishes to maintain that if
God knows that it is now t1 and not t2 and then
knows that it is now t2 and not t1, God first
knows two propositions and then knows two different propositions and, therefore, changes. The
trouble with this formulation is that indexical
terms in indirect discourse express indexical
references of the speaker, and leave it open
as to whether the person spoken about made an
indexical reference or not. What has been said
does not, therefore, preclude the possibility
that the four propositions God knows are non-
indexical, in which case all four propositions
could be known by God both at t1 and at t2.
At the end of the article, Castañeda draws several
conclusions from his discussion. These include
the claim that an immutable knower cannot formulate indexical propositions, and the claim
that an omniscient being could not know every
true proposition in direct discourse (e.g., "I
am ill") although it could know related "quasi-
indexical propositions" (e.g., "At t1, William
knows that he is ill").

115 Fitzgerald, Paul. "Relativity Physics and the
God of Process Philosophy," Process Stud, 2
(Winter, 1972), 251-76.

A critical examination of proposed solutions to
the problem raised by John Wilcox (#157 below).
It is argued that a solution may require

supposing that God is composed of a number of
different streams of consciousness which inter-
lock at various points (a moment of divine experience could be a member of several series of
divine experiences), which share a common aim,
and which share the same "primordial nature."
Alternatively, we can think of God as one everlasting entity (rather than as a set of different
series of "occasions") which embraces within
its single synoptic vision each occurrence as
it occurs. According to this conception, God
"physically prehends" the world from each spatio-
temporal location and, as such, directly experiences temporality. He also, however, non-tem-
porally prehends everything which happens within
Himself including all of His physical prehensions.
The existence of this non-temporal prehension
ensures that all of the elements in God's life
are connected so as to form one total mental
state. (The first approach is connected with
the conception of God as a society of occasions
which has been advocated by Charles Hartshorne
and John Cobb. The second approach is connected
with the conception of God as a single everlasting
process of "concrescence," a view adopted by
William Christian, Lewis Ford and -- apparently --
Whitehead himself.) An interesting examination
of certain issues in Process Theism.

116 Ford, Lewis Stanley. "Is Process Theism Compatible
    with Relativity Theory?" J Relig, 48 (April,
    1968), 124-35.

Ford addresses himself to the difficulty raised
by John Wilcox (#157 below). The solution which
is developed by Ford in this and two related
essays ("Boethius and Whitehead on Time and

Eternity" and "Whitehead's Conception of Divine
Spatiality," [#36 above and #161 below]) depends
upon Whitehead's metaphysics. Ford maintains
that God prehends, from the standpoint of each
occasion, whatever is to be prehended from the
standpoint of that occasion. This includes
everything in the occasion's causal past but it
does not include its contemporaries. God, thus,
prehends from the "point of view" of each occasion as that occasion comes into being, and all
occasions are eventually prehended, but in pre-
hending from any given "point of view" God never
prehends what is occurring contemporaneously
with the occasion with which He shares that "point
of view." Ford's solution is (as he admits)
similar to the solution of William Christian
(#5 above). It is unclear whether a modified
version of this solution could be adopted by
someone who was not a Whiteheadian.

117 Garrigou-Lagrange, Reginald Marie. God, His Exis-
     tence and Nature; A Thomistic Solution of Certain
     Agnostic Antinomies. Vol. II. Translated from
     the fifth French edition by Dom Bede Rose. St.
     Louis and London: B. Herder Book Co., 1936.
     Pp. 59-95 and 465-562.

     Section 49 contains a Thomistic account of divine
     omniscience and foreknowledge. The discussion
     of Molinist "Middle Knowledge" (the knowledge
     of what free creatures will freely do if placed
     in various circumstances) is particularly in-
     teresting. Middle knowledge is rejected for
     three reasons. (1) Because it is impossible.
     A free act cannot be known in its causes for if
     it were known in its causes it would not (accord-
     ing to the Molinist) be free. Nor is the Molinist
     correct when he argues that these acts can be

known by God because it is objectively true that
free creatures <u>will</u> freely do certain things if
placed in appropriate circumstances for propositions about future contingents are neither true
nor false. (2) Because, if the Molinist is
correct, God's knowledge of free actions is passive, dependent upon facts which are extrinsic
to Him and which do not fully depend upon Him.
(3) Because, if the Molinist is correct, God is
not the cause of our free acts and is, therefore,
not a completely universal cause. Garrigou-
Lagrange contends that God knows what free actions
will take place because He is the cause of free
actions. These matters are again discussed in
Appendix IV and the Epilogue.

118 Haack, Susan. "On a Theological Argument for
     Fatalism," <u>Phil</u> <u>Quart</u>, 24 (April, 1974), 156-9.

     Haack presents a standard argument for "theolo-
     gical fatalism," and argues that the principle
     of bivalence ("it is either true or false at tl
     that e will occur at t2") is essential to the
     argument, but that its theological premiss ("God
     is omniscient") is not. Interesting. See Helm's
     reply and Haack's rejoinder to that reply (#s 123
     and 119 below).

119 _____. "On 'On Theological Fatalism Again'
     Again," <u>Phil</u> <u>Quart</u>, 25 (April, 1975), 159-61.

     A rejoinder to Helm (# 123 below). The logical
     argument for fatalism confuses L(pɔq) with pɔLq.
     It is (according to Haack) possible that a theo-
     logical argument for fatalism which proceeded
     from "God is necessarily omniscient" rather than
     from "God is omniscient" could not be reduced to

the logical argument for fatalism, and would
not make this mistake. See Helm's reply, (# 122
below).

120 Hartshorne, Charles. Man's Vision of God and the
    Logic of Theism. New York: Harper and Row,
    Inc., 1941. Pp. 98-104.

    Chapter III contains a good informal defense of
    the claim that since the details of the future
    are indeterminate they are unknowable, and that,
    therefore, not even an omniscient being can
    know them.

121 Helm, Paul. "Divine Foreknowledge and Facts,"
    Can J Phil, IV (December, 1974), 305-15.

    Since God's foreknowledge is past and therefore
    necessary and since what is entailed by a necessary
    fact is necessary, what is foreknown must also
    be necessary. The first part of the essay ad-
    dresses itself to Kenny's attempt (# 123 below)
    to evade this difficulty. If God has grounds for
    His beliefs about the future, then it is diffi-
    cult to see how those grounds can be adequate
    if they do not necessitate the future. But
    suppose there are no (antecedent) grounds.
    Couldn't we say that our present actions bring
    about God's prior knowledge (rather than the
    other way around)? We cannot say this because
    we cannot now bring about something which is
    already the case. (Is this because one cannot
    bring about or cause something which has already
    been brought about or caused by oneself or some-
    thing else [I can't, e.g., write a book which
    has already been written] or because future states
    of affairs cannot be the cause of past states of

affairs? It is the latter which is at issue,
and to assert that it is impossible begs the
question.) The second part of Helm's essay
addresses itself to Nelson Pike's argument
(# 141 below), and to Marilyn McCord Adams'
reply to that argument (# 111 above). Helm
maintains that the latter's distinction between
hard and soft facts about the past is unsound.
Helm's objections at this point seem to be
vitiated by (1) a failure to remember that the
power to bring it about that a soft fact about
the past (e.g., that Napoleon died before I
finish this sentence) does not obtain is not a
power to change the past but rather a power
to bring it about that a fact about the past
which in fact obtains never obtained, by (2) a
failure to recognize that soft facts are not
unreal facts, and by (3) a failure to realize
that soft facts about the past are facts about
the past which logically, and not merely causally,
involve facts about the future. Helm also contends that the argument for theological fatalism
is generated by the fact that foreknowledge is
past and that Pike is, therefore, mistaken when
he supposes that the problem crucially depends
upon the fact that God is necessarily omniscient.

122 _____. "Fatalism Once More," Phil Quart,
25 (October, 1975), 355-6.

A reply to Susan Haack's "On 'On Theological
Fatalism Again' Again" (# 119 above). A minor
addendum to an interesting discussion.

123   _____ . "On Theological Fatalism Again,"
    <u>Phil Quart</u>, 24 (October, 1974), 56-8.

    A critique of Susan Haack's "On a Theological
    Argument for Fatalism" (# 118 above). See her
    rejoinder (# 119 above).

124   _____ . "Timelessness and Foreknowledge,"
    <u>Mind</u>, LXXXIV (October, 1975), 516-27.

    The coherence of the notion of timeless omni-
    science is defended against A. N. Prior (#s 146
    and 147 below), Martha Kneale (# 41 above),
    Norman Kretzmann (# 130 below), and Anthony
    Kenny (# 128 below). A timeless being can be
    said to foreknow certain events. While "I fore-
    know that A" is necessarily false for such a
    being, "He (the timeless being) foreknows A"
    may be true when uttered by a temporal being,
    for the sentence means "Before t (**where** t is the
    present), the statement that the timeless being
    (timelessly) knows that A (where A occurs after
    t) is true." Helm argues, however, that even
    though the notion of God's timeless knowledge
    makes sense, it will not enable us to escape
    theological fatalism. It **was** true yesterday
    that God timelessly knows that B occurs today.
    This fact about the past entails that B occurs
    today and, since it is about the past, it is a
    necessary fact. Hence, B too must be necessary.
    This problem could, perhaps, be resolved by
    introducing the concept of "soft facts" about
    the past. Helm would, however, reject this
    solution. (See his "Divine Foreknowledge and
    Facts," # 121 above.)

125 Hutchings, P. Ae. "Can We Say That Omniscience
       is Impossible?" Austl J Phil, 41 (December,
       1963), 394-6.

     A reply to Puccetti (# 149 below).

126 Iseminger, Gary. "Foreknowledge and Necessity,"
       Midwest Stud Phil, I (1976), 5-12.

       "S knows at t1 that e (e.g., a human action)
       will occur at t2" entails "it is true at t1
       that e will occur at t2." If the first pro-
       position is necessary, the second proposition
       is also necessary, in which case e's occurrence
       at t2 would appear to be "unpreventable." Ise-
       minger appeals to an "Aristotelian" concept
       of necessity according to which whatever is
       present or past is necessary (unalterable),
       and argues that if foreknowledge (or foretruth)
       is a fact, it is a necessary fact. Aquinas
       attempts to evade the force of this argument
       by distinguishing between propositions as objects
       of God's foreknowledge and propositions in
       themselves, arguing that from the necessity of
       the former, we cannot infer the necessity of the
       latter. Iseminger admits that an object of
       thought may have properties (e.g., immateriality)
       which the object in itself lacks, but suggests
       that if necessity (or truth) characterizes a
       proposition as thought, it must also characterize
       that proposition in itself. See the replies
       of Langerak, Mavrodes and Rosenthal (#s 135,
       137 and 151 below).

127   Joyce, George Hayward. Principles of Natural
       Theology. (Stonyhurst Philosophical Series.)
       London, New York [etc.]: Longmans, Green and
       Co., 1923; New York: AMS Press, 1972. Pp.
       333-71.

       Chapter XI contains a valuable discussion of
       divine foreknowledge. After providing arguments
       for divine foreknowledge, Joyce proceeds to
       ask how such foreknowledge is possible. He
       rejects the Thomistic view that God foreknows
       free acts because He predetermines them, and
       defends the view that God possesses "mediate"
       knowledge. God not only knows what is possible
       and what is actual but also knows what free
       choices would be made in all the situations in
       which free agents might be placed. Since God
       also knows (because He determines) the condi-
       tions under which free agents act, He knows
       what free choices will actually be made. Joyce
       maintains that if God's foreknowledge is com-
       patible with human freedom, then it must be
       understood in this way.

128   Kenny, Anthony John Patrick. "Divine Foreknow-
       ledge and Human Freedom," Aquinas, A Collection
       of Critical Essays. Edited by Anthony Kenny.
       Garden City, New York: Anchor Books, Double-
       day & Co., Inc., 1969. Pp. 255-70.

       Aquinas argues that if divine foreknowledge
       occurs in the past it is necessary, from which
       it follows that the events foreknown are neces-
       sary as well. He attempts to solve this problem
       by asserting that God is outside of time, that
       the whole of time is simultaneously present to
       Him and that, therefore, God does not know the
       future qua future. Kenny points out that, strict-
       ly speaking, this solution abandons the notion

that God foreknows the future. What is more
important, it is incoherent. If God's eternity
is simultaneous with two temporally separated
events, then those events are simultaneous with
each other. (This is not clear. "Simultaneous"
may refer to the manner in which God knows --
God grasps all things in one intuition as we
grasp several successive things in one specious
present -- rather than to what God knows.)
Kenny suggests that the problem can be resolved
in another way. Specifically, (1) he denies
that the past is necessary in any sense which
precludes future contingency, (2) argues that
in certain cases present actions can affect
the past (what I do now can, e.g., make it the
case that certain beliefs about what I would
do were true), (3) and argues that because it
is not clear that knowledge must always be based
on evidence or grounds (cf. our knowledge of
our own actions), it is not clear that God needs
present or past grounds for His beliefs about
the future in order for those beliefs about the
future to constitute knowledge of the future.

129 Khamara, Edward J. "Eternity and Omniscience,"
     Phil Quart, 24 (July, 1974), 204-19.

     Khamara argues that because he mistakenly assumed
     that present knowledge must be simultaneous
     with the event known (as perception must be
     [nearly] simultaneous with what is perceived),
     Boethius concluded that an omniscient being
     (which knows past, present, and future at once)
     must be outside time. Khamara also argues that
     knowledge is, in principle, datable although
     his argument is unconvincing since it appears
     to assume that any knower endures through time

97

and this is precisely what is at issue. In
the latter part of his essay the author suggests
that we should distinguish the question as to
what it means to say _that_ God knows, from the
question as to _how_ God knows. We may be able
to answer the first question without being able
to answer the second. Khamara, then, proceeds
to critically examine two accounts of the manner
in which God knows -- the account of Berkeley,
Newton and Clarke which assimilates God's knowledge to human perception, and the account of
Leibniz which assimilates God's knowledge to
our knowledge of necessary truths.

130 Kretzmann, Norman. "Omniscience and Immutability,"
     J _Phil_, LXIII (July 14, 1966), 409-21.

This very interesting article contains two arguments. The first is designed to show that omniscience and immutability are incompatible. A
being which knows everything must know what
time it is, but a being which (always) knows
what time it is changes and is, therefore, not
immutable. The second argument is sketched
very briefly at the end of the essay. Jones's
knowledge that he is in the hospital must be
distinguished from Jones's knowledge that Jones
is in the hospital. (Jones might have amnesia.)
God cannot know what Jones knows in the first
case unless He is Jones. Hence, if God is distinct from other persons, He cannot know everything. See Castañeda's discussion of the second
argument (# 114 above), Pike's discussion of
the first point (# 142 below), and Kretzmann's
University Lecture (# 44 above).

131 Lachs, John. "Professor Prior on Omniscience,"
    Philosophy, XXXVIII (October, 1963), 361-4.

A reply to "The Formalities of Omniscience"
(# 146 below). Prior offers the following
formalization of the claim that God is omniscient: "For every p, if p then God knows that
p." This is inadequate on two counts. (1)
Knowing what it is to (e.g.) love or feel sorrow
cannot be reduced to knowing that certain things
are the case. Since Prior's formalization ignores
knowing what, it is insufficiently inclusive.
(2) A being which knows all truths cannot doubt
any proposition. But since "no one can know
the meaning of 'doubt' unless he is having or
has had the experience of doubting," it follows
that a being which knows all truths does not
understand and, therefore, does not know the
truth of any proposition in which the term
"doubt" occurs. Hence, a being which knows all
truths does not know all truths, i.e., the concept of omniscience is incoherent. See Prior's
reply (# 148 below).

132 Lackey, Douglas Paul. "A New Disproof of the
    Compatibility of Foreknowledge and Free Choice,"
    Relig Stud, 10 (September, 1974), 313-8.

Edmund Gettier has shown that justified true
belief does not always constitute knowledge,
and A. I. Goldman has suggested that "if there
is to be knowledge, the fact believed must be
causally connected to the belief in the fact."
If this is correct, it follows that if God knows
what choices will be made, then either those
choices modify God or God modifies those choices.
The first alternative is impossible because "God

causes but is Himself uncaused," and the only way in which God can "modify" a state of affairs is by producing it (sic!). Therefore, if God knows what choices will be made, He produces them and, if He produces them, they are not free.

133 La Croix, Richard Ray. "Omniprescience and Divine Determinism," Relig Stud, 12 (September, 1976), 365-81.

La Croix argues that if God has foreknowledge and is omniscient, immutable and eternal, then He cannot freely decide "to perform the acts He does perform." La Croix maintains that this, in turn, entails that God is not omnipotent (in any significant sense), that He is not intrinsically good, that He is not a person, and that there is no problem of evil. This is an interesting paper. In drawing his conclusions, however, La Croix employs two questionable premisses: (1) "If God knows at t1, that He will do . . . a at t3, then at t2 or t3 it is not possible for God to refrain from doing . . . a at t3," and (2) it is a logically necessary feature of a decision to do a that it be made at a particular time and be preceded by a period in which the decision to do a has not yet been made. La Croix's argument for the first premiss is fallacious. He assumes that the denial of the first premiss is "It is possible that (God knows at t1 . . ., etc., and God refrains from doing a at t3)." Its denial, however, is either "God knows at t1 . . . etc., and it is possible at t2 or t3 that God refrains from doing a at t3" or (if the conditional is necessary) "It is possible that (God knows at t1 . . . etc., and it is possible at t2 or t3 that God refrains

from doing a at t3)." On the other hand, it
should be conceded that some of the arguments
which have been used to (allegedly) show that
God's foreknowledge is incompatible with human
freedom could be used to show that God's foreknowledge is incompatible with His own freedom.
The second premiss is plausible but implicitly
rules out the possibility of eternally deciding
that a certain state of affairs shall occur at
tn. (For a discussion of this possibility see
Kretzmann, # 44 above.)

134 Lacy, William Larry. "Aquinas and God's Knowledge
     of the Creature," S J Phil, 2 (Summer, 1964),
     43-8.

Aquinas maintains that, since God knows things
in so far as He creates them, His knowledge of
them is not dependent upon what He knows. This
thesis, however, leads to a dilemma. Either
God creates all things including free actions
or (if He does not create free actions) either
He does not know free actions or His knowledge
of free actions is dependent upon those actions.
Lacy attempts to show that in ascribing the
kind of dependence which is involved in knowledge to God we do not ascribe any imperfection
to God. Unless the doctrine of divine simplicity is true, God can be fully independent and
unmoved in one aspect of His being and yet be
dependent or caused in another aspect of His
being. God's knowledge of creation is not included in His knowledge of Himself. His knowledge (of actual things) is, therefore, "extended"
by creation. Furthermore, God is in potentiality
with respect to the created objects which He
knows (for He might not have created them).

These points, however, do not imply that God's
act of knowledge is in any way imperfect. Although not exciting, this article is of some
interest.

135 Langerak, Edward. "Of Foreknowledge and Necessity,"
     Midwest Stud Phil, I (1976), 12-6.

     A reply to Iseminger (# 126 above). Langerak's
     most important point is that classical theists
     should be bothered by the notion that propositions
     about future contingents are neither true nor
     false, for if propositions about future contin-
     gents are neither true nor false, God cannot
     foreknow them and the doctrine of providence
     is endangered.

136 Lucas, John Randolph. The Freedom of the Will.
     Oxford: Clarendon Press, 1970. Pp. 71-7.

     "Theological determinism" is briefly discussed
     in chapter 14. After examining several standard
     solutions, Lucas concludes that the conflict
     between divine omniscience and human freedom
     can only be resolved if we suppose that God
     "limit[s] His infallible knowledge as He does
     His power, in order to let us be independent
     of Him." This suggestion is not worked out in
     any detail. See Purtill's reply, # 150 below.

137 Mavrodes, George Ion. "Aristotelian Necessity and
     Freedom," Midwest Stud Phil, I (1976), 16-21.

     A reply to Iseminger (# 126 above). Mavrodes
     suggests that "Aristotelian" necessity is ex-
     pressed in the claim that it is necessarily
     true that what obtains obtains when it obtains,

and argues that the existence of this sort of
necessity or of a necessity which is temporally
coextensive with the events which are said to
be necessary, has no interesting implications
for human freedom.

138   Matson, Wallace I.   "An Introduction to Omni-
        science," _Analysis_, 29 (New Series), (October,
        1968), 8-12.

In this interesting but rather curious essay,
Matson argues (1) that unless the world is finite
or such that "knowledge of a finite number of
items entails knowledge of all the rest of the
items," an omniscient being must have "infinite
storage capacity" and thus be immaterial, and
(2) that because a being must be connected with
the world in order to know it, it must either
be related to the world as effect to cause or
be identical with the world.   (Matson does not
try to show that these are the only alternatives.)
Since it is difficult to see how infinite omniscience could be causally acted upon (for it
is immaterial), "infinite omniscience entails
Pantheism."

139   Phillips, Richard Percival.   _Modern Thomistic
        Philosophy_, An Explanation for Students. Vol. II.
        London: Burns, Oates and Washbourne, Ltd.,
        1935. Pp. 312-28.

Chapter V, Part III, provides an account of the
points at issue between Thomists and Molinists
with respect to God's foreknowledge of future
contingents. While this chapter contains little
which cannot be found in the more extended discussions of Garrigou-Lagrange and Joyce (#s 117
and 127 above), its summary of the controversy

is useful and, on the whole, lucid.

140   Pike, Nelson Craft. "Divine Foreknowledge, Human
       Freedom and Possible Worlds," Phil Rev, LXXXVI
       (April, 1977), 209-16.

       A reply to Plantinga (# 144 below). According
       to Pike, Plantinga believes that it is within
       my power to refrain from doing x if there is
       a possible world in which I refrain from doing
       x. (It is doubtful that Plantinga actually
       believes this.) He thus ignores the fact that
       what is within my power is determined by a number
       of things including my abilities, opportunities,
       etc. To say that it is within my power to re-
       frain from doing x is to say that the subset of
       possible worlds in which these and other condi-
       tions obtain includes a world in which I refrain
       from doing x. Pike moves from this contention
       (which is surely correct) to the further conten-
       tion that the relevant subset of possible worlds
       "will have to be worlds in which what has hap-
       pened in the past relative to the given moment
       is precisely what has happened in the past re-
       lative to that moment in the actual world."
       Since (in the case with which we are concerned)
       God foresees that I will do x, the relevant
       worlds will all be worlds in which God foresees
       that I will do x. Hence, no world in the rele-
       vant subset is a world in which I refrain from
       doing x. It follows that I do not have the
       power to refrain from doing x. Unfortunately,
       Pike's contention is dubious. If someone had
       truly believed that I would write this biblio-
       graphy, then all worlds with a past history
       indistinguishable from that of the actual world
       would have contained this fact and, hence, in

all those worlds I would have written this
bibliography. If Pike is correct it would
follow that it was not within my power to refrain from writing it (which is absurd). The
moral appears to be that the past included in
the relevant subset of possible worlds must
be distinguishable in at least some respects
(e.g., with respect to "soft facts") from the
past of the actual world.

141 _____. "Divine Omniscience and Voluntary
     Action," Phil Rev, LXXIV (January, 1965),
     27-46.

A very interesting and much discussed attempt
to show that given certain assumptions (that
God is in time, that God is necessarily omniscient, that we cannot bring it about that a
belief which was held at a past time was not
held at that time, that we cannot bring it about
that a person who existed at a past time did
not exist at that time, etc.), God's foreknowledge and human freedom are incompatible. We
are not free unless we possess the power to
refrain from acting in those ways in which we
do in fact act. However, if God exists and
foreknows what we will do, exercising that power
would involve bringing it about either that
God did not exist, or that He did not believe
that we would do what we will in fact do, or
that His beliefs were false. Since it is impossible for us to bring about any of these
things, we have no power to refrain from acting in the ways in which we do in fact act.
See the replies of Adams (# 111 above), Plantinga
(# 144 below), and Saunders (# 153 below).
Pike reformulated the argument in God and

105

<u>Timelessness</u> (# 142 below). For another dis-
cussion of Pike's argument, see Young (# 158
below).

142 _____. <u>God</u> and <u>Timelessness</u>. (Studies in
Ethics and the Philosophy of Religion.) London:
Routledge & Kegan Paul; New York: Schocken Books,
1970. Pp. 53-96 and 121-9.

Chapter 4 provides a reformulation of the argument which was first presented in "Divine
Omniscience and Voluntary Action" (# 141 above).
This reformulation is superior to the original
because it more clearly brings out the fact
that we are required to suppose that the being
who is God (e.g., Yahweh) is essentially God or
essentially omniscient (and not merely that it
is necessary that whatever being happens to
be God is omniscient). This blocks the move
made by Marilyn Adams (# 111 above), for if
the individual who is named "Yahweh" is necessarily God or necessarily omniscient, then, in
bringing it about that Yahweh was never God or
never omniscient we would be bringing it about
that that individual never existed which (given
that Yahweh did exist) is impossible. In chapter 5, Pike turns his attention to the claim
that a timeless being cannot know such facts
as the fact that today is the twenty-seventh of
February. Pike argues that although a timeless
knower could not truly say that he knows p where
p is a true statement which includes temporal
indexical terms, it does not follow that he
does not know the fact expressed by p. In
chapter 7, Pike argues that even though a timeless being could not remember, anticipate or
deliberate, it is not clear that such a being

would be unable to know anything, for "x knows
∅" does not appear to entail "x is temporally
related to ∅." On the other hand, Pike thinks
that he has shown (in chapter 6) that a timeless
being cannot produce anything, and is bothered
by the fact that a timeless being cannot, therefore, produce circumstances which would show
that he knew something.

143 _____. "Of God and Freedom: A Rejoinder,"
      Phil Rev, LXXV (July, 1966), 369-79.

A reply to John Turk Saunders (# 153 below).
Pike concedes that we often have the power to
perform actions which are such that if we were
to perform them "soft" facts about the past
(facts about the past which include facts about
the future) would be different than they in
fact are, but insists that believing at some
time in the past is a "hard" fact about the
past, and that it is not within anyone's power
to perform an action which would bring it about
that someone who held a certain belief in the
past did not hold that belief in the past. In
discussing the case (described by Saunders)
in which I decide to skip at t1 and skip at
t2, Pike asserts that since the decision to
skip causally guarantees that I will skip, it
is not clear that I do have the power not to
skip at t2, but that in any case the counter
example is not relevant. If I am free at t2,
it is because the determining cause is my decision to skip. In the case which concerns us,
however, my decision is not among the determining
conditions of my behavior. The determining
conditions are, instead, God's beliefs. In
the second part of his reply, Pike concedes

that if truth is analytically tied to God's
beliefs or if believing truly is analytically
tied to being God, then it may be the case that
we have the power to bring it about that beliefs
which God held at an earlier time were not held
by Him at that time or that the divine person
who existed at an earlier time did not exist
at that time. However, Pike maintains that
if we do have these powers, God's beliefs are
not beliefs in the normal sense, and the person
called "God" is not a person in the normal sense.

144 Plantinga, Alvin Carl. God, Freedom and Evil.
     New York: Harper and Row, Publishers, Inc.,
     1974. Pp. 67-72.

This section is concerned with Nelson Pike's
attempt (# 141 above) to show that God's necessary omniscience is incompatible with human
freedom. Essential to Pike's argument is the
claim that if God believes we will do x and we
have the power to refrain from doing x, then
either (1) we have the power to bring it about
that God held a false belief or (2) we have
the power to bring about that He did not hold
the belief which He in fact held, or (3) we
have the power to bring it about that God did
not exist. Pike maintains that each of these
alternatives is impossible. Plantinga argues
that (1) and (3) do not follow, and that (2),
when correctly understood, is innocuous. See
Pike's reply, #140 above.

145 Poteat, William H. "Foreknowledge and Foreordina-
     tion: A Critique of Models of Knowledge," J
     Relig, XL (January, 1960), 18-26.

According to the Platonic model, the object of

knowledge is eternal and unchanging being.
Becoming is the object of mere opinion. If a
theologian adopts this model, he will be driven
to conclude that God's knowledge of the future
is -- since it is knowledge -- a knowledge of
what eternally is. From this it is natural
to infer that the future already is what it
will be, i.e., that the future is fixed or
"determined." According to a second model, God
foreknows the future as an agent knows his own
intentions. Since a knowledge of one's intentions
is compatible with the contingency of what is
intended, foreknowledge is compatible with human
freedom. A third model of knowledge is provided
by contexts of love, faith and encounter. (Cf.
the use of "know" in "She doesn't even know that
I exist," or its biblical use as a synonym for
sexual intercourse.) It may be doubted whether
an appeal to either of these last two models
solves any problems. (If what we do expresses
the intentions of an omnipotent agent, then
even though our actions may be contingent [for
God could have chosen otherwise], it is difficult to see how they can be free. Nor is it
clear that the third model is relevant to the
problem of foreknowledge and human freedom.)
Nevertheless, this article is suggestive and
Poteat is probably correct in contending that
these diverse models have influenced Christian
formulations of the doctrine of God's foreknowledge.

146 Prior, Arthur Norman. "The Formalities of Omni-
      science," Philosophy, XXXVII (April, 1962),
      114-29.

      Prior argues that propositions about future

contingents are neither true nor false. Since
no one can know a proposition which is neither
true nor false, not even an omniscient being
can know future contingents. Prior examines
medieval discussions, presents a number of interesting arguments, and formalizes some of the
major points. This influential and important
essay is reprinted in the author's Papers on
Time and Tense (Oxford, 1968).

147 _____. Past, Present and Future. Oxford:
The Clarendon Press, 1967. Pp. 113-36.

It is often asserted that there is some sense
in which the past is necessary. If the past
(e.g., the foreknowledge that something will
occur, or the mere fact that something will be
the case) is necessarily connected with the
future, then the future is necessary as well.
The Ockhamist response involves asserting that
past tense propositions are only necessary when
they do not include future-tense subordinate
clauses within them. The Peircean response involves denying that the fact that something is the
case today entails that it was true that it
would be the case today. In chapter VII, Prior
attempts to formalize the argument for the incompatibility of foreknowledge or foretruth
and indeterminism, and these two responses.

148 _____. "Rejoinder to Professor Lachs on
Omniscience," Philosophy, XXXVIII (October,
1963), 365-6.

A reply to # 131 above. (1) "Knowing what" is
not "anything different in itself from 'knowing
that'." For example, knowing what 2 and 2 are,

is knowing that 2 and 2 are 4. (2) "To doubt
whether p is simply not to know that p and not
to know that not p." Hence, anyone who has
had experience of knowledge can understand
"doubt." Prior concedes that there are cases
in which knowing does appear to presuppose having certain experiences. It would seem that
God cannot know "that a toothache feels to me
like this" if He has never had a toothache.
What follows, however, is not that the concept
of omniscience is incoherent but that omniscience
may be incompatible "with other attributes
traditionally ascribed to divine beings."

149 Puccetti, Roland. "Is Omniscience Possible?"
     Austl J Phil, 41 (May, 1963), 92-3.

     Puccetti argues that an omniscient being must
     know everything that is the case and must, there-
     fore, know that it knows everything that is the
     case. It is impossible, however, to know that
     there are no facts unknown to one, because in
     order to know this one would have to step over
     the boundary circumscribing the set of facts
     which one knows and determine that there are
     no unknown facts on the other side of that boun-
     dary. (A confusion appears to occur at this
     point. Knowing that there is nothing on the
     other side of the "boundary" separating the
     known from the unknown does not entail knowing
     some [unknown] fact on the other side of that
     boundary.) See Hutchings' reply, # 125 above.

150 Purtill, Richard L. "Foreknowledge and Fatalism,"
     Relig Stud, 10 (September, 1974), 319-24.

     A response to Lucas (# 136 above). It is clear

that if God were to overtly predict what we will do, then (since divine predictions are infallible, and since once overt predictions have been made they are unchangeable) no genuine alternatives would be open to us. It is less clear (though probable) that divine foreknowledge precludes genuine alternatives. Purtill tries to solve the problem by appealing to the notion that God is outside of time and that, therefore, God's beliefs do not antedate the facts which He believes to be true. Purtill attempts to make this notion plausible by calling our attention to parallels between God's spatial transcendence and His temporal transcendence, arguing that if the first is intelligible the second is intelligible. Purtill's defense of the notion of God's atemporality is superior to most.

151 Rosenthal, David Michael. "The Necessity of Fore-knowledge," Midwest Stud Phil, I (1976), 22-5.

Rosenthal attempts to show that the necessity attributed to events by Iseminger's argument (# 126 above) amounts to "no more than the concept of truth at a particular time."

152 Rowe, William Leonard. "Augustine on Foreknowledge and Free Will," Rev Metaph, XVIII (December, 1964), 356-63.

Augustine argues that divine foreknowledge makes human choices necessary, but insists that this necessity is compatible with the voluntary character of those choices. Our choices are voluntary because they are within our power, and they are within our power because they would

not occur unless we made them. Rowe accuses
Augustine of overlooking the distinction between
"I will to sin even though I do not will to
sin," and "I will to sin even though I do not
will to will to sin." From the fact that the
first is impossible, Augustine concludes that
willing to sin is always in our power. But
(given Augustine's own analysis of "in our
power"), it is the second proposition which
must be shown to be impossible if the argument
is to go through. Augustine is also accused
of illicitly confusing "Necessarily (if God
foreknows p, p will happen)," and "if God foreknows p, p will happen necessarily."

153 Saunders, John Turk. "Of God and Freedom," Phil
     Rev, LXXV (April, 1966), 219-25.

A reply to Pike's "Divine Omniscience and Voluntary Action" (# 141 above). Saunders argues
that even though we never have the power to
causally produce states of affairs in the past,
we often have the power to (non-causally) bring
it about that "earlier situations would be different from what they in fact are." Thus, suppose
the world is so constituted that my decision
to skip at t1 is a causally sufficient condition of my skipping at t2. Given normal conditions (I have not been drugged, threatened,
etc.), I have the power to run rather than skip
at t2. However, if I exercised this power, I
would not at t1 have decided to skip at t2.
Therefore, my power to run at t2 includes a
"power so to act that an earlier situation would
be other than it in fact is." Of more interest
is Saunders' observation that certain propositions which appear to be about the past are

about the future as well. Even though the facts
described by these propositions are (partly) about
the past, we sometimes have the power so to act
that these facts which do obtain never obtained.
Significantly, the proposition that an essentially
omniscient God believes at t1 that Jones will
do x at t2, is a proposition of the relevant
type. See Pike's response (# 143 above).

154   _____. "The Temptations of 'Powerlessness',"
         Amer Phil Quart, 5 (April, 1968), pp. 104-7.

In section III Saunders returns to some of the
issues discussed in his earlier essay, (# 153
above). He accepts the distinction between
soft and hard facts about the past. (See
Adams, # 111 above.) That a being was God or
omniscient is a soft fact about the past and,
like other soft facts about the past, is such
that one can so act that this fact would never
have obtained. (Acting so that this fact would
never have obtained does not involve either
causing the past or changing the past.) Saunders
also argues that it is possible to possess a
power to so act that hard facts about the past
would never have obtained. Thus, if Ben Franklin
would have been President only if George Washington had not existed, and if I am the sort of
person who would assert that Franklin was President only if Franklin had been President, then
I would assert that Franklin was President only
if George Washington had not existed. I clearly
have the power to make this assertion. Hence,
I have the power to so act that a person who
did exist would not have existed. The past
existence of George Washington (unlike the past
existence of God who is essentially everlasting)

114

is a hard fact about the past. It follows that
I have the power to so act that hard facts about
the past which did obtain would not have obtained.

155 Streveler, Paul Andrew. "The Problem of Future
     Contingents: A Medieval Discussion," New Scholas,
     XLVII (Spring, 1973), 233-47.

An excellent critical exposition of medieval
discussions of the problems involved in reconciling foreknowledge and human freedom. In
the course of his article, Streveler comments
on the arguments of Kenny, Pike and Prior (#s
128, 141, 146 and 147 above). One thing which
clearly emerges is that the alleged necessity
of propositions about the past lies at the heart
of the problem. Streveler favors the Occamist
solution according to which statements which
assert that God foreknew something involve a
reference to the future and are, therefore,
contingent. While future contingents are not
necessitated by anything in their past, it is
false that God has no grounds for His beliefs
about the future. The grounds for His beliefs
(what makes them true) are the future facts
which He foreknows.

156 Unger, Peter. "An Analysis of Factual Knowledge,"
     J Phil, LXV (March 21, 1968), 157-70.

While this article does not address itself to
issues of philosophical theology, it has important implications for those issues. One of the
principal objections to the claim that God foreknows future contingents is that if those events
are genuinely contingent, God can have no reason
for His belief that they will occur. Unger

argues that one need not possess evidence or
grounds in order to be entitled to say that
one knows. Knowledge is, instead, a correct
belief, where the correctness of the belief
is not merely an accident. If Unger is right,
the problem of God's foreknowledge becomes more
managable, for it is surely not merely an accident that the beliefs of an omnipresent,
creative spirit, who is free from the physical
and psychological limitations which render our
knowledge imperfect, are correct.

157 Wilcox, John Thomas. "A Question from Physics
     for Certain Theists," J Relig, XLI (October,
     1961), 293-300.

If the theory of relativity is correct, simul-
taneity is relative. Contemporary events which
are so situated that a light signal leaving one
cannot reach the other before it occurs are
causally independent of one another. Whether
or not those events are calculated to be simultaneous will depend upon the observer's state
of motion. A problem, thus, arises for those
theists who believe both that God is situated
in time and that His knowledge increases as He
moves through time, for given any two contemporary and causally independent events it would
seem that God must either know one before the
other or experience both at once. Either alternative appears to arbitrarily privilege the
position of some observers by identifying their
position with that of God. In the last part of
his essay, Wilcox examines William Christian's
attempt (# 5 above, pp. 330 ff.) to provide a
solution to this problem from the standpoint
of Whitehead's metaphysics. Although the problem

has been discussed almost exclusively by Process Philosophers (See, e.g., Fitzgerald and Ford, #s 115 and 116 above) it would seem to be a problem for any theist who believes that God cannot know future contingents until those contingents become actual.

158 Young, Robert. Freedom, Responsibility and God. (Library of Philosophy and Religion.) London & Basingstoke: The Macmillan Press Ltd., 1975. Pp. 169-85.

Chapter 12 discusses Pike's attempt (#s 141 above) to show that divine foreknowledge and human freedom are incompatible.

God's Relation to the World

(See also #s 3, 4, 5, 10, 13, 15, 17, 25, 29, 30, 33, 36, 39, 44, 49, 55, 61, 504, 896 and 919)

159 Cobb, John B., Jr. "Natural Causality and Divine Action," Ideal Stud, III (September, 1973), 207-22.

Some modern theologians construe God as a formal cause. Thus, Wieman appears to identify God with the common form of the processes of creative interchange through which good increases. Theologians who, like Tillich, identify God with being-as-such come close to regarding God as a material cause. Pannenberg, Moltmann and the Theologians of Hope treat God as a final cause. Apart from their intrinsic difficulties, these positions involve a radical departure from "biblical and traditional notions of God's agency" as involving efficient causality. There are at least three conceptions of efficient causality. According to the "Newtonian" view, causes necessitate their effects. "The Humean view sees cause and effect in terms of regular succession of observable states of affairs." A third conception interprets efficient causality as the "real influence" of the past. Cobb suggests (1) that the real influence of the past is directly experienced by us and/or (2) that the conviction that the past really influences us is built into ordinary experience. (It is not clear whether Cobb sees that [1] and [2] are not equivalent.) Cobb argues that God's efficient causality cannot be understood in either of the first two ways, but that we can make sense of God's efficient causality if we interpret it as "real influence." Just as our anger or resolve exerts a real influence upon our future experience, so God constitutes Himself in such a way as to influence the future. (Although his article does not make this entirely clear, what Cobb has in mind is the "persuasive power" of Process Philosophy, by which God presents ideals to actual occasions.) Cobb's essay is suggestive even though it raises more questions than it resolves. See Lachs' reply, # 168 below.

160 Dyck, Grace M. "Omnipresence and Incorporeality,"
     Relig Stud, 13 (March, 1977), 85-91.

Dyck argues that "presence" must be understood in terms of awareness and influence as well as physical location. (We are not present only "inside our own skin." I am, e.g., present in my study even though I do not physically permeate the whole room.) If God's influence and awareness were universal He would be omnipresent

even if He had a body which was located at a
particular place.

161   Ford, Lewis Stanley. "Whitehead's Conception of
Divine Spatiality," S J Phil, VI (Spring, 1968),
1-13.

It is argued that God's spatio-temporal region
or standpoint includes every spatio-temporal
region or standpoint. "God is situated at every
standpoint" and, thus, experiences actuality
from every perspective. Whitehead's conception
of God as a single actual entity is defended
against the contention (made by Hartshorne and
Cobb) that God is a society of actual occasions.
This essay should be read in conjunction with
two others ("Boethius and Whitehead on Time and
Eternity" and "Is Process Theism Compatible
with Relativity Theory?", #s 36 and 116 above)
in which the author develops related themes.

162   Geach, Peter Thomas. "Causality and Creation,"
Sophia, I (April, 1962), 1-8.

"God brought it about that x is A" should be
understood as "God brought it about that
($\exists$x)(x is an A)" rather than as "($\exists$x)(God brought
it about that x is an A)" for the latter, but
not the former, "implies that God makes into
an A some entity presupposed to his action."
God's creating an individual c can be construed
in the following way: "There is just one A;
and God brought it about that ($\exists$x)(x is an A);
and for no x did God bring it about that x is
an A; and c is an A." The third conjunct denies
that in creating God acted upon an already existing individual. The creative act is expressed

119

in the first three conjuncts which do not mention
c. Since no relation is asserted to hold between
God and c, we can "see how in creation there
is no real relation of God to the creature."
Reprinted as chapter 6 in God and the Soul.
(See # 163 below.)

163 _____. God and the Soul. (Studies in Ethics
and the Philosophy of Religion.) London: Routledge & Kegan Paul; New York: Schocken Books,
1969. Pp. 75-99.

Chapter 6 ("Causality and Creation") originally
appeared in Sophia. (See # 162 above.) Chapter 7
explores the notion that God sometimes brings
things about because we pray for them. Geach
argues (against C. S. Lewis, # 169 below) that
it is absurd to pray for something which is
now past and, therefore, decided even if we
are ignorant of how the issue was decided.
Again, miracles aside, it is only reasonable
to pray for future issues which are not determinate in their causes. See Helm's response
(# 165 below).

164 Griffen, David Ray. "Schubert Ogden's Christology
and the Possibilities of Process Philosophy,"
Christian Schol, L (Fall, 1967), 290-313.

Ogden has suggested (# 172 below) that a public
act expresses a person's inner being if it leads
someone to believe that it manifests a feature
of that person's inner being, and if that person's
inner being in fact possesses that feature.
Griffen provides an effective counter example,
and suggests that in order for an act to express
a person's inner being it must fulfill that
person's intentions and those intentions must

be of an "appropriate nature." (The intention
expressed in the act of tying my shoe laces
"will generally not do much" towards displaying
my inner being. The intentions expressed in
my behavior towards my wife may do so.) If events
in world history can be regarded as God's acts,
then a special act of God can be understood as
an event which fully expresses God's intentions
for it and which is such that the intentions
which it expresses are peculiarly expressive
of His character. It is worth observing that
although Griffen's account of divine activity
is presented within a Whiteheadian framework,
it can be abstracted from that framework without serious distortion.

165 Helm, Paul. "Omnipotence and Change," Philosophy,
     51 (October, 1976), 454-61.

     Helm argues that Geach (# 163 above) is mistaken
     in supposing that "God can answer petitionary
     prayer only in a world of two-way contingency."
     Petitionary prayer is reasonable if it is reason-
     able to believe that there is a set of conditions
     which is necessary and, together with the request,
     possibly sufficient for the bringing about of
     a certain state of affairs. The practice of
     petitionary prayer is consistent with God's
     unchanging will provided that God's intentions
     are complex, where "B is a complex thing to
     intend when B is some action the attempt to
     do which is suspended upon the action of another,"
     and provided that God possesses foreknowledge
     and thus knows from eternity what actions others
     will perform.

166   Jones, Owen Roger. The Concept of Holiness.
        London: George Allen & Unwin; New York: The
        Macmillan Co., 1961. Pp. 157-82.

        In chapter X, Jones argues that the distinctive
        feature of any act of artistic creation is the
        expression of the artist's vision. One views
        the world as a divine creation if one regards
        it as an expression of a perfect vision. Fairly
        suggestive.

167   Kaufman, Gordon D. "On the Meaning of 'Act of
        God'," Harvard Theol Rev, 61 (April, 1968),
        175-201.

        Kaufman's problem is created by the necessary
        (sic) assumption that all events are "interre-
        lated and interconnected" "in an unbroken web."
        If we are forced to view the world in this way,
        then it is difficult to see how a particular
        event (e.g., the Exodus) can be regarded as an
        act of God, for if we regard that event as an
        act of God it would seem that we must suppose
        that it has no natural antecedents. The clue
        to a solution is provided by the notion of a
        "master act" (e.g., building a house) which
        includes subordinate acts (e.g., driving nails).
        Kaufman suggests that the history of the world
        as a whole can be regarded as God's master act,
        and particular events "which move the creation
        forward a step toward the realization of God's
        purposes" can be regarded as subordinate acts
        within this master act. Other events may be
        said to be caused by God, but should not be
        regarded as acts of God since "to be regarded
        as an act, the movement must realize some posited
        objective." (Similarly, not every physical
        movement which occurs in the process of building

can be said to be an <u>act</u> of the builder.) See
Mason's reply (# 170 below).

168 Lachs, John. "God's Action and Nature's Ways,"
     <u>Ideal Stud</u>, III (September, 1973), 223-8.

     A reply to Cobb's "Natural Causality and Divine
     Action" (# 159 above). The author's most signifi-
     cant claim is that Cobb's third sort of efficient
     causality is not directly experienced, and that
     in suggesting that it is Cobb has confused "the
     derivation of experience (the [indisputable]
     fact that experience is causally influenced
     by the past) with the experience of derivation."
     (It is more likely that Cobb has confused the
     [alleged] fact that a conviction that experience
     is derived is built into our experience with
     an experience of derivation.)

169 Lewis, Clive Staples. <u>Miracles, A Preliminary</u>
     <u>Study</u>. London: G. Bles, The Centenary Press;
     New York: Macmillan Co., 1947. Pp. 208-16.

     Appendix B contains a rather interesting discus-
     sion of "special providence," which includes
     the claim that prayers made at time tn can be
     partial causes of events occurring at some earlier
     time tn - 1. (God, who is a-temporally related
     to temporal events, takes these prayers into
     account in determining the course of temporal
     events.) See Geach's critique of this position
     (# 163 above).

170 Mason, David R. "Can We Speculate on How God
     Acts?" <u>J Relig</u>, 57 (January, 1977), 16-32,
     esp. 17-26.

     A reply to Kaufman (# 167 above). Mason's most

important objections are perhaps the following:
(1) The world described by modern evolutionary
theory does not possess sufficient unity to be
regarded as a single act. (2) (Given Kaufman's
concept of an act) the world can only be regarded
as God's "master act" if it has both a beginning
and an end, and yet Kaufman believes that every
event has temporal antecedents and consequents
from which it follows that the world has neither
beginning nor end. In the final section Mason
argues that the Whiteheadian theory according
to which God is an agent who supplies ideals
or aims to actual events, provides a viable
alternative to Kaufman.

171 Mavrodes, George Ion. "Real and More Real," <u>Int</u>
<u>Phil</u> <u>Quart</u>, IV (December, 1964), 554-61.

There is a point of view from which we can truly
say that Eisenhower is real and MacBeth is not,
and there is a point of view from which we can
truly say that MacBeth is real but that the
dagger which he thinks he sees is not. There
are no points of view from which we can truly
say that MacBeth is real and Eisenhower is not,
or that MacBeth's dagger is real but not MacBeth.
These facts suggest the notion of hierarchically
ordered levels of reality. Two things are on
the same level if there is no point of view from
which one is real and the other is not. One thing
occupies a higher level of reality than another
if there is a point of view from which the first
is real and the second is not (but no point of
view from which the second is real and the first
is not?). The notion of levels of reality appears
to be connected with the notion of dependence.
(Things at any one level depend upon things

at a higher level, the dependence relation
being asymmetrical and transitive.) In the light
of these considerations, the claim that God is
more real than anything else can be explicated
in the following way: Everything else is related
to God as things on MacBeth's level are related
to things on Eisenhower's level, and nothing is
such that there is some point of view from which
it is real and God is unreal. Compare this analysis with Ross's explication of the same notion
(# 176 below).

172 Ogden, Schubert Miles. "What Sense Does It Make
     to Say 'God Acts in History'?" J Relig, XLIII
     (January, 1963), 1-19.

If God is related to all events in the same
kind of way, what sense does it make to speak
of a particular event or set of events as a
special act of God? Ogden points out that while
all of our bodily acts are our acts, some of
these acts reveal our character or inner being
in a way in which others do not. Hartshorne
and others have suggested that the world is
related to God as our bodies are related to our
inner being. If this is correct, then a special
act of God can be understood as a world event
which reveals God's inner being to us more clearly
than other world events. This essay is reprinted
in the author's The Reality of God (New York:
Harper and Row, 1966). See the replies of Griffen
and Peters (# 164 above and # 173 below).

173 Peters, Eugene Herbert. "A Framework for Christian
     Thought," J Relig, XLVI (July, 1966), 374-85,
     esp. 379-80.

The author has several criticisms of Ogden's

account (# 172 above) of God's special activity.
The most damaging of these criticisms is the
following: Ogden's account presupposes that
events in world history can be regarded as God's
acts in a sense analogous to the sense in which
our bodily acts are our acts. It is difficult,
however, to see how (e.g.) Paul's freely resisting
temptation can be God's act, both because that
act is free and because God cannot be tempted.

174 Phillips, Richard Percival. Modern Thomistic
     Philosophy, An Explanation for Students. Vol.
     II. London: Burns, Oates and Washbourne, Ltd.,
     1935. Pp. 329-63.

Part III, chapter VI, provides a brief but reasonably clear account of creation as a relation
of dependence (with respect to being). This
relation is real in the contingent, mutable
and temporal effect but not in the necessary,
immutable and non-temporal cause. Chapter VII
examines God's relation to finite activity.
Since God is the ground of all being, He must
be the ground of finite activity. Occasionalism
is rejected because it preserves God's causal
primacy but denies the real causality and (since
being expresses itself in activity), by implication, the real being of creatures. Molinism
maintains that the agent moves itself to act
but that God concurs with the agent to produce
the effect (viz., the agent's action and its
term). This doctrine preserves the real causality
of creatures but denies that God is totally
responsible for the effect. Thomists maintain
that God moves the agent to act and determines
the action, and also determines whether its mode
is necessary or free. Phillips makes the usual

moves when he attempts to show that this divine
"premotion" is compatible with human liberty.
While it is impossible for God to premove the
will in a certain direction and for the will
not to move in that direction, it is nevertheless
possible that the will be determined otherwise
(for the will has the power to move in different
directions and God could have premoved it in a
direction different from the direction in which
He did in fact premove it). Again, God's action
upon the will is "intrinsic," not "extrinsic."
He moves it "from within." In section II of
chapter VIII, Phillips attempts to explain how
God can be the cause of sinful acts without
being responsible for sin. (God premoves the
will to choose this rather than that, and is
the cause of all that is positive in the act.
Its badness springs from an inattention to the
good, a deficiency or privation which God permits
but which -- since it lacks being -- God does
not cause.) A good brief presentation of an
influential but very problematic position.

175 Poteat, William H. "Birth, Suicide, and the Doc-
    trine of Creation: An Exploration of Analogies,"
    Mind, LXVIII (July, 1959), 309-21.

    Suicide, construed as the destruction of my
    world -- the world as it is for me -- provides
    an analogue for God's creation of the world ex
    nihilo. In suicide I do not merely destroy this
    or that thing in my world, but my world as a
    whole. "In this sense, I stand to the world
    in my act of radical destruction, as God seems
    to be thought to stand in his act of radical
    creation." Again, the coming into being of a
    world for me (a world which can only be described

127

with the help of first person pronouns) provides
a model for God's creation of the world out of
nothing. Suggestive.

176 Ross, James Francis. Philosophical Theology.
     Indianapolis and New York: The Bobbs-Merrill
     Co., Inc., 1969. Pp. 254-78.

     In chapter 6, Ross explicates the notion of de-
     grees or levels of reality and the claim that
     God exists at a higher level of reality than
     anything else. For a further description of
     this attempt see # 532 below. Compare this analy-
     sis with Mavrodes' explication of the same no-
     tion (# 171 above).

177 Smart, Ninian. "Myth and Transcendence," Monist,
     50 (October, 1966), 475-87.

     Smart argues that the concept of divine tran-
     scendence embraces five elements -- the concept
     of non-spatiality, independence and creativity,
     the notion that God is concealed behind every-
     thing, and the idea that God is specially present
     in certain things. Smart demonstrates the logical
     copossibility of these elements. He also attempts
     to prove that these elements are coherent (are
     internally related) by showing how all of these
     elements are suggested by numinous and mystical
     experience. An interesting treatment of the
     concept of transcendence.

178 Stokes, Walter Elliott. "Is God Really Related
     to the World?" Proc Cath Phil Ass, XXXIX (1965),
     145-51.

     Stokes attempts to show how (within an Augus-
     tinian-Thomistic framework) God can be understood
     to be really related to the world. Both Thomas

and Augustine recognize that being a person involves both existing in one's own right and being related to another. As a person God, in part, "is what He is eternally. . . by a free decision to create the world." This decision is a "free self-giving" or "self-relating." Since this decision is eternal, it does not involve mutability or the acquisition of a new perfection. Since creation is a free self-giving, it does not entail any "dependence involving imperfection." The proposal under consideration is, however, incompatible with the notion that "a being is more perfect. . . when it is wholly by necessity rather than by any kind of spontaneity." (While creation, on this account, does not involve the acquisition of a new perfection, it is not clear whether or not Stokes believes that a God who eternally decides to create is more perfect than a God who eternally decides not to do so. If he does believe this, then his position is less traditional than he admits.)

179 Wainwright, William Judson. "God's Body," JAAR, XLII (September, 1974), 470-81.

In sections I and II, Wainwright critically examines two sets of arguments -- arguments designed to show that God is not a body, and arguments designed to show that God does not have a particular body distinct from other bodies. Some of these arguments turn out to be sound. Sections III and IV explore the contention that the world is related to God as bodies are related to souls. It is argued that classical theism can only accept this contention if it adopts a Platonic view of the soul-body

relationship, but that the contention can be
rather easily assimilated by Process Theology.

God's Moral Attributes

(See also #s 448, 449, 450, 484,
495, 552, 677 and 955)

Note: Many discussions of the Problem of Evil contain
useful observations on God's moral attributes.

180 Gingell, John. "Forgiveness and Power," Analysis,
34 (New Series, 162), (June, 1974), 180-3.

Gingell argues that since one cannot forgive
offenses which are committed against another
person, God can completely forgive all sins
only if all sins are offenses against God and
no one else. See Hughes' reply (# 182 below).

181 Hughes, George E. "Mr. Martin on the Incarnation:
A Reply to Mr. Plantinga and Mr. Rowe," Austl
J Phil, 40 (August, 1962), 208-11.

A reply to #s 188 and 190 below. Hughes maintains that Martin's argument can be rehabilitated
if "It is necessary that God is good" is replaced
by "Any being which is God is a necessarily
good being." Many theologians wish to assert
this, and if this premiss is added to "Jesus
is God," we can validly deduce "Jesus is a necessarily good being" (which contradicts the claim
that it is conceivable that Jesus sin). Hughes
thinks that the trouble with both Martin's argument and his own rehabilitated version of that
argument is that "Jesus is God" is construed
as a straightforward identity statement when
it is clear that it is not. The orthodox believe that God possesses many characteristics

130

which are not possessed by Jesus (e.g., omnipresence in space and time). Since "Jesus is
God" is not a straightforward identity statement,
the fact that God has some property P (e.g.,
necessary goodness) does not entitle us to infer
that Jesus has P. Hughes' general point is
well taken. The orthodox would not, e.g., infer
Jesus's immutability and aspatiality from God's
immutability and aspatiality. On the other
hand, Martin, Plantinga, Rowe and Hughes may
all be mistaken when they assume that the orthodox believe that Jesus is contingently good.
(It is important to remember that, according
to the orthodox, the "subject" of Jesus's human
nature is the second person of the trinity.
It is, therefore, not clear that Jesus can sin
[even in His human nature].)

182   Hughes, Martin.   "Forgiveness," Analysis, 35 (New
      Series, 166), (March, 1975), 113-7.

      A reply to Gingell's "Forgiveness and Power"
      (# 180 above).

183   Jones, Owen Roger.   The Concept of Holiness.
      London: George Allen & Unwin; New York: The
      Macmillan Co., 1961.   200 pp.

The awareness of holiness is more like the discernment of a pattern or relationship, or like
the discernment of the significance of a whole
complex of facts, than it is like sense perception.   "Fear of the holy" has both an emotional
and dispositional sense.   In both senses, the
sort of fear involved is best understood as fear
of a person with great power and authority,
where the dangers and benefits at stake are

not scientifically calculable. The power of
the holy is related to, and can be discerned
in, but is distinguishable from, ordinary power.
Its relation to the will power needed to live
a godly life, and to completely selfless love,
is particularly important. Will power and love
provide a model for holy power. Furthermore,
when will power and love become extraordinary,
there is a tendency to identify them with holy
power. People, places, actions and objects
become holy by participation in God's own personal unity and wholeness. (An analogy is provided by the way in which a person's possessions,
the gifts which he bestows, or his family, can
come to be regarded as an extension of his personality.) Jones adds that the fact that the
physically and morally unclean or unhealthy or
abnormal cannot be easily incorporated into
"God's personal whole" tells us something significant about the nature of His holiness. Jones
concludes that holiness is God's essence, and
that holiness logically implies personality of
a rather extraordinary sort. (In the last two
chapters Jones tries to explicate the extraordinary nature of God's personality by introducing
the notion of a perfect creative vision.) Jones'
book is a fairly successful attempt to combine
the insights of one style of analytic philosophy
(the author expresses his indebtedness to I. T.
Ramsey) and the insights of modern biblical
scholarship.

184   Martin, Charles Burton. _Religious Belief_. (Con-
      temporary Philosophy.)   Ithaca, New York: Cornell
      University Press, 1959. Pp. 17-63, esp. 33-63.

The third and fourth chapters discuss "God's

perfect goodness." Chapter three contains a pedestrian examination of the claim that God is the ground of moral value. Chapter four is of more interest. As theologians use the terms "God" and "good," it is necessarily true that any being who is God is good. (Either "x is good" is part of the meaning of "x is God" or, if "God" is a proper name and not a descriptive expression, the meaning instructions for the use of the name includes the demand that the being to whom the name is applied be good.) If, however, it is inconceivable that the being who is God (Yahweh, Jesus, etc.) is not good, then the application of "good" to that being is vacuous. While Martin's discussion is of some interest, his central argument appears to be confused. He appears to wish to say that although "goodness" is analytically connected with "God," that "God" (or "good") applies to a being is logically contingent. If this is correct, there is no problem. "It is inconceivable that God not be good, i.e., 'God' cannot properly be applied to a non-good being" is consistent with "It is conceivable that (the being who is) God is not good," provided that it is logically contingent that the being who is God (Yahweh, Jesus) is God. Martin could have strengthened his case if he had had a firmer grasp of traditional theology. It has normally been supposed that the application of "God" to Yahweh or Jesus is not logically contingent. The being who is God (e.g., Yahweh) is essentially God (i.e., if Yahweh is God, it is necessary that He is God), and if "Jesus" refers to the divine hypostasis which bears the human nature (and not merely to the human nature) then Jesus is essentially

133

divine as well. It follows that there is <u>no</u>
significant sense in which God or Jesus could
conceivably have acted badly. Does it follow
that the application of "good" is vacuous?
Martin thinks that it does, apparently on the
grounds that the use of "good" has ceased to
mark a significant contrast between instances
of good behavior and instances of bad behavior.
His argument, however, is unconvincing. If we
are using the term significantly, then there
must be some contrast between behavior which
we are willing to call "good" and behavior which
we are not willing to call "good." What is
<u>not</u> clear is that "good" can be applied to an
individual only if there is a contrast between
behavior which is logically possible for that
individual which we are willing to call "good,"
and behavior which is logically possible <u>for</u>
<u>that</u> <u>same</u> <u>individual</u> which we are not willing
to call "good." --These chapters employ material
which originally appeared as "The Perfect Good"
(<u>Australasian</u> <u>Journal</u> <u>of</u> <u>Philosophy</u>, 1955, reprinted in #923 below, pp. 212-26). Martin's
argument has been effectively criticized by
Plantinga and Rowe (#s 188 and 190 below), and
defended by Hughes (# 181 above).

185 Mayberry, Thomas. "Standards and Criteria," <u>Mind</u>,
     LXXXI (January, 1972), 87-91.

     Mayberry explores the claim that God is the (a)
     standard of goodness. Standard examples (e.g., a
     given loudspeaker) must be distinguished from
     criteria which tell us how to apply those stan-
     dards (e.g., "the criterion of excellence in
     a loudspeaker is the fidelity with which it
     reproduces the sound of live music"). If God

is a standard example of goodness, then, while He can meaningfully be said to be good, there must be a criterion of goodness which is independent of God. If, on the other hand, God is a criterion of goodness (and it is not clear what it would mean to say this), God is not an example of goodness and, therefore, cannot be said to be good.

186 Minas, Anne C. "God and Forgiveness," Phil Quart, 25 (April, 1975), 138-50.

Minas considers several senses of "forgives" and concludes that it is absurd to say that God forgives in any of these senses. While not particularly original, her essay does succeed in showing that in many standard senses, "forgives" cannot be applied to God and that the concept of divine forgiveness is, therefore, problematic.

187 Nygren, Anders. Agape and Eros: Part I, A Study of the Christian Idea of Love; Part II, The History of the Christian Idea of Love. Authorized translation by Philip S. Watson. London: S.P.C.K., 1957. xxvi + 764 pp.

The two parts of this very influential study originally appeared in Sweden in 1930 and 1936 respectively. Eros is a love of the lower for the higher. It presupposes a certain need or lack, and -- since it seeks to achieve satisfaction by possessing the good -- is subtly egoistic. Agape is spontaneous and unmotivated. It is not elicited by the value of its object, but creates or bestows value in the very act of loving. In Christianity, both God's love and the Christian's love for his neighbor are

interpreted as agape. Platonic eros is rejected
in spite of its nobility. Augustine introduced
the "caritas synthesis" which dominates medieval
Christianity. Human love is an acquisitive love
which can only be satisfied by God who is the
supreme good. Neighbor love should be directed
towards God (The Good) as reflected in the neighbor. (The "eros motif.") A rightly ordered
human love is, however, only made possible by
God's free grace. (The "agape motif.") Luther
repudiates the caritas synthesis, rejects eros,
and restores agape to its proper place. Many
of Nygren's theses are tendentious (e.g., the
thesis that the caritas synthesis is not properly Christian, or the thesis that Luther restores
the New Testament conception of love). Nevertheless, his analyses of the various types of
love, and his exploration of Augustine, Luther,
and others have permanent value. Part One (which
analyzes the eros motif and the agape motif),
Part Two, section II (which examines the caritas
synthesis), and the concluding chapters on Luther
are of special interest. The importance of
Nygren's study (and of Singer's study, #191 below)
for the philosopher of religion lies in the
fact that philosophers typically construe God's
goodness as moral righteousness (à la Kant, or
Mill, etc.) and/or as rational benevolence,
whereas the Christian typically construes it as
gratuitous love. The failure to notice this
can vitiate the treatment of certain philosophical
problems. For example, this feature of traditional Christianity is usually ignored in treatments of the Problem of Evil and yet it is surely
relevant. (Robert Adams [# 435 below], and
Charles Journet [# 482 below] provide notable

exceptions to this generalization.)

188 Plantinga, Alvin Carl. "The Perfect Goodness of
God," *Austl J Phil*, 40 (May, 1962), 70-5.

C.B. Martin has claimed (# 184 above) that (1)
"It is impossible that God is non-good" and (2)
"Christ is God" entail (3) "It is impossible
that Christ is non-good," and that this is incompatible with (4) "It is possible that Christ
is non-good." Plantinga points out that "Christ"
can either be interpreted as (a) "The Second
Person of the Trinity" or as (b) a proper name
for Jesus. Interpreted in the first way, (1)
and (2) do entail (3), but (4) is false. Interpreted in the second way, (2) is not a
necessary truth and, therefore, (1) and (2) do
not entail (3).

189 Robbins, J. Wesley. "Moral Standards and the
Application of the Term 'God': A Response to
Kai Nielsen's *Ethics Without God*," *JAAR*, XLIII
(September, 1975), 591-7.

Robbins argues that in judging something to
be God, we judge it to be a suitable standard
or model for human conduct and character. Nielsen
(and others) are mistaken when they suppose that
judgments of this sort must involve the application of independent standards. In selecting
a certain piece of metal as "a suitable standard for being a yard long," or in deciding
that (e.g.) the sort of person who acts out of
respect for the moral law is a "suitable standard for conduct and character," we are not
employing independent standards and saying that
that piece of metal is a yard long or that that
sort of person is good because they measure up

137

to the appropriate standards. On the other
hand, the selection of these (concrete) standards is not necessarily arbitrary. Reasons
can be provided for deciding as we did. This
article should be compared with Mayberry's
article (# 185 above). Analytically minded
philosophers of religion have, perhaps, paid
insufficient attention to the traditional claim
that God is not only good but a (the) standard
or model of goodness. The sort of criticisms
made by Mayberry must be met if any progress
is to be made in explicating this notion in
an intelligible manner. Robbins' remarks provide a good start.

190   Rowe, William Leonard. "C. B. Martin's Contra-
      diction in Theology," Austl J Phil, 40 (May,
      1962), 75-9.

      A reply to # 184 above. Rowe points out that
      (1) "It is not logically possible that God did
      evil," (2) "Christ is God," and (3) "It is logi-
      cally possible that Christ did evil" will only
      yield a contradiction if (2) is necessarily
      true, and that (since Martin uses "Christ" as
      the name of a historical figure), (2) is not
      necessarily true.

191   Singer, Irving. The Nature of Love: Plato to
      Luther. New York and Toronto: Random House,
      1966. xiii + 395 pp.

      In the first part of his book, Singer charac-
      terizes love as a positive valuation which
      gratuitously bestows value upon the beloved
      and is, therefore, not simply a response to
      those valuable features which the beloved
      possesses in its own right. The second part

is devoted to a critical discussion of the views
of Plato, Plotinus, Aristotle, Lucretius, and
Ovid. The third part discusses the medieval
conception of Christian love. This conception
synthesizes four elements: Eros is a love of
God as a person and the highest good, God being
valued both for His own sake and because He
bestows beatitude. The aim of Christian love
is philia, a friendship or wedding between God
and man. The soul in its ascent to, and union
with, God exhibits nomos, a total submission
to God's will. God's love is agape, a free
and unmotivated love which gratuitously bestows
value on its objects. God's agape is the ground
of the other three sorts of love. Luther rejects this synthesis retaining only agape.
Singer criticizes these religious idealizations
on a number of counts -- that human love cannot
be free and meritorious if it is caused by God's
love, that in insisting that human beings should
be loved only in so far as they are ordered to
and manifest God's goodness we distort human
love, that anyone who prizes persons only because
they are ordered to and manifest God treats them
as a mere means (does he, however, manipulate
them or neglect their interests which is what
is normally meant by "treating someone as a
mere means"?), and that an eros which seeks
beatitude is paradoxically combined with a nomos
which is willing to abandon it if God so wills.
Singer provides a rich and suggestive philosophical discussion of ideas which must be grasped
if the Christian conception of God's goodness
is to be fully understood. Although his discussion owes a great deal to Nygren (# 187 above),
it is not derivative. It is worth noting that

implicit defenses of what Nygren calls the
"caritas synthesis" and Singer identifies as
the religious love of the middle ages can be
found in Neo-Scholastic treatises on grace and
mysticism. Particularly noteworthy in this
connection are Gilson's The Mystical Theology
of St. Bernard and Maritain's The Degrees of
Knowledge, #s 610 and 656 below.

The Divine Perfection

Note: Many discussions of the ontological argument
contain useful observations on the nature of
perfection. See especially #s 212, 225, 231,
250 and 260.

192   Coval, Samuel Charles. "Worship, Superlatives
and Concept Confusion," Mind, LXVIII (April,
1959), 218-22.

Coval argues that the concept of an object of
worship includes the concept of omniperfection
and the concept of being. Not exciting but
of some interest.

193   Findley, John Niemeyer. "Can God's Existence
Be Disproved?" Mind, LVII (April, 1948), 176-83.
(Reprinted in # 278 below, pp. 111-22, and in
923 below, pp. 47-56.

Findley defines a religious attitude as one
in which we tend "to abase ourselves before
some object, to defer to it wholly, to devote
ourselves to it with unquestioning enthusiasm,
to bend the knee before it whether literally
or metaphorically." Findley argues that an
appropriate object of these attitudes must be
unlimited in every respect. Findley's remarks
have been very influential. (For a discussion

of other aspects of Findley's article, see # 66
above.)

194　Foss, Martin. The Idea of Perfection in the Western
World. Princeton, N.J.: Princeton University
Press, 1946. 102 pp.

Perfection is "the conformity of a reality to
its concept" (cf. "that's a perfect example
of Gothic architecture"), or the conformity of
a means to a specific and limited end. (No
defense of this claim is provided.) Foss attempts
to show that in Greek philosophy the idealization of perfection leads to a preference for
limit, totality, and completeness, and that
this in turn leads either to pantheism or to
the divinization of being qua being. The Greek
idealization of perfection culminates in
Aristotle's Unmoved Mover -- "an end which is
its own realization" (so there can be no question of a means being imperfectly adapted to
this end), and "a form which absorbs its own
content." (Since Aristotle's God is pure form,
there is no danger of its failing to approximate
to its concept.) Perfection understood as conformity to a concept or as the adequate fulfillment of a function (Foss runs these things together) is always the perfection of a thing.
(According to Foss, a smoothly operating machine
thus provides the best image of perfection.)
Hence, "God in all philosophies of perfection
is a mere thing." The God of the Bible (and
of religion in general) is living and dynamic,
cannot be named, and transcends all limits.
The attempt to express this God in the categories
of Greek thought leads to the interpretation
of perfection as excellence and the transformation

141

of "is perfect" into a comparative (Anselm),
to the idea that God continually surpasses Himself and, thus, grows in perfection (Hegel,
Hartshorne), and to efforts to distinguish a
perfect infinity which can be ascribed to God
from imperfect infinities. The results of these
attempts are hopelessly paradoxical because
the Greek concept of perfection (a totality
of conditions, the limited, complete, and comprehensible) cannot be combined with the notion
of that which transcends not only all conditions
and limitations, but the power of reason itself.
Foss's critique is guided by a conviction of
the importance and value of will, force and
personality, and of the intellect's inability
to capture these things in a net of concepts.
The argument of this little book is excessively
impressionistic, frequently implausible, and
often obscure. Nevertheless, the first two
of its three chapters deserve a cursory examination both because they are occasionally suggestive and because surprisingly little explicit
attention has been devoted to this topic.

195   Hartshorne, Charles.   "The Idea of a Worshipful
      Being," S J Phil, 2 (Winter, 1964), 165-7.

A fairly interesting reply to McCloskey (# 196
below). Hartshorne argues that a God who is
surpassible by Himself, but not by another, is
worthy of worship, and that although the objections raised by McCloskey cannot be adequately
met by classical theism, they can be met by
Process Theism.

196   McCloskey, Henry John. "Would Any Being Merit
      Worship?" S J Phil, 2 (Winter, 1964), 157-64.

McCloskey argues that no possible being is worthy
of worship. While most of McCloskey's points
are familiar, two of his arguments deserve some
attention. (1) If God's goodness is not necessary, then God can cease to be good and, if
God can cease to be good, then it is not proper
to yield our will to God's will. "Yet the
yielding of one's will to God's will is a vital
part of worship." If, on the other hand, God's
goodness is necessary, then God is not virtuous
and so, once again, God is not worthy of worship.
(2) If God creates free beings, He divests Himself of some of His power and control and is,
therefore, no longer worthy of worship. If, however, God does not create free beings, He cannot
be worshiped. (McCloskey apparently assumes
that worship is a moral act, and that moral
acts cannot be performed by beings who are not
free.) See Hartshorne's reply, # 195 above.

197   Mann, William Edward. "The Divine Attributes,
      Amer Phil Quart, 12 (April, 1975), 151-9.

Mann addresses himself to the objection that
the concept of a perfect or supreme being (a
being than which a more perfect is impossible)
is incoherent since some of the perfections
ascribed to such a being have no maxima. Mann
shows that at least three of the most important
perfections ascribed to a perfect being (knowledge, power, and benevolence) do have maxima.

198 Mason, David R. "An Examination of 'Worship'
      as a Key for Re-examining the God Problem,"
      J Relig, 55 (January, 1975), 76-94.

A further exploration of two concepts of worship. (See the author's "Three Recent Treatments of the Ontological Argument," # 196 below.)
Both Findley and Hartshorne define worship as
an unqualified devotion, commitment, or concern,
but while for Findley the heart of this concern
is self-abasement before the wholly other, for
Hartshorne its heart is love. Since God is
defined as the appropriate object of worship,
these differences lead to differences in their
concepts of God. Mason criticizes Findley's
concept of worship, and attempts to explain
how love can include elements of contrition
and awe. It is worth observing that there are
several concepts of love, and that in order to
get from the claim that love is the heart of
worship to the claim that the God of Process
Theology is the only appropriate object of worship, love must be identified with a sympathetic
and loving interaction in which both partners
act and react, grow and are modified in the
course of their relationship, and not with (e.g.)
Platonic eros or delight in the good.

199 _____. "Three Recent Treatments of the Ontologi-
      cal Argument," Ohio J Relig Stud, 2 (April, 1974),
      28-43.

An examination of Findley, Malcolm, and Hartshorne. While the article does not make a substantial contribution to our understanding of
the ontological argument, its section on Hartshorne does provide a useful comparison of
Findley's and Hartshorne's concepts of worship

and perfection. Mason suggests (1) that a concept of worship which stresses self-abasement
(Findley, # 193 above) is connected with the
concept of a statically perfect being who is
in all respects complete and necessary, and
(2) that a concept of worship which stresses
love and service (Hartshorne) is connected with
the concept of a dynamically perfect being who
is in some respects incomplete and contingent,
and who cannot be surpassed by others but can
be surpassed by himself. An examination of
these differences is important in view of the
logical connections which seem to exist between
"God is perfect" and "God is worthy of worship."

200 Moulder, James. "What Counts as a God?" Sophia,
     XIII (July, 1974), 5-18.

A critical discussion of certain issues raised
by Smart's The Concept of Worship (# 202 below).
Moulder argues that "god" is a dyadic predicate,
and explores the analogy between "x is y's god"
and "x is y's wife." This article is worth
examining though Moulder's argument does raise
a number of serious questions. For example:
(1) Smart is taken to task for making "god" a
monadic predicate, but Smart's point is not
that "god" is not a relational term, but that
a god's existence does not depend upon its being
worshiped. This is related to the major weakness of Moulder's proposal. If "god" behaves
like "wife," then nothing can be a god if there
are no worshipers. It is more plausible to
suppose that a god is a being who can or should
be appropriately worshiped (if there is anyone
to worship it). "God" is thus defined in terms
of worship, but the existence of a god is not

made dependent upon the existence of creatures.
(2) Moulder correctly argues that the choice of
a wife is a-rational and idiosyncratic. (One
does not have to provide non-idiosyncratic reasons for marrying, or for choosing one women
rather than another as one's wife.) It is not
clear, however, that a decision to worship is,
or should be, similarly a-rational and idiosyncratic.

201 Pike, Nelson Craft. God and Timelessness. (Studies
in Ethics and the Philosophy of Religion.)
London: Routledge & Kegan Paul; New York:
Schocken Books, 1970. Pp. 130-66.

Chapter 8 contains an important examination of
the concept of a being greater than which none
can be conceived. Anselm wishes to construe
perfections as qualities which make a thing
better as a thing rather than as a thing of a
certain kind. A certain amount of sense can
be made of this, if "greater than" is interpreted
as "more worthy of preservation than." This
interpretation, nevertheless, proves to be
inadequate, for on this interpretation certain
properties which Anselm wishes to count as perfections (power) turn out not to be perfections,
and other properties which Anselm would not wish
to count as perfections (sweet-smelling) turn
out to be perfections. Pike then explores the
suggestion that "greater than" can be interpreted
as "more worthy of worship than," and examines
ways in which the formulae "x is worthy of worship" and "x is more worthy of worship than any
other possible being" can be used to derive "x
is conscious," "x is benevolent," etc.

202 Smart, Ninian. The Concept of Worship. (New
Studies in the Philosophy of Religion.) London
and Basingstoke: The Macmillan Press Ltd.;
New York: St. Martin's Press, 1972. ix + 77 pp.

Smart argues that "worship is relational,"
"typically involves ritual," expresses the
superiority of the Focus" (object of worship),
"sustains or is part of the power of the Focus,"
involves praise of the Focus, expresses the experience of the numinous described by Rudolf
Otto and thus perceives the Focus as awe-inspir-
ing, and that the Focus of worship transcends
its manifestations. "God" is a relational concept
for a god is (analytically) something to be
worshiped. Certain features of God can be
elicited from an analysis of the concept of worship (e.g., personality and transcendence),
but Findley (# 66 above) is criticized for arguing that a necessary being is alone worthy
of worship. It is suggested that goodness (as
contrasted with numinosity of benificence towards
its worshipers) may not be analytically connected
with the notion of God (defined as an appropriate
object of worship). The attempt to define God
(or God's perfection) in terms of worship is
not uncommon. Smart's examination of these
issues is, however, unique in two (related)
respects. (1) Smart is concerned with the concept of worship which is actually employed in
concrete religions (and not with some abstract
"essence" of worship). (2) This concern leads
Smart to emphasize the importance to worship
of overt ritual activity. Though "numinous
experience is in a sense definitive of worship,"
Smart cautions us against minimizing the importance of the ritual acts which express that

147

experience and suggests that attempts to define
God in terms of some inner experience or attitude will be unsuccessful. (See Moulder's reply,
200 above.)

203 Srzednicki, Jan. "The Ontological Proof and the
Concept of 'Absolute'," Sophia, IV (October,
1965), 28-32.

The ontological argument must either assume
that God possesses all perfections or that nothing can be more perfect than God. Both notions
are incoherent, for some perfections (e.g., perfect justice and perfect mercy) are incompatible
with one another and some perfections (e.g.,
truthfulness) do not clearly have a maximum
degree. (On this last point see Mann, # 197
above.)

II   ARGUMENTS FOR THE EXISTENCE OF GOD

The Ontological Argument

(See also #s 35, 66 and 203)

204 Adams, Robert Merrihew. "The Logical Structure
of Anselm's Arguments," Phil Rev, LXXX (January,
1971), 28-54.

A valuable article. Offers a valid formalization
of Anselm's Proslogion II argument, in which
the variables range over non-actual as well as
actual beings and "real existence" is construed
as a predicate. A formalization of Gaunilo's
perfect island objection is provided and it is
argued that Anselm can escape the thrust of
his objection if the assumption that there must
be something (real or unreal) to which consistent

descriptions apply is modified so as to be restricted to (consistent) descriptions "containing only properties which necessarily belong to their common subject." A formalization of the modal argument found in Anselm's reply to Gaunilo is offered which is very similar to that provided by Hartshorne in The Logic of Perfection (# 245 below) pp. 50-1. Adams points out that it is simpler to derive God's existence from the assumption that God's existence is possibly necessary. The article concludes with a discussion of Proslogion III.

205 _____. "The Modal Argument for the Existence of God." Doctoral Dissertation: Cornell University, 1969. 232 pp.

A modal argument is defined as an argument which infers God's existence from the claim that it is a necessary truth that if God exists it is necessarily true that He exists and from the claim that it is logically possible that God exists. It is argued (chapters one through three) that the argument is formally valid. The first premiss is examined in chapters four through six (with special attention to Hartshorne, Malcolm and Plantinga), and the second premiss is examined in chapters seven through eleven. "The principal conclusion of the dissertation is that it has not been proved that the modal argument adds anything to whatever other grounds there may be for believing in the existence of God."

206 Alston, William P. "The Ontological Argument
Revisited," _Phil Rev_, LXIX (October, 1960),
452-74. (Reprinted in # 278 below, pp. 86-110.)

An important article. According to Alston,
existential statements set up subjects for predication, and the sort of existence (real, fictional, mental, etc.) presupposed by the use of
the subject term determines the logical status
of the predicate. Thus fictional existence is
presupposed by the use of "Ivan Karamazov" in
"Ivan Karamazov had two brothers" and "had two
brothers" only applies to Ivan within the realm
of fiction. Anselm's conclusion "The Perfect
Being exists in reality" ascribes a predicate
to a subject. However, in the context of the
argument it is clear that the sort of existence
presupposed by the use of the subject term is
mental existence (existence in the understanding).
Hence, the use of the predicate "exists in
reality" can have no implications with respect
to the real world. See Plantinga's critique
and Yandell's critique (#s 274 and 301 below).

207 Barnes, Jonathan. _The Ontological Argument_ (New
Studies in the Philosophy of Religion). London
and Basingstoke: The Macmillan Press, Ltd.,
New York: St. Martin's Press, 1972, viii + 98 pp.

Good discussions of Anselm's argument, the argument found in Descartes' fifth meditation, and
the modal arguments of Malcolm and Hartshorne
(chapter 1). Barnes provides an interesting
critique of the claim that existential propositions can't be necessary (chapter 2) and of the
claim that existence isn't a predicate (chapter 3,
especially sections I, II, III and VI). In
chapter 4 section III, Barnes discusses the

"Pseudo-Cartesian Argument." This argument
has the following form: (1) God is F, (2) Everything F exists, therefore (3) God exists. Barnes'
discussion is interesting but it should be noted
that his criticism of the "first pattern of
interpretation" (in which the conclusion is
construed as "all Gods exist") loses its force
if the variables are allowed to range over possibles as well as actuals and if "God is a
possible being" is added as a premiss. There
is a useful bibliography containing many cita-
tions of articles which examine the logical
status of "exists."

208   Barth, Karl. Anselm: Fides Quaerens Intellectum,
      Anselm's Proof of the Existence of God in the
      context of his theological scheme. Translated
      by Ian W. Robertson from the second German edi-
      tion. London: SCM Press; Richmond, Virginia:
      John Knox Press, 1960. 173 pp.

      A very interesting and controversial interpre-
      tation of Anselm's argument. Barth contends
      that (as in the Cur Deus Homo) Anselm is arguing
      from one revealed proposition (or more accurate-
      ly, a revealed name of God, viz., "A being greater
      than which none can be thought") to another (that
      God exists). The argument is therefore addressed
      to the believer rather than to the man of mere
      reason. The first German edition appeared in
      1931, and the second German edition in 1958.
      See the essays contained in the first part of
      The Many-Faced Argument (# 248 below) and Potter's
      critique (# 281 below).

209   Basham, Ronald Robert, Jr. "The 'Second Version'
      of Anselm's Ontological Argument," <u>Can</u> <u>J</u> <u>Phil</u>,
      VI (December, 1976), 665-83.

         Basham attempts to show that there is no non-
         question begging way of establishing "If God's
         existence is conceptually possible, then God's
         existence is conceptually necessary."

210   Blumenfeld, David. "Leibniz's Modal Proof of the
      Possibility of God," <u>Stud</u> <u>Leibniz</u>, IV (1972),
      132-40.

         Leibniz recognized that the ontological argument
         presupposes that God is possible, and offered two
         proofs of God's possibility. He argued that
         God is the sum of all perfections and that all
         perfections are co-possible. This article,
         however, is devoted to Leibniz's second proof
         which rests upon the assumption that if the
         necessary being is not possible, no being is
         possible. The falsity of the consequent can
         be established in two ways: (1) By presenting
         examples of concepts containing no contradictions
         and (2) by showing that it is necessary that
         the domain of possibles be non-empty (in which
         case there is at least one possible being).

211   Brecher, R. "Pure Objects and the Ontological
      Argument," <u>Sophia</u>, XIV (October, 1975), 10-18.

         Argues that since Meinong defines pure objects
         as "conglomerations of properties," and believes
         that (real) existence is not a property, he
         would not classify existent golden mountains
         as pure objects. Hence, he is not forced to
         infer that golden mountains exist from the
         fact that some pure objects are existent golden

mountains. Brecher observes, however, that
Meinong did believe that non-existence could
be deduced from certain natures (e.g., round
squares) in spite of the fact that those natures
contain neither (real) existence nor non-existence. He suggests that Anselm's (first) argument might be regarded as a parallel attempt to
deduce (real) existence from a nature which
contains the property of being such that a
greater cannot be thought. In the case of both
deductions a further (a priori) principle must
be introduced to deduce the ontological status
of the object in question. The first deduction
employs the principle that objects with incompatible properties can't really exist. The
second deduction employs the principle that if
God's nature exists in the understanding, then
it can be thought to exist in reality as well,
which is greater. An interesting article.

212 Broad, Charlie Dunbar. "Arguments for the Existence of God," Religion, Philosophy and Psychical
Research: Selected Essays by C. D. Broad.
(International Library of Psychology, Philosophy
and Scientific Method.) London: Routledge &
Kegan Paul Limited, 1953. Pp. 175-201, esp.
177-83.

After some useful observations on the concept
of a perfect being, Broad rejects the ontological argument on the grounds that it makes
an illicit comparison between a possible being
and an actual being. A possible being cannot
be compared with an actual being except upon
the hypothesis that it (the possible being)
exists, in which case it is "meaningless to
compare it with anything in respect of the
presence or absence of existence." This essay

originally appeared in the _Journal of Theological Studies_ (1939). See Plantinga's critique (# 274 below).

213 Brown, T. Patterson. "Professor Malcolm on 'Anselm's Ontological Arguments'." _Analysis_, 22 (October, 1961), 12-14.

It is argued that Malcolm's ontological argument (see # 260 below) fails because it confuses the impossibility of God's existing at some (other) time _if_ He does not presently exist, with the impossibility of God's ever existing.

214 Campbell, Richard. _From Belief to Understanding, A Study of Anselm's Proslogion Argument on the Existence of God_. Canberra: The Australian National University Press, 1976. 229 pp.

According to Campbell, the argument presented by Anselm in _Proslogion_ II and III is a single argument with three stages. Anselm first establishes that something than which nothing greater can be thought exists in reality as well as in the understanding. He then shows that something than which nothing greater can be thought cannot be thought not to be, and concludes by proving that God and God alone is something than which nothing greater can be thought. The argument which Campbell finds in Anselm has several significant features. (1) It rests upon a speech act -- Anselm's utterance of "something than which nothing greater can be thought." It is (correctly) presupposed that the terms employed in this expression are part of public language and that someone who hears it, therefore, has such a thing in his understanding. The argument does not need a premiss

154

which asserts that it is logically possible
that there be something than which a greater
cannot be thought. (2) What cannot be thought
not to be might nevertheless not be. It follows
that the second stage does not by itself establish an existential conclusion. (3) The argument
does not begin with a definition. That God is
a being greater than which none can be thought
is established by the argument. It is not a
presupposition of it. In the course of this
book, Campbell considers most of the problems
associated with ontological arguments. His
comments are original, suggestive and often
persuasive. A significant contribution to the
study of Anselm and the ontological argument.

215   Cargile, James. "The Ontological Argument," _Philos-
      ophy_, 50 (January, 1975), 69-80.

      Whether existence or necessary existence is or is
      not a perfection is irrelevant to an evaluation
      of the argument. The soundness of the argument
      depends solely upon whether "God" or "a supreme
      being" is consistent.

216   Charlesworth, Maxwell John. "St. Anselm's Argu-
      ment," _Sophia_, I (July, 1962), 25-36.

      Discusses a number of points. Charlesworth
      argues that the argument does not crucially
      depend upon the assumption that existence is
      a predicate, attempts to determine whether com-
      parisons can be made between conceptual and
      real existence and, if so, whether real exis-
      tence has some sort of priority over concep-
      tual existence, and contends that, while what
      _is_ crucial is the meaningfulness of such

expressions as "a being greater than which none
can be thought," "what exists necessarily is
greater than what exists contingently," etc.,
it is unclear whether the burden of proof lies
on theists who believe that these expressions
are meaningful, or whether it lies on those
atheists who believe that they are meaningless.

217   _____. St. Anselm's _Proslogion_ with a _Reply_
on Behalf of the Fool by Gaunilo and the Author's
Reply to Gaunilo. Translated with an introduction
and philosophical commentary by M. J. Charlesworth. Oxford: The Clarenden Press, 1965.
vi + 196 pp.

Latin text with English translation. The extensive introduction is devoted to Anselm's
life, his relation to Augustine, faith and reason in the _Cur Deus Homo_, and Barth's interpretation of Anselm. The commentary (which extends
from pages 49 to 99) is primarily concerned with
the ontological argument and incorporates the
author's "St. Anselm's Argument" (# 216 above).

218 Clarke, Bowman Lafayette. "Modal Disproofs and
Proofs for God," _S J Phil_, 9 (Fall, 1971), 247-58.

Where $(\exists x)Gx$ is interpreted as "God exists,"
we can construct valid arguments from $M(\exists x)Gx$ to
$(\exists x)Gx$, and from $M-(\exists x)Gx$ to $-(\exists x)Gx$. Leibniz
justifies $M(\exists x)Gx$ by arguing that $(\exists x)Gx$ is not
inconsistent. Hume and Kant justify $M-(\exists x)Gx$ by
pointing out that $(\exists x)Gx$ is not a tautology. All
parties to the dispute appear to assume that
something is possible if and only if its description is not self-contradictory and that it
is possible for something not to be if and
only if the claim that it exists is not

156

tautologous. Clarke argues that this assumption
is suspect and proposes that "possibility,"
"necessity," etc., be defined in terms of the
axioms of some appropriate system.

219 Coburn, Robert Craig. "Animadversions on Plantin-
     ga's Kant," J Phil, LXIII (October 13, 1966),
     546-8.

Abstract of a reply to Plantinga's "Kant's Objection to the Ontological Argument" (# 276
below). Argues that Plantinga's interpretation
of Kant is implausible since it would involve
ascribing to Kant the view that existence (while
not a "real predicate") is a property which
can be annexed to a concept -- a view which
Kant almost certainly did not hold.

220 _____. "Professor Malcolm on God," Austl
     J Phil, 41 (August, 1963), 143-62.

In the paper's first section, Coburn defends
the plausibility of Malcolm's ontological argument. In its second section he argues that
since the being whose necessary existence has
been established is non-temporal, he (it?) cannot be a person (for persons remember, anticipate, deliberate, decide, etc., i.e., do things
which imply temporality) and is therefore not
the God of the Judeo-Christian tradition. Coburn
also argues (rather plausibly) that the consistency of "God," which is essential to the argument, cannot be established by appealing to
ordinary religious usage and (less plausibly)
that it cannot be defended by taking terms desig-
nating personal attributes in extended senses.

221 Cock, Albert A. "The Ontological Argument for the existence of God," _Proc Aris Soc_, XVIII (1917-1918), 363-84.

Section II contains a rather interesting discussion of Kant's criticism in which it is argued that, given his theory of knowledge, Kant is simply not equipped to fairly assess the ontological argument. Section V provides an ontological "proof" of the devil, defined as a being than which a worse is inconceivable. Cock suggests that the ontological argument fails to produce conviction because it appeals to the intellect rather than the whole person and "only a whole person can worship."

222 Collingwood, Robin George. _An Essay on Philosophical Method_. Oxford: The Clarenden Press, 1933. Pp. 123-36.

Philosophy as a form of thought guarantees the existence of its subject matter. Thus, metaphysics guarantees the existence of Being, the Good, or God. (No argument is given for this.) Logic guarantees the existence of its subject matter because logic is a set of propositions reached through inference whose subject matter is the nature of propositions and inference. Moral philosophy is concerned with ideals ("essences") in so far as these wholly or partially exist in the minds of moral agents and effect action. Here too "essence involves existence." (It should be noted that according to Collingwood metaphysics, logic and moral philosophy are concerned with three aspects of the same subject matter, viz., being, truth and goodness.) See Ryle's critique (# 292 below).

158

223 Corr, Charles A. "The Existence of God, Natural
Theology and Christian Wolff," _Int J Phil Relig_,
IV (Summer, 1973), 105-18, esp. 113-5.

Section 3 contains a sketch of Wolff's ontological
argument. God contains compossible realities
in the highest degree. Existence is a reality
which is compatible with the other realities
contained in God. (Since these other realities
are mutually compatible, it is possible that
they exist together and hence existence is compatible with them.) Therefore, existence is
contained in God. The highest degree of existence is necessary existence. Therefore, God
necessarily exists.

224 Cosgrove, Matthew R. "Thomas Aquinas on Anselm's
Argument," _Rev Metaph_, XXVII (March, 1974),
513-30.

It is argued that Aquinas believes Anselm's
argument (in both its non-modal and in its modal
form) to be ineffective because the "fool" can
reply that a being greater than which none can
be thought exists neither in reality _nor in_
the understanding. The position which Aquinas
attributes to the "fool" and which he believes
to have a certain plausibility is not that God
is logically impossible but that God is so great
that he cannot be conceived by us. An interesting
article.

225 Crittendon, Charles. "The Argument from Perfection
to Existence," _Relig Stud_, 4 (October, 1968)
123-32.

Argues that there is no coherent concept of a
perfect being. We need criteria which can be

used to rank beings of different kinds. The
degree of dependence and mutability won't do
for dependence and mutability aren't always
imperfections. We can't argue that a perfect
being possesses all perfections because some
perfections are incompatible. And so on. The
questions which Crittendon raises need to be
raised but his answers are not wholly convincing.
(In particular, notice that when we say that
dependency or mutability are imperfections we
do not imply that it would be better for dependent and mutable things to be independent
and unchanging. An absolutely independent or
immutable human life would not be a better human
life for an absolutely independent and immutable
human life is logically impossible. Nevertheless,
one might argue that human life is less perfect
than divine life because it is dependent and
mutable.)

226   Crocker, Sylvia Fleming.   "Descartes' Ontological
      Argument and the Existing Thinker," Mod Sch,
      LIII (May, 1966). 347-77.

This examination of Descartes' argument has
several interesting features, including the
following: (1) Crocker contends that Descartes
is not arguing from the meaning of "God" but
from His "true and immutable nature," that he
realizes that the character of this nature must
be determined by investigation, and that this
investigation occurs in Meditation III.   (2)
She argues that the concept of perfection primarily refers to "ontological completeness [where
a thing is complete if it perfectly expresses
its essence] and underivedness, understood in
terms of God's 'inexhaustible power'," and

that existence is a perfection in the sense
that it is a necessary condition of perfection.
(Unrealized perfections are merely possible
perfections.) On the other hand, Crocker's
interpretation of the argument in Meditation V
(as a movement from a system of possible existence
to a ground of that system) is both confusing
and inadequately supported by the text.

227 Davis, Stephen Thane. "Anselm and Gaunilo on
     the 'Lost Island'," S J Phil, XIII (Winter,
     1975), 435-48.

Gaunilo attempts to construct an argument which
(1) is formally similar to Anselm's argument
but which (2) leads to an absurd conclusion
because an expression referring to an obviously
non-existent entity is substituted for "greatest
conceivable being." According to Davis, an argument of this type can fail for a number of reasons. If the substituted expression refers to
a contingent being, the argument which results
from the substitution will be unsuccessful because no a priori argument can establish the
existence or non-existence of a contingent being.
If the substituted expression (e.g., "a necessarily existing lion") refers to a necessary
being whose necessity is incompatible with its
other properties, the argument which results
from the substitution fails because a crucial
premiss in any argument of this type asserts
that the entity whose existence we are trying
to prove is a possible entity. If the substituted expression (e.g., "a necessary being which
can perform any action except the most trivial
action") refers to a necessary being whose other
properties cannot be coherently specified, the

argument which results from the substitution
fails for the same reason. An argument will
fail if it results from substituting an expression
(e.g., "a necessary but non-omnipotent being")
which refers to a being which is not the greatest
conceivable member of some set since the original
argument rests upon the absurdity of asserting
that we can conceive of something greater than
that than which a greater is inconceivable.
Davis concludes by suggesting that the only
expressions which will prove to be satisfactory
will be those which refer to God himself. Very
interesting.

228 _____. "Anselm and Question-Begging: A
     Reply to William Rowe," Int J Phil Relig, VII
     (1976), 448-57.

A reply to Rowe (# 287 below). Davis's most
important contention is the following: Concepts
(e.g., the concept of a unicornex, where "unicornex" is defined as an existing unicorn) which
conjoin existence with a set of properties the
exemplification of which is contingent are not
coherent. If Davis is correct, Rowe's argument
loses its plausibility for there is no longer
any reason to suppose that there are coherent
concepts which are not exemplified by any possible object. (According to Davis, if "unicornex"
is defined as an existing unicorn, then existence
must be regarded as an essential feature of
unicornexes. However, existence cannot be an
essential feature of unicornexes because the
existence of unicornexes is, as Rowe maintains,
contingent, and existence cannot be an essential
property of a contingently existing thing.)

229   _____. "Does the Ontological Argument Beg
the Question?" Int J Phil Rel, VII (1976),
433-42.

A reply to Rowe's "The Ontological Argument
and Question-Begging" (# 290 below). Davis
argues that Rowe has failed to show that Anselm's
argument begs the question. See Rowe's response
(# 287 below).

230 Devine, Philip Edwards. "Does St. Anselm Beg the
Question?" Philosophy, 50 (July, 1975), 271-81.

It is sometimes argued that the first premiss
of Anselm's argument, viz., "God is a being
greater than which none can be thought," begs
the question for the proper use of "God" presupposes that that to which it refers (God)
exists. Devine rather plausibly argues that
we can both talk about and refer to objects
without committing ourselves to the existence
of these objects. The article is drawn from
Devine's doctoral dissertation, "The Very Idea
of Ontological Argument" (University of California, Berkeley, 1972).

231   _____. "The Perfect Island, the Devil, and
Existing Unicorns," Amer Phil Quart, 12 (July,
1975) 255-60.

A fairly interesting discussion of several
loosely related points. Devine attempts to
show that the notion of a perfect island is
incoherent, and that it may make perfectly good
sense to speak not merely of perfection of a
certain kind but of absolute perfection. He
argues that the concept of a being worse than
which none can be conceived may be incoherent

and that we cannot, therefore, construct an
ontological proof of the existence of an absolutely evil being. Devine concludes by contending
that the ontological argument does not simply
extract existence from a concept in which it
has been arbitrarily included (as one might
extract existence from the concept of an existent
unicorn). To say that God's nature entails
existence is not to say that the attributes
which comprise that nature can be analyzed
into p1, p2. . . etc., + exists. (Cf. to say
that being red entails being colored is not to
say that red can be analyzed into some set of
properties + being colored.)

232 _____. "The Religious Significance of the
     Ontological Argument," Relig Stud, 11 (March,
     1975), 97-116.

     Argues that even if some ontological arguments
     are sound, they do not establish the truth of
     religion for (1) all religious systems include
     contingent truths and no necessary proposition
     (and, therefore, no conclusion of a sound onto-
     logical argument) entails a contingent proposi-
     tion, and (2) while the proposition that the
     concept of God is coherent is essential to the
     argument, a person's acceptance or rejection of
     that proposition is largely determined by whether
     or not he has already committed himself to a
     religious position.

233 Donceel, Joseph. "Can We Still Make a Case in
     Reason for the Existence of God?" God Knowable
     and Unknowable. Edited by Robert J. Roth. New
     York: Fordham University Press, 1973. Pp.
     159-86.

This rather interesting article presents an ontological argument for God's existence which employs material drawn from recent Roman Catholic philosophical speculation concerning the intentional character of human consciousness and knowledge, and the relation of these intentions to the infinite. Donceel maintains that Hartshorne, Findley, and others have shown that if God is possible He exists. What must be established, therefore, is God's possibility. According to Donceel, the dynamism of the human intellect drives it beyond every limit. What we know or want is "projected against the horizon of infinity." Since the object of an aim which is an ineradicable feature of human nature must be logically possible, God (the Infinite or Unlimited) must be logically possible.

234 Dore, Clement Joseph, Jr. "Examination of an Ontological Argument," Phil Stud, XXVIII (November, 1975), 345-56, esp. 350-5.

A defense of the modal argument. In section III, Dore argues that, since there are apparent perceptions of God and since one cannot seem to perceive what is logically impossible, God is logically possible. (Dore is aware that this argument commits him to the [implausible] contention that some people seem to perceive the necessary possession of God-attributes.) In section IV, Dore shows that modal arguments similar to the argument which establishes God's existence cannot be used to demonstrate the existence of several Gods or the existence of one or more near-Gods.

235   Dupré, Louis. "The Moral Argument, the Religious
      Experience, and the Basic Meaning of the Onto-
      logical Argument," Ideal Stud, III (September,
      1973), 266-76.

      Suggests that the ontological argument is an
      attempt to articulate the believer's spontaneous
      transition from "immanent experience to tran-
      scendent reality."

236   Edwards, Rem B.   Reason and Religion: An Intro-
      duction to the Philosophy of Religion. New York:
      Harcourt Brace Jovanovich, Inc., 1972. Pp. 219-
      53, esp. 238-40 and 244-51.

      Edwards' defense of the ontological argument
      contains worthwhile discussions of several ob-
      jections -- that existence is not a predicate
      (238-40), that the argument confuses ontological
      and logical necessity (244-45), and that even
      if the argument shows that a necessary being
      exists, it doesn't show that God exists (245-51).

237   Fitch, Frederic B.   "The Perfection of Perfection,"
      Process and Divinity. Edited by William Reese
      and Eugene Freeman. LaSalle, Illinois: Open
      Court Pub. Co., 1964. Pp. 529-32.

      Fitch argues that unless the attribute of perfec-
      tion is itself perfect, then anything which has
      that attribute is less perfect than it might
      be (for it enjoys an "imperfect kind of perfec-
      tion," "lacks the fullest sort of perfection")
      and is, therefore, not perfect after all. If,
      however, the attribute of perfection is "empty,"
      it falls short of perfection. Therefore, a
      perfect being exists.

238 Forest, Aimé. "St. Anselm's Argument in Reflexive
     Philosophy," in # 248 below, pp. 275-300.

     In "reflexive philosophy," God or the Absolute
     is said to be given in self-reflection as "a
     presence that sustains our intellectual process-
     es." In reflection, the soul discerns not only
     itself "but also, at its foundation," the ab-
     solute from which it emanates. Maurice Blondel,
     Jacques Paliard, Louis Lavelle and Ferdinand
     Alguie are discussed. This article illustrates
     the fact that modern continental philosophy
     interprets the ontological argument in a very
     different way from the way in which it is inter-
     preted in analytical philosophy. Rather than
     deriving God's existence from an examination
     of the concept of God (or deducing God's exis-
     tence from certain necessary truths), reflexive
     philosophy discerns the infinite in the very act
     of thinking the infinite (or in any act of think-
     ing). The ontological argument is seen as a
     movement from the thought of God (= the act of
     thinking God) to the reality of God, rather
     than as a movement from the thought of God (=
     the concept of God) to the reality of God. A
     translation, by Arthur McGill, of "L'Argument
     de S. Anselme dans la philosophie reflexive,"
     (Spicilegium Beccense, Paris: J. Vrin, 1959,
     pp. 273-94).

239 Forgie, James William. "Frege's Objection to the
     Ontological Argument," Nous VI (September, 1972),
     251-63.

     Frege argues that (1) in making an existence
     claim we are ascribing a second order property
     (non-emptiness) to a first order concept, that

consequently (2) existence is a second order
property, and that, therefore, (3) the ontological argument, which assumes that existence is
a first order property, fails. Forgie expresses
some doubts about the third point, argues against
(1), and attempts to show that (2) does not follow
from (1).

240 _____. "Is the Cartesian Ontological Argument
Defensible?" New Scholas, L (Winter, 1976),
108-21.

It is sometimes argued that the first premiss of
Descartes' argument ("God is a supremely perfect
being") is either a disguised hypothetical, in
which case the conclusion is also hypothetical,
or categorical, in which case it presupposes
that God exists, and, thus, begs the question.
Forgie addresses himself to the second alternative and explores the suggestion that the sort
of existence which is presupposed is not actual
existence but either fictional existence, existence in the understanding, or the sort of existence enjoyed by a Meinongian pure object and
that, therefore, no questions are begged. Forgie
argues that if the premiss is understood in the
first of these ways, then the argument can only
establish that God exists in the relevant fictional world, that if the premiss is understood
in the second way, the argument can only show
that God exists in the "world of the understanding," etc. This objection is familiar and lucidly presented but we are essentially being asked
to simply see that it is correct. (Forgie maintains that if we are not careful Cartesian type
arguments can be used to establish the real
existence of such things as "the existent Emperor
of Idaho." His objection does not, however,

rest upon this possibility.)

241 Grant, C. K. "The Ontological Disproof of the
      Devil," Analysis, XVII (January, 1957), 71-2.

      Since existence is a perfection, an absolutely
      imperfect being cannot exist. Hence the devil
      cannot exist. (Grant acknowledges that a being
      with no moral perfections but some ontological
      perfections might exist.)

242 Harris, Errol E. "Mr. Collingwood and the Onto-
      logical Argument: Reply to G. Ryle," Mind,
      XLV (October, 1936), 474-80. (Reprinted in # 248
      below, pp. 261-8.)

      A defense of an "Hegelian form" of the ontological
      argument. Whether thoughts are true or false
      and whether facts exist or do not exist is deter-
      mined by whether they do or do not fit into
      the whole of thought and being. Hence, God
      (defined as this all-inclusive whole) is a pre-
      supposition of all thought and being. Harris
      does not discuss Collingwood's own formulation
      of the ontological argument (# 222 above). See
      Ryle's response to Harris (# 291 below).

243 _____. Revelation Through Reason. New Haven:
      Yale University Press, 1958. Pp. 53-63 and
      82-94.

      In these sections, Harris presents an "Hegelian
      version" of the ontological argument. God (de-
      fined as a perfected system of knowledge and
      reality -- a suprapersonal whole which includes
      the temporal order) must be thought of as exist-
      ing, for God so-conceived is a presupposition
      of all discourse and thought. The world process

and the stages within it cannot be thought without thinking their end, viz., God, the completed whole of things. Therefore, God must be thought to exist.

244 Hartshorne, Charles. Anselm's Discovery: A Re-examination of the Ontological Proof for God's Existence. (The Open Court Library of Philosophy.) LaSalle, Illinois: Open Court Pub. Co., 1965. xvi + 333 pp.

An elaborate defense of the modal version of the ontological argument presented by Hartshorne in the long second chapter of The Logic of Perfection (# 245 below). Contains many interesting observations.

245 _____. "Ten Ontological or Modal Proofs for God's Existence," The Logic of Perfection and Other Essays in Neo Classical Metaphysics by Charles Hartshorne. LaSalle, Illinois: Open Court Pub. Co., 1962. Pp. 28-117.

A very important essay. Charles Hartshorne and Norman Malcolm are largely responsible for the renewed interest in the ontological argument. Hartshorne (like Malcolm) distinguishes modal from non-modal versions of the ontological argument, argues that necessary existence is a predicate, that it must be ascribed to God, and that (given that God is possible) "if God exists, He necessarily exists" entails "God exists." See the responses by Hick, Pailin and Purtill (#s 247, 272 and 282 below).

246 Henle, Paul. "Uses of the Ontological Argument," Phil Rev, LXX (January, 1961), 102-9. (Reprinted in # 278 below, pp. 172-80.)

An interesting response to Malcolm (# 260 below).

Henle (1) introduces a variant of Gaunilo's perfect island objection, (2) argues that if the second form of the argument is to be distinguished from the first, "necessarily" must be supposed to modify "exists" rather than the whole proposition "God exists" and that this supposition commits one to the unacceptable position that necessary existence is a special kind of existence which is different from ordinary existence, (3) that since proper names usually imply or presuppose existence, the use of "God" (which sometimes functions as a proper name) lends a specious plausibility to the argument, and (4) that the purpose of the argument is not to establish something new but "to summarize and encapsulate what was proved before."

247 Hick, John Harwood. "A Critique of the 'Second Argument'," in # 248 below, pp. 341-56.

Hick distinguishes the logical necessity of propositions from ontological necessity (a being is ontologically necessary if it is eternal, independent, indestructible, etc.) and argues that the "second ontological argument" of Hartshorne and Malcolm fails because it sometimes employs "necessity" in one sense and sometimes in the other. Thus, there are two crucial premisses in Hartshorne's argument: (1) $(\exists x)Px \supset L(\exists x)Px$ (where Px = x is Perfect), and (2) $-L-(\exists x)Px$. The first is only plausible if interpreted as "if perfection exists, it is ontologically necessary," (for, according to Hick, existential propositions cannot be logically necessary), while the second is interpreted as "It is not logically necessary that perfection does not exist." Malcolm's argument is

said to be open to a similar objection. See
Nasser's reply (# 268 below).

248 _____ and Arthur C. McGill, eds. The Many
Faced Argument, Recent Studies on the Ontolo-
gical Argument for the Existence of God. New
York: The Macmillan Co., 1967. vii + 373 pp.

The first part of this excellent anthology consists of papers which are concerned with the
interpretation of Anselm's argument. McGill's
essay ("Recent Discussions of Anselm's Argument")
is particularly valuable. The second part contains a number of important recent papers (see
#s 247, 260 and 293), and several papers devoted
to the "Hegelian version" of the argument (see
#s 238, 242, 291 and 292). This version of
the ontological argument, which attempts to
show that God is presupposed in all rational
thinking, has been neglected by analytic philosophers. Includes a useful bibliography.

249 Hopkins, Jasper. A Companion to the Study of
St. Anselm. Minneapolis: University of Minnesota Press, 1972. Pp. 67-89 and 260-75 (bibliography).

While, taken as a whole, this is a useful book,
its discussion of the ontological argument is
rather pedestrian. The bibliography contains
a list of articles about the ontological argument which have appeared since 1945.

250 Howe, Leroy Thomas. "The Ambiguity of 'Perfection'
in the Ontological Argument," Proc Cath Phil Ass,
46 (1972), 58-70.

This is a suggestive essay even though its argument is sometimes opaque. Howe makes three

major points. (1) Necessary existence is included in some concepts of perfection (e.g., in the concept of perfection construed as completeness) and not in others. (2) Howe argues that "the concept of perfection includes (necessary) existence" is a warrant in Toulmin's sense, and discusses the ways in which backing might be provided for it. (He suggests that certain concepts of perfection are rooted in the "boundary experiences" of death, meaninglessness and guilt discussed by Tillich and Jaspers.) (3) The ontological argument may depend on postulates whose function is to govern a "field of discourse" and which, like other postulates of this kind, are less than self-evidently true. In this sense, the necessity of its conclusion may be a hypothetical one.

251 _____. "Conceivability and the Ontological Argument," Sophia, V (April, 1966), 3-8.

Both Leibniz and Hartshorne mistakenly suppose that because their concepts of God are not self-evidently contradictory, no contradictions are present. That "God" has a use in religious discourse does establish God's conceivability. On the other hand, the fact that "God exists" expresses a tautology in religious discourse is not sufficient to establish the claim that "God exists" expresses a tautology in all "spheres of discourse."

252 Johnson, Clark B. "Why the Atheist is not a Fool," Int J Phil Relig, IV (Spring, 1973), 53-8.

Argues that Anselm is mistaken in supposing that if a word (e.g., "a being greater than which

none can be thought") is understood, the concept which that word signifies invariably exists
in the understanding.

253 Kapitan, Tomis. "Perfection and Modality: Charles
Hartshorne's Ontological Proof," _Int_ _J_ _Phil_ _Relig_,
VII (1976), 379-85.

(1) The first premiss of Hartshorne's proof is
"$(\exists x)Px \supset L(\exists x)Px$," where "$Px$" is to be construed
as "x is perfect." Kapitan points out that
Hartshorne doesn't adequately distinguish this
proposition from "$(x)(Px \supset LPx)$" (and its derivative, "$(\exists x)Px \supset (\exists x)LPx$"), and that the arguments
which Hartshorne offers for the former are in
fact arguments for the latter. (2) Kapitan
attempts to show that given the premisses of
Hartshorne's modal argument, his doctrine of
"modal coincidence" (viz., that a perfect being
is the actual knower of all actual states of
affairs and the possible knower of all possible
states of affairs), standard logical rules, and
Hartshorne's own interpretation of "necessity,"
it follows that no actual state of affairs is
contingent. Kapitan's argument is not implausible
although it should be noted that it rests upon
a controversial interpretation of the claim
that a perfect being knows all actual states
of affairs. (Kapitan interprets this claim
as "if x is perfect, then [where $\underline{p}$ ranges over
actual states of affairs] $(\underline{p})(x$ knows $\underline{p})$."
If we let p range over possibles we can, how-
ever, interpret Hartshorne's claim as "if x
is perfect, then $(p)(if$ p is actual, x knows
$p)$," and avoid Kapitan's paradox.)

254 Kenny, Anthony John Patrick, Norman Malcolm, Terence
     Penelhum, Bernard Williams, and Ernest Sosa.
     "Descartes' Ontological Argument," _Fact and
     Existence_. Edited by J. Margolis. Oxford:
     Basil Blackwell, 1969. Pp. 18-62.

In his very significant lead essay Kenny shows
that Descartes' argument presupposes that there
are something like Meinongian pure objects.
Kenny's paper may be profitably compared with
Robert Adams' attempt to show that Anselm's
first argument works if we assume that there
are non-actual objects of certain sorts (see
204 above). The replies of Williams and Sosa,
together with Kenny's rejoinder to those replies,
are important. Malcolm's reply is not only a
comment on Kenny but a contribution in its own
right and is, therefore, discussed separately
(see # 261 below). Kenny's essay is reprinted
(with some modifications) in his _Descartes: A
Study of his Philosophy_ (New York: Random House,
1968).

255 La Croix, Richard Ray. _Proslogion II and III:
     A Third Interpretation of Anselm's Argument_.
     Leiden: E. J. Brill, 1972. xii + 137 pp.

In _Proslogion_ II, Anselm deduces that a being
than which a greater cannot be thought exists.
In _Proslogion_ III, Anselm deduces that a being
than which a greater cannot be thought cannot
be thought not to exist, and in the subsequent
chapters, he shows that the being than which
a greater cannot be thought "bears the properties
traditionally attributed to God." It is, thus,
the _Proslogion_ as a whole (and not simply _Proslo-
gion_ II and III) which "establish that God exists
where . . . 'God exists' is taken to mean 'the

175

being bearing the properties traditionally attributed to God exists'."

256 Lewis, David. "Anselm and Actuality," <u>Nous</u>, IV (May, 1970), 175-88.

Discusses a version of the argument which is valid if its third premiss is interpreted as (roughly) (1) There is a member of the actual world whose greatness is unsurpassed by the greatness of any member of any possible world, or (roughly) (2) There is a being which exists in each possible world and which is such that its greatness in each world is unsurpassed by the greatness of any member of any possible world, or (roughly) (3) Each possible world includes a being whose greatness in that world is unsurpassed by the greatness of any being in any possible world. Lewis argues that the third premiss is implausible on any of these interpretations. This interesting article makes a number of valuable points.

257 Lochhead, David Morgan. "Is Existence a Predicate in Anselm's Argument?" <u>Relig Stud</u>, 2 (October, 1966), 121-7.

Argues (1) that there is little basis for supposing that Anselm believed that real existence was always better than conceptual existence and (2) that if we were to attribute any general view about the value of existence to Anselm, it would be preferable to attribute to him the view that real existence "makes goodness greater and evil worse."

258 Lomasky, Loren E. "Leibniz and the Modal Argument for God's Existence," Monist, 54 (April, 1970), 250-60.

It is generally admitted that "God is possible" must be included as a premiss in any sound ontological argument. This article discusses the possibility premiss with particular reference to Leibniz.

259 Lycan, William G. "Eternal Existence and Necessary Existence," Notre Dame J Form Log, XVII (April, 1976), 286-90.

Both Malcolm (# 260 below) and Hartshorne (# 244 above) offer arguments for "if God does exist, then it is necessary that God exists" which depend upon the claim that "if God does not exist in our world but does exist in some other possible world [i.e., if God's non-existence is contingent], then it possible that He will come into existence." Lycan argues that this claim is only plausible if we assume that "any temporal slice of a possible world w ($w \neq$ our world α) is a possible future slice of α," but that this assumption is false. (If it were true, then, since there are no eternally existing gavels in our world, it follows that an eternally existing gavel is impossible; for if such an object were possible, then, given our assumption, it could come into existence in which case it would not be an eternally existing gavel.)

260 Malcolm, Norman. "Anselm's Ontological Arguments," Phil Rev, LXIX (January, 1960), 41-62. (Reprinted in # 248 above, pp. 301-20, and in # 278 below, pp. 136-59.)

A very influential article in which an ontological

argument which construes existence as a perfection is distinguished from another ontological
argument which construes necessary existence as
the relevant perfection. The first argument
is rejected on the grounds that existence isn't
a perfection, but according to Malcolm the second argument is sound. While Hartshorne's
version of the second argument is superior to
Malcolm's, Malcolm's essay is a very rich and
suggestive one. It has evoked a number of replies. (See especially #s 213 and 246 above
and #s 273 and 280 below.)

261 _____. "Descartes' Ontological Proof," Fact
and Existence. Edited by J. Margolis. Oxford:
Basil Blackwell, 1969. Pp. 36-43.

A reply to Kenny's paper on Descartes' ontological argument (# 254 above). Sections IV and
V are of special interest. In section IV Malcolm
argues that according to Descartes, the ontological argument "reveals a synthetic (although
necessary) truth about reality." In section
V, Malcolm again defends his version of Anselm's
second ontological argument. See Kenny's response to Malcolm (# 254 above), and Tomberlin's
critique of section V (# 298 below).

262 Mann, William Edward. "The Ontological Presuppositions of the Ontological Argument," Rev Metaph,
XXVI (December, 1972), 260-77.

Considers a non-modal version of Anselm's first
argument and argues that the crucial difficulty
lies in its first premise (viz., "Whatever is
understood is in the understanding").

263 Matthews, Gareth Blanc. "On Conceivability in Anselm," _Phil Rev_, LXX (January, 1961), 110-1.

Argues that in the _Proslogion_ "conceivable" and "inconceivable" cannot always be equated with "logically possible" and "logically impossible" respectively and that, therefore, some interpretations of Anselm's argument appear to rest upon a mistake.

264 Mavrodes, George Ion. "Properties, Predicates, and the Ontological Argument," _J Phil_, LXIII (October 13, 1966), 549-50.

Abstract of a paper presented to the American Philosophical Association which argues (1) that eminence or perfection is a second order property which cannot, therefore, be _contained_ in a first order concept, though a first order concept may have that property if the first order properties which it _contains_ are of the right sort. Mavrodes also argues (2) that if existence is a second order property then we cannot simply include it in a concept by stipulation (as we can arbitrarily combine first order properties to form a concept by stipulation) and that, hence, we cannot follow Anselm's invitation to conceive that the eminent being which exists in our understanding also exists in reality. (Is Anselm asking us to include existence in our concept of a being greater than which none can be thought or to form a new concept from the conjunction of that concept and the concept of existence?)

265 _____ "Some Recent Philosophical Theology,"
Rev Metaph, XXIV (September, 1970), pp. 93-102.

Section II discusses the two "ontological type
arguments" which Ross presents in his Philosophical Theology Chapter 4, section 4 (# 286
below). Mavrodes makes a number of decent points
but his basic objection is that arguments of this
type "tend to fall prey to . . . the 'Gaunilo
strategy'," i.e., the principles employed in
these arguments can be used to establish the
existence of problematic entities of one type
or another. On page 94 Mavrodes says that Ross's
statement of the first argument can be found
on p. 115 of Philosophical Theology. The reference should be to p. 174.

266 Miethe, T. L. "The Ontological Argument: A Research Bibliography," Mod Sch, LIV (January,
1977), 148-67.

The topics covered in this bibliography include
"The Argument in Anselm," "The Argument from
Descartes to Kant," "The Hegelian and Idealistic
Use of the Argument," "The Argument in Conti-
nental Philosophy," "The Argument in British and
American Philosophy," "The Logic of 'Exists',"
and "The Concept of Necessary Being." The bib-
liography is not annotated.

267 Nakhnikian, George. "St. Anselm's Four Ontological Arguments," Art, Mind and Religion. Proceedings of the 1965 Oberlin Colloquium in Philosophy. Edited by W. H. Capitan and D. D. Merrill.
Pittsburgh: University of Pittsburgh Press,
1967. Pp. 29-36.

A discussion and criticism of four ontological
arguments suggested by the remarks of Anselm.

Interesting, although in disposing of these versions of the argument Nakhnikian has not, of course, disposed of the argument itself.

268 Nasser, Alan George. "Factual and Logical Necessity and the Ontological Argument," Int Phil Quart, XI (September, 1971), 385-402.

This essay contains plausible replies to Hick's criticisms of Hartshorne's ontological argument (see # 247 above) but at its heart is an attempt to show that if God's existence is ontologically or factually necessary (if God is eternal and independent, etc.) then it is logically necessary as well. Nasser argues that if God is really independent, then His existence is compatible with all possible contingent states of affairs in which case God could exist in all possible worlds, i.e., God's existence could be logically necessary. Since whatever is possibly necessary is actually necessary it follows that if God is genuinely independent, God's existence is logically necessary.

269 Oakes, Robert Aaron. "Containment, Analyticity, and the Ontological Argument," Thomist, XXXIX (April, 1975), 319-31.

Oakes argues that conceptual containment is not a necessary condition of analyticity. Consider "If this object is a cup, it is not a speck of radioactive cloud dust." "Being a cup" entails "not being a speck of radioactive cloud dust" and that this is the case can be determined by considering the meanings of "cup" and "speck of radioactive cloud dust." Nevertheless, not being a speck of radioactive cloud dust is not contained in the concept of a cup. (For it is

not part of the meaning of "cup.") Our statement is therefore analytic but does not involve
conceptual containment. It follows that those
who maintain that "God exists" is analytic need
not argue that existence is contained in the
concept of God.

270 _____. "God, Electrons and Professor Plantinga," Phil Stud, XXV (February, 1974), 143-6.

Argues that Plantinga's criticism of Malcolm's
ontological argument (# 280 below) is unsound.
While it is true that an electron could be eternal, non-dependent and contingent, it does not
follow that God can be eternal, non-dependent
and contingent. The cases are dissimilar.
Independence and eternity are at best contingent
features of electrons whereas God is necessarily
independent and eternal. Therefore, from the
fact that we cannot move from eternity and independence to necessary existence in the first
case, it does not clearly follow that we cannot do
so in the second case.

271 _____. "Logical Necessity, Self-Evidence
and 'God Exists'," Man World, 5 (August, 1972),
327-34.

Distinguishes between necessity and self-evidence,
pointing out that necessarily true propositions
may not in fact be evident. According to Oakes,
it is a mistake to argue that if contingent
"premises are required to support the truth of
'God exists,' it thereby follows that it is not
a necessary truth." "Nondefinitional premises"
can be employed to enable someone to come to
see the truth (but not the logical necessity)

of a proposition which is necessary but not
self-evident.

272 Pailin, David Arthur. "Some Comments on Hart-
       shorne's Presentation of the Ontological Argu-
       ment," Relig Stud, 4 (October, 1968), 103-22.

       Pailin argues that "necessary existence" is a
       predicate which indicates the kind of being
       God has but implies nothing about the contents
       of reality, considers the possibility that the
       necessity of God in Hartshorne's metaphysics
       is the necessity of a regulative idea, and sug-
       gests that although the religious significance
       of the conclusion that perfection is necessarily
       instantiated depends upon the sort of perfection
       which is instantiated, the ontological argument
       does not itself provide an answer to the question
       as to just what this perfection is like.

273 Penelhum, Terence. "On the Second Ontological
       Argument," Phil Rev, LXX (January, 1961), 85-92.

       A reply to Malcolm's "Anselm's Ontological Argu-
       ments" (# 260 above). A number of questions
       are raised, perhaps the most significant of
       which are whether necessary existence can be a
       perfection, if existence is not a perfection,
       and whether necessary existence can be contained
       in the concept of God if existence is not a
       property.

274 Plantinga, Alvin Carl. God and Other Minds, A
       Study of the Rational Justification of Belief
       in God. (Contemporary Philosophy.) Ithaca,
       New York: Cornell University Press, 1967.
       Pp. 26-94.

       Chapter 2 contains acute criticisms of several

objections to the ontological argument. (Kant, Broad [# 212 above], Shaffer [# 293 below], and Alston [# 206 above] are discussed.) In Chapter 3 Plantinga (1) attempts to reformulate Anselm's first ontological argument but is driven to the conclusion that it is unsound and (2) examines Malcolm's version of Anselm's "second" ontological argument. (This portion of Chapter 3 is identical with # 280 below.) See Rowe's critique of Plantinga's argument (# 288 below).

275 _____. God, Freedom and Evil. New York: Harper and Row Pub., Inc., 1974. Pp. 85-112.

The book's concluding discussion of the ontological argument is a somewhat simplified but useful presentation of points made in God and Other Minds (# 274 above) and The Nature of Necessity (# 277 below).

276 _____. "Kant's Objection to the Ontological Argument," J Phil, LXIII (October 13, 1966), 537-46.

(1) Attempts to show how existence differs from other predicates but suggests that this difference has no bearing on Anselm's argument (cf. God and Other Minds, chapter 2 [# 274 above]) and (2) discusses the claim that existence is a property of concepts not of objects, concluding that even if the claim is true it has no obvious relevance to Anselm's argument. See Coburn's response (# 219 above).

277   . The Nature of Necessity. (Clarendon
Library of Logic and Philosophy.) Oxford:
The Clarendon Press, 1974. Pp. 196-221.

Chapter X ("God and Necessity") is a very important contribution to the discussion of the ontological argument. Several versions of the
argument (including one which rests upon the
notion that God is a being possessing maximal
greatness in some world or other) are discussed
and rejected. It is pointed out that many versions of the argument rest on the suspect assumption that there are possible but non-existent
objects. Plantinga concludes by defending a
version of the argument which construes God
as a being which possesses maximal excellence
in every possible world.

278   , ed. The Ontological Argument from
St. Anselm to Contemporary Philosophers with
an introduction by Richard Taylor. Garden City,
New York: Anchor Books, Doubleday and Co.,
Inc., 1965. xviii + 180 pp.

The second part of this anthology contains several
important papers, including William Alston's
"The Ontological Argument Revisited," J. N.
Findley's "Can God's Existence be Disproved?"
and Norman Malcolm's "Anselm's Ontological Arguments" together with Henle's and Plantinga's
replies. (See #s 206, 66, 260, 246 and 280.)

279   . Review of Philosophical Theology by
James F. Ross. Phil Rev, LXXXI (October, 1972),
509-11.

Ross's a priori argument for God's existence
(see #286 below) employs the principle that
every contingent state of affairs is explicable

185

in the sense that it is possible that it have an explanation. Plantinga points out a serious difficulty in Ross's formulation of that principle.

280 _____. "A Valid Ontological Argument?" Phil Rev, LXX (January, 1961), 93-101. (Reprint- ed in # 274 above, pp. 82-94 and in # 278 above, pp. 160-71.)

A reply to Malcolm's "Anselm's Ontological Argu- ments" (# 260 above). It is pointed out that "God cannot begin to exist or cease to exist" only entails that "if God exists, He always exists" and "if God does not exist, He never exists." It does not entail that God's existence is either logically necessary or logically im- possible. Futhermore, the claim that God just happens to exist entails neither that God is not eternal nor that God is dependent. See Oakes' reply (# 270 above).

281 Potter, Vincent G. "Karl Barth and the Ontologi- cal Argument," J Relig, XLV (October, 1965), 309-25.

A presentation of ideas developed by Henri Bouil- lard in Part II of his Karl Barth: Parole de Dieu et existence humaine. (Paris: Aubier, 1957). Bouillard concedes that the ontological argument is developed in the community of faith and can only be "effectively understood" within that community. Nevertheless, he argues that Barth (# 208 above) is mistaken when he supposes that Anselm was not attempting to present a proof the soundness of which could, in principle, be recognized by any rational being regardless of his faith or lack of faith.

186

282 Purtill, Richard L. "Hartshorne's Modal Proof,"
J Phil, LXIII (July 14, 1966), 397-409.

In this interesting essay Purtill argues (1)
that Hartshorne's argument (see #s 244 and 245
above) is valid, (2) that the objections of
Hume and Kant can't be effectively deployed
against Hartshorne's argument, but (3) that
there is no interpretation of "'necessity' for
which Hartshorne's modal proof is both valid
and sound." Perhaps the most interesting point
made in this last section is that if we construe
necessity as logical necessity and assert
"($\exists$x)Px$\supset$L($\exists$x)Px", then we imply that what is logically necessary is determined by the existence of
something which "seems to be contrary to our
idea of logical necessity." (It should be pointed
out in reply (1) that "$\supset$" does not mean "determines," and (2) that the existence in question
is the existence of something which the argument
shows to be logically necessary, and that any
logically necessary fact is entailed and, in
that sense, "determined" by everything.)

283 _____. "Three Ontological Arguments," Int
J Phil Relig, VI (Summer, 1975), 102-10.

Purtill examines Anselm's (first) argument, and
the arguments of Charles Hartshorne and James
Ross (#s 244 and 245 above and 286 below).
Purtill contends that these arguments are sound
if "God" has a referent (which may be either
an actual or a possible being) but that no absurdity is involved in denying that "God" has
a referent. Purtill points out that, if he is
right, it would follow that the ontological
argument is sound if the cosmological argument

187

is sound. This would in turn entail that if
the ontological argument is unsound, the cosmological argument is also unsound. Kant was,
therefore, correct.

284   Richman, Robert J. "A Serious Look at the Onto-
      logical Argument," Ratio, XVIII (June, 1976),
      85-9.

The second part of this article contains an
interesting argument. Anselm's alleged proof
employs the principle that it is better to exist
in intellectu and in re than to exist in intellectu alone. Clearly, if one state is better
than another, the states must be distinct. It
follows that existence in intellectu alone is
distinct from existence in intellectu and in re.
If, however, the ontological argument is valid,
"God exists in intellectu" entails "God exists
in intellectu and in re." Since it is clearly
true that the latter trivially entails the former,
"God exists in intellectu" is logically equivalent to "God exists in intellectu and in re,"
from which it follows that God's existing in
intellectu and His existing in intellectu and
in re are not distinct states. The ontological
argument is, therefore, incoherent. (One might
reply that two states can be logically equivalent
without being identical or, alternatively, one
might argue that the states which are being
compared and contrasted are not God's existing
in intellectu and God's existing in intellectu
and in re but God's only existing in intellectu
and God's existing in intellectu and in re.)

285 Ross, James Francis. "On Proofs for the Existence
     of God," Monist, 54 (April, 1970), 201-17.

An informal and useful presentation of the modal
proof for God's existence first presented by
Ross in Chapter 3 of his Philosophical Theology
(# 286 below). The article also contains suggestive observations about the nature of "God-
proofs."

286 _____. Philosophical Theology. Indianapolis
     and New York: The Bobbs-Merrill Co., Inc.,
     1969. Pp. 86-139 and 173-82.

Chapter 3 sets out a modal argument for God's
existence which depends upon the description
of God as an unproducible and unpreventable
being, the assumption that it is logically possible for any logically contingent state of
affairs to be explained by a logically distinct
state of affairs, and the assumption that the
existence of an unproducible and unpreventable
being is a logically consistent state of affairs.
This argument deserves much more attention than
it has received. One should also examine the
modal arguments defended by Ross in Chapter 4,
section 4. See Plantinga's review (# 279 above).

287 Rowe, William Leonard. "Comments on Professor
     Davis' 'Does the Ontological Argument Beg the
     Question?" Int J Phil Relig, VII (1976), 443-7.

This response to # 229 above makes it clear
that Rowe's defense of the contention that
Anselm's argument begs the question depends
upon the truth of the (paradoxical) claim that
some coherent concepts (e.g., the concept of
a unicornex, where "unicornex" is defined as

189

an existing unicorn) are not exemplified by
any possible object. (Since unicorns do not
exist, no existing being exemplifies the concept.
Since unicornexes are _existing_ unicorns, no
being which is merely possible exemplifies the
concept either. Hence, no possible being exemplifies the concept.) In order to show that
these concepts are concepts of possible things
one must show that these concepts are actually
exemplified. See Davis's reply (# 228 above).

288 _____. "God and Other Minds," Nous, III
(September, 1969), pp. 264-70.

A discussion of the second and third chapters
of # 274 above. Rowe argues (1) that Plantinga
has not succeeded in showing how existence differs
from other predicates, and (2) argues that the
version of Anselm's argument considered in the
third chapter can be re-formulated so as to
evade Plantinga's major objection to that argument.

289 _____. "The Ontological Argument," Reason
and Responsibility: Readings in Some Basic
Problems of Philosophy. 3d edition. Edited
by Joel Feinberg. Encino and Belmont, California:
Dickenson Pub. Co., Inc., 1975. Pp. 8-17.

A good discussion of Anselm's argument. (See,
for example, Rowe's remarks on Gaunilo's perfect
island objection in section III.) Section IV
is especially interesting. Rowe argues that
Anselm's reasoning proves that his concept of
God can only be applied to an existing thing
but does not prove that it _does_ apply to an
existing thing. Rowe shows that Anselm's premisses imply that if a perfect being does not

exist, no possible thing is God. It follows
that if God is a possible thing, a perfect being
exists and, therefore, God exists. At this
point, according to Rowe, it becomes clear that
in order to establish the conclusion that God
exists, we must show that God is a possible thing.
Since to show this we must show not only that
the concept of God is coherent but also that a
perfect being exists, our argument begs the
question -- God can be shown to exist only if
we have already established (what is virtually
the same thing) that a perfect being exists.

290 _____. "The Ontological Argument and Question-Begging," Int J Phil Relig, VII (1976),
425-32.

"A condensation of some points [principally
those presented in section IV] developed in
. . . 'The Ontological Argument'" (# 289 above).
See Davis's reply (# 229 above).

291 Ryle, Gilbert. "Back to the Ontological Argument,"
Mind, XLVI (January, 1937), 53-7. (Reprinted
in # 248 above, pp. 269-74.)

A rejoinder to Harris's reply to Ryle's "Mr.
Collingwood and the Ontological Argument" (# 242
above). Ryle points out that Harris's "ontological argument" is really a cosmological argument, and wonders how one could show that our
experience or a thought (or whatever) is a part
or aspect of a greater whole.

292 _____. "Mr. Collingwood and the Ontological
Argument," Mind, XLIV (April, 1935), 137-51.
(Reprinted in # 248 above, pp. 246-60.)

A discussion of the views advanced in Collingwood's An Essay on Philosophical Method (# 222
above). The most incisive part of the essay
is devoted to Collingwood's most plausible contention, viz., that logic guarantees the existence of its own subject matter.

293 Shaffer, Jerome. "Existence, Predication and the
       Ontological Argument," Mind, LXXI (July, 1962),
       307-25. (Reprinted in # 248 above, pp. 226-45.)

(1) Examines and dismisses Kant's reasons for
supposing that existence isn't a predicate,
(2) criticizes the claim that "exists" isn't
an ordinary predicate since if it were, e.g.,
"crows exist" would be equivalent to "if there
exists anything which is a crow, then that thing
exists," and (3) rejects the view (held by Nakhnikian and Salmon) that "exists" is a necessary
predicate of everything conceivable, arguing
that such a view will not allow us to make sense
of negative existentials. (4) He concludes
that "God" can be defined so that "God exists"
is a tautology, but argues that it fails to
follow that there is some actual being which
meets the specifications of that concept. When
"God exists" is tautologous, it makes a remark
about the intension of the concept of God.
Whether the concept has extension is still an
open question. See Plantinga's critique of
Shaffer (God and Other Minds, chapter 2, #274
above).

294 Smart, John Jamieson Carswell. "The Existence
       of God." Public Lecture: University of Adelaide,
       1951. (Reprinted in # 923 below, pp. 28-46.)

After some general remarks on metaphysical

arguments (they are -- according to Smart --
either invalid or rest upon controversial premisses), Smart briefly discusses the ontological,
cosmological and teleological arguments. While
this lecture is frequently referred to and has
been reprinted in a number of places, its principle value lies in the fact that it briefly
articulates some standard modern objections
to these arguments. It is not an original
contribution, and Smart's main objection to the
first two arguments ("Existential propositions
can't be necessary") is beginning to appear to
many philosophers to be no more than an unjustified dogma.

295 Sommers, Fred. "Why Is There Something and Not
     Nothing?" Analysis, 26 (New Series 114), (June,
     1966), 177-81.

In the last part of this essay Sommers offers
"an odd [but interesting] form of the ontological
argument." His argument is roughly as follows:
Assume that God is possible. It follows that
if R is a divine attribute, then it is possible
that something is R. However, "If R-things
are possible, they are categorically possible,"
i.e., either something is R or something fails
to be R. Therefore, something is R-or-$\bar{R}$. But
R and R-or-$\bar{R}$ entail each other (because "in
God there is no distinction between potency and
act," i.e., no distinction between possessing
P-or-$\bar{P}$ and possessing P). It follows that there
is something that is R. Moreover, the divine
attributes entail one another. We are, therefore, entitled to conclude that there is something which possesses not only R but all the
divine attributes. (For Sommers' account of

God's simplicity, see # 54 above.)

296   Sontag, Frederick. "The Meaning of 'Argument'
       in Anselm's Ontological 'Proof'," J Phil, LXIV
       (August 10, 1967), 459-86.

       In this interesting article Sontag attempts to
       show that Anselm was in fact offering an "Hege-
       lian" version of the ontological argument.
       According to Sontag, Anselm's argument is not
       a logical demonstration but a bit of dialectical
       reasoning which proceeds by hints, suggestions
       and questions to a direct and immediate appre-
       hension of God whose nature is never fully known
       -- an apprehension made possible by the fact
       that the mind is in some sense already acquainted
       with the divine.

297   Tillich, Paul Johannes Oskar. "The Two Types of
       Philosophy of Religion," Theology of Culture.
       Edited by Robert C. Kimbell. New York: Oxford
       University Press, 1959. Pp. 10-29.

       This very influential essay first appeared in
       the Union Seminary Quarterly Review I (May,
       1946), and provides another version of the
       "Hegelian" form of the ontological argument.
       According to Tillich, the reality of God is a
       presupposition of all thinking and inquiry and,
       therefore, of all thinking about God. As Tillich
       says, "God is the presupposition of the question
       of God." God can no more be coherently denied
       than the skeptic can coherently deny that there
       is such a thing as truth. Tillich maintains
       that the function of the argument is to arti-
       culate the immediate awareness of the Absolute
       which underlies all reflection. The "ontological
       approach" is contrasted with the "cosmological

approach" which introduces a cleavage between
man and the Absolute, and it is argued that
the latter must be subordinated to the former.

298 Tomberlin, James Edward. "Malcolm on the Ontological Argument," Relig Stud, 8 (March, 1972),
65-70.

A reply to Malcolm's "Descartes' Ontological
Proof" (# 261 above). It is argued that the
"rather ingenious version of St. Anselm's ontological argument" which is presented in that
paper may not be open to Kenny's criticism but
is guilty of begging the question. (A minor
point: Tomberlin argues that Malcolm's premisses
entail "God exists" but not "necessarily, God
exists." However, if the premisses are true
at all, they are presumably necessarily true.
Hence, if they entail "God exists," it follows
that God necessarily exists.)

299 Wald, Albert W. "The Fool and the Ontological
Status of St. Anselm's Argument," Heythrop J,
15 (October, 1974), 406-22.

Wald maintains that some of the argument's premisses would appear to be empirical and, therefore, contingent (e.g., that the fool has such
and such a conception). Wald shows that the
argument is, nevertheless, an ontological one.

300 Wilbanks, Jan Joseph. "Some (Logical) Trouble
for St. Anselm," New Scholas, XLVII (Summer,
1973), 361-5.

Wilbanks attempts to show that if Anselm's first
argument is cogent then another argument can be
constructed which is equally cogent and which

has for its conclusion the denial of Anselm's second premiss (viz., that whatever is understood exists in the understanding). Wilbanks concludes that if Anselm's argument is cogent it isn't cogent, from which it follows that it isn't cogent. Original if not entirely convincing.

301 Yandell, Keith Edward. Basic Issues in the Philosophy of Religion. Boston: Allyn and Bacon, Inc., 1973. Pp. 95-101.

A discussion of Anselm's alleged proof. Yandell provides an argument to show that "God necessarily exists" is not logically equivalent to "if God exists, then God necessarily exists," and criticizes Alston's "The Ontological Argument Revisited" (# 206 above).

The Cosmological Argument

(See also # 294)

302 Broad, Charlie Dunbar. "Arguments for the Existence of God," Religion, Philosophy and Psychical Research: Selected Essays by C. D. Broad. (International Library of Psychology, Philosophy and Scientific Method.) London: Routledge & Kegan Paul Limited, 1953. Pp. 175-201, esp. 183-9.

Broad contends that the cosmological argument presupposes "that nature must be . . . capable of satisfying the intellect in the way in which it can be satisfied in pure mathematics," and that for this satisfaction to be obtainable there must be intrinsically necessary existential facts which are such that all other facts are necessary consequences of these facts. According to Broad there is no reason to suppose that nature provides this kind of satisfaction.

303 Brown, T. Patterson. "Infinite Causal Regression,"
      Phil Rev, LXXV (October, 1966), 510-25.

Brown points out that medieval versions of the
cosmological argument only assume that all
infinite causal regressions of essentially ordered causes are impossible. An essentially
ordered series of causes exhibits three features:
(1) Its members depend upon their causes for
their exertion of causal efficacy. (2) The
members of an essentially ordered series act
simultaneously. (3) Causes in such a series
are more perfect than their effects. Brown
argues (1) that the salient feature of an essentially ordered series is the fact that in such
a series the causal relation is transitive, and
(2) that one might be led to conclude that an
essentially ordered series of causes must be
finite if one were to interpret "cause" in a
quasi-legal sense as that which is responsible
for its effect. See Wengert's comments (# 351
below).

304 _____. "St. Thomas' Doctrine of Necessary
      Being," Phil Rev, LXXIII (January, 1964), 76-90.

Brown persuasively argues that Aquinas did not
believe "that everything in the world around
us is or must be contingent," and did not believe
that a necessary being must be infinitely perfect.
Furthermore, by "necessary being" Aquinas did
not mean "logically necessary being." It is,
therefore, historically inaccurate to construe
the Third Way as an argument from "something
exists" to "a logically necessary being exists."

197

The argument instead proceeds from the existence
of generable and corruptible beings to the existence of an ungenerable, incorruptible, absolutely
immutable, and uncreated being.

305   Caputo, John David. "Kant's Refutation of the
      Cosmological Argument," _JAAR_, XLII (December,
      1974), 686-91.

Caputo argues that Kant does not succeed in reducing the cosmological argument to the ontological argument, and that in his concern to provide
a systematic refutation of all proofs for the
existence of God, Kant neglects more substantial
criticisms of the cosmological argument (e.g.,
the illicit extension of the category of causality
beyond the limits of experience).

306   Clarke, W. Norris. "A Curious Blindspot in the
      Anglo-American Tradition of Antitheistic Argu-
      ment," _Monist_, 54 (April, 1970), 181-200.

It is frequently argued that the cosmological
argument is incoherent because it assumes that
every being has a cause but concludes to a being
which has no cause. Clarke shows that this
assumption is not made by advocates of the cosmological argument. What _is_ assumed is that
every being must either have a sufficient reason
for its existence in itself or in another, and
that this sufficient reason may be an internal
principle of intelligibility rather than a cause.
Interesting.

307 _____. "How the Philosopher Can Give Meaning
to Language About God," The Idea of God: Philosophical Perspectives. Compiled and edited by
Edward H. Madden, Rollo Handy and Marvin Farber.
(American Lecture Series, 731.) Springfield,
Illinois: Charles C. Thomas, 1968. Pp. 1-27
and 37-42.

God's existence must be posited if the world
and our experience of it are to be made intelligible. The most interesting feature of this
essay is the discussion of the Principle of
Sufficient Reason (the claim that reality is
intelligible). Clarke maintains that this principle can neither be established by demonstration
nor by intuition. It expresses a commitment,
albeit a commitment which is eminently reasonable
since it is an expression of the fundamental
"pull of our very intelligence itself."

308 Conway, David Alton. "Possibility and Infinite
Time: A Logical Paradox in St. Thomas's Third
Way," Int Phil Quart, XIV (June, 1974), 201-8.

It is often argued that the Third Way contains
a suppressed premiss, viz., that all possibilities
are actualized during the course of an infinite
period of time. Conway shows that this premiss,
together with the assumptions that it is possible
that nothing exist, that an infinite period of
time has already passed, and that every moment
of time prior to now occurred a finite period
of time ago, leads to the contradictory conclusion that the state of affairs described by
"nothing exists" occurred at some time which
was a finite period of time ago, and yet occurred
prior to that time. Conway's argument hinges
on the notion that, since an infinite time has
already transpired before any past time, the

state of affairs in question must have already occurred before any past time and, therefore, cannot have taken place at any past time.

309   Copleston, Frederick Charles. _Aquinas_. Harmondsworth, Middlesex: Penguin Books, 1955. Pp. 110-26.

Chapter 3 contains a brief discussion of the Five Ways. This discussion is frequently alluded to and has proved to be rather influential. (It has, for example, helped to popularize the notion that in the Third Way Aquinas is assuming that if past time is infinite all possibilities will have been realized.) It is not, however, particularly original.

310   Duff-Forbes, Donald R.   "Hick, Necessary Being, and the Cosmological Argument," _Can J Phil_, I (June, 1972), 473-83.

A logically necessary being cannot have an explanation since its existence is not a contingent state of affairs which might not have obtained. A factually necessary being cannot have an explanation because it is (by definition) eternal and independent. Hick (#s 69 and 70 above) is, however, mistaken in supposing that a factually necessary being can put an end to the regress of questions and explanations, and that the cosmological argument does not, therefore, need to employ the notion of a logically necessary being. The existence of a factually necessary being is a brute fact, and the appeal to such a being is no more and no less satisfactory than the appeal to a fundamental scientific law which has no further explanation but

just happens to obtain. See Hick's reply (#
317 below).

311 Edwards, Paul. "The Cosmological Argument," The
     Rationalist Annual, 1959, 63-77. Reprinted in
     The Cosmological Arguments, A Spectrum of Opinion.
     Edited by Donald R. Burrill. Garden City, N. Y.:
     Anchor Books, Doubleday and Co., Inc., 1967.
     Pp. 101-23.)

     A lucid presentation of standard objections to
     the cosmological argument. Edwards is primarily
     concerned with the claim that causal series
     require a first member, with the claim that the
     collection of causes has not been explained
     when each part has been explained, and with the
     claim that explanations which account for one
     contingent state of affairs by adducing another
     contingent state of affairs are somehow defec-
     tive or incomplete.

312 Farrer, Austin Marsden. Finite and Infinite,
     A Philosophical Essay. 2d ed. London: Dacre
     Press, 1959. xvi + 300 pp.

     God's existence cannot be legitimately inferred
     but God can be apprehended "in and through"
     or "along with" creatures. Cosmological argu-
     ments articulate this awareness or apprehension.
     Farrer contends that the argument is most ef-
     fective if it begins with selves rather than
     with other creatures. It is within the self
     that the dependence relation between finite and
     infinite can be most clearly apprehended, and
     this is because only our own existence or activity
     can be apprehended directly. Interesting though
     sometimes obscure. The notion that cosmological
     arguments evoke or express an intuition continues
     to enjoy some currency. The first edition

appeared in 1943. For a description of the
section on analogy, see # 972 below.

313   Garrigou-Lagrange, Reginald Marie. God, His Exis-
      tence and his Nature; A Thomistic Solution of
      Certain Agnostic Antinomies. Vol. I. Translated
      from the fifth French edition by Dom Bede Rose.
      St. Louis and London: B. Herder Book Co., 1934.
      Pp. 242-392.

      Volume I, chapter III contains a detailed account
      of the Five Ways and provides an excellent example
      of the way in which these arguments are inter-
      preted by modern Thomists. The discussion of
      the First Way (which addresses itself to objec-
      tions based on non-Aristotelian conceptions of
      change and motion) is particularly interesting.
      The discussion of the Fourth Way is also of
      interest although it deviates from the argument
      of Aquinas and is ultimately unconvincing.

314   Geach, Peter Thomas. "Aquinas," Three Philoso-
      phers by G. E. M. Anscombe and P. T. Geach.
      Oxford: Basil Blackwell, 1961. Pp. 109-17.

      A brief but good discussion of the Five Ways.

315   Gurr, John Edwin. The Principle of Sufficient
      Reason in Some Scholastic Systems, 1750-1900.
      Milwaukee, Wisconsin: The Marquette University
      Press, 1959. 196 pp.

      A historical examination of the Principle of
      Sufficient Reason (PSR) as understood by Leib-
      niz, Wolff and the 18th and 19th century scholas-
      tics. It is argued that, in spite of the re-
      newal of Thomism, scholastic manual writers
      remained under the influence of the rationalism
      of Leibniz and Wolff. This tradition is faulted
      for its concern with essences and its neglect

202

of existence. Gurr's book is of interest, not
because of its principle thesis but because of
the incidental light which it throws on the
PSR. (Gurr shows, e.g., that there were many
attempts to deduce the PSR from the Principle
of Non-Contradiction, and that the PSR was clearly
distinguished from the principle that everything
must have a cause.) Unfortunately these portions of Gurr's book are not developed in as
much detail as one would like.

316 Hepburn, Ronald William. Christianity and Paradox,
     Critical Studies in Twentieth-Century Theology.
     London: C. A. Watts and Co. Ltd., 1958. Pp.
     155-85.

     The cosmological argument is discussed in chapters
     IX and X. Hepburn's principal objection is that
     the argument must use "cause" in a stretched
     sense which is not clearly coherent.

317 Hick, John Harwood. "Comment," Can J Phil, I
     (June, 1972), 485-7.

     A reply to Duff-Forbes (# 310 above). The exis-
     tence of a factually necessary being and the
     fundamental scientific law(s) to which some
     atheists appeal are both contingent states of
     affairs which have no further explanation.
     The first state of affairs nevertheless enjoys
     an explanatory ultimacy which the second lacks.
     (1) The nature of a factually necessary being
     is such that it cannot have an explanation,
     i.e., it is necessarily independent. The phy-
     sical universe or the fundamental laws which
     govern it can have explanations even if they
     do not in fact have them, i.e., they may in
     fact be independent but they are not necessarily

independent. (2) Explanations which appeal
to conscious acts of will possess a psychological
ultimacy which is not possessed by explanations
which appeal to "states or movements of unconscious matter."

318 Joyce, George Hayward. Principles of Natural
     Theology. (Stonyhurst Philosophical Series.)
     London, New York [etc.]: Longmans, Green and
     Co., 1923; New York: AMS Press, 1972. Pp.
     56-115.

     Chapter III provides an excellent exposition
     and defense of the first four Ways as those
     four Ways are understood by many modern Thomists.
     Joyce's discussion may be usefully compared
     with that of Garrigou-Lagrange (# 313 above).
     Both discussions are valuable but Joyce's pre-
     sentation of the first four Ways is on the whole
     clearer and more effective.

319 Kennick, William E. "A New Way with the Five
     Ways," Austl J Phil, XXXVIII (December, 1960),
     225-33.

     An excellent critique of the interpretation of
     the cosmological argument proposed by Farrer
     (# 312 above) and Mascall (#s 326, 327 and 328
     below), with particular attention to Mascall.
     The latter has suggested that this "proof" can
     be used to evoke a "contuition" of "God-and-
     the-creature-in-the-cosmological relation."
     Kennick's most important point is, perhaps,
     the following: Since Mascall rejects the pos-
     sibility of a direct sensible or intellectual
     intuition of God, it is difficult to see how
     he can admit the existence of a direct intuition
     of "God-together-with-the world." There can,

of course, be an _inference_ from the world to
God, but Mascall denies that inference is involved. Kennick is aware that Mascall or Farrer
might wish to speak of an _indirect_ apprehension
of God through finite objects, but argues that
this is not a genuine alternative (to direct
intuition or inference). Kennick's remarks on
this point are persuasive although not a knock-
down-drag-out refutation.

320 Kenny, Anthony John Patrick. The _Five Ways_, St.
     Thomas Aquinas' Proofs of God's Existence.
     (Studies in Ethics and the Philosophy of Reli-
     gion.) London: Routledge & Kegan Paul; New
     York: Schocken Books, 1969. vii + 131 pp.

     Separate chapters are devoted to critical analyses
     of each of the Five Ways. Kenny is to be com-
     mended for focusing his attention upon Aquinas's
     versions of these arguments instead of upon the
     versions of later commentators and disciples.
     He argues that "the Five Ways fail . . . prin-
     cipally because it is much more difficult than
     it at first appears to separate them from their
     background in medieval cosmology." The discus-
     sions of the first three Ways are especially
     interesting. This is an important book which
     does succeed in showing that Aquinas's formula-
     tions of the cosmological argument are unsound.
     Other versions of the argument (e.g., that of
     Samuel Clarke) would appear, however, to be
     substantially unaffected by Kenny's criticism.

321 King-Farlow, John. "The First Way in Physical
     and Moral Space," _Thomist_, XXXIX (April, 1975),
     349-74.

     King-Farlow argues that the First Way crucially

depends upon the assumption that space is finite
and that it is impossible for there to be "infinitely many actual co-existents." He concludes
by suggesting that, in the First Way, Aquinas
abstracts a concept of "change" from a world
characterized by value, and that this is unfortunate because it is precisely a world characterized by value which the theist is trying to
explain.

322 Laver, Rosemary. "The Notion of Efficient Cause
in the Secunda Via," Thomist, XXXVIII (October,
1974), 754-67.

An interesting historical comment on Aquinas's
use of "efficient cause."

323 Leahy, Louis. "Contingency in the Cosmological
Argument," Relig Stud, 12 (March, 1976), 93-100.

Leahy first attempts to show that the cosmological argument does not involve a fallacious
inference to the contingency of the universe
from the contingency of its parts. In the second,
and more interesting, part of his essay, Leahy
argues the universe as a whole cannot be a necessary and self-sufficient reality which provides
a sufficient reason for the existence of its
parts. (The principal reason provided for this
contention is that wholes are constituted by
their parts and cannot, therefore, be self-sufficient.)

324 McTaggart, John McTaggart Ellis. Some Dogmas of
Religion. London: Edward Arnold, 1906; New
York: Kraus Reprint Co., 1969. Pp. 190-6.

The "first cause argument" traces the series

of temporal events to a divine volition.
McTaggart's objection to this argument is
(roughly) this: Either this event (the divine
volition) is caused by a second event which is
in turn caused by a third event and so on ad
infinitum, or the volition or one of its causal
predecessors is uncaused, or the volition (or
its effect if the volition is regarded as timeless) is caused by something which is not an
event but unchanging. The advocate of the argument must reject the first two alternatives
(because he rejects the notion of an infinite
causal regress and insists that every event
has a cause), and yet the third alternative
is equally unattractive. A change cannot be
fully accounted for by something which changes
neither before nor after the change occurs.
Whatever objections one may have to McTaggart's
critique, he has made an important and often
neglected point. The cosmological argument
traces contingent, changing and dependent being
back to the volition of a necessary, unchanging
and independent being. While the explaining
being may be (e.g.) necessary it is difficult
to see how its volition can be necessary. If,
however, its creative volition is contingent
the explicans would appear to exhibit the very
feature to be explained. Cf. James Ross, Philosophical Theology, chapter 7 (# 338 below).

325 Maritain, Jacques. Approaches to God. Translated
    from the French by Peter O'Reilly. (World Per-
    spectives, 1.) New York: Harper, 1954. Pp.
    1-71, esp. 16-71.

    Chapter 2 defends the Five Ways. Maritain follows
    in the footsteps of Garrigou-Lagrange, Joyce and

other modern Neo-Scholastics. Although his defense is not particularly innovative it does contain several points of interest (see, e.g., his discussion of the First Way and its relation to modern science), and should be examined by those interested in this approach to these arguments. Maritain maintains that philosophic proofs of God's existence are a "development and unfolding" of a natural knowledge of God which consists of an intuition of being, and a "prompt, spontaneous reasoning" which is "more or less involved in it" and concludes that being which is threatened by nothingness depends upon and is activated by self-existent being. (This "natural knowledge" is discussed in chapter 1.) Maritain's position should be compared with the positions of Farrer (# 312 above) and Mascall (#s 326, 327 and 328 below). However, whereas Mascall and Farrer tend to reduce the proofs to an intuition, maintaining that the proofs articulate our intuitive grasp of contingent being as grounded in self-existing being, Maritain appears to regard the intuition as an implicit and inarticulate proof.

326 Mascall, Eric Lionel. Existence and Analogy, A
      Sequel to "He Who Is." London and New York:
      Longmans, Green and Co., Ltd. 1949; Hamden,
      Connecticut: Archon Books, 1967. Pp. 65-91.

In chapter 4, Mascall argues that the Five Ways are "not so much five different demonstrations of the existence of God as five different ways of manifesting the radical dependence of finite being upon God." The Five Ways "exhibit . . . five different characteristics of finite beings, all of which show that it [sic] does not account

for its own existence," and thus provide "five
different aids to the apprehension of God and
the creature in the cosmological relation."
"The existence of God is [thus] not inferred
by a logical process but apprehended in a cognitive act." The object of this apprehension
"is not God in his naked reality but God as
manifested in his creative activity in finite
being." See Kennick's critique of this position
(# 319 above).

327   . He Who Is, A Study in Traditional
Theism. London, New York, Toronto: Longmans,
Green and Co., 1943. Pp. 40-82.

The Five Ways are examined in chapters V and
VI. At the heart of Mascall's discussion is
the contention that "in practise the argument
is either accepted or rejected as a whole,"
depending upon whether we have or have not grasped finite beings as they are, viz., as creatures
of God. The arguments are expressions of an
intuitive apprehension of "the fact of God's
existence as the ground of the existence of finite
beings" and not pieces of discursive reasoning.
This thesis is developed further in the author's
Existence and Analogy (# 326 above) and Words
and Images (# 328 below).

328   . Words and Images, A Study in Theological Discourse. London, New York, Toronto:
Longmans, Green and Co., 1957. Pp. 76-87.

In chapter IV section 3, Mascall reverts to the
idea that the Five Ways "direct the attention
. . . to certain features of finite beings . . .
from which the existence of God can be seen
without a discursive process." There is a

"contuition" of God as cause of a perceived effect, an apprehension which is "direct . . . but
not immediate, for it is mediated by and in
our apprehension of finite beings."

329 Matson, Wallace I. The Existence of God. Ithaca,
     New York: Cornell University Press, 1965.
     Pp. 56-86.

A rather decent discussion of the cosmological
argument construed as an attempt to find a sufficient reason for the world in a perfectly
rational choice. Matson has several criticisms
of the argument perhaps the most interesting
of which is his contention that explaining things
in terms of causes and explaining things in terms
of purposes (i.e., finding a justification or
excuse) are two quite different sorts of activity,
and that hence "the reasoning 'the universe can't
be explained causally; therefore if it is to
be explained at all, it must be explained pur-
posively' really rests on a sort of pun."

330 Mautner, Thomas. "Aquinas's Third Way," Amer
     Phil Quart, 6 (October, 1969), 298-304.

The Third Way commits two fallacies. (1) It
infers "if there is a time u, at which something
begins to be, then at any time before u something is" from "what is not only begins to be
by something which is." (2) It infers "if everything need not be, then at some time nothing
was" from "what need not be at some time is
not." (This involves an illicit quantifier
shift from $(x)(\exists t)$ to $(\exists t)(x)$.) A version of
the Third Way which treats the world as one big
object is attributed to Mascall and Geach, and

dismissed as fallacious. This section is less
convincing than the preceding ones. Mautner
appears to assume that the world so-conceived
is either a mere collection of objects (in which
case it cannot instantiate the variable in
(x)-(x need be)) or else it is simply one object
alongside other objects (in which case "at some
time the world is not" does not imply "at that
time nothing is"). There is, however, a third
possibility, viz., that the world is a real
object composed of all other objects (as an
automobile engine is an object composed of pis-
tons, rods, etc.).

331 Morillo, Carolyn R. "The Logic of Arguments from
     Contingency," Phil Phenomenol Res, XXXVII (March,
     1977), 408-17.

While not original, this essay provides a clear
statement of an objection which deserves more
attention than it has received. The connection
between necessary and contingent being is itself either necessary or contingent. If it is
necessary, then contingent being is not contingent. If it is contingent, then there is at
least one unexplained contingent fact. For
a fuller discussion of this difficulty see Ross,
338 below.

332 Munitz, Milton Karl. The Mystery of Existence,
     An Essay in Philosophical Theology. (Century
     Philosophy Series.) New York: Appleton-Century
     Crofts, 1965. xii + 270 pp.

A fairly interesting discussion of a number of
related issues such as the meaning of "world"
and "the world exists," whether or not it makes
sense to speak of the origin of the world or

to say that the world might not have been, and whether or not the world can have a reason for its existence. Munitz concludes that "the mystery of existence consists in the fact that we have no rational method by which we can know whether there is" a reason for the existence of the world in any sense of "reason."

333 Penelhum, Terence. "Divine Necessity," _Mind_, LXIX (April, 1960), 175-86.

The questions "why does anything exist?" and "why does anything have P?" are spurious questions. The only thing which could provide an answer to these questions would be a thing which is such that both its existence and its possession of P is self-explanatory, but existential propositions cannot be necessarily true and although the concept of a being may contain P, that being's possession of P is not self-explanatory unless it is logically necessary that that concept be instantiated. Penelhum concludes by suggesting that it does make sense to suppose that God is "factually necessary," i.e., to suppose that God depends on nothing while everything else depends upon Him. That there is such a being is, however, contingent and the appeal to such a being will not provide an answer to the questions which lie behind the cosmological argument. Although this article has been fairly influential, it is not particularly original.

334 _____. _Religion and Rationality, An Introduction to the Philosophy of Religion_. New York: Random House, Inc., 1971. Pp. 19-47 and 373-80.

The cosmological argument is discussed in chapters
3 and 4, and in Appendix B. Fairly pedestrian
although Penelhum's remarks on the Fourth and
Fifth Ways (pp. 28-33), and on Mascall, Patterson
Brown, etc. (pp. 373-79) are of some interest.

335 Phillips, Richard Percival. Modern Thomistic
     Philosophy, An Explanation for Students. Vol.
     II. London: Burns, Oates and Washbourne, Ltd.,
     1935. Pp. 277-98.

     Part III, chapters II and III contain a succinct
     discussion of the Five Ways. Phillips' discus-
     sion is heavily dependent upon the more complete
     discussion of Garrigou-Lagrange (# 313 above).

336 Plantinga, Alvin Carl. God and Other Minds, A
     Study of the Rational Justification of Belief
     in God. (Contemporary Philosophy.) Ithaca, New
     York: Cornell University Press, 1967. Pp. 3-25.

     Chapter 1 contains an excellent discussion of
     the Third Way. Plantinga considers the possi-
     bility that the argument is sound given the
     assumption that all posibilities will be realized
     in an infinite stretch of time. Several inter-
     pretations of this assumption are considered,
     and it is shown that their truth implies that
     past time is not infinite. It follows that if
     the Third Way is sound, it can be shown that
     past time is not infinite. This creates a prob-
     lem for Aquinas who believed both that the Third
     Way is sound and that it cannot be shown that
     past time is not infinite. See Rowe's response
     (# 342 below).

337 Reichenbach, Bruce Robert. The Cosmological Argu-
     ment: A Reassessment. Springfield, Illinois:
     Charles C. Thomas, 1972. xiv + 150 pp.

     Includes chapters on causation, on the Principle
     of Sufficient Reason, on whether we can speak
     of the totality of contingent beings as caused,
     on the meaning of "necessary being," on the sup-
     posed dependence of the cosmological argument
     on the ontological argument, etc. Reichenbach
     defends a version of the Third Way which is simi-
     lar to that offered by some modern Thomists but
     addresses himself to criticisms which have arisen
     within the Anglo-American analytic tradition.
     The book is not without interest. However,
     even those who are sympathetic to the cosmolo-
     gical argument will be suspicious of several of
     his theses (e.g., that cause and effect must
     be simultaneous, or that God can be really neces-
     sary -- providing a sufficient reason for His
     own existence -- even though His existence is
     not logically necessary), and will not always
     be convinced by the arguments offered for those
     theses which they do accept (e.g., the arguments
     offered for the Principle of Sufficient Reason).

338 Ross, James Francis. Philosophical Theology.
     Indianapolis and New York: The Bobbs-Merrill
     Co., Inc., 1969. Pp. 159-73 and 279-319.

     Some significant criticisms of the Five Ways
     can be found in chapter 4. The discussion of
     the Principle of Sufficient Reason in chapter
     7 is of particular importance. The principle
     states that there is a sufficient reason for
     every contingent state of affairs and is employed
     in most modern versions of the cosmological
     argument. Ross shows that those who defend

214

these versions are involved in an inconsistency. The free decision of a necessary being is introduced to provide a sufficient reason for contingent being and yet, since this free decision is a contingent state of affairs for which there is no sufficient reason, the principle is violated. It follows that they must either abandon the principle or conclude that contingent being necessarily follows from the activity of a necessary being and is, therefore, not genuinely contingent. (Ross neglects another possibility. One might modify the principle or replace it. One might, e.g., suggest that every contingent state of affairs which requires a sufficient reason has one, and go on to argue that free choices do not require sufficient conditions [perhaps because they cannot both have causally sufficient conditions and be free decisions]. Or one might [à la Hartshorne] suggest that although things can exist for which there is no sufficient reason, nothing [e.g., a world] can exist for which there is no reason at all.)

339 Rowe, William Leonard. "The Cosmological Argument," Nous, V (February, 1971), 49-61.

Rowe distinguishes between medieval versions of the cosmological argument which rest upon the impossibility of an infinite regress of essentially ordered causes, and modern versions of the argument which rest upon the Principle of Sufficient Reason. He discusses the latter arguing that the proponents of the argument "are right in contending that if every being is dependent there will be no explanation of the existence of the collection of dependent beings," but that the Principle of Sufficient

Reason is not known to be true.

340 _____. The Cosmological Argument. Princeton
and London: The Princeton University Press,
1975. 273 pp.

This is the best work on the cosmological argument to appear in recent years. In the first
chapter Rowe discusses 13th century versions of
the argument. These versions are not clearly
unsound but do suffer from two deficiencies.
They employ the (possibly suspect) notion of an
essentially ordered causal series, and their
appeal to the Principle of Sufficient Reason
(an appeal which must be made in order to show
that essentially ordered causal series are grounded in a first cause) is only implicit. The
rest of the book is devoted to a discussion of
Samuel Clarke's cosmological argument. As in
other 18th century versions of the argument,
the appeal to the Principle of Sufficient Reason
is explicit and no distinction is made between
accidentally and essentially ordered causal
series. Clarke's argument has two parts. The
first part is designed to show that since (1)
every being either depends for its existence upon
some other being or contains the reason for
its existence within its own nature and since
(2) it is false that every being is dependent,
(3) there exists a being which contains the reason for its existence within its own nature
and (4) this being must be a logically necessary
being. Chapters II and III are devoted to the
first three steps and chapter IV examines the
inference from (3) to (4). (These chapters
incorporate major portions of Rowe's articles
on the cosmological argument but also introduce

significant new material.) Rowe argues, roughly,
that the inferences (from [1] and [2] to [3], and
from [3] to [4]) are valid, that the Principle
of Sufficient Reason provides a good reason for
(1) and (2), that the Principle of Sufficient
Reason is not clearly false, and that the major
criticisms of the first part of the cosmological
argument are unsound. The second part of Clarke's
argument attempts to show that any self-existent
(logically necessary) being which accounts for
the fact that there are dependent beings must
be God. In chapter V, Rowe examines Clarke's
attempts to show that a self-existent being upon
which other beings depend for their existence
must be eternal, omnipresent, omniscient, omnipotent and infinitely good. He concludes that
Clarke's attempt to show that the being in question is eternal and omnipresent is rather convincing, that his attempt to show that it is intelligent and powerful is plausible but does not succeed in establishing infinite power and intelligence, and that his attempt to show that this
being is infinitely good is only plausible if we
accept Clarke's belief that moral principles
are objectively grounded in the nature of things
and are intuitively evident to the rational
intellect. Rowe's final conclusion is that
although the cosmological argument may be sound
(it is valid and its premises have not been
shown to be false), it is not a proof of God's
existence because it rests upon the Principle
of Sufficient Reason and that Principle is not
known to be true. He suggests, however, that
the argument might establish the reasonableness
of theistic belief. Whether it does so depends
upon whether it is reasonable to believe in

the Principle of Sufficient Reason.

341 _____. "The Cosmological Argument and the
Principle of Sufficient Reason," Man World,
1 (May, 1968), 278-92.

Rowe argues that the Principle of Sufficient
Reason is not known to be true, for (1) no one
has succeeded in demonstrating it, (2) it is
neither analytic nor a synthetic necessary truth,
and (3) it is not clearly a presupposition of
reason. A very good discussion.

342 _____. "God and Other Minds," Nous, III
(September, 1969), pp. 261-4.

A good critical discussion of Plantinga's treatment of the Third Way (# 336 above). Rowe argues
that although Plantinga has shown that Aquinas
is inconsistent, he has not shown that the Third
Way is unsound.

343 _____. "Two Criticisms of the Cosmological
Argument," Monist, 54 (July, 1970), 441-59.

It has been argued that "the notion of cause or
explanation" cannot be applied "to the totality
of things." Others have maintained that "it
is intelligible to ask for an explanation of
the existence of an infinite collection of dependent beings [but that] the answer to this
question . . . is provided once we learn that
each member of the infinite collection has an
explanation of its existence." Rowe effectively
argues that neither of these objections is sound.

344 Smart, Ninian. _Philosophers and Religious Truth_.
London: SCM Press, Ltd., 1964. Pp. 88-129.

The cosmological argument is discussed in chapter
IV. The cosmological question is not why _any_
thing exists but why a _cosmos_ exists. In its
most plausible form, the argument is not deductive
but involves an "imaginative leap" which posits a
creative act of will in order to solve the problem of the contingency of the cosmos. The
"Explanatory Principle" ("in general, contingent events, etc. can be explained") justifies
this attempt to explain the cosmos. The teleological argument may then be introduced, not as
an independent argument, but as a means of ascer-
taining the nature of the creative will which
has been postulated to explain the existence
of a contingent world.

345 Swinburne, Richard G. "Whole and Part in Cosmological Arguments," _Philosophy_, XLIV (October,
1969), 339-40.

It is argued that the causes (in the scientific
sense) of a set of states cannot themselves
be members of that set of states. It follows
that "whether finite or infinite, the series
of past states of the universe has no cause
in the scientific sense, and so is scientifically
inexplicable."

346 Taylor, Richard. _Metaphysics_. 2d ed. Englewood
Cliffs, New Jersey: Prentice-Hall, Inc., 1974.
Pp. 103-12.

An effective presentation of the "modern" version
of the cosmological argument (see Rowe, # 339
above). This essay contains little which is new,
and issues are not discussed in depth.

Nevertheless, Taylor's exposition is clear and balanced. His discussion has been frequently referred to since the appearance of the first edition in 1963.

347   Thompson, Samuel Martin. A Modern Philosophy of Religion. Chicago: Henry Regnery Co., 1955. Pp. 284-358.

Part Six contains a frequently cited presentation of the cosmological argument. This presentation is not without interest but is ultimately less persuasive than other presentations of the same argument. "Contingency" is defined as "dependency," and it is argued that the world is contingent because it is temporal. (According to Thompson, temporality implies change, and change implies a movement from potentiality to actuality, which in turn implies an external mover and, hence, dependency. [While Thompson shows that temporality involves a "Cambridge" change, viz., existing at two different times, he does not show that it involves any real change.]) The author argues that there cannot be an infinite series of actually existing things. (It is not entirely clear whether he means that there cannot be an infinite series of essentially ordered agents or whether he means that there cannot be any kind of infinite series of actually existing things. It appears, however, that he means the latter.) More time is spent defending the reality of causality than in defending the claim that the world (the whole of contingent being) must have a cause. Thompson argues that because things act in accordance with their nature, they can only give what is in their nature (sic!). Since existence is not included in

the essence of contingent beings, contingent
beings cannot bestow existence. In chapter
21, Thompson attempts to show that the self-
existent cause of dependent being is one, intelligent and purposive, and to explain how the
world depends upon this being. This is perhaps
the most interesting part of Thompson's discussion.

348   Tooley, Michael. "Does the Cosmological Argument
       Entail the Ontological Argument?" Monist, 54
       (July, 1970), 416-26.

Tooley argues (1) that Kant did not show that
the cosmological argument presupposes the ontological argument, but (2) that a cosmological
argument which attempts to show that the necessary being which is the cause of contingent
beings is a perfect being, entails an ontological
argument in the sense that there is a valid
ontological argument each premiss of which is
either deducible from premisses of the cosmological argument together with the fact that it
is a cosmological argument or "can be shown
independently to be an a priori truth." This
article is interesting and Tooley's argument
appears to be sound. It is doubtful, however,
that its conclusion should bother a proponent
of the cosmological argument.

349   Wallace, William A. "Newtonian Antimonies and
       the Prima Via," Thomist, XIX (April, 1956),
       151-92.

Wallace attempts to show that Newtonian physics
is compatible with the Aristotelian-Thomistic
account of motion and, therefore, with the First
Way. Intelligent and well argued although

something of a tour de force.

350   Weber, Stephen Lewis. "Concerning the Impossi-
        bility of A Posteriori Arguments for the Existence
        of God," J Relig, 53 (January, 1973), 83-98.

Cosmological arguments purport to be a posteriori
in two senses -- they proceed from an effect
to God as cause, and at least one of their premisses allegedly depends upon experiential verification. Weber argues that cosmological proofs
cannot be a posteriori in both senses. The effect
which God is introduced to explain is contingent
being, but the contingency of being is not revealed to experience and, therefore, that there
is contingent being is not experientially verifiable. Weber's paper is interesting but it is
not clear that he has succeeded in establishing
his thesis. That a thing is contingent must
perhaps be determined by examining its concept.
Even so, that the concept (which has been determined by analysis to be the concept of a contingent thing) applies can, in many cases, be
experientially verified. Hence, "there are contingent beings" can (pace Weber) be partially
verified by experience.

351   Wengert, Robert G. "The Logic of Essentially
        Ordered Causes," Notre Dame J Form Log, XII
        (October, 1971), 406-22.

When the medievals assert that an infinite causal
regress is impossible they are referring to a
series of essentially ordered causes. Wengert
attempts to explicate this concept borrowing some
"logical notions that can be found in introductory texts." The article includes some apprecia-
tive but critical comments on Brown's "Infinite

Causal Regression" (# 303 above).

352 Williams, C. J. F. "Hic auten non est procedere
       in infinitum . . . (St. Thomas Aquinas)," _Mind_,
       LXIX (July, 1960), 403-5.

       In arguing for the impossibility of an infinite
       regress, Aquinas asserts that without a first
       mover there would be no second movers. This
       begs the question. We are only entitled to
       speak of first and second movers if the series
       is finite, and this is precisely what is at issue.

353 Wolfe, Julian. "Infinite Regress and the Cosmo-
       logical Argument," _Int_ _J_ _Phil_ _Relig_, II (Winter,
       1971), 246-9.

       It is sometimes argued that an infinite causal
       series is impossible because an infinite time
       cannot elapse. Wolfe shows that if nothing
       can come into being without a cause, then, if
       an uncaused cause exists, an infinite time has
       elapsed. (If nothing comes into being without
       a cause, an uncaused cause could not have come
       into being and must, therefore, have always
       existed.) Since the series of causes is either
       finite (in which case there is an uncaused cause)
       or infinite, it follows that an infinite time
       has elapsed. Wolfe implicitly assumes that an
       uncaused cause would be in time, and that an
       infinite causal series would occupy an infinite
       length of time. Given these assumptions his
       argument appears to be sound.

354 Yandell, Keith Edward. _Basic_ _Issues_ _in_ _the_ _Philo-_
       sophy _of_ _Religion_. Boston: _Allyn_ _and_ _Bacon,_
       Inc., _1971._ Pp. 67-95.

This section contains a very decent critical discussion of the first three Ways, and a plausible formulation of the argument from the existence of contingent entities. Yandell suggests that proponents and critics of the cosmological argument disagree about the nature of explanation, and proceeds to defend the use of the Principle of Sufficient Reason in the cosmological argument by presenting a pattern of reasoning which is similar to that employed in the cosmological argument, and which is (according to Yandell) clearly cogent.

The Argument From Design

(See also # 294)

355 Alston, William P. "Teleological Argument for the Existence of God," The Encyclopedia of Philosophy. Vol 8. Edited by Paul Edwards. New York: Macmillan, 1967. Pp. 84-8

Alston begins with some valuable observations on the nature of teleological order and then proceeds to distinguish between the argument from particular cases of teleological order (e.g., the eye) and the argument from the teleological order of the universe as a whole. The first type of argument is employed by William Paley. The second sort of argument is employed by F. R. Tennant. Science may provide alternative explanations (e.g., the theory of evolution) in the first case but it cannot do so in the second. Alston presents several standard criticisms of these arguments.

356 Bertocci, Peter Anthony. Introduction to the
     Philosophy of Religion. (Prentice-Hall Philo-
     sophy Series.) Englewood Cliffs, New Jersey:
     Prentice-Hall, Inc., 1951. Pp. 329-88.

     Chapters 13-15 present what Bertocci calls "the
     wider teleological argument" -- a cumulative
     argument from certain general features of the
     cosmos which should be distinguished from narrower
     arguments based upon the apparent design of
     specific items within the cosmos. The wider
     argument appeals to seven things: (1) The
     emergence, in the course of cosmic evolution,
     of new things which "advance the quality of
     existence," (2) the existence of minds which
     can penetrate the secrets of nature, (3) the
     existence of an ordered, predictable world within
     which rational moral activity is possible, (4)
     the fact that the world can be modified in ac-
     cordance with moral ideals, (5) the fact that
     the world is a "vale of soul making" in which
     we can help to determine the quality of our own
     lives, and a moral order in which love and well-
     doing tend to produce happiness while selfishness
     and ill-doing tend to produce misery, (6) the
     beauty of the world, and (7) the existence of
     religious experiences. No one of these things
     is sufficient, but (according to Bertocci) when
     taken together they create a strong presumption
     in favor of the existence of a benevolent crea-
     tive intelligence directing the processes of na-
     ture. Bertocci quite properly acknowledges
     his debt to F. R. Tennant (# 388 below).

357 Bowler, Peter John. "Sir Francis Palgrave on
     Natural Theology," J Hist Ideas, XXXV (January-
     March, 1974), 144-7.

The design argument rests upon the assumption
of the goodness of the world. This assumption
conflicts with the traditional Christian claim
that the world is spoiled by sin.

358   Clarke, Bowman Lafayette. "The Argument from
      Design -- A Piece of Abductive Reasoning,"
      Int J Phil Relig, V (Summer, 1974), 65-78.

An abductive inference has the form "C, If A
then C, therefore (probably) A." Clarke argues
that regarding the design argument as an abductive rather then an inductive inference has
several advantages. For example, since an abductive inference does not move from the consideration of the constitution of a sample to a
conclusion about the constitution of the class
from which that sample is drawn, many potentially
embarrassing questions ("How many worlds have
been observed to be designed?" "Is there one
class which contains both artifacts and the
world as a whole?") prove to be irrelevant.

359   Edwards, Rem B. Reason and Religion, An Introduc-
      tion to the Philosophy of Religion. New York:
      Harcourt Brace Jovanovich, Inc., 1972. Pp.
      272-87.

Chapter 11 contains a fairly interesting discussion of the design argument. The principle that
governs the design argument (viz., "what resembles the products of purposive intelligence may
be inferred to be a product of purposive intelligence") is employed in many cases including the
argument to other minds, an argument which is
in many respects similar to the design argument.
Edwards responds to several standard criticisms.
For example, it is sometimes asserted that any

connection which we infer must be a new instance
of a connection which we have observed in several
other instances. (Hence, it is said that we
are entitled to infer a connection between a
watchmaker and a specific watch, or a designer
and the cosmos only if we have observed several
instances of the connection between watchmakers
and watches, or designers and worlds.) Edwards
points out that, since we have not observed
connections between other minds and other bodies,
an insistence upon this requirement would force
us to reject the inference to other minds (or
more exactly, to reject the connection between
the behavior of other bodies and other minds).

360   Gaskin, John C. A. "The Design Argument: Hume's
        Critique of Poor Reason," Relig Stud, 12 (Septem-
        ber, 1976), 331-45.

        A reply to Swinburne (#s 383 and 384 below).
        Gaskin (1) defends the claim that we must not
        ascribe more to the cause than is warranted by
        the effect, (2) accuses Swinburne of deliberately
        ignoring the crucial question as to whether
        or not artifacts and the universe (or its parts)
        are in fact similar, and (3) argues that the
        introduction of an agent explanation of the
        world's order does not increase our understanding
        of that order. Gaskin's points are well developed
        though familiar (which is, of course, what one
        would expect in an avowed defense of Hume).

361   Hendel, Charles William. Studies in the Philosophy
        of David Hume. 2d ed. Indianapolis: Bobbs-
        Merrill, 1963. Pp. 267-358.

        The first edition was published in 1925 by Prince-
        ton University Press. Chapters X-XII discuss

the <u>Dialogues</u> <u>Concerning</u> <u>Natural</u> <u>Religion</u>.
Hendel's most interesting contention is that
Hume views the design argument not as a scientific argument but as the expression of a natural
or spontaneous movement of thought which deserves
to be called rational, and which is akin to the
movement of thought which leads to belief in
other minds. This point is developed in Pike's
commentary on the <u>Dialogues</u> (# 375 below).
(Pike acknowledges his debt to Hendel.) For
a somewhat similar view see Plantinga's <u>God</u>
<u>and</u> <u>Other</u> <u>Minds</u>, chapter 10 (# 376 below).
Further discussion of the contention that Hume
regards religious belief as spontaneous, natural,
and not irrational can be found in R. J. Butler's
"Natural Belief and the Enigma of Hume," and
in J. C. A. Gaskin's "God, Hume and Natural
Belief" (#s 1039 and 1049 below).

362   Hinton, R. T.   "God and the Possibility of Science,"
      <u>Sophia</u>, XII (April, 1973), 25-9.

      Hinton attacks a premiss which plays a role in
      some versions of the design argument, viz.,
      that it is improbable that a law governed universe
      would occur by chance. The author argues that
      there are an infinite number of possible worlds
      which are law-governed, but only one possible
      world which can be described as a chaos (since
      there is no way of distinguishing chaotic uni-
      verses[?]). The odds in favor of a law-governed
      universe are, therefore, overwhelming.

363   Hurlbutt, Robert H., III.   <u>Hume</u>, <u>Newton</u> <u>and</u> <u>the</u> <u>De-</u>
      <u>sign</u> <u>Argument</u>.   Lincoln, Nebraska: University
      of Nebraska Press, 1965.   xiv + 221 pp.

The first part of this book explores the form
which the argument assumed under the influence
of the new science and the second part examines
ancient and medieval versions of the argument.
(One interesting difference is that classical
versions of the argument more frequently compare
the world to a work of art than to a machine.)
The third and last part is devoted to Hume's
critique and to the recent history of the argument. Those familiar with Hume and the argument's
modern history will find little to interest
them in this section.

364 Jeffner, Anders. Butler and Hume on Religion, A
     Comparative Analysis. Translated by Keith Brad-
     field, notes translated by James Stewart.
     (Studia Doctrinae Christiane Upsaliensia, 7.)
     Stockholm: Diakonistyrelsens Bokförlag, 1966.
     Pp. 131-71.

Chapter VI contains a good discussion of the
design argument. Three types of natural system
are distinguished: (Roughly) systems whose
components interact in lawlike ways, systems the
components of which interact in such a way as
to maintain a certain organization, and systems
the components of which interact in such a way
as to maintain an organization and which are
also such that the organization in question
is a unique consequence of just those parts
interacting in just those ways. Jeffner shows
that proponents of the design argument sometimes
appealed to one type of system and sometimes
to another, and considers the ways in which Hume's
objections affect design arguments which appeal
to these different sorts of system. He concludes
that Hume has succeeded in showing that design
arguments which attempt to explain systems

within nature are bad scientific arguments,
and that the design argument which attempts to
explain the apparent design of nature as a whole
is not a scientific argument at all.

365   Joyce, George Hayward. Principles of Natural
      Theology. (Stonyhurst Philosophical Series.)
      London, New York [etc.]: Longmans, Green and
      Co., 1923; New York: AMS Press, 1972. Pp.
      116-44.

In chapter IV, one of the better Neo-Scholastics
defends the design argument against standard
objections. It is worth observing that Aquinas's
Fifth Way can be interpreted as an argument from
order and final causation, order and final causation being construed as features which must be
exhibited by any world of created beings. Understood in this fashion, the Fifth Way is a cosmological argument. The Fifth Way can also be
interpreted as an argument from the specific
sort of design which happens to be found in our
world. This is the design argument proper.
Thomists sometimes interpret the Fifth Way in
the first fashion, sometimes in the second,
and sometimes appear to be unclear as to which
interpretation they are proposing. Joyce is
clear about the distinction and chooses to interpret the argument in the second fashion.

366   Laird, John. Theism and Cosmology, Being the First
      Series of a Course of Gifford Lectures on the
      General Subject of Metaphysics and Theism Given
      in the University of Glasgow in 1939. New York:
      Philosophical Library and Alliance Book Corp.,
      1942. Pp. 261-90.

Chapter IX contains an extended critique of the
design argument. While his comments are not

particularly original, Laird does effectively
present the case against the hypothesis that
the cosmos as a whole is designed. Although
he is referred to only once, Laird's criticisms
appear to be specifically directed against the
sort of design argument presented by Tennant
(see # 388 below).

367 McPherson, Thomas. The Argument from Design.
(New Studies in the Philosophy of Religion.)
London and Basingstoke: The Macmillan Press,
Ltd.; New York: St. Martin's Press, 1972.
ix + 78 pp.

This little book contains a number of good things.
Three chapters are of particular interest:
chapter 2 which discusses the question as to
whether the proponent of the argument discovers
apparent design in nature or imposes design
upon nature, chapter 5 in which McPherson gives
reasons for concluding that the argument from
design is an empirical argument but not a scientific one, and chapter 6 in which McPherson argues that even if the design argument fails
to conclusively establish its conclusion, it
can confirm faith and help believers "to see
design in the things about them," and in which
he also suggests that (since the argument depends upon the assumption that machines, artifacts, human bodies, etc., are correlated with
minds which are distinct from them, and which
explain them) "the future of the Argument from
Design depends upon the refutation of mechanism."

368   McTaggart, John McTaggart Ellis. Some Dogmas of
      Religion. London: Edward Arnold, 1906; New
      York: Kraus Reprint Co., 1969. Pp. 196-202
      and 238-60.

The design argument is first discussed in sections
161-165, where it is contended that since the
argument commits one to the position that the
designer employs means, its premises not only
fail to establish an omnipotent designer, but
are actually incompatible with the omnipotence
of the designer whose existence they allegedly
establish. The argument is discussed again in
sections 196-215, where it is argued that the
hypothesis of a designer has some plausibility
if matter is real and independent, but is unnecessary if certain forms of idealism are true (if,
e.g., reality is a unified society of finite
selves). Interesting.

369   Matson, Wallace I. The Existence of God. Ithaca,
      New York: Cornell University Press, 1965.
      Pp. 87-131.

(1) Probabilistic versions of the design argument
are dismissed on the grounds that we have no
way of calculating the relevant probabilities.
(2) The hypothesis that evolutionary processes
are anti-entropic and, therefore, require a
designer is effectively criticized. (3) It
is argued that at least some forms of the design
argument rest upon the false assumption that
the "curious adaptation of means to ends" is
the criterion which we use in ordinary contexts
to distinguish artifacts from natural objects.

370 Mellor, D. Hugh. "God and Probability," <u>Relig</u> <u>Stud</u>,
     5 (December, 1969), 223-34.

     Mellor argues that the notions of statistical
     probability, subjective probability, and induc-
     tive probability cannot be "properly applied
     to matters of religious belief." Section II
     possesses the most interest. In that section,
     Tennant is accused of committing a fallacy simi-
     lar to the fallacy committed by someone who
     examines a deal in a card game, constructs the
     hypothesis that the cards were deliberately
     arranged in that way by the dealer, and then
     proceeds to argue that since the probability
     of the arrangement which in fact occurred is
     higher upon that hypothesis than upon the hy-
     pothesis that the arrangement in question was
     the result of an honest shuffle, the dealer
     cheated. See Sturch's reply (# 382 below).

371 O'Briant, Walter Herbert. "A New Argument from
     Design," <u>Sophia</u>, VI (April, 1967), 30-4.

     A criticism of Richard Taylor's design argument
     (# 387 below). It is suggested that Taylor's
     analogies are defective because the connection
     between the arrangement of stones or the pattern
     of marks, and the messages which they convey
     depends upon linguistic convention. Since the
     connection is conventional we are entitled to
     infer a designer(s). The connection between
     our sensory and cognitive faculties and the
     truths which they reveal is not conventional,
     however, and the inference to a designer(s) is,
     therefore, unwarranted.

372   Olding, A.   "The Argument from Design -- A Reply
          to R. G. Swinburne," Relig Stud, 7 (December,
          1971), 361-73.

          A reply to # 383 below. (1) Olding attacks
          the contention that the designer hypothesis
          simplifies explanation by reducing all explana-
          tions to personal explanations, arguing that
          because we are not told how the designer acts
          we do not understand the hypothesis clearly
          enough to determine whether it is simpler than
          alternative hypotheses or not.   (2) Swinburne's
          argument presupposes mind-body dualism. If,
          however, the designer acts on the world as we
          act on our brains or bodies, the designer must
          be unconscious of what he is doing.   (3) The
          designer initiates regularities of succession
          while human minds only modify such regularities.
          Hence the analogy breaks down. See Swinburne's
          reply (# 384 below), and Oldings response to
          that reply (# 373 below).

373   _____.   "Design -- A Further Reply to R. G.
          Swinburne," Relig Stud, 9 (June, 1973), 229-32.

          A reply to # 384 below. Olding responds to
          the charge that he has overlooked the fact that
          a difference in effects may require us to pos-
          tulate a difference in causes, and to the charge
          that he mistakenly believes that C has not ex-
          plained E unless C has itself been explained
          and it has been explained how C caused E.   In
          the course of this reply it becomes increasingly
          clear that at the heart of Olding's objection
          to Swinburne is the contention that the rele-
          vant analogy is with the mind's action on the
          brain rather than with intentional bodily

behavior (e.g., singing or dancing).

374 Pearl, Leon. "Hume's Criticism of the Argument from Design," _Monist_, 54 (April, 1970), 270-84.

The proponent of the design argument normally wishes to draw two conclusions -- that the universe probably originated from intelligent design, and that the designer is probably "somewhat similar to the mind of man though possessed of much larger faculties." Pearl admits that Hume has presented good reasons for supposing that the proponent of the design argument is not entitled to draw the second conclusion, but effectively argues that Hume's criticisms of the first inference are unsound. A good article.

375 Pike, Nelson Craft. _Dialogues Concerning Natural Religion by David Hume._ Edited and with commen- by Nelson Pike. (The Bobbs-Merrill Text and Commentary Series.) Indianapolis and New York: The Bobbs-Merrill Co., Inc., 1970. Pp. ix-xix and 127-238.

Pike's extensive commentary provides a detailed and astute examination of the arguments presented by Cleanthes and Philo. Pike provides evidence for the claim that Hume believed that the design argument was unsound if regarded as a piece of scientific reasoning, but thought that the design argument was worthy of respect if regarded as an immediate inference from the impression of apparent design which nature creates within us. Pike's commentary is an important and original contribution to the discussion of the teleological argument.

376 Plantinga, Alvin Carl. God and Other Minds, A
    Study of the Rational Justification of Belief
    in God. (Contemporary Philosophy.) Ithaca,
    New York: Cornell University Press, 1967.
    Pp. 95-111 and 268-71.

In chapter 4, Plantinga suggests that the design
argument should be construed as an inductive
argument in which the sample class is the class
of things which exhibit the adaption of means
to ends and which are such that we know whether
or not they are the product of intelligent design,
and in which the reference class is the class
of those things which exhibit the adaption of
means to ends, a class which includes the universe and organisms as well as human artifacts.
Plantinga considers the objection that there
is no appropriate reference class for the argument, contends that the criteria for "appropriate
reference class" are unclear, and concludes
that Hume provides no conclusive reason for
supposing that the reference class which is
used in the design argument is in fact inappropriate. He then proceeds to argue that although
there may be some evidence for design, the total
evidence provides as much support for the claim
that there are several embodied and limited
designers as it does for the claim that there
is one, disembodied, unlimited designer. Since
God is one, disembodied and unlimited, the total
evidence does not make God's existence more probable than not. See also the last section of
chapter 10 in which the design argument is compared with the analogical argument for other
minds, and it is concluded that the two arguments
share similar defects. Plantinga suggests,
however, that just as our belief in other minds
is nevertheless a rational belief, so too is

our belief in God. (For a discussion of this
contention, see #s 1045, 1057, 1075 and 1079
below.)

377 Richman, Robert J. "Plantinga, God and (Yet)
     Other Minds," <u>Austl</u> <u>J</u> <u>Phil</u>, 50 (May, 1972),
     40-54.

     Richman takes exception to Plantinga's formulation
     of the design argument (see # 376 above). (1)
     The first premiss ("Everything which exhibits
     a means-end relationship and concerning which
     we know whether it is designed or not, is in
     fact designed") is unfalsifiable. This is odd
     because the argument purports to be an inductive
     one. (2) Consider the following argument:
     "Every person of whom we know whether they have
     a body or not, has one; God is a person, there-
     fore, God has a body." The conclusion is self-
     contradictory (for God is necessarily immaterial);
     but "surely an inductive principle [viz., if
     every K of which we know whether or not it has
     P, has P, then all K's have P] that yields such
     conclusions is unacceptable." It is not clear
     that these objections are sound. Some empirical
     statements are strictly unfalsifiable (e.g.,
     "There are unicorns"). Again, given that God
     is necessarily a disembodied person, and that
     we know this, then there is at least one person
     of whom we know whether he has a body or not,
     who does not have one. The first premiss of
     Richman's argument, unlike the first premiss
     of the design argument, is known to be false,
     and, hence, we are not forced to conclude that
     God has a body.

378   Ruse, Michael. "William Whewell and the Argument from Design," <u>Monist</u>, 60 (April, 1977), 244-68.

An interesting historical and critical examination of a version of the Design Argument. Whewell inferred a Designer from apparent design by eliminating three alternative hypotheses, viz., chance, necessity and evolution. The force of Whewell's argument is compromised (1) by his insistence that many natural laws are necessary (in the sense that their denials are inconceivable!), and (2) by his recognition that the world contains many things which are "not designed for organisms in general and man in particular." Ruse concludes by suggesting that even though Darwin's theory can accomodate the hypothesis of design, it removed what was thought to be an insurmountable obstacle to the <u>rejection</u> of that hypothesis by providing an alternative account of adaptation.

379   Salmon, Wesley C. "A Modern Analysis of the Design Argument," <u>Research Studies of the State College of Washington</u>, XIX (December, 1951), 207-20.

It is argued that "inferences by indirect evidence [such as the design argument] are schematized, that is their form is explicitly stated by," Baye's theorem. Salmon estimates the relevant probabilities on the basis of Hume's arguments and concludes that the design argument fails. In particular: (1) The probability that given the existence of God a world which contains as much evil as ours would exist is low. (2) Since there are alternative hypotheses which plausibly explain apparent design, the probability that given God's non-existence a world such as the

present one would exist is rather high. (3)
Because science is abandoning teleological explanations, the antecedent probability of a
teleological hypothesis must be regarded as
quite low. For a different estimate of these
probabilities see Schlesinger (# 380 below).

380 Schlesinger, George. "Probabilistic Arguments
for Divine Design," Philosophia (Israel),
3 (January, 1973), 1-16.

This article may be usefully compared with # 379
above. Probabilistic versions of the argument
are based upon the assumption that the actual
state of the universe is a rare kind of state
rather than upon the assumption that the universe
exhibits design. These versions (unlike versions
based upon the second assumption?) can be explicated with the help of Baye's theorem. Given
a suitably formulated God-hypothesis, the probability of the actual state of affairs occurring
is 1. The probability of (e.g.) conditions
occurring which produce human life is very low
on alternative hypotheses. Therefore, even
if the antecedent probability of the God-hypothesis is low, if it is higher than the probability of the actual state of affairs occurring
upon alternative hypotheses, then the overall
probability of the God-hypothesis will be higher
than the overall probability of the alternative
hypotheses. An interesting article.

381 Smith, Norman Kemp. Dialogues Concerning Natural
Religion by David Hume. Edited and with an
introduction by Norman Kemp Smith. 2d ed. with
supplement. Edinburgh and London: Thomas Nelson
and Sons, Ltd., 1947. Pp. 1-123.

The extended introduction and appendices contain discussions of Hume's religious views, a consideration of the dates of composition and revision, an analysis of the main argument, an examination of the question "Who is Hume's spokesman in the Dialogues?," etc. While it does not have the philosophical value of Pike's commentary (# 375 above), Smith's edition should interest anyone concerned with the Dialogues. (The first edition was published by the Clarendon Press [Oxford] in 1935.)

382 Sturch, Richard Lyman. "God and Probability," Relig Stud, 8 (December, 1972), 351-4.

A reply to Mellor (# 370 above).

383 Swinburne, Richard G. "The Argument from Design," Philosophy, XLIII (July, 1968), 199-212.

Regularities of copresence (e.g., the arrangement of books in a library or parts in the eye) are distinguished from regularities of succession (e.g., the movements of a dance, or a pattern of behavior in accordance with natural law). While most design arguments have been based upon regularities of copresence, it would be better to base the design argument upon regularities of succession. The design argument moves, by analogy, to a conclusion which simplifies our account of empirical matters since it reduces all explanation to personal explanation. Swinburne maintains that the argument has no formal weaknesses. The only issue of significance is whether the analogy between natural regularities and those regularities which we know are produced by human agents is

sufficiently close. Hume's objections are discussed. This is an important article. See
Olding's reply (# 372 above), Swinburne's response
(# 384 below), and Olding's reply to that response
(# 373 above). Also see Gaskin (# 360 above).

384   . "The Argument from Design -- A De-
     fence," Relig Stud, 8 (September, 1972), 193-206.

A reply to Olding (# 372 above). Swinburne agrees
that he is committed to the possibility of disembodied mental existence, and defends that possibility. He argues that whereas a similarity
in effects requires us to postulate a corresponding similarity in causes, a difference in effects
should lead us to postulate a difference in
causes. Thus, the fact that the designer produces all natural regularities should lead us
to conclude that the designer is disembodied.
Again, an explanation of E by C cannot be faulted
simply because we cannot explain C or how C
produces E. Several other objections are briefly
considered. Swinburne concludes by suggesting
that in order to see the force of the various
God arguments, we must take them cumulatively
rather than individually. See Olding's response
(#373 above).

385 Taylor, Alfred Edward. Does God Exist? London:
     Macmillan & Co., Ltd., 1945. Pp. 36-113.

Chapter IV contains an intelligent, though not
particularly original, exposition and defense
of the argument from the apparent design of the
cosmos to an "intelligence at work in nature."
In chapter V, the design argument is supplemented
by a moral argument. It is suggested that the

objectivity of values, etc., provides a reason
for supposing that the purpose to which nature
is subservient is the development of moral personality. In chapter VI, Taylor argues that we
are sometimes justified in inferring a designer
even though we do not understand the purposes
for which the apparently designed object was
constructed, and that the existence of human
agency shows that physical events can have non-
physical causes.

386 _____. "The Present-Day Relevance of Hume's
Dialogues Concerning Natural Religion," Proceed-
ings of the Aristotelian Society, Supplementary
Volume XVIII (1939), 179-205.

Taylor finds the Dialogues "wanting in high
seriousness and logical coherency," and asserts
"that their permanent worth is commonly over-
estimated." While it is difficult to agree with
Taylor's assessment, his essay does make a number
of suggestive points. Among these are (1) that
the sort of teleological order which the world
displays might be more aptly compared with the
order found in a work of art or a well lived
life than with the order found in a machine,
and (2) that in order to determine the character
of the designer, the design argument must be
supplemented by another argument which establishes
that moral personality is the end for which nature
exists. (Taylor's argument for this conclusion
appears, however, to be defective. He seems to
confuse the claim that moral laws are part of
nature in the sense that they are objectively
valid with the claim that moral laws are part
of nature in the sense that they determine its
actual operations.)

387   Taylor, Richard. <u>Metaphysics</u>. 2d ed. Englewood
       Cliffs, New Jersey: Prentice-Hall, Inc., 1974.
       Pp. 112-9.

       Taylor has a very interesting design argument.
       Suppose that we encounter a pattern of stones,
       or marks, which appear to spell out a message
       informing us of some fact. It would be irra-
       tional for us to accept these patterns as evidence
       for this fact, and yet deny that the patterns
       were produced by intelligent and purposeful
       beings. Similarly, it would be irrational for us
       to assume that "our sensory and cognitive facul-
       ties . . . reveal some truth with respect to
       something other than themselves," and yet deny
       that those faculties were produced by one or
       more intelligent and purposeful beings. This
       argument has provoked several replies since its
       appearance in the first edition (1963). For one
       of the better replies see # **371** above.

388   Tennant, Frederick Robert. <u>Philosophical</u> <u>Theology</u>.
       Vol. II: <u>The World, the Soul, and God</u>. Cam-
       bridge: Cambridge University Press, 1930. Pp.
       78-120.

       Chapter IV contains one of the most significant
       modern versions of the design argument. Tennant's
       argument is based upon certain pervasive features
       of the cosmos rather than upon "particular cases
       of adaptedness." These features are (1) that
       the world is intelligible when it might have
       been a chaos providing no foothold for the cate-
       gories of reason, (2) that the process of organic
       evolution exhibits "directivity . . . and plan
       in the primary collocations," (3) that the inor-
       ganic world is adapted to the emergence of life,
       (4) that nature is "saturated" with beauty, and

(5) that nature is a theatre within which moral action is possible and moral values are realized. When all these features are taken together, and we consider the progressiveness of the world together with the "intricate and harmonious interconnexion" which make this progress possible, purpose is inevitably suggested. Objections are raised to the notion of an unconscious purpose pervading nature, and the nature of purpose is discussed.

Other Arguments for the Existence of God (The Moral Argument, The Argument from the World's Intelligibility, etc.)

389 Baillie, Donald Macpherson. Faith in God and its Christian Consummation, The Kerr Lectures for 1926. New edition with a foreword by John McIntyre. London: Faber and Faber, 1964. Pp. 164-96.

Chapter V defends the moral argument. According to Baillie many people have discovered that "the way out of doubt to faith is by the moral consciousness." It is misleading to speak of our being entitled to argue from moral facts to religious beliefs. The point is rather that moral beliefs are implicitly religious beliefs, carrying with them the conviction that "goodness is at the heart of the universe, or that our ideals are laid upon us by One in whom they are somehow realized," or that "values are the shadowings of a perfect divine Reality." Baillie's weakness (and the weakness of other attempts of this sort) is his failure to show precisely how moral beliefs imply religious beliefs. We are told that if values are objective they provide a clue to the nature of reality and/or are

grounded in reality, but we are neither shown
that this is the case nor why (if it is the case)
theism must be true. (The first edition was
published by T. & T. Clark [Edinburgh, 1927].)

390 Baillie, John. The Interpretation of Religion.
     New York: Charles Scribner's Sons, 1928; Nash-
     ville, Tennessee: Abingdon Press, 1965. Pp.
     256-380.

Chapters V-VII develop a moral argument for
God's existence. Religion is defined as a moral
trust in reality -- a conviction that "the inner
core of reality must be continuous with the moral
consciousness," that moral purpose provides a
clue to a Purpose at the very heart of things.
Baillie argues that even though values can be
discerned without discerning any cosmological
or theological facts, values presuppose such
facts. Although he does not clearly explain how
they do so, what seems to be involved is a move
from the authoritative or absolute character
of values to a ground of that authority or absoluteness, or a move from the fact that certain
moral demands are made upon us to the claim that
reality demands these things of us and must,
therefore, itself be moral. Baillie believes
that people reject this argument because they
fail to fully appreciate the absolute and objective character of value. (John Hick echoes
this in his Arguments for the Existence of God,
1053 below.) Many philosophers, however, are
instead disturbed by the transition from the
objectivity and authority of values to the claim
that the world is a "home" for moral agents
which supports and nurtures the values recognized by conscience. This is, in short, an

attractive and rather persuasive but insufficiently rigorous presentation of the moral argument.

391 Bobik, Joseph. "The Sixth Way," Mod Sch, LI
     (January, 1974), 91-116.

     An interesting critical discussion of Maritain's
     argument (see # 402 below) from the pure activity
     of the intellect to God. Maritain's "Sixth
     Way" is compared with the traditional Five Ways,
     and a number of objections to his argument are
     considered.

392 Broad, Charlie Dunbar. Review of The Faith of a
     Moralist by A. E. Taylor. Mind, XL (July, 1931),
     364-75.

     This review contains a number of interesting
     observations. Perhaps Broad's most important
     point is that the moral views which are most
     plausibly regarded as implying religious beliefs
     may be such that it is reasonable to hold them
     only if one already knows that the religious
     beliefs in question are true. If this is the
     case, then moral arguments for theological con-
     clusions are, epistemically circular.

393 Ewing, Alfred Cyril. "The Autonomy of Ethics,"
     Prospect for Metaphysics, Essays of Metaphysical
     Exploration. Edited by Ian Ramsey. London:
     George Allen & Unwin Ltd., 1961. Pp. 33-49.

     Ewing offers standard arguments for supposing
     that theological concepts should not be intro-
     duced into our analysis of ethical terms. He
     nevertheless contends that even though the concept
     of God is not included in ethical concepts, and
     even though ethical knowledge does not depend

upon theological knowledge, it may still be
the case that an argument for the existence
of God can be constructed upon the basis of
our ethical knowledge (just as, even though
biological concepts can be analyzed without
introducing the concept of God and even though
biological knowledge does not rest upon theological knowledge, certain versions of the design
argument are constructed on the basis of that
knowledge). However, he concedes that he is
unable to produce such an argument.

394 Farrer, Austin Marsden. "A Starting Point for
the Philosophical Examination of Theological
Belief," Faith and Logic, Oxford Essays in
Philosophical Theology. Edited by Basil Mitchell.
London: Allen & Unwin; Boston: The Beacon
Press, 1957. Pp. 9-30.

Our moral regard for persons must be distinguished
from our evaluation of their lives. Farrer
argues that moral regard for personality as
such can best be explained within a theistic
framework.

395 Hartshorne, Charles. A Natural Theology for Our
Time. LaSalle, Illinois: Open Court, 1967.
Pp. 29-89.

Chapter two contains an interesting, though
perhaps not fully convincing, discussion of
several proofs, including an argument from order
(roughly, to be real is to be ordered and order
entails an orderer) and an argument which purports to show that the life of God, "to which
all creatures in their measure contribute,"
is the only thing which can provide a fully
rational aim for rational beings. In chapter
three, Hartshorne argues that because God exists

necessarily, there can be no empirical proofs
of God's existence. God, being necessary, is
exemplified in every fact and every experience
but there is no contingent state of affairs
(e.g., the existence of a particular sort of
world) which is such that its existence would
provide a good reason for God's existence and
its nonexistence would weaken or destroy the
case for God's existence.

396   . "Six Theistic Proofs," <u>Monist</u>, 54
(April, 1970), 159-80.

This very interesting essay is reprinted in
Hartshorne's <u>Creative Synthesis and Philosophic
Method</u> (LaSalle, Illinois: Open Court, 1970,
pp. 275-97). Hartshorne presents a version
of the ontological argument which is similar
to the version of James Ross (# 286 above),
a cosmological argument, a design argument (which
is really an argument from the existence of
order), an argument from truth or reality which
hinges upon the notion that truth or reality
must be defined in terms of God's knowledge,
an argument which contends that value implies
a supreme value which can only be the enrichment
of God's life, and an argument which moves from
beauty to the existence of a divine being who
fully enjoys that beauty. All of these arguments are regarded as a priori. (Thus, the
first premiss of the cosmological argument --
"something is" -- and the first premiss of the
design argument -- "order is exemplified" --
are both regarded as necessarily true. According
to Hartshorne, something must necessarily be
and be ordered.) The six arguments are phases
of what Hartshorne calls the "global argument,"

viz., that a "properly formulated" theism is "the most intelligible, self-consistent and satisfactory" view of "life and reality," and that alternative views are fundamentally incoherent. All arguments except the ontological "may be interpreted as showing that the idea of God, taken as true, is required for the interpretation of some fundamental aspect of life or existence." They can also be regarded as proofs of a premiss which is crucial to the ontological argument, viz., that deity can be consistently conceived.

397 Hepburn, Ronald William. "Moral Arguments for the Existence of God," The Encyclopedia of Philosophy. Vol. 5. Edited by Paul Edwards. New York: Macmillan, 1967. Pp. 381-5.

A good brief discussion of the arguments from "moral commands" to a divine commander, the argument from "moral laws" to a divine lawgiver, the argument from moral consensus to a God who is responsible for that consensus, and the positions of Farrer, Kant, Sorley, and A. E. Taylor. (See # 394 above and #s 411 and 413 below.)

398 Joyce, George Hayward. Principles of Natural Theology. (Stonyhurst Philosophical Series.) London, New York [etc.]: Longmans, Green and Co., 1923; New York: AMS Press, 1972. Pp. 166-79.

A lucid statement of the argument from the desire for happiness (beatitude) to the existence of an object (viz., God, or goodness-itself) which can satisfy that desire.

399 Klocker, Harry R. "The Personal God of John
Henry Newman," Personalist, 57 (Spring, 1976),
145-61.

A good explication of Newman's argument from
our sense of guilt and responsibility to a Lawgiver and Judge before whom we are responsible,
and of the relation of that argument to Newman's
views on inference and assent. The article is
expository, not critical.

400 Lonergan, Bernard Joseph Francis. Insight, A
Study of Human Understanding. London: Longmans,
Green and Co., Ltd.; New York: Philosophical
Library, 1957. Pp. 634-86.

Chapter XIX attempts to prove the existence of
God by moving from the unrestricted desire to
know to the affirmation of the perfect intelligibility of reality, and from the perfect intelligibility of reality to the existence of
an unrestricted act of understanding. The author
attempts to show that the latter is self-existent,
that it is the ground of contingent being, and
that it possesses the other attributes (simplicity, immutability, goodness, etc.) attributed
to God by classical theism. Lonergan has been
a major influence on recent Roman Catholic philosophy, and his argument should interest philosophers in other traditions. It is in essence,
however, (as Lonergan seems to recognize) a
cosmological argument. The appeal to the Principle of Sufficient Reason or to the Causal
Principle is replaced by the assertion that
reality is intelligible (an assertion which is
said to be a necessary or inevitable consequence
of our unrestricted desire to know). That an
unrestricted act of understanding must be posited

if existence is to be intelligible bears a
family resemblance to the claims that change,
causality, contingent being, value and order
presuppose the reality of an Unchanged Changer,
an Uncaused Cause, a Necessary Being, a Supreme
Good and an Ordering Intelligence, respectively.
There is also a certain similarity between Lonergan's argument and the Idealist argument that
since reality is only intelligible in so far
as it is understood by mind, its perfect intelligibility presupposes the existence of an Absolute Mind which fully understands it. It
should be asked whether or in what way Lonergan's argument is an advance upon these more
traditional arguments.

401 Maclagen, William Gauld. The Theological Fron-
     tier of Ethics, An Essay Based on the Edward
     Cadbury Lectures in the University of Birming-
     ham 1955-56. (The Muirhead Library of Philo-
     sophy.) London: George Allen & Unwin Ltd.;
     New York: The Macmillan Co., 1961. Pp. 50-94
     and 170-81.

     This book contains interesting discussions of
     a number of issues including the notion of prayer,
     the relation between freedom and grace, etc.
     Chapters III and VI have an important bearing
     upon one's assessment of the moral argument
     for God's existence. Maclagen assumes that
     there is an objective order of values but ar-
     gues that far from an objective order of values
     presupposing a divine claimant or lawgiver, its
     very nature is such as to be incompatible with
     its being grounded in God. Maclagen also argues
     that theists are driven to inconsistently think
     of God as both a person and an impersonal order
     of values. (Maclagen assumes [perhaps wrongly]

that an impersonal order of values cannot be
independent of God. Since, as he has argued,
an impersonal order of values cannot be grounded
in God, it follows that, if God exists, it must
be God.) See Owen's critique (# 405 below).

402 Maritain, Jacques. Approaches to God. Translated
     from the French by Peter O'Reilly. (World Per-
     spectives, 1.) New York: Harper, 1954. Pp.
     72-108.

     Chapter 3 presents a "Sixth Way" which moves
     from finite "spiritual acts of intellection"
     which in transcending sensing and imagining in
     a sense transcend time, to something which is
     Being in pure act, Thought in pure act and Self
     in pure act, and from which these finite intel-
     lectual acts derive their reality. Chapter 4
     discusses three ways ("which are not demonstra-
     tions") by which the "practical intellect" ap-
     proaches God. The artist who responds to the
     demands of beauty, and the person who chooses
     to do the morally right thing because it is the
     right thing, implicitly know God who is Beauty
     itself and Goodness itself. The sanctity of the
     saints also attests to the reality of that to
     which they have dedicated their lives. Mari-
     tain's discussion in these two chapters is in-
     teresting though not fully convincing. For a
     criticism of the "Sixth Way," see # 391 above.

403 Muyskens, James Leroy. "Kant's Moral Argument,"
     S J Phil, XII (Winter, 1974), 425-34.

     Muyskens argues that one cannot rationally re-
     cognize a duty to pursue the highest good, be-
     lieve that in order for the highest good to
     obtain it is necessary that God exist and that

the soul be immortal, and yet <u>deny</u> that God exists
and that the soul is immortal. One can, however,
recognize such a duty, believe that God's existence and the soul's immortality are necessary
if the highest good is to obtain, and yet not
<u>believe</u> that God exists and that the soul is
immortal. The considerations adduced by Kant
only show that a <u>hope</u> that God exists and that
the soul is immortal is required or at least
reasonable. They do not justify a belief that
these things are the case. (The only belief
which is necessary is a belief in the <u>possibility</u>
of God's existence and of the soul's immortality.)

404 Newman, Jay Alan. "Cardinal Newman's 'Factory-
Girl' Argument," <u>Proc</u> <u>Cath</u> <u>Phil</u> <u>Ass</u>, 46 (1972),
71-7.

The factory girl, dying in miserable surround-
ings, argues that this can't be all there is
and that there must be a "God to wipe away all
tears from all eyes." Newman maintained that
this is a legitimate informal inference. The
test of its validity, and the validity of similar inferences, rests upon "the judgment of
those who have a right to judge, and . . . the
agreement of many private judgments in one and
the same view of it." The author shows that
the factory girl's argument can be easily recast
as a formal argument. He calls our attention
to the fact that Newman at one place asserts
that those who have a right to judge are the
gifted or educated or well prepared, and argues
that it is neither clear that the factory girl
meets these conditions nor that those who do
so will accept her argument. Neither is it
clear that many private judgments will converge

with that of the factory girl. It is concluded
that Newman is exposed to charges of subjectivism
and relativism.

405   Owen, Huw Parri. The Moral Argument for Christian
      Theism. London: George Allen & Unwin, Ltd.,
      1965. 128 pp.

The best recent defense of the moral argument
for God's existence. Although moral facts can
be known without knowing any theistic facts,
theism makes the best sense of such facts as
our awareness of moral claims and of "the obedience that the categorical imperative requires,"
the dignity of persons, the experience of responsibility and guilt, the fact that values oblige
us as well as attract us, etc. At the heart of
many of Owen's arguments is the insistence that
notions of responsibility, claim, and obligation
are inseparably bound up with the notion of a
person to whom we are responsible, who makes
claims, and to whom we are obligated. This
contention is familar and, to many, unconvincing.
Owen's presentation of these arguments is, nevertheless, as effective as any and more effective
than most. W. G. Maclagen's objections to the
moral argument (# 401 above) are discussed at
some length but Owen's response to one major
point is inadequate. He agrees that the order
of values must be identified with God but does
not explain how this is possible. Toward the end
of the book, Owen introduces an argument of a
different type: We are unable to achieve either
perfection or well-being in this life. Hence,
immortality is necessary if we are to discharge
our obligation to achieve perfection and if our
desire for well-being is to be fulfilled.

However, (if immortality is construed as an unending progress toward a finite human perfection) immortality alone is not enough. Our obligation can be discharged only through a participation in, and a reflection of, God's own perfection. Furthermore, the achievement of a finite human perfection will not satisfy the heart's desire. Only a participation in God's infinite perfection will do so. God must, therefore, be postulated as well as immortality. (In assessing these arguments it is important to remember that Owen does not claim that the facts which he adduces entail theism but only that theism best explains them.)

406 Paton, Herbert James. The Modern Predicament, A Study in the Philosophy of Religion Based on Gifford Lectures Delivered in the University of St. Andrews. (The Muirhead Library of Philosophy.) London: George Allen & Unwin, Ltd.; New York: The Macmillan Co., 1955. Pp. 317-36.

John Hick commends this "important . . . sympathetic treatment of the moral argument" to our attention. In chapter XXI, Paton examines an argument which proceeds from a recognition of the duty to seek "an ideal society in which the good will of its citizens may be fully effective," to the postulation of the existence of a God who ensures that this ideal can be realized. This argument is an expression of "the drive of reason towards wholeness or completeness in thought and action." It is not a proof and does not lead to knowledge, but does show that religious faith is reasonable. Paton's treatment of (this version of) the moral argument is not particularly rigorous.

407   Rashdall, Hastings. <u>Philosophy</u> <u>of</u> <u>Religion,</u> <u>Six</u>
       <u>Lectures</u> <u>Delivered</u> <u>at</u> <u>Cambridge.</u> New York:
       Charles Scribner's Sons, 1910; Westport, Conn.:
       Greenwood Press, 1970. Pp. 58-86.

       In Lecture III, Rashdall argues that if the moral
       law is objective, it is "part of the ultimate
       nature of things." Unlike physical laws, it
       cannot be supposed to exist in matter. It must,
       therefore, exist in mind. Since our apprehension
       of the moral law is imperfect and partial, the
       moral law must exist independently of human
       thinking about it. It, therefore, exists in
       a mind which is free from the imperfections
       which beset human understanding. Furthermore,
       since the moral law is part of the very nature
       of things, it must exist in a mind which deter-
       mines the nature of things. (Rashdall never
       explains how the fact that the moral law is
       objective implies that it must exist <u>in</u> some-
       thing.)

408   _____. "The Ultimate Basis of Theism," <u>God</u>
       <u>and</u> <u>Man.</u> Selected and edited by H. D. A. Major
       and <u>F.</u> L. Cross. Oxford: Basil Blackwell, 1930.
       Pp. 13-67.

       This essay first appeared in the collective
       volume <u>Contentio</u> <u>Veritatis</u> (London: John Murry,
       1902). After arguing that a consistent idealism
       must postulate an eternal mind to account for the
       fact that things exist independently of human
       consciousness and for the fact that many of our
       experiences do not spring from our own volition,
       Rashdall turns his attention to the moral argu-
       ment. The objectivity of our moral judgments
       can only be explained if God's "thought and
       . . . will, his ultimate purpose" is regarded

as the reality of which our moral judgments
are "the more or less inadequate representations."
Moral value is objective only if "one and the
same 'idea [thought] of the Good'" is the source
of both reality and morality. Although interesting, Rashdall's discussion suffers from the
imprecision which infects so many presentations
of the moral argument.

409 Sherry, Patrick J. "Philosophy and the Saints,"
Heythrop J, 18 (January, 1977), 23-37.

An intelligent examination of the "argument
from sanctity." Sherry concludes (1) that
sanctity can be (but need not be) interpreted
by a theory which links it to other actual and
alleged historical facts (e.g., Christ's work
and death, and eschatological facts) and to
certain alleged "ontological" facts (God's grace
and forgiveness), and (2) that it is more plausible to suppose that the failure of Christianity
to produce sanctity would falsify Christian
theism than to suppose that the occurrence of
sanctity verifies Christian claims. (But if
q̃ disconfirms p, why doesn't q confirm it?
By "verifies," Sherry presumably means "establishes" and, of course, "q confirms p" does not
entail "q establishes p.")

410 Silber, John Robert. "Kant's Conception of the
Highest Good as Immanent and Transcendent,"
Phil Rev, LXVIII (October, 1959), 469-92.

Kant maintains that we are obligated to attain
the highest good, that ought implies can, and
that because of our weakness we cannot attain
the highest good. The postulates of God and

immortality are introduced to resolve the problem
created by this inconsistent triad. Silber
shows that the contradiction cannot be resolved
in this way. That God can attain the highest
good does not imply that we can do so. Furthermore, if the introduction of these postulates
did show that we could attain the highest good,
they would thereby show that one of the premisses
necessary to Kant's moral argument is false,
viz., that we cannot attain the highest good.
Silber suggests that what Kant was driving at
is that although we have a "constitutive" or
actual obligation to promote the highest good,
the obligation to attain the highest good is a
regulative ideal which must be employed as a
spur to moral activity.

411   Sorley, William Ritchie. Moral Values and the
      Idea of God: The Gifford Lectures Delivered
      in the University of Aberdeen in 1914 and 1915.
      Cambridge [Eng.]: The University Press, 1918.
      Pp. 331-57.

      Chapter XIII contains a defense of the moral
      argument for God's existence. Like Rashdall,
      Sorley argues that since moral laws and values
      are eternal and objective they must "exist some-
      where." Because they are imperfectly exempli-
      fied in nature and human thought we must place
      them in the mind of God. In the course of his
      argument, Sorley moves from the claim that moral
      laws and values are "valid for existents" to the
      claim that they are either fully exemplified
      in existents and/or fully known by some exis-
      tents -- a move which is surely suspect.

412 Stainsby, Harold V. "Descartes' Argument for
God," _Sophia_, VI (October, 1967), 11-6.

An interesting examination of the argument which
occurs in Meditation III. Stainsby suggests
that Descartes is not so much arguing to a God
who has produced the idea of God which is in
him as he is to a God who is "the indispensable
model of this idea." Descartes is assuming that
complex ideas can be resolved into simple ideas,
and that simple ideas are derived from objects
whose properties serve as the models for our
ideas of those properties. Since Descartes regards the idea of God as a simple idea, he is
forced to conclude that a divine being actually
exists and provides the model for his idea of
God.

413 Taylor, Alfred Edward. _The Faith of a Moralist_:
Gifford Lectures Delivered in the University
of St. Andrews, 1926-28. Series I: The Theo-
logical Implications of Morality. London:
Macmillan and Co., Ltd., 1930. xx + 437 pp.

According to Taylor, it is irrational to suppose
that moral facts throw no light upon the nature
of reality. In chapter III, he argues that we
cannot content ourselves with goods which are
superceded and left behind, but that our hearts
are set on "that simultaneous and complete
fruition of a life without bounds of which Boethius speaks." (Faint images of this life are
provided by moments of aesthetic contemplation
and intellectual satisfaction. In these moments
there is a "before and after" but no sense of
a good which is no longer or a good which is
not yet.) Since it is reasonable to argue from
"the existence of a function to the reality

of an environment in which the function can
find adequate exercise" and since temporal and
secular goods cannot satisfy our aspiration,
we must suppose that there is an eternal good
which is able to satisfy us. In chapter IV,
Taylor argues that the fact that we reverence
the moral law and the fact that our moral reason
grows and develops, implies that our practical
reason is not the source of the moral law but
instead originates "in a supreme and absolute
reason into likeness with which I have to grow,
but which remains always beyond me." At the
end of chapter V, Taylor maintains that intense
moral guilt is experienced as a form of disloyalty
or betrayal. This can only be adequately explained if we think of our ideals "as already
embodied in the living and personal God." Again,
only a person can awaken the devotion characteristic of moral life at its best. In chapter VI,
Taylor argues that the ideal could not draw
us "with an overwhelming force" if it was not
"an efficient as well as a final cause." It is
because it is actual that it motivates us.
While far from rigorous, this is an effective
presentation of the theistic "implications"
(or, perhaps more accurately, a theistic interpretation) of one view of the moral life (a
non-utilitarian view which emphasizes growth,
heroism, struggle, self sacrifice, and giving).
See Broad's review (# 392 above).

414 _____. "The Vindication of Religion," Essays
Catholic and Critical by Members of the Anglican
Communion. 2d ed. Edited by Edward Gordon
Selwyn. London: Society for Promoting Christian
Knowledge; New York and Toronto: The Macmillan
Co., 1926. Pp. 29-81.

Taylor argues that those philosophers who, like
Kant and Plato, have taken morality most seriously
have invariably supposed that man belongs to a
supranatural as well as to a natural environment. Taylor is eloquent but the relevant portions of his essay are a bit long on assertion
and short on argument.

415   Van Wyk, Robert Nicholas. "Michael Novak on the
      Existence of God," Int J Phil Relig, V (Spring,
      1974), 61-3.

An examination of an argument which Van Wyk
thinks he finds on page 125 of Belief and Unbelief (New York: Macmillan, 1965), and which
moves from the claim that the real is the intelligible to the claim that God exists. Van Wyk
presents the argument with more clarity than
usual. This particular version of the argument
hinges upon the claim that unless God is the
source of the world's intelligibility, the fact
that the world is intelligible is itself unintelligible, from which it follows that at least
one real fact is unintelligible. Van Wyk criticizes the argument on the grounds that no real
support has been offered for the claim that
whatever is real is intelligible.

416   Wood, Allen William. Kant's Moral Religion.
      Ithaca, New York: Cornell University Press,
      1970. Pp. 10-37 and 100-52.

Chapters 1 and 4 contain an interesting exposition and defense of Kant's arguments for God
and immortality. Wood's discussion of the argument for immortality is noteworthy because of
the way in which he explicates the claim that
holiness of will is impossible if we are not

immortal by Kant's doctrine of radical evil and
grace. (Wood treats those notions at more length
in chapter 6.)

417 Yandell, Keith Edward. Basic Issues in the Philo-
     sophy of Religion. Boston: Allyn and Bacon,
     Inc., 1971. Pp. 156-80.

An interesting reconstruction and discussion of
Kant's moral argument. Yandell concludes that
moral evaluations (e.g., "rational personality
is intrinsically valuable") and the metaphysical
setting of these evaluations (e.g., God and
immortality) are interdependent, and that, therefore, arguments from the first to the second
tend to beg the question.

The Nature of "God-Proofs"

(See also #s 285 and 663)

418 Hartshorne, Charles. "Can There Be Proofs for
     the Existence of God?" Religious Language and
     Knowledge. Edited by Robert H. Ayers and William
     T. Blackstone. (Essays originally presented in
     the 1965 Great Thinkers Forum sponsored by the
     Department of Philosophy and Religion at the
     University of Georgia.) Athens, Georgia: Uni-
     versity of Georgia Press, 1972. Pp. 62-75.

Hartshorne maintains that any interesting philosophical argument rests on premises which are
more or less controversial. The value of a
theistic proof (or of any argument) is found in
the fact "that it establishes a logical price for
rejecting a certain conclusion," viz., the rejection of one or more of the premises from which
the conclusion follows, the price increasing
with the plausibility of those premises. Some

examples of theistic proofs are given -- an argument from order, and a rather dubious attempt
to show that unless our good actions enrich
God's life they cannot have the value which we
ascribe to them. (The second argument is dubious
for it would seem that our actions enrich God's
life because they are good. They do not derive
their goodness from the fact that they enrich
God's life.)

419 Hick, John Harwood. Faith and Knowledge, A Modern
     Introduction to the Problem of Religious Know-
     ledge. 2d ed. Ithaca, New York: Cornell Univer-
     sity Press, 1966. Pp. 151-6.

It is sometimes argued that, given the relevant
evidence as a whole, theism is more probable
than its alternatives. Hick contends that talk
of probability is out of place. (1) The frequency concept of probability is inapplicable
because we are interpreting the universe and
the universe is not a member of a class of uni-
verses. (2) Theism cannot be said to be reasonable in relation to a prior set of evidence-
stating propositions for, since theism is a
"total interpretation" of the universe, there
can "be no data outside the interpretand."
(3) We cannot appeal (à la Tennant) to an a-
logical judgment of probability which rests
upon our assessment of the relevant evidence
since there are no common standards for assessing
the strength of the evidence. Although Hick's
argument is important and has won adherents, his
first two points are clearly suspect. The universe would appear to be a member of other relevant classes with multiple instances, e.g., the
class of ordered things. If Hick's second

263

contention were sound, it would follow that
judgments concerning the nature and value of
a person's life could not be said to be authorized
by statements about his thoughts, feelings, and
actions since the data in question are included
in the interpretand. As to his third point,
one should notice both that there is some agreement as to what counts strongly for theism (e.g.,
apparent design) and what counts strongly against
it (e.g., evil), and that there are no standards
for determining the precise strength of relevant
evidence in other areas in which we use probably." (Consider, e.g., determinations of
guilt and innocence.) See Oakes' reply, # 424
below.

420   Iseminger, Gary. "Successful Argument and Rational
      Belief," Phil Rhet, 7 (Winter, 1974), 47-57.

      George Mavrodes (# 422 below) is criticized for
      maintaining that person-relative concepts are
      subjective. "Worthy of belief" is a concept
      which is person-relative ("p is worthy of belief"
      should be expanded to "p is worthy of belief
      by . . .") but not subjective (for "p is worthy
      of belief" does not entail that anyone is in a
      psychological state or has a psychological at-
      titude relative to p). The most interesting
      feature of this article is the distinction
      between successful arguments and proofs. To
      give a successful argument for the existence
      of God, one must produce a set of premises and
      show that "God exists" follows from them, and
      for each of the premises either it is believed
      by nearly every sane man or one must show that
      it is necessarily true. In producing a successful
      argument one establishes the rationality of

believing in its conclusion. A successful argument may not be a proof, however, because
it may not be sound. (What is believed by nearly
every sane man could be false.)

421 Kennick, William E. "On Proving that God Exists,"
     Religious Experience and Truth, A Symposium.
     Edited by Sidney Hook. New York: New York
     University Press, 1961. Pp. 261-9.

Kennick argues that if "God exists" is an a
priori truth, then (1) since that proposition
is entailed by all propositions, no contingent
proposition can provide evidence for it, and
(2) the conclusion of a non-ontological argument for God's existence provides no more information about the world than its premisses.
(Kennick's second point rests upon the dogma
that a priori propositions are not factually
informative. His first point is more interesting.
According to Kennick if everything is evidence
for p, then nothing is evidence for p. While
this may seem plausible, similar considerations
would show that [since true mathematical propositions are a priori, and therefore entailed by
all propositions] sound mathematical demonstrations provide no evidence for their conclusions.)

422 Mavrodes, George Ion. Belief in God, A Study
     in the Epistemology of Religion. (Studies in
     Philosophy.) New York: Random House, 1970.
     Pp. 17-48.

Chapter II contains an important discussion of
the nature of proof in general, and the nature
of proofs for the existence of God in particular.
Mavrodes shows that it is possible to construct
a trivial but sound argument for any true

proposition and that, therefore, (1) to show
that there cannot be a sound argument for God's
existence one must show that "God exists" is
false, and (2) to prove "God exists" (or any
other proposition) one must do more than produce
a sound argument for it. Mavrodes contends
that the notion of proof is "person-relative."
An argument is good ("convincing") for a person N if and only if it is sound, N knows it
to be sound, and N's knowledge of the truth
of the premisses is not derived from his knowledge of the truth of the conclusion. Because
what is known varies radically from person to
person and because only the simplist propositions
are known to everyone, it is a mistake to suppose (as Plantinga and others do suppose [see
50 above, p. 4]), that the natural theologian
must produce arguments whose premisses are either
necessarily true or "obviously true and accepted
by nearly every sane man." See Iseminger's
reply (# 420 above).

423 _____ . "Some Recent Philosophical Theology,"
Rev Metaph, XXIV (September, 1970), Pp. 83-93.

Part I criticizes two notions of proof. Plantinga
is criticized for contending that a proof of
God's existence must show that God's existence
validly follows from premisses which are necessarily true, or "obviously true and accepted
by nearly every sane man." Mavrodes shows that
if God's existence is necessary this demand
can be trivially met, and that in any case it
is not clear why premisses cannot be used which
are only known to some people. James Ross (#
426 below) contends that the premisses of a
good philosophical argument must be assessable

by methods generally accepted in the philosophical community. Mavrodes replies that there
are no such methods, and that there are probably
no decidable truths which aren't decidable by
the methods used by some philosopher or other.
Both Plantinga and Ross are criticized for failing
to make the notion of proof person-relative.
It is argued that neglect of this factor leads
to the proposal of criteria which are either
trivial or impossible to satisfy.

424 Oakes, Robert Aaron. "Theistic Antiprobabilism
     and Possible Worlds," S J Phil, XII (Winter,
     1974), 449-54.

     Oakes argues that Hick (# 419 above) is mistaken
     in supposing that we cannot intelligibly say that
     God's existence is either probable or improbable.
     "It is probable that God exists" is intelligible
     because a possible world can be described in
     which it is true. Hick is accused of overlooking
     the fact that the statistical concept of prob-
     ability applies to empirical generalizations
     but not to theoretical hypotheses such as the
     atomic theory of matter, Freud's theory of the
     unconscious, and -- possibly -- theism.

425 Penelhum, Terence. Problems of Religious Know-
     ledge. (Philosophy of Religion Series.) London:
     Macmillan, 1971; New York: Herder and Herder,
     1972. Pp. 21-65.

     Chapter 2 discusses the nature of proof. Penel-
     hum's conditions (that the premisses can be
     stated without stating the conclusion, that they
     are known by the hearer to be true, and that
     they entail the conclusion or make it overwhelm-
     ingly probable) are too generous for they do

not clearly exclude such "proofs" as "Either
unicorns exist or God does, but unicorns do
not exist so God exists." Nevertheless, Penelhum
makes a number of valuable observations in the
course of this chapter. In chapter 3, Penelhum
argues (1) that the impossibility of proving
God's existence cannot be established by appealing
to general epistemological principles, (2) that
because of the possibility of irrationally rejecting conclusions which follow from premises
which are known to be true, a proof of God's
existence would not coerce belief and would be
compatible with faith in its conclusion, and
(3) that while there may in fact be no non-
theistic evidence which establishes theistic
statements, there are no convincing general
considerations which show that there could not
be non-theistic evidence which establishes
theistic statements.

426   Ross, James Francis. Philosophical Theology.
      Indianapolis and New York: The Bobbs-Merrill
      Co., Inc., 1969. Pp. 3-34.

      Chapter 1 contains an important discussion of
      the nature of philosophical proofs in general,
      and of philosophical proofs of theistic proposi-
      tions in particular. Ross contends that a good
      philosophical argument must be sound, and that
      its premises must either be generally acknow-
      ledged or such that others are able to determine
      their truth for themselves by employing "some
      method which is generally followed in the [ap-
      propriate] science." In spite of the fact that
      the methods of philosophical "science" are noto-
      riously unclear (is there, for example, a "gener-
      ally followed" method employed by both Carnap

and Heidegger?), Ross's contention is a significant one, and the chapter contains a number
of valuable observations. See Mavrodes' critique, # 423 above.

427 Rowe, William Leonard. The Cosmological Argument.
     Princeton and London: The Princeton University
     Press, 1975. Pp. 249-69.

     In his final chapter, Rowe distinguishes between
     a proof, a proof for someone, and an acceptable
     argument. A proof is a sound argument the pre-
     misses of which are known to be true by some
     person independently of that person's knowledge
     of the conclusion. An argument is a proof for
     x only if its premisses are known by x indepen-
     dently of any knowledge x has of the conclusion.
     An argument is acceptable only if its conclusion
     follows from its premisses, and it is reasonable
     for someone to believe that its premisses are
     true. While some distinctions of this sort
     are clearly necessary, one may wonder whether
     they should be drawn in precisely the way in
     which Rowe draws them. (Why, for example, must
     the premisses of a proof be known to someone?
     Wouldn't it be sufficient if the premisses were
     capable of being known by some generally accept-
     able philosophical or scientific method?)

428 Scriven, Michael. Primary Philosophy. New York:
     McGraw-Hill Book Co., 1966. Pp. 87-167, esp.
     102-10.

     Scriven's discussion of the standard arguments
     for and against God's existence is of some inter-
     est though on the whole not particularly original
     and often superficial. Of more interest are
     his remarks (pp. 107-10, 152 ff.) about the

cumulative argument for God's existence (which
rests upon the contention that the bits of
evidence cited in the standard arguments may be
individually insufficient but cumulatively
sufficient to establish God's existence), and
his contention that if the arguments for God's
existence fail, atheism, and not agnosticism,
is the only rational conclusion (pp. 102-7).

429 Spade, Paul Vincent. "What is a Proof for the
     Existence of God?" Int J Phil Relig, VI (Winter,
     1975), 234-42.

A proof of God's existence in the context of
a specific doctrinal scheme would be a proof
of "there exists an x such that   x" where (a)
the doctrinal scheme in question entails "God
is identical with the x such that   x" and where
(b) "there are no philosophical proofs of sentences which together with 'there exists an x
such that   x' entail that" that doctrinal scheme
is false. If one assumes (as a theologian would
assume) that the doctrinal scheme is true, one
can conclude that condition b is satisfied.
There cannot, however, be a philosophical proof
that it is satisfied and hence "the question
whether a given philosophical proof constitutes
a proof for the existence of God is not in general
philosophically decidable."

430 Tillich, Paul Johannes Oskar. Systematic Theology.
     Vol. I. Chicago: The University of Chicago
     Press, 1951. Pp. 204-10.

Many contemporary theologians maintain that the
very nature of God precludes the possibility
of proving His existence. Tillich is one of
the few theologians to offer reasons for this

270

contention. He claims that arguments for God's
existence fail because "both the concept of
existence and the method of arguing to a conclusion are inadequate for the idea of God."
The conclusion of these arguments ("God exists")
is illicit because it construes God as a being
and ascribes existence to a reality which transcends it. The method of arguing to a conclusion
"contradicts the idea of God" because it involves
a denial of God's transcendence. The traditional
arguments are not really arguments at all but
misleading attempts to articulate some aspect
of reality, and/or the question of God, and/or
an immediate awareness of Being-itself. In
spite of its inadequacies (see Wainwright, #
431 below), Tillich's discussion has proved
to be very influential.

431 Wainwright, William Judson. "Paul Tillich and
     Arguments for the Existence of God," JAAR, XXXIX
     (June, 1971), 171-85.

     Wainwright first shows that several arguments
     for God's existence can be constructed from
     Tillich's remarks. These arguments are valid
     and have premisses which Tillich believes to
     be true. The second section examines Tillich's
     reasons (see # 430 above) for supposing that
     there is something illegitimate about any argu-
     ment for the existence of God. It is maintained
     that Tillich has failed to establish his position.
     Section III attempts to reconcile the fact that
     arguments for God's existence can be found in
     Tillich's work with Tillich's contention that any
     argument for God's existence is necessarily
     illegitimate. It is suggested that Tillich
     would not regard these arguments as good arguments

or proofs because knowledge of their premisses is based upon knowledge of their conclusion, and because their premisses are no more obvious than their conclusion. Step 9 of the argument found on p. 174 should read: "Therefore, _being is_ is either necessary or impossible or contingently false." Step 12 follows from 9, 10 and 11, and footnote 7 should be deleted.

III THE PROBLEM OF EVIL

(See also #s 10, 39, 52 and 1032)

432 Adams, Marilyn McCord. "Hell and the God of Justice," _Relig Stud_, 11 (December, 1975), 433-47.

It has often been supposed that the doctrine of hell follows from the doctrine of God's perfect justice, the latter being understood to imply that God treats persons no better and no worse than they deserve. The implication does not hold, however, unless "there is some sound principle about what people deserve, according to which a man could, by his actions in this world, earn eternal damnation." Three sorts of principle are examined: (1) versions of the "eye for an eye" principle, (2) the principle that liability to punishment is proportional to the worth of the offended party, and (3) the principle that it is as intrinsically bad to will evil as to do evil. Adams attempts to show that (1) does not support the doctrine of hell, and that although (2) and (3) can be used to do so, (2) and (3) are false. Interesting.

433   Adams, Robert Merrihew.   "Middle Knowledge," J
        Phil, LXX (October 11, 1973), 552-4.

        Abstract of a reply to Plantinga's "Which Worlds
        Could God Have Created?"   (# 522 below).   Plan-
        tinga assumes that God possesses "middle know-
        ledge," i.e., knows what free action would be
        performed by each possible free being in each
        possible situation.   Adams argues that, given
        Plantinga's radical indeterminism, middle know-
        ledge is impossible.   The relevant counterfac-
        tuals cannot be known unless they are true and
        it is unclear what it would be like for them
        to be true.   They are not true because they
        correspond to the actual course of events, nor
        are they true in virtue of any logical or causal
        connection between antecedent and consequent.
        Furthermore, given Plantinga's account of coun-
        terfactuals, the truth of counterfactuals partly
        depends upon what world is actual.   (A counter-
        factual is said to be true if its antecedent
        and consequent hold in a world which is more
        like ours than any possible world in which its
        antecedent holds and its consequent does not
        hold.)   What world is actual, however, partly
        depends on God's choice.   The relevant counter-
        factuals are, therefore, posterior to God's
        choices rather than prior to them as is usually
        supposed.   For a further development of this
        argument, see # 434 below.

434   _____.   "Middle Knowledge and the Problem
        of Evil," Amer Phil Quart, 14 (April, 1977),
        109-17.

        A later version of a paper presented to the
        American Philosophical Association in 1973.

(See # 433 above.) Middle knowledge is impossible
since it is not clear what it would be like
for (e.g.) (1) "If David stayed in Keilah, Saul
would freely besiege the city" to be true.
(2) "If David stayed in Keilah, Saul would probably besiege the city" is true in virtue of
Saul's character and intentions, but (2) is
a different proposition. Two objections are
considered. (a) It could be said that in asserting (2) I am asserting that (1) is probably true,
and that I cannot both assert this and claim
that there is no way in which (1) can be true.
(Adams replies that in asserting [2] I am not
asserting "Probably [1]" but rather that the
consequent of [1] would be probable given "facts
which would obtain if David stayed in Keilah.")
(b) Apparent counter examples are considered and
dismissed. (It is argued, e.g., that knowing
that the butcher would sell me meat if I asked
him to do so amounts to knowing that he would
probably do so if he were asked, the probability
that he would not do so being so slight that
it can be ignored for all practical purposes.)
Plantinga (#s 517 and 521 below) argues that
it is logically possible that (3) all free persons would freely fail if God created them.
Adams agrees that this is logically possible
but adds that because of the infinite resources
of God's grace (the many influences God can
bring to bear without coercing the will) (3) is
very implausible. Adams also points out that
given his own view about subjunctive conditionals
it cannot be true that (4) if God had acted
differently, he would have had creatures who
make free choices but never make wrong choices.
It could, however, be true that (5) if God had

274

acted differently he would probably have had
creatures who make free choices but never make
wrong choices, and it could be true that (6)
if God had acted differently he would probably
have had better behaved free creatures than
he has. Adams suggests that (5) is implausible
(because of the enormous number of free choices
involved, the risk of failure is enormous) but
that (6) is plausible.

435 _____. "Must God Create the Best?" Phil
    Rev, LXXXI (July, 1972), 317-32.

In this very interesting article, Adams argues
that God need not create the best world. Suppose
that God creates a world, w, which is not the
best world but is such that all of its members
live lives which when taken in their entirety
(including post-mortem periods, if any) are
happy on the whole. Creatures which do not
belong to w are not wronged because they are
not actual. Nor is it clear that the members
of w can legitimately complain of being wronged
even if there are alternative worlds in which
they would have been happier. (Worlds in which
they would have been happier might, for example,
be worlds in which others would be less happy.)
Again, since all lives are happy, God is kind
to all. Furthermore, the creation of w can be
seen as an expression of grace (which, according
to the Judeo-Christian view, is itself a desirable
character trait). In short, God may be justified
in creating w, even though w is not the best
possible world. See the reply by Quinn (# 525
below).

436 _____. "Self-Identity, Self Interest, and the Problem of Evil." (Paper.) The American Philosophical Association, Western Division: St. Louis, April, 1974.

Adams distinguishes the "personal unity relation" between possible lives ("the relation of being possible lives of one person") from the "self-interest relation" between possible lives. (A possible life is related to my life by the self-interest relation if it is appropriate for me "to regard it with the peculiar interest, pride, shame, guilt, desire, regret with which I regard my own life.") Evils similar to those we actually experience may quite possibly be indispensable ingredients of all lives which bear a self-interest relation to our actual lives. Therefore, if our lives (including our after-lives) are happy on the whole, it is probably unreasonable for us to complain that God has behaved unjustly or unlovingly by bringing about or permitting those evils which our lives include. Again, just as lives which we (legitimately) prize may not be the best possible lives (for the best possible lives may not stand in the self-interest relation to our actual lives), so it may not be wrong for God to prize and create lives which are good but not the best possible.

437 Ahern, M. B. "The Nature of Evil," *Sophia*, V (October, 1966), 35-44.

A response to McCloskey's criticism (# 496 below) of Ahern's defense of the privation theory. This response does not substantially advance the discussion.

438 _____. "A Note on the Nature of Evil,"
Sophia, IV (July, 1965), 17-25.

A reply to some remarks made by H.J. McCloskey
in "The Problem of Evil" (# 499 below). According to the privation theory, evil is the absence
of a good which ought to be present. The theory
is an analysis of the nature of evil, not an
explanation of its existence. Ahern attempts
to make the theory plausible by applying it to
three cases: germs, a toothache, and an act of
murder. See McCloskey's reply (# 496 below)
and Ahern's response to that reply (# 437 above).

439 _____. The Problem of Evil. (Studies in
Ethics and the Philosophy of Religion.) London:
Routledge and Kegan Paul; New York: Schocken
Books, 1971. xiv + 85 pp.

Ahern's argument is rather belabored and does
not break new ground. Nevertheless, it is cogent and deserves some attention. Three problems
of evil are distinguished: (1) The general problem, viz., "is the existence of God compatible
with any evil?" (2) The specific abstract problems, viz., "is the existence of God compatible
with such and such a kind of evil, with such
and such a degree of intensity of that kind of
evil, and with such and such a number of instances
of evil of that kind?" (3) The concrete problems
of evil, viz., "are conditions under which God's
existence would be compatible with actual evil
in fact met?" The general problem can be resolved in two ways: (1) By introducing principles (e.g., "a moral agent is justified in permitting evils which are necessary to goods which
outweigh them") which would justify God's crea--
tion or permission of evil. (2) By showing

that principles which critics have introduced
to elicit a contradiction from "God exists"
and "evil exists" (e.g., "a morally good being
will eliminate all the evil it can") are not
analytically true. Similar considerations establish the fact that it is impossible to show
that God's existence is logically incompatible
with the kinds of evil which actually exist or
with the intensity or extent of that evil.
The concrete problems cannot be completely resolved because we do not know all actual evils,
all actual goods and the relations between them,
and because of "our imperfect knowledge of the
logically possible" and hence of the limits of
God's power.

440 Aiken, Henry David. "God and Evil: A Study of
     Some Relations Between Faith and Morals," Ethics,
     LXVIII (January, 1958), 77-97.

The "monotheistic syndrome" involves three elements -- a metaphysical belief in an all-powerful
and all-knowing creator, the claim that this
being is a morally good personality, and the
belief that the being in question is God, i.e.,
worthy of worship. While these elements are
logically independent of one another, their
connection has the status of a fundamental principle within monotheistic traditions. The clash
between the theological thesis (that an all-
powerful, all-knowing and all-good God exists)
and the ethical thesis (that evil exists) is
a clash "of attitudes towards reality and the
conduct of life rather than a contradiction in
our beliefs about the nature of what exists."
Aiken attempts to show that in resolving the
conflict, standard "solutions" radically modify

the attitudes expressed by these two theses.
This article is of some interest though it may
be doubted whether Aiken's re-interpretation
of the problem of evil as a practical or existential problem succeeds in casting new light
upon it. See Nelson Pike's reply (# 514 below).

441   Atkins, Anselm. "Caprice: The Myth of the Fall in
      Anselm and Dostoevsky," J Relig, 47 (October,
      1967), 295-312.

      The notion of a deliberate choice of evil by
      beings who are defective in neither knowledge,
      intelligence, temperament, nor disposition plays
      a role in several versions of Free Will Defense.
      Atkins brings out the fact that the concept of
      a perverse, unmotivated choice has been treated
      more fully in literature than in philosophy.
      The theme is traced in Poe, Dostoevsky and other
      authors as well as in Anselm, Kierkegaard and
      recent existentialists. Of interest.

442   Benditt, Theodore. "A Problem for Theodicists,"
      Philosophy, 50 (October, 1975), 470-4.

      We are asked to consider three states of affairs:
      (1) A is in pain, B believes that A is in pain,
      and is unhappy about it. (2) A is not in pain,
      B does not believe that A is in pain, and so is
      not unhappy about it. (3) A is not in pain, B
      believes that A is in pain, and is unhappy about
      A's supposed pain. (2) is better than (3), and
      (3) is better than (1). Hence, contrary to cer-
      tain theodicists, (2) is better than (1). Benditt
      defends the contention that (3) is better than
      (1) by arguing that if the desirability of a
      virtuous response is able to make pain

desirable, then it is also able to make believing
falsely desirable. Benditt considers but dismisses the claim that the fact that the virtuous
response is appropriate in (1) but not in (3),
makes (1) better than (3). (2) is said to be
better than (3) because if we were to encounter
(3) we would judge it incumbent upon us to correct
B's false belief (thus producing [2]). (This
is not conclusive. Correcting B's false belief
replaces a virtuous response to an apparent
evil with a virtuous response [the correction
of B's false belief] to a real evil [B's false
belief]. Therefore, the fact that we judge it
good to do so does not constitute a decisive
objection to the type of theodicy in question.)

443   Bertocci, Peter Anthony. Introduction to the Philo-
      sophy of Religion. (Prentice-Hall Philosophy
      Series.) Englewood Cliffs, New Jersey: Prentice-
      Hall, Inc., 1951. Pp. 389-441.

In chapter 16, Bertocci argues that the extent
and nature of evil cannot be reconciled with
the omnipotent, omniscient, omni-good God of
classical theism. Chapter 17 defends the suggestion that the facts can be accounted for if
we suppose that God is unlimited in goodness
and knowledge, but limited in power. Bertocci
rejects the notion that God is limited by an
external "environment" or "matrix" which He
did not create (Plato), or by an uncreated "internal environment" or "body" consisting of a
plurality of good, bad and indifferent beings
(Montague). These views make the disparity
between God and His environment so great that
it becomes difficult to explain God's ability
to shape this environment to His own purposes.

Brightman's view (# 447 below) is adopted.
God's mental life (like ours) contains a non-
rational Given (sensations, impulses) which His
perfect will to goodness cannot completely
dominate. This recalcitrant element in God's
own life explains the slowness of the world's
growth toward goodness and the occurrence of
"excess evil."

444 Blumenfeld, David. "Is the Best Possible World
     Possible?" Phil Rev, LXXXIV (April, 1975),
     163-77.

The author contends that Leibniz has an implicit
argument for the consistency of the concept
of the best possible world, and that this argument fails because of Leibniz' claim that
God freely subscribes to the principle of perfection (the principle that His will shall always
be determined by the best). He suggests an
alternative line of argument which Leibniz might
have employed and which rests upon the (possibly
suspect) idea that the concept of God includes
the notion of God's freely subscribing to the
principle of perfection.

445 Botterill, George. "Falsification and the Exis-
     tence of God: A Discussion of Plantinga's Free
     Will Defense," Phil Quart, 27 (April, 1977),
     114-34.

(1) "There is a good, omnipotent, omniscient
God" is a high-level theoretical statement and
it is permissible to introduce auxiliary hypothesis in order to square this statement with such
apparent anomolies as evil. It is reasonable
to retain belief in God, however, only if we
have some reason to believe that these auxiliary

hypotheses are true. It is not enough that they be (merely) possible. (2) According to Botterill, God could prevent the occurrence of particularly heinous actions by taking away the freedom which he foresees will be abused. Botterill thinks that this is compatible with freedom because it does not involve causing free actions, and is convinced that if God were to act in this way there would be a more favorable balance of good over evil. (3) Botterill argues that Plantinga (# 521 below) is unable to provide an adequate account of the truth of the relevant counterfactuals (that A would freely do x in circumstances C) and that, therefore, he is not entitled to say that God knows them. (This important objection is developed more fully by Adams, #s 433 and 444 above.)

446 Bowker, John. Problems of Suffering in the Religions of the World. Cambridge: Cambridge University Press, 1970. xii + 318 pp.

A comparative study of the ways in which suffering is treated by Judaism, Christianity, Islam, Marxism, Hinduism, Buddhism, and the dualistic religions (Zoroastrianism, Manichaeism, and Jainism). This is not a philosophical book, but Bowker's material should interest philosophers who are concerned with the problem of evil.

447 Brightman, Edgar Sheffield. A Philosophy of Religion. (Prentice-Hall Philosophy Series.) New York: Prentice-Hall, Inc., 1940. Pp. 240-341.

In chapters eight, nine and ten, Brightman argues that classical theism cannot adequately accommodate the sort of evil which our world contains. Our experience of good and evil can, however,

be adequately explained if we suppose that although God's goodness is unlimited, His power
is not. It is suggested that God's power is
limited both by "the eternal, uncreated laws
of reason," and by the "equally eternal and
uncreated processes of non-rational consciousness." (Brightman refers to the latter as "The
Given," and says that it includes "the ultimate
qualities of sense objects [qualia], disorderly
impulses and desires, such experiences as pain
and suffering, the forms of space and time,
and whatever in God is the source of such evil.")
Dualism is avoided by including both the laws
of reason and The Given within God. Brightman
attempts to show both that his "finite God"
explains the facts and provides an adequate
object of religious attitudes. One of the most
interesting attempts to defend a view of this
kind. See Knudson's and Stahl's discussions
of Brightman's position (#s 491 and 547 below).

448   Brown, T. Patterson. "God and the Good," Relig
      Stud, 2 (April, 1967), 269-76.

      A further development of points initially made
      in the author's "Religious Morality" (# 449
      below). The meaning of a term does not always
      include criteria for its application. Thus,
      the meaning of "metre" is "a unit of length
      in the metric system" but that the metre bar
      in Paris provides the appropriate standard "is
      simply stipulated to be true as it were synthe-
      tic a priori." "Good," "right," etc., function
      in a similar way. Theists adopt God's will
      as their moral standard. (Brown attempts to
      show that theists appeal to God's will in order
      to settle moral disputes but that they do so

could be conceded by Brown's opponents. God's
will may be appealed to because it is believed
to be an expression of His perfect goodness and
wisdom, and not because His will has been adopted
as the standard of right and wrong.) Against
this background, the problem of evil dissolves.
If God's will is adopted as the standard of
good and evil, then the judgment that something
is evil presupposes the reality of that standard and, thus, that God exists. If some other
standard is employed, "then nothing concerning
the existence of . . . God can be inferred.
For it is no part of orthodox theology that
God must be perfectly good according to any
secular criteria." Brown admits that a residual
puzzle may remain, viz., how can God tolerate
the existence of what displeases Him? (See
Dore's reply, # 458 below.)

449 _____. "Religious Morality," Mind, LXXII
     (April, 1963), 234-44.

According to Brown, Christianity cannot be falsified by the existence of evil because its
doctrine of sin and redemption entails that
evil exists. Furthermore, within Christianity,
God is the standard of goodness. Consequently,
God's existence is compatible with the existence
of evil. Brown is arguing in one or both of
the following two ways: (1) In judging anything
to be evil we presuppose certain standards.
Since the Christian's standard is God, he presupposes that God exists whenever he judges
something to be evil. He cannot, therefore,
allow evil to count against God's existence.
(2) If God's will is the standard of goodness,
then everything God wills (including suffering,

etc.) must be good and, therefore, its existence cannot count against His goodness. The most suspect part of this interesting essay is the claim that, within Christianity, God is the standard of goodness. This is clearly false if it means that most Christian theists accept God's will as their ultimate standard of goodness. Catholic Christianity has generally supposed that moral standards are rationally necessary and, hence, valid in their own right. (Although to avoid compromising God's independence, these standards have usually been "placed" within God's intellect.) See the replies by Campbell and Flew (#s 452 and 465 below), and Brown's response to these replies (# 450 below).

450 _____. "Religious Morality: A Reply to Flew and Campbell," Mind, LXXVII (October, 1968), 577-80.

A defense of the author's "Religious Morality" (# 449 above). Its most interesting points are developed at more length in "God and the Good" (# 448 above). Brown argues that Campbell's position (see # 452 below) commits him to an infinite regress. If the rational adoption of a criterion of goodness presupposes a prior system of evaluation, then the (rational) adoption of that "prior system" would in its turn appear to presuppose a still more ultimate system of evaluation, and so on ad infinitum.

451 Calvert, Brian. "Descartes and the Problem of Evil," Can J Phil, II (September, 1972), 117-26.

Calvert argues that in Meditation IV, Descartes rejects the Free Will Defense for the same reason

as Flew and Mackie, viz., because God could
bring about sinless free actions. He instead
appeals to the Principle of Plenitude (according
to which it is good to maximize the number of
types of beings that exist) in constructing
his theodicy.

452 Campbell, Keith. "Patterson Brown on God and
Evil," Mind, LXXIV (October, 1965), 582-4.

A reply to # 449 above. It is argued that either
the Christian has a reason for adopting God's
will as his criterion of goodness or he does
not. The only reason that he could have would
be the discovery that God's judgment is superior
to our own. However, in order to discover this
he would need "a prior system of evaluation"
against which he could measure the word of God,
in which case God's will would not be his ultimate criterion. If he has no reason, then
he is frankly irrational and will not (or should
not) be bothered by the Problem of Evil or by
any other intellectual difficulty. See Brown's
reply (# 450 above).

453 Capitan, William Henry. "Part X of Hume's Dialogues," Amer Phil Quart, 3 (January, 1966),
82-5.

Capitan argues that Hume is not trying to prove
that a benevolent God does not exist. Philo
concedes that a benevolent deity and evil are
logically compatible. He does, however, try
to show that the facts of common experience
provide us with no reason for supposing that the
cause of the world (which is admitted to exist)
is benevolent. Cleanthes concedes that the only

fact of common experience which would establish the benevolence of that cause is the happiness of creatures. Philo then argues that the happiness of creatures cannot be established and that, therefore, the divine benevolence cannot be established either.

454 Chisholm, Roderick Milton. "The Defeat of Good and Evil," Proc Amer Phil Ass, XLII (1968-69), 21-38.

"When the badness of a state of affairs p is defeated by a wider state of affairs q, then the following is true: q obtains; q entails p; p is bad; q is not bad; and it is not the case that q entails an r such that p does not entail r, r does not entail p, and r is better than q." "A state of affairs p is absolutely good provided . . . that p is good and . . . that any possible state of affairs entailing p is better than any possible state of affairs not entailing p." Evil would be justified if it were defeated by an absolute good. The theodicist is, therefore, entitled to say that it is at least possible that God is justified in creating a world which contains evil.

455 Davis, Stephen Thane. "A Defence of the Free Will Defence," Relig Stud, 8 (December, 1972), 335-43.

Davis argues that although it is logically possible for Adam to be free and yet always choose the good, it is not possible for God to create Adam such that he is free and such that he always chooses the good. "x is ø" is said to be inconsistent with "x can be either ø or not-ø," for the latter implies that either disjunct

is (still) a real possibility while the former
implies that one of the disjuncts has been
realized and that, therefore, the other disjunct
is not (any longer) a real possibility. (x
cannot be not-$\emptyset$ if it is in fact $\emptyset$.) If we
accept this, it follows that "Adam is a person
who always chooses the good" is incompatible
with "Adam can either be a person who always
chooses the good or a person who does not do so"
and that, therefore, "God created Adam such
that Adam is a person who always chooses the
good" is incompatible with "God created Adam such
that Adam can either be a person who always
chooses the good or a person who does not do
so." Since the latter must be true if God creates
Adam such that Adam is free, we may conclude
that God cannot consistently create Adam free
and also guarantee his goodness. See Walton's
discussion (# 557 below) of the claim that "x
is $\emptyset$" is inconsistent with "x can be either
$\emptyset$ or not-$\emptyset$."

456 Dore, Clement Joseph, Jr. "Do Theists Need to
     Solve the Problem of Evil?" Relig Stud, 12
     (September, 1976), 383-9.

A (very) qualified defense of the claim that
it is rational to believe that God has a property which we are unable to specify precisely
but in virtue of which God's refusal to eliminate
evil is not morally reprehensible. (An example
of such a property might be the knowledge that
the elimination of evil would bring about an
undesirable state of affairs which human beings
cannot precisely specify and which is such that
the rational belief that the elimination of that
evil would produce that state of affairs would

justify any person's refusal to eliminate it.)

457 _____. "Do Theodicists Mean What They Say?"
Philosophy, 49 (October, 1974), 357-74.

Dore returns to some of the issues raised in
his "An Examination of the 'Soul-Making' Theodicy"
(# 459 below). He argues that if we knew that
all suffering was an indispensable means to
an overwhelming good, then we would be justified
in producing or permitting it, is spite of its
prima facie badness. We do not, however, know
this though we may believe it and have some
grounds for it. If it is true, God knows that
it is true, and therefore our situation and
God's situation are relevantly dissimilar, in
which case God is justified in bringing about
evil so that good may occur even though we are
not justified in doing so. (Again, -- see section
V -- because of our sin and ignorance, it is
dangerous for us to act upon the maxim that the
end justifies the means. Hence, as a matter
of policy, we should not do so. God, on the
other hand, is neither sinful nor ignorant.
It is, therefore, not dangerous for him to act
upon that maxim.)

458 _____. "Ethical Supernaturalism and the
Problem of Evil," Relig Stud, 8 (June, 1972),
97-113.

A reply to Patterson Brown's "God and the Good"
(# 448 above). Dore argues (1) that theists
who derive their knowledge of God's will from
the Bible or some similar source cannot base
their acceptance of that source on its morally
significant character and at the same time be

"ethical supernaturalists" (persons who identify
the good with God's will) with respect to all
their moral judgments, (2) that in the absence
of convincing reasons for believing that there
are morally relevant differences which explain
why God can permit suffering which is destructive
of character although we cannot do so, the ethical
supernaturalist may be forced to choose between
his belief that we can be blamed for failing
to prevent such suffering, and his belief in
the existence of an omnipotent, omniscient and
perfectly good God, and (3) that, for certain
sorts of ethical supernaturalists, that God
wants us to prevent destructive suffering but
does not want Himself to do so, is not a morally
relevant difference. This article is of some
interest although its effectiveness may be questioned. What Dore succeeds in showing is that
under certain conditions (e.g., if there are
no morally relevant differences which would
explain why God, unlike us, is not to be blamed
for permitting destructive suffering) evil is
a problem for some ethical supernaturalists
(e.g., those who believe that God's wanting
someone to do something is a sufficient reason
for blaming that person for not doing it only
if, under similar conditions, God would want
all other persons to do it as well).

459 _____. "An Examination of the 'Soul Making'
    Theodicy," Amer Phil Quart, 7 (April, 1970),
    119-30.

An interesting and important defense of the view
that suffering is justified by the virtuous
responses which it elicits. The greater part
of this article is devoted to a discussion of

two objections. (1) If suffering is justified
because it evokes (or tends to evoke) valuable
responses, why should we relieve it? We might
reply that in relieving suffering we are simply
replacing one valuable state of affairs with
another (viz., our own virtuous response), and
therefore no loss of value results. Or we might
reply that we have a deontological obligation
to remove or prevent suffering even where it
would be anti-utilitarian to do so. One may
of course object that if we have a deontological
obligation to relieve suffering even though
that suffering evokes (or tends to evoke) valuable
responses, then God does so as well, in which
case God's permission of suffering cannot be
justified by the valuable responses which suffering evokes (or tends to evoke). However, the
cases are not parallel. In God's case an obligation of this sort would be vastly anti-utilitarian. (If God were to act in this way, there
would be no suffering, and therefore no "vale
of soul-making.") In our case, an obligation
of this type is (in view of the relatively small
amount of suffering we can prevent or remove)
not vastly anti-utilitarian. (2) Dore suggests
that alternative worlds in which God eliminates
or reduces suffering which does not lead to a
virtuous response may (in spite of appearances)
be less valuable than our own -- either because
the virtuous responses to suffering which would
occur would not be morally praiseworthy (if God
were to relieve suffering whenever we did not,
then our responses would be unnecessary), or
because our virtuous responses to suffering
would not be free (if God were to prevent
suffering from occurring which he foresaw would

not be the occasion of a virtuous response,
it would then be impossible for us to choose
not to relieve suffering), or because our moral
obligations to relieve suffering would be less
stringent (if God were to reduce the frequency,
intensity and duration of suffering, suffering
would not be as serious a matter as it is in
our world).

460 _____. "Plantinga on the Free Will Defense,"
Rev Metaph, XXIV (June, 1971), 690-706.

After criticizing Plantinga's formulation of the
Free Will Defense (# 517 below) Dore offers
the following argument: (1) In order for people
who always act well to be free, God must not
be disposed to prevent their existence if He
had foreseen that they would freely fail if they
were created. (If God is so disposed, then
there is no genuine alternative to their always
acting well.) (2) God would not be reprehensible
if He were to lack this disposition, for freedom
is a great value. Therefore, (3) God could
not be blamed if it were the case that He would
not have prevented the existence of these sinless creatures even if He had foreseen that they
would freely fail if He created them. Therefore,
(4) God cannot be blamed for not having prevented
the existence of beings whose free failure He
did in fact foresee (viz., us).

461 Downing, F. Gerald. "God and the Problems of
Evils," Sophia VII (April, 1968), 12-8.

Downing argues that because theism is introduced
to deal with practical problems of good and evil,
it is unlikely that the existence of evil will

be found to be incompatible with it.

462 Farrer, Austin Marsden. Love Almighty and Ills
Unlimited, An Essay on Providence and Evil Con-
taining the Nathaniel Taylor Lectures for 1961.
(Christian Faith Series.) Garden City, New York:
Doubleday and Co., Inc., 1961. 168 pp.

This book contains a number of interesting discussions including (1) a better than average
defense of the claim that evil is parasitic
upon good (chapter II), (2) a persuasive demonstration of the incoherency of the suggestion
that evil is to be explained by a recalcitrant
stuff or matter which imposes limits upon what
God can do (chapter III), (3) an attempt (in
chapter IV) to show that "physical accident"
(which occurs when one system thwarts another)
is inevitable in a physical universe, because
the nature of any system is to radiate its influence and "absolutize itself, so far as in
it lies," and (4) an attempt (in chapter VI)
to combine aspects of the Soul-Making Theodicy
with the view that those people whose lives are
spiritually stunted or crippled in this world
will be redeemed in the next. (According to
Farrer, they will be redeemed through the medium
of Christ's mystical body which is composed of
souls which have successfully met the challenges
imposed by the evils of this world.) Not nearly
as successful are Farrer's treatments of animal
pain (chapter V), his account of perverse choice,
original sin and devils (chapter VII), and his
attempt to show how God brings good out of evil
even though God does not use evils as "means
perfectly calculated to produce ulterior ends"
(chapter VIII).

463 Flew, Antony Garrard Newton. "Are Ninian Smart's
     Temptations Irresistible?" Philosophy, XXXVII
     (January, 1962), 57-60.

     A reply to Smart's "Omnipotence, Evil and Super-
     men" (# 543 below). Flew argues that Smart
     has overlooked the most obvious possibility,
     viz., that God ensures that men always act well
     not by altering their dispositions or circum-
     stances so that they are never tempted, but
     by strengthening their character and sense of
     duty so that they always succeed in resisting
     temptation. See Smart's reply (# 545 below).

464 _____. "Divine Omnipotence and Human Free-
     dom," in # 923 below. Pp. 144-69.

     This widely discussed article is an expanded
     version of a paper published in The Hibbert
     Journal (January, 1955). If we examine paradig-
     matic cases of free behavior, we discover that
     actions are said to be free when certain familiar
     conditions obtain (the agent was not acting
     under pressure or coercion, alternatives within
     the agent's capacities were open to the agent,
     etc.). These conditions can be fulfilled even
     if the action is predictable or "explicable in
     terms of caused causes." It follows that deter-
     minism and freedom are compatible and that God
     could, therefore, bring it about that everyone
     always freely did the right thing. It may be
     objected that from the fact that freedom and
     determinism are compatible, it does not follow
     that freedom and divine determination are com-
     patible. A God who predetermines everything
     we do would be something like a "master-hypno-
     tist," and hypnotism is, or may be, an excusing

condition. Flew suggests (though with some
hesitation) that his paradigm case argument
shows that whether or not our actions are divinely
determined, they are (since the relevant conditions are fulfilled in some cases) sometimes free.
Nevertheless, if God has determined our behavior,
He cannot (according to Flew) legitimately blame
or punish us for it. Flew adds that if divine
determination and human freedom are incompatible,
then the advocate of the Free Will Defense must
abandon his belief in an omnipotent creator.
(Flew is assuming that "x is an omnipotent creator" entails "x determines everything.") This
essay provides one of the best statements of
a familiar position. (Interwoven with the main
argument are a number of lucid observations upon
the claim that pain, suffering, etc., are logically necessary conditions of such goods as
courage, compassion and perseverance.)

465 _____. "The 'Religious Morality' of Mr.
Patterson Brown," Mind, LXXIV (October, 1965),
578-81.

A reply to Brown (# 449 above). Flew concedes
that if God's will is adopted as the standard
of value, the Problem of Evil as usually understood dissolves. However, Brown's thesis is
said to be subject to three difficulties. (1)
It follows that all the time and effort which
Christians have devoted to the solution of the
Problem of Evil rests upon a misunderstanding
of their own position. (2) The view that Brown
ascribes to Christians leads to a worship of
naked power. (3) Brown asserts that God's choices
will not be arbitrary, for they are expressions
of His intelligence, knowledge and love. This

re-introduces the Problem of Evil in a new form, since we may now ask how the existence of suffering, frustration, and so on, is compatible with God's love. See Brown's reply (# 450 above).

466   Ford, Lewis Stanley. "Divine Persuasion and the Triumph of Good," Christian Schol, L (Fall, 1967), 235-50.

An excellent example of the way in which Process Philosophy attempts to handle the Problem of Evil. On a Whiteheadian view God is not the only being responsible for what transpires. (God does not know future contingents, and is only one power among others.) Evil occurs when an "occasion" freely refuses to accept and enact the initial aim which God proposes for it. (The Free Will Defense is thus extended to embrace not only rational agents but the "occasions" out of which everything else is "constructed.") Ford explicates this view, and responds to the accusation that Process Theology provides no real assurance of the triumph of good. (Belief in a guaranteed triumph is incompatible with human endeavor, and Process Theology does provide a conditional guarantee, viz., that the good will triumph if we cooperate with God.) Ford concludes by explaining how (upon a Process view) evil and suffering enter into God's own life but are integrated with other elements to produce a beautiful whole -- a creative and harmonious vision of reality which transfigures its constituents in the way in which Oedipus Rex transfigures parricide and incest. This divine satisfaction concerns us in two ways. The evil of perishing is overcome in so far as things are preserved and transformed in the divine

memory, and God's creative vision of reality
at any given point causally influences all subsequent actualities.

467   Geach, Peter Thomas.   "An Irrelevance of Omnipo-
      tence," Philosophy, 48 (October, 1973), 327-33.

McTaggart has suggested "that a being to whose
antecedent will much in this universe were not
repugnant would not be perfectly good." Geach
agrees that in God's case it is difficult to
draw a distinction between an antecedent will
and a consequent will. (God cannot, e.g., be
said to be frustrated by circumstances like the
ship captain who antecedently wills to bring
his goods to port but consequently upon a storm
wills to throw them overboard.) It may be objected to Geach that, given certain versions
of the Free Will Defense, the distinction makes
excellent sense. God antecedently wills that
the free persons He creates always choose the
good, but given certain facts about how persons
would freely behave if they were created, He
may consequently will to create free persons
whom He foresees will sometimes fail. (See
Dore, Plantinga, and Wainwright [# 460 above and
#s 517, 521 and 553 below] on the Free Will
Defense.)

468   Grave, Selwyn A.   "On Evil and Omnipotence," Mind,
      LXV (April, 1956), 63-6.

A reply to Mackie (# 501 below). Grave defends
the claim that God (logically) cannot bring it
about that everyone freely chooses the good.

297

469 Griffen, David Ray. God, Power, and Evil: A
     Process Theodicy. Philadelphia: Westminster
     Press, 1976. 336 pp.

Having reviewed traditional theodicies, Griffen
turns to his own position in the last two chapters (pp. 251-310). Previous writers are accused
of illicitly moving from the claim that it is
logically possible that there be a state of
affairs which includes no evil to the claim
that it is logically possible for some being
to bring this state of affairs about, and of
mistakenly supposing that it is possible for
one being to completely control another. (Griffen
argues that anything which is actual must have
a certain independence, some power of its own.)
Since no being can completely control another,
God cannot do so and, therefore, even though
a world without evil may be intrinsically possible God cannot guarantee such a world. These
considerations do not imply that God's power
is defective. Since a power to determine everything is impossible, God's lack of a power of
this sort is not an imperfection. Griffen maintains that if God is good, He will act in such
a way as to maximize the likelihood of intrinsic
good, where the criteria of intrinsic good are
harmony and intensity, and where intensity in
turn is a function of complexity. He attempts
to show that in order to maximize the likelihood
of good, God must maximize novelty or "freedom"
as well as order, and that the very conditions
which make for the emergence of intrinsic goods
of great value also make for the emergence of
intrinsic evils of great disvalue. Is God,
then, morally indictable for "having urged the
creation forward to those states in which

discordant feelings could be felt with great
intensity?" In particular, is God morally defective because He regards aesthetic considerations as primary, because evil is only overcome
in His own experience, and because "while lacking
the power to prevent discord, [He] has nevertheless led the creation to a stage where horrendous
evils . . . can occur?" Griffen replies that
aesthetic good (as understood by Whitehead)
includes moral good, that part of what Whitehead
means by God's overcoming evil is that God "provides ideal aims for the next stage of the world
designed to overcome the evil in the world,"
that if God is good, He must not only act in
such a way as to minimize disorder but must
also act in such a way as to minimize triviality,
and that since God suffers with the world, "the
risks which God asks the creation to take are
also risks for God." While not highly original
(Griffen's views are modifications of the views
of Whitehead and Hartshorne), this is the most
lucid presentation of Process theodicy yet to
appear.

470 Hare, Peter Hewitt and Edward H. Madden. "Evil
     and Persuasive Power," Process Stud, 2 (Spring,
     1972), 44-8.

A critique of the way in which Process Theology
attempts to handle the Problem of Evil. This
essay makes a number of points, including the
following: (1) Coercive power (which determines
its object) is sometimes legitimate. Whiteheadians are therefore wrong when they insist that
the only legitimate power is persuasive power
(which merely influences its object). (2) The
amount of evil in the world suggests that God's

299

persuasive power is not unlimited or perfect.
(3) If it "is in principle impossible" to experen-
tially estimate the "nature and extent" of God's
persuasive power, then the notion of God's persuasive power may be incoherent. These objections are significant but not conclusive. (1)
The authors are aware that Process philosophers
regard coercive power as metaphysically impossible. However, if coercive power is metaphysically impossible, its exercise cannot be
required and it is odd to say that it is sometimes
legitimate. (2) Since (as the authors admit)
unlimited persuasive power (unlike unlimited
coercive power) need not always be effective,
the fact that God's persuasive power appears
to be frequently ineffective does not entitle
us to conclude that it is limited or imperfect.
(3) Some Whiteheadians (e.g., Hartshorne) would
insist that the nature and extent of God's persuasive power can be determined a priori.

471 _____. Evil and the Concept of God. (American Lectures in Philosophy.) Springfield,
Illinois: Charles C. Thomas, Publishers, 1968.
vii + 142 pp.

A critique of classical and modern treatments
of the Problem of Evil. Attempts to evade or
deny the problem (Barth, Tillich, George
Schlesinger, Patterson Brown, Charles Hartshorne)
are discussed in chapters two and three. Classical solutions are discussed in chapter four,
and the views of John Hick and Ian Ramsey are
examined in chapter five. The sixth chapter
is devoted to the "Quasi-Theism" of Royce, Brightman and the Process philosophers. This chapter
is particularly valuable since attempts to solve

the Problem of Evil by limiting God's power
or by including a principle of limitation within
God are usually neglected altogether or dismissed
with a few general remarks. The authors' arguments are sometimes facile and frequently familar.
Many of their responses are vitiated by the assumption that it is incumbent upon the theist
to provide an explanation of every evil that
occurs. (It is just not clear that an explanation of the existence of a given kind of evil
fails if it is unable to account for the amount
of evil of that type.) Nevertheless, the authors'
remarks are often interesting and perceptive.
Taken as a whole, their book succeeds in providing
one of the better statements of the case against
theism.

472   Hartshorne, Charles. "A New Look at the Problem
      of Evil," Current Philosophical Issues: Essays
      in Honor of Curt John Ducasse. Edited by Freder-
      ick C. Dommeyer. Springfield, Illinois: Charles
      C. Thomas, Publisher, 1966. Pp. 201-12.

      Hartshorne argues that because "God exists"
      is a necessary truth, it holds in all possible
      worlds and is, therefore, compatible with any
      empirical (or contingent) state of affairs.
      Since any evil state of affairs is an empirical
      (or contingent) state of affairs, God's existence
      is compatible with any evil state of affairs.
      Thus, the Problem of Evil dissolves. According
      to Process Philosophy, all individuals are free.
      Evil is the result of free decisions made by
      human and non-human individuals. God in "en-
      acting" natural laws determines the limits within
      which these individuals must make their decisions
      but although He does so in such as way as to
      maximize opportunities and minimize risks, He

301

cannot eliminate great risks without eliminating
precious opportunities. (It should be noted,
that other Process philosophers reject the thesis
that God, in determining natural law, provides
the limits within which freedom must operate.)

473　Herman, Arthur Ludwig. "Indian Theodicy: Śaṁkara
　　　and Rāmāuja on Brahma Sūtra II. 1. 32-36,
　　　Phil East West, XXI (July, 1971), 265-81.

This interesting article provides a critical
analysis of the way in which the Problem of
Evil has been handled in the Vendānta tradition
by Samkara and Rāmānuja. Their "solution" has
two parts. (1) Brahman created the world in play
(līlā). (2) The evils we experience can be
accounted for in terms of the transmigration
of souls, and the operation of the law of Karman.
Herman shows that this is not satisfactory.
(1) Although play is purposeless, we are held
responsible for evils caused by our playful
activity. (2) If Brahman is limited by the law
of Karman his power is imperfect. If he is not
limited by the law of Karman he must be held
responsible for the evils which its operation
occasions. Herman's essay is drawn from his
thesis ("The Problem of Evil and Indian Thought,"
University of Minnesota, 1970).

474　Hick, John Harwood. Evil and the God of Love.
　　　New York: Harper and Row, Publishers, 1966.
　　　xii + 404 pp.

In this important and influential book Hick
distinguishes Augustinian-type theodicies from
Irenaean-type theodicies. The former are traced
from Augustine through Aquinas to the optimistic
theodicies of the 18th century. They are

characterized by the equation of being and goodness, the notion that evil is a privation of
being and goodness, an appeal to the Principle
of Plenitude (according to which it is good
that all kinds of things be created), the claim
that evil contributes to the aesthetic value
of the created universe, a version of the Free
Will Defense which involves the assertion that
finitely perfect beings freely and perversely
choose evil, and so on. Hick argues that the
fact that many kinds of being were not created
shows either that God does not act in accordance
with the Principle of Plenitude or that God
is not omnipotent, that although the aesthetic
defense may justify some kinds of decay and de-
generation, e.g., that of inanimate and vegetable
nature) it cannot justify suffering and moral
evil, that the fall of a finitely perfect being
is impossible (in what sense?), etc. Hick's
major criticism is, however, this: In Augustinian-type theodicies, God's love and goodness
are construed as "creative fecundity, His bestowing of the boon of existence as widely as
possible." Man is created to fill "a gap in the
great chain of being," and evil is understood
as a privation of being. Hick maintains that
this conception is not sufficiently personal
and ethical and is, therefore, an inadequate
interpretation of the Christian tradition in
which God's love is construed as a personal
relationship to the "finite persons whom He
has created," in which finite personality is
believed to be made in God's image and to be
"of unique significance to Him" (and not merely
a link in the chain of being), and in which sin
is interpreted as a "failure in personal

relationship." Hick traces theodicies of the
second type from Irenaeus through Schleiermacher
to F. R. Tennant and other modern theologians
and philosophers. At the heart of these theodicies is the notion that this world is "a vale
of soul-making" in which, through their encounter
with hardships, challenges and defeats, human
beings are prepared, trained and educated for
fellowship with God. In spite of the fact that
these theodicies are sometimes insufficiently
Christocentric and occasionally fail to appreciate the terrifying power of evil, Hick concludes
that they are distinctly preferable to Augustinian
type theodicies. Hick's positive contributions
are contained in the final section. He argues
that God prizes our free and loving responses
to Him. In order to ensure that we possess
sufficient independence and autonomy to enter
into this kind of relationship, God creates an
epistemic distance between Himself and us, by
placing us in a world which can (because of
its evils and the fact that it has its own structures and laws) be interpreted atheistically as
well as theistically. Freedom is secured in
this fashion, but sin is made virtually inevitable. This last section also contains interesting discussions of pain, of gratuitous and
excessive suffering (it helps to maintain epistemic distance between God and man), and a defense of the claim that any viable theodicy
must include a doctrine of universal redemption.
Hick's book has evoked many responses. See,
for example, the critiques of Howe, Kane, Puccetti, and Trethowan (#s 478, 485, 524 and 551
below).

475 _____. "God, Evil and Mystery," <u>Relig Stud</u>,
  3 (April, 1968), 539-46.

A reply to Puccetti (# 524 below). Hick returns
to two points made in <u>Evil</u> <u>and</u> <u>the</u> <u>God</u> <u>of</u> <u>Love</u>
(# 474 above). (1) Placing apparently pointless
suffering in an eschatological context should
affect our evaluation of it. (2) Apparently
random and meaningless suffering may be a necessary feature of a "vale of soul-making." If
suffering and happiness were distributed according
to desert, it would be impossible (in what sense?)
to perform one's duty for its own sake. If
suffering "could always be seen to work for
the good of the sufferer," there would be no
place for "personal sympathy or . . . sacrificial
help." Furthermore, the "accidental" character
of evil helps to maintain the epistemic distance
between God and man which is necessary if human
nature is to develop freely.

476 _____. "The Problem of Evil in the First
  and Last Things," <u>J Theol Stud</u>, XIX (New Series),
  (October, 1968), 591-602.

This reply to Trethowan (# 551 below) is reprinted
in the author's <u>God</u> <u>and</u> <u>the</u> <u>Universe</u> <u>of</u> <u>Faiths</u>,
<u>Essays</u> <u>in</u> <u>the</u> <u>Philosophy</u> <u>of</u> <u>Religion</u> (London and
Basingstoke: The Macmillan Press, Ltd., 1973,
pp. 62-74). Hick attempts to defend the notion
that it is impossible for a finitely perfect
being to choose evil, and returns to the claim
that a viable theodicy must include a doctrine
of universal redemption. Hell stands "before
all men as a terrible possibility" but because
of God's love and power, it is "morally and prac-
tically certain" that He will redeem each of

of us without destroying our freedom. Hick
admits that it is difficult to see how the doctrine of universal redemption is compatible
with human freedom. It should be added that it
is also difficult to see how hell can be a
"terrible possibility" if the nature of things
(God's love and power) precludes it.

477 Hoitenga, Dewey James, Jr. "Logic and the Problem
     of Evil," Amer Phil Quart, 4 (April, 1967),
     114-26.

Although frequently cited, this article suffers
from several weaknesses. In part I, the author
argues that the claim that evil is necessary
to a higher good involves a peculiar conception
of good which ultimately rests upon the notion
that what is good is determined by God's will.
Hoitenga appears to believe that the "higher
good defense" involves the claim that God could
produce good without evil, but that even though
human beings might think that it would be better
if God were to do so, it really is not. But
this misses the point. The "higher good defense"
does not deny that it would be better to have
the good without the evil; it simply insists
that it is not possible to have the good without
the evil and that, therefore, God cannot act
for the best unless He permits evil. In part
II, Hoitenga argues that the Free Will Defense
conflicts with certain tenets of classical Christian theism, e.g., that God and the blessed are
both free and unable to sin, that God is wholly
responsible for our good acts, and that God's
power and control are unlimited. Although
Hoitenga rightly sees a problem here, his observations are not particularly original. See

Yandell's reply (# 564 below).

478   Howe, Leroy Thomas.   "Leibniz on Evil," _Sophia_,
       X (October, 1971), 8-17.

       Howe argues that "best" in the expression "best
       world" must be understood in terms of the meaning
       of "perfection" in the expression "divine per-
       fection." God's being is perfect because it
       is compatible with all possibilities and thus
       retains its identity in all situations. The
       world which contains "the greatest variety of
       phenomena consonant with the simplist scheme
       of arrangement" provides the best created image
       of this perfection. Howe also addresses himself
       to Hick's contention (# 474 above) that theodicies
       of this type are invariably sub-personal and
       sub-ethical.

479   Hudson, William Donald.   "An Attempt to Defend
       Theism," _Philosophy_, XXXIX (January, 1964),
       18-28.

       It is part of our ordinary notion of freedom
       that the agent "is a centre of determination
       ultimately distinct from . . . all other selves."
       It follows that God cannot fully determine free
       actions. Although the Free Will Defense implies
       that God is not the sufficient causal ground
       of everything that obtains, it is compatible
       with the belief that God influences everything
       we do and with the belief that everything good
       in us is a result of such influences. Pontifex
       (# 523 below) is criticized for arguing that
       because failure is negative it requires no cause,
       and that, therefore, our freedom to reject good-
       ness is compatible with God's complete deter-

mination of all real events. As Hudson points
out, the fact that moral failure has negative
value does not imply that it does not exist
or is not a real event.

480   Jefferson, Howard Bonar. "Royce on the Problem of
        Evil," J Relig, XI (July, 1931), 359-77.

This critique is drawn from the author's doctoral
dissertation ("The Problem of Evil in the Philosophy of Josiah Royce," Yale, 1929). Among
Jefferson's more significant contentions are
the following: (1) Since the Absolute experiences
the triumph over an evil as well as the evil
itself, it does not experience that evil as
we do. Therefore either our experience of evil
is unreal or there are certain experiences which
lie outside the Absolute -- both of which Royce
denies. (2) While evil is transcended in the
experience of the Absolute it is not normally
transcended in our own experience. Therefore,
even though the problem may be solved for the
Absolute, it is not solved for us. On the other
hand, in so far as we do experience the triumph
over evil it becomes unnecessary for us to postulate the Absolute as that in which a fulfilment
which we cannot achieve in our own fragmentary
experience is secured. (3) Royce is wrong when
he asserts that good (logically) must involve
the conquest of evil. There are both moral
and natural goods which do not do so.

481   Joad, Edwin Mitchinson and Clive Staples Lewis.
        "The Pains of Animals: A Problem in Theology,"
        Month, CLXXXIX (February, 1950), 95-104.

Joad criticizes the suggestions about animal

pain made by Lewis in The Problem of Pain (#
495 below). The fact that some animals are not
self-conscious does not alter the fact that
they feel pain. The theory that domestic animals
achieve a kind of immortality in conjunction
with their masters has no bearing on the problem
created by the suffering of non-domestic animals
and involves interesting difficulties in those
cases in which the animals' masters are thoroughly
bad people. The notion that animal creation
has been corrupted by fallen angelic beings and
is for that reason "red in tooth and claw" is
incredible and, in any case, cannot explain
all animal suffering. Lewis provides cogent
replies to some of the points made by Joad and
emphasizes the provisional and speculative nature
of his original remarks. This interesting exchange is reprinted in God in the Dock, a collection of Lewis's essays edited by Walter Hooper
(Grand Rapids, Michigan: William B. Eerdmans
Pub. Co., 1970).

482 Journet, Charles. The Meaning of Evil. Translated
     by Michael Barry. London: Geoffrey Chapman;
     New York: P. J. Kenedy, 1963. 299 pp.

     Originally published in French under the title
     Le Mal (1961). "The mystery of evil is considered
     in this book from the theological [and specifi-
     cally Neo-Thomist] viewpoint." Journet's book
     is an excellent specimen of its kind. His de-
     fense of the privation theory of evil (chapter
     two) and his presentation of the Thomistic
     version of the Free Will Defense (chapter six)
     are unusually lucid. The chapter on hell (chap-
     ter seven) is also of interest. The most signi-
     ficant philosophical discussion occurs in

chapter four where Journet examines and rejects
the notion that God was obligated to create
the best possible world. There are an infinite
number of possible worlds each of which provides
an image of God's perfections and each of which
is surpassed in value by some other world.
There is, therefore, no best world to create.
God is only obligated to create a world in which
good is victorious. This defense is not original but it is well presented and deserves to
be better known by those who stand outside the
Thomistic tradition. Journet's presentation may
be usefully compared with that of Joyce (# 483
below) and Schlesinger (# 540 below) who employs
what is essentially a non-Thomistic version of
the same defense.

483   Joyce, George Hayward. Principles of Natural
      Theology. (Stonyhurst Philosophical Series.)
      London, New York [etc.]: Longmans, Green and
      Co., 1923; New York: AMS Press, 1972. Pp.
      557-606.

      Chapter XVII provides a Scholastic account of
      providence and evil. While most of Joyce's
      remarks are familiar, they are developed with
      typical lucidity. The key to his solution is
      found on pages 577-583. For every world which
      provides an image of God's perfection, there is
      another possible world which provides a still
      more adequate image of that perfection. Since
      there is no best possible world, God cannot
      be faulted for not creating the best possible
      world, and no evil state of affairs is a logi-
      cally necessary condition of the best possible
      total state of affairs. God is only obligated
      to create a good world and to bring good out
      of evil. This contention, if sound, undercuts

a standard objection to many of Joyce's other
remarks. Joyce contends, for example, that as
a matter of empirical fact pain serves useful
purposes. The usual response to this defense
is that it is irrelevant because God is not
limited by empirical necessity. If Joyce's
position is sound, however, then even though
God is not constrained by empirical necessity,
He is not morally bound to permit only those
evils which are logically indispensable to an
unsurpassable state of affairs. He is only
obligated to produce a world in which good outweighs evil and in which no evil is pointless.
To show that pain serves useful purposes has a
direct logical bearing upon this later contention.
Joyce's solution (which goes back to Aquinas)
is similar to that of other modern Thomists
(e.g., Journet, # 482 above), and may be usefully compared with the solution recently developed by Schlesinger (# 540 below). Joyce's
remarks on moral evil are also of more than
average interest.

484 Kane, Gordon Stanley. "The Concept of Divine
Goodness and the Problem of Evil," Relig Stud,
11 (March, 1975), 49-71.

Kane criticizes arguments designed to show that
God's goodness bears no relation to what we
mean by goodness and/or that it is inappropriate
to apply our standards of value to God. He concludes that the Problem of Evil cannot be evaded
by arguing that God's standards of value differ
from our standards of value.

485 _____ . "The Failure of Soul-Making Theodicy,"
Int J Phil Relig, VI (Spring, 1975), 1-22.

A very interesting critique of John Hick's version
of the Soul-Making Theodicy. (See # 474 above)
Kane makes five points. (1) Persistence, stead-
fastness, sympathy and other virtues analogous
to courage and compassion could be displayed
in a world which required effort but did not
include pain and suffering. (2) Evil is not
necessary for the existence of an "epistemic
distance" between God and man. All that is necessary is a world which "operates according to
its own internal set of general causal laws"
and is, thus, apparently self-sufficient. (3)
Kane suggests that the existence of "epistemic
distance" implies that people cannot be blamed
for their failure to recognize God. (4) The
fact that there will be no room for the exercise
of courage, compassion, etc., in the eschaton,
implies that these virtues cannot have the great
value which is placed upon them by advocates
of the Soul-Making Theodicy. (5) Evil establishes
an epistemic distance between God and man only
if it is evidence against theism. However, if
any theodicy is successful, evil is not evidence
against theism. (Kane appears to assume that if
e can be shown to be compatible with p, then
e is not evidence against p.) Although Kane's
last point is questionable and although Kane
may exaggerate the extent to which the notion
of "epistemic distance" plays a role in Soul-
Making Theodicies, his article is worth examining
with some care. It accentuates the fact that
what is fundamentally at issue are value judgments which the theist is prepared to make (e.g.,
about the intrinsic value of moral struggle)

but which the critic is not willing to make.
Kane's article is valuable because it clearly
articulates reasons for questioning the evaluations made by theists.

486 _____. "The Free-Will Defense Defended,"
New Scholas, L (Autumn, 1976), 435-46.

Kane argues that if men are contra-deterministically free, then even if they had been created
with "the strongest possible inclination to do
what is right that is consistent with their
being free, there is no reason for thinking
that the amount of moral evil" would have been
less. Kane points out (1) that "Augustinian"
Christians have supposed that man was created
with such an inclination, (2) that if men are
contra-deterministically free good inclinations
do not necessarily lead to good actions, (3)
that the fact that our inclinations to the good
are now weaker than they might be does not imply
that man was not created with strong inclinations
to the good, and (4) that moral evil, once introduced, would so corrupt our inclinations that
"the sort of situation that exists in the world
today" could develop in relatively little time.
It follows that it is possible for the Free-Will
theodicist to maintain that man was created with
strong inclinations to the good and that God
cannot, therefore, be faulted for having failed
to do so.

487 _____. "Theism and Evil," Sophia, IX (March,
1970), 14-21.

Although this reply to Yandell's "Ethics, Evils,
and Theism" (# 562 below) possesses little

intrinsic interest, Yandell's response (# 566
below) is worth examining.

488   Kellner, Menachen Marc. "Gersonides, Providence,
      and the Rabbinic Tradition," JAAR, XLII (December,
      1974), 673-85.

      A rather interesting account of an attempt to
      accommodate the fact that evil exists by limiting
      God's providence.

489   Khatchadourian, Haig. "God, Happiness and Evil,"
      Relig Stud, 2 (October, 1966), 109-19.

      A critical discussion of Schlesinger's "The
      Problem of Evil and the Problem of Suffering"
      (# 540 below) and of LaPara's "Suffering, Hap-
      piness, Evil" (# 494 below). A number of points
      are made. It is argued against Schlesinger that
      it is not clear that there is no upper logical
      limit to happiness. Reasons are offered for
      believing that LaPara is mistaken when he sup-
      poses that God cannot have an obligation to
      create someone just because that person would
      be happy. The most serious objection is the
      following: While there may be no upper logical
      limit to happiness, there does appear to be a
      lower logical limit to suffering, viz., its com-
      plete absence. Since God could have created
      a world without suffering, He should be faulted
      for having failed to do so. This criticism
      may be effective against Schlesinger's argument
      as it stands. It is not so clearly effective
      if that argument is reformulated by replacing
      "happiness" and "suffering" with "good" and
      "bad." From the fact that there is a lower
      logical limit to suffering (viz., the complete

absence of suffering), it does not follow that
there is a lower logical limit to badness (viz.,
the complete absence of badness). The mere
absence of pleasure or happiness is not pain or
suffering, but it can be argued that the absence
of a possible good is bad. While "x is more
pleasurable than y" does not entail "y is more
painful than x," "x is better than y" does appear
to entail "y is worse than x." If there is no
lower logical limit to evil, a Schlesinger-type
argument can be used to show that God cannot
be faulted simply because He could have created
a world with less evil in it.

490 Kielkopf, Charles Francis. "Emotivism as the
     Solution to the Problem of Evil," Sophia, IX
     (July, 1970), 34-8

     If non-cognitivist analyses of value judgments
     are correct, sentences of the form "x is good"
     and "x is bad" have no truth value. It follows
     that "there is evil" is neither true nor false,
     in which case it cannot logically conflict with
     "God exists," and at least one form of the Pro-
     blem of Evil dissolves.

491 Knudson, Albert Cornelius. The Doctrine of Redemp-
     tion. New York, Nashville: Abingdon-Cokesbury
     Press, 1933. Pp. 204-12.

     A brief but rather effective critique of Bright-
     man's attempt (# 447 above) to solve the Problem
     of Evil. According to Knudson, Brightman's
     "solution" compromises the divine unity, fails
     to meet the demand of religious faith for an
     effective goodness, introduces "an unduly anthro-
     pomorphic concept of God," postulates the exis-
     tence of something (the Given) which is neither

315

self-explanatory nor capable of being explained
in terms of anything else, etc. Brightman regarded Knudson as his most searching critic.

492 Kondoleon, Theodore J. "Moral Evil and the Exis-
    tence of God: A Reply," New Scholas, XLVII
    (Summer, 1973), 366-74.

This reply to Oakes' "Actualities, Possibilities
and Free Will Theodicy" (# 508 below) and to
Walter's "Are Actualities Prior to Possibilities?"
(# 556 below) makes several interesting points.
Oakes' thesis is incoherent. On the one hand,
Oakes contends that moral agency requires a knowledge of the possibility of moral evil which
in turn rests upon a knowledge of its actuality
and, on the other hand, Oakes maintains that
the existence of moral evil presupposes moral
agency. Moral evil is thus logically prior to
moral agency (since it is required for the knowledge of the possibility of moral evil upon
which moral agency depends) and yet moral agency
is logically prior to the commission of morally
evil acts. Kondoleon also contends that Oakes
and Walter are mistaken in supposing that moral
agents must be able to sin. God is a moral
agent (since He knowingly and willingly does
the good), and God is free (to choose between
goods). He cannot, however, sin.

493 La Croix, Richard Ray. "Unjustified Evil and God's
    Choice," Sophia, (April, 1974), 20-8.

A reply to Plantinga (# 518 below). Theists
assume that God is so great a good that the
addition of created goods does not produce an
increase in value, that God is so great a moral

good that the addition of finite moral goods
does not result in increased moral value, and
that God need not have created. It follows from
these assumptions, according to La Croix, that
evil is not necessary to goodness and the permission of evil is not necessary to the possibility of moral goodness. More precisely, there
is a maximal good -- God himself -- which outweighs any of the goods which entail evil and
which does not itself entail it, and -- since
preventing evil (by not creating) will not
diminish moral goodness -- the permission of evil
is not necessary for a maximal moral good and,
therefore, is not necessary for the possibility
of a maximal moral good. It is difficult to
believe that a total state of affairs which includes created goods as well as non-created
goods is no better than a total state of affairs
which contains only non-created goods but, in
fairness to La Croix, it must be admitted that
many classical theists do appear to believe
this to be the case. (There is, however, no
indication that Plantinga does so.)

494   LaPara, Nicholas. "Suffering, Happiness, Evil,"
      Sophia, IV (July, 1965), 10-6.

This reply to Schlesinger's "The Problem of
Evil and the Problem of Suffering" (# 540 below),
contains a number of interesting points. (1)
LaPara argues that even if an overall task (e.g.,
producing the maximum amount of happiness) is
impossible, one is not excused from performing
parts of the task (e.g., eliminating all suffering) if those parts are possible and valuable.
(2) It is argued that God can be blamed for
creating beings which are less happy than

conditions of the world which they inhabit allow.
(3) For any world there is a better. Hence,
since every world is worse than some other world,
there is an objection to creating any particular
world. God has no obligation to create. It
would, therefore, seem to follow that God ought
not to create. See Schlesinger's response to
the first and third point (# 538 below), and
Khatchadourian's response to the third point
(# 489 above).

495   Lewis, Clive Staples. The Problem of Pain. London:
      Centenary Press, 1940. ix + 148 pp.

      This "popular" discussion of the Problem of
      Evil contains much which should interest philo-
      sophers. For example, in chapter 2, Lewis ar-
      gues that a society of free beings logically
      requires a common environment governed by rela-
      tively stable laws, and that the operation of
      these laws accounts for much of the evil which
      exists. While this argument is familiar, it
      is well presented. In chapter 3 Lewis discusses
      God's goodness, attempting to explain how God's
      standards can differ from ours without reversing
      them, distinguishing kindness from love, and
      arguing that since God has no wants and no in-
      terests which can conflict with the wants and
      interests of others, the distinction between
      egoism and altruism does not apply to Him.
      The chapters on hell and animal pain are specu-
      lative (some would say fanciful) but of more
      than ordinary interest.

496 McCloskey, Henry John. "Evil and the Problem of
     Evil," Sophia, V (April, 1966), 14-9.

        A response to M. B. Ahern's defense of the pri-
        vation theory (# 438 above). McCloskey attempts
        to show that Ahern's analyses of pain and moral
        evil are implausible. See Ahern's reply (# 437
        above).

497 _____. "God and Evil," Phil Quart, X (April,
     1960), 97-114. (Reprinted in # 515 below, pp.
     61-84.)

        This article and Mackie's "Evil and Omnipotence"
        (# 501 below) provide the most influential recent
        defenses of the claim that theism is unable to
        cope successfully with the Problem of Evil.
        A number of things are discussed -- the claims
        that evil is an illusion or a mere privation
        of good, that pleasure and pain are correlatives
        which entail each other, that suffering can be
        regarded as a punishment, and that pain and
        suffering are a consequence of the operation
        of natural laws. The article also includes
        some rather uninteresting remarks on the Free
        Will Defense. McCloskey's more significant con-
        tentions include the following: (1) That the
        theist cannot both argue that physical evil is
        justified by a greater good which it makes pos-
        sible and at the same time recognize an obligation
        to eliminate or reduce physical evil. (For an
        attempted refutation of this argument see Wain-
        wright, # 554 below.) (2) That God can be blamed
        for creating a society in which some are favored
        at the expense of others since He does not Him-
        self share in the risks of that society.

498   . God and Evil. The Hague: Martinus
Nijhoff, 1974. viii + 132 pp.

Although this book is, on the whole, somewhat
disappointing, it does contain a few interesting
discussions. Consider, e.g., McCloskey's criticism of the privation theory of evil (pp. 31-41),
and his attempt (in chapter IV) to show that
if one does not take the predicates which one
applies to God literally, one commits oneself
to the doctrine of a finite and limited God.
(If, e.g., God is not literally all knowing,
then He is not all knowing and is, therefore,
finite in that respect.) A number of McCloskey's
remarks are just, and his objections are sometimes effectively stated. (See, e.g., his criticism of the theory that pain is a warning
system.) However, for the most part little
is new, many of McCloskey's points have been
better expressed elsewhere, and his arguments
are often facile. Thus, proposed solutions
are dismissed because they fail to explain all
evil (even though it is not clear that they are
intended to do so). Or solutions are dismissed
on the grounds that they rest on false or incredible moral evaluations although little is
said to support the charge that the evaluations
are misguided. (One notable exception is his
discussion of the supposed intrinsic value of
freedom which occurs on page 121 ff.) This
is not one of the better books on the Problem
of Evil, but it should not be ignored.

499   . "The Problem of Evil," J Bible Relig,
XXX (July, 1962), 187-97.

Most of the points made in this article were

previously made in "God and Evil," (# 497 above).
There are, however, two new points. (1) Evil
can be morally justified as a means to good
but not as a part of it. To suppose that it
can is to confuse moral justification and aesthetic justification. (2) We are quite willing to
interfere with freedom and to tolerate interferences with freedom, in order to secure peace,
happiness, etc. We do not, then, in fact place
the value upon freedom which is ascribed to
it by the Free Will Defense. Both of these points
are interesting but both are questionable. (1)
While not all means are parts of the goods to
which they contribute, it is not clear that parts
of good wholes cannot be regarded as means to
the overall effect. Furthermore, it is not clear
why an appeal to a parts-whole relation cannot
play a role in moral justification and, in any
case, the production of aesthetically good wholes
may have moral value. (2) Freedom from causal
necessity must not be confused with social and
political freedom. The fact that we tolerate
interferences with the latter does not imply
that we would be willing to tolerate interferences with the former. (Most of us, for example,
would heartily disapprove of turning people
into automata through the use of drugs and sur-
gical techniques.)

500　McCullough, H. B. "Theodicy and Mary Baker Eddy,"
　　　Sophia, XIV (March, 1975), 12-8.

A defense of the proposition that (the practice
of) such virtues as compassion, sympathy and
mercy logically entails the existence of real
evils. It is argued, e.g., that given the "cri-
terial connection between mental states and

behavior" it is impossible to be systematically deceived in supposing that those who appear to suffer actually do suffer and that, hence, the mere appearance of evil is not sufficient for the existence of these virtues. It is conceded that these virtues might be practiced in a world in which there was no pain if those who practiced these virtues were irrational or defective in some other way. It is suggested, however, that it is by no means clear that a world of this sort would be preferable to the world which God has actually created.

501   Mackie, John Leslie. "Evil and Omnipotence," Mind, LXIV (April, 1955), 200-12. (Reprinted in # 515 below, pp. 46-60.)

This article and McCloskey's "God and Evil" (# 497 above) provide the most influential recent defenses of the claim that theism is unable to successfully cope with the Problem of Evil. "God exists and is omnipotent, omniscient and all good" is said to be logically incompatible with "evil exists." A number of theistic defenses are discussed -- the claim that evil is merely an illusion or the privation of good, the claim that good and evil are correlatives which logically presuppose each other, etc. The most original features of this article are the following: (1) An argument that first order evils (pain and suffering) cannot be justified by second order goods (e.g., courage and compassion) which entail and outweigh them because, if there are second order goods, there are also second order evils which must be justified by third order goods -- and so on ad infinitum. (Mackie's argument seems to require an assumption which

is not obviously true, viz., that if we posit
a good of order n, then we must also posit an
evil of order n which is neither justified by
a good of order n nor by a good of any lower
order.) (2) Mackie argues that since worlds
in which (causally) free beings always act well
are logically possible and since an omnipotent
God can instantiate any logically possible state
of affairs, evil cannot be justified by arguing
that its permission is necessary for freedom.
(Plantinga's work on the Free Will Defense [#s
517, 521 and 522 below] can be regarded as an
answer to this objection.) (3) A new formulation
of the "Paradox of Omnipotence." (This is discussed under the appropriate heading. See #
94 above.)

502 _____. "Theism and Utopia," Philosophy,
XXXVII (April, 1962), 153-8.

This reply to Smart's "Omnipotence, Evil, and
Supermen" (# 543 below) is of most interest because of its clarification of the author's criticism of the Free Will Defense. It is argued
that if free choices are not determined by the
nature and character of the agent, then either
they occur randomly or else they are determined
by the "substance qua substance and not through
its characteristics." In either case, freedom
appears to have little value. If, on the other
hand, free choices are determined by the nature
and character of the agent, it is very difficult
to see why God could not have made men such that
they would always freely choose the good, by
providing them with the right sort of nature
and character.

503 McTaggart, John McTaggart Ellis. Some Dogmas
     of Religion. London: Edward Arnold, 1906;
     New York: Kraus Reprint Co., 1969. Pp. 208-37.

Sections 171-194 contain an interesting and
original discussion of the Problem of Evil.
(1) McTaggart considers the possibility that
when "good" is applied to God it means something different from what it means when it is
applied to men, and attempts to determine whether
it might, in certain circumstances, be reasonable
to worship a being who was evil by our standards
but who possessed unlimited power. (2) It is
argued that if "omnipotence" is construed literally, then God can perform logically impossible tasks, from which it follows that evils
cannot be justified on the grounds that they
are necessary to some good. McTaggart contends
that there are religious motivations for con-
struing "omnipotence" literally. (These include
the desire to magnify God and the desire to show
that the universe is good on the whole.) If
we suppose that God's power is limited in certain ways (e.g., by logical necessity), we are
confronted with another difficulty. If God is
good, the evil which occurs must be contrary
to His antecedent will, but in God's case no
viable distinction can be drawn between an antecedent will to goodness and His choice, which
is consequent upon circumstances, of a state
of affairs which includes evil. The distinction
between an antecedent and consequent will depends
upon the existence of external constraints which
prevent the agent from doing what he (antecedently) wants to do, whereas any limitations
to which an omnipotent creator is subject must
be internal rather than external (otherwise,

324

his sovereignty is compromised). McTaggart can
see how these internal constraints could prevent
God from willing (e.g.) a logically impossible
state of affairs, but he cannot see how they could
prevent Him from carrying out something which
He does in fact will. McTaggart's argument is
interesting although one may wonder how logical
facts and value facts (both of which may be
said to be necessary and to limit God) can be
parts of God's nature. One may also wonder
whether the fact that a being who actually wills
the best logically possible state of affairs,
but does not will a logically impossible state
of affairs which contains no evil and which
is better than the state of affairs which he
does will provides us with any reason for concluding that that being is not good.

504 Maritain, Jacques. God and the Permission of
    Evil. Translated by Joseph W. Evans. (Chris-
    tian Culture and Philosophy Series.) Milwaukee:
    Bruce Publishing Co., 1966. ix + 121 pp.

A very interesting little book. Since goodness
and being are convertible and since God is the
source of being but not of non-being, (1) God
is the first cause of freely chosen good actions
while we are only the secondary causes of these
same actions and, (2) we are the first causes
of freely chosen bad actions, God merely permitting then to occur. We are, then, (causally)
free in so far as we are able to decline from
the good or refuse grace. Maritain claims to
be explicating the thought of Aquinas. Whether
or not he is doing so accurately, Maritain is
departing from the Dominican tradition. According
to this tradition there are (roughly speaking)

two levels of causality -- divine and natural.
While some things which occur on the natural
level (e.g., human choices of good and evil)
are not causally determined by other things
on that level, everything that occurs is causally
determined either by God's acting or by His
refusing to act in certain ways (e.g., by His
bestowing or refusing to bestow efficacious
grace). Maritain, on the other hand, at least
appears to be saying that certain contingent
occurrences (free choices of evil) are not causally determined by God in any sense. Maritain's
"innovation" can be viewed as a reflection of
modern Christian theism's insistence upon the
radical character of human freedom. (Cf. Christian Existentialism, modern Christian Liberalism,
etc.)

505 _____. St. Thomas and the Problem of Evil;
Under the Auspices of the Aristotelian Society
of Marquette University, by Jacques Maritain.
(The Aquinas Lecture, 1942.) Translated by Mrs.
Gordon Andison. Milwaukee: Marquette University
Press, 1942. 46 pp.

Maritain first considers evil which occurs in
the order of nature. Aquinas justifies this
evil by arguing that God must create corruptible
beings in order to fill out every degree of
being, and by arguing that the evil of the part
is necessary for the good of the whole. Leibniz's theodicy is said to be a rationalistic
caricature of this aspect of Aquinas. What
Leibniz neglects, and Thomas sees, is that there
is an order of freedom and grace as well as an
order of nature. This has several important
implications. For one thing, since free persons
are wholes in their own right, the evil which

326

infects them cannot be completely justified
by the role which it plays in some larger whole.
For another, nature as a whole is ordered toward grace, and the permission of sin can only
be understood as a necessary condition of a
supernatural good -- an "outpouring of creative
goodness" in which God gives Himself to those
who freely love Him. The second part of Maritain's lecture is devoted to a theme which is
developed at more length in the author's God
and the Permission of Evil (# 504 above), viz.,
that evil choice proceeds from a voluntary (but
not sinful) inattention to the rule for human
action.

506 Mavrodes, George Ion. Belief in God, A Study
     in the Epistemology of Religion. (Studies in
     Philosophy.) New York: Random House, 1970.
     Pp. 90-111.

The Problem of Evil is discussed in chapter IV.
Mavrodes argues that nothing of significance
follows from the alleged fact that theologians
cannot tell us what reasons God has for permitting
evil, unless we add either that if there are such
reasons the theologian will know them or that
if someone knows that God has a good reason for
permitting evil he must know what that reason
is. Neither of these propositions is clearly
true. Furthermore, it is possible that the
theologian may have a good reason for his belief
that there is a justification and yet not know
what that reason is, or he may infer the existence
of such a justification from God's omnipotence
and goodness without any obvious circularity.
In the second part of this chapter, Mavrodes
argues that the problem is more aptly thought

327

of as an epistemic problem rather than as a
logical problem. What is at issue is not simply
the relationships between the members of a set
of propositions. The Problem of Evil is an
epistemic dilemma, where an epistemic dilemma
is a problem arising for someone who is inclined
to believe a set of propositions but is also
inclined to believe that that set is inconsistent. Since the problem is person-relative,
the solution must also be person-relative, satisfying requirements of psychological effectiveness
as well as requirements of "epistemic propriety
involving truth and logic."

507 _____. "Some Recent Philosophical Theology,"
Rev Metaph, XXIV (September, 1970), pp. 103-11.

Section III discusses the Problem of Evil.
Mavrodes argues that neither the truth of theism
nor the rationality of belief in theism entails
that any human being will know what God's reason
for permitting evil is. James Ross's dissolution of the Problem of Evil (# 532 below) is
examined and found wanting, though it is not
clear that Mavrodes has succeeded in showing
precisely what is wrong with it.

508 Oakes, Robert Aaron. "Actualities, Possibilities
and Free Will Theodicy," New Scholas, XLVI
(Spring, 1972), 191-201.

Oakes argues that in order to know that something is possible, we must experience it. Since
moral agents must know that evil is possible,
there must be actual evils which they experience.
Hence, if there are moral agents, evil must exist.
See Walter's reply (# 556 below), and Kondoleon's

response to both Oakes and Walter (# 492 above).

509 _____. "God, Evil and Professor Ross,"·Phil
Phenomenol Res, XXXV (December, 1974), 261-7.

It is sometimes argued that if God is a causally
necessary and sufficient condition of human
behavior (as classical Christian theism appears
to maintain), then it is God -- not we -- who
is responsible for our moral failings, from which
it follows that God is culpable. James Ross
(# 532 below) maintains that this argument is
confused. If we are not responsible there is
no moral fault, in which case God cannot be held
responsible for our moral faults. Oakes replies
that while (1) "God's causal sufficiency exoner-
ates His creatures from moral responsibility
for their actions" is incompatible with (2)
"God is morally responsible for the morally evil
actions of His creatures," it is not incompatible
with (3) "God is responsible for the moral evil
in the world." On the view under consideration,
God is the voluntary cause of the injuries which
we inflict. Hence, while there may be no moral
evil in the world for which we are responsible,
there appears to be moral evil in the world for
which God-is responsible, viz., that which He
commits through us. Hence, the problem is not
resolved.

510 _____. "God, Suffering and Conclusive Evidence," Sophia, XIV (July, 1975), 16-20.

Consider the following triad: (1) Evil exists,
(2) God exists, (3) God does not have a morally
sufficient reason for permitting evil. Pike
(# 516 below) argues that (3) entails the falsity

of the conjunction of (1) and (2). Hence, if (3)
was logically necessary, (1) and (2) would be
logically incompatible, and so evil would constitute a conclusive objection to God's existence.
Since, however, (3) is not necessary, (1) does
not provide a conclusive reason for rejecting
(2). Oakes points out that even if (3) is contingent, it still follows that the conjunction
of (1) and (2) is false (though not logically
false), and that, therefore, if (1) is true,
(2) is false. Hence, even if (3) is not necessary, (1) can still provide a conclusive reason
for rejecting (2) (and will do so if [3] is true).
It may of course be impossible for us to come
to know that (3) is true and that evil is, therefore, a conclusive objection to God's existence,
but epistemic impossibility should not be confused with logical impossibility.

511 Olding, A. "Finite and Infinite Gods," Sophia,
     VI (April, 1967), 3-7.

This essay contains a rather curious argument.
God can create more than one world. One would,
therefore, expect Him to create not only the
best world but also all good worlds. It follows
that if our world is a good world, the fact
that it is not the best world does not count
against God's goodness. ("World" is being used
in the sense of "cosmos" -- a set of things and
events which are lawfully interconnected in a
common space and time -- and not in the sense
of "logically possible world.")

512 Penelhum, Terence. "Divine Goodness and the Problem of Evil," _Relig Stud_, 2 (October, 1966),
95-107.

Penelhum argues that it is not enough for the
theist to show that the existence of God and
the existence of evil are logically compatible,
and to adopt an agnostic attitude towards any
particular theodicy. The very nature of his
position precludes certain theodicies (e.g.,
those which would limit God's power). In particular, the theist is logically forced to interpret God's goodness in terms of his own moral
standards. It follows that not only is the
theist committed to saying that God has a good
reason for permitting evil, he is also committed
to the view that these reasons are the sorts
of reasons which are acceptable within the
theist's moral system. All of this is rather
plausible. What is less plausible is Penelhum's
contention that these considerations imply that
the theist is committed to the view that evils
are necessary for "certain spiritual states in
his creatures, who have, to participate in these
states, to be capable of free choice."

513 _____. _Religion and Rationality, An Introduction to the Philosophy of Religion._ New
York: Random House, 1971. Pp. 223-52, esp.
237-40 and 247-51.

The Problem of Evil is discussed in chapters
sixteen and seventeen. While the discussion
as a whole is not particularly original, two
sections are worth examining. Pages 237-240
contain some astute observations on the claim
that evils are necessary conditions of certain
character traits which are highly valued in

331

the Christian tradition, and pages 247-251 summarize the argument presented in the author's
"Divine Goodness and the Problem of Evil" (#
512 above).

514 Pike, Nelson Craft. "God and Evil: A Reconsid-
      eration," Ethics, LXVIII (January, 1958), 116-24.

      A reply to Aiken's "God and Evil" (# 440 above).
      The "theological thesis" and the "ethical thesis"
      are not inconsistent if, e.g., the existence of
      some evil is logically necessary or if God has
      or can have a good reason for permitting evil.
      Within a theological context, the theological
      and ethical theses are axiomatic. It follows
      from these axioms that there is a good reason
      for evil whether we can discover it or not.
      The discovery of that reason is not, however,
      crucial for theology. Within a philosophical
      context, we must weigh the considerations for the
      theological thesis against the fact that we are
      unable to explain many evils. Whether the fact
      that we are unable to explain many evils should
      lead us to reject the theological thesis depends
      upon the strength of the arguments for the exis-
      tence of God. Pike concludes by observing that
      since the two theses are consistent there is,
      or should be, no conflict of attitudes in a
      person who adheres to both of them.

515 _____, ed. God and Evil, Readings on the
      Theological Problem of Evil. (Contemporary
      Perspectives in Philosophy Series.) Englewood
      Cliffs, New Jersey: Prentice-Hall, Inc., 1964.
      viii + 114 pp.

      This useful anthology reproduces four important
      recent essays -- McCloskey's "God and Evil,"

Mackie's "Evil and Omnipotence," Pike's "Hume on Evil," and Smart's "Omnipotence, Evil and Supermen" (#s 497 and 501 above and #s 516 and 543 below).

516   . "Hume on Evil," Phil Rev, LXXII (April, 1963), 180-97. (Reprinted in # 515 above, pp. 85-102.)

In this rather widely discussed essay, Pike argues that in order to show that the theist is inconsistent when he asserts both that evil exists and that God exists, the critic must show that it is necessarily true that God has no morally sufficient reasons 'for permitting evil. It is also argued that if the theist has independent reasons for believing that God exists (an a priori proof or "reasons of the heart"), then the search for God's (morally sufficient) reasons has no crucial importance for the theist. If, on the other hand, theism is regarded as an explanatory hypothesis which is introduced to account for the facts of common experience, then evil is a recalcitrant datum and the search for a plausible account of God's (morally sufficient) reasons is crucially important.

517 Plantinga, Alvin Carl. "The Free Will Defense," Philosophy in America. Edited by Max Black. (Muirhead Library of Philosophy.) London: Allen and Unwin; Ithaca, New York: Cornell University Press, 1965. Pp. 204-20.

Perhaps the most carefully worked out and important modern version of the Free Will Defense. If freedom involves indeterminism, God cannot without contradiction determine or bring it about that a person always freely does what

is right. Why, though, doesn't God instantiate
free beings who He foresees would freely (and,
therefore, independently of His determination)
act well if they were created? Plantinga points
out that whether or not a possible person would
freely do so and so if he were created is contingent. Hence, it is logically possible that
it be contingently true that all possible persons
would freely fail if they were created. If this
contingent fact were to obtain, God could not
create persons who would always freely act well.
Plantinga's argument has many merits not the
least of which is that it clearly brings out
the fact that the Free Will Defense must employ
the indeterminist's concept of freedom, and the
fact that the Free Will Defense introduces certain contingent limitations which make it impossible for God to do certain things which it is
logically possible for Him to do and which He
might wish to do (e.g., create beings who always
freely act well). In evaluating Plantinga's
argument it is important to remember that he
is not asserting that it is in fact contingently
true that all possible persons would freely
fail if they were created. He is only arguing
that since this statement is possibly true and
since if it were true God would (given the value
of free persons and the good which they bring
about) have a good reason for creating a world
which contains evil, the existence of God and
the existence of evil are logically compatible.
Plantinga's versions of the Free Will Defense
have evoked many responses. See especially those
of Adams, Botterill, Rowe, Steuer, Wainwright
and Windt (#s 433, 434 and 445 above, and #s
533, 548, 553 and 559 below). "The Free Will

Defense" is reprinted in God and Other Minds
(# 518 below).

518 _____. God and Other Minds, A Study of the
Rational Justification of Belief in God. (Con-
temporary Philosophy.) Ithaca, New York: Cornell
University Press, 1967. Pp. 115-55.

Chapter 5 discusses the claim that the existence
of God and the existence of evil are logically
incompatible. "God exists and is omnipotent,
omniscient and all good" and "evil exists" are
not themselves formally incompatible. To show
that theism is logically incoherent, the "atheologian" must introduce a proposition which is
either necessary or essential to theism, and
which, when taken together with the proposition
that God exists, is omnipotent, omniscient and
all good, entails either that evil does not exist
or that some unjustified evil exists. Plantinga
considers several propositions of this sort
(e.g., "A good being elimates all the evil it
can," "Any good G which entails an evil E is
or is equivalent to a conjunctive state of affairs
of which one conjunct is E and the other a good
that [1] outweighs and is logically independent
of E, and [2] is better than G"). In each case,
Plantinga succeeds in showing that the proposition
in question is neither necessary nor essential
to theism. Chapter 6 reproduces "The Free Will
Defense" (# 517 above) and concludes with an
interesting section in which Plantinga argues
that since evil is logically compatible with
God's existence the existence of evil does not
disconfirm God's existence. (To reach this result Plantinga employs the principle that if
p disconfirms q it disconfirms the conjunction

of q with any other proposition. Hence, if "evil
exists" disconfirms "God exists," it disconfirms
"God exists and evil exists and a world containing
moral good is better that one which does not and
all possible sets of free persons whose members
freely perform more good than evil has members
who perform evil." Since "evil exists" does
not disconfirm the latter, it does not disconfirm
the former. For a critique of this argument
see Richman, # 528 below.)

519 _____. God, Freedom and Evil. New York:
Harper and Row Pub., Inc., 1974. Pp. 7-64.

The first half of this book contains a useful
but simplified presentation of the author's work
on the Problem of Evil. Most of this section
is devoted to an explication of the version of the
Free Will Defense which appears in The Nature
of Necessity (# 521 below).

520 _____. "The Incompatibility of Freedom with
Determinism: A Reply," Phil Forum, II (New
Series), (Fall, 1970), 141-8.

Plantinga argues that Tomberlin (# 550 below)
has failed to show that freedom and causal determinism are compatible. In order for an action
to be free either it or one of its causal ances=
tors must be undetermined. Hence, although for
any action it is perhaps possible that it be both
free and causally determined (suppose it is causally determined by some preceding choice or performance which is itself undetermined), it does
not follow that it is possible that all of an
agent's actions are causally determined and yet
that some actions of that agent are free.

521 _____. The Nature of Necessity. (Clarendon
    Library of Logic and Philosophy.) Oxford: The
    Clarendon Press, 1974. Pp. 164-95.

    Chapter IX contains a significant development
    of the argument originally presented in the au-
    thor's "The Free Will Defense" (# 517 above).
    This new formulation employs ideas about possible
    worlds developed in the book's earlier chapters.
    Of particular interest are the proof that given
    the contingent truth (or falsity) of counterfac-
    tuals stating what individuals would freely do
    in various circumstances, there are possible
    worlds which God could not have actualized, and
    the introduction of the notion of trans-world
    depravity. (Roughly, an individual exhibits
    trans-world depravity if it would act badly in
    any situation in which God is able to place it.)

522 _____. "Which Worlds Could God Have Created?"
    J Phil, LXX (October 11, 1973), 539-52.

    This very interesting paper was presented at the
    Eastern Division meetings of the American Philo-
    sophical Association on December 29, 1973. The
    argument of this paper is developed more complete-
    ly in The Nature of Necessity, chapter IX (# 521
    above). (Most of this paper is reproduced ver-
    batim in the latter.) See the replies of Rowe
    (# 534 below) and Adams (# 433 above).

523 Pontifex, Mark. "The Question of Evil," Prospects
    for Metaphysics, Essays of Metaphysical explora-
    tion. Edited by Ian Ramsey. London: George
    Allen & Unwin Ltd., 1961. Pp. 121-37.

    Pontifex argues that while God is the ultimate
    cause of good, moral evil or failure is

                        337

essentially negative and, therefore, requires
no cause. It is initiated by the creature and
permitted by God. For a fuller and more adequate
statement of this thesis see (e.g.) Maritain's
God and the Permission of Evil (# 504 above).
Also see Hudson's reply (# 479 above).

524 Puccetti, Roland. "The Loving God -- Some Obser-
     vations on John Hick's Evil and the God of Love,"
     Relig Stud, 2 (April, 1967), 255-68.

Puccetti describes four cases of innocent suffering and argues (1) that this suffering cannot
be justified by any morally good consequences
which it has for the sufferer (for it has no
such consequences), (2) that the fact that the
sufferers will be compensated in another life does
nothing to alter the fact that they have been
treated unjustly, and (3) that even if a world
with some dangers and evils is better than a world
without them, it does not follow that our world
is better than a world without the evils which
he has described. Finally, just as the goodness
of Eichmann cannot be defended by appealing to
the logical possibility that he had morally good
reasons for the evil which he committed, so the
goodness of God cannot be defended by appealing
to the logical possibility that God has a morally
sufficient reason for permitting the innocent
to suffer. (It is not clear, however, that the
cases are parallel. Some theists believe that
they have good independent reasons for believing
that God exists and is good, and they believe
that they are able to supply theodicies which
provide plausible explanations of much apparently
unjustified suffering. If these theists are
correct, then the fact that they are unable to

provide plausible explanations for all evils
may not present an insoluble difficulty.) Puccetti's overall argument is weakened by his failure to consider the fact that innocent suffering
may have morally good consequences for others.
See the responses by John Hick (# 475 above)
and Keith Yandell (# 565 below).

525 Quinn, Michael Sean. "Mustn't God Create for the
     Best?" J Crit Anal, V (July/October, 1973),
     2-8.

A reply to Robert Adams' "Must God Create for the
Best?" (# 435 above). Quinn concedes that the
creation of a world which is less than the best
may be the expression of a virtue (viz., grace),
but argues that to show this is insufficient.
One must also show that there is no other virtue
which is such that God's creating a world which
is less than the best would provide evidence
that He does not possess that virtue. "Benevolence" is defined as the disposition to choose the
morally best action of any given type, and it
is argued that if God creates a world which is
less than the best, then He cannot be said to
possess that virtue in its perfection. Quinn
assumes that the moral value of creative acts
is solely determined by the value of what is
created and this may, of course, be questioned.

526 Reichenbach, Bruce Robert. "Natural Evils and
     Natural Law: A Theodicy for Natural Evils,"
     Int Phil Quart, XVI (June, 1976), 179-96.

Although not highly original, this is a better
than average defense of the contention that God
is justified in permitting natural evil because
the occurrence of natural evil is a necessary

339

consequence of the operation of natural laws.
The principal objections to this defense are
(1) that God could have prevented natural evil
by miraculously intervening in nature, and (2)
that God could have prevented natural evil by
creating a different natural order. Reichenbach
has no difficulty in showing that rational foresight and moral action would be impossible if
the world exhibited no regularity. It would
seem, however, that it would be possible for
God to intervene frequently enough to either
eliminate or significantly curtail natural evil
and at the same time preserve sufficient regularity to make rational foresight and moral action
possible. Reichenbach replies that the atheologian wants to have it two ways. When he first
raises the Problem of Evil, the atheologian
emphasizes the tremendous quantity of natural
evil and yet when he formulates the present objection the atheologian minimizes the quantity
of natural evil, arguing that it could be prevented by miraculous intervention "without [sig-
nificantly] altering rational predictibility."
Reichenbach makes two points with respect to
the second objection. (1) To be human is to
be part of a natural order. If man is part of
a natural order he will interact with other elements in that order and the interaction with
these elements will sometimes be propitious and
sometimes non-propitious. (How does Reichenbach
know this?) (2) We simply do not know that there
are alternative natural systems which would if
instantiated both contain sentient and physical
moral agents and result in less natural evil.

527   Resnick, Lawrence.   "God and the Best Possible
      World," <u>Amer</u> <u>Phil</u> <u>Quart</u>, 10 (October, 1973),
      313-7.

Resnick presents the following argument: If
God exists, He necessarily creates the best possible world. God necessarily exists. Hence,
the best possible world necessarily exists and
all other worlds are impossible. An yet, "if
this is the best of all possible worlds, then
worlds worse than this one are logically possible." It follows that (a certain form of)
classical theism is incoherent. Resnick's argument is not fully persuasive. If "best possible
world" is construed as "a world than which none
is better," then from the fact that there is a
best possible world, it does not follow that
there is a worse one. While Resnick admits that
"best possible world" can be construed in this
way, it is not clear that he sees that this concession damages his argument. Resnick also fails
to consider the possibility that the notion of
a best possible world is incoherent. (Many classical theists -- e.g., Aquinas -- supposed that
for any world there is a better.) Nevertheless,
Resnick does have hold of a real problem. It
would seem that if God is to be an approriate
subject of moral praise, He must choose between
alternatives which are genuinely possible and
which are unequal in moral value, and yet if
theists like Leibniz are correct, there are no
such alternatives. (This appears to be one form
of a more general problem -- how can God be a
praiseworthy moral agent if He <u>cannot</u> act immoral-
ly?)

528 Richman, Robert. "Plantinga, God and (Yet) Other
      Minds," <u>Austl J Phil</u>, 50 (May, 1972), pp. 46-50.

      Plantinga has argued (# 518 above) that if <u>q</u>
      disconfirms <u>p</u>, then it disconfirms any proposi-
      tion that entails <u>p</u>. Since "evil exists" does
      not disconfirm the conjunction of "God exists"
      and certain other propositions (those employed
      in the Free Will Defense) and since that conjunc-
      tion entails "God exists," it follows that "evil
      exists" does not disconfirm "God exists." Richman
      points out that this pattern of reasoning leads
      to apparently absurd results. Since "John has
      a heavy beard" does not disconfirm "John shaved
      this morning and John applied a new preparation
      which grows a beard in twenty minutes," it follows
      (if Plantinga is correct) that "John has a heavy
      beard" does not disconfirm "John shaved this
      morning."

529 Ricoeur, Paul. "Guilt, Ethics and Religion," <u>Talk
      of God</u>. (Royal Institute of Philosophy Lectures,
      <u>Vol. 2</u>, 1967-1968.) London, Melbourne [etc.]:
      Macmillan; New York: St. Martin's Press, 1969.
      Pp. 100-17. (Reprinted in # 1012 below, pp.
      425-39.)

      An examination of (1) the symbolism of stain,
      sin and guilt, (2) of a type of ethical reflection
      which (a) interprets evil as a consequence of
      freedom and discovers its freedom in reflecting
      upon evil, which (b) discovers the relation be-
      tween obligation and freedom, and which (c)(à la
      Kant in <u>Religion Within the Limits of Reason
      Alone</u>) finds that an evil for which one is somehow
      responsible precedes each act of freedom, and
      (3) a type of religious reflection which thinks
      of freedom and evil "under the sign of hope,"

i.e., which envisages an eschatological conquest
of evil and the "achievement of totality."

530 _____. The Symbolism of Evil. Translated
from the French by Emerson Buchanan. (Religious
Perspectives Series, 17.) New York: Harper and
Row Publishers, Inc., 1967. xv + 357 pp.

Ricoeur (1) examines the notion of confession,
the symbol of defilement, the idea of sin and
the concept of guilt, and (2) considers myths
which have been introduced to account for the
origin of evil -- stories of struggles between
a divine king and chaos, the tragic theology of
Aeschylus and the Greeks, the story of Adam,
and the "Orphic" myth of the exiled soul. While
this brilliant study does not attempt to provide
a philosophical solution to the Problem of Evil,
it deepens our understanding of the ways in which
evil has been interpreted in the religious traditions of the West.

531 Rosenberg, Jay Frank. "The Problem of Evil Revisited, A Reply to Schlesinger," J Value Inq, IV
(Fall, 1970), 212-8.

A critique of the argument presented by Schlesinger in "the Problem of Evil and the Problem of
Suffering" (# 540 below). It is argued that although Schlesinger has shown that God cannot be
faulted for having failed to create a world which
he ought to have created, He can be faulted for
having created a world which He ought not to
have created. Even though the prescriptive standards which are to be applied to God's creative
activity are unclear, the principles of prohi-
bition which are to be applied to God's creative
activity are clear. God ought not to create

intrinsic bads (e.g., suffering) and yet He has
done so. God ought not to create worlds in which
creatures exist who are not only less happy than
other possible beings but who are also less happy
than they themselves might be. Again, God has
done so. See Schlesinger's reply (# 539 below).

532   Ross, James Francis. Philosophical Theology.
      Indianapolis and New York: The Bobbs-Merrill
      Co., Inc., 1969. Pp. 222-78.

Chapter 6 contains a very interesting dissolution
of the Problem of Evil. Levels of reality are
distinguished. Roughly, a is on a lower level
of reality than b if and only if a belongs to
a class of things each member of which depends
for its existence and qualities upon some member
of a class including b. Dreams are on a lower
level of reality than dreamers, Mr. Pickwick
belongs to a lower level of reality than Dickens,
and (according to classical theism) the world
is on a lower level of reality than God. Now,
it appears to be false that b is accountable
for the evil which he has produced at a lower
level if b could have prevented it from occurring
and if the situation which would have obtained
if b had done so would be better than the situation which does in fact obtain. (A novelist,
for example, is not held morally accountable
for the wicked deeds of his characters or for the
suffering and ugliness which characterize the
world which his characters inhabit even though
he could have written a story in which these
things did not occur and even though such a story
might have been as good or better than the story
he did write.) It would seem to follow that
God cannot be held accountable for the evil which

the world contains even though he could have
prevented it from occurring and even though he
could have created a better world. There have
been several attacks on Ross's position. (See,
for example, Mavrodes and Oakes, #s 507 and 509
above). However, even though Ross's argument
may be unpersuasive, it is not clear that these
attacks have been successful.

533   Rowe, William Leonard. "God and Other Minds,"
       Nous, III (September, 1969), pp. 271-7.

Section II discusses Plantinga's solution of the
Problem of Evil (# 518 above). Rowe constructs
a version of Mackie's argument which is designed
to show that (1) "God is omnipotent, omniscient
and good" entails (2) "No free person created
by God ever performs a morally evil action,"
and which employs the following premiss: (3)
If God is omnipotent, then God can instantiate
persons containing the property of always freely
doing what is right. Rowe argues that although
Plantinga has shown that this premiss's consequent is contingent, he has not shown that the
premiss as a whole is contingent. (If [3] must
be added to [1] in order to deduce [2] from [1]
and if [3] is contingent, then [1] does not entail
[2].) Indeed, given his definition of "omnipotence" (God can do whatever is such that the proposition that He does it is consistent), (3) is
necessarily true. Two comments are in order.
First, it is not clear that Plantinga wishes to
adhere to this definition of omnipotence. Second-
ly, given classical theism which insists that
God exists necessarily and possesses His properties necessarily, the antecedent of (3) is necessary. If follows that if the consequent is

indeed contingent, then the consequent is not entailed by the antecedent and so (3) is not necessary.

534 _____. "Plantinga on Possible Worlds and Evil," J Phil, LXX (October 11, 1973), 554-5.

Abstract of a reply to Plantinga's "Which Worlds Could God Have Created?" (# 522 above). Rowe points out that Plantinga's argument rests upon the controversial assumption that compatibilism is false, and that it is necessarily true that whatever a person is caused to do, he does not do freely. Rowe distinguishes the logical Problem of Evil from the epistemological Problem of Evil. One should concede that "God exists" and "evil exists" are consistent. However, even though it is possible that any other world which God could have actualized would be worse that our own, it is highly implausible. The "variety and profusion of evil" together with "our reasonable judgments as to what the free agents in our world would have done under slightly different circumstances provide rational grounds" for believing that theism is false.

535 Royce, Josiah. The Problem of Christianity. Lectures Delivered at the Lowell Institute in Boston, and at Manchester College, Oxford, by Josiah Royce. 2 vols. New York: The Macmillan Company, 1913.

An interesting attempt to demythologize the Christian drama of sin and atonement. (See especially Lectures III, IV, V and VI.) Conflict between the individual and social will is inevitable, but this form of "original" sin can be overcome by freely given loyalty to a beloved community.

346

Betrayal or treason then appears as the one un-
forgivable sin. The sin of treason can, however,
be atoned for provided that someone makes the
act of betrayal a condition of good, provided
that just this sin is necessary to the good in
question, and provided that "the world as transformed by this creative deed is better than it
would have been . . . had that deed of treason
not been done at all." It is a "postulate of the
highest form of human spirituality" that "no
baseness or cruelty of treason [is] so deep or
so tragic but that loyal love shall be able in
due time to oppose to just that deed of treason
its fitting deed of atonement."

536 _____. The Sources of Religious Insight,
Lectures Delivered before Lake Forest College
on the Foundation of the late William Bross,
by Josiah Royce. New York: Charles Scribner's
Sons, 1912. Pp. 213-54.

Lecture VI returns to the Problem of Evil. We
experience evil in two ways. Some evils appear
to us to be unmitigated surds which should simply
be eliminated. There are other ills, however,
which "we remove only in so far as we assimilate
them, idealize them, take them up into the plan
of our lives, give them meaning, set them in
their place in the whole." The second sort of
experience provides some insight into the way
in which all evils may be transformed and spiritualized by a "world-embracing insight."

537 _____. The World and the Individual: Gifford
Lectures Delivered before the University of Aber-
deen. Second Series: Nature, Man and the Moral
Order. London: Macmillan and Co., Ltd; New York:
The Macmillan Company, 1901. Pp.·335-452.

In lectures VIII, IX and X one of the major Absolute Idealists provides an interesting treatment of the Problem of Evil. All finite facts
are evil when viewed in detachment from the whole
of experience, for when considered by themselves
these facts are partial and their meaning is
incomplete. On the other hand, since each finite
fact belongs to the whole, no finite fact is
totally evil. Evil is rooted in the finite will
-- more specifically, in the gap between a plan
or ideal and its fulfilment, or in evil intent
(a deliberate shifting of attention from the
good as one knows it). While these evils are
real, they are justified by their place in the
whole. Finality (the attainment of a goal) "means
a consciousness that a certain process wins its
own completion. But this process is essentially
a struggle towards the goal." Hence, the consciousness of completeness presupposes a prior
consciousness of incompleteness or dissatisfaction
(and, thus, natural evil). A morally evil deed
is evil in so far as it expresses the agent's
will, but this same moral evil is good in so
far as it is "supplemented" and "overruled" by
some other will. Perfection is won "through the
conquest . . . [-- by the agent himself or by
some other agent -- of the] evil doer and his
deed." Thus, cowardly dread is "atoned for"
by the courage which endures and overcomes it.
Since a complex state of affairs which consists
of an evil "being held by the throat" is more
valuable than related goods which do not involve
the conquest of evil, the evil which is a logically necessary component of that complex state of
affairs contributes to the perfection of the
whole. Royce's "solution" to the Problem of Evil

348

is characterized by one more significant feature. Since the Absolute is self-conscious and includes the finite self-consciousness of each of us, the Absolute includes our suffering and evil and in that sense shares it. At the same time, because the Absolute comprehends the whole of experience and not a mere fragment of the whole, it also includes the victory over those evils. See Jefferson's critique of Royce (# 480 above).

538 Schlesinger, George. "Omnipotence and Evil: An Incoherent Problem," Sophia, IV (October, 1965), 21-4.

A response to LaPara's criticism (# 494 above) of his "The Problem of Evil and the Problem of Suffering" (# 540 below). Schlesinger suggests that LaPara's first point rests upon an arbitrary distinction between positive and negative evil, and that his third point paradoxically implies that God would be blameworthy for doing what is more desirable (creating a world) but not blameworthy for doing what is less desirable (refusing to create).

539 _____. "On the Possibility of the Best of All Possible Worlds," J Value Inq, IV (Fall, 1970), 229-32.

This reply to Shea and Rosenberg (# 542 below and # 531 above) concentrates upon the latter. The most important thing to emerge from Schlesinger's discussion is his admission that the argument which he presented in "The Problem of Evil and the Problem of Suffering" (# 540 below) may not provide a complete solution to the Problem of Evil. While that argument disposes of the claim that God should be faulted simply because

349

He did not create a better or happier world,
one must at least consider the possibility that
God should be faulted for violating some other
norm (e.g., norms of justice or truthfulness).
God is not obligated to maximize happiness or
intrinsic value, but He is obligated to be just,
truthful, etc.

540 _____. "The Problem of Evil and the Problem
of Suffering," Amer Phil Quart, 1 (July, 1964),
244-7.

A very important paper. Schlesinger argues that
for any world which exhibits a certain degree
of happiness, there is another world which exhibits a greater degree of happiness. Since it
is logically impossible to produce a world with
an unsurpassable degree of happiness, God cannot
be faulted for having failed to do so. Nor can
God be faulted for having failed to create a
world which is happier than the world which He
did create. Since any world can be surpassed
with respect to happiness, no matter what world
God created, God could be criticized for having
failed to create a world which is happier than
the world which He in fact created. A criticism
which is always in place (which it is impossible
to evade) is never in place. It follows that
God cannot be faulted for having created a world
which exhibits just that degree of happiness which
this world exhibits. It is worth observing that
if for every possible world there is another
possible world which is better, Schlesinger's
argument can be generalized to dispose of the
claim that God should be faulted because He could
have produced a better world than He in fact
produced. See the critical responses of

Khatchadourian, LaPara, Rosenberg and Shea (#s 489, 494 and 531 above and # 542 below), and Schlesinger's responses to the last three of these critiques (#s 538 and 539 above). Cf. the "Thomistic" solutions of Journet and Joyce (#s 482 and 483 above).

541 Scriven, Michael. Primary Philosophy. New York: McGraw-Hill Book Co., 1966. Pp. 158-64.

While Scriven's discussion is unoriginal, it is an effective expression of the incredulity with which the standard defenses are often met. Scriven insists that theists employ a double standard, tolerating behavior in God which they would not tolerate in human beings.

542 Shea, Winslow. "God, Evil and Professor Schlesinger," J Value Inq, IV (Fall, 1970), 219-28.

A critique of the argument which Schlesinger presents in "The Problem of Evil and the Problem of Suffering," and defends in "Omnipotence and Evil: An Incoherent Problem" (#s 540 and 538 above). Shea's two most telling points are the following: (1) If there is no upper logical limit to happiness, then classical theism is mistaken when it supposes that God's happiness cannot be surpassed. (But cf. Hartshorne's notion that God's present happiness can indeed be surpassed but only by His own future happiness.) (2) If for every world there is a world which is better and a world which is worse (or a world which is happier and a world which is less happy) then while it may be true that God cannot be blamed for not having created a world which is better than the world which He did create, it

is also true that He cannot be praised for having
created a world which is better than other worlds
which He might have created. Just as blame which
is always in order is never in order, so praise
which is always in order is never in order.

543   Smart, Ninian. "Omnipotence, Evil and Supermen,"
      Philosophy, XXXVI (April and July, 1961), 188-95.
      (Reprinted in #515 above, pp. 103-12.)

      This interesting article has been widely dis-
      cussed. Smart distinguishes the thesis that
      determinism is compatible with free will (the
      Compatibility Thesis) from the thesis that God
      could have created men wholly good (the Utopia
      Thesis), and argues that the Compatibility Thesis
      does not entail the Utopia Thesis. Moral concepts
      are embedded in the "cosmic status quo." There
      may appear to be no contradiction in the idea
      of a world constructed so as to ensure that men
      always act well. However, as soon as we begin
      to fill in the details and attempt to concretely
      imagine what these worlds would be like, it be-
      comes increasingly less clear that the concepts
      of goodness or humanity apply to the creatures
      which inhabit them. If "men" were built differ-
      ently or if the world was governed by radically
      different laws, the concepts of goodness and
      humanity would have no purchase. See Flew's
      discussion of this article (# 463 above), and
      Smart's reply (# 545 below).

544   _____. Philosophers and Religious Truth.
      London: SCM Press Ltd., 1964. Pp. 167-96.

      Chapter VI contains a moderately interesting
      exposition of the thesis that evil is an

inevitable product of an evolving cosmos which exhibits a certain amount of regularity and autonomy, and which is able to serve as a theatre for the creation of value.

545 _____. "Probably," Philosophy, XXXVII (January, 1962), 60.

A reply to Flew's "Are Ninian Smart's Temptations Irresistible?" (# 463 above). Smart's most significant point is, perhaps, the following. If temptations were always successfully overcome, agents would be sure of the outcome in advance, from which it would follow that their struggles against temptation would be unreal. If, however, their struggles against temptation are unreal, their temptations are not genuine.

546 Sontag, Frederick. The God of Evil: An Argument for the Existence of the Devil. New York, Evanston and London: Harper and Row, Publishers, 1970. x + 173 pp.

It is suggested that instead of accepting negativity and evil as evidence against God, we should allow a consideration of these things to determine our concept of God, asking "what sort of God could hide Himself behind evil and negativity?" If we ask this question it becomes immediately clear that any God who exists is a God who does not depend upon us (and, therefore, need not make His existence plain to us), who rejects "simple clarity" and prefers indirection, who can tolerate the existence of unnecessary suffering, violence and destruction, etc. A consideration of the roots of atheism leads to a conception of God in which "non-being is discovered to be the foundation of being." It is

because of the presence of non-being in God that
non-being can appear in the world. This non-
being is to be understood in terms of God's radical freedom, -- a freedom to give being to any
possibility. Since what is actual, the nature
of the laws which govern being, and the relative
priority of values are all determined by God's
decision, non-being (or possibility), freedom,
and "existence" (in the Existentialist's sense)
may be said to be prior to being, necessity and
essence. (The world's radical contingency -- the
fact that other orders of being, necessity and
value are equally possible -- can lead to atheism
[cf. Sartre's experience of meaninglessness or
nausea in the face of the given, or the anguished
recognition that a better world is just as possible as our own] but it can also lead to belief
in a God who is able to account for its existence.) A consideration of evil suggests the
conception of a God who is subject to anguish
in the face of possibility, who confronts real
evil and suffering, but whose power and control
are so great that He is neither overcome by anguish in the face of possibility nor by evil.
Sontag's book has met with very mixed reactions.
However, in spite of a certain looseness of argument, it is suggestive. In its exaltation of
God's power and will and in its claim that God's
decision determines even such necessities as the
Principle of Non-Contradiction, Sontag's book
belongs to the Voluntarist tradition in theology.
(In view of Sontag's insistence that we must
begin with the fact of evil, it is worth observing
that the Voluntarist tradition frequently paints
a very stark picture of the misery, horror, and
sinfulness of human existence.)

547 Stahl, Roland. "Professor Brightman's Theory of
the Given," Relig Life, XXIII (1954), 537-48.

This article provides a good account of the
sources of Brightman's concept of a finite God.
(See # 447 above.) These include a consideration
of the waste which occurs in the process of evolution, the notion that personality must be finite, the conviction that life necessarily
involves tension and struggle, and the belief
that the concept of a finite God is an appropriate
expression of at least some varieties of religious experience.

548 Steuer, Axel D. "Once More on the Free Will Defence," Relig Stud, 10 (September, 1974), 301-11.

Steuer argues that the versions of the Free Will
Defense which have been provided by Alvin Plantinga and Stephen T. Davis (#s 517 and 455 above)
employ the indeterminists' conception of freedom and, thus, suppose that in creating free
beings, God creates beings which He cannot subsequently control. This would appear to be incompatible with His omnipotence. Mackie's paradox (# 94 above) has not been fully faced, viz.,
that if God cannot create beings He cannot control, then He is not omnipotent, and if He can
create such beings, then -- once again -- He
is not omnipotent (presumably because if He can
create such beings they are possible, and the
possibility of beings which He cannot control
is precluded by His omnipotence). Steuer points
out that proposed solutions of the paradox concentrate on the first horn of the dilemma, arguing
that since it is logically impossible for there
to be beings which God (an essentially omnipotent

being) cannot control, it is logically impossible
for God to create such beings and that, hence,
the fact that God cannot do so does not count
against His omnipotence. Steuer argues that
this solution is not available to Plantinga or
Davis. If it is impossible for there to be beings
which God cannot control, then free beings are
impossible and the Free Will Defense collapses.
(Notice an ambiguity: God cannot control free
beings while at the same time preserving their
freedom, but He can control the beings who happen
to be free even though if he were to control them,
He would destroy their freedom. Hence, the identification of free beings and beings which God
cannot control, is suspect.) Steuer, in effect,
proposes that we concentrate on the second horn
of the dilemma, arguing that the task which God
is unable to perform (upon the supposition that
He creates beings which He cannot control, viz.,
free beings) is not a logically possible task.
To control these beings God would have to make
their decisions for them, in which case they would
not be genuinely independent (or better: in which
case their decisions would not be genuinely free).
Hence, God's inability to perform the relevant
task is compatible with His omnipotence.

549 Tennant, Frederick Robert. Philosophical Theology.
     Vol. II. The World, the Soul and God. Cambridge:
     Cambridge University Press, 1930. Pp. 180-208.

     Chapter VII contains an influential discussion
     of the Problem of Evil. Recognizing the neces-
     sity of a plausible theodicy for any sort of
     "empirical theism" (on this point see Pike's
     "Hume on Evil," # 516 above), Tennant proceeds
     to argue (1) that the best world is not the

happiest world but a world which exhibits developing moral life, (2) that such a world must
be an evolutionary world which is characterized
by uniformity and which contains genuinely free
agents, and (3) that evil will be necessarily
included in any world which exhibits these features.

550   Tomberlin, James Edward.   "Plantinga's Puzzles
      about God and Other Minds," Phil Forum, I (New
      Series), (Spring, 1969), pp. 372-5.

      A discussion of Plantinga's Free Will Defense
      (# 517 above). Tomberlin attempts to show that,
      contrary to Plantinga, it is possible for an
      action to be both causally determined and free.
      See Plantinga's reply (# 520 above).

551   Trethowan, Illtyd.   "Dr. Hick and the Problem of
      Evil," J Theol Stud, XVIII (New Series), (October,
      1967), 407-16.

      Trethowan argues (1) that Hick makes an unduly
      sharp distinction between Augustinian-type theo-
      dicies and Irenaean-type theodicies in view of
      the fact that one rarely appears in total isola-
      tion from the other, and (2) that Hick is not
      totally fair to Augustinian-type theodicies.
      His main objection to Hick's Irenaean-type theo-
      dicy is that it involves the contention that
      God arranges evil in order to produce a great
      good. Of some interest. See Hick's reply (#
      476 above).

552   Wainwright, William Judson.   "Christian Theism and
      the Free Will Defense: A Problem," Int J Phil
      Relig, VI (Winter, 1975), 243-50.

The Free Will Defense, as normally presented,
presupposes that moral agency involves the freedom to act badly. This is incompatible with classical theism which insists that God is a moral
agent who is unable to sin. Several arguments
for the assertion that God is unable to sin are
examined and found wanting. It is conceded,
however, that if classical theism is correct
in supposing that any being who is God is essentially divine, then it does indeed follow that
God cannot sin. The Free Will Defense can be
modified to accommodate the doctrine of God's
essential sinlessness, but when modified it loses
at least some of its plausibility.

553   _____. "Freedom and Omnipotence," Nous, II
     (August, 1968), 293-301.

If Plantinga's Free Will Defense (# 517 above)
is correct, then, for any possible free person,
it is contingently true that that person will
freely act in certain ways if it is created.
Wainwright argues (1) that God cannot constitute
contingent facts of this sort, (2) that although
it is logically necessary that there be some
facts of this sort, it is simply a "brute fact"
that the particular set of facts of this kind
which does obtain obtains, and (3) that while
facts of this sort impose limits upon what God
can do, it is not clear that their existence is
incompatible with His omnipotence.

554   _____. "God and the Necessity of Physical
     Evil," Sophia, XI (July, 1972), 16-9.

In "God and Evil" (# 497 above) H. J. McCloskey
presents an argument which purports to show that

the theist is inconsistent if he maintains both
that we have an obligation to reduce physical
evil and increase the amount of physical good
and that physical evil is necessary for a greater
good. This paper attempts to establish the un-
soundness of McCloskey's argument. It is also
suggested that if McCloskey is correct, and "all
physical evil is necessary to a greater good"
is incompatible with "the struggle against physical evil is morally legitimate," then a God who
prizes moral struggle and moral endeavor should
permit the existence of physical evils which are
not specifically necessary to any good result.

555 Wallace, Gerald. "The Problems of Moral and Phy-
     sical Evil," Philosophy, XLVI (October, 1971),
     349-51.

     Wallace argues that it is not clear that the
     Free Will Defense can be successfully combined
     with the thesis that physical evil (defined as
     any pain, suffering, etc., which is produced
     by non-moral causes) is a logically necessary
     condition of such moral goods as compassion, cour-
     age and so on. The Free Will Defense ascribes
     much suffering and pain to the wicked choices of
     moral agents. Since the suffering and pain which
     are produced in this manner would appear to pro-
     vide a sufficient occasion for virtuous responses,
     it would seem that physical evil is not logically
     necessary for these responses.

556 Walter, Edward. "Are Actualities Prior to Possi-
     bilities?" New Scholas, XLVI (Spring, 1972),
     202-9.

     A reply to Oakes' "Actualities, Possibilities
     and Free Will Theodicy" (# 508 above). Walter

denies that our knowledge of actuality is (necessarily) epistemically prior to our knowledge of possibility.

557 Walton, Douglas Niel. "Modalities in the Free Will Defense," Relig Stud, 10 (September, 1974), 325-31.

Walton explores a contention made by Stephen T. Davis in "A Defence of the Free Will Defence" (# 455 above), viz., that "x is ∅" is incompatible with "x can be either ∅ or not-∅." Walton argues that this contention can only be made good if we employ "a deviant alethic modal logic" which contains the theorem "L*p≡p," where L* is a deviant type of necessity.

558 Watkin, Edward Ingram. "The Problem of Evil," God and the Supernatural, A Catholic Statement of the Christian Faith. Edited by Fr. Cuthbert, O.S.F.C. London, New York, [etc.]: Longmans, Green and Co., 1920. Pp. 119-62.

A better than average examination of the Problem of Evil from the standpoint of classical Roman Catholic theology. Its more interesting features include (1) a development of the claim that modern Western man is more acutely conscious of physical evil than his predecessors but less acutely conscious of the horror of moral evil, (2) a decent discussion of the contention that the universe contains more good than evil, and (3) an attempt to weave together an Augustinian-type theodicy and an Ireneaen-type theodicy. (The terms are Hick's. Watkin's attempt is of interest in view of Hick's insistence that these two theodicies are fundamentally incompatible.)

559 Windt, Peter Yale. "Plantinga's Unfortunate God,"
Phil Stud, 24 (September, 1973), 335-42.

Plantinga's Free Will Defense (# 517 above) introduces the notion that God's choices are limited
by a set of contingent facts -- the fact that
the instantiation of free person P^1 would freely
do A if it were created, the fact that the instantiation of free person P^2 would freely refrain from B if it were created, etc., etc.
These facts are not chosen by God. Neither are
they chosen by us. (While we are the authors
of those things which we freely decide to do,
we are not "responsible for the sins which other
possible persons would have committed had they
been created.") Nor are merely possible persons
the author of these facts. (Since merely possible
persons are not actual, they cannot be the authors
of anything.) It follows from these considerations that what facts of this sort obtain is a
matter of luck, fortune or fate. (This objection goes back at least to Jonathan Edwards'
Freedom of the Will.) Windt maintains that
Wainwright (# 553 above) is mistaken in supposing
that this state of affairs is compatible with
God's omnipotence. He does not, however, provide any argument to show that this is the case.

560 Wisdom, John. "God and Evil," Mind, XLIV (January,
1935), 1-20.

In this interesting and rather important essay,
Wisdom argues that evil is compatible with divine
perfection and omnipotence if the evils which
exist are logically necessary parts of good
wholes, if the goodness of these wholes is not
entirely derived from the goodness of their parts

and if the substitution of other wholes containing less evil would result in a loss of value.
Some wholes (e.g., "A's being sorry because he
believes B to have a headache") possess a value
which is not entirely derived from the value
of their parts, but do not clearly include evils.
Other wholes (e.g., "A's being sorry because B
has a headache") include evils but do not clearly
possess a value over and above the values of
their parts (which, in the example cited are
the positive value of A's being sorry because
he believes B to have a headache and the negative
value of B's headache). There are other wholes
(e.g., "A's affectionate sorrow for B's headache,"
or friends empathizing with one another's fear)
which seem to possess a value which is not entirely derived from the value of their parts
and which do include evils, but which (it would
seem) could be replaced by other wholes without
a loss in total value. There are still other
wholes (e.g., "A and B happily and affectionately
remembering the trials and triumphs of an Arctic
expedition," and certain sorts of friendship)
which include evils, possess a value which is
not entirely derived from the value of their
parts, and are among the best possible wholes.
(Wisdom observes that it is not clear that the
best world will contain only the best wholes.)

561 Yandell, Keith Edward. Basic Issues in the Philo-
     sophy of Religion. Boston: Allyn and Bacon,
     Inc., 1971. Pp. 43-65.

Chapter II contains a fairly interesting although
somewhat rambling discussion of the Problem of
Evil. (1) In a manner reminiscent of Plantinga
(# 518 above), Yandell argues that there is no

proposition which is either essential to theism, necessary, or obviously true, and which when added to the proposition that both God and evil exist, yields a contradiction. For example, "It is always good to prevent evil" is not a proposition of the required sort because there are conditions under which evils are justified. (2) Yandell argues that it is not clear that God can be faulted for not having created the best possible world because it is not clear that the concept of the best possible world is coherent. (3) Finally, it is not clear that there is a good reason for concluding that it is probable that some evil is unjustified and, therefore, probable that God does not exist. (Yandell shows this to be the case both when probability is construed statistically and when it is construed as an "a-logical" probability which rests upon our impressions of what is reasonable on the evidence.)

562 _____. "Ethics, Evils and Theism," Sophia, VIII (July, 1969), 18-28.

Yandell attempts to resolve the apparent incompatibility of "Evils are justified" and "We have an obligation to eliminate evils." The contradiction is only apparent, for it can be argued that some evils are justified precisely in so far as they provide opportunities for moral struggle and victory. Of these evils we can consistently say both that they are justified and that we ought to eliminate them The essay also includes a useful distinction between several patterns of justification. (Evils may be justified by showing that they are logically necessary conditions of goods which counterbalance them,

or by showing that they belong to classes of
evil the existence of some members of which is
a logically necessary condition of goods which
counterbalance them, or by showing that they are
the consequences of the free choices of rational
beings where it is the case that these evils are
counterbalanced by the good of free agency together with the good choices which those free
agents make.) See Kane's critique (# 487 above)
and Yandell's reply (# 566 below).

563   _____ . "The Greater Good Defense," Sophia,
    XIII (October, 1974), 1-16.

Yandell argues that the theist is committed to
the "greater good defense" where that is defined
as "Every evil is logically necessary to some good
which either counterbalances or overbalances it,
and some evil is overbalanced by the good to
which it is logically necessary." It is not
clear that Yandell succeeds in showing that
the theist's commitment to the claim that God
has morally sufficient reasons for permitting
evil commits him to the greater good defense.
The Free Will Defense appears to provide a morally
sufficient reason for the permission of evil and
yet (pace Yandell) it is by no means clear that
it can be subsumed under the greater good defense.
Given certain contingent facts about how free
persons would behave if they were created, it
may be impossible for God to create moral agents
without creating worlds in which moral evil
occurs. While the evil in question is a contingently necessary condition of the relevant
goods (viz., the existence of certain moral agents
and their morally good actions) it is not a logically necessary condition of those goods. Again,

a Schlesinger-type defense does not fit Yandell's
formula. If a good world has been produced,
and if for every world there is a better (in
which case one cannot produce the best), and
if God has not violated norms of justice, truthfulness, etc., then it is not clear that God can
be faulted even if He produces a world which contains evil which is not logically necessary to
a greater good. In the second half of this essay,
Yandell defends the claim that evils are justified by the moral goods which they make possible.
Several interesting points are made. It is argued
that the only evidence which we have for what
possible free persons would do if they were created is what actual free persons have done, viz.,
act badly. There is a discussion of the claim
that infant mortality and geriatric disability
count against the contention that God prizes
moral maturity. Yandell also shows that the fact
that God is praised for doing things for which
we would be blamed does not entail that man and
God are good in different senses since our circumstances may differ in morally relevant ways.

564 _____. "Logic and the Problem of Evil: A
Response to Hoitenga," God, Man and Religion.
Edited by Keith E. Yandell. New York, [etc.]:
McGraw-Hill Book Co., 1973. Pp. 351-64.

This essay is largely devoted to a consideration
of Hoitenga's contention that the belief that
evil is a logically necessary condition of a
greater good is incompatible with ordinary moral
notions, and to a consideration of Hoitenga's
objections to the Free Will Defense. (For a
description of Hoitenga's position, see # 477
above.) Yandell has little difficulty in showing

that Hoitenga's first point lacks any solid
foundation. His apology for the Free Will Defense is plausible though not particularly original. It is, perhaps, worth observing that in
the course of his defense Yandell rejects the
traditional notion that God and the blessed are
unable to sin. This is, probably, the most
straightforward course for the advocate of the
Free Will Defense, for it is natural to suppose
both that God and the blessed are moral agents
and that the ability to sin is a necessary condition of moral agency. For a further discussion
of this issue see Wainwright (# 552 above).

565 _____. "A Premature Farewell to Theism (A
Reply to Roland Puccetti)," Relig Stud, 5 (December, 1969), 251-5.

A reply to Puccetti (# 524 above). It is argued
that the fact that the theist is unable to provide morally good reasons for God's permission
of certain evils is not a decisive reason against
theism unless there are some grounds for supposing
that the theist's inability to do so implies
that there is no such reason.

566 _____. "Theism and Evil: A Reply," Sophia,
XI (April, 1972), 1-7.

An interesting response to G. Stanley Kane (#
487 above). A number of points are made in defense of the claim that certain types of evil
are necessary conditions of certain moral goods
(opportunities for moral struggle, the possession
and exercise of certain virtues, the development
of moral character, etc.). Perhaps the most interesting and controversial claim which Yandell

makes is that the possession of character traits
logically entails the possession of "some epi-
sodic character-relevant property or other."
If this contention is true we must consider the
possibility that some virtuous responses to evil
are necessary for the possession of a fully virtuous character even if one can possess certain
virtues without exercising them.

567   Young, Robert. Freedom, Responsibility and God.
      London and Basingstoke: The Macmillan Press,
      Ltd., 1975. Pp. 201-24.

Chapter 14 argues (1) that given the libertarian
conception of freedom Plantinga's Free Will Defense (# 517 above) is successful, and (2) that
although God could, given a compatibilist view
of freedom, create worlds in which free beings
never act badly, it is unclear that these worlds
would be better than our own. The second part
of this chapter is more original and more interesting than the first.

IV MYSTICISM AND RELIGIOUS EXPERIENCE

(See also #s 810, 843, 844 and 955)

568   Alston, William P. "Ineffability," Phil Rev, LXV
      (October, 1956), 506-22.

This is an important examination of the assertion that the object of mystical experience is
ineffable. Alston argues that "God is ineffable"
is self-stultifying both because it involves
predicating ineffability of God, and because a
meaningful use of its subject term presupposes
that one is in possession of an identifying

phrase which characterizes God in some fashion.
He concludes that statements of the form "x is
ineffable" cannot be taken literally.

569 _____. "Psychoanalytic Theory and Theistic
Belief," Faith and the Philosophers. Edited by
John Hick. New York: St. Martin's Press, Inc.,
1964. Pp. 63-102, esp. 87-90.

On page 87 ff. Alston argues that the existence
of an adequate natural explanation of religious
experience would be incompatible with the validity
of religious experience. See Wainwright's reply
(# 726 below).

570 _____, ed. Religious Belief and Philosophical
Thought: Readings in the Philosophy of Religion.
New York and Burlingame: Harcourt, Brace & World,
Inc., 1963. Pp. 117-125.

Alston makes a number of interesting points in
his introduction to the section on religious
experience. The most significant feature of
this essay is a criticism of C. B. Martin (#
658 below) for his failure to recognize that,
since the objects of religious experience and
sense experience are radically different, the
nature of the tests appropriate to each experience must be different as well.

571 Baillie, John. Our Knowledge of God. London:
Oxford University Press, H. Milford; New York:
Charles Scribner's Sons, 1939. Pp. 147-258.

Chapters IV and V argue that God is immediately
known in and through our experience of ourselves,
others, and nature as an absolute subject or
Thou. (Cf. the way in which finite persons are
"immediately" known through words, gestures,

facial expressions, etc.) Baillie's position
is somewhat similar to the position of Martin
Buber. However, his presentation is more lucid.

572 Bastow, David. "Otto and Numinous Experience,"
Relig Stud, 12 (June, 1976), 159-76.

A useful examination of the relation between
the Neo-Kantian philosophical system of Fries
adopted by Otto and the phenomenological theses
advanced in The Idea of the Holy. According to
Fries, the possibility of a feeling or intuition
(Ahnung) of Reality is inherent in human consciousness. Bastow suggests that this thesis
may have influenced Otto's contention that a
single type of religious experience underlies
all religion, but shows that numinous experience
and Fries's Ahnung are formally dissimilar.

573 Beatie, William J. "Von Hügel's 'Sense of the
Infinite'," Heythrop J, 16 (April, 1975), 149-73.

A lucid and interesting account of the nature
and development of Von Hügel's theory of religious
experience. Of particular value is the attempt
to relate that theory to Von Hügel's general
epistemological position -- a position which
stresses the "givenness" of objective reality
in human experience. According to Von Hügel,
the (apparent) givenness of an external world
in sense experience or of the divine in religious
experience warrants belief in an external world
or in God, once objections to those beliefs have
been adequately dealt with.

574   Bennett, Charles Andrew Armstrong. "An Approach
      to Mysticism," Phil Rev, XXVII (July, 1918),
      392-404.

      Bennett draws analogies between features of mys-
      tical consciousness (emptiness, passivity, opti-
      mism, noetic character) and features of more
      familiar experiences (freeing oneself from old
      ideas, the natural and apparently spontaneous
      performance of difficult tasks, "moral holidays"
      in which we step back from our specific tasks
      and view the whole, having familiar truths come
      home to us).

575   _____. A Philosophical Study of Mysticism.
      New Haven: Yale University Press, 1923. 194 pp.

      Of some interest. Chapters VII and VIII develop
      the thesis that mystical experience is a synthetic
      grasp of the world-whole, which precedes any dis-
      cernment of detail. It is analogous to the syn-
      thetic vision of the artist which precedes the
      articulated work of art.

576   Bergson, Henri. The Two Sources of Morality and
      Religion. Translated by R. Ashley Audra and
      Cloudesley Brereton, with the assistance of W.
      Horsfall Carter. London: Macmillan and Co.,
      Ltd.; New York: Holt and Co., 1935, viii +
      308 pp.

      This influential book first appeared in 1932.
      Its third part ("Dynamic Religion") contains
      Bergson's interpretation of mysticism. Mystical
      consciousness is essentially a joyful and con-
      scious experience of, and contact with, the
      "creative impetus" or "élan vital" which expresses
      itself in the emergence of matter, the evolution
      of the species, and the life of the mystic

himself. Loving the principle behind the creative advance of evolution and the emergence of
humanity, the mystic becomes a source of creative
energy and embraces humanity in active love.
The mystic's love differs from the affection
which binds limited societies together in scope
and in kind. The dynamic nature of mysticism
stands in sharp contrast with the static but
socially useful nature of institutionalized religion.

577 Bertocci, Peter Anthony. Introduction to the Phi-
losophy of Religion. (Prentice-Hall Philosophy
Series.) Englewood Cliffs, New Jersey: Prentice-
Hall, Inc., 1951. Pp. 82-120.

Chapter 4 contains a rather decent discussion
of religious experience. It is argued that religious experiences may confirm religious beliefs
but do not provide an independent source of religious knowledge. According to Bertocci, the
essential problem is that these experiences have
no clear common core. There is no datum which
has "a steadiness, a refractoriness, which . . .
[could] serve to ground and control the thinking
of the experients." (But, see p. 114 where Bertocci seems to describe what is in fact a common
core.) These experiences are, however, "a source
of moral power and inspiration" and worth having
for their intrinsic value.

578 Bishop, Donald H. "Some Aspects of Western Mystical
Ethics," Brahmavadin, 7 (July-October, 1972),
138-48.

An accurate description of the moral valuations
of classical Christian mystics. The author fails
to observe that these valuations are, for the

371

most part, those of classical Christianity in
general.

579 Bouquet, Alan Coates. Religious Experience, Its
Nature, Types and Validity. 2d ed. Cambridge:
W. Heffer & Sons Ltd., 1968. viii + 140 pp.

This is an extensively revised version of a work
which first appeared in 1932. It contains discussions of the nature of religious experience,
revelation, Christian experience, and other related topics. Of most interest are the sections
entitled "Validity of Immediate Experience" and
"Theory of Immediate Experience" (pp. 56-97) in
which Bouquet argues that religious experiences
are best explained as glimpses of a divine order.
His discussion is marred by his failure to distinguish between mystical experiences, numinous
experiences, visionary experiences, obscure in-
timations of religious truth, and other types
of religious experience.

580 Brenner, William. "George Mavrodes on the Epistemology of Religion," Int J Phil Relig, II (Fall,
1971), 172-82.

A moderately interesting criticism of Mavrodes'
defense (# 662 below) of the validity of religious
experience.

581 Bridges, Leonard Hal. American Mysticism from
William James to Zen. New York: Harper & Row,
1970. xi + 208 pp.

A good historical treatment of William James,
Rufus Jones, Thomas Merton, Aldous Huxley, Alan
Watts and other figures. Includes an extensive
bibliography.

582 Broad, Charlie Dunbar. "Arguments for the Existence of God," Religion, Philosophy and Psychical Research: Selected Essays by C. D. Broad. (International Library of Psychology, Philosophy and Scientific Method.) London: Routledge & Kegan Paul, Limited, 1953. Pp. 175-201, esp. 190-201.

The last part of the essay includes a good brief discussion of the cognitive status of mystical experience. Special attention is paid to the relation between interpretation and immediacy in religious experience, the agreement among mystics, and the connection between the genetic origins of the experience and its validity.

583 Browne, Henry. Darkness or Light, An Essay in the Theory of Divine Contemplation. St. Louis, Mo. and London: B. Herder Book Co., 1925. vii + 286 pp.

A Catholic theologian argues that mystical knowledge is not direct or intuitive and that, therefore, "touching God," "seeing God," etc., are mere metaphors. Mystical contemplation is an act of faith not vision, but whereas ordinary exercises of faith have both a primary object (God) and a secondary object (the truth which God reveals), the exercise of faith which lies at the heart of mystical prayer is exclusively directed to faith's primary object.

584 Buber, Martin. "Dialogue," Between Man and Man by Martin Buber. Translated by Ronald Gregor Smith. New York: Macmillan Co., 1948. Pp. 1-39.

This essay elaborates and clarifies a number of themes first presented in I and Thou, including the author's sharp distinction between monistic mysticism and the I-Thou experience. "Dialogue" originally appeared in 1929.

585 _____. I and Thou. Translated by Ronald
Gregor Smith. Edinburgh: T. & T. Clark; New
York: Charles Scribner's Sons, 1937. xiii +
120 pp.

This modern classic explores the I-Thou and I-It
relationships between persons, between man and
nature, and between man and God. The discussion
of the self's relation to the eternal Thou in
Part Three (which repudiates a mysticism which
would blur the distinction between man and God)
has been a major influence on contemporary
accounts of religious experience. Buber's discussion remains suggestive although it is gnomic
and frequently obscure. I and Thou first appeared
in 1923.

586 Bucke, Richard Maurice. Cosmic Consciousness,
A Study in the Evolution of the Human Mind.
Philadelphia: Innes & Sons, 1901. xviii +
318 pp.

Bucke argues that there is an evolutionary movement from simple consciousness, through self-
consciousness, to cosmic consciousness (roughly,
the consciousness of the nature mystic) -- the
great mystics and spiritual leaders being fore-
runners of the next major evolutionary advance.
Widely read, influential, occasionally interesting, but on the whole rather shoddy. See
Zaehner's critique in Concordant Discord chapter
III (# 737 below).

587 Burr, Ronald. "Wittgenstein's Later Language-Phi-
losophy and Some Issues in Philosophy of Mysticism," Int J Phil Relig, VII (1976), 261-87.

Stace (#s 716 and 717 below) attempts to discover the essence of mysticism by isolating features common and peculiar to a certain kind of inner experience. Burr maintains that Stace's project is misconceived because (1) we cannot discover "essences" by examing the features of things but only by attending to the logical grammar of the expressions we use, and because (2) the meaning of terms for inner experiences can only be determined by examining their criteria and by exploring the role which these terms play in the lives of those who employ them. Many of Burr's criticisms of Stace are well taken. (E.g., Stace attempts to abstract the essence of mysticism by isolating features common and peculiar to typical cases of mysticism but fails to provide criteria for determining when a case of mysticism is or is not typical. Again, Stace's cavalier attitude towards borderline cases is unfortunate because the existence of instances of mystical experience which fail to exhibit some of his defining features casts doubt upon his claim to have discovered the essence of mysticism.) Is Burr's central thesis correct? A Wittgensteinian approach to the language of mysticism might succeed in deepening our understanding of that language even if Wittgenstein's theory of language is not entirely adequate. Whether it will in fact succeed in doing so cannot be determined until we are provided with specific analyses of mystical terms and sentences.

588 Butler, Edward Cuthbert. Western Mysticism, The Teaching of Augustine, Gregory and Bernard on Contemplation and the Contemplative Life, 2d ed. with Afterthoughts. London: Constable and Co., 1927. xci + 344 pp.

The first edition appeared in 1922. A valuable
introduction was added to the second edition
(1927) providing a balanced discussion of issues
being debated by Farges, Poulain, Saudreau (#s
604, 695 and 703 below) and other French Catholics
in the early part of this century. These issues
include the question of the degree to which the
self is passive in contemplation, whether contemplation always involves an "experimental perception" of divine reality, whether such perception involves an intuition of God's essence, and
whether the mystical state is extraordinary or,
on the contrary, a normal part of a life of sanctity.

589 Clark, Walter Houston. Chemical Ecstasy, Psyche-
     delic Drugs and Religion. New York: Sheed &
     Ward, 1969. ix + 179 pp.

The most interesting chapters are 6 and 7 in
which Clark provides empirical evidence for the
claim that hallucinogens sometimes induce mystical
experiences and for the claim that drug induced
religious experiences frequently bring about
beneficial personality changes. Chapter 8 contains a sympathetic but judicious evaluation of
the benefits and dangers of drug mysticism, and
is also of some interest.

590 Clarke, W. Norris. "Some Criteria Offered," Faith
     and the Philosophers. Edited by John Hick.
     New York: St. Martin's Press, Inc., 1964. Pp.
     58-60.

Clarke suggests that there are criteria which
may be used to determine whether an experience
is an experience of God. These include the impression of being acted upon, and nourished by,

the (apparent) object of the experience.

591 Cobb, John B., Jr. A Christian Natural Theology,
     Based on the Thought of Alfred North Whitehead.
     Philadelphia: The Westminster Press, 1965.
     Pp. 225-46.

     Chapter VI, section 2 ("Religious Belief and
     Religious Experience") contains an examination
     of religious experience by a prominent disciple
     of Charles Hartshorne. This is the best treat-
     ment of religious experience yet offered by a
     process theologian.

592 Coe, George Albert. "The Sources of the Mystical
     Revelation," Hibb J, VI (1907-8), 359-72.

     Mystical experience is traced to auto-suggestion
     (which causes us to confuse beliefs with percep-
     tions) and self-hypnosis. Religious experience
     in general, and mystical experience in particular,
     has no metaphysical significance. The mystic
     "brings his theological beliefs to the mystical
     experience; he does not derive them from it."

593 Conway, David Alton. "Mavrodes, Martin and the
     Verification of Religious Experience," Int J Phil
     Relig, II (Fall, 1971), 156-71.

     Conway criticizes Mavrodes (# 662 below) and
     provides a qualified defense of C.B. Martin (#
     658 below). The second section of this rather
     interesting article is weakened by the assumption
     that no tests are employed within religious com-
     munities to distinguish veridical religious ex-
     periences from those which are not veridical.

377

594 Copleston, Frederick Charles. Religion and Philosophy. Dublin: Gill and Macmillan, Ltd.; New
York: Harper and Row, 1974. Pp. 73-91.

Chapter 5 contains one of a series of lectures
delivered in 1969 at the University of Dundee.
A persuasive deductive argument can't be based
on religious experience nor, given that alternative (naturalistic) explanations are available,
can religious experience be made the basis of
a strong non-deductive argument. On the other
hand, a person who is already predisposed to
believe in God (perhaps because of his own more
ordinary religious experiences) may find that
mysticism not only confirms his belief but that
it provides further insight into the nature of
the object of that belief. Again, reflections
upon mysticism may play a role in deciding between
competing world views. Finally, the lives and
writings of the mystics may provide an occasion
not for an inference but for one's own personal
awareness of God. This is a lucid and intelligent, if not strikingly original, essay.

595 Danto, Arthur Coleman. "Ethical Theory and Mystical
Experience: A Response to Professors Proudfoot
and Wainwright," J Relig Ethics, 4 (Spring, 1976),
37-46.

A response to Wainwright's "Morality and Mysticism" (# 724 below) and Wayne Proudfoot's "Mysticism, The Numinous, and the Moral" (Journal
of Religious Ethics, 4 [1976], 3-28) which contains a very interesting account (pp. 43-6) of
the uniqueness and apparent ineffability of mystical experience. (Danto's idea is, roughly,
that mystical experience cannot be neatly com-
partmentalized. It affects, colors and transforms

our other experiences, attitudes and ways of
regarding things. The mystic thus lives in a
different world incommensurable with the familiar
world.)

596 _____. "Language and the Tao: Some Reflections on Ineffability," J Chin Phil, 1 (December,
1973), 45-55.

This is an interesting exploration of different
sorts of ineffability though, as Danto recognizes,
it is doubtful whether the senses of "ineffable"
which are isolated can be used to explicate the
statement that the Tao is ineffable.

597 _____. Mysticism and Morality: Oriental
Thought and Moral Philosophy. New York: Basic
Books, 1972. xiv + 127 pp.

In this interesting book Danto argues that mysticism and/or those oriental philosophies which
are rooted in mysticism (Danto does not distinguish between the two) are incompatible with the
presuppositions of morality. No attention is
paid to Western mysticism or to the theistic
mystical traditions of India.

598 De Boer, Jesse. "First Steps in Mysticism," Faith
and Philosophy, Philosophical Studies in Religion
and Ethics. Edited by Alvin Plantinga. Grand
Rapids, Michigan: William B. Eerdmans Pub. Co.,
1964. Pp. 53-93.

An examination of monism (which the author equates
with mysticism). Considered as an examination
of (Advaita) Vedānta, the article is reasonably
accurate and has some value, but it errs not only
in neglecting non-monistic mysticism, but in
failing to consider other types of monism (e.g.,

Buddhist monisms which dispense with any notion of self).

599 Deikman, Arthur J. "Bimodal Consciousness," Archiv Gen Psychiat, 25 (December, 1971), 481-9. (Reprinted in The Nature of Human Consciousness. Edited by Robert E. Ornstein. San Francisco: W. H. Freeman and Co., 1973. Pp. 67-86.)

In this interesting article, Deikman distinguishes between "two primary modes of organization." "The action mode is a state organized to manipulate the environment" and is characterized by muscle tension, "focal attention, object based logic, heightened boundary perception, and the dominance of formal characteristics over the sensory." "The EEG shows beta waves." The receptive mode is "organized around intake of the environment rather than manipulation." In this mode, the sensory-perceptual system is dominant, attention is diffuse, thought is paralogical, there is a decrease in boundary perception and the sensory dominates the formal. The EEG shows alpha waves. Deikman employs these models to illuminate certain clinical findings, experimental studies of mysticism, Zen consciousness, schizophrenia and LSD experiences. He concludes by suggesting that there is no good reason to reject the possibility that the receptive mode provides "a way of 'knowing' certain aspects of reality not accessible to the action mode."

600 Dhavamony, Mariasusai. Love of God According to Śaiva Siddhānta: A Study in the Mysticism and Theology of Śaivism. Oxford: The Clarenden Press, 1971. xvii + 402 pp.

This contains an interesting account of a form of theistic mysticism found in Southern India.

Pp. 367-74 provide reasons for distinguishing
monistic mysticism from theistic mysticism.
Monistic experiences should be distinguished
from theistic experiences because they differ
in aim, object and method of attainment, and
because the former are analogous to knowledge
experiences while the latter are analogous to
love experiences.

601 Eliade, Mircea. The Sacred and the Profane: The
     Nature of Religion. Translated from the French
     by Willard R. Trask. New York: Harcourt, Brace
     and Company, Inc., 1959. 256 pp.

A deservedly influential and richly suggestive
account of the ways in which the sacred (apparently) manifests itself in ordinary objects and
in the cosmos as a whole. Eliade discusses sacred
space, sacred time, initiation rites, etc., and
contrasts the sacralized world of premodern man
with the desacralized world of modern man. There
would be value in determining the relation between
the experience of the cosmos (or a part of the
cosmos) as sacred and those numinous experiences
which are focussed upon ordinary objects, and
between the experience of the sacred and nature
mysticism. (Jesus and the Buddha are numinous
objects for some people. Are their experiences
qualitatively similar to the experiences of those
who celebrate the New Year, ritually representing,
and thereby participating in, the archetypal creative act which these festivities celebrate?
Is there any reason to believe that those who
inhabit a sacralized cosmos are normally nature
mystics? Although it is not clear that the answer
to either question is "yes," there would appear to
be important relations between these experiences.)

See also #s 1000, 1001 and 1002 below.

602 Ewing, Alfred Cyril. "Awareness of God," Philo-
     sophy, XL (January, 1965), 1-17.

     An interesting defense of the validity of reli-
     gious experience against the charge that it does
     not exhibit the characteristics of a cognitive
     experience, that its occurrence can be explained
     by psychology, that there are no intuitions dis-
     tinct from sense perception, introspection and
     memory, that it is private, that religious in-
     tuitions can't be veridical because they conflict
     with one another, etc.

603 Fakhry, Majid. "Three Varieties of Mysticism in
     Islam," Int J Phil Relig, II (Winter, 1971),
     193-207.

     Three types of mysticism or mystical theology
     are distinguished: (1) Philosophical mysticism,
     a sort of intellectual union or conjunction with
     the active intellect which emanates from God and
     is the immediate ground of the world's order
     and human intellection, (2) a vision or apprehen-
     sion of God which involves epistemic but not
     ontological union, and (3) ontological union
     or identification with God.

604 Farges, Albert. Mystical Phenomena Compared with
     their Human and Diabolical Counterfeits, a Trea-
     tise on Mystical Theology in Agreement with the
     Principles of St. Teresa set forth by the Car-
     melite Congress of 1923 at Madrid . . . Trans-
     lated by S. P. Jacques from the 2d French edition.
     New York, Cincinnati and Chicago: Benziger Bros.,
     1925. xvi + 668 pp.

     Part I provides a valuable discussion of Christian
     mystical phenomena. Pp. 50-86, chapters IX and

XI of the section entitled "Reply to Controversies," and appendix IV are of particular interest. They develop and defend the notion that God is directly and intuitively perceived through the medium of his action upon our souls. The effects of God's action within our souls perform a function analogous to that which is performed by the sensible effects produced in our souls by sense objects during sense perception. In both cases, the effects produced by the object of perception are media through which the object of perception is directly perceived.

605 Feigl, Herbert. "Critique of Intuition According to Scientific Empiricism," Phil East West, VIII (April-July, 1958), 1-16.

Feigl distinguishes various senses of "intuition" and argues that the mystic's supposed intuition of a transempirical reality should be discredited because a naturalistic account of mystical experience is available (Freud's), and because the mystic's intuition is not certified by the "criteria of the inductive or hypothetico-deductive methods." See P. T. Raju's reply (# 699 below).

606 Flew, Antony Garrard Newton. God and Philosophy. London: Hutchinson; New York: Harcourt, Brace & World, 1966. Pp. 124-39.

Chapter 6 contains a discussion of religious experience. A great deal of space is devoted to establishing the claim that religious experience is not self-authenticating. Flew then argues that an independent warrant for, or proof of, the validity of these experiences is necessary (why?) and that it cannot be provided.

607 Fromm, Erich, ed. <u>Zen and Psychoanalysis</u> by D. T.
    Suzuki, Erich Fromm and Richard De Martino.
    London: G. Allen; New York: Harper, 1960.
    vii + 180 pp.

    The three long essays contained in this book
    resulted from a conference on Zen and psycho-
    analysis held at Autonomous National University
    of Mexico in 1957. Fromm's contribution contains
    a significant and sympathetic attempt to inter-
    pret satori as the same sort of attunement to
    external and internal reality which is the aim
    of "humanistic psychoanalysis." Fromm's essay
    should interest those who can neither dismiss
    mysticism as illusory nor accept the supranatu-
    ralistic accounts of mystical experiences which
    are typically given by those who have them.
    The other two essays are of less interest.

608 Gale, Richard. "Mysticism and Philosophy," <u>J Phil</u>,
    LVII (July 7, 1960), 471-81.

    Gale discusses several points made by Walter
    Stace in <u>Time and Eternity</u> (# 717 below). The
    first section contains a discussion of the al-
    leged ineffability of mystical experience and
    is of some interest.

609 Garside, Bruce. "Language and the Interpretation
    of Mystical Experience," <u>Int J Phil Relig</u>, III
    (Summer, 1972), 93-102.

    This interesting article attacks the notion
    (shared by Stace and others) that a clear dis-
    tinction can be drawn between the description
    of a mystical experience and its interpretation.
    Garside maintains that, since an experience is
    always a joint product of the setting in which

384

that experience occurs and the conceptual structures, predispositions and expectations which
one brings to that setting, no clear distinction
can be drawn between the description of an experience and its interpretation. (This argument
is enthymatic. How does it follow from the fact
that interpretive structures are partial causes
of an experience, that the experience which is
partially caused by those structures cannot be
described in a neutral fashion or that we cannot
distinguish between a description of that experience and an interpretation of it?)

610 Gilson, Etienne. The Mystical Theology of St.
     Bernard. Translated by A. H. C. Downes. New
     York: Sheed & Ward, 1940. ix + 226 pp.

     According to Gilson, Bernard believes that the
     ecstatic love of the introverted contemplative
     is an image or mirror in which God is known.
     A very interesting study. See Wainwright's cri-
     tical discussion of this theory (# 728 below).

611 Gordon, Ruth M. "Has Mysticism a Moral Value?"
     Int J Ethics, XXXI (October, 1920), 66-83.

     Mysticism is indicted for its egocentricity and
     self-absorption, its stress on emotion at the
     expense of intellect, its refusal to adopt a
     melioristic attitude towards the world, etc.
     The charges are familiar and not entirely fair,
     but they are lucidly presented and supported
     by a number of telling illustrations.

612 Henle, Paul. "Mysticism and Semantics," Phil Phe-
     nomenol Res, IX (March, 1949), 416-22.

     This is a very significant attempt to show that

certain truths are ineffable in relation to
certain languages and that, therefore, it is at
least possible that the mystic does indeed acquire an insight into truths which are ineffable
in relation to known symbolic systems.

613 Hepburn, Ronald William. Christianity and Paradox:
     Critical Studies in Twentieth-Century Theology.
     London: C. A. Watts & Co. Ltd., 1958. Pp. 24-59.

     Chapters III and IV ("Encounters") contain an
     interesting and important exploration of the
     ways in which I-thou relationships presuppose
     knowledge about the persons to whom one is so
     related, of the disanalogies between human en-
     counters and the (putative) encounter with a
     divine Thou, and of the hazards involved in moving
     from a sense of presence and encounter to the
     conclusion that God exists. See Shiner's cri-
     tique (# 706 below).

614 _____. "From World to God," Mind, LXII (Jan-
     uary, 1963), 40-50.

     Hepburn argues that (1) because of the logical
     gap between the occurrence of numinous experiences
     and the existence of God, we are not in a posi-
     tion to conclude that numinous experiences are
     cognitive, and that (2) the incommunicability
     of numinous experience and the increasing refine-
     ment of the sense of the numinous through the
     course of history provide inadequate reasons for
     supposing that numinous experiences are valid.

615 _____. "Mysticism, Nature and Assessment
     of," The Encyclopedia of Philosophy. Vol. 5.
     Edited by Paul Edwards. New York: Macmillan,
     1967. Pp. 429-34.

A sympathetic but critical discussion of several
issues, including the paradoxes of mystical language and the epistemological status of mystical
experience.

616 _____. "Religious Experience, Argument for
the Existence of God," The Encyclopedia of Philosophy. Vol. 7. Edited by Paul Edwards. New
York: Macmillan, 1967. Pp. 163-8.

This article contains interesting remarks on the
history of the argument, on the many types of
religious experience, and on the effect which
psychological explanation should have upon our
assessment of the argument's validity. It also
includes a brief but lucid statement of standard
objections to the argument.

617 Hocking, William Ernest. The Meaning of God in
Human Experience, A Philosophic Study of Religion.
New Haven: Yale University Press, 1912. xxxix
+ 586 pp.

Feeling issues in idea and is inseparable from
it. Religious feeling or idea is the feeling
or idea of the whole of reality as divine. It
involves the experience of a subject which communicates itself in nature and whose unity or
permanence is the ground of the unity and permanence of nature (a nature which lies at the
heart of the social world as the common object
of finite selves). In worship God is appropriated
by the self. Mystics are specialists in worship.
Worship in general, and mysticism in particular,
involves turning from the parts to the whole.
The best life alternates between contemplation
which attends to the whole and action which attends to the parts, for each of these is

necessary to the other. Parts V and VI (which
deal with mysticism and its fruits) and chapter
IV (which discusses the increased emphasis on
feeling in modern discussions of the nature and
value of religion) should interest both those
philosophers who are attracted to Hocking's
metaphysics and those who are not.

618 Hospers, John. An Introduction to Philosophical
     Analysis. 2d ed. Englewood Cliffs, New Jersey:
     Prentice-Hall, Inc., 1967. Pp. 444-8.

Hospers' brief discussion of religious experience
(chapter 7, section 21.D.) provides a clear
statement of the objection that religious experiences can't be cognitive because they provide
(apparent) support for logically incompatible
claims. (In assessing this argument one must
be careful to specify those experiences for which
cognitive claims are made. Voices and visions
do conflict with one another. It is less clear
that mystical experiences and numinous experiences
do so. Again, it should be noted that interpretations can conflict even though the experiences
which are being interpreted do not conflict.)

619 Hügel, Frederick von, Baron. The Mystical Element
     of Religion as Studied in Saint Catherine of
     Genoa and her Friends. 2d ed. 2 vols. London:
     J. M. Dent and Co.; New York: E. P. Dutton and
     Co., 1923.

Evelyn Underhill referred to this as "the best
work on mysticism in the English language."
While this judgment would be hard to sustain,
von Hügel's work is still of interest. His philosophical reflections are contained in the second
volume. Von Hügel argues that we all enjoy the

sense of the infinite but that this sense is most
highly developed in the mystics. He opposes
quietism and a mystical otherworldliness which
abstracts from the things of time and space.
Genuine mysticism combines time and eternity,
the visible and invisible, activity and contemplation, and the mystical element in religion
must be integrated with its institutional and
intellectual elements. The first edition appeared
in 1909.

620   Huxley, Aldous Leonard. The Devils of Loudun.
      New York: Harper & Bros., 1952. 340 pp.

This study of the cases of demonic possession
which occurred at Loudun in the 17th century
contains many observations on religious psychology and the nature of mysticism. Of particular
interest is Huxley's discussion of the morally
suspect role played in the affair by Jean-Joseph
Surin, a contemplative of some note, and his
ensuing mental and spiritual derangement. The
epilogue contains a discussion of drugs, sex,
"herd intoxication" and other forms of "downward
transcendence."

621   _____ . The Doors of Perception. London:
      Chatto & Windus; New York: Harper, 1954. 79 pp.

Huxley's famous reflections upon the drug experience which, he says, enabled him to understand
what Christians mean by "the beatific vision"
and what Hindus mean by "being-awareness-bliss."
Not silly although somewhat over exuberant.

622   _____. Gray Eminence. London: Chatto &
Windus; New York and London: Harper and Brothers,
1941. 342 pp.

A study of Father Joseph, Richelieu's "confiden-
tial advisor and right-hand man." This study
of a genuine comtemplative who engaged in Machia-
vellian power politics is of importance because
of its implications for the relations between
mystical consciousness and morality. Also worth
noting is the discussion (in chapter III) of the
mystical teachings of Benet of Canfield and Pierre
de Berulle both of whom attempted to combine
a high mysticism of the Dionysian sort (which
involves the complete annihilation of images
and concepts) with contemplation of the humanity
of Jesus, the Virgin, etc. Huxley argues that
this combination is impossible.

623   _____. Heaven and Hell. London: Chatto &
Windus; New York: Harper, 1956. 103 pp.

A discussion of visionary experiences -- which
Huxley distinguishes from mystical experiences
-- and their relation to art. Of interest.

624   _____. Letters of Aldous Huxley. Edited
by Grover Smith. London: Chatto & Windus, 1969;
New York: Harper and Row, 1970. 992 pp.

A number of the letters to Dr. Henry Osmond and
others provide additional insight into Huxley's
views on chemical mysticism. See especially
Nos. 623, 676, 724, 725, 730, 749, 808, 818,
842 and 902.

625   _____.   The Perennial Philosophy. New York
      and London: Harper & Bros., 1945. xi + 312 pp.

    A widely read work which argues that mystical
    experience is everywhere the same, and that one
    can distill a common philosophy from the remarks
    of the mystics. The "perennial philosophy" iso-
    lated by Huxley is most similar to Advaita Vedānta
    and neo-Platonism. Huxley's claim is a very
    contentious one because it is not clear that all
    mystical experiences are similar, and because
    mystics have endorsed systems which are very
    different from the one described by Huxley (e.g.,
    Theravāda Buddhism).

626   Hyers, Conrad M. "Prophet and Mystic: Toward a
     Phenomenological Foundation for a World Ecumeni-
     city," Cross Currents, XX (Fall, 1970), 435-54.

    A rather interesting comparison of prophetic and
    mystical consciousness which argues that they
    are expressions of two different responses to
    the sacred. Prophetic consciousness is grounded
    in the experience of awe and humility before
    a transcendent other (Otto's mysterium tremendum).
    Mystical consciousness is grounded in an ecstatic
    participation in divine reality (Otto's mysterium
    fascinans).

627   James, William. "A Suggestion about Mysticism,"
     J Phil, VII (February 17, 1910), 85-92.

    James suggests that in mystical experience, con-
    sciousness is widened so that knowledge which
    is ordinarily transmarginal becomes included
    within the field of consciousness.

628   . The Varieties of Religious Experience, A Study in Human Nature Being the Gifford Lectures on Natural Religion Delivered at Edinburgh in 1901-02. New York [etc.]: Longmans, Green & Co., 1902. xii + 534 pp.

Although James' work has been superseded in some respects, it remains a classic.

629 Johnston, William. The Mysticism of the Cloud of Unknowing: A Modern Interpretation, with a foreword by Thomas Merton. New York: Desclee, 1967. xvi + 285 pp.

This analysis of a mystical classic of the English Middle Ages provides an excellent introduction to western mysticism.

630   . The Still Point, Reflections on Zen and Christian Mysticism. New York: Fordham University Press, 1970. xiii + 193 pp.

A valuable collection of essays originally published in a number of relatively inaccessible sources. In the course of his examination of Zen, Christian mysticism and the relation between the two, the author discusses the psychology of mysticism, mysticism's connections with reason and virtue, the problem of defining mysticism, and other topics.

631 Jones, Rufus Matthew. New Studies in Mystical Religion, The Ely Lectures Delivered at Union Theological Seminary, New York, 1927 by Rufus Jones. New York: The Macmillan Co., 1927. 205 pp.

These studies tend to be somewhat long on inspiration and short on argument. Among the more interesting chapters are II in which Jones suggests that the ascetic extremes which characterize

the history of mysticism are the consequence
of mental instability, an over-emphasis on the
image of the suffering Christ, and two false
theories -- a dualism which rejects this world
as evil or illusory, and a "black theology" which
invests God with our own cruel instincts and
passions. Chapters IV and V argue that Christianity begins in a "novel experience of God,"
a release of new spiritual energies, and that
religious organizations must be judged by whether
they are penetrated by this experience and pro-
pogate it or whether they "tend to arrest it."
Only "organic" and unstructured organizations
such as those of the Quakers can be deemed successful. It is suggested that the success of
these groups shows that mysticism can be communal
and socially active.

632 _____. Studies in Mystical Religion. London:
Macmillan and Co. Ltd., 1909. xxxviii + 518 pp.

Studies in the history of Christian mysticism
and "inward religion" which are guided by the
conviction that mysticism as a "direct and intimate consciousness of the divine presence . . .
is religion in its most acute, intense and living
stage." The introduction contains a general account of the nature and value of mysticism.
Jones attempts to distinguish the healthy from the
abnormal, and concludes both that mystics are
aware of "wider spheres of Reality" and that
"such experiences minister to life . . . and
conduce to the increased power of the race."
His views are colored by his suspicion of the
via negativa -- the mysticism of "withdrawal
and negation." Jones' studies of mysticism are
not without value but on the whole his reputation

appears to be somewhat inflated.

633 Jordan, G. Ray, Jr. "LSD and Mystical Experiences,"
J Bible Relig, XXXI (April, 1963), 114-23.

Argues that under favorable conditions LSD can
produce each type of mystical experience.

634 Kellenberger, Bertram James. "God and Mystery,"
Amer Phil Quart, 11 (April, 1974), 93-102.

In section II, Kellenberger argues that Stace
is mistaken in supposing that mystical language
is self-contradictory. Although it is sometimes
self-contradictory in form, it is not normally
self-contradictory in meaning. To suppose (as
Stace did in Time and Eternity) that mystical
language is purely evocative conflicts with the
fact that mystics clearly believe themselves to
be uttering truths. Sections III and V argue
that the sense of mystery and numinous awe is
not only compatible with belief and conceptuali-
zation, but includes it.

635 Kennick, William E. Review of Mysticism and Philosophy by W. T. Stace. Phil Rev, LXXI (July,
1962), 387-90.

Kennick suggests that mystical experiences are
not perceptions but states of mind, and that the
paradoxical language of mysticism is not descriptive but a symptom or expression of these states.

636 Knox, Ronald Arbuthnott. Enthusiasm, A Chapter
in the History of Religion with Special Reference
to the XVII and XVIII Centuries. New York:
Oxford University Press, 1950. viii + 662 pp.

Discussions of the Quakers, Jansenism, Quietism,
Wesley, etc. Polemical but interesting.

637 Koestler, Arthur. The Lotus and the Robot. New
York: The Macmillan Co., 1961. 296 pp.

A thoughtful, anecdotal and jaundiced view of
Yoga, Zen and Eastern mysticism in general.

638 Kordig, Carl R. "Proclus on the One," Ideal Stud,
3 (Summer, 1973), 229-37.

A useful exhibition of the incoherencies involved
in asserting that the One (or anything else)
is literally ineffable.

639 Krimerman, Leonard Isaiah. "The Negative Divine,"
S J Phil, 2 (Summer, 1964), 70-4.

Mystics and their spokesmen sometimes say that
no predicates can be ascribed to God. However,
if no predicates can be ascribed to God, "God"
is not a logical subject and if "God" is not
a logical subject, "God" does not refer to anything. It is sometimes suggested that the mystics
and theologians in question merely mean to say
that no positive and/or literal terms can be
applied to God, but, apart from its intrinsic
difficulties, this position fails to take the
relevant utterances seriously. What is claimed
is that no descriptive or assertive language is
in order and not merely that some selected sub-
class of descriptive or assertive language is
not in order.

640   Kvastad, Nils Bjorn. "Pantheism and Mysticism,"
      Sophia, XIV (July, 1975 and October, 1975), 1-
      15 and 19-30.

      A fairly interesting examination of the relation
      between different types of pantheism and mystical
      experiences. (Stace's classification of mystical
      experiences is adopted.) Part I includes an in-
      vestigation of the alleged objectivity of extro-
      vertive experiences, but this is of less interest.
      On the whole, Kvastad's critical observations
      are neither profound nor original.

641   _____. "Philosophical Problems of Mysticism,"
      Int Phil Quart, XIII (June, 1973), 191-207.

      Fairly interesting discussions of the ineffability
      of mystical experience, and of the ethical im-
      plications of mystical consciousness.

642   Léonard, Augustin. "Phenomenological Inquiries
      into Mystical Experience," Cross Currents, III
      (Spring, 1953), 231-50.

      Erwin W. Geissman's translation of the first
      part of an article which appeared in La Vie
      Spirituelle (Supplément, No. 23, Nov. 15, 1952).
      Contains comments on Delacroix's distinction be-
      tween Christian and non-Christian elements in
      the mysticism of Teresa of Avila, Soderblom's
      contrast between prophetism and mysticism, von
      Hügel's claim that some degree of mystical in-
      tuition lies at the heart of all religious at-
      titudes, and a number of other topics. (See
      # 643 below.)

643 _____. "Phenomenological Introduction to
Catholic Mysticism," Cross Currents, III (Summer,
1953), 307-28.

Translation of the second part of an essay ap-
pearing originally in La Vie Spirituelle (see
642 above). A generally balanced attempt to
demonstrate the specifically Christian character
of Christian mysticism. Léonard's claim that
Christian mystics do not seek mystical knowledge
is a questionable one.

644 Leuba, James Henry. The Psychology of Religious
Mysticism. London: K. Paul, Trench, Trubner
& Co., Ltd.; New York: Harcourt Brace & Co.,
Inc., 1925. xii +·336 pp.

A very skeptical account of the nature and cognitive pretensions of mystical experience. For
a criticism of Leuba's position see Maréchal
(# 655 below).

645 Lewis, Hywel David. "The Cognitive Factor in Religious Experience," Proc Aris Soc, Supplementary
Volume XXIX (1955), 59-84.

Religious experience in general is construed
by Lewis as an intuitive grasp of existence as
rooted in an "overwhelming mystery." Specific
religious experiences occur when this intuition
is brought into conjunction with secular features
of our experience (e.g., moral ones).

646 _____. "Mysticism," London Quart, 189 (July,
1964), 190-7.

While not discounting the claim that mystics have
experienced God, Lewis argues that these experiences cannot be immediate, cannot involve a total

obliteration of the subject-object distinction,
and cannot literally involve an absorption into
deity.

647 _____ . Our Experience of God. (The Muirhead
Library of Philosophy.) London: George Allen
& Unwin; New York: The Macmillan Co., 1959.
301 pp.

A general account of the nature of religion which
finds its essence in an intuitive apprehension
of the fact that the world is grounded in an
unconditioned being. This intuition is mediated
through finite data. It combines with other
experiences (e.g., experiences of defeat and
triumph, acts of moral discernment, etc.) to
yield the rich variety of religious experience.
Lewis discusses the ways in which religious experience is related to imagination, the formulation of dogma, worship, art, morality, etc.
There is no detailed discussion of mysticism
or of the epistemological issues normally considered in examinations of the validity of religious experience.

648 Londis, James J. "'Mediated Immediacy' in the
Thought of John E. Smith: A Critique," Relig
Stud, 11 (December, 1975), 473-80.

According to Smith (#s 713 and 714 below), both
our experience of other persons and our experience
of God are direct but not immediate. We experience God in and through the medium of other
things, just as we experience persons in and
through their speech, gestures, expressions, etc.
These experiences involve interpretation and
judgment but not inference. Londis argues (1)
that the distinction between interpretation and

inference is unclear, (2) that Smith cannot
adequately explain error in religious experience
unless he can explain what it would be like to
discover that God had not been present in and
through the medium (notice that we do know what
it would be like to discover that what we had
taken to be a person was not a person but, e.g.,
a robot), and (3) questions Smith's apparent
assumption that in an experience or encounter
that something is present is given and what is
at issue is only the nature of what is given,
since this assumption prejudges the question
as to whether or not anything is given in religious experience.

649 Ludovic de Besse, father. The Science of Prayer.
London: Burns, Oates and Washbourne Ltd., 1925.
x + 189 pp.

Translated from the French. An interesting account of the nature of Christian contemplation,
particularly of the prayer of Faith (or Quiet,
or Recollection) in which grace acts upon the
will rather than upon the intellectual or emotional faculties, and God is obscurely touched.

650 McCready, William Charles. "A Survey of Mystical
Experiences: A Research Note," Listenings, 9
(Autumn, 1974), 55-70.

Description of the results of a recent statistical study which indicates that mystical experiences occur with some frequency among the general
population (35% of the sample reported that they
had had at least one mystical experience), and
that these "mystics" are more likely to be Black,
Protestant, older and college educated. Although
this study is interesting it should be noted

that "mystics" were distinguished from non-mystics
on the basis of their affirmative response to
the question, "Have you ever felt very close to
a powerful spiritual force that seemed to lift
you out of yourself?" While an attempt was made
to determine the qualities of these experiences
and while some of these qualities (e.g., a "sense
of unity," ineffability, etc.) are indeed correlated with mysticism, it is clear that not only
classical mystical experiences but intense de-
votional experiences, numinous experiences and
"pentecostal experiences" would justify an affirmative answer to the crucial question. The
results of the study are, therefore, ambiguous.
Nevertheless, the study does have an important
bearing on the claim (made by a number of philosophers) that mystical consciousness is a normal
human possibility.

651   MacIntyre, Alasdair C. Difficulties in Christian
      Belief. London: SCM Press Ltd., 1959. Pp.
      66-73.

      Chapter VII ("The Argument from Religious Experi-
      ence") offers a skeptical view of the argument
      from religious experience. While somewhat super-
      ficial this chapter does contain a few interesting
      observations.

652   _____. "Visions," in # 923 below, pp. 245-60.

      Argues that if any religious experience were to
      provide evidence for religious claims, visions
      would do so (sic!), but that visions fail to
      provide such evidence because we do not experience
      the connection between the vision and its supposed
      object, because visions conflict, and because

there are no criteria for sorting out veridical
visions from those which are not veridical.

653 McPherson, Thomas. The Philosophy of Religion.
     London: D. Van Nostrand Co. Ltd., 1965. Pp.
     101-24.

     Chapter 8 ("Religious Experience") contains use-
     ful comments on the meaning of "experience" and
     "religious experience," argues that the proof
     from religious experience is weakened if a good
     empirical explanation of religious experience
     can be provided, and concludes with a somewhat
     pedestrian discussion of the criteria of a genuine
     religious experience and of the difficulty of
     inferring God's existence from the fact that
     people have these experiences.

654 McTaggart, John McTaggart Ellis. "Mysticism,"
     Philosophical Studies by the Late J. McT. Ellis
     McTaggart. Edited with an introduction by S. V.
     Keeling. London: E. Arnold & Co.; New York:
     Longmans, Green & Co., 1934; Freeport, N. Y.:
     Libraries Press, 1966. Pp. 46-68.

     This essay explores the nature and value of the
     unity which mystics claim to intuit.

655 Maréchal, Joseph. Studies in the Psychology of
     the Mystics. Translated with an introductory
     foreward by Algar Thorold. London: Burns, Oates
     & Washbourne, Ltd., 1927. vii + 344 pp.

     Delacroix, Leuba and other psychologists are cri-
     ticized for proposing theories of mystical con-
     sciousness which (1) do not fit the descriptions
     which mystics have provided of their experiences,
     and which (2) are based upon certain a priori
     assumptions about the nature of human conscious-
     ness. These essays contain much which is of

     401

philosophical interest. The second, third and fourth (on the feeling of presence, Christian mysticism, and Leuba, respectively) are particularly noteworthy.

656   Maritain, Jacques. Distinguish to Unite, or the Degrees of Knowledge. Newly translated from the 4th French edition under the supervision of Gerald B. Phelan. New York: Charles Scribner's Sons, 1959. Pp. 247-470.

The Second Part ("The Degrees of Supernatural Knowledge") provides a very interesting account of the nature of mystical knowledge. The consciously experienced effects of the charity which God infuses in the soul function as a medium (analogous to the sensible species involved in sense perception) through which God is directly (non-inferentially) though obscurely grasped. See Wainwright's critique of this theory (# 728 below). The 1st French edition appeared in 1932.

657   _____. "The Natural Mystical Experience and the Void," Ransoming the Time. Translated by Harry Lorin Binnse. New York: Charles Scribner's Sons, 1941; New York: Gordian Press, 1969. Pp. 255-89.

This essay is based on a communication delivered to the Fourth Congress of Religious Psychology in 1938. It supplements the theory developed in Distinguish to Unite by adding an account of non-theistic mysticism. Since a direct intuitive vision of the soul's essence is impossible so long as the soul remains united to a body, the soul must grasp itself through the medium of its various acts. In natural contemplation the mystic non-conceptually apprehends his soul's substantial existence or being through the medium

402

of the act which empties the mind of ordinary
contents and suspends all normal mental activity.
This is the purest experience of the self possible to us.

658 Martin, Charles Burton. Religious Belief. (Con-
     temporary Philosophy.) Ithaca, New York: Cornell
     University Press, 1959. Pp. 64-94.

An earlier version of chapter five ("'Seeing'
God") appeared under the title "A Religious Way
of Knowing" (Mind, 1952, reprinted in # 923 below). Martin argues that while ordinary perceptual claims are subject to public "tests and
checkup procedures," claims to have directly
experienced God are suspiciously like first
person psychological reports. This important
essay suffers from an exaggerated emphasis on
the alleged incorrigibility of the mystic's
claims. Martin's arguments have evoked a number
of replies. See especially Alston (# 570 above),
Pletcher (# 693 below), and Robbins (# 701 below).

659 Maslow, Abraham Harold. Religious, Values, and
     Peak Experiences. (The Kappa Delta Pi Lecture
     Series.) Columbus: Ohio State University Press,
     1964. xx + 123 pp.

A very influential examination of "transcendent"
experiences which argues that "mystery, ambiguity,
illogic, contradiction, mystic and transcendent
experiences may now be considered to lie well
within the realm of nature" and that a humanistic
science can, therefore, appropriate the insights
and values which have historically been associated with organized religion. Maslow's psychological investigations are significant in spite
of sloppy philosophizing, a rather elastic

understanding of "science" and "nature," and
a tendency to blur the distinction between various sorts of "transcendent" experience.

660 Masters, Robert E. L. and Jean Houston. The Varieties of Psychedelic Experience. New York:
Holt, Rinehart & Winston, Inc., 1966. Pp.
247-313.

Chapter nine ("Religious and Mystical Experience")
contains the most balanced discussion of the relation between drugs and religious experience
yet to appear in print.

661 Matson, Wallace I. The Existence of God. Ithaca,
New York: Cornell University Press, 1965. Pp.
10-40.

A discussion of visions and mystical experience.
It is argued (1) that visions have no evidential
value because they are not public, (2) that "it
is not unreasonable to suspect that mysticism
is insanity," (3) that while both mystics and
physicists make claims which are vague to most
people and appeal to evidence which is inaccessible to most people, there are important disanalogies between the two cases, and (4) that,
unless the mystic makes claims which can be independently checked by the non-mystic the non-
mystic has no reason to credit the mystic with
anything like a sixth sense.

662 Mavrodes, George Ion. Belief in God, A Study in
the Epistemology of Religion. (Studies in Philosophy.) New York: Random House, Inc., 1970.
Pp. 49-89.

Chapter III ("The Experience of God") defends
the claim that the experience of ordinary objects

can mediate an experience of God, explores the
analogy between the experience of God and sense
experiences, and criticizes the position of C. B.
Martin (# 658 above). Well worth examining.

663 _____. "The Concept of a Direct Experience
of God." Doctoral Dissertation: University
of Michigan, 1961. 247 pp.

Mavrodes argues that if Christian doctrine is
true, (1) it is in principle possible to construct
a proof of God's existence, (2) "every part of
the world has sufficient relation to God to function as the mediator of an experience of Him,"
and (3) "every element of the world has characteristics . . . which could serve as the basis
of a satisfactory proof of God's existence."

664 Merton, Thomas. _Mystics and Zen Masters_. New York:
Farrar, Straus and Giroux, 1967. x + 303 pp.

A collection of essays on Christian mysticism
and asceticism, and Zen. Many of the essays
are excellent (see, for example, "Mystics and
Zen Masters," "From Pilgrimage to Crusade,"
"Virginity and Humanism in the Western Fathers,"
and "The Zen Koan") but the relation between
Zen's alleged insight into Being and/or the Ground
of being and the (Christian) mysticism of love
and grace is never adequately defined.

665 _____. _Zen and the Birds of Appetite_. New
York: New Directions, 1968. ix + 141 pp.

A collection of essays previously published in a
number of places. Of most interest are "The New
Consciousness," "A Christian Looks at Zen,"
"Transcendental Experience," and "The Recovery

405

of Paradise" (Merton's response to Suzuki).

666   Moore, John Morrison. <u>Theories</u> <u>of</u> <u>Religious</u> <u>Ex-</u>
       <u>perience</u> <u>with</u> <u>Special</u> <u>Reference</u> <u>to</u> <u>James,</u> <u>Otto</u>
       <u>and</u> <u>Bergson.</u> New York: Round Table Press, Inc.
       1938. xi + 253 pp.

       Moore's doctoral dissertation. Still of some
       interest.

667   Moore, Peter G. "Recent Studies of Mysticism:
       A Critical Survey," <u>Religion</u>, 3 (Autumn, 1973),
       146-56.

       This helpful bibliographical essay critically
       surveys "studies in English published since about
       1955," and contains a number of astute observa-
       tions concerning the difficulties involved in
       distinguishing interpretations of mystical ex-
       perience from descriptions of mystical experience.

668   Moraczewski, Albert S. "Mescaline, Madness and
       Mysticism," <u>Thought</u>, XLII (Fall, 1967), 358-82.

       Argues that psychedelic experiences must be dis-
       tinguished from genuine mysticism.

669   Oakes, Robert Aaron. "Biochemistry and Theistic
       Mysticism," <u>Sophia</u>, XV (July, 1976), 10-6.

       Oakes argues that the concept of a drug induced
       experience of God is problematic. It is a con-
       ceptual truth that God cannot be experienced
       except when He chooses to be experienced and
       that His will cannot be determined by anything
       outside Himself. It follows that the ingestion
       of a drug cannot be a causally sufficient condi-
       tion of an experience of God. While it is logi-
       cally possible that the ingestion of a drug

406

induces God to reveal Himself, it is implausible
to suppose it ever in fact does so. God may
reveal Himself to a person who takes drugs, but
He does not do so because that person takes drugs.

670 _____. "'Epistemic Constitutivity' and Sensible Experience of God," New Scholas, XLVIII
(Spring, 1974), 171-84.

A further (see # 674 below) exploration and defense of the possibility of experiencing God
through sensible phenomena.

671 _____. "'God': An Observation Term?" Mod
Sch, LIV (November, 1976), 43-56.

"This paper is intended to constitute a coherent
finalization" of what the author attempted in
670 above and #s 673 and 674 below. Oakes ar-
gues that epistemological dualism should be construed as the view "that physical objects are
perceived [not inferred] -- albeit indirectly
on the basis of . . . sense data caused by those
objects." Although sense data and physical objects are numerically distinct, the experience
of the sense data caused by a physical object
is (numerically the same as) the experience of
that object. Whether or not this view is true,
it is (according to Oakes) intelligible. Since
God can bring it about that some physical event
or object mediates His presence, He can bring
it about that He is indirectly perceived on the
basis of physical phenomena which He causes.
Furthermore, because the experience of a physical object is a sense experience, and because
-- given that the physical object mediates God's
presence in the way suggested -- the experience

of that object is (numerically the same as) an
experience of God, the experience in question
would be a sense experience of God (even though
God is not Himself a physical object).

672 _____. "Is Self-validating Religious Experience Logically Possible?" Thomist, XXXVI (April,
1972), 256-66.

Oakes argues that if God exists, He can -- being
omnipotent -- bring about a self-validating religious experience.

673 _____. "Mediation, Encounter, and God," Int
J Phil Relig, II (Fall, 1971), 148-55.

Oakes argues that it is the nature of perception
to grasp its object through a medium. Therefore,
a perception of God could only occur if God was
mediated through some other datum. While it is
often claimed that an experience of finite things
can also, under certain circumstances, be an experience of God, the author wonders "how an experience of something finite could be revelatory
of that which transcends all finitude."

674 _____. "Noumena, Phenomena, and God," Int
J Phil Relig, IV (Spring, 1973), 30-8.

Oakes argues that whether or not an immediate
intuition of God as a noumenal object is possible,
it is possible for there to be a sensible intuition of God -- a perceptual encounter in which
the experience of God "supervenes upon" an experience of some sensible object.

675 _____. "Religious Experience and Rational
Certainty," _Relig Stud_, 12 (September, 1976),
311-8.

Oakes argues that (1) a self-authenticating experience should be construed as a veridical experience which is such that the person who has
that experience is rationally certain that it is
veridical, rather than as an experience which
cannot be delusive, and that (2) since it would
appear that God can produce experiences of Himself which exhibit these characteristics, self-
authenticating religious experiences are logically possible.

676 Osborn, Catherine B. "Artificial Paradises, Baudelaire and the Psychedelic Experience," _Amer
Schol_, 36 (Autumn, 1967), 660-8.

Consists largely of passages from "On Wine and
Hashish, compared as ways to the Multiplication
of the Personality" and _Artificial Paradises_,
Opium and Hashish, in which Baudelaire discusses
his drug experiences (which were very similar
to those sometimes induced by LSD and psilocybin)
and comes to the conclusion that these experiences
lead to a self-absorption and inflation of the
personality which is spiritually and morally
harmful. Interesting.

677 Otto, Rudolf. _The Idea of the Holy: An Inquiry
into the Non-rational Factor in the Idea of the
Divine and its Relation to the Rational_. Revised
with additions. Translated by John W. Harvey.
London: Oxford University Press, H. Milford,
1936. xix + 239 pp.

This classic, which first appeared in German in
1917, introduced the concept of numinous feelings.

In addition to its very influential description
of these feelings, there is a further development
of ideas presented in Otto's earlier works.
Numinous feelings disclose a numinous reality
(which is identical with or part of the noumenal
world), are the source of the concept of the
numinous, and provide the warrant for synthetic
a priori judgments which apply certain concepts
(necessity, goodness, completeness, etc.) to
the numinous reality.

678 _____. Mysticism East and West, A Comparative
Analysis of the Nature of Mysticism. Translated
by Bertha L. Bracey and Richenda C. Payne. New
York: Macmillan Co., 1932. xvii + 262 pp.

A comparison of Śankara and Eckhart which contains
many interesting observations on the nature of
mysticism.

679 _____. Naturalism and Religion. Translated
by J. Arthur Thomson and Margaret R. Thomson.
Edited with an introduction by the Rev. W. D.
Morrison, LL. D. London: Williams & Norgate;
New York: G. P. Putnam's Sons, 1907. xi +
374 pp.

Argues that the truths of religion rest upon
heart, conscience, feeling and intuition rather
than upon reason.

680 _____. The Philosophy of Religion based on
Kant and Fries. Translated by E. B. Dicker with
a foreword by W. Tudor Jones. London: Williams
& Norgate, 1931. 231 pp.

Originally appeared in German in 1909. Otto
argues that while reason can only ascertain what
the noumenal world is not, positive knowledge of
the noumenal world is provided by the feeling

of beauty, the feeling of the sublime, and religious feelings.

681 _____ . Religious Essays; A Supplement to
"The Idea of the Holy." Translated by Brian
Lunn. London: Oxford University Press, H.
Milford, 1931. vii + 160 pp.

Consists primarily of translations of essays found
in Das Gefühl des Überweltlichen (Sensus Numinis)
(Munich, 1932) and Sunde und Urshuld und andere
Aufsätze zur Theologie (Munich, 1932), the first
of which is the first part of the 5th and 6th
editions of Aufsätze das Numinose betreffend
(Stuttgart and Gotha, 1923) with some added material, and the second of which is the second
part of the 5th and 6th editions of the Aufsätze
with some added material. Of interest.

682 Owen, Huw Parri. The Christian Knowledge of God.
London: University of London, The Athlone Press,
1960. Pp. 178-205 and 269-81.

Interesting discussions of the nature of experience, the relation between interpretation and
religious experience, and a defense of the validity of religious experience against the charge
that it is private, that reductive explanations
of religious experience can be provided, that
its validity cannot be proved, etc. Owen compares religious experience with our (objectively
valid) experiences of goodness and beauty, and
insists that the differences between sense experience and religious experience can be explained
by differences in the nature of their objects.

683 Owens, Claire Myers. "The Mystical Experience:
     Facts and Values," Main Currents, 23 (March-April,
     1967), 93-9. (Reprinted in # 731 below, pp.
     135-52.)

     A critical examination of "Mystical States and
     the Concept of Regression" by Prince and Savage
     (see # 697 below).

684 Ozment, Steven E. Mysticism and Dissent: Reli-
     gious Ideology and Social Protest in the Sixteenth
     Century. New Haven: Yale University Press,
     1973. 270 pp.

     A study of Hans Denk, Sebastian Franck, and others
     which argues that their radical religious and
     political views are grounded in late medieval
     mysticism. The author contends that mysticism's
     "understanding of the penultimate character of
     all worldly power and authority" can provide a
     justification for "dissent, reform or revolu-
     tionary activity."

685 Pahnke, Walter Norman. "Drugs and Mysticism," Int
     J Parapsychology, VIII (Spring, 1966), 295-320.
     (Reprinted with some minor excisions in # 731
     below, pp. 257-77.)

     Substantially identical with "The Contribution
     of the Psychology of Religion to the Therapeutic
     Use of the Psychedelic Substances" in The Uses
     of LSD in Psychotherapy and Alcoholism, edited
     by Harold Abramson (Indianapolis: Bobbs-Merrill
     Co., 1967). An account of the nature of Pahnke's
     Harvard experiment, its results, and its impli-
     cations.

412

686 _____. "Drugs and Mysticism: An Analysis
of the Relationship between Psychedelic Drugs
and the Mystical Consciousness." Doctoral Dissertation: Harvard University, 1964. 153 pp.

Pahnke reports that a significant number of the
subjects who received psilocybin in his experiment enjoyed experiences which satisfy Stace's
criteria for a mystical experience. Pahnke's
experiment and conclusions have been frequently
discussed in the literature.

687 _____ and William A. Richards. "Implications
of LSD and Experimental Mysticism," J Relig
Health, 5 (July, 1966), 175-208.

Discusses the typology of mysticism used in
Pahnke's Harvard experiment, types of psychedelic
experience, and the implications of the investigation of these experiences for theology,
psychiatry and society.

688 _____. "LSD and Religious Experience," LSD,
Man and Society. Edited by R. C. Debold and
R. C. Leaf. Middletown: Wesleyan University
Press, 1967. Pp. 60-84.

Discusses types of psychedelic experiences, research projects designed to explore the connection between psychedelic drugs and religious
experience, psychedelic churches and other matters.

689 Penelhum, Terrence. Religion and Rationality, An
Introduction to the Philosophy of Religion.
New York: Random House, 1971. Pp. 163-83.

Chapter 13 provides a sympathetic but skeptical
examination of the claim that religious experiences have cognitive value. Of some interest.

413

690 Pensa, Corrado. "On the Purification Concept in
Indian Tradition, with Special Regard to Yoga,"
East West, 19 (1969), 194-228.

That there is a sharp distinction between mysticism, on the one hand, and magic and occult
phenomena, on the other, has become part of the
received wisdom on the subject of mysticism.
(Cf., e.g., Stace.) Pensa rather plausibly
argues that a careful and unbiased examination
of Yoga, Buddhism and Neoplatonism will show
that while "magical" and "occult" powers are
not cultivated for their own sake, they are believed to be both a sign of increased spiritual
power and a means to enlightenment. They are,
thus, an integral part of these mystical paths.

691 Pepler, Conrad. "The Unity of Mystical Experience,"
Blackfriars, 31 (April, 1950), 204-219.

While not a philosophical essay, Pepler's article
is of interest because it presents an alternative
both to the thesis that mysticism is everywhere
the same (Huxley, Stace, Suzuki) and to the
thesis that theistic mysticism must be distinguished from non-theistic mysticisms (Zaehner).
According to Pepler, a theoretical distinction
can be made between supernatural and natural
mysticism, but as a matter of fact all mysticism
is implicitly and by intention theistic and supernatural. Pepler thus preserves the unity of
mystical experience by baptizing non-Christian
mysticisms.

692 Pletcher, Galen Kenneth. "Agreement Among Mystics,"
Sophia, XI (July, 1972), 5-15.

An interesting defense of the proposition that
agreement among mystics provides impressive
support for the validity of their experiences.

693 _____. "Mysticism and Knowledge." Doctoral
Dissertation: The University of Michigan, 1971.
169 pp.

A defense of "mystical experience as a way of
knowing." C. B. Martin (# 658 above) is criticized for requiring stricter tests for religious
experience than are required for ordinary perceptual experience, and for undervaluing the importance of "coherence content checks," i.e.,
checks which attempt to determine the degree of
agreement and coherence within the same mode of
experience. After examining other difficulties
Pletcher concludes that if most mystics are in
agreement, it should be granted that "mystical
experience is a way of knowing those propositions
on which they agree."

694 _____. "Mysticism, Contradiction, and Ineffability," Amer Phil Quart, 10 (July, 1973),
201-11.

The author develops Paul Henle's thesis (see
612 above). Although no new ground is broken,
Pletcher does provide a persuasive presentation
of the position in question.

695 Poulain, Auguste. The Graces of Interior Prayer
(Des Graces d'Oraison). A Treatise on Mystical
Theology. Translated from the 6th edition by
Leonora L. Yorke Smith and corrected to accord
with the 10th French edition with an introduction
by J. V. Bainvel. St. Louis: B. Herder Book
Co., 1950. cxii + 665 pp.

415

This book appeared in France in 1901 and was one
of several works responsible for the revival
of interest in mystical contemplation among
Catholics in the latter part of the 19th century
and in the earlier part of the 20th century.
Contains an examination of the "experimental
perception of divinity" which lies at the heart
of contemplation, the "spiritual senses," and a
number of other topics. Well worth looking at.

696 Pratt, James Bissett. The Religious Consciousness,
     A Psychological Study. New York: The Macmillan
     Co., 1920. viii + 488 pp.

The last five chapters (pp. 337-479) contain a
sympathetic and balanced account of the nature
and value of mysticism. The final chapter, which
discusses the origin of mysticism and attempts
to assess its worth, should be of most interest
to philosophers.

697 Prince, Raymond and Charles Savage. "Mystical
     States and the Concept of Repression," Psyche-
     delic Rev, No. 8 (1966), 59-75. (Reprinted in
     # 731 below, pp. 114-34.)

An interesting attempt to explain mysticism as
a controlled regression to early pre-conceptual
experience, undertaken in the service of the ego.
For a critical examination of the authors' thesis
see Owens' "The Mystical Experience: Facts and
Values" (# 683 above).

698 Proudfoot, Wayne and Phillip Shaver. "Attribution
     Theory and the Psychology of Religion," J Scien
     Stud Relig, 14 (December, 1975), 317-30.

The authors discuss experiments which suggest
that emotions are partly determined by the way

in which subjects interpret certain physiological
states, or in which people's "attitudes, emotions
and other internal states" are known "partially
by inferring them from observations of their own
overt behavior and/or the circumstances in which
the behavior occurs." It is suggested that religious phenomena can be understood in a similar
way. This is an interesting paper but it is
not entirely clear whether the authors are arguing
that religion includes interpretation (and, thus,
a cognitive element), or that interpretations
placed upon feelings, physiological changes,
overt behavior, etc., (partially) <u>cause</u> religious
experience, or that inferences drawn from these
things (partially) <u>constitute</u> religious experience. It should be noted that the authors concentrate on cases in which some fairly neutral
internal or external change is <u>followed</u> by a
religious inference or interpretation rather
than on quasi-perceptual religious experiences
(viz., numinous experiences and classical mystical
experiences).

699 Raju, Poolla Tirupati. "Feigl on Intuition," <u>Phil</u>
     <u>East</u> <u>West</u>, VIII (October, 1958 and January, <u>1959</u>),
     <u>149-63</u>.

     A reply to Feigl's "Critique of Intuition Accord-
     ing to Scientific Empiricism," (# 605 above).
     The most interesting feature of this reply is
     the author's observations on knowledge by acquain-
     tance.

700 Regis, Edward, Jr. "A Dismissal of Mysticism,"
     <u>Relig</u> <u>Hum</u>, 9 (Autumn, 1975), 162-6.

     Regis defines mysticism as "the doctrine which

asserts the existence of a means of knowledge
which operates independent of reason and the
senses and provides access to truths which are
denied to them." To substantiate the doctrine
one would have to employ reason or the senses
to establish the truth of the propositions which
the mystic claims to know. Since, however, the
truth of these propositions is not (by definition)
within the purview of reason and the senses, one
cannot establish their truth in this way. It
follows that the doctrine of mysticism cannot
be substantiated and should be rejected. This
article is not without interest though it should
be noted that mystics do not always claim to
be aware of truths which cannot be known in other
ways. They sometimes claim to be <u>directly</u> ac-
<u>quainted</u> with truths or realities which are only
indirectly known (e.g., by inference or authority)
by non-mystics.

701 Robbins, J. Wesley. "C. B. Martin on Religious
     Experience," <u>Mod</u> <u>Sch</u>, LIII (January, 1976),
     167-71.

According to Martin, "objective" experiences
meet what might be called the "correlation condition." Objective visual experiences are, for
example, supported and corroborated by other
sense experiences. Religious experiences are
not correlated with <u>sense</u> experiences but this
(given the nature of their putative object) is
hardly surprising. On the other hand, if Otto
is even roughly correct, religious experience
is a complex of feeling states and conceptual
states which can occur in isolation, but which
often occur together and mutually support one
another. Martin's "correlation condition" is,

thus, in fact met though he fails to see that
this is the case.

702 _____. "John Hick on Religious Experience
and Perception," Int J Phil Relig, V (Summer,
1974), 108-18.

Hick (# 810 below) maintains that just as our
experience of physical objects is mediated through
sense impressions, so our experience of God is
mediated through finite realities. An interpretive activity is involved in both cases, and in
both cases it is impossible to prove that what
we take to be the ultimate object of the experience (physical objects, God) actually exists.
Robbins argues that the analogy breaks down because reference to an interpretive activity need
not be included in an analysis of sense perception.

703 Saudreau, Auguste. The Mystical State, Its Nature
and Phases. Translated by D. M. B. London:
Burns, Oates & Washbourne, Ltd., 1924. xvi +
204 pp.

One of the works responsible for the renewed interest in mysticism among Catholics in the late
19th century and early 20th century. Saudreau
(unlike most mystical theologians) maintains
that mystical contemplation does not typically
involve an "experimental perception" of divine
things. Rather, God's presence is inferred from
effects which God produces in the soul (feelings
of love, delight, etc.), and sometimes a conviction (but not a perception) of God's presence
is divinely infused. For a criticism of this
position see Farges' Mystical Phenomena (# 604

above) and Butler's <u>Western</u> <u>Mysticism</u> (# 588
above).

704 Scharfstein, Ben-Ami. <u>Mystical</u> <u>Experience</u>. Oxford:
     Basil Blackwell, 1973. 195 pp.

     Scharfstein's treatment of purely philosophical
     topics (e.g., the cognitive status of mystical
     experience, the metaphysical claims of mystical
     theologians like Proclus and Nāgārjuna) is su-
     perficial. Nevertheless, this book contains
     interesting discussions of a number of topics
     including mystical techniques, the relation be-
     tween Freudian analysis and Patanjali's yoga,
     and "psychotic mysticism."

705 Schmidt, Paul F. <u>Religious</u> <u>Knowledge</u>. Glencoe,
     Illinois: The Free Press of Glencoe, Inc., 1961.
     Pp. 113-36.

     In spite of an unpersuasive treatment of knowledge
     by acquaintance, chapter VIII provides a clear
     statement of a standard objection to the cogni-
     tive claims of religious experience, viz., that
     religious experiences are not evidence for the
     existence of supernatural reality unless one has
     independently (of these experiences) established
     the existence of these experiences and their
     alleged object, and shown that a correlation
     exists between the occurrence of these experi-
     ences and the presence of that object. For a
     critique of this claim see Wainwright, # 725
     below.

706 Shiner, Roger A. "A Defence of Encounters," <u>Sophia</u>,
     XII (October, 1973), 1-6.

     Hepburn has argued (# 613 above) that because

of the logical gap between encounter-experiences
and statements about reality which are based
upon them, one must remain skeptical of any claim
to have encountered God. Shiner argues that
a similar gap occurs between ordinary perceptual
experiences and claims based upon those experiences and that, therefore, there is no more reason
to be skeptical of the former than of the latter.

707 Smart, Ninian. A Dialogue of Religious. (The
     Library of Philosophy and Theology.) London:
     SCM Press, Ltd., 1960. Pp. 23-4, 46-60 and 71-2.

     Smart makes an important distinction between
     numinous feelings and mystical experiences, ar-
     guing that the former tends to express itself
     in theistic concepts and the latter in non-per-
     sonal concepts (e.g., the concepts of Advaita
     Vedānta or Theravāda Buddhism). This book was re-
     issued under the title World Religions, A Dialogue
     (Baltimore: Penguin Books, 1966).

708 _____. "Interpretation and Mystical Experi-
     ence," Relig Stud, 1 (October, 1965), 75-87.

     An important article which attacks Zaehner's
     distinction between monistic mysticism and the-
     istic mysticism, and proposes criteria by means
     of which descriptions of mystical experiences
     can be distinguished from interpretations of those
     experiences. Second hand accounts of mystical
     experiences and accounts which employ concepts
     with many theoretical ramifications are more
     plausibly construed as interpretations than as
     descriptions.

709   _____. "Mystical Experience," Sophia, I
      (April, 1962), 19-26.

Interesting criticism of a number of points made
in Stace's Mysticism and Philosophy (# 716 below).
Smart also considers how theism can accommodate
mysticism, and the objection that there can be
no perception of objects which transcend the
world.

710   _____, Nelson Craft Pike and Paul F. Schmidt.
    "Mystical Experience," Art, Mind and Religion,
    Proceedings of the 1965 Oberlin Colloquium in Phi-
    losophy. Edited by W. H. Capitan and D. D.
    Merrill. Pittsburgh: University of Pittsburgh
    Press, 1967. Pp. 133-58.

Smart's paper is an abbreviated version of # 708
above. Pike's response is the more interesting
of the two, and includes a number of observations
about the nature of phenomenological descriptions.
Smart's rejoinder to Pike and Schmidt is also
included.

711   _____. Philosophers and Religious Truth.
    London: SCM Press, Ltd., 1964. Pp. 130-66.

Chapter V contains a discussion of Rudolf Otto
and religious experience. Interesting observations on the validity of religious experience
and a number of other topics.

712 Smith, Huston. "Do Drugs Have Religious Import?"
    J Phil, LXI (October 1, 1964), 517-30.

Often reprinted, this important article maintains
that drugs can, under favorable conditions, induce
all varieties of mystical experience. Smith's
argument is partially vitiated by overstatement

and by the fact that he appears to equate theistic mysticism with visionary experiences and/or experiences in which the empirical personality enjoys a passionate or sentimental relationship to God. Smith defends the possibility that drug-induced religious experiences incorporate valid intuitions of reality, and discusses the relation between religious experiences and a religious life.

713 Smith, John Edwin. Experience and God. New York: Oxford University Press, 1968. viii + 209 pp.

In this book Smith develops what is becoming a rather influential account of religious experience. The first three chapters are particularly important. Religion can only be rooted in experience if experience is properly understood. It is a mistake to suppose that experience consists of sensory contents and feelings located within the private consciousness of isolated subjects. Experience occurs when we "encounter what is there," and is a joint product of the nature of what is encountered and of the nature, purposes, and interests of the encounterer. Experience is not an isolated momentary occurrence but social, involving the interpretation and comparison of encounters. Furthermore, its contents are not restricted to sense data or "raw feels" but include "events and things, . . . hopes and fears, . . . persons and places." What is true of experience in general is true of religious experience in particular. It is a mistake to concentrate on the idiosyncratic religious experiences of mystics and visionaries rather than on the religious dimension of experience. The "material" of this dimension is

provided by our awareness of dependence and
limitation and the need to find an object of
supreme worth to which we can devote ourselves.
This material emerges particularly clearly at
times of "crisis," and can become the medium
through which we encounter a reality upon whom
we depend for our being, purpose and fulfillment.
(Much of what Smith says suggests that it is the
generic concept or idea of God which is disclosed
through this medium rather than the actuality
which is the object of that idea or concept,
but apparently he wants to say both.) The specific God of the religious traditions is disclosed
through the medium of particular events, persons,
etc. God is neither immediately experienced
(as sensory qualities are experienced) nor inferred from experience, but is directly encountered in a mediated or interpreted experience.
Thus, the experience of God is also an "experience
of something else at the same time" through which
God is disclosed. In this respect, our experience of God is like our experience of other persons who reveal themselves to us through speech,
expressions, gestures, etc. (It is worth noting
that, according to Smith, in both cases the problem is not whether or not we are encountering
something -- that we are doing so is given -- but
the nature of that which is encountered.) See
Londis's critique of this position (# 648 above).

714 _____. "In What Sense Can We Speak of Experiencing God?" J Relig, 50 (July, 1970), 229-44.

A development of some of the themes of Experience
and God (# 713 above). There is, e.g., a clear
statement of the claim that experience involves
a "co-presence" which "is the warrant for the is

of what is . . . encountered," and a discussion
of the way in which experience includes inference.

715 Staal, Frits. Exploring Mysticism, A Methodological Essay. Berkeley, Los Angeles, London:
University of California Press, 1975. xix +
230 pp.

Eastern religious traditions, such as Mādhyamika,
are defended against the charge of irrationalism
on the grounds that although they may reject the
law of excluded middle and deny that any predicates apply to reality, they do accept the law
of non-contradiction. It is admitted that someone
like Nāgārjuna may occasionally get caught in
contradictions, but Staal contends that he is
not an irrationalist because he does not "desire
to be illogical." Western religion, on the other
hand, is irrational. Staal arrives at this conclusion by making Tertullian, Pascal and Kierkegaard speak for the whole western tradition,
and by calling attention to Christianity's acceptance of the doctrines of the Trinity and
Incarnation. Buddhist paradoxes are explained
away as merely apparent contradictions but Christian paradoxes are taken at face value. These
sections of Staal's book are primarily noteworthy
for providing a paradigmatic example of special
pleading. Staal next proceeds to examine various
approaches to the study of mysticism. Theological approaches are invalid because of dogmatic
bias. Philological and historical approaches
are unsatisfactory because they concentrate on
terms and texts rather than experiences. Phenomenology does not raise the question of validity
and is often infected by bias. The investigation
of the physiology of mysticism merely provides

information about its incidental effects. The
psychological approach is the most promising
but the psychological studies which have been
constructed up to this point are useless. While
many of Staal's judgments are undoubtedly correct,
they are inadequately supported by argument.
(Thus, in attacking Zaehner, Staal calls attention to some historical errors in his work, but
does not provide any arguments against Zaehner's
central thesis, viz., that a distinction can be
drawn between nature mysticism, monistic mysticism, and theistic mysticism.) Staal concludes
that to study mysticism we must observe mystical
experiences at first hand (i.e., we must have
them), points out that this may involve placing
ourselves in the hands of a guru, sympathetically
considers the possibility that drugs may provide
useful tools under certain conditions, calls our
attention to the difficulties involved in distinguishing interpretation from experience, etc.
The argument in these final sections contains
little which is new. This book will probably
become influential because of its author's schol-
arly reputation, and, in spite of its weaknesses,
it does contain much interesting incidental information. Chapter 2 (which examines the claim
that Buddhists knowingly accepted contradictions)
is of special interest.

716 Stace, Walter Terence. Mysticism and Philosophy.
     Philadelphia & New York: J. B. Lippincott Co.,
     1960. 349 pp.

Perhaps the best philosophical book on mysticism
to appear in this century. Stace's distinction
between extrovertive and introvertive mysticism
has been widely influential. Contains a number of

interesting arguments. Particularly noteworthy
are arguments which purport to show that mystical
experiences are neither subjective nor objective,
that they are experiences of a Universal Self
which transcends the empirical personality, and
that because logic only applies where duality
obtains, neither mystical experiences nor mystical
claims can be evaluated by logical criteria. For
a criticism of these positions see Smart (# 709
above, Watkin (# 729 below), and, especially,
Wainwright (# 727 below).

717   _____. Time and Eternity, An Essay in the
Philosophy of Religion. Princeton, N. J.:
Princeton University Press, 1952. vii + 169 pp.

At the heart of religion is a mystical intuition
which (since it involves no distinction between
subject and object) can be referred to either
by "mystical experience" or by "God." This intuition is unconceptualizable because it is in-
divisible and unrelated to anything else. Affirmative religious statements are not literally
true. They merely evoke the experience. (In
Mysticism and Philosophy Stace will argue that
some of these affirmative statements are literally
true in spite of the fact that they are self-
contradictory.) Mystical experience is the in-
tersection of an eternal and a temporal order
of being. Seen from within, the experience
(=God) is non-conceptualizable, infinite, eternal,
and the only reality. Seen from without, it is
located in space and time, has causes and effects,
and can be conceptualized.

718 Suzuki, Daisetz Teitaro. Mysticism: Christian
     and Buddhist, The Eastern and Western Way. (World
     Perspectives Series, 12.) New York: Harper
     and Bros., 1957. 214 pp.

     A comparative study which focuses on Eckhart
     and Zen. In this study Suzuki articulates cer-
     tain familiar and influential theses -- that
     all mysticism is essentially the same (a seeing
     into the "suchness of things"), that conceptual
     thought is necessarily dualistic and presents a
     distorted picture of reality, that experience
     is at the heart of religion, etc., etc.

719 _____. Zen Buddhism: Selected Writings.
     Edited by William Barrett. Garden City, New
     York: Doubleday and Co., Inc., 1956. 294 pp.

     A collection of representative essays. It should
     be noted that Suzuki presents Zen from the stand-
     point of its Rinzai school. A useful corrective
     to his influential but somewhat one sided charac-
     terization can be found in Heinrich Doumoulin's A
     History of Zen Buddhism (translated by Paul
     Peachy, New York: Random House, 1963). Essays
     of special interest to philosophers are "The
     Sense of Zen," "Satori, or Enlightenment," "The
     Role of Nature in Zen Buddhism," and "Existen-
     tialism, Pragmatism and Zen."

720 Tennant, Frederick Robert. Philosophical Theology.
     Vol. I: The Soul and Its Faculties. Cambridge:
     Cambridge University Press, 1928. Pp. 306-22.

     Tennant argues that religious experience can't
     provide a basis for theology. There are too many
     disanalogies between mystical experience and
     sense experience (e.g., the absence, in the
     former case, of anything corresponding to sensa).

The alleged truths of mysticism cannot simply
be read off mystical experience. They are either
inferred from the experience or are an interpretation placed upon it. (Thus, what appears to
be a perceptual experience is not actually a
perceptual experience.) While religious experience can be interpreted or explained theistically,
there is nothing about it which demands such
an interpretation or explanation.

721   Underhill, Evelyn. The Essentials of Mysticism
      and Other Essays. London & Toronto: J. M. Dent
      & Sons, Ltd.; New York: E. P. Dutton & Co., 1920.
      vii + 245 pp.

      Essays on Plotinus, three medieval mystics, three
      modern French mystics, and a number of other
      subjects. The most interesting are "The Mystic
      as Creative Artist" and "The Mystic and the Cor-
      porate Life." The latter discusses the value of
      the corporate religious life for the mystic and
      helps to correct a onesided emphasis on the mystic
      as a religious individualist or spiritual anar-
      chist who stands outside of, and is opposed to,
      institutional religion. (The first of these es-
      says originally appeared in The Quest 4 [July,
      1913], pp. 629-52. The second originally appeared
      in The Interpreter 11 [January, 1915], pp.
      143-60.)

722   _____. Mysticism, A Study in the Nature and
      Development of Man's Spiritual Consciousness.
      12th ed., revised. London: Methuen and Co.;
      New York: E. P. Dutton & Co., Inc., 1930. xviii
      + 515 pp.

      The first edition was published in 1911. The
      first part of Underhill's book contains discus-
      sions of the nature and psychology of mysticism,

its expression in philosophy and psychology,
symbolic expressions of the mystical life (the
Pilgrimage or Quest, the Spiritual Marriage, and
the "Great Work" of the alchemists), and mysticism's relation to magic and the occult. The
second part provides a very valuable account of
the stages (Purgation, Illumination, etc.) through
which a mystic passes in his quest for perfect
union with the divine. Includes an extensive
bibliography. Underhill tends to restrict her
attention to theistic and specifically Christian
mysticism, and was strongly influenced by Bergson
and other "vitalists." Nevertheless, her book
is still valuable. Mysticism was revised twice.
(The third edition, which appeared in 1912, and
the 12th edition, which appeared in 1930, incorporate slight but significant changes. For example, phrases which might suggest identity between the mystic and God are altered in the 1912
edition.)

723 _____. The Mystic Way: A Psychological Study
in Christian Origins. London & Toronto: J. M.
Dent & Sons, Ltd.; New York: E. P. Dutton &
Co., 1913. xiv + 395 pp.

Underhill (influenced by Bergson and others)
develops an evolutionary theory according to
which life as a whole is irresistably moving
towards the Transcendent, and mystics are a "new
species" in which the urge toward the Absolute
is most fully realized. All mysticism seeks unity
with God, but God is a whole which combines Being
and Becoming, Rest and Motion, etc. The mysticism identified with the via negativa identifies
God with Being, and the soul with only one of
its own aspects (being), and is thus a

subtraction from life, an escape. The other
mysticism is a dynamic love mysticism which embraces the whole in its fullness, which transmutes
the personality rather than subtracts from it,
and is active as well as contemplative. The
greatest part of this book is devoted to a justification of the claim that this sort of mysticism emerges with Christianity and can be traced
in the life of Jesus, the writings of Paul and
John, the early church, and in the liturgy.
While interesting -- and not untraditional --
this portion of Underhill's book is historically
contentious.

724 Wainwright, William Judson. "Morality and Mysti-
     cism," J Relig Ethics, 4 (Spring, 1976), 29-36.

     Stace (# 716 above) and others maintain that
     mystical consciousness reveals the identity of
     selves and, therefore, provides a justification
     for altruism. Zaehner (# 741 below) argues that
     some types of mystical consciousness seem to re-
     veal the identity of such opposites as good and
     evil, and Danto (# 597 above) asserts that mysti-
     cal consciousness involves a transcendence of
     all distinctions including moral distinctions.
     In either case, morality collapses. Wainwright
     attempts to show that these arguments are defec-
     tive, and suggests that there are probably no
     important epistemic or lógical connections be-
     tween mystical consciousness and morality.

725 _____. "Mysticism and Sense Perception,"
     Relig Stud, 9 (September, 1973), 257-78.

     Explores the analogy between mystical experiences
     and sense experiences and argues that the

similarity between the two modes of experience
is greater than C. B. Martin and other skeptics
would allow.

726 _____. "Natural Explanations and Religious
Experience," Ratio, XV (June, 1973), 98-101.

A reply to Alston (# 569 above). Wainwright argues
that the existence of a complete scientific explanation of religious experience is compatible
with the validity of religious experience.

727 _____. "Stace and Mysticism," J Relig, 50
(April, 1970), 139-54.

Argues that Stace (see # 716 above) has failed
to show (1) that mystical experiences are neither
objective nor subjective, (2) that there is one
universal Self, and (3) that logic does not apply
to mystical experiences and mystical claims.

728 _____. "Two Theories of Mysticism: Gilson
and Maritain," Mod Sch, LII (May, 1975), 405-26.

A critical analysis of the theory that God can
be experimentally perceived through the effects
(felt love and delight) which He creates in the
soul. Among other things, this article contains
an examination of arguments which purport to show
that mystical perception must employ a medium
through which God is apprehended. These arguments are shown to be unsound.

729 Watkin, Edward Ingram. "Beyond All Utterance,"
Month, 28 (Summer, 1962), 168-71.

Critical discussion of some points made in Stace's
Mysticism and Philosophy (# 716 above).

432

730 _____. The Philosophy of Mysticism. London:
G. Richards, Ltd.; New York: Harcourt, Brace
and Howe, 1920. 412 pp.

A study of "the metaphysic implied in mystical
experience," and of the stages through which
the object of that experience is attained. Watkin states that he has selected St. John of the
Cross as his guide. While not particularly original, this readable book provides a good example
of a type of Roman Catholic interpretation of
mysticism common in the earlier part of this
century. (It belongs to the same milieu as the
work of Browne, Butler, Farges, Poulain, Saudreau,
etc.).

731 White, John, ed. The Highest State of Consciousness. Garden City, New York: Anchor Books,
Doubleday & Co., Inc., 1972. vii + 512 pp.

Essays by Huxley, Laing, Maslow, Watts and others
on higher states of consciousness. Reprints
articles which should interest philosophers,
but which are drawn from journals which philosophers would not normally examine.

732 Wiebe, D. "The Religious Experience Argument,"
Sophia, XIV (March, 1975), 19-28.

A reply to Lawrence C. Becker, "A Note on Religious Experience Arguments" (Religious Studies,
7, March, 1971, 63-8). While Becker's article
is of little interest, Wiebe makes a valuable
point in his response to Becker. The appeal to
religious experience is designed to replace the
traditional rational arguments. Hence, it must
not be construed as an inference from subjective
data to God (i.e., as an argument), but rather

as an appeal to a "perception" or "intuition" or "awareness" of divinity. Argument only appears at a second level at which we attempt to vindicate this intuition (or our reliance upon it).

733 Wilson, John Cook. "Rational Grounds of Belief in God," Statement and Inference, with Other Philosophical Papers by John Cook Wilson. Edited from the mss. &c. by A. S. L. Farquharson, with a Portrait, Memoir, and Selected Correspondance. Vol. II. Oxford: The Clarendon Press, 1926. Pp. 835-67.

This essay provides a better than average discussion of the claim that belief in God is a consequence of direct experience. The experience of reverence and awe may be compared with other experiences (e.g., the experience of gratitude) but is sui generis. Furthermore, the uniqueness of the idea of the object of the experience can only be adequately explained if we assume that the experience is what it purports to be, viz., the experience of an eternal spirit. The most interesting feature of this essay is Wilson's attempt to show that we can be directly conscious of things (e.g., causality, the self) whose existence we do not implicitly acknowledge and may even doubt.

734 Yandell, Keith Edward. "Religious Experience and Rational Appraisal," Relig Stud, 10 (June, 1974), 173-87.

Yandell (1) analyzes "someone having an experience of something" and argues that the concept applies to numinous but not to monistic experiences, (2) analyzes "self-authenticating experience" and argues that religious experiences aren't self-authenticating, and (3) discusses the

conditions under which an experience can be said
to provide evidence for a claim.

735 _____. "Some Varieties of Ineffability,"
Int J Phil Relig, VI (Fall, 1975), 167-79.

Yandell argues that religious experience is not
ineffable in any interesting sense. Both "experience-entailed concepts" (e.g., "experience,"
"'owned' by someone," "having only consistent
properties") and non-["experience-entailed concepts"] (e.g., "experience central to at least
one religious tradition") apply to religious
experience. Religious experiences may have features which can only be discerned by those who
have them, but the same is true of (e.g.) the
experience of tasting a pineapple. Yandell concludes by suggesting that if religious experience
were genuinely ineffable it "would contain nothing
to render any [belief,] rite, practice, institution, or attitude somehow more appropriate
than any other."

736 Zaehner, Robert Charles. At Sundry Times, An Essay
in the Comparison of Religions. London: Faber
& Faber Ltd., 1958. 230 pp.

Published in the U.S. as The Comparison of Religions (Boston: Beacon Press, 1962). Contains
discussions of the mysticisms of India, and of
the prophetic religions of Zoroaster and Muhammad.
The discussion of nature mysticism in chapter 3
is particularly interesting. Zaehner argues that
since the nature mystic is not literally identical
with nature, he can't (veridically) experience
identity with nature, and that in fact what nature
mysticism actually involves is a union with the

435

"imago mundi" which Zaehner somehow manages to
identify with Jung's collective unconscious.

737 _____. Concordant Discord, The Interdepen-
dence of Faiths, Being the Gifford Lectures on
Natural Religion Delivered at St. Andrews in
1967-1969 by R. C. Zaehner. Oxford: The Clarendon Press, 1970. ix + 464 pp.

A major work which discusses the mystical strand
in eastern and western religion, religion's ethical strand (with special reference to the Mahāb-
hārata and Chinese religion), the Fall (with
special reference to Rousseau), the Incarnation,
the relation of matter and spirit, and other
topics. Of special interest are the discussion
of cosmic consciousness (=nature mysticism) in
chapter III, the discussion of types of mysticism
and of the annihilation of the ego in chapter X
(where Zaehner, for the first time, distinguishes
four forms of mystical consciousness -- the
transcendence of space, the transcendence of time,
monistic mysticism and theistic mysticism), and
the discussion of theistic mysticism in chapter
XV.

738 _____. Drugs, Mysticism and Make-Believe.
London: William Collins Sons & Co. Ltd., 1972.
223 pp.

Published in the U.S. as Zen, Drugs and Mysticism
(New York: Pantheon Books, 1973). Very interesting discussions of nature mysticism and "negative mysticism" with special reference to Ber-
nanos' Monsieur Ouine. While Zaehner's earlier
attitude toward nature mysticism was somewhat
ambiguous (though on the whole negative), nature
mysticism is now clearly condemned as both

intellectually and morally suspect. Negative
mysticism is a mysticism of "death" and "ice"
in which the world is stripped of value and robbed
of meaning. (These experiences may be compared
with the experience of "nausea" described by
Sartre, and with the "psychotic mysticism" discussed by Scharfstein [#704 above]. Insufficient
attention has been paid to these experiences.
In particular, it is necessary to ask whether
the considerations which are introduced to show
that ["positive"] mystical and numinous experiences are veridical would also show that these
experiences are veridical.)

739   . Hindu and Muslim Mysticism. (Jordan
Lectures in Comparative Religion, 5.) London:
University of London, The Athlone Press, 1960.
234 pp.

An interesting study of the monistic and theistic
mystical strands, and the relationship between
them. Zaehner's discussion in this book and
elsewhere provides a helpful corrective to the
simplistic identification of monistic and theistic
mysticism with eastern and western mysticism
respectively.

740   . Mysticism: Sacred and Profane, An
Inquiry into Some Varieties of Praeternatural
Experience. Oxford: The Clarendon Press, 1957.
xviii + 256 pp.

In this important and influential book, Zaehner
distinguishes between nature mysticism (an experience of the unity of the phenomenal world in
which the empirical ego loses itself in nature),
monistic mysticism (an experience of undifferen-
tiated unity which transcends space and time),

and theistic mysticism (an experience in which
the transcendental self, free from space and time,
lovingly unites with its divine ground).

741 _____. Our Savage God. London: William
Collins Sons & Co. Ltd., 1974. 319 pp.

Contains a moral indictment of nature mysticism
or cosmic consciousness because of its indif-
ference to the distinction between good and evil,
a sympathetic discussion of the way in which the
rational and contemplative strands are combined
in the Aristotelian tradition, and a discussion
of the "anti-rational" or "savage" God of the
Bible, Islam, and (parts of) the Bhagavad-Gītā.
Zaehner is prone to exaggeration and is often
polemical, dogmatic and unfair. These faults are
particularly characteristic of his last works.
Zaehner continues, however, to be very suggestive
and his theses, although overstated, must be
taken seriously.

V MIRACLES

742 Ahern, Dennis Michael. "Hume on the Evidential
Impossibility of Miracles," Studies in Epistemology. (American Philosophical Quarterly Series,
9.) Oxford: Basil Blackwell, 1975. Pp. 1-31.

In this very interesting paper, Ahern argues
that Hume intended to show not only that there is
no good evidence for miracles but that there can
be no good evidence for miracles. The clue to
the correct interpretation of Hume's essay is
provided by the fact that Hume claims to be employing an argument similar to that used by
Tillotson against the doctrine of transubstantiation. Ahern shows that Hume mis-states

Tillotson's argument which is in essence as follows: If transubstantiation were true and what appears to be bread and wine were not really bread and wine, we would have no grounds for ever relying on our senses. However, "sensory evidence in the form of observation of miracles is the main evidence for" Christianity, and one must rely on the senses in order to determine the contents of scripture. It follows that if transubstantiation were true, no grounds could be provided for it "that relied upon miracles, the authority of scripture, or any kind of empirical evidence." Hence, the doctrine cannot be established "either by empirical evidence or by the authority of scripture." According to Ahern, Tillotson is not arguing that transubstantiation is conceptually impossible or even physically impossible but that transubstantiation is evidentially impossible where "p is evidentially impossible if and only if alleged evidence for the truth of p would not be evidence for p were the truth of p established." Ahern suggests that Hume's insistence that no proof can establish a miracle should be understood in a similar way. (1) A proof of the occurrence of a miracle would undermine the proof of the natural law which the alleged miracle is supposed to violate. Since the event in question is only a miracle if that natural law holds, the proof destroys itself. (2) If miracles were to occur, causal judgments concerning the capacities of nature would be unreliable but since we must possess a reliable understanding of the capacities of nature if we are to reliably judge that a miracle has occurred, it follows that if miracles occur judgments that they have occurred are unreliable.

(As Ahern points out, the second argument is closer to Tillotson.) One may doubt whether Ahern has correctly interpreted Hume. (The fact that Hume mis-states Tillotson's argument and never explicitly formulates the arguments which Ahern ascribes to him would seem to count rather strongly against Ahern's interpretation.) The argument which Ahern finds in Tillotson and the somewhat similar arguments which Ahern ascribes to Hume are, however, of considerable intrinsic interest even though each of these arguments contains a questionable premiss. (Thus, as Ahern points out, it is just not clear that if miracles were to occur all causal judgments would be un-reliable.)

743   _____. "Miracles and Physical Impossibility,"
         Can J Phil, VII (March, 1977), 71-9.

Natural laws are nomologicals which entail coun-terfactuals. These counterfactuals can be un-derstood in either of two ways: (1) as asserting that were c to occur e would occur, if "there are no other causally relevant (natural or super-natural) forces present," or (2) as asserting that were c to occur e would occur, if "there are no other causally relevant natural forces pre-sent." If the relevant counterfactuals are understood in the first way, then it is impossible for events to occur which are incompatible with natural law. (Even if, e.g., the presence of supernatural forces were to prevent the occurrence of e in circumstances c, nothing would have hap-pened which was incompatible with the relevant counterfactual.) If the relevant counterfactuals are understood in the second way, then if natural laws are true, events incompatible with natural law will not occur. (If the presence of supernatural forces were to prevent the occurrence of e in circumstances c, the relevant counterfactual would be false.) Ahern suggests that instead of understanding "physically impossible events" or "violations of natural law" as events which are logically incompatible with the laws of nature, we should instead understand them as events "which can be explained only by reference to the intervention of a supernatural force."

744 Boden, Margaret A. "Miracles and Scientific Explanation," Ratio, XI (December, 1969), 137-44.

A reply to Robinson (# 767 below). Boden asks us to imagine a case in which we and others observe someone fully restore a leper's lost fingers in ten seconds by saying "caramba." "This would surely be an example of an event which was conceptually of a type to be explained by science (i.e., an observable event) but permanently and contingently inexplicable by science." The occurrence of this event "conflicts with so many of our basic scientific beliefs" that a belief in its scientific explicability is "as blatant an act of faith as the wildest claim ever made in the name of religion."

745 Broad, Charlie Dunbar. "Hume's Theory of the Credibility of Miracles," Proc Aris Soc, XVIII (New Series), (1916-1917), 77-94.

According to Broad, Hume's essay on miracles is "an over-rated work" which falls below his usual high standards. Hume intends to show two things -- that even if the testimony for a miracle is as good as possible we ought not to believe that

a miracle has occurred, and that in fact the
testimony for miracles never is the best possible.
Broad agrees with Hume's second contention, but
maintains that Hume has not established the first
contention. Hume in effect argues that we should
reject testimony when there is a uniform experience against the occurrence of the events to
which that testimony bears witness. According
to Broad, if one were to accept Hume's recommendation he would not only reject reports of alleged
miracles but would also reject reports of alleged
counter-instances to formulae which are believed
to be laws of nature. This policy would, if
generally followed, bring science to a standstill.
Broad also contends that Hume's psychological
account of the belief in induction vitiates his
argument. The belief in continued uniformity
cannot be logically justified although it can
be psychologically explained by the "natural
tendency to pass from the constant experience
of A followed by B to the belief that A will always be followed by B." Similarly, the enthusiast's belief in miracles cannot be logically
justified although it can be psychologically
explained by "his natural tendency to believe
what is wonderful and what makes for the credit
of his religion." "Hence the enthusiast's belief
in miracles and Hume's belief in natural laws
(and consequent disbelief in miracles) stand on
precisely the same logical footing." This is a
significant and rather influential article.

746 Cherry, Christopher. "Miracles and Creation,"
    Int J Phil Relig, V (Winter, 1974), 234-45.

    Cherry argues that a miraculous intervention must
    be understood as the creation of a new state of

affairs rather than as the "harnessing and de-
ployment of natural resources in some supernaturally sophisticated manner." On the latter
view, God employs empirical means to produce
the desired effect. Since the empirical conditions which God deploys as means are sufficient
to bring about the event it is false that the
occurrence can only be understood supernaturally,
and from this it follows that there is no reason
to suppose that the event must be understood
supernaturally.

747 Dietl, Paul. "On Miracles," Amer Phil Quart, 5
     (October, 1967), 130-4.

A defense of the coherence of the concept of
miracle. An event is described which clearly
appears to be an exception to natural law. Dietl
makes a number of useful observations, perhaps
the most significant of which is the following:
Explanations do not always rest upon laws. In
particular, explanations of actions do not always
do so. To explain an event by interpreting it
as a miracle involves regarding that event as an
action. Therefore, the fact that such explanations do not rest upon laws is (pace Nowell-Smith
[# 766 below]) irrelevant.

748 Dubs, Homer H. "Miracles -- A Contemporary Atti-
     tude," Hibb J, XLVIII (January, 1950), 159-62.

Dubs argues that intelligent Christians can no
longer believe in miracles if miracles are construed as violations of natural law. Miracles
should rather be construed "as any act of God,"
where "all events that are truly good are, at
least in part, God's acts." This article

443

illustrates an attitude towards miracles which
is fairly widespread among modern Christians.
Its primary interest, however, consists in the
fact that it is the first in a series of papers
which concludes with Nowell-Smith's well known
essay on miracles. See Lunn's reply (# 762
below).

749 Farmer, Herbert Henry. The World and God, A Study
     of Prayer, Providence and Miracle in Christian
     Experience. London: James Nisbet & Co., Ltd.;
     New York: Harper and Row, 1935. Pp. 107-27
     and 145-79.

In chapter VII, Farmer explicates the concept
of miracle. A miracle is an event through which
God reveals Himself, and -- because it reveals
God -- is an occasion of wonder and awe. Miracles are distinguished from other revelatory
events in virtue of the fact that they reveal
God "as actively succoring human life." The
term is most appropriately used when this succor
is felt to be most "intensely personal and individual," i.e., when an event answers "a prayer
for succor in a situation apprehended as being
peculiarly critical in personal destiny." Farmer
wishes to ground these events in special divine
volitions while at the same time avoiding the
notion that miracles violate natural law. In
chapters IX and X, Farmer argues that the initiation of particular events by divine volition
is, scientifically, no more problematic than
the initiation of particular events by human
volition. These chapters are interesting but
confusing. Farmer appears to be saying two rather
different things: (1) Scientific "laws" are
statements of observed regularities and/or statistical generalizations. Scientific predictions

444

are probabilistic. Hence, science cannot exclude the possibility that a special divine intervention operates as a causal factor in any concrete situation, although it does not need to take account of this possibility. (2) "Nature" is the phenomenal expression of the routine activity of a society of finite wills. God "intervenes" by redirecting this routine activity. Since God's intervention (as distinguished from the effects of His intervention) occurs at the noumenal level, it is of no concern to science. Farmer's discussion has the merit of stressing the connection between the concept of miracle and the concept of an active, holy will. He may be correct in maintaining that this concept is a particularly apt expression of a theism which clings to the idea of a personal God who stands in personal relation to other free beings.

750   Fethe, Charles B. "Miracles and Action Explanations," Phil Phenomenol Res, XXXVI (March, 1976), 415-22.

It has been suggested that the theistic explanation of miraculous occurrences should be assimilated to action explanations rather than to scientific explanations. Fethe argues that action explanations are causal explanations, and that it is incumbent upon anyone who denies that this type of causal explanation presupposes the existence of a law-like relation between the cause and its effect to (1) explain the difference between the causal connection to which he is appealing and a mere conjunction, and (2) defend himself against the charge that his explanation is ex post facto, "uselessly tacked on to past somethings." According to Fethe, theists are unable to do either of these things.

751   Flew, Antony Garrard Newton. Hume's Philosophy of
      Belief, A Study of His First Inquiry. (Inter-
      national Library of Philosophy and Scientific
      Method.) London: Routledge & Kegan Paul; New
      York: The Humanities Press, 1961. Pp. 166-213.

      Chapter VIII contains a sympathetic but not en-
      tirely uncritical discussion of Hume's essay
      on miracles. Hume is defended against several
      objections. Flew concedes that even though Hume's
      argument is only designed to show that we cannot
      have good evidence for the occurrence of miracles,
      Hume may in fact have thought that as violations
      of natural law, miracles are intrinsically impos-
      sible, and that this fact complicates the inter-
      pretation of the essay at certain points. Flew
      also argues that Hume could have strengthened
      his argument if he had recognized that natural
      laws are nomologicals and not (mere) statements
      of constant conjunction.

752   Gaskin, John C. A. "Miracles and the Religiously
      Significant Coincidence," Ratio, XVII (June,
      1975), 72-81.

      Extraordinary and impressive coincidence should
      be distinguished from events which involve an
      apparent violation of natural law. Unlike the
      latter, the former can be fully explained by
      natural factors. Consequently, while extraor-
      dinary coincidences can be regarded as the acts
      of a god if they are compatible with his charac-
      ter, they do not (like "violation miracles")
      provide evidence for the existence of an invisible
      agent. Furthermore, since "coincidence miracles"
      are the result of natural factors it is difficult

446

to explain why a "coincidence miracle" should be regarded as a special act of God, or why it should be thought to reveal God's character or purposes more clearly than other events.

753 Grant, Robert McQueen. Miracle and Natural Law in Graeco-Roman and Early Christian Thought. Amsterdam: North Holland Pub. Co., 1952. 293 pp.

Grant's theme is the credulity, scientific ignorance, and lack of firm critical standards which mar the work of early Christian intellectuals and their non-Christian counterparts. This theme is illustrated by a vast amount of material drawn from Christian and non-Christian sources. Whether this material establishes the author's thesis is, however, a moot point. (Science was admittedly primitive and stagnant, but was the Christian belief in Christ's resurrection a consequence of scientific ignorance? Were no critical standards employed or is it simply that the critical standards which were employed are not those of a modern biblical scholar? Is "credulity" the right word to apply to, e.g., the early Fathers or the Middle and Late Platonists?) The material which Grant introduces to support his conclusion possesses considerable intrinsic interest although his presentation of philosophical and theological arguments is often too sketchy to be helpful.

754 Hardon, John A. "The Concept of Miracle from St. Augustine to Modern Apologetics," Theol Stud, XV (June, 1954), 229-57.

Its title notwithstanding, most of this essay is concerned with comparatively recent Roman Catholic theology. Of special interest is Hardon's

447

discussion of the work of Pope Benedict XIV which
"remains . . . the standard reference at the
Roman Curia in the processes of beatification
and canonization." In spite of its intrinsic
interest, Benedict's account of miracles has
been largely ignored by philosophers. (R. G.
Swinburne is a notable exception.) The concluding
pages, in which the author comments on the way in
which miracles function as signs, are also of
interest. The article as a whole has a direct
and important bearing on the question of the proper definition of "miracle."

755 Holland, R. F. "The Miraculous," Amer Phil Quart,
     2 (January, 1965), 43-51.

Holland first argues that coincidences can be
viewed as miracles when they are significant
because of "their relation to human needs and
hopes and fears." To regard a coincidence as a
miracle involves regarding it as something for
which God is to be thanked, something which could
be prayed for, something which could "be taken
as a sign or made the subject of a vow," etc.
Miracles of this sort must be sharply distinguished
from those which involve an interference in the
natural order. The remainder of the article is
devoted to an examination of the concept of miracle
as a violation of natural law. Holland describes
three events (one of which is the alleged miracle
at Cana) and contends that, under the described
conditions, one should assert both that the occurrence of those events is empirically certain
and that the occurrence of those events is conceptually impossible (from which it follows that
it is not always true that to be is to be possible). Holland's remarks are misleading for

by "conceptually impossible" he simply means "imcompatible with well-established scientific conceptions."

756 Jeffner, Anders. Butler and Hume on Religion, A Comparative Analysis. Translated by Keith Brad-field, notes translated by James Stewart. (Studia Doctrinae Christiane Upsaliensia, 7.) Stockholm: Diakonistyrelsens Bokförlag, 1966. Pp. 112-25.

Chapter V section A considers several definitions of "miracle." It is argued that, defined in these ways, miracles are either of such a nature that is is impossible to provide adequate empirical evidence for their occurrence or of such a nature that an inference from their occurrence to divine intervention is unwarranted. Jeffner concludes by suggesting that if we possessed independent reasons for supposing that God acted directly through Christ, we would have reason to believe both that we were dealing with a situation which was unique and that the standards in terms of which we ordinarily assess probabilities do not apply. In these circumstances it would be rea-sonable to base our judgment as to the probability or improbability of the occurrence of miracles on considerations of testimony alone.

757 Keller, Ernst and Marie-Luise. Miracles in Dispute, A Continuing Debate. Translated by Margaret Kohl from the German Der Streit um die Wunder. London: S. C. M. Press; Philadelphia: Fortress Press, 1969. 256 pp.

The first (and longest) part of this book provides a historical account of the ways in which Chris-tian scholars and their critics have handled the subject of miracles. Biblical and medieval views are perfunctorily examined in the first

two chapters. The last ten chapters of the first
part are devoted to Post-Reformation (principally
German) discussions of miracles. The authors
show how criticisms of traditional supernaturalism
first led to attempts to explain biblical miracles
naturalistically, and how the failure of these
attempts led Strauss and Feuerbach (and, more
recently, Bultmann and Bloch) to treat miracle
stories as significant myths. This section of
the book is of some interest. In the second
part, the authors argue that the mythical point
of view is the only point of view compatible
with a modern Christian consciousness which regards nature and history as an interconnected
whole that precludes any invasions from without
or the suspension of its natural processes. The
mythical point of view is also the only point
of view which is compatible with the belief in
a God who -- instead of being the direct and
immediate ruler of nature -- works (only) through
the heart and conscience. (This rather telling
admission calls our attention to the fact that
a change in the doctrine of miracles may be connected with a change in the doctrine of God.)
The case for the mythical point of view is presented at more length than is now customary.
(Cf. the accounts of MacQuarrie and Tillich, #s
764 and 775 below. That this case is usually
presented so perfunctorily is a reflection of the
fact that the mythical point of view is no longer
seriously questioned by those who stand in the
mainstream of modern Christian thought.) The
authors' defense is, however, philosophically
disappointing. For example, although a chapter
is devoted to C. S. Lewis (# 761 below), his
book is dismissed as a "forced and artificial

. . . <u>tour de force</u>" which demands "the total 'eradication' of the kind of thinking customary in modern times." The authors' judgment may be sound but it is not supported by any attempt to come to grips with Lewis's argument.

758 Landrum, George. "What a Miracle Really Is," <u>Relig Stud</u>, 12 (March, 1976), 49-57.

Landrum argues that the notion of a violation of natural law is incoherent, that Hume was mistaken in supposing that the occurrence of miracles of a given type must be rare, and that one can conceive of worlds in which miracles occur according to non-scientific laws. (If, for example, in a world otherwise like ours, angels always punish heretics, then that they do so will be a law. It will not, however, be a natural law since "angel" and "punish" are not natural predicates, and since the law neither follows from more basic scientific laws nor is itself a brute scientific fact. [It cannot be regarded as a brute scientific fact because it does not deal with the sorts of things which science considers basic.]) Landrum concludes by suggesting that miracles must either be regarded as events which are not covered by law or as events which are only covered by non-natural laws.

759 Langtry, Bruce. "Hume on Miracles and Contrary Religions," <u>Sophia</u>, XIV (March, 1975), 29-34.

Langtry argues that Hume is mistaken when he supposes that the miracles which support one religion are necessarily evidence against contrary religions, or the miracles which support them, or the testimony which is evidence for those miracles.

451

760 _____. "Hume on Testimony to the Miraculous,"
Sophia, XI (April, 1972), 20-5.

According to Langtry, Hume mistakenly supposed
that the relevant question is (e.g.) whether a
generalization like "Those who die remain dead"
is more strongly supported by mankind's apparently
uniform experience of the finality of death than
"In some cases, the dead are restored to life"
is supported by (e.g.) the witness of the apostles
to the Resurrection. Langtry argues that the
question should rather be: which of the two
competing hypotheses receives the most support
from the _total_ body of evidence (which in this
case includes both the vast amount of testimony
to the finality of death _and_ the testimony of
the apostles)?

761 Lewis, Clive Staples. _Miracles_, _A Preliminary Study_.
London: G. Bles, The Centenary Press; New York:
The Macmillan Co., 1947. 220 pp.

This is, perhaps, the best popular defense of the
traditional Christian conception of miracles.
Lewis observes that the manner in which one as-
sesses the relevant historical evidence will
be largely determined by one's judgment as to
the intrinsic likelihood of miracles occurring.
His book attempts to show that the intrinsic
probability of the Christian miracles is not
so low that historical evidence which suggests
that they have occurred can be safely ignored.
Of particular interest are: (1) Lewis's reply
to the charge that a belief in miracles is a consequence of scientific ignorance (chapter 7).
Lewis points out that a belief in miracles presupposes knowledge of how the world (normally)

452

operates, and distinguishes a belief in miracles
from belief in the fabulous (dragons, floating
islands, etc.). Miracles are exceptions to natural laws. The fabulous is (if real at all)
part of nature. It follows that belief in the
latter, but not in the former, can be upset by
advances in our knowledge of nature's regular
operations. (2) In chapter 8, Lewis argues that
miracles do not violate natural laws. Scientific
laws assert that other things being equal such and
such is the case, but when God intervenes other
things are not equal. He adds that miracles
are not uncaused events, and that the supernaturalist will reject miracles which are simply
"stuck on" and cannot be reconciled with the
"texture of total reality." (3) In chapter 12,
Lewis argues that miracles may be compared with
the licenses taken by great artists who depart
from formal rules in the interest of the beauty
and integrity of the work as a whole. (4) Lewis
argues (chapter 13) that in determining the antecedent probability of a miracle, calculations
based upon the assumption of the absolute uniformity of nature are irrelevant because that
assumption is itself in question. He suggests
that in fact even the skeptic judges some miracle
stories to be intrinsically more implausible
than others, and that this judgment is based
upon his "innate sense of the fitness of things."
The remaining chapters explore ways in which the
Christian miracles can be regarded as fitting
or appropriate.

762　Lunn, Arnold. "Miracles -- The Scientific Ap-
　　　proach," Hibb J, XLVIII (April, 1950), 240-6.

　　　A reply to Dubs (# 748 above) which attacks

liberal Christianity for its dogmatic refusal
to consider the possibility of miracles as traditionally understood, and which contends that
miracles (so understood) are essential to Christianity. This article is of little intrinsic
interest but is important because it provided
the immediate occasion for Nowell-Smith's attack
on the logical coherence of the concept of miracle. (See # 766 below.)

763 McKinnon, Alastair. "'Miracle' and 'Paradox',"
    Amer Phil Quart, 4 (October, 1967), 308-14.

McKinnon contends that miracles are events "involving the suspension of natural law," events
which are discrepant with a true and adequate
conception of nature. Natural law, on the other
hand, is identical with "the actual course of
events" or "the way in which things actually
happen," and an adequate conception of nature is
one "which takes account of . . . all real
events." It follows that miracles are impossible
since no real event can be discrepant with the
way in which things actually happen or with a
conception of nature which takes account of all
real events. This article has received some attention and is not without interest. However,
miracles have not been traditionally believed
to be outside nature, if nature is understood as
the totality of all that happens, nor have miracles been thought to involve a suspension of
natural law if natural law is understood as the
order of all events. Miracles have only been
supposed to be discrepant with conceptions of
nature which appear to be adequate from the scientific point of view but are not fully adequate
precisely because they fail to take account of

454

these events. McKinnon assumes that the totality
of events is the set of scientifically explicable
events, and that true and adequate accounts of
nature must be scientific ones, but these assumptions are question begging since they are denied
by the traditionalists whom he is attacking.

764 Macquarrie, John. Principles of Christian Theology.
New York: Charles Scribner's Sons, 1966. Pp.
225-32.

Section 38 provides a discussion of miracles.
The traditional concept "is irreconcilable with
our modern understanding of both science and
history" according to which any event within
the world can be explained by other events within
the world. It is also theologically objectionable
because "it goes back to a mythological outlook"
and regards miracles as "magic signs." A miracle
is instead any (natural) event that "opens up
Being and becomes a vehicle for Being's revelation
or grace or judgment or address." Macquarrie's
analysis of the concept of miracle may be usefully
compared with that of Paul Tillich (# 775 below).
Both Macquarrie and Tillich speak as if they
were simply clarifying the concept of miracle.
They are in fact recommending new uses of the
term.

765 Moule, Charles Francis Digbey, ed. Miracles, Cambridge Studies in their Philosophy and History.
London: A. R. Mowbray & Co. Ltd., 1965. viii
+ 245 pp.

Only two of these essays are of immediate philosophical relevance: "The Evidential Value of
the Biblical Miracles" by G. F. Woods is of little
interest, and Mary Hesse's "Miracles and the

Laws of Nature" is disappointing. One should
glance at the remarks made by Moule towards the
end of his introduction concerning the ways in
which miracles can be integrated into a coherent
view of the universe. A number of the historical
essays are worth examining: "Some Notes on Miracle in the Old Testament" by J. P. Ross, "Plutarch
and the Miraculous" by B. S. Mackay, "The Theory
of Miracles and the Wisdom of Solomon" by J. P.
M. Sweet, "Miracles in The Antiquities of Jose-
phus" by G. MacRae, "'John Did No Miracle':
John 10:41" by E. Bammel, and especially G. W.
H. Lampe's "Miracles and Early Christian Apolo-
getic" and "Miracles in the Early Church" by
M. F. Wiles. Excursus 1 ("The Vocabulary of Miracle") is also of interest.

766 Nowell-Smith, Patrick. "Miracles -- The Philoso-
      phical Approach, A Reply to Arnold Lunn," Hibb J,
      XLVIII (July, 1950), 354-60. (Reprinted in #
      923 below, pp. 243-53.)

A miracle is an event which is "above or contrary
to nature," and "which is explicable only as a
direct act of God." To explain an event as a
miracle is, however, otiose since "E is a miracle"
is related to "E occurred but is at present scientifically inexplicable" as "opium has dormative
power" is related to "opium puts people to sleep."
Nowell-Smith's point appears to be that because
the empirically verifiable and falsifiable consequences of the two statements are the same, their
informative or factual meaning is identical, and
that, therefore, a scientifically inexplicable
event cannot be explained by interpreting it as
a miracle and ascribing it to divine intervention.
In a similar vein, Nowell-Smith argues that

because these "explanations" do not employ laws
which can be used to make empirically testable
predictions, they are not genuine explanations.
It is clear that the plausibility of the author's
argument rests squarely upon the plausibility
of verificationism, and upon the plausibility
of the assumption that the only genuine explanations are scientific explanations. Nowell-Smith's
essay is a reply to # 762 above.

767 Robinson, Guy. "Miracles," Ratio, IX (December,
     1967), 155-66.

Robinson maintains that the concept of a scientifically inexplicable event is incoherent. His
principal arguments are the following: (1) An
event to which the concept of miracle applies
is "of the right type for scientific explanation"
and, therefore, it is logically possible that
it be scientifically explained, but since it is
a miracle it is "permanently excluded from scientific explicability" and, there, it is not logically possible that it be scientifically explained. (This last inference is suspect. Even
if no law in fact accounts for an event it may
still be the case that there could have been a
law which accounted for it [i.e., that a law
accounts for it is logically possible]. In these
circumstances the event would be permanently but
contingently excluded from scientific explanation.) (2) A class has a complement only if
either it is finite or the class has "a criterion
that unambiguously settles its membership."
The class of scientifically explicable events is
not finite, and "there is no criterion that
settles whether something is [scientifically]
explicable or not, only whether it is explained."

457

(This last contention is not clearly true. For
example, in describing conditions under which
it would be reasonable to assert that a particular occurrence violated the laws of nature,
Swinburne [# 770 below] has in effect provided
criteria which can be used to exclude an event
from the class of scientifically explicable
events.)

768 Schlesinger, George. "The Confirmation of Scienti-
     fic and Theistic Hypotheses," Relig Stud, 13
     (March, 1977), 17-28.

The occurrence of the ten plagues of Egypt would
confirm theism. Since the events recorded in
Exodus are more probable on the theistic hypothesis than on the naturalistic hypothesis, their
occurrence would support the theistic hypothesis
more strongly than it would support the naturalistic hypothesis. One can devise fanciful alternative hypotheses upon which the events in question
are as probable as they are upon the theistic
hypothesis, but these alternatives can be excluded
on the grounds of intrinsic inadequacy. Schlesinger maintains (1) that the principles which he
is invoking lie at the heart of scientific confirmation, (2) that the fact that the occurrence
of miracles would confirm theism has nothing to
do with the fact that the events in question are
contrary to natural law (but rather with the fact
that their occurrence is less probable on the
naturalistic hypothesis than on the theistic hypothesis), and (3) that such non-miraculous facts
as the existence of human beings can (on the
basis of similar considerations) be regarded as
confirming the theistic hypothesis. The weakest
part of this very interesting essay is its

cavalier response to the question "How, in the relevant cases, does one determine the intrinsic adequacy of competing hypotheses?." (In effect, Schlesinger simply dismisses the question.)

769 Smart, Ninian. Philosophers and Religious Truth. London: SCM Press Ltd., 1964. Pp. 26-56.

Chapter II is a rather good essay on miracles. Smart's most important contribution is his distinction between repeatable and non-repeatable counter-instances to scientific law. The former are incompatible with the truth of the generalization with which they conflict. The latter are not. Since miracles are non-repeatable counter-instances, it makes sense to speak of them as exceptions to, or violations of, genuine scientific laws. This notion is developed in more detail by Swinburne (# 770 below). Also of value is Smart's discussion of the charge that one does not really explain an event by interpreting it as a miracle because no laws are involved in the alleged explanation and because the alleged explanation has no predictive power. Smart points out that in interpreting an event as a miracle, one links that event up with a number of other facts and alleged facts. By placing the event in this wider context one offers a kind of explanation of it. Furthermore, one links the event to a whole body of doctrine which speaks of the future (among other things) and, thus, does have predictive power.

770 Swinburne, Richard G. The Concept of Miracle. (New Studies in the Philosophy of Religion.) London and Basingstoke: Macmillan and Co. Ltd.; New York: St. Martin's Press, 1970. ix + 76 pp.

This is, perhaps, the best sustained study of
the concept of miracle to have appeared in a
number of years. It begins with a useful examination of the problem of defining "miracle," and
concludes that a miracle is best understood as
the violation of natural law by a god. Swinburne's most significant contribution is to be
found in his account of the meaning of "a violation of natural law," and of the conditions
under which it would be reasonable to conclude
that a violation had occurred: Let L be any universal generalization which is a law of nature.
An event E is a violation of L provided that
(1) L predicts that E will not occur in the circumstances in which it did occur, (2) there is
very good evidence for L, (3) E occurs and is
a non-repeatable counter-instance to L, i.e.,
E occurs but E-type events will not occur in
circumstances similar to those in which E occurred (the occurrence of E should not, therefore,
affect our assessment of the likelihood of past
and future events of that type), (4) L cannot
be modified to take account of E (because E is
non-repeatable), and (5) L will predict correctly
in all other instances. Swinburne argues that
if an occurrence, E, is a counter-instance to
a formula L which is reasonably believed to be
a law of nature, and if any proposed rival formula L' which takes account of E is so clumsy
and ad hoc that there is no reason to believe
that its untested predictions will prove to be
successful, then we have a good reason for concluding that there is no alternative law under
which E can be subsumed, hence, for regarding
E as a non-repeatable counter-instance to a law
of nature (viz., L) and, thus, as a violation

460

of natural law. Swinburne provides a similar
account of the violation of statistical generalizations which are laws of nature. This excellent
little book also contains a number of astute
criticisms of Hume, a discussion of historical
evidence, a description of conditions under which
it would be reasonable to ascribe an event to
the intervention of a god, and a judicious examination of the effect which independent evidence
for God's existence should have upon our assessment of the evidence for miracles.

771 _____. "Miracles," Phil Quart, XVIII (October,
1968), 320-8.

The substance of this essay is incorporated in
the author's The Concept of Miracle (# 770 above).

772 Taylor, Alfred Edward. David Hume and the Miraculous. (The Leslie Stephen Lecture, 1927.) Cambridge: Cambridge University Press, 1927. 54 pp.
(Reprinted in A. E. Taylor, Philosophical Studies,
New York: Macmillan, 1934, pp. 330-65.)

After calling our attention to several (alleged)
difficulties in Hume's essay on miracles, Taylor
proceeds to "re-state Hume's main argument in
the terms of his own philosophy": The repeated
experience of A's followed by B's creates a habit
of expectation, a particularly "lively idea"
or belief that all A's will be followed by B's.
The more frequently A's are observed to be followed by B's, the stronger the habit and the
livelier the idea. An (apparently) uniform experience of A's followed by B's will lead to a
habit which is so strong that the ideas which
are excited by opposing testimony will not in
fact be sufficiently lively to amount to belief.

461

Taylor's point is that Hume's argument leads
to a psychological conclusion and not to a conclusion about what ought to be believed. Similarly, Hume's concluding remark about the "miracle
of faith" simply calls our attention to the fact
that religious belief has other psychological
roots than those which lead to our "beliefs about
the majority of things." Taylor concludes by
arguing that one's metaphysical views must largely
determine one's estimate of the antecedent probability of miracles. Taylor's discussion of
Hume is neither sympathetic nor entirely fair.
(Hume is, for example, clearly trying to establish
conclusions about what ought to be believed.)
Nevertheless, this lecture continues to be of
interest.

773   . The Faith of a Moralist, Gifford Lectures Delivered in the University of St. Andrews,
1926-28. Series II. Natural Theology and the
Positive Religions. London: Macmillan and Co.,
Ltd., 1930. Pp. 150-96.

In chapter IV, Taylor argues that the occurrence
of miracles does not necessarily imply that the
universe is irrational. Miracles may be compared
with the "surprises" which appear in the lives
of heros and saints, and in the works of great
artists. They cannot be anticipated but are
seen to be eminently rational after the fact.
Miracles may be defined as startling events which
disclose the divine purpose. Since what is startling in one state of knowledge may not be startling in another state of knowledge, "miracle"
is a relative term.

774 Tennant, Frederick Robert. Miracle and Its Philosophical Presuppositions: Three Lectures Delivered in the University of London, 1924. Cambridge [Eng.]: The University Press, 1925.
103 pp.

The 18th century mistakenly assumed that natural
laws are necessary, and the 19th century mistakenly assumed that the uniformity of nature was not
merely "an irresistible belief for certain minds"
but a "self-evident and demonstrable truth."
Natural laws are in fact "empirically devised
descriptions" which may "undergo remodelling
as knowledge increases." Furthermore, if theism
is true a viable distinction can, in principle,
be drawn between those events which are the outcome of "nature's potencies" and those which are
instead produced by divine intervention. Divine
intervention would be in some respects analogous
to those human activities which combine "forces
each of which is purely natural, and which Nature
herself does not combine . . . in order to produce an effect which Nature herself does not
produce." The production of miracles may also
be analogous to the act of creation which the
theist postulates in order to explain the origin
of nature. Tennant concludes that miracles are
ontologically possible. However, because our
knowledge of the potentialities of nature is incomplete, we can never be certain that an event
which conflicts with our current scientific conceptions exceeds the potentialities of nature
and is produced by God's intervention. We cannot,
therefore, appeal to miracles to establish the
truth of either natural or revealed religion,
although events which appear to exceed the potentialities of nature (and, thus, may actually

be miracles) can, by their wonderfulness, <u>suggest</u>
divine intervention.

775 Tillich, Paul Johannes Oskar. <u>Systematic Theology</u>,
     Vol. I. Chicago: The University of Chicago
     Press, 1951. Pp. 115-8.

A short but important discussion of the concept
of miracle. Tillich defines a miracle as an
event which is "astonishing, unusual, shaking
without contradicting the rational structure of
reality," which "points to the mystery of being,"
and is ecstatically experienced as a "sign-event."
Swinburne has pointed out (# 770 above) that
Tillich blurs the distinction between miracles
and what were traditionally called "signs."
By re-interpreting the concept in this way, the
theologian succeeds in avoiding potential conflicts with science, but at the cost of making
a major departure from the very tradition which
he is trying to protect. These few pages provide
an excellent example of the sort of account which
has become standard among liberal Christian theologians.

776 Yandell, Keith Edward. "Miracles, Epistemology
     and Hume's Barrier," <u>Int J Phil Relig</u>, VII (1976),
     391-417.

If miracles are violations of natural law, then
whatever difficulties are involved in identifying
real natural laws will also be involved in identifying real miracles. Hume believed that the
identification of real natural laws was comparatively easy. From a Kuhnian perspective laws
are always in the process of being superseded
and the distinction between apparent **and** real
natural laws becomes elusive if not incoherent.

464

After a workmanlike discussion of Hume's arguments, Yandell concludes that miracles should
be understood as events whose known truth would
require the revision of a "true garden-variety
generalization" (e.g., "water quenches fire," or
"dead bodies stay dead"). These generalizations
survive scientific paradigm shifts. (Indeed,
any adequate scientific theory must "fit" the
facts described by such generalizations.) If
"miracle" is not understood in this (or some
similar) way, then talk of miracles and observing
miracles is vacuous. If, on the other hand,
"miracle" is understood in this way, then there
is no a priori reason to suppose that miracles
cannot be known to occur.

777 Young, Robert. "Miracles and Epistemology," Relig
     Stud, 8 (June, 1972), 115-26.

Young rejects the "violation concept" of miracles
and points out that there are "laws whose antecedent does not specify a genuine sufficient
condition of the effect (for the other conditions
of the effect are only tacitly specified)."
Miracles occur when, because God intervenes as
a causal agent, some of these tacit conditions
are not satisfied. (Young acknowledges that his
view implies that God is not "active as a causal
agent in every event.") The author concludes
with some general remarks on the assessment of
evidence for the occurrence of miracles.

(See also #s 1030, 1033, 1059, 1068 and 1074)

778   Abelson, Raziel. "The Logic of Faith and Belief,"
      <u>Religious Experience and Truth, A Symposium</u>.
      Edited by Sidney Hook. New York: New York Uni-
      versity Press, 1961. Pp. 116-29.

"I know that p," "I believe that p," and "I have
faith that p" are performatives. "I believe
that p" makes a tentative truth claim, disclaims
present backing although it implies that "we
expect the backing to be forthcoming," and is
"secondarily, a more or less definite commitment
to action." "I have faith that p" makes an even
weaker truth claim, disclaims all reliable backing, and involves a strong commitment to action.
Because these utterances disclaim all reliable
backing, they are always unreasonable. Therefore,
religious "faith that" is always unreasonable.
"I have faith in x" implies a risk, involves a
strong commitment to action, and presupposes a
personal experience of x. While "faith in" is
reasonable in some cases, faith in God is not
reasonable. "Faith in" is reasonable only where
it is <u>preceded</u> by an experience of its object,
but faith in God is not (normally) preceded by an
encounter with God. (Faith is in fact generally
considered to be a normal <u>precondition</u> of such
encounters.) Abelson's analysis is suggestive
but questionable. When (e.g.) devout Christians
say that they believe that Christ rose from the
dead, their truth claim is not made tentatively.
Nor do they disclaim all present backing for they
are prepared to support their claim by appealing
to the authority of church or scripture.

Furthermore, even if one were to concede that
Abelson's distinction between "belief that" and
"faith that" is sound, it would still not be
clear that religious faith should be assimilated
to the latter and not to the former.

779 Ammerman, Robert Ray. "Ethics and Belief," Proc
     Aris Soc, LXV (New Series), (1964-65), 257-66.

Since we can try to believe or refrain from believing it makes sense to talk about duties with
respect to belief. Whether we actually have such
duties is another matter, but Ammerman maintains
that we sometimes do. One has a secondary duty
to do those things which will enable him to perform his primary duties. It follows that if holding a certain belief is necessary in order to
perform one's duty, then one has a secondary duty
to do what he can to acquire that belief. Thus,
if a man's jealousy leads him to beat his wife,
it may be his duty to curb that jealousy by trying
to believe in his wife's faithfulness. Ammerman
concludes that because Clifford did not show that
believing on insufficient evidence always interferes with our duty, he should not have maintained
that we ought never to believe on insufficient
evidence, and because James did not show that
believing on passional grounds never interferes
with our duty he should not have maintained that
we always have a right to believe on passional
grounds.

780 Arberry, Arthur John. Revelation and Reason in
     Islam, the Forwood Lectures for 1956 Delivered
     in the University of Liverpool. London: George
     Allen & Unwin Ltd., 1957. 122 pp.

An examination of the relations between

467

"orthodoxy," "philosophy" and mysticism. Tension
between these approaches to religion characterizes
classical Christianity, but is especially acute
in Islam because of the extremity of some of the
positions which were adopted by their adherents.
(Thus, some of the orthodox insisted that even
the anthropomorphic imagery of the Qurān must
be taken literally. Philosophers introduced a
distinction between esoteric and exoteric truth,
identifying the former with philosophy and the
latter with revelation as expounded by the orthodox. Several Sufi mystics appeared to claim out-
right identity with God.) These lectures contain many quotations and a mass of illustrative
material.

781 Baillie, John. The Idea of Revelation in Recent
     Thought. (The Bampton Lectures in America, 7.)
     New York and London: Columbia University Press,
     1956. 151 pp.

This is an excellent presentation of what is
becoming the standard theological view of revelation. See especially chapters II, III and IV.
When we speak of an object disclosing or revealing
itself, we are speaking metaphorically since the
standard use of "revelation" and "self-disclosure"
is to be found in the field of personal relations.
Persons reveal themselves to one another in their
words and actions. (When we attempt to convey
what was revealed, we must either list some of
the qualities which we found in the person who
disclosed himself to us, or recount a few of his
more revealing actions. These descriptions will
not, however, be exhaustive.) Divine revelation
is analogous to cases in which a person reveals
"his character and mind and will to another,"

468

and not to cases in which a person reveals "certain items of knowledge other than knowledge of himself." The content of revelation is not a body of information but God Himself and the new life which He provides in communicating Himself. Revelation is given through historical events but only occurs when those events are interpreted as acts of God, the interpretation itself being grounded in God's activity. Revelation thus includes selected historical events together with the mind's interpretation of those events. It should be pointed out that if revelation includes interpretation, then (in spite of what was said earlier) revelation does include a propositional element. Baillie's discussion in the concluding chapters confirms this point. Thus, in chapter V he argues that although faith (the human response to revelation) is primarily trust, this trust involves an assent to certain propositions about the person who is trusted. These assents may be initially implicit but are articulated by theology. In chapter VI, Baillie admits that God would not have "left the prophetic and apostolic testimony to itself . . . the Biblical writers were divinely assisted in their attempt to communicate" the illumination which they had received. (The only question is whether this testimony is inerrant.) These are significant concessions to the theory that revelation consists in the communication of propositions and that faith is an obedient assent to those propositions. Baillie maintains that those who adopt the newer account of faith and revelation are, in general, willing to make these concessions but, as a matter of fact, they have not usually done so. The "new theory," as presented by

469

Baillie, is distinguished from the older theory
by virtue of the fact that revelation is construed
as primarily the self-disclosure of a person and
not the disclosure of a set of propositions,
and by its insistence upon the difficulty of
isolating a set of propositions which can be
said with certainty to be implicit in that self-
disclosure.

782 _____. The Interpretation of Religion. New
York: Charles Scribner's Sons, 1928; Edinburgh:
T. & T. Clark, 1929; Nashville, Tennessee: Abing-
don Press, 1965. Pp. 448-70.

With the advent of Kant and Schleiermacher, the
opposition between natural insight and revelation
has been transcended. It is now believed that
"an entirely unaided reason can discover nothing
about God at all, while . . . it is only to the
. . . seeker than any aid from Heaven ever comes."
Baillie endorses this view, arguing that "the
entire process by which men become aware of God
may be described in terms of human seeking and
finding," but can and must also "be described
in terms of divine self-disclosure." (This position should be distinguished both from the position that natural insight and revelation conflict
with one another and from the position that natural insight and revelation provide different,
though complementary, insights.) In particular
man's apprehension of moral value can be (correctly) interpreted both as a human discovery
and as a divine self-disclosure. Our experience
of moral obligation involves a knowledge of "a
Beyond that is in some sort actively striving
to make itself known to us." This higher order
of value discloses itself in our conscience but

470

more clearly in the lives of saintly human beings
and preeminently in Jesus.

783 Barth, Karl. Church Dogmatics, A Selection. With
an introduction by Helmut Gollwitzer. Translated
and edited by G. W. Bromiley. Edinburgh: T. &
T. Clark, 1961; New York: Harper and Row, 1962.
Pp. 29-86.

A useful selection of extracts from various volumes of the Church Dogmatics on the subject of
our knowledge of God.

784 _____. The Doctrine of God. Vol. I. Translated by T. H. L. Parker [and others]. Edinburgh:
T. & T. Clark, 1957. Pp. 3-254.

The first part of the first volume of this translation of Die Kirchliche Dogmatik II contains a
very influential discussion of faith and revelation. Among Barth's more important points are
the following: (1) Faith is a knowledge of (as
well as a love of, trust in, and obedience to)
God as God is revealed in created objects and
events. All human knowledge of God is, thus,
mediate. God is both revealed through, and concealed by, these signs. This is, of course, a
familiar point. Barth's position is, however,
distinguished from a number of similar positions
by its insistence that faith does not involve any
transcendence of the subject-object relation, and
by its insistence that the vehicles of revelation
do not function as signs in virtue of any inherent
power which they possess but only because God
has freely selected these events and objects as
media through which He will reveal Himself.
(Both of these points reflect Barth's rejection
of any kind of "mysticism" or religion of

immanence.) (2) This knowledge of God is not at our disposal. God is known only in so far as He freely chooses to reveal Himself. Natural theology is a sinful expression of the belief in human self-sufficiency (and, specifically, of the belief in our ability to know God apart from God's own gracious self-disclosure). Man as such lacks the capacity to apprehend God. He lacks this capacity because: (a) Man does not resemble God. (b) God cannot be mastered. To apprehend, however, is to encompass, and "we are superior to, and spiritually masters of, what we can encompass." (Since this argument rather obviously rests upon a pun [on "masters"], it is surprising how often it appears in contemporary theology.) (c) To apprehend is to possess and possession implies an "original and proper unity between possessor and possessed." (Sic!) There is thus an "irrevocable otherness" between God and man. Only through grace do we become like God, "master" of God, one with God, and, there-fore, capable of knowing God. According to Barth, it follows from these considerations that man as such (the man who lacks faith) lacks the capacity to even conceive God. (What he conceives is always something other than God -- a philosophical idol, a projection of himself, etc.) This in turn implies that the unbeliever does not under-stand Christian claims. Barth's position as a whole entails that the knowledge of God (revela-tion and its reception in faith) can be neither understood nor assessed from the outside, and that it neither needs nor can receive any sort of external confirmation.

785 _____ . The Doctrine of the Word of God.
(Prolegomena to Church Dogmatics . . .). 2
vols. Authorized translation by G. T. Thomson.
Edinburgh: T. & T. Clark, 1936, 1956.

These two volumes comprise the first full volume
of Church Dogmatics. Neither scripture nor the
proclamation which is based upon scripture can be
identified with revelation. These only become
revelation when God speaks to us through them,
and we succeed in seeing and hearing what (e.g.)
John saw and heard. Through God's grace the
human words become God's word. Revelation is a
free and gracious act of sovereignty, an address
to particular individuals. It is a mystery because in revelation God is veiled (by the human
medium through which He reveals Himself) and
unveiled at the same time. The Incarnation is
the objective ground of revelation and the Holy
Spirit its subjective ground. The authority
of the Bible is derived from the fact that it
is the primary witness to the Incarnation (which
is the central mystery, viz., that God is with
us). The capacity to grasp revelation (faith)
is not inherent in human nature but is bestowed
by the Word itself. No analysis of human capacities or states of mind will disclose the nature
of faith. It can only be understood theologically. And so on. Many of these themes are by
now quite familiar. Nevertheless, Barth's treatment of them is seminal and superior to most,
though unnecessarily prolix. Particularly noteworthy is Barth's attempt to combine an orthodox
(Protestant) conception of revelation and the
authority of scripture, with an acceptance of
the methods and results of modern biblical scholarship.

786 _____. The Knowledge of God and the Service of
God According to the Teaching of the Reformation,
Recalling the Scottish Confession of 1560. The
Gifford Lectures Delivered in the University of
Aberdeen in 1937 and 1938. Translated by J. L.
M. Haire and Ian Henderson. London: Holder and
Stoughton Publishers, 1938. xxix + 255 pp.

After declaring that natural theology is impossible since God is known only in so far as He reveals Himself in Jesus Christ, Barth proceeds to
explicate revealed theology by commenting upon the
Scottish confession of 1560. The first part of
these lectures is most directly relevant to the
topics of faith and revelation, and their relation
to reason. As one would expect (given the nature
of his thesis), Barth states and expounds but
offers little by way of argument.

787 Brunner, Heinrich Emil. Revelation and Reason, the
Christian Doctrine of Faith and Knowledge. Translated by Olive Wyon. Philadelphia: The Westminster Press, 1946. xii + 440 pp.

The German original appeared in 1941. Revelation
is the self-manifestation of God. The response
to this self-manifestation (faith) is itself included in the event of revelation (for one cannot
reveal anything without revealing it to someone),
and involves recognition, obedience and trust.
A sharp distinction must be drawn between revelation and natural knowledge. (1) "Secular" or
"objective" knowledge "remains master" of what
is known "but through revelation God became Lord
[master] over me." (Notice the pun.) (2) Ordinary knowledge enlarges us and enriches us but,
unlike the knowledge of revelation, cannot transform us. (Is this true?) (3) "Objective" knowledge is a feature of isolated subjects, for it

can in principle be acquired without the aid
of another. On the other hand, revelation as
the self-disclosure of a person creates community
between revealer and revealed and in so doing
communicates life and salvation. God is, in
principle, inaccessible to autonomous reason.
Brunner offers several reasons for this contention. (1) Persons are known as persons -- and
not as mere objects -- only in so far as they
reveal themselves to others. God is the "Absolute Person" or "Unconditional Subject." Since
God is not an object in any sense (sic!), He can
be known only in so far as He reveals Himself.
(Brunner occasionally confuses "knowing a person
objectively" and "treating a person as an object.") (2) Because God is absolutely unique
(sic!), He can be compared with nothing else.
(3) The intellect proceeds by abstractions and
"every abstraction means a moving away from the
personal to the impersonal." (4) The world is
the "appropriate" or "normal" object of man's
natural faculties. As Lord and Creator, God
transcends the world and, therefore, cannot be
known by these faculties as such. -- The presupposition of the occurrence of historical revelation is, however, not only finitude and natural incapacity. It is also sin. According
to Brunner, sin as a rebellion against God can
only be understood if we postulate an original
self-disclosure which is rejected and denied.
God has revealed Himself in creation and conscience. As a rational creature man is, in principle, capable of recognizing this self-disclosure. Since, however, man is sinful and his
reason corrupt, this original revelation does
not in fact lead to knowledge of God but to

475

distortion and illusion. Hence, natural theology
is impossible and non-Christian religions are
idolatrous. (However, a reason which is healed
by the grace mediated through the particular
historic revelation in Christ can rightly understand the law which God has written in our hearts
and perceive the world as a manifestation of
His power and wisdom.) Another important feature
of Brunner's theory is presented in chapter 11.
Our acceptance of scripture is based neither
upon reason nor upon external authority but upon
the testimony of the Holy Spirit. In one act,
Christ is accepted as God's word together with
scripture as witnessing to that word. Faith, so
understood, is a form of knowledge. Its evidence
"is no whit inferior to that of rational knowledge but it is evidence of a different kind."
One is illuminated and can see for himself. It
is "knowledge in the dimension of personal encounter." Proof is neither possible nor fitting
because this form of knowledge involves trust,
decision and obedience. The certainty of faith
has to be continually regained for it is a "continued decision" and (from the point of view of
unbelief) a venture. (Brunner would appear to
want to have it two ways. Faith is, on the one
hand, an interior illumination, a kind of seeing.
On the other hand, faith is a free decision un-
coerced by any evidence. It is not clear that
these contentions are compatible.) A major work.

788 Buber, Martin. Two Types of Faith. Translated by
Norman P. Goldmark. London: Routledge & Kegan
Paul, 1951. 177 pp.

The first form of faith occurs when one trusts
someone without being able to provide sufficient

476

reasons for that trust. The second form of faith
occurs when someone believes something without
being able to provide sufficient reasons for
that belief. The first type of faith arises
within a covenant community. It is exemplified
in the early history of Israel. The second type
of faith involves the conversion of individuals
who then join together to create a community.
A classical illustration of this sort of faith
is provided by the early Christian church.
Buber's general thesis is articulated in the
foreword and concluding chapter. The other
chapters attempt to substantiate this thesis
by closely examining biblical and rabbinic material. These chapters are interesting but not
fully convincing. (Consider, e.g., Buber's sharp
distinction between Jesus's understanding of
faith -- which he claims is essentially Jewish --
and Paul's understanding of faith, and contrast
this with [e.g.] Bultmann on the relation between
Jesus and Paul.)

789 Bultmann, Rudolf Karl. Existence and Faith, Shorter
     Writings of Rudolf Bultmann. Selected, trans-
     lated and introduced by Schubert M. Ogden. New
     York: Meridian Books, 1960. 320 pp.

     Several of these essays examine the nature of
     faith and revelation. (See, e.g., "The Concept
     of Revelation in the New Testament," and "The
     Historicity of Man and Faith.") Revelation and
     faith should not be understood as the communi-
     cation and reception of information. Revelation
     is an event which communicates a new mode of
     existence and faith is the appropriation of that
     mode of existence. This new mode of existence
     is a gift which, in freeing one from the past,

frees one for love. Faith is said to involve
a noetic element although its importance is mini-
mized. The advent of faith involves a rejection
of the sinful belief in one's ability to secure
one's own existence, and the acquisition of a
new self-understanding which recognizes that only
God can secure one's existence. (At one point,
Bultmann compares the noetic element in faith
to the way in which the meaning of friendship
comes home to a person who finds a friend. No
new information is acquired but his life is
"qualified in a new way." This would suggest
that the reality of the new mode of existence
can be discerned apart from faith, and that faith
merely involves its personal appropriation.
Bultmann does sometimes speak in this way but
his considered view appears to be that while
philosophy [more specifically Heideggerianism]
can "demonstrate" the possibility of this new
mode of existence, its reality is only disclosed
in revelation.) Bultmann's discussions of faith
have proved to be very influential.

790 _____. Theology of the New Testament. 2 vols.
Translated by Kendrick Grobel. New York: Charles
Scribner's Sons, 1951, 1955. London: SCM Press
Ltd., 1952, 1955.

The Pauline concept of faith is examined in the
first volume and the Johannine concept of faith
is examined in the second volume. These very
influential discussions are of interest not only
because they illuminate the New Testament material
but also because they cast light upon Bultmann's
own "existentialist" interpretation of faith.

478

791 Chisholm, Roderick Milton. "Lewis' Ethics of Belief," The Philosophy of C. S. Lewis. Edited
by Paul Arthur Schilpp. LaSalle, Illinois:
Open Court, 1968. Pp. 223-42.

The first section of this paper contains a fairly
interesting defense of the claim that terms of
ethical appraisal can be appropriately applied
to beliefs. Section III argues that "all of
ethics, on Lewis' view, presupposes the ethics
of belief." This controversy has important implications for the philosophy of religion. If
beliefs cannot be ethically appraised, then faith
as traditionally understood is not a virtue, and
it is illegitimate to either speak of a right
to religious belief (James) or to regard religious belief as a vice (Clifford).

792 Davis, Stephen Thane. "Faith and Evidence: An
Epistemological Study of the Nature of Religious
Faith." Doctoral Dissertation: Claremont Gra-
duate School, 1970. 309 pp.

"Public evidence" is defined as "any proposition
which would normally produce belief in a rational
man." "Private evidence" is defined as "a proposition which will produce belief in a given
man but not necessarily in any other man." Faith
can be construed as a conviction based upon private evidence. According to Davis, faith so-
defined is sometimes rationally warranted.

793 Demos, Raphael. "Religious Faith and Scientific
Faith," Religious Experience and Truth, A Sym-
posium. Edited by Sidney Hook. New York: New
York University Press, 1961. Pp. 130-6.

Religious faith is compared with a scientist's
commitment to the uniformity of nature, the

principle of simplicity, etc. Although popular,
this comparison is suspect. It is simply not
clear that a commitment to methodological principles is relevantly similar to factual beliefs
such as (e.g.) the belief that God exists and
providentially governs the world. For a rather
effective criticism of this position see Zimmerman, # 853 below.

794 Dodd, Charles Harold. The Authority of the Bible.
     London: James Nisbet & Co., Ltd., 1928; New York:
     Harper and Bros., 1929. xv + 310 pp.

Dodd compares scriptural authority with authority
in science and, more especially, art. Authorities
provide "stimulus, support, and direction" but
do not absolve the individual of responsibility
for his own judgment. The authority of the prophets and saints who speak to us through scripture is the "authority which belongs intrinsically
to genius." When we say that they are inspired
we do not refer to any mechanism of production
but "to a quality in the product which has a
certain effect in those who experience it."
The authority of these figures is based upon
the fact that their experience of divine reality
is "fuller, deeper, and more compelling" than
our own. Their apprehension of the "thought
of God" is, nevertheless, mediated through their
historically conditioned and (with the exception
of Jesus) morally imperfect personalities. We
should not, therefore, "submit to them blindly
or expect them to be infallible" but instead
follow their guidance to see if what they say can
be verified in our own experience. The Bible also
possesses another kind of "authority." It mediates truth in so far as it records the

"appropriation of 'inspired' ideas by a whole
community whose experience, through many genera-
tions, tests, confirms and revises them." ·(Dodd
appears to have two things in mind. He believes
that the history of inspiration and its appropriation which culminates in Jesus is itself a
revelation of God to man. Again, he believes that
the inspired ideas of the prophets and saints
are confirmed by the fact -- to which scripture
attests -- that the lives of those who adopt
them become fuller and deeper and more adequately
attuned to wider stretches of reality.) A very
readable presentation of a "liberal" Christian
theory of revelation.

795   Duff-Forbes, Donald R.   "Faith, Evidence and Coer-
      cion," Austl J Phil, 47 (August, 1969), 209-15.

An important critique of Hick's claim (see #s
810 and 813 below) that the existence of coercive
evidence for God's existence is incompatible
with human autonomy. His two most important
points are the following: (1) Hick has admitted
that one can believe that God exists without
having faith in Him but if so, "God could bring
it about that evidence for His existence is as
. . . conclusive as one could wish . . . without
forcing from his creatures the religiously appropriate response of trust and love." (Hick
concedes that this is possible if the evidence
is not experiential or immediate but indirect,
requiring an inference from the evidence to God's
existence. It is only a "coercive" experience
of God which is incompatible with autonomy.)
(2) Hick has asserted that for the "paradigmatic
men of faith religious experience is as 'coercive'
as sense perception," and yet he surely does

481

not believe that the experiences of these men
destroy their autonomy. See Hick's reply, # 811
below.

796 Dulles, A. "Revelation," New Catholic Encyclopedia.
     Vol. 12. Prepared by an editorial staff at the
     Catholic University of America. New York:
     McGraw-Hill, 1976. Pp. 440-4.

     While this article has little intrinsic interest,
     it may be profitably compared with the article
     by Joyce (# 816 below) which appeared fifty years
     earlier. A comparison of the two articles re-
     veals the extent to which recent Roman Catholic
     thought has adopted views which originated in
     modern Protestant theology and biblical scholar-
     ship. While the notion that revelation consists
     in God's disclosure of certain propositions is
     not altogether abandoned, primary emphasis is
     placed upon God's self-disclosure in the events
     of salvation history.

797 Evans, Donald Dwight. "Faith and Belief," Relig
     Stud, 10 (March and June, 1974), 1-19 and 199-212.

     A valuable critical analysis of ten concepts of
     faith employed in contemporary Christian theology.
     Evans argues that while "love and ultimate concern
     and authenticity are of immense importance in
     faith," faith cannot be exhaustively analyzed
     in these terms. "Christian faith is faith in
     God, and . . . such faith presupposes that God
     . . . actually exists." It may be true that what
     is believed can only be fully understood if one
     shares certain "existential" attitudes and experi-
     ences (e.g., an I-Thou encounter, or a numinous
     experience, or a mystical experience, or "courage
     in the face of meaninglessness"). Nevertheless,

"existential meaning" (existential meaning is,
presumably, what is grasped in the appropriate
existential experience) presupposes "some framework of public meaning." And so on. While all
of the views call our attention to certain aspects
of faith, they fail to isolate the element which
distinguishes religious faith from other faith,
viz., its transcendent reference. This transcendence is dual. The object of faith transcends,
and must be understood by analogy with, ordinary
objects, and faith's attitude towards this object
(worship, a sense of absolute dependence, etc.)
transcends, and must be understood by analogy
with, ordinary attitudes.

798 Fabro, Cornelio. "Faith and Reason in Kierkegaard's
     Dialectic," A Kierkegaard Critique, An interna-
     tional selection of essays interpreting Kierke-
     gaard by F. J. Billeskov Jansen et al. Edited
     by Howard A Johnson and Niels Thulstrug. New
     York: Harper & Brothers, Publishers, 1962.
     Pp. 156-206.

     Fabro attempts to show that Kierkegaard's attitude
     towards reason is more positive than is sometimes
     admitted. Reason may, for example, be used to
     prepare the ground for faith, to support the
     claims of religious authority, and to establish
     the fact that certain things, while not nonsense,
     cannot be understood by reason. Fabro constructs
     a plausible case. This article is significant
     because it raises the question as to the extent
     to which theological "enemies of reason" are
     actually opposed to its use in religious contexts.

799 Farmer, Herbert Henry. <u>The</u> <u>World</u> and <u>God</u>: A <u>Study</u>
of <u>Prayer</u>, <u>Providence</u> and <u>Miracle</u> <u>in</u> <u>Christian</u>
<u>Experience</u>. (The Library of Constructive Theo-
logy.) London: James Nisbet & Co. Ltd.; New
York: Harper and Row, 1935. Pp. 13-31 and 68-91.

Chapter V contains an excellent discussion of the
concept of revelation. "Revelation" is distinguished from "discovery." Farmer argues that,
in ordinary language, the former is primarily
used in interpersonal relationships to refer to
those cases in which one person actively imparts
himself to another through speech or some other
medium, "thrusting his mind . . . into yours,
his values and purposes among yours." Revelation
in the religious sense occurs when God thrusts
Himself into our own immediate situation "as
active personal will," making an absolute demand
and promising final succor. The primary sense
of "revelation" must be distinguished from two
secondary senses -- an acquisition of knowledge
which appears to be unconnected with previous
efforts and researches, and the discernment of
"a deeper, more permanent and more orderly reality" beneath the surface of things. ("Revelation"
is employed in religious and non-religious contexts in both of these secondary senses.) While
chapters I and IV are not themselves concerned
with revelation, they are directly relevant to
the discussion of revelation in chapter V. (In
chapter I, Farmer discusses the nature of interpersonal relationships, and argues that "the
awareness of God as personal will is given immediately in the impact of unconditional value" in
the midst of [some of] the concrete situations
in which I find myself. In chapter IV, Farmer
argues that the way in which the world or selected
aspects of it express God is analogous to the

way in which bodily gestures, facial expressions,
and other non-conventional signs express our
own inner being.)

800   Farrer, Austin Marsden. Faith and Speculation,
An Essay in Philosophical Theology containing
the Deems Lectures delivered at New York University in 1964. New York: New York University
Press, 1967. Pp. 86-103.

In chapter VI, Farrer argues that the popular
distinction between a pure datum of revelation
and a fallible reflection upon that datum is
untenable. Although revelation involves God's
activity and man's response, it is impossible
to disentangle a pure given from the fallible
human response to that activity.

801   _____. The Glass of Vision. (The Bampton
Lectures, 1948.) Westminster [London]: Dacre
Press, 1948. xii + 151 pp.

The events through which God reveals Himself are
only revelatory when properly interpreted. The
apostolic interpretation of these events is indeed
uniquely inspired but the "product" of divine
inspiration is a set of images (the Kingdom of
God, the Son of Man, Israel, the Atoning Sacrifice, etc.) and not a set of propositions. This
comparatively unusual interpretation of revelation
is developed with care and sophistication. Farrer
explores the connections between revealed images
and the "natural analogies" employed by classical metaphysics, and compares the inspiration
of the prophets and apostles with poetic inspiration. Throughout these lectures, Farrer worries
over the question as to how, if God is only given
to us through images, true images can be

distinguished from false images. His answer
seems to be that revealed "master images" can
be used to interpret other less important images,
that the systematically developed analogies of
natural theology provide another set of controls,
and that we are able to make discriminations because we have an imperfect but quasi-experiential
awareness of what is shadowed forth by these
analogies and images (an awareness of finite
being as grounded in infinite being in the case
of natural theology, and an awareness of God
supernaturally acting within the soul in the case
of revealed theology). This suggestive work
deserves more attention. (But see Hepburn's
critique, # 926 below).

802   Gibson, Alexander Boyce. Theism and Empiricism.
      London: SCM Press; New York: Schocken Books,
      1970. Pp. 159-207.

In chapter VII, Gibson distinguishes "first
faith," "faith in," and "faith that." "Faith
that" is implicit in the more fundamental "faith
in." Gibson's most original contention is that
faith in God is a natural development of "first
faith," which he defines as a faith in the openness of the future in the face of seemingly
insurmountable obstacles. According to Gibson,
first faith pervades human activity and makes
it possible.

803   Gilson, Etienne. Reason and Revelation in the
      Middle Ages. (The Richard Lectures in the Uni-
      versity of Virginia, 1937.) New York: Charles
      Scribner's Sons, 1938. 114 pp.

The first lecture is devoted to the Augustinian
tradition which regards faith as a presupposition

of understanding or rational inquiry. The second lecture discusses the Averroists who either
(1) (like Averroes himself) argue that religious
belief is merely an approximation to philosophical
truth, or (2) find the conclusions of natural
reason and revealed theology incompatible
but sincerely adhere to the latter (this, according to Gilson, was the actual position of those
who are said to have adhered to the doctrine of
two-fold truth), or (3) accept the conclusions
of philosophy and (more or less covertly) adopt
a wholly skeptical attitude towards revelation.
The third and final lecture is concerned with
Aquinas's accommodation of faith and reason, and
the breakdown of this synthesis in the following
centuries. An excellent study.

804 Govier, Trudy. "Belief, Values and the Will,"
Dialogue, XV (December, 1976), 642-63.

Govier distinguishes between (1) belief by fiat
(simply deciding to believe something which one
wishes to believe), (2) the attempt to alter
one's beliefs by taking steps which one has reason to believe will over a period of time produce
the desired change, and (3) indirectly controlling
one's beliefs by deciding what norms to apply,
choosing whether to seek further evidence, determining what one shall attend to, etc. Govier
argues (1) that while believing by fiat may be
psychologically impossible, it is logically possible, and (2) that (because willing is connected
with believing in the second and third of these
ways) epistemic, logical, moral, and prudential
norms can be applied to believing. A good discussion of issues which have an important bearing
upon the nature of faith and its justification.

805 Grant, C. K. Belief and Action, Inaugural Lecture
of the Professor of Philosophy. Delivered in
the Appleby Lecture Theatre on 31 May, 1960.
Durham, England: University of Durham, 1960.
23 pp.

Grant concedes that a person can be praised or
blamed for his moral beliefs but argues that one
cannot legitimately be praised or blamed for
factual beliefs because beliefs are not actions
or datable performances. Furthermore, if beliefs
were actions they would be determined by our
wills instead of by the evidence and, thus, could
not be rational. (These same considerations
would appear to count equally against the claim
that a person can be blamed for his moral beliefs.)
The activities by which we form our beliefs, on
the other hand, are voluntary and, as such, are
logically appropriate objects of moral appraisal.
Noting that it is sometimes claimed that we have
a moral obligation to arrive at our beliefs in
accordance with the evidence, Grant argues (1)
that a person who forms his beliefs irrationally
may be imprudent but is not clearly blameworthy on
any other grounds, and (2) that other obligations
may sometimes take precedence over our obligation
to form our beliefs in accordance with the evidence. This could happen, e.g., if a belief
that another person is better than he is would
help to transform that person's character for the
better. See Harvey's critique of Grant's position
(# 807 below).

806 Hare, Peter Hewitt and Peter Kauber. "The Right
and Duty to Will to Believe," Can J Phil, IV
(December, 1974), 327-43.

A philosophically interesting exploration of

William James' ethics of belief. Among other
things, the authors argue that James' ultimate
reluctance to speak of either a duty to believe
or a will to believe but only of a right to believe is misplaced. Since James construes belief as an act or disposition to act, it is possible to will to believe. But if it is possible
to will to believe and one has a right to believe,
willing to believe cannot be illegitimate. Again,
our primary duties generate secondary duties to
secure the conditions which will best enable us
to fulfill our primary duties. Among these conditions is (according to James) the belief in
meliorism. Since we can acquire this belief,
and since the acquisition of this belief will
help us to better fulfill our primary duties, we
have a secondary duty to believe (or acquire
the belief) in meliorism. See Wernham's reply,
851 below.

807 Harvey, Van Austin. "Is There an Ethics of Belief?"
     J Relig, 49 (January, 1969), 41-58.

     Harvey argues that whether or not believing is
     a voluntary action is essentially irrelevant.
     Since the way in which we go about forming our
     beliefs is within our control, it makes sense
     to speak of an ethics of belief. Price (# 839
     below) and Grant (# 805 above) have argued that
     we only have a prudential obligation to adopt a
     policy of believing reasonably. Harvey points
     out that if a moral virtue is a habit which we have
     a duty to inculcate in ourselves and others, then
     it is at least arguable that prudence is itself
     a moral virtue. Harvey next considers the possi-
     bility that believing reasonably is a duty but
     only with respect to certain roles (lawyer,

newspaper reporter, university professor, etc.)
and concedes that he is not quite sure how to
handle this suggestion. He concludes by examining
a contention made by Grant. A belief in the
fidelity or goodness of another can sometimes
(help to) create its own object. It would, therefore, seem that we could sometimes have a duty
to believe in another person's goodness or fidelity
in spite of the evidence against it. Harvey replies that although we might have a duty to express
such a belief it is by no means clear that we
would have a duty to hold that belief. Harvey's
reflections are inconclusive but not without
interest. (A distinction which is often ignored
in these discussions is the distinction between
believing against the evidence, believing in the
absence of evidence, and believing more strongly
than is warranted by the evidence. Harvey and
others lump these together, but it is not immediately clear that they are equally legitimate or
equally illegitimate.)

808 Henze, Donald F. "Faith, Evidence and Coercion,"
     Philosophy, XLII (January, 1967), 78-85.

Hick, MacIntyre and others (e.g., Emil Brunner)
have argued that the presence of conclusive evidence for God's existence would preclude the free
response of faith. Henze maintains that this
argument derives its force from a misuse of such
expressions as "free," "coercive," "compulsion,"
etc. Thus, Hick's contrast (see #s 810 and 813
below) between the freedom which is characteristic
of faith and the coercive character of sense perception rests upon an illicit inference from the
claim that sense perception is indubitable or
involuntary to the claim that it is coercive

or compelled. Similarly, Alasdair MacIntyre
(Difficulties in Christian Belief [London: SCM
Press, 1959], pp. 76-77) speaks of being compelled
by proofs, ignoring the fact that "compelled"
(in the sense in which "compelled" contrasts with
"free") is properly applied to actions and choices
but not to beliefs. See Hick's reply (# 809
below).

809 Hick, John Harwood. "Faith and Coercion," Philo-
     sophy, XLII (July, 1967), 272-3.

A reply to Henze (# 808 above). Hick concedes
that when he speaks of sense perception as coercive, he is using "coercive" in an extended sense,
but argues that this is not relevant to his main
point, viz., that it is not left "to our choice
whether we shall believe in the reality of the
physical world" whereas belief in God is, "to
some extent at least," left to our choice, and the
fact that God has "set us at an 'epistemic distance' from himself" is a necessary condition of
our autonomy. Hick makes one important concession.
"Valid theistic proofs" (as distinguished from
coercive religious experiences) would be compatible with our freedom, but this is because they
would compel "a merely notional assent . . . [and]
could not bring about a distinctively religious
and worshipping response." (Doesn't this give
the case away? If theistic proofs are compatible
with human freedom, why hasn't God provided them?)

810 _____. Faith and Knowledge, A Modern Intro-
     duction to the Problem of Religious Knowledge.
     London: Oxford University Press; Ithaca, New York;
     Cornell University Press, 1957. xix + 221 pp.
     2nd ed. Ithaca, New York: Cornell University
     Press, 1966. x + 268 pp.

491

The first two parts of the first edition of this
very influential book provided an analysis of
the concepts of knowledge and belief (knowledge
was equated with rational certainty), and critical
discussions of several influential positions.
"Voluntarist" theories of faith (James, Ward,
Tennant) were criticized for using pragmatic results as a criterion of truth, and for failing to
take account of the psychological certainty of
the religious believer. Hick criticized Donald
Baillie for contending that religious belief is
implicit in moral experience, and offered an essentially sympathetic account of Newman's illative
sense. These sections are of minor interest.
(Hick's analyses are implausible and his critical
observations are neither novel nor penetrating.)
The third and longest part of the first edition
made a major contribution to the study of the
epistemology of religion. In this section, Hick
argued for the following contentions: (1) Belief
in an orderly external world, belief in the reality
of moral relationships and obligations, and belief in God are all interpretations of experience.
(2) Theism interprets "the world as a whole as
mediating a divine presence and purpose." Like
belief in an external world, belief in God is a
total interpretation of the whole of experience.
Since total interpretations are interpretations
of the whole of experience, there are no independent data in terms of which they can be said to
be either probable or improbable. The decision
to adopt one interpretation rather than another
rests upon private judgment; there is no "calculus"
which could be employed to determine the issue.
(Must the evidence for an interpretation be altogether independent of that which is interpreted?

It would seem not. A person's behavior is [e.g.] evidence for his moral character even though it is part of what is interpreted. Again, Hick fails to consider the possibility that there are relevant criteria of assessment, e.g., coherence or simplicity, which [should] guide these judgments. If there are criteria then the determination to adopt an interpretation may not entirely rest upon private judgment even though no mechanical decision procedure exists which can be used to reach an unambiguous decision.) (3) The ambiguous character of experience, which permits both theistic and non-theistic interpretations, protects our autonomy and thus ensures that the response of faith will be free. The second edition incorporates the following changes: (1) The chapter on belief is omitted altogether and the chapter on knowledge is replaced by a chapter entitled "Faith and Knowledge." Hick now maintains that a distinction must be made between the definition of knowledge and those conditions which justify a claim to know. ("There can only be knowledge of p when p is true, but a claim to know p is justified by a rational certainty that p.") He argues that "a sufficiently vivid religious experience would entitle a man to claim to know that God is real." (2) Hick adds a chapter on the "Thomistic-Catholic view of faith." Aquinas's theory is clearly stated but Hick's response to that theory is inadequate. (It consists in observing that the theory is "intellectualistic," and that there is an alternative theory, viz., that "revelation consists in the conjunction of God's activity within our human experience, with the human recognition that the events in question are God's actions." A theory which has dominated Christian thought throughout

493

most of its history deserves a more extensive
critical treatment.) (3) The chapter on Christian
faith which concluded the first edition is now
followed by a chapter ("Faith and Works") in
which Hick discusses the relation between religious
belief and moral action. Neither chapter possesses
much interest. For a discussion of the section
on eschatological verification, see #s 870 and
871 below.

811   _____. "Faith, Evidence, Coercion Again,"
         Austl J Phil, 49 (May, 1971), 78-81.

A reply to Duff-Forbes (# 795 above) which essentially consists in a clarification of his own
position. One important point does emerge. If
a person is to retain his autonomy, the process
of becoming aware of God must be free and unco-
erced. But once he "has become aware of God
that awareness can be as vivid and unescapable
as . . . awareness of the physical world" without
destroying his freedom.

812   _____. "Revelation," The Encyclopedia of
         Philosophy. Vol. 7. Edited by Paul Edwards.
         New York: Macmillan, 1967. Pp. 189-91.

An exceptionally lucid explication of two concepts
of faith and revelation. In classical Christianity, revelation was normally understood as God's
communication of truths which could not be made
out by reason alone, and faith was regarded as
the acceptance of those propositions on the authority of the proposer. This conception of revelation
and faith is in the process of being replaced by
another in which revelation is interpreted as
God's self-disclosure in and through (non-

494

miraculous) events, and faith is construed as
the religious interpretation or appreciation of
those events.

813 _____ . "Skeptics and Believers," Faith and
the Philosophers. Edited by John Hick. New York:
St. Martin's Press, Inc., 1964. Pp. 235-50.

Hick briefly explicates some of the theses first
presented in Faith and Knowledge (# 810 above).
Two important points emerge. (1) Religious experience (which always involves an interpretation
of data) varies in intensity. At its most intense
it is as coercive as sense perception and those
who have it cannot help but believe in God's
reality. On the other hand, the process of coming
to consciousness of God involves "the individual's
own free receptivity or responsiveness." "God
does not force Himself upon our attention as does
the physical environment," and refusal is always
possible. (2) God cannot force Himself upon
our attention without destroying our autonomy
although our physical environment can do so.
This difference is a reflection of differences
in the nature of the two objects.

814 Hook, Sidney, ed. Religious Experience and Truth,
A Symposium. New York: New York University Press,
1961. Pp. 91-191.

Part II contains papers on the nature of religious
faith by Arthur Danto, Richard Taylor and others.
The most interesting papers are those of Abelson,
Demos, Kennedy, Niebuhr and Zimmerman. These
are described separately (#s 778 and 793 above
and #s 822, 831 and 853 below).

815 Jaspers, Karl. Philosophical Faith and Revelation. Translated by E. B. Ashton. (Religious Perspectives Series, 18.) New York: Harper and Row, Pub., 1967. xxiii + 368 pp.

This book is of some interest because even though there are significant similarities between Jaspers' system (which speaks of a Transcendence which is non-objectifiable and can only be expressed in "ciphers" [symbols]) and the systems of several important Christian theologians (e.g., Tillich and Macquarrie), Jaspers rejects revelation. He rejects (alleged) revelations because their acceptance involves the abdication of rational autonomy, because they exclude all but their own privileged "ciphers," and because they fail to recognize that the accounts which they provide of God's nature and activity should be construed as "ciphers." It would be valuable to determine the real differences (if any) between Jaspers, on the one hand, and theologians like Macquarrie and Tillich (#s 825, 849 and 850 below), on the other. A study of this kind might provide an accurate estimate of the precise extent to which these theologians have departed from more traditional concepts of revelation.

816 Joyce, George Hayward. "Revelation," The Catholic Encyclopedia, An International Work of Reference on the Constitution, Doctrine, Discipline and History of the Catholic Church. Vol. XIII. Edited by Charles G. Habermann . . . Edward A Pace . . . Conde B. Pallen . . . Thomas J. Shahan, D. D., John J. Wynne, S. J., assisted by numerous collaborators. New York: Robert Appleton Co., 1907-12. Pp. 1-5.

A good exposition of the classical Roman Catholic doctrine of revelation. Joyce discusses the meaning of "revelation" ("revelation" is defined

as "the communication of some truth by God to
a rational creature through means which are beyond
the ordinary course of nature"), the possibility
and necessity of revelation, and the nature of
Christian revelation. The most interesting section
is the section on criteria. (External criteria
include miracles, fulfilled prophecy, and the
history of the Church. Negative internal criteria
include the absence of "any teaching . . . which
is manifestly erroneous or self-contradictory,
the absence of all fraud on the part of those
who deliver it," etc. Internal positive criteria
include "the beneficent effects of the doctrine
and . . . its power to meet even the highest aspirations . . . [and] the internal conviction
felt by the soul as to the truth of the doctrine.")

817　Kauber, Peter. "Does James's Ethics of Belief
　　　Rest on a Mistake?" S J Phil, XII (Summer, 1974),
　　　201-14.

　　　"Ethics of belief talk" makes sense if beliefs
　　　are either external actions ("philosophical behav-
　　　iorism") or internal actions ("the belief-as-
　　　assent theory"). James appears to adopt both
　　　views at different points. On the whole, however,
　　　James identifies beliefs with dispositions to act.
　　　James provided two different accounts of the will
　　　to believe: (1) While many of our beliefs are
　　　simply "given," choice becomes relevant where
　　　beliefs which tempt the will are incompatible.
　　　In these cases we must decide which we shall
　　　assent to (i.e., believe). (2) The will can ini-
　　　tiate a course of action which will lead to belief
　　　(construed as a habit or disposition to act). A
　　　similar ambiguity infects contemporary discussions.
　　　Some, like Chisholm (# 791 above), identify belief

with assent. Others, like Price (# 839 below),
interpret belief dispositionally, and argue that
the ethics of belief is not concerned with belief
as such (for beliefs are not acts) but rather with
coming to believe, i.e., with the process by which
we form or cultivate our beliefs.

818 _____. "The Foundation of James's Ethics of
    Belief," Ethics, 84 (January, 1974), 151-66.

Among the points made in this helpful essay are the
following: (1) By 1870, James had adopted two
views of Alexander Bain -- an analysis of belief
as "action and preparedness to act," and the
"theory of primitive credulity," viz., that belief
(i.e., action) legitimately precedes doubt. (2)
James attempted (in 1870) to induce in himself
a "belief in freedom and moral endeavor by fiat."
(3) At one point James maintained that we have a
duty to believe where "it makes a practical difference (whether of motive to action or mental
peace)." In the face of Chauncey Wright's criticism, James retreated to the position that the
only duty we have with regard to belief is a
duty to attend to the evidence.

819 Kaufman, Gordon D. "Philosophy of Religion and
    Christian Theology," J Relig, XXXVII (October,
    1957), 233-45.

Revelation is (by definition) a divine act disclosing something which is in principle hidden
from us. It, thus, exceeds all human capacities
and possibilities. Our "criteria of knowledge
on the other hand must be defined in terms of the
normal patterns of logic and experience." Any
standard which we can successfully employ to

distinguish true claims to knowledge from false
claims to knowledge must obviously lie within
the bounds of human possibility. It follows
that revelation will inevitably "be regarded as
absurdity or illusion from the point of view of
all humanly elaborated canons of truth." It also
follows that "the marks by means of which revelation is recognized to be true revelation could
not be determined or expressed before or apart
from the revelation itself," that "revelation
can never be proved to be true," and that faith
is a gift rather than "a simple human possibility." The thrust of Kaufman's argument is that
because the apparent irrationality of revelation
is a consequence of the very nature of revelation,
the apparent irrationality of revelation cannot
be used as an argument against the reality of
revelation. The author then proceeds to examine
the relation between philosophy and theology.
See Nielsen's reply, # 833 below.

820 Kellenberger, Bertram James. "God and Mystery,"
     Amer Phil Quart, 11 (April, 1974), Pp. 99-101.

     Hick (#s 810 and 813 above) and others have ar-
     gued that if the case for God's existence was
     conclusive or if our awareness of God was as
     coercive as sense perception, then our autonomy
     would be endangered. In section VI, Kellenberger
     distinguishes three models of faith. The biblical
     model is provided by Job for whom God's presence
     was certain, and who neither chose to believe
     nor was forced to believe against his will.
     According to the Absurd model (Kierkegaard), the
     man of faith believes in the absence of evidence
     or even against the evidence. "With the Paradox
     model the man of faith does not have faith; yet

he tries with every fiber to believe, and so affirms the faith he does not have." In all three cases the man of faith chooses to act in ways appropriate to his belief but only in the last two cases can the man of faith be said to have chosen to believe. Since the last two models articulate real possibilities, faith can be chosen. Since, on the other hand, biblical faith is also a real possibility choosing to believe is not necessary for faith.

821 _____. "Problems of Faith," Can J Phil, VI (September, 1976), 417-42.

Kellenberger makes a plausible case for several related contentions. (1) Religious faith can be supported by reasons and yet not be indifferent, tentative, uncommitted, and devoid of risks. (According to Kellenberger the contrary view is at least partly based upon a failure to see that rational religious belief arises through discovery rather than through an investigative process.) (2) There are two models of faith. The biblical model of faith is exemplified by Abraham whose faith was certain. Faith which exemplifies the existentialist model is characterized by radical uncertainty. (3) If faith is compatible with the possession of reasons and with certainty, it would appear to be compatible with knowledge. Kellenberger also argues in the following way: A believer (first model) feels certain that p. Since he feels certain, he sees the matter as certain (he cannot say "I am certain that p, but p is not certain") and, since he sees the matter as certain, he sees himself as knowing p (he cannot say "It's certain that p, but I don't know p"). The believer thus regards

himself as having faith that p and as knowing
p. Given that fully committed faith is conceptually coherent, it follows that the way in which
the believer regards himself is coherent. Hence,
faith and knowledge are compatible. (This argument may be vitiated by an ambiguity. "The matter
is uncertain" may mean "The matter is doubtful
[is or should be doubted by me and by others]"
or it may mean "The matter is inadequately supported by evidence.") (4) Although religious
faith (first model) does not involve a free
choice, it is not coerced if the believer wants
to believe and "would choose to believe [even]
if the surrounding signs of God's presence were
lacking." Futhermore, commitment and love are
not excluded by the first model since commitment
and love do not presuppose that one has chosen
to believe.

822 Kennedy, Gail. "Some Meanings of 'Faith'," Reli-
     gious Experience and Truth, A Symposium. Edited
     by Sidney Hook. New York: New York University
     Press, 1961. Pp. 109-115.

     A reply to Niebuhr (# 831 below). Kennedy argues
     that Niebuhr's two senses of "faith" cannot be
     neatly separated (e.g., accepting a proposition
     on authority involves trust), that "faith" is
     not applicable in many cases where there is a
     high degree of subjective assurance, and that
     "faith" is not always applicable to a commitment
     to first principles.

823 Livingston, James Craig. The Ethics of Belief,
     An Essay on the Victorian Religious Conscience.
     (AAR Studies in Religion, 9.) Tallahassee,
     Florida: American Academy of Religion; Missoula,
     Montana: Distributed by Scholar's Press, 1974.
     60 pp.

An account of the debate concerning the ethics
of believing more than is warranted by objectively
stateable and publicly testable evidence. The
arguments of J. S. Mill, J. H. Newman, W. K.
Clifford, W. G. Ward, Fitzjames Stephen, Henry
Sidgwick, and others are placed in their historical setting, viz., the controversies over sub-
scription to and conformity with the creeds and
formulae of the Church of England. Livingston's
treatment of these arguments is somewhat cursory.
Nevertheless, this is a valuable monograph.

824 MacIntosh, J. J. "Belief In," Mind, LXXIX (July,
1970), 395-407.

According to MacIntosh, "I believe in X" has
at least two uses. "I believe in capital punishment (or our legal system, John's innocence,
etc.)" is used to commend capital punishment and
also to report one's attitude toward it. "I
believe in Santa Claus (or goblins, devils, etc.)"
is used to make an existential claim but implies
that there is some doubt as to whether this claim
can be upheld. MacIntosh's analysis pays close
attention to actual usage and is of considerable
interest. In the second half of his paper, the
author attempts to show that there are no good
reasons for theism, and some good reasons (viz.,
particular cases of apparently unjustified evil)
against theism. This section of MacIntosh's paper
is neither original nor interesting.

825 Macquarrie, John. Principles of Christian Theology.
New York: Charles Scribner's Sons, 1966. Pp.
75-93.

The concept of revelation is discussed in chapter

IV. Revelation is the self-disclosure of Being
"present and manifest in, with, and through . . .
particular beings." Being appears in such ontological moods as anxiety, awe, etc. The encounter
with Being is not adequately described as a personal (I-Thou) encounter. Personal relations are
relations between particular embodied beings
and are characterized by reciprocity. Being,
on the other hand, is neither embodied nor particular, and in the experience in which Being reveals itself we are "transcended" or "mastered"
or "subjected" by that which appears to us. The
sort of mental activity involved in the reception
of revelation is similar to Heidegger's primordial thinking and analogous to the aesthetic
experiences of beauty and the sublime. Although
Macquarrie is heavily influenced by Heidegger,
his account has two merits. It is presented as
clearly as a position of this sort could be presented. Furthermore, Macquarrie (unlike others
who espouse similar positions) is aware that the
relevant experiences are not self-authenticating,
and that their credentials must be carefully
scrutinized.

826 McTaggart, John McTaggart Ellis. Some Dogmas of
     Religion. London: Edward Arnold, 1906; New York:
     Kraus Reprint Co., 1969. Pp. 48-52 and 66-74.

Chapter II contains objections to the claim that
miracles could substantiate dogma (sections 41-
43), to the attempt to justify faith by appealing
to human ignorance (sections 53-54), and to the
contention that because faith in God is analogous
to faith in the goodness of another human being,
it can be reasonable (sections 55-58). McTaggart's objections are (roughly) that the

occurrence of miracles cannot provide a logically
conclusive reason for the acceptance of dogma,
that if we are truly ignorant we should suspend
judgment rather than believe, and that those
circumstances which justify trust in another human
being (e.g., detailed knowledge of his previous
behavior) are absent in the case which is under
consideration. McTaggart's presentation of these
familiar points is lucid and sophisticated.

827 Matthysse, Steven. "Faith and Evidence," Relig
     Stud, 4 (April, 1969), 253-8.

Both Aquinas and Calvin speak of an interior
illumination ("the interior testimony of the
Holy Spirit," "the light of faith") which attests
to revelation's divine origin. This notion can
be interpreted in three ways: (1) as an apprehension of the holiness of the doctrine from which
we infer its divine origin (Jonathan Edwards),
or (2) as an act by which the intellect organizes
the evidential "signs that it already knows, so
as to see that they all point to the divinity of
the doctrine" (Pierre Rousselot), or (3) as a
"veiled glimpse of God authorizing the doctrine"
(Illtyd Trethowan). The problem with the doctrine
of interior illumination is that it is very difficult to discover criteria which can be used
to distinguish genuine illuminations from spurious
ones. Matthysse concludes by suggesting that
faith is a complex state of mind which includes
(1) an intuition that the doctrine is true, (2)
"doubt-free states in which doubts are banished
to the periphery of consciousness, [and which]
make possible untroubled acts of devotion," and
(3) "an additional intuition [which] makes the

504

believer certain that he is required to accept
the doubt-free state."

828 Murty, K. Satchidananda. *Reason* and *Revelation*
     in *Advaita Vedānta*. Waltair: *Andhra* University;
     New York: Columbia University Press, 1959.
     365 pp.

This is an interesting book for several reasons.
(1) Advaita Vedānta accepts revealed scriptures
(the Vedas) but denies that a divine person has
revealed them. This has important implications
for those who maintain that revelation is necessarily a theistic concept. (2) Advaita Vedānta
regards scripture as its primary authority. An
examination of the role of scripture in Advaita
Vedānta thus provides a valuable corrective to
the simpleminded contrast between theistic western
religions which rely on external authority, and
mystical and non-theistic eastern religions which
allegedly rest upon reason and personal experience. (3) Murty provides a detailed account of
the different ways in which reason plays an an-
cillary role in Advaita Vedānta. The use of
reason in Advaita Vedānta can be profitably compared with the use of reason in Augustine,
Aquinas, Al Ghazzali and other theistic divines.

829 Newman, Jay Alan. "Newman on the Strength of Be-
     liefs," *Thomist*, 41 (January, 1977), 131-47.

Locke maintains that assent is illegitimate when
it is stronger than the evidence warrants. John
Henry Newman attacks a presupposition of this
position, arguing that assent does not admit of
degrees. According to Cardinal Newman, assent
must be dissociated from its grounds. We assent
or we do not assent. What is called a "strong"

assent to "p" is either an assent in which our
apprehension of "p" is associated with powerful
images, or an assent to "p" as distinguished from
an assent to "probably p." After sympathetically
but critically explicating these notions, the
author concludes that Newman has not really succeeded in escaping the burden of Locke's criticism
for, within Newman's framework, it is still possible to ask whether (in view of the evidence) the
untutored believer who assents to "God exists"
should assent to that proposition rather than
to (e.g.) "There is some slight probability that
God exists."

830 Niebuhr, Helmut Richard. The Meaning of Revelation.
     New York: The Macmillan Co., 1941. x + 196 pp.

Revelation must be understood in relation to a
historical confessional community which preserves
in its memory those events which were decisive
for its existence and which make its history intelligible. Events appear as revelatory only when
viewed from within by the believing community.
Although the perspective of the believing community is unavoidably particular and relativistic,
it proceeds "with confidence in the independent
reality of what is seen." According to Niebuhr,
the believer's perspective is the perspective of
an evaluating agent who does not simply observe
human affairs but participates in them, responding
to others as persons. He insists that this perspective is both legitimate and necessary. (Niebuhr apparently fails to notice that the fact
that an agent perspective is necessary and legitimate does not imply that a religious perspective
is either necessary or legitimate.) The content
of revelation is a sovereign love which judges

506

us, claims us, and calls all that we are, have,
and do into question. Niebuhr is not the only
modern theologian to draw a distinction between
the absoluteness of what is revealed and the
relative and fragmentary character of every attempt to express that revelation. (Tillich [# 850
below] makes a similar distinction.) Whether
this distinction is viable is not entirely clear.
(For one thing, Niebuhr's position implies that
his own statement of the distinction is relative
and fragmentary.)

831 _____. "On the Nature of Faith," Religious
Experience and Truth, A Symposium. Edited by
Sidney Hook. New York: New York University
Press, 1961. Pp. 93-102.

Niebuhr distinguishes noetic senses of "faith"
(the acceptance of a proposition on authority,
the subjective assurance of the truth of a proposition, the belief in first principles, the acceptance of a proposition for "reasons of the
heart," etc.) from senses which the term has
when it is used to indicate a quality of interpersonal relations (loyalty, trust, fidelity,
etc.). See Kennedy's critique (# 822 above).

832 Niebuhr, Reinhold. The Nature and Destiny of Man,
A Christian Interpretation. Vol. I. London:
Nisbet & Co. Ltd.; New York: Charles Scribner's
Sons, 1941. Pp. 123-49.

Chapter V contrasts general or private revelation
with special or public or historical revelation.
The former consists of the soul's obscure awareness of its dependence, its "sense of moral obligation laid upon one from beyond itself and of
moral unworthiness before a judge," and (less

clearly) its longing for forgiveness. The latter consists in God's self-disclosure in the events of Israel's history and (pre-eminently) in Jesus Christ. Without private revelation, "historical revelation would not gain credence." Without public revelation private revelation "would remain poorly defined and subject to caprice." It is worth observing that there is a decided tendency in modern theology to substitute a distinction between general revelation and special revelation for the more traditional distinction between reason and revelation or natural theology and revealed theology. (This tendency appears to be partly a consequence of the belief that the traditional "proofs" are discredited, partly a consequence of the modern emphasis upon religious experience, and partly a consequence of the insistence that God can only be known in so far as He chooses to disclose Himself.)

833   Nielsen, Kai.   "On the Logic of 'Revelation'," Sophia, IX (March, 1970), 8-13.

Gordon Kaufman (# 819 above) has argued that it is a conceptual truth that there is no higher standpoint from which revelation can be assessed. Nielsen concedes this point but contends that its admission is compatible with the insistence that reason must judge whether or not the concept of revelation has application. (This implies that there is no inconsistency in asserting "there are good reasons for believing that this is a revelation, but this revelation cannot be assessed by human standards." Nielsen does not make it clear whether "revelation" in its second occurrence refers to what is revealed or to the fact that this particular revelation has occurred.

However, if the sentence is to be consistent,
"revelation" [in its second occurrence] must
refer to the content of revelation. Kaufman,
on the other hand, appears to be saying that neither the content of revelation nor the [alleged]
fact that revelation has taken place can be assessed by human standards.)

834 Owen, Huw Parri. The Christian Knowledge of God.
     London: University of London, The Athlone Press,
     1960. Pp. 26-70 and 153-77.

Revelation and faith are discussed in chapters
2, 3, and 7. Owen's theses include the following:
(1) The distinction between special revelation
(pre-eminently the Incarnation) and general revelation (which includes knowledge of God acquired
through rational reflection) is more adequate
than the distinction between revealed knowledge
and rational knowledge. (2) While what is revealed is primarily God, and not a body of propositions, revelation does have propositional
content. (3) Reason must be employed to understand what is revealed, to provide grounds for the
claim that a revelation has occurred, and to articulate revelation and demonstrate its coherence
with the rest of human experience. (4) Faith
includes an intuitive apprehension of God.
Owen's arguments for the second thesis are on
the whole convincing. They are of particular
interest in view of the fashionable contention
that in revelation it is God Himself that is
revealed and not a set of propositions. Owen's
case for his fourth and most significant thesis
is less convincing. It consists in alleged inadequacies in alternative views, and in the claim
that the full assurance of faith can only be

explained upon the supposition that it includes an intuitive apprehension of God. These chapters contain several interesting arguments and a number of sound observations, but (as is so often the case with Owen) they are not always developed in sufficient detail or with sufficient precision.

835   Penelhum, Terence. "The Analysis of Faith in St. Thomas Aquinas," Relig Stud, 13 (June, 1977), 133-54.

Most of this article is devoted to a detailed and workmanlike explication of Aquinas's position on faith. Penelhum concludes by arguing that Aquinas cannot accommodate the fact that believers frequently experience doubt and feel obligated to struggle against it. This feeling of obligation makes sense only if doubts can be regarded as a "test of trust," but Aquinas has separated faith from trust. Aquinas also maintains that an act of assent cannot be meritorious if it is commanded by the evidence. Penelhum professes not to understand how the will can command assent, and argues that, even if the evidence is conclusive, faith can be meritorious if men are free to accept the conclusions to which the evidence points either grudgingly, or ungrudgingly, and if "men are free to deceive themselves" by refusing to admit that the evidence is conclusive.

836   _____. Problems of Religious Knowledge. (Philosophy of Religion Series.) London: Macmillan, 1971; New York: Herder and Herder, 1972. ix + 186 pp.

A fairly interesting discussion of the nature of faith and its relation to religious knowledge. Penelum's discussion is predicated upon the assumption that theism is coherent, and that neither theism nor atheism can be established by non-theistic facts. Among Penelhum's more significant contentions are (1) that because of the ever present possibility of human irrationality faith is compatible with the acceptance of proofs, and (2) that any adequate analysis of the concept of faith must take account of the fact that (many of) those who have faith think that they do not merely believe but know that certain propositions are true. Penelhum argues that faith and knowledge are, as a matter of fact, not exclusive. Chapters 2 and 3 (on proof) and chapter 4 (on verification) are discussed elsewhere (# 425 above and # 888 below).

837 Persson, Per Erik. Sacra Doctrina: Reason and
     Revelation in Aquinas. Translated by Ross Mac-
     Kenzie. Oxford: Basil Blackwell; Philadelphia:
     Fortress Press, 1970. xii + 317 pp.

This book was originally published in Sweden in 1957. Its first chapter contains a very interesting discussion of Aquinas's theory of revelation, and his views on the nature and function of scripture. Among the points which Persson makes in this chapter are the following: (1) In its primary sense, revelation is knowledge which is supernaturally bestowed upon the prophets and apostles. This knowledge involves two components: (a) either an external event, or an image or concept directly infused in the soul, and (b) an intellectual light granted by God which surpasses and perfects the light of natural reason, and enables the prophet or apostle to understand that event or image or concept. One implication of this characterization of revelation is that

an uninterpreted event is not revelation. Another
implication is that because scripture is only
the verbal expression of revelation in the primary sense, it is not itself revelation in the
primary sense. (It should be noticed that although revelation is knowledge, faith is not
knowledge but a cognitive act based upon the knowledge of another.) (2) Scripture provides the
norm of faith for Aquinas. Tradition is not a
second source of revealed knowledge. Tradition
and the church's magisterium merely interpret,
expound and protect the content of faith as preserved in scripture. Aquinas's view of scripture
and tradition must, therefore, be distinguished
from the view of post-Tridentine Roman Catholi-
cism. The first section of the book's third and
concluding chapter provides a clear and accurate
(albeit familiar) account of the role which Aquinas assigns to reason. The remainder of the
book is of less interest. (Persson examines the
interplay between revelation [i.e., biblical
ideas] and reason [i.e., Greek philosophical
ideas], and shows that biblical ideas shape and
determine the way in which Aquinas uses philosophical ideas, and that philosophical ideas
shape and determine the way in which Aquinas
uses biblical ideas.)

838 Pieper, Josef. Belief and Faith: A Philosophical
     Tract. Translated from the German by Richard
     and Clara Winston. London: Faber and Faber;
     New York: Pantheon Books, 1963. 106 pp.

     Pieper's principal points are the following:
     (1) Belief is defined as the unconditional assent
     to a proposition as true on the testimony of
     another. Belief, thus, involves both believing

something (believing in the truth of what is said) and believing someone (trusting the witness). In the most extreme case one accepts what is said "for the simple reason that the trusted person said it," and not because of the antecedent probability of the events reported, their agreement with what one already knows, or any other reason. (Pieper adds that while it may be appropriate for a child to believe what its mother says for the sole reason that she says it, a belief of this sort is not appropriate for a mature person except where the witness "stands incomparably higher than the believer.") (2) Belief involves knowledge. (a) Belief is a participation in the knowledge of the witness. In accepting another as a competent witness one comes to share in his vision, and indirectly sees what he sees directly. (b) Legitimate belief presupposes a knowledge that the witness exists, is trustworthy, and has indeed declared what is proposed for belief. Pieper suggests that this knowledge need not be argumentative, but can be the "intuitive" sort which is involved in interpersonal relations. (3) Reason can, sometimes convince us that we ought to believe but belief itself cannot occur without an act of will. "Belief rests upon volition." The object of this free act of will is not a proposition but the person who bears witness, and its character is love or trust in that person. (4) Belief involves an absolutely firm assent. Certainty is elicited by the trustworthiness of the witness. (Certainty excludes doubt but not "mental unrest." The object of belief is not a report but the reality which that report describes. "The believer partakes truly of this reality; he

touches it, and it becomes present to him."
Nevertheless, because his vision of this reality
is indirect, his "intellect is not readily satisfied" and he is "tormented by the need" to
better understand what is both revealed to him
and concealed from him.) (5) What differentiates
religious belief from other belief is the fact
that God is both witness and content. God reveals "His own Being and works" to us. The only
analogous case is the case in which one believes
a declaration of love. A declaration of love
reveals and communicates the love of the lover
to the beloved, thus allowing the beloved to
partake in the love of the lover. In a similar
way, God's self-disclosure reveals and communicates His own being to the believer. -- Pieper's
book also contains brief discussions of the possibility and necessity of revelation (according
to Pieper, if God is personal, "divine speech"
is possible), modern unbelief (which he attributes principally to "inattention"), the proper
method for establishing the credentials of an
alleged revelation (one must first establish
its possibility and our need for it; we must
be receptive and open; our investigation must
be a cooperative rather than an isolated endeavor,
etc.), and other topics. This is an excellent
presentation of a version of the traditional
Roman Catholic interpretation of faith. It provides a useful corrective to the caricature of
the classical position found in so much contemporary Protestant theology. It is simply wrong
to say that, on the classical view, a set of
propositions and not God is the primary object
of faith, or that the act of faith involves only
the intellect (or the intellect as moved by the

514

will) and not the whole person, or that faith
is not a personal relation between God and the
believer.

839 Price, Henry Habberly. "Belief and Will," Proc
Aris Soc, Supplementary Volume XXVIII (1954),
1-26.

In this interesting essay, Price (1) considers
a family of expressions ("can believe," "easy
to believe," "difficult to believe," "almost
impossible to believe," "cannot believe," "will
not believe," "quite willing to believe") which
suggest that belief is voluntary, (2) argues
that (in spite of such expressions as "I decided
that p" or "I made up my mind that p") we cannot
directly and immediately produce belief by an
effort of will but that we can (by directing
our attention towards the evidence or away from
it, by dwelling on the proposition we wish to
believe, by acting as if we believed), indirectly
and over a period of time manage to partially
determine what we believe, (3) concludes that
even though it makes sense to speak of moral
duties to believe, we probably have no such
duties, and (4) suggests that, since believing
reasonably is advantageous in the long run, we
may have a prudential obligation to believe reasonably.

840 _____. "Belief 'in' and Belief 'that'," Relig
Stud, 1 (October, 1965), 5-28.

A valuable analysis of the relations between
believing in and believing that. Evaluative
believing in ("I believe in my doctor") must
be distinguished from factual believing in ("I

515

believe in the Loch Ness monster"). The latter
is reducible to believing that, but the former
is not. Nevertheless, evaluative believing in
does presuppose the belief that certain things
are the case. (These beliefs are not always
existential beliefs. Thus, a belief in the ideal
of complete unselfishness may presuppose a belief
that approximations to that ideal are practica-
ble. It does not, however, presuppose a belief
in the real or even possible existence of complete
unselfishness.) It is not entirely implausible
to suppose that evaluative belief in can be reduced to the belief that certain value statements
are true. E.g., one might argue that believing
in one's doctor is equivalent to believing that
one's doctor is good at curing diseases and believing that it is a good thing that diseases
be cured. However, the proposed reduction does
not provide for the element of trust which is
an essential part of a belief in one's doctor.
A reduction of this type is even less plausible
where the evaluative belief in is belief in a
friend, for one can believe in a friend without
believing that he is good at anything.

841 Purtill, Richard L. Reason to Believe. Grand
     Rapids: William B. Eerdmans, 1974. Pp. 71-9.

In chapter 6, Purtill argues that "belief in
the stronger sense, where we are confident in
what we believe and would be astounded if we
were wrong," implies some understanding of what
is believed, a readiness to act upon what is
believed, and some reason for what is believed.
Religious faith exhibits these characteristics.
Religious belief differs from other beliefs
(strong sense) in four ways: (1) It is more

516

unquestioning and more personal than other beliefs. (2) What is believed is only partly understood. (3) It involves a willingness to suffer
and die for what is believed. (4) "In a sense
the evidence for a belief of this kind is everything the man knows." World views are accepted
because they make sense of the whole of things.
(Notice that, e.g., a strong commitment to Marxism exhibits at least the first, third and fourth
of these characteristics.)

842 Reid, Louis Arnaud. *Preface* to *Faith*. London:
George Allen & Unwin, Ltd., 1939. Pp. 155-61.

In chapter X, Reid argues that "faith" should
be applied to a belief when there is some uncertainty as to the truth of what is believed, and
a strong disposition to act upon that belief
even if risks are involved in doing so. There
can obviously be many variations in the uncertainty of what is believed and in the strength
of the disposition to act upon that belief. A
sound religious faith is based upon good reasons
and involves a strong disposition to act.

843 Ross, James Francis. *Introduction* to the *Philosophy*
of Religion. New York: The Macmillan Co., 1969.
Pp. 73-111.

In chapter II, Ross argues that faith (understood
as the acceptance of certain propositions on the
word of another) can be knowledge. Faith is
knowledge when the trust upon which it is based
is reasonable. If "an act of trust is to result
in knowledge," several conditions must be met.
E.g., "the person we trust should be in a position to know what he claims to know, and he should

have "acquired his belief about what he conveys
to us by virtue of his having been in a position
to come to know." What he says must be true,
and we must have reason to believe that he is
speaking truthfully. Ross concludes that since
the appropriate conditions sometimes are fulfilled, sometimes faith is knowledge. (Ross's
position is very similar to that of Thomas Aquinas
but appears to depart from it in one minor respect. Aquinas reserves "knowledge" for cases
in which one has direct evidence for the truth
of what he believes. Ross's usage is preferable.
It is, e.g., perfectly legitimate for me to say
that I know the date of my birth even though the
only basis for my belief is a reasonable trust
in authority.) Religious faith is, in principle,
no more problematic than non-religious faith.
It is based upon a chain of testimony which begins with humans who are believed to have directly
encountered God. The two basic questions are
(1) whether the chain of testimony is reliable
and (2) whether religious experience can be a
source of knowledge. In principle no more difficulty is involved in the transmission of religious testimony than in the transmission of
non-religious testimony, and, in principle,
religious experience is no more problematic than
other sorts of experience. Seeing that (e.g.,
seeing that a metallic object is a watch or that
God has acted in certain historical events) is
a function of seeing as (seeing the object as a
watch or seeing a historical event as an act
of God). Seeing as is determined both by the
sensory data and by the "perceptual sets" which
one brings to the data and which dispose one to
assign specific sorts of significance to it.

In both religious and non-religious contexts,
new perceptual sets are sometimes acquired through
disclosures in which the data are seen in new
ways. In both contexts, the experiences of others
can confirm one's own. -- As we have seen, Ross's
account of faith is similar to that of Aquinas.
His remarks on "seeing-as" and disclosure are
reminiscent of John Wisdom and Ian Ramsey. One
must not, however, overlook the provocative
character of Ross's thesis, viz., that, in principle, religious faith and religious experience
are no more problematic than forms of secular
knowledge which everyone regards as legitimate.

844   _____ . "Religious Knowledge," Proc Cath Phil
           Ass, 46 (1972), 29-42.

A further development of the argument presented
in # 843 above. Among its more interesting features is a discussion of the role played by the
community in creating and sustaining perceptual
sets.

845 Smith, George Duncan. "Faith and Revealed Truth,"
     The Teaching of the Catholic Church, A Summary
     of Catholic Doctrine. Vol. I. Edited by George
     D. Smith. London: Burns, Oates & Washbourne,
     1948; New York: The Macmillan Company, 1950.
     Pp. 1-37.

This essay contains an interesting exposition
of a version of the traditional Roman Catholic
doctrine of faith. Faith is an act of intellectual assent. This act is reasonable because
God's existence and truthfulness can be established by natural theology, and because the fact
that God has revealed the propositions which
faith believes is attested by miracles, fulfilled

519

prophecy, and the fact that the church "bears upon her unmistakable marks of her divine institution." (It should be noted, however, that those who cannot attend to this evidence may reasonably base their conviction upon [e.g.] the teaching of their parents or a parish priest, just as those who are unable to attend to scientific evidence because they lack time or ability may reasonably base their scientific beliefs upon the teaching of a schoolmaster.) These "motives of credibility" lead to the judgment that we ought to believe what has been revealed. An act of will (which is both free and caused by grace) must then move the intellect to actually assent to what has been revealed. Although the act of faith is reasonable because of the presence of "motives of credibility," the motive for the act of faith is not this evidence but the authority of God, i.e., in making an act of faith one does not advert to the "motives of credibility" but simply believes because God (who can neither deceive nor be deceived) has spoken. (Similarly, a child's trust in its mother may be reasonable, i.e., there may be reasons which the child has for its trust, and these reasons may be good ones. Nevertheless, when the child believes his mother "he does not advert to these reasons." "He believes simply and solely because his mother has said it.") This distinction between the "motives of credibility" which provide the basis for the judgment that we ought to believe and the authority of God which provides the motive for the act of faith, allows us to regard faith as a virtue and accounts for its certainty. Faith is a virtue because it is not compelled by the evidence but is a free response

to God's authority, and faith is certain because
it is based upon God's authority and not upon
a set of more or less probable arguments.

846   Taylor, Alfred Edward. The Faith of a Moralist,
Gifford Lectures Delivered in the University of
St. Andrews, 1926-1928. Series II: Natural
Theology and the Positive Religions. London:
Macmillan and Co., Ltd., 1930. Pp. 43-108.

In chapter II, Taylor attempts to show that there
is nothing inherently absurd in the notion of
a historical revelation valid for all times and
all places. Among the objections discussed by
Taylor are the following: (1) "Salvation cannot
reasonably be made dependent upon a historical
event of which many are ignorant." Taylor admits
that this is true but maintains that it does not
follow that a special revelation cannot occur.
The occurrence of special revelation is no more
problematic than the uneven distribution of other
goods. (2) "A particular revelation must be
adapted to the minds of its recipients and will,
therefore, be unintelligible to people of other
times and other cultures. Since a final revelation must be universally intelligible, no particular revelation can be final." Taylor replies
that revelations should be compared with master-
pieces of philosophy or art. These works have
universal appeal in spite of the fact that they
are organically rooted in a particular time, place
and culture. (3) "If revelation does not conflict
with reason, its insights can in principle be
discerned and assimilated by reason. Revelation
is, therefore, irrational or unnecessary." Taylor
points out that, by parity of reasoning, it could
be argued that great poets and artists are superfluous since we can come to see what they see

for ourselves. They are not, of course, superfluous because it is only with their help that
we come to see what they see, and because their
vision is never assimilated so thoroughly that
they have no more to teach us. While what we
learn from these artists cannot be inferred from
our own experience, it does not conflict with
our experience but instead supplements, enriches
and completes it. A literate and intelligent
discussion.

847 Temple, William. Nature, Man and God; Being the
     Gifford Lectures Delivered in the University of
     Glasgow in the Academical Years 1932-1933 and
     1933-1934 by William Temple. London: Macmillan
     and Co., Ltd., 1935. Pp. 301-27.

     Lecture XII contains an influential but rather
     commonplace account of the nature of revelation.
     The world as a whole is grounded in the activity
     of a transcendent person. It follows, according
     to Temple, that everything is (potentially?)
     revelation. However, revelation in its fullest
     sense only occurs when an event which is especial-
     ly indicative of God's character is conjoined
     with a mind's appreciation of that event, both
     the event and the mind's appreciation of it being
     grounded in and guided by God. Doctrine expresses,
     assists, and issues from man's fellowship with
     God, but revelation is not doctrine.

848 Tennant, Frederick Robert. Philosophical Theology.
     Vol. II: The World, The Soul, and God. Cam-
     bridge: Cambridge University Press, 1930. Pp.
     209-45.

     In chapter VIII, Tennant argues that if revela-
     tion is construed either as the divine inspiration
     or guidance of human minds, or as the

communication "in propositional form of ready-made truth or information," then revelation is incompatible with human freedom. The former involves a non-personal or non-moral causal action upon persons (moral agents), and the latter involves a heteronomous submission to external authority. Tennant is willing to speak of revelation if what is meant by "revelation" is man's (unassisted) discovery of religious truths.

849 Tillich, Paul Johannes Oskar. Dynamics of Faith.
     (World Perspectives Series, 10.) New York:
     Harper and Brothers, Publishers, 1956[^c1957].
     xix + 127 pp.

A very influential account of the nature of faith. Faith is ultimate concern, a state of utter devotion or complete commitment. "It is an act of the total personality" in which all dimensions of our nature (will, intellect, emotions, the unconscious) participate. The primary object of ultimate concern is the truly ultimate (the infinite, the Unconditioned) which demands total surrender and promises total fulfillment. Or (alternatively) the primary object of ultimate concern is the Holy (in Rudolf Otto's sense). The Unconditioned expresses itself in symbols. The secondary objects of faith are those concrete contents through which the Holy appears. In so far as faith is related to the truly ultimate, it is certain, but in so far as faith adopts a particular set of symbols for the truly ultimate it involves risk or uncertainty. Idolatry occurs when concrete expressions of the Unconditioned are treated as if they were themselves ultimate or inherently holy. (The claim that faith contains an element of certainty is partly explained by

two other theses. Tillich appears to believe
that all religious symbols -- even idolatrous
ones -- point to Being-itself, and also that
each of us enjoys an immediate awareness of Being-
itself.) A feature of Tillich's theory which
has received considerable attention is the claim
that everyone has faith. Tillich appears to
be trading on an ambiguity. It may be true (though
it is probably false) that each of us is ultimately concerned in the sense that there is some
one thing -- God, the nation, success -- around
which we integrate our lives, and in relation
to which all other concerns become peripheral.
It does not, however, follow that we are all ultimately concerned about the Unconditioned and
as such have (religious) faith. What entitles
Tillich to infer the second from the first of
these two claims is his thesis that concrete objects of ultimate concern (God, the nation, success, etc.) are symbols of Being-itself and that,
therefore, ultimate concern about some concrete
content is always implicitly concern about the
Unconditioned.

850 _____. Systematic **Theology**. Vol. I. Chicago:
        The University of Chicago Press, 1951. Pp. 71-159.

Reason (which Tillich distinguishes from the
"technical reasoning" employed in, e.g., engineer-
ing or analytic philosophy) is in essence "transparent toward its depth" (Being-itself), although
this depth cannot become an object of reason.
(Being-itself cannot become an object of reason
because the categories of reason can only be
symbolically applied to it.) Under the conditions
of actual existence, however, reason is distorted,
and "this transparency is replaced by myth and

cult." Reason tends to either abdicate to external authority, or to lose its depth in pursuit of autonomy. Furthermore, it tends to either absolutize forms and principles which possess only partial validity, or to slip into an empty relativism. Finally, reason tends to either degenerate into an empty formalism, or to reject form altogether, thus falling prey to various irrationalisms. The distortions to which reason is subject create an existential problem which is answered by revelation, "for revelation means the reintegration of reason." Revelation occurs when the Ground of being and meaning discloses itself through an astonishing event, and that event is grasped by the mind in "ecstasy." (Ecstasy is a state in which the mind transcends its subject-object structure, and in this sense stands outside itself.) That which is revealed (Being-itself) is in principle mysterious since it cannot be grasped as an object. This mystery has both a negative and positive side, for what appears is both the "abyss" which proceeds reason, order and structure and the "power of being, conquering non-being." Revelation is not opposed to reason because the "sign-events" through which the mystery discloses itself conform to the laws of nature, and because in receiving revelation reason transcends but "does not deny itself." (Reason is characterized by a subject-object structure. Since the mind in "ecstasy" transcends that structure, a conflict between reason and "ecstasy" cannot occur. Again, "revelation does not increase our knowledge about the structures of nature, history and man." Since these are the proper objects of reason, a conflict with reason is impossible.) Because everything

participates in Being-itself, everything is
potentially a medium of revelation. Nevertheless,
the qualities and characteristics of being are
more clearly exemplified in certain things (e.g.,
persons) that in others (e.g., stones), and, therefore, a revelation which employs the former as
its vehicle will generally be "truer" or "more
significant" than one which employs the latter.
For the Christian, Christ is the "final revelation" (the decisive revelation which serves as
a norm for all other revelations). Christ has
this decisive quality because in His perfect
self-abandonment He negates Himself as finite,
thus becoming "completely transparent to the
mystery He reveals." Through His self-negation,
Christ forestalls an idolatry which would treat
the medium, rather than the mystery which discloses itself through the medium, as ultimate.
In spite of its obscurities, Tillich's account
of revelation has proved to be very influential.

851 Wernham, James C. S. "Did James Have an Ethics of
     Belief?" Can J Phil, VI (June, 1976), 287-97.

A reply to Kauber and Hare (# 806 above). Wernham
argues (1) that James' position does not commit
him to the claim that there are duties to believe,
(2) that James maintained that in the appropriate
circumstances we have a moral right to believe
and also a moral right not to believe even if
believing is more prudent than not believing,
and (3) that although James is in fact entitled
to assert that there is a will to believe, that
there is a will to believe does not follow from the
right to believe. (Ought implies can, but from the
fact that we have a right to do something it does
not follow that we can do it.)

852 Williams, C. J. F. "Believing in God and Knowing
     that God Exists," Nous, VIII (September, 1974),
     273-82.

     Aristotle maintains that knowing p and believing
     p are incompatible because "x knows that p" en-
     tails "x judges that necessarily p," while "x
     believes that p" entails "x judges that not neces-
     sarily p." According to Aquinas, knowing p and
     believing p are incompatible because "if x knows
     that p, the fact that p is what causes x to as-
     sent; if x believes that p, the fact that p, if
     it is a fact, leaves x free to assent or not
     to assent." Williams maintains that a person
     who said that he both knew and believed that
     p would not be contradicting himself, but con-
     cedes that it is odd to say "I believe that p"
     when one knows that p. (It is misleading to as-
     sert a weaker claim when one is entitled to assert
     a stronger one.) There are, nevertheless, con-
     texts in which this usage is appropriate. Williams
     attempts to show that the baptismal rite in which
     the Creed originated is one such context. (His
     point is, roughly, that in certain situations
     "I believe that p" simply signifies assent and
     carries no implications with respect to the grounds
     for one's assent.)

853 Zimmerman, Marvin. "Faith, Hope and Clarity,"
     Religious Experience and Truth, A Symposium.
     Edited by Sidney Hook. New York: New York Uni-
     versity Press, 1961. Pp. 187-91.

     A critique of the popular comparison between
     religious faith and "scientific faith." The
     devout also believe in the uniformity of nature.
     It follows that the devout make more unwarranted
     assertions than are made by those who do not

share their belief. Again, while it would be
difficult to survive without belief in the principle of induction, the same cannot be said of
religious belief. Finally, although a belief
in the principle of induction may go beyond the
evidence it does not go against the evidence,
whereas religious belief appears to do so.

VII   RELIGIOUS LANGUAGE

The Verification Controversy

(See also #s 902, 912, 913, 914, 920, 925,
938, 939, 946 and 964)

854   Austin, William Harvey. "Religious Commitment and
the Logical Status of Doctrines," Relig Stud,
9 (March, 1973), 39-48.

According to Lakatos, we must distinguish between
"a research programme such as Descartes' programme
of explaining the universe as a great mechanism
in which the push of one thing against another
is the only cause of motion," and the series of
theories and hypotheses which are generated by
a research program. The latter are held tentatively, and are subject to falsification in a
relatively straightforward manner. The former
are relatively immune from falsification although
a research program will be abandoned if it stalls,
or if the new theories put forward "run afoul
of the same problems, or generate new and equally
bad ones, without scoring new successes." Austin
suggests that religious belief is neither an
unconditional commitment which is immune to counter
evidence nor an adoption of a tentative hypothesis.

It is instead similar to a commitment to a research program.

855 Ayer, Alfred Jules. Language, Truth and Logic.
     2d rev. ed. London: Gollancz, 1946. Pp. 5-16,
     35-45, and 114-20.

The first edition of this very influential book
appeared in 1936. In it, Ayer argued that genuine propositions are either tautologies or empirical hypotheses. An empirical hypothesis
was defined as a proposition which when conjoined
with other propositions entails observation statements not entailed by these other propositions
alone. (This form of the Verification Principle
was drastically revised in the introduction which
Ayer added to the second edition.) Metaphysical
propositions are neither tautologies nor empirical
hypotheses but pseudo-propositions. Since statements about God are metaphysical propositions,
they too have no literal significance. Church
and Hempel have shown that Ayer's second formulation of the Verification Principle is inadequate. (See #s 860 and 868 below.)

856 _____ and Frederick Charles Copleston. "Logi-
     cal Positivism -- A Debate," Third Program, BBC
     (June 13, 1949). (Reprinted in A Modern Intro-
     duction to Philosophy. 2d ed. rev. Edited by
     Paul Edwards and Arthur Pap. New York: The
     Free Press, 1965. Pp. 726-56.)

Copleston argues that Ayer's definition of "cognitive meaning" is arbitrary, and presupposes
the truth of Positivism. Ayer attempts to show
that his definition is grounded in an analysis
of sentences whose cognitive meaningfulness is
not in dispute (the sentences of mathematics,
science, and common sense) and of sentences which

529

are clearly meaningless (e.g., "There's a drogulus over there," where "drogulus" is defined
as an undetectible being). He concludes that
his definition is not arbitrary but "can be derived from an analysis of understanding."

857 Bean, William. "Eschatological Verification . . .
     Fortress or Fairyland?" Methedos, XVI (1964),
     91-107.

A criticism of Hick's appeal to eschatological
verification (see #s 870 and 871 below). Bean
argues that Hick's description of the eschatological state of affairs which would verify theistic
assertions moves through three stages, and at
each stage proves inadequate. (1) "Conscious
existence continues after death" can only be
verified if "some conscious sentient being will
be on hand" to verify it. To assume that this
condition is met, or can be met, is to assume precisely what is at issue, viz., that post-mortem
existence is possible. (Couldn't one argue, in
a similar way, that "there are verifiers" can
only be verified if verifiers are on hand to
verify it, and that to assume that this condition
is, or can be, met is to assume precisely what
is at issue, viz., that "there are verifiers"
is [factually] meaningful?) (2) Hick's "description" of the Resurrection world (with its talk of
"other" space and "other" bodies) is too imprecise and incomplete to be susceptible to verification. (3) Hick is unable to describe in non-
theological language post-mortem experiences which
would verify God claims.

858 Berthold, Fred, Jr. "Empirical Propositions and
     Explanations in Theology," The Future of Empirical
     Theology by Fred Berthold, Jr. [and others].
     Edited by Bernard E. Meland. Chicago and London:
     The University of Chicago Press, 1969. Pp.
     103-28.

     A critique of MacIntyre (# 934 below). Berthold
     makes several sound points, the most important
     of which is the following: A statement like
     "God loves us" cannot be understood in isolation.
     In order to determine the empirical implications
     of this statement (if any) we must connect it
     with other "statements regarding the nature and
     (possible) limits of God's power, some doctrine
     concerning His purposes, some specification of
     the nature and meaning of the term 'love' when
     viewed Christologically," etc. Even if empirical
     consequences follow from this system of statements
     when taken as a whole (and Berthold believes that
     they do), the failure of these consequences would
     not entail the falsity of "God loves us" but
     would only indicate that something is wrong some-
     where -- that some statement in the system is
     false, that a mistake was made in observation,
     that some relevant factor was overlooked, etc.
     It does not follow from these considerations
     that "God loves us" is not an empirical statement
     (any more than from similar considerations it
     would follow that high-level scientific generali-
     zations are not empirical statements).

859 Blackstone, William Thomas. The Problem of Religious
     Knowledge: The Impact of Philosophical Analysis
     on the Question of Religious Knowledge. Englewood
     Cliffs, N. J.: Prentice-Hall, Inc., 1963. xii +
     175 pp.

Most of this book is devoted to a discussion
of the verificationist challenge. The "Left-
Wing Response" (Hare, Braithwaite, MacIntyre, etc.)
fails because it offers analyses of religious
language which neglect the fact that those who
use religious language intend to make factual
assertions. The "Right-Wing Response" (Mitchell,
Hick, and Crombie) fails because it does not succeed in showing that religious utterances are
verifiable or falsifiable and, therefore, genuinely factual. Blackstone argues that many religious utterances which purport to be cognitive
are not cognitive because they are neither analytic nor empirically testable. Since these
utterances are not cognitive, it is logically
impossible to know what is expressed by them.
Other religious utterances are cognitively significant but the propositions which they express
are not known since they cannot be established
by either deduction, induction or observation.
Blackstone admits that his criteria for knowledge
and factual significance can be challenged but
argues that a person will adopt these criteria if
he is concerned with truth and consistency, and
suggests that religious people reject these criteria because they are only concerned with ful-
filling "certain of man's psychic needs." Blackstone's argument for this conclusion is inadequate.
(The chapters in which Blackstone discusses "Right-
Wing" and "Left-Wing" responses to the verificationist's challenge [pp. 73-124] possess more
interest than the rest of the book.)

860   Church, Alonzo.   Review of Language, Truth and Logic
      (2d ed.) by A. J. Ayer.   J Sym Log, 14 (March,
      1949), 52-3.

This review contains an important criticism of
Ayer's second formulation of the Verification
Principle (# 855 above). Church argues that,
if we adopt Ayer's formulation, it can be shown
"of any statement S whatever that either it or its
negation is verifiable." See Nidditch's rebuttal
(# 879 below).

861 Davis, Stephen Thane. "Theology, Verification
and Falsification," Int J Phil Relig, VI (Spring,
1975), 23-39.

It is argued that Flew (# 866 below) confuses
the notion of a psychological limit (a point
at which a believer will modify or abandon his
belief) and the notion of an evidential limit
(a degree of evidence which actually falsifies
a statement). There are psychological limits
for many believers. An evidential limit may be
construed as a degree of evidence which would
convince everyone, or as a degree of evidence
which has been conventionally accepted as sufficient. Very few statements have evidential limits
in the first sense. Theological statements are
verifiable (e.g., the discovery of a sound proof
would verify them) though not falsifiable. Hence,
the denials of theological statements have evidential limits.

862 Demos, Raphael. "The Meaningfulness of Religious
Language," Phil Phenomenol Res, XVIII (September,
1957), 96-106.

A response to New Essays in Philosophical Theology
(# 923 below). Demos raises objections to the
claim that "all and only analytic statements are
necessary while all existential (synthetic) statements are contingent," and to the Verification

Principle. He concludes that religious sentences
have not been shown to be meaningless. Familiar
but not without interest.

863 Diamond, Malcolm Luria and Thomas Vernon Litzenburg,
Jr., eds. The Logic of God: Theology and Verification. Indianapolis: The Bobbs-Merrill Company, Inc., 1975. (Bibliography, 527-52.)

864 Duff-Forbes, Donald R. "Theology and Falsification
Again," Austl J Phil, 39 (August, 1961), 143-54.

A critique of Hare, Mitchell and Crombie (#s
866 and 914 below). (1) Hare wishes to distinguish between right and wrong "bliks." Duff-
Forbes argues that one cannot make this distinction
if "bliks" are unfalsifiable as Hare maintains.
He also argues that some of the examples of sane
"bliks" provided by Hare (the belief that dons
are not murderous and the belief that steel is
normally reliable) are in fact falsifiable and,
therefore, not "bliks" at all. (2) According
to Mitchell, things count against religious beliefs but nothing decisively counts against them.
Duff-Forbes replies that if nothing decisively
counts against religious beliefs, religious beliefs are unfalsifiable. He also argues that
religious belief (as described by Mitchell) is
suspiciously like the insane "bliks" described
by Hare. (3) Crombie's appeal to eschatological
verification is unsuccessful for the claim that
we survive death is itself a religious assertion
whose factual meaning is in doubt. In any case,
its truth cannot be established. (It is not,
however, an assertion of the same logical type
as assertions about God. Furthermore, Duff-Forbes
assumes that in order to show that eschatological
verification is possible, we must prove that

we do in fact survive death -- an assumption
whose truth is by no means obvious.)

865 Flew, Antony Garrard Newton. "'Theology and Falsi-
fication' in Retrospect," The Logic of God:
Theology and Verification. Edited by Malcolm L.
Diamond and Thomas V. Litzenburg, Jr. Indiana-
polis: The Bobbs-Merrill Company, Inc., 1975.
Pp. 269-83.

Flew reviews the University discussion (# 866
below) and replies to some of his critics. Even
though this essay possesses comparatively little
significance in its own right, it is of interest
because of the importance of Flew's original
contribution.

866 _____, Richard Mervyn Hare and Basil Mitchell.
"Theology and Falsification: (1) The University
Discussion," in # 923 below, pp. 96-108.

Flew argues that a meaningful factual assertion
must exclude some state of affairs, infers from
this that factual assertions must be empirically
falsifiable, and concludes that, since religious
assertions are not empirically falsifiable, they
are not factual assertions. Hare concedes that
religious statements do not make assertions.
He suggests, however, that these statements express
"bliks." (The paranoid's belief that all dons
are out to murder him is an insane "blik." Our
belief in the uniformity of nature is a sane
"blik.") Since a "blik" is unfalsifiable, it is
not a genuine assertion. On the other hand,
"bliks" influence our expectations and behavior
and determine what we count as explanations.
It is, thus, "very important to have the right
'blik'." (Unfortunately, Hare does not tell us

how to determine which "bliks" <u>are</u> the right
"bliks.") (See Gibson"s, Matson's and Passmore's
critiques of Hare, #s 925, 937 and 887 below.)
Mitchell's response to Flew is quite different.
The religious believer allows (e.g.) the fact
of pain to count against his assertion that God
loves us, but because he trusts God, he will
(as long as he retains that trust) allow nothing
to count decisively against that assertion.
Because the believer allows things to count against
his belief, and because he has a reason for that
belief (viz., whatever provides the basis for
his trust in God), his utterances must be regarded as genuine assertions. The discussion
concludes with Flew's rejoinder. Its most important point is that those who employ religious
utterances intend to make factual assertions and
not to (e.g.) express "bliks." Unfortunately,
(according to Flew) their utterances are "bogus
assertions" since they are unfalsifiable. --
These four papers originally appeared in the now
defunct <u>University</u> (1 [1950-1], pp. 1-8, 16-20,
93-95, and 143-46.) Their influence has been
substantial. See the reply by Duff-Forbes (#
864 above).

867 Heimbeck, Raeburne Seeley. <u>Theology</u> and <u>Meaning</u>:
     A <u>Critique</u> of <u>Metatheological Scepticism</u>. Stan-
     ford, California: Stanford University Press,
     1969. 276 pp.

In chapter II, Heimbeck argues that truth conditions (criteria) must be distinguished from checking procedures, that the truth conditions (or
meaning) of a statement are displayed by its
entailments and incompatibles, and that a statement therefore has cognitive meaning if it has

entailments and incompatibles. (It can be argued that imperatives have entailments and incompatibles. Does it follow that imperatives are
cognitively meaningful?) Heimbeck maintains
that knowing a statement's checking procedures
is neither a necessary nor sufficient condition
of knowing its meaning and that, while all checkable sentences express cognitively significant
statements, checkability is not a logically necessary condition of cognitive meaningfulness.
Chapters III and IV discuss Flew (# 866 above)
and Braithwaite (# 903 below). (Heimbeck's critique of Flew's Gardener Parable [pp. 78-87]
is excellent.) Verification and falsification
("checkability") are examined in chapters V and
VI. There are certain God-statements (e.g.,
"God raised Jesus from the dead") which have empirical entailments and incompatibles, and "have
only empirical evidence as their primary ultimate
data." These statements are "in some sense foun-
dational to the [Christian] system," and provide
the backing for those God-statements (e.g., "God
is love") which have only other God-statements
for their entailments, and incompatibles. First
order God-claims are conclusively falsifiable if
their empirical entailments are conclusively
falsifiable. They are also checkable in another
manner. The concept of God is associated with
the model of certain patterns which should be
found in experience if that experience is an
experience of God. These patterns include such
things as "tremendous power, preternaturalness,
numinousness, mind likeness, [and] redemptive
activity." The discovery of these patterns in
experience verifies first order God-claims.
The absence of these patterns "disverifies" these

claims, and the presence of conflicting patterns
falsifies them. (Compare this with the way in
which a pattern is detected in the facts when
we "discern Mary's true feelings toward John."
There are certain patterns of behavior associated
with hatred. In so far as one of these patterns
is actually found in a cluster of facts, those
facts may be said to verify "Mary hates John.")
-- Heimbeck's theses are not particularly novel
but they are very well presented.

868　Hempel, Carl Gustav. "Problems and Changes in the
　　　　Empiricist Criterion of Meaning," Rev Int Phil,
　　　　IV (Janvier, 1950), 41-63. (Reprinted in Semantics
　　　　and the Philosophy of Language, A Collection of
　　　　Readings. Edited by Leonard Linsky. Urbana, Illi-
　　　　nois: The University of Illinois Press, 1952.
　　　　Pp. 168-85.)

Hempel examines several attempts to formulate
the Verification Principle and shows that each
is inadequate. He then suggests that a statement is cognitively meaningful if and only if
it can be translated into an empiricist language
which includes not only logical terms and observation predicates, but terms for theoretical constructs which cannot be reduced to observation
predicates. The statements in which these terms
occur are cognitively significant because they
belong to theories which, when taken as a whole,
entail observation statements. (It is at least
arguable that [e.g.] classical Christian theology
which speaks of miracles, special interventions,
a general resurrection, and so on -- satisfies
Hempel's criterion of cognitive significance.)

869　Hick, John Harwood. "Eschatological Verification
　　　　Reconsidered," Relig Stud, 13 (June, 1977),
　　　　189-202.

In this reply to his critics, Hick makes several
important points. (1) The proposition which
eschatological facts verify is not "God exists"
but "the theistic account of the character of
the universe, and what is taking place in history,
is true." Since we do not need to appeal to infinite wisdom, power, etc., in order to explain
either the universe or its history, infinite
attributes play no role in this account. Consequently, we are not faced with "the impossible
task of verifying the infinite nature of God's
attributes." (However, Hick thinks that certain
arguments show that God's attributes are infinite.)
(2) This-worldly experiences can warrant religious
belief (and even justify a claim to knowledge)
but they do not establish verifiability. (But
why not? Because they do not exclude all rational
doubt? And yet, if they do not exclude all rational doubt, how can a claim to knowledge be
legitimately based upon them?) (3) The appeal to
eschatological facts is not intended to explain
the meaning of religious utterances to a person
who professes not to understand them; it is only
intended to insure their factual meaningfulness.
Hence, the fact that the description of these
states is couched in religious terms is irrelevant. (4) Since belief in "the life everlasting"
is an essential component of Christian theism,
it is necessarily the case that if Christian theism
is true, it will be eschatologically verified.
If theism is false, it may or may not be falsified. (If materialistic naturalism is true, and
consciousness ends at death, it is unfalsifiable.
However, the occurrence of post-mortem experiences of a malevolent sort would falsify it.)

Points (1) and (4) involve departures from Hick's earlier position.

870 _____. Faith and Knowledge, A Modern Introduction to the Problem of Religious Knowledge.
2d ed. Ithaca, New York: Cornell University
Press, 1966. Pp. 151-99.

In chapter 7 of the first edition (Cornell University Press, 1957), Hick argued that although
theistic assertions are not falsifiable, they
are verifiable. Theistic assertions would be
verified by certain types of post-mortem experiences. This discussion proved to be very influential. The issue of verification is again examined
in chapters 7 and 8 of the second edition. Hick
retains part of chapter 7 of the first edition,
incorporates "Theology and Verification" (# 871
below), and responds to his critics by providing
some additional clarifications. (For example:
Although the possibility of eschatological verification ensures the factual meaningfulness of
"God exists," the eschatological situations which
would verify "God exists" do not exhaust the
meaning of "God exists" since they provide only
some of its truth conditions. Furthermore, these
situations are not the only things which would
provide a good reason for "God exists." Present
experience can, if sufficiently vivid, provide
an adequate warrant for belief in God.) See the
discussions of Bean (# 857 above), Kavka, Nielsen,
Penelhum and Tooley (#s 872, 880, 882, 888 and
891 below).

871 _____. "Theology and Verification," Theol
Today, XVII (April, 1960), 12-31.

A further development of ideas originally presented in the first edition of Faith and Knowledge (see # 870 above). The notion of verification is discussed. (Hick shows that statements
can be verifiable without being falsifiable,
and maintains that verification consists in the
exclusion of rational doubt and not the exclusion
of the logical possibility of error.) Hick
attempts to explicate the notion of survival in
a "resurrection-world" which stands in no spatial
relations to our own, and argues that theism
would be verified if existence in that world
involved "an experience of the fulfillment of
God's purpose for ourselves, as this has been
disclosed in the Christian revelation; in conjunction . . . with an experience of communion with
God as he has revealed himself in the person of
Christ." This article is incorporated in the
second edition of Faith and Knowledge.

872 Kavka, Gregory Stephen. "Eschatological Falsifi-
       cation," Relig Stud, 12 (June, 1976), 201-5.

Hick (#s 870 and 871 above) has argued that even
though "God exists" is unfalsifiable, it would be
verified if certain post-mortem experiences were
to occur. Hick construes verification as the
exclusion of rational doubt. Kavka shows that
there are Satanic post-mortem experiences the
occurrence of which would exclude any rational
doubts about the non-existence of God. It follows
that "God exists" is falsifiable as well as verifiable.

873 Kellenberger, Bertram James. <u>Religious Discovery</u>,
<u>Faith</u>, <u>and</u> <u>Knowledge</u>. Englewood Cliffs, New
Jersey: Prentice-Hall, Inc., 1972. Pp. 155-93.

The first two appendices reprint "The Falsifi-
cation Challenge" and "More on the Falsification
Challenge." (The latter is a reply to Antony
Flew's "The Falsification Response" and Thomas
McPherson's "The Falsification Challenge: A
Comment." All four articles appeared in <u>Religious</u>
<u>Studies</u>, 5, 1969.) Empirical denials are distin-
guished from logical and syntactical denials.
(The syntactical denial of "God exists" is "God
does not exist." Its logical denial, e.g., "The
God of the old and new covenants does not exist,"
fills out the syntactical denial.) Empirical
denials are empirical, determinable and conclusively falsify the statements which they deny.
Religious statements are similar to such statements as "John loves Mary." These statements
are meaningful and have logical denials. Things
in the world count for and against them. However, they have no empirical denial. The third
appendix attempts to show that God-predicates
need not be taken in stretched or extended senses.
Kellenberger examines arguments which have been
used to show that they must. (E.g., that if
God-predicates are taken in the ordinary sense,
religious statements are false; that if God-
predicates are taken literally, God will be
thought of anthropomorphically; that God's activity differs from ours, etc.) He concludes that
all of these arguments rest upon controversial
philosophical theses (e.g., that bodily continuity
is needed for personal identity, a verificationist
theory of meaning, etc.).

874 Klein, Kenneth. Positivism and Christianity:
A Study of Theism and Verifiability. The Hague:
Martinus Nijhoff, 1974. xi + 183 pp.

A qualified defense of the claims (1) that theological sentences are characteristically used to
make factual assertions, (2) that the Verification
Principle is a legitimate criterion of factual
significance, and (3) that theological sentences
fail to satisfy that criterion. Klein's discussion of the relevant literature is thorough, but
unexciting. His defense of the Verification
Principle is particularly weak. Klein adopts
a version of that principle originally proposed
by David Rynin in "Vindication of L*G*C*L*P*S*
T*V*SM" (Proceedings and Addresses of the American
Philosophical Association, XXX [1956-57], pp.
45-67), viz., that a sentence is factually meaningful if and only if there is either a (finite)
set of observation statements which entails its
truth or a (finite) set of observation statements
which entails its falsity, and argues that we
should accept it in spite of the fact that it
rules out sentences involving mixed quantification. His discussion (in chapter IV) of Hick
(#s 870 and 871 above) is also revealing. In
chapter I, Klein distinguishes between states of
affairs which verify a statement and states of
affairs which merely "attest to" or "certify"
its truth. What verifies a statement is what
"shows it to be true," and what "shows it to be
true" is a direct "confrontation" with the fact
which it asserts. It follows that if the statement that a state of affairs obtains is not part
of the meaning of a sentence, the experience of
that state of affairs fails to verify it. Since
the statement that eschatological states of

affairs obtain is not part of the meaning of
theistic sentences, eschatological states of
affairs will not verify them. (And, more generally, since one cannot confront a transcendent
deity, no observable state of affairs could verify
theistic claims.) Unfortunately, it is unreasonable to demand that factual assertions be verifiable in the specified sense. It would seem,
e.g., that we cannot "confront" the facts described by scientific statements about theoretical entities, and when Klein defends the Verification Principle in chapter III he only insists
that such statements be parts of theories which
are falsifiable when taken as a whole. Klein's
criticism of Hick is, therefore, inappropriate.

875 Mascall, Eric Lionel. Words and Images, A Study in
     Theological Discourse. London, New York and
     Toronto: Longmans, Green and Co., 1957. Pp.
     1-14.

A reply to Ayer (# 855 above) by one of the more
able Thomists. Mascall suggests that when Ayer
revises the Verification Principle in order to
accommodate those sentences whose meaningfulness
he wishes to preserve, he is employing a criterion
of significance which is independent of the Verification Principle. Mascall points out that the
Verification Principle is itself neither analytic
nor empirical but a definition, and attempts to
show that that definition is arbitrary. He concludes by accusing Ayer of arbitrarily restricting
experience to sense experience. See Nielsen's
reply (# 880 below).

876 Matthews, Gareth Blanc. "Theology and Natural
     Theology," J Phil, LXI (January 30, 1964), 99-108.

Matthews makes several significant points. (1)
The demand for the non-theological consequences
of theological assertions would be reasonable
if it could be shown that geometrical assertions
have non-geometrical consequences, physical assertions have non-physical consequences, etc.
This has not been shown. (2) It can be conceded
that if theological assertions are compatible
with every conceivable empirical state of affairs,
then theological assertions say nothing about
the empirical world. However, from the fact
that a theological assertion is incompatible
with some empirical state of affairs, it does
not follow that we know what empirical state of
affairs that assertion is incompatible with,
and if we do not know this, "we could not conceivably falsify it empirically." (3) It is a
mistake to suppose that if a term like "love"
is employed in both an empirical and a non-empirical assertion, it must express two different
concepts. ("Cube" does not express different
concepts in "Susan's building block is a cube"
and "all cubes have twelve edges.") See Nielsen's reply (# 944 below).

877 Mavrodes, George Ion. "God and Verification," Can
J Theol, X (July, 1964), 187-91.

In this reply to Nielsen's "Eschatological Verification" (# 882 below), Mavrodes argues that
the test proposed by the verificationist exhibits
the following incoherence: In order to determine
the meaningfulness of some statement p, we are
told that we must show that there is some conceivable state of affairs, E, such that "E verifies p" is true. Unfortunately, we will be unable

to determine the truth of "E̲ verifies p̲" unless
we already understand p̲ and we do not understand
p̲. (If we knew what p̲ meant, we would know that
p̲ is meaningful yet, by hypothesis, the meaningfulness of p̲ is just what is at issue.) See
Nielsen's reply (# 883 below).

878 Miller, John Franklin, III. "Science and Religion:
     Their Logical Similarity," Relig Stud, 5 (October,
     1969), 49-68.

Miller argues that statements like "There is a
God" and "God loves mankind" are formally similar
to the principle of causality and the law of
conservation of energy. These statements and
principles are fundamental to certain world views.
They are not themselves verifiable or falsifiable
but are "principles in accordance with which
inferences are drawn and evidence is advanced."
Miller offers a number of considerations designed
to show that certain scientific statements should
be understood in this way, but the only reason
which he gives for interpreting theistic statements in a similar manner is their alleged un-
falsifiability.

879 Nidditch, Peter. "A Defence of Ayer's Verifiability
     Principle Against Church's Criticism," Mind,
     LXX (January, 1961), 88-9.

A response to Church's critique of Ayer (# 860
above). Church is accused of overlooking Ayer's
second requirement, viz., that the statements
conjoined with the statement whose factual significance is in dispute must be analytic or verifiable. See Plantinga's reply (# 889 below).

880 Nielsen, Kai. *Contemporary Critiques of Religion*.
     (Philosophy of Religion Series.) London and
     Basingstoke: Macmillan; New York: Herder and
     Herder, 1971. Pp. 31-93.

Nielsen responds to critics of Verificationism
in chapters 2 and 3. (1) Mascall (# 875 above)
is mistaken when he supposes that if the Verification Principle in neither empirical nor analytic it must either be a metaphysical assertion
or a (mere) stipulative definition. The Verification Principle is a persuasive definition.
It is reasonable to accept this definition because
it is based upon the meanings which words like
"understand" and "know" have in science and
everyday life (which presumably implies that
religion is not part of everyday life!), and
because it is useful in ruling out modes of
thought (e.g., metaphysics) for which there are
no clear rules. Nielsen concedes that the experiences which test our claims should not be
arbitrarily restricted to sense experiences,
but argues that mystical experience is "neutral
with respect to . . . theological and religious
truth claims." (This is surely mistaken. Mystical experience may be neutral with respect
to the truth claims of any particular religion
or type of religion. Nevertheless, the impression
of contact with an "objective" and non-empirical
order of reality appears to be constitutive of
both extrovertive and introvertive mysticism.)
(2) Responding to Plantinga (# 889 below), Nielsen
admits that the verificationist should not insist
upon decisive verification and falsification as
a criterion of factual significance, but maintains that theological assertions are not even
weakly confirmable or infirmable. Nielsen's

argument at this point is revealing. Nielsen
contends that if an assertion is factually significant, there must be some empirical state
of affairs which counts for (against) that assertion and against (for) its denial. (Does this
contention reflect the assumption that assertions
with the same observational consequences have
the same factual significance? See Salmon and
Tooley [#s 890 and 891 below] on the importance
of this principle.) Since theological assertions
and their denials are equally compatible with the
evidence which is alleged to be relevant to them,
theological assertions are devoid of factual
significance. (The antecedent of this conditional
is only [clearly] true if by "compatible" we
mean "logically compatible." If, however, this
is what Nielsen means, then he is in fact demand-
ing that theists specify empirical states of
affairs which entail their claims and is, therefore, insisting on decisive confirmation and
infirmation after all.) In response to the charge
that he is conflating the demand that something
must count for or against factual assertions
with the demand that empirical states of affairs
must count for or against factual assertions,
Nielsen argues that the only alternative to empirical tests is the appeal to non-sensory intuitions. (Nielsen thus ignores the role which
various sorts of arguments have traditionally
played in metaphysics and theology. See, e.g.,
Mitchell, # 1065 below.) (3) Nielsen argues that
Hick (#s 870 and 871 above) has not succeeded
in providing a description of an experiential
state of affairs which would verify theistic
assertions. The descriptions which Hick has
offered covertly include theistic assertions.

If these assertions are abstracted from his descriptions, what remains is compatible with
atheism. (4) Nielsen rejects the notion that
the empiricist critique of religion is vitiated
by the (alleged) fact that no distinction can
be drawn between fact and metaphor, description
and interpretation, seeing and seeing us, etc.,
and by the (alleged) fact that there is no direct
relation between language and the world.

881 _____ . "Empiricism, Theoretical Constructs
and God," J Relig, 54 (July, 1974), 199-217.

It is sometimes argued that "there is a God"
is logically similar to "there are photons."
Neither statement is directly verifiable but
both are indirectly verifiable because they belong to systems of statements which are confirmable or infirmable when taken as a whole. (1)
Nielsen argues that in order for "indirect confirmation of 'God exists'" to make sense it must
have an "intelligible opposite." ("Indirect
confirmation or infirmation" is not intelligible
unless "direct confirmation or infirmation" is
intelligible. It is less clear that "direct
confirmation or infirmation of p" must be intelligible in order for "indirect confirmation or
infirmation of p" to be intelligible.) (2) Nielsen also maintains that because religious sentences are loosely related to one another, it
is not clear that religious sentences form a
system in the sense in which the scientific sentences which constitute a theory form a system.
(3) According to Nielsen, (e.g.) photons are
"mere" theoretical constructs which are not "part
of the furniture of the universe." On the other
hand, "God" does not designate a theoretical

construct but (allegedly) stands for a reality "whose existence cannot depend on human conventions."

882 _____. "Eschatological Verification," <u>Can J Theol</u>, IX (October, 1963), 271-81.

A significant critique of Hick's notion of eschatological verification. (See #s 870 and 871 above.) Nielsen argues that Hick's description of the post-mortem experiences which would verify theism incorporates theological concepts and, thus, presupposes their meaningfulness. (Hick's description does in fact incorporate theological concepts. It is not, however, clear that he needs to use these concepts.) Nielsen agrees that the existence of such things as magnetic fields and superegos can be indirectly verified but denies that post-mortem experiences can indirectly verify theism. While the concepts of a magnetic field or superego are only "useful devices," the concept of God is not merely heuristic. Since the existence of an objective reality can be indirectly verified only if it can be directly verified (sic!), and since the existence of God cannot (by Hick's own admission) be directly verified, it follows that God's existence cannot be indirectly verified.

883 _____. "God and Verification Again," <u>Can J Theol</u>, XI (April, 1965), 135-41.

A reply to Mavrodes (# 877 above). Nielsen makes three points. (1) We are sometimes able to employ a concept even though we are unable to provide a satisfactory analysis of it. Hence, the fact that no one has succeeded in providing an

adequate statement of the Verification Principle
does not show that we cannot employ the concept
of verification. (However, to employ the notion
of verification is one thing; to appeal to verification as a criterion of factual significance
is quite another.) Nielsen realizes that a theist
might reply that in this unanalyzed sense of
"verify" there are many things which would verify
"God exists," but contends that this reply is
unsatisfactory because there are no descriptions
of observable states of affairs which entail
"God exists." (2) Nielsen protests that he is
not making verifiability a criterion of cognitive
meaningfulness but only of "factual intelligibility." (Ethical statements are cognitively
meaningful but non-factual, according to Nielsen.)
(3) Nielsen points out that because he is not
making verifiability a criterion of cognitive
meaningfulness, Mavrodes' argument cannot be
used to show that he begs the question.

884   _____. "Metaphysics and Verification Revis-
        ited," SW J Phil, VI (Fall, 1975), 75-93.

Although (as Nielsen admits) this essay moves
"over some well-trodden ground," it does provide
a decent statement of a prominent verificationist's response to some standard objections.
The author examines the claim that statements
about the past, such statements as "There is no
sentient life," universal and existential generalizations, and statements involving mixed
quantification are factually meaningful in spite
of the fact that they fail to satisfy the Verification Principle. Nielsen concludes that statements are factually meaningful if there is, in

principle, empirical evidence which counts for
or against them (though perhaps not conclusively).
To the objection that this statement of the
Verification Principle is so weak that it fails
to exclude metaphysical and religious assertions,
Nielsen rather lamely responds that it at least
"makes the theologian or metaphysician put his
cards on the table," and explain what counts for
or against his utterances. This essay is of
interest because it enables us to discern certain
assumptions which lie behind Nielsen's arguments
and undoubtedly behind the arguments of other
verificationists as well. Among these assumptions are (1) that if it is logically possible
to indirectly verify a statement, it is logically
possible to directly verify it, (2) that if
statements (such as "There are no sentient
beings") cannot be truly stated, they cannot be
true and so are not genuine statements, and (3)
that evidence and empirical evidence are coextensive. (Nielsen does not tell us whether
empirical evidence is to be restricted to what
can be observed by our senses or whether it is
to be construed more broadly. If we adopt the
first alternative, what he says is not obviously
true. If we adopt the second alternative, it
is relatively innocuous.)

885   _____ . Reason and Practice: A Modern Intro-
        duction to Philosophy. New York [etc]: Harper
        and Row Publishers, 1971. Pp. 393-491, esp.
        420-35.

A very lucid presentation of the case for Verificationism. Two features of Nielsen's discussion
deserve special attention. (1) There is an almost unnoticed transition from (a) "factually

552

significant sentences are true or false," to
(b) "In order to understand a factually significant sentence, one must have some grasp of those
conditions under which that sentence would be
true and of those conditions under which that
sentence would be false," to (c) "In order to
understand a factually significant sentence, one
must know what would count for and against its
truth," to (d) "In order to understand a factually
significant sentence, one must know what empirically experiencable states of affairs would
count for or against its truth," to (e) "In order
to show that a sentence is factually significant,
one must show that a set of observation statements
entails its truth or falsity." Although the
last two (and, perhaps, the last three) moves
are suspect, Verificationism gains a specious
plausibility from its conflation of these five
claims. Nielsen recognizes the difficulties
which beset (e) and explicitly rejects it. Nevertheless, he asserts that if p and its denial are
factually meaningful "it must be possible at
least in principle to state certain empirically
determinable states of affairs that would justify
p and certain contrasting states of affairs in
which one will be justified in asserting not-p."
Furthermore, theological and metaphysical sentences are denied factual meaning because there
is a logical gap between any allegedly relevant
empirical evidence and what those sentences purport to assert. (Thus, "there is a God" and
"it is not the case that there is a God" are
said to be factually meaningless because they
"are equally compatible with any conceivable
bit of empirical evidence.") It is difficult to
avoid the conclusion that even though Nielsen

explicitly adopts (d), he in fact employs (e)
when he engages in the investigation of theological and metaphysical sentences. (2) Nielsen
concedes that the Verification Principle is not
a factual or analytic statement, but only a
recommendation. However, he argues (following
Ayer, # 856 above) that we should accept the
recommendation because those sentences which
are clearly factual are empirically verifiable
while those sentences which are clearly non-
factual are not. (But clear to whom? Many
theists [e.g., Hartshorne] are firmly convinced
that some [empirically] non-verifiable sentences
are factually significant. It is true that there
are no non-verifiable sentences which everyone
finds factually significant since verificationists
deny that such sentences are factually significant. Nevertheless, it is difficult to see how
this fact can be used to support Verificationism.)

886 Owen, Huw Parri. The Christian Knowledge of God.
     London: University of London, The Athlone Press,
     1960. Pp. 260-9.

Owen argues that theistic claims can be eschatologically verified and falsified, that although
the theist does qualify the meaning of terms like
"love" when he applies those terms to God, the
qualifications which he introduces are (pace
Flew) reasonable, and that there are two important differences between the theist's decision
to believe in God and a decision to believe in
an invisible gardener. (1) Theism explains facts
(e.g., the existence of contingent being) which
can only be explained in terms of a transcendent
God, while the arrangement of the plants can be
explained without appealing to a gardener. (2)

Although the invisible gardener cannot be experienced, God can be experienced.

887 Passmore, John Arthur. "Christianity and Positivism," Austl J Phil, 35 (August, 1957), 125-36.

This frequently cited review article discusses Braithwaite's response to the verificationist challenge (# 903 below) and the responses contained in New Essays in Philosophical Theology (# 923 below). Passmore finds these responses inadequate. His critical remarks are, on the whole, fair but unexciting. His remarks on Hare (# 866 above) are of some value. He argues that the beliefs which Hare regards as "bliks" are in fact falsifiable and are, therefore, not "bliks" but factual assertions.

888 Penelhum, Terence. Problems of Religious Knowledge. (Philosophy of Religion Series.) London: Macmillan, 1971; New York: Herder and Herder, 1972. Pp. 66-86.

Chapter 4 provides a defense of John Hick's theory of eschatological verification (#s 870 and 871 above). The concept of verification is compared with the concept of proof. It is argued that there are statements which employ religious concepts but are non-theistic in the sense that they can be known to be true without knowing that God exists, and which are such that the ascertainment of their truth would verify theistic statements. (An example of such a statement is "There is a community of persons whose personalities are as they would be if they were infused by grace.") Penelhum concludes that even though it may be unreasonable to insist that meaningful theistic statements must be verifiable by

non-theistic statements, the requirement can
be met. It is conceded, however, that these
considerations presuppose the meaningfulness
of religious concepts (since religious concepts
are employed in those non-theistic statements
which verify theistic statements).

889   Plantinga, Alvin Carl. God and Other Minds, A
      Study of the Rational Justification of Belief
      in God. (Contemporary Philosophy.) Ithaca,
      New York: Cornell University Press, 1967. Pp.
      156-68.

      An important critique of Verificationism. Plan-
      tinga shows that Flew's formulation of the falsi-
      fication requirement (# 866 above) is confused,
      shows that attempts to formulate the Verification
      Principle (see #s 855 and 879 above) have been
      unsuccessful, and argues that if the verification-
      ist's demand is only that possible empirical
      states of affairs be described which could serve
      as non-deductive evidence against religious as-
      sertions, then that demand is easily met.

890   Salmon, Wesley C. "Verifiability and Logic," Mind,
      Matter and Method. Edited by P. K. Feyerabend
      and G. Maxwell. Minneapolis: University of
      Minnesota Press, 1966. Pp. 354-76.

      Salmon argues that we must distinguish between
      the question as to whether empirical verifiability
      is an adequate criterion of cognitive signifi-
      cance and the question of how the notion of
      empirical verification is to be understood. The
      failure to provide an adequate formulation of
      the Verification Principle (see Hempel and Plan-
      tinga, #s 868 and 889 above) shows that the con-
      cept has not yet been adequately analyzed. It
      does not show that the concept is incoherent,

or that empirical verifiability is not a criterion
of cognitive significance. Salmon also suggests
that any attempt to explicate the notion of verifiability must consider inductive as well as deductive relations between sentences, and that in
order to avoid problems "the verifiability criterion of cognitive meaningfulness needs to be
supplemented with a verifiability criterion of
sameness of cognitive meaning."

891 Tooley, Michael. "John Hick and the Concept of Es-
      chatological Verification," Relig Stud, 12 (June,
      1976), 177-99.

According to Tooley, Hick's attempt (#s 870 and
871 above) to establish the meaningfulness of
theological statements by appealing to the possibility of eschatological verification is both
unnecessary and inadequate. (1) Hick maintains
that the believer "can already have, on the basis
of his religious experience, a warrant as to the
reality of God," and appears to imply that although our present this-worldly situation happens
to be ambiguous ("one which seems in some ways
to confirm and in other ways to contradict the
truth of theism") it could have been unambiguous.
Since the religious experiences of believers do
verify theological statements and since there
are possible this-worldly situations which would
verify theological statements if they were to
occur, there is no need to appeal to eschatological experiences to establish the verifiability
of theological statements. (2) The verificationist maintains that if the observational consequences of a pair of statements are the same,
then those statements have the same factual
meaning. "S" ("There exists a religiously

557

unambiguous eschatological situation") and "T"
("There exists a religiously unambiguous eschatological situation, together with a transcendent
person who is the cause of that situation") would
appear to have the same observational consequences. It follows that, if Verificationism
is correct, "S" and "T" have the same factual
meaning. Therefore, "since sentence 'S' does
not assert the existence of a transcendent person,
neither does sentence 'T'." Hick cannot both
adhere to Verificationism and give meaning to
talk about a transcendent person. (Or, more accurately, Hick cannot adhere to the sort of
Verificationism described by Tooley [does he?],
and give meaning to talk about a transcendent
person.) This is a suggestive essay.

892 _____. "Theological Statements and the Ques-
tion of the Empiricist Criterion of Cognitive
Significance," The Logic of God: Theology and
Verification. Edited by Malcolm L. Diamond and
Thomas V. Litzenburg, Jr. Indianapolis: The
Bobbs-Merrill Company, Inc., 1975. Pp. 481-524.

Tooley distinguishes "the falsifiability challenge
argument" (which he ascribes to Flew) from "the
translatability challenge argument" (which he ascribes to Ayer and Carnap). The former can be
countered by showing that theological sentences
are in fact falsifiable. The latter cannot be
countered in this way. The translatability challenge argument rests upon the assumption that a
pair of sentences which entail the same observation sentences have the same cognitive content. A
sentence, S, which purports to refer to something
which transcends the physical world will entail the
same observation sentences as a sentence, T, which
is equivalent to the conjunction of the observation

558

sentences entailed by S. It follows that S and
T have the same cognitive significance. Since T
is clearly an empirical sentence (i.e., a sentence
[solely] about the physical world or the experiences of physical organisms), S does not succeed
in making a reference to anything which transcends
the physical world. (Tooley later modifies this
argument in order to take account of inductive as
well as deductive relations between sentences.)
Tooley provides reasons for believing that any
properly selected set of basic observation sentences must include sentences which describe the
experiences of (embodied or disembodied) persons.
However, because these experiences need not be
experiences of the physical world (cf. "I am in
pain") and because these experiences need not be
the experiences of any physical organism, "there
will be sentences that can be constructed from the
basic observation sentences which will not be empirical sentences" (e.g., God says "I am God").
Since the translatability challenge argument assumes that any sentence constructed from basic observation sentences is an empirical sentence, the
translatability challenge argument is unsound.

893 Wainwright, William Judson. "The Presence of Evil
     and the Falsification of Theistic Assertions,"
     Relig Stud, 4 (April, 1969), 213-6.

     It is sometimes claimed that the theist will allow
     no amount of evil to falsify his assertions. This
     essay attempts to show that the reasons offered
     for this view are far from conclusive.

894 Wilson, John. Language and Christian Belief.
     London: Macmillan & Co., Ltd.; New York: St.
     Martin's Press, 1958. xvi + 136 pp.

Wilson argues that genuine assertions must be verifiable, and that (some) religious sentences express assertions which are verified by religious experiences. Wilson appears at times to speak as if assertions about God are really assertions about (actual and possible) religious experiences. If assertions about God are (only) assertions about religious experiences, then they are clearly verifiable. Unfortunately, this sort of reductionism is not particularly plausible.

895   . Philosophy and Religion, the Logic of Religious Belief. London: Oxford University Press, 1961. xii + 119 pp.

A further development of themes which first appeared in Language and Christian Belief (# 894 above).

Explications of Religious Language
in Recent Analytic Philosophy

(See also #s 854, 866, 867, 878, 894, 895, 1044, 1050, 1051, 1100, 1101, 1102, 1103, 1104, 1105, 1106, 1107 and 1108)

896 Alston, William P. "Elucidation of Religious Statements," Process and Divinity. Edited by William Reese and Eugene Freeman. LaSalle, Illinois: Open Court Pub. Co., 1964. Pp. 429-43.

Alston examines "God forgives our sins" in order to elucidate the difficulties which beset action-sentences which have "God" as their subject. Our understanding of this sentence is parasitic upon our understanding of sentences which assert that some human being forgives another. The latter entail claims to the effect that the person who forgives another will perform overt acts of "an

appropriate sort . . . in the absence of special
reasons to the contrary." These acts involve
"essential connections with bodily activity."
Since God is disembodied, we must prescind from
these implications, but if we prescind from these
implications, we are reduced to asserting that
God experiences certain private mental states.
Alston (not very surprisingly) concludes that if
we construe the test sentence as the expression
of an assertion about God's private mental states,
we will find ourselves unable to answer the following four questions: (1) How can I know whether
it is true? (2) How can I tell whether I believe
it? (3) How do I go about truly turning to God?
(4) Why should I care whether it is true? This
interesting paper is vulnerable at two points.
(1) Alston isolates the test sentence from its
context. But this won't do. If we were to abstract "atoms have no diameter" from its (scientific, or poetic, or metaphysical) context, from
arguments offered for it, from the reactions which
its use evokes, etc., we would be unable to answer
the first two questions. (The other two questions
are not clearly applicable.) It does not follow
that the sentence is suspect. (2) Alston is
aware that one might want to introduce causal
connections between God's inner states and certain empirical states of affairs but dismisses
this suggestion with the remark that "God forgives
A" does not entail "A feels forgiven." This is
unsatisfactory for two reasons. (a) The effects
are construed too narrowly. (Why not include
pronouncements of forgiveness by Jesus or by
the church, an altered personal destiny, etc.,
as well as subjective states?) (b) The causal
relation provides an analogue to the overt bodily

561

activity typically involved in human forgiveness. It may, therefore, be essential to include it.

897 Attfield, Robin. "The Lord is God: There is No Other," Relig Stud, 13 (March, 1977), 73-84.

A reply to Durrant (# 917 below). Attfield argues (1) that "God is a member of a sort" (characterized by immateriality, non-spatiality and non-temporality, omnipotence, etc.), (2) that God can be identified ("as the creator of any material object we care to select") and (since He is unique) re-identified, (3) that Durrant is correct in maintaining that Aquinas is confused when he speaks of "God" as an abstract noun, and (4) that "God" can be used as a proper name. Attfield's response is an expression of what might be called "theistic common sense." Just as the burden of proof is upon those philosophers who take exception to such widely accepted beliefs as our belief in the reality of an external world, our belief in other minds, and our belief in the coherence and reality of moral obligation, so the burden of proof would appear to be upon Durrant when he argues that the concept of God is incoherent. Attfield's responses to Durrant's questions have a certain prima facie plausibility. If Durrant is to establish his case, he must base cogent arguments upon premises which not only have a certain plausibility but are clearly true.

898 Austin, William Harvey. "Models, Mystery and Paradox in Ian Ramsey," J Scien Stud Relig, VII (Spring, 1968), 41-55.

Austin argues that according to Ramsey (#s 948,

949, 950, 951 and 952 below) models not only evoke disclosures, they also articulate the mystery which is disclosed and interpret experience. It is, therefore, important that these models cohere. Unfortunately Ramsey pays little attention to the problem of their coherence. (When faced with a conflict, Ramsey simply suggests that we should look for the common basis of these conflicting models in disclosure.)

899 _____. The Relevance of Natural Science to Theology. (Library of Philosophy and Religion.) London and Basingstoke: The Macmillan Press, Ltd., 1976. Pp. 32-47.

Chapter 3 contains what is, perhaps, the best discussion of Braithwaite's theory of religious language. (See # 903 below.) It includes a helpful account of the role which stories play according to that theory, and a critical analysis of the arguments which Braithwaite provides for it (viz., that it accounts for the way in which religious belief involves a way of life, that it allows freedom in the interpretation of doctrine, and that it explains such facts as the fact that conduct is a test for the sincerity of a person's belief.) Austin concludes that the arguments are "too weak to compensate for the initial implausibility of his position."

900 Bambrough, Renford. Reason, Truth and God. London: Methuen, 1969. vii + 164 pp.

Bambrough begins by asking what it means to say that Poseidon is angry, and points out that in so far as the assertion expresses a religious belief it provides an explanation (and not merely a

metaphysical description) of certain familiar
facts. We must understand beliefs of this sort
in order to understand more sophisticated beliefs because the latter develop from, and are
still influenced by, the former. A consideration
of the Poseidon case suggests that three features
are essential to religious belief. They are
(1) assertions of fact, (2) which rest upon features of our experience, and (3) claim that "something over and above those features exists and
can be known." According to Bambrough, any account of Christian belief which eliminates reference to a transcendent substance distorts it.
Even John Wisdom, with whom he is otherwise in
sympathy, is accused of failing to preserve "God
exists" "as the kind of assertion it is . . .
namely, an assertion of the existence of a substance, and, what is more, of a personal substance." On the other hand, if we regard God
as a transcendent substance, we sever God's connections with the world and, thus, with those
features which provide evidence for His existence.
Furthermore, recent philosophy has shown that
the postulation of transcendent entities (immaterial souls, Platonic forms, etc.) is an error.
(Bambrough does not establish either of these
contentions.) If the dogmas of religion (with
their reference to a transcendent substance)
are eliminated, we no longer have Christian belief
but what remains can be used to illuminate human
life and its problems. (Consider, e.g., the
way in which Greek mythology has been used to do
this.) According to Bambrough, "literature is
concerned with truth and knowledge." There are
correct answers to the problems of human life,
and the issues of human life are properly subject

to rational discussion. Furthermore, it is precisely within literature and theology that much
of this discussion goes on. These problems are
not solved by adducing facts but by illuminating
facts with which we are already familiar, thus enabling us to see them in a new way. -- Bambrough's
account of religious belief is clearly reductive,
but it is one of the more attractive proposals
of its kind.

901 Bendall, Kent. "Propositions, Belief, and Christian
     Faith," Exploring the Logic of Faith, A Dialogue
     on the Relation of Modern Philosophy to Christian
     Faith., by Kent Bendall and Frederick Ferré.
     New York: Association Press, 1962. Pp. 182-201.

A fairly decent discussion of the cognitive status
of models. Bendall argues that adopting the
Christian model (cf. Ferré, #s 921, 922 and 1046
below) should not be identified with believing
Christian claims (e.g., that God was in Christ
reconciling the world to Himself). While Bendall
is specifically concerned with Ferré, his remarks
are more generally applicable. (Ferré replies to
Bendall on pp. 204-6 of the same volume where
he argues that the adoption of the [a?] set of
Christian metaphysical propositions includes the
adoption of each member of that set and, thus,
the adoption of "God was in Christ reconciling
the world to Himself." Unfortunately, Ferré's
reply is only to the point if the adoption of
a model is equivalent to the adoption of the
[a?] set of propositions which explicate it,
and Ferré denies that this is the case.)

902 Bocheński, Innocent Marie Joseph. The Logic of
     Religion. New York: New York University Press,
     1965. x + 179 pp.

Chapter II argues (1) that the religious object
is not unspeakable, and (2) that religious discourse is communicative, includes a propositional
element, and is such that logic applies to it.
Chapter III explores the logical structure of
religious discourse and concludes that there
are formal similarities between religious discourse and the discourse of the natural sciences.
(Observation sentences are formally analogous
to credal sentences, scientific hypotheses to
non-credal theological sentences, etc.) Chapter
IV discusses the meaning of religious sentences.
Their meaning is problematic because they refer
to a transcendent object. Bocheński maintains
that a sentence is (factually) meaningful if and
only if there is some method of determining its
truth or falsity. Although Bocheński distinguishes
between meaning and verification, he does appear
to equate the meaning of religious sentences with
certain types of verification. While religious
sentences can be verified by appealing to authority, authority cannot supply meaning to religious
sentences. In order to be meaningful religious
sentences must be directly verifiable. Bocheński
suggests that they can be directly verified by
"a non-natural experience of some intelligent
agent." Does this imply that only those who
have had these experiences (and thus know what
they are like) are able to understand the meaning
of religious sentences? Presumably not, since
Bocheński thinks that while all believers understand these sentences, many believers accept
them on authority. The meaning which religious
sentences have for these believers is apparently
analogical (although this seems to conflict with
the claim that a certain type of direct

566

verification supplies meaning to religious sentences). Unfortunately, Bocheński's theory of analogy has at least two questionable features. (1) It is assumed that when a term is employed analogically part of its meaning is <u>identical</u> with (part of) its ordinary meaning. (2) When terms are analogically applied to God "what is common in the two meanings are just the formal properties of relations" such as symmetry, transitivity, etc. Chapter V addresses itself to the logic of justification. Bocheński argues that believers offer partial justifications for their basic dogma, viz., that all statements in a certain context (creed, scripture, etc.) are true, and that these justifications are typically of two kinds -- an appeal to authority, and a claim that the basic dogma makes sense of their experience. Analogy and justification by authority are examined at more length in the appendix. -- Although Bocheński's book is worth examining it is disappointing. His analysis is most aptly applied to traditional Roman Catholic discourse with its clearly defined lines of authority, well articulated rules for determining the truth or falsity of religious assertions, etc. Furthermore, in concentrating on the formal features of religious discourse, Bocheński tends both to belabor the obvious, and to ignore its richness and complexity. (For a fuller statement of Bocheński's theory of analogy, see # 967 below.) See Christian, # 905 below.

903 Braithwaite, Richard Bevan. <u>An Empiricist's View</u>
     <u>of the Nature of Religious Belief</u>. (Arthur Stanley
     Eddington Memorial Lecture, 9.) Cambridge:
     Cambridge University Press, 1955. v + 34 pp.

Moral expressions are used to subscribe to a
policy of action and are, therefore, neither
true nor false. Religious expressions are moral
expressions which are used to subscribe to a
general policy of behavior. For example, Christian
claims are employed to express one's commitment
to an "agapeistic" way of life. Religious claims
are associated with stories. The sentences in
these stories can be construed as ordinary empirical propositions but these propositions are
not (or need not be) believed or put forward as
true. They are instead entertained by the "believer" in order to reinforce his intention to
subscribe to the appropriate way of life. Whatever Braithwaite's intentions may have been,
this widely discussed essay must clearly be
regarded as a recommendation to use religious
expressions in a certain way and not as an analysis
of their actual use. See the critiques of Austin,
Ewing, Horsburgh and Yandell (# 899 above and
#s 920, 929 and 963 below).

904 Bramann, Jorn Karl Roy. "Kafka and Wittgenstein
on Religious Language," Sophia, XIV (October,
1975), 1-9.

A rather interesting exploration of Wittgenstein
and some remarks of Kafka. According to Bramann,
both suggest that we miss the point of religious
language (or the "words of the wise") if we suppose
that we are being provided with a metaphysical
description of a transcendental reality rather
than a path to be followed. Practice, and not
belief, is the heart of religion.

905 Christian, William Armistead, Jr. "Bochenski on
     the Structure of Schemes of Doctrines," Relig
     Stud, 13 (June, 1977), 203-19.

     A sympathetic but not uncritical examination of
     three claims of Bocheński (# 902 above): that
     in each religious community there are (1) a set
     of sentences about the object of religion, (2)
     a "heuristic rule" indicating which sentences are
     doctrines, and (3) a "meta-logical rule" according
     to which each sentence picked out by means of the
     heuristic rule as a doctrinal sentence is true.
     (Most attention is devoted to the second claim.)
     Christian's discussion has merits which Bocheń-
     ski's discussion lacks. It is detailed, deploys
     significant examples, and takes account of the
     complexity of religious discourse.

906 _____. Meaning and Truth in Religion. Prince-
     ton, New Jersey: Princeton University Press,
     1964. ix + 273 pp.

     Although it has not been entirely neglected, this
     book deserves more attention than it has received.
     "Doctrinal proposals" (e.g., "God acts in history")
     are distinguished from "basic proposals" (e.g.,
     "God is the source of our being"). Basic pro-
     posals are of the form Fm where F takes as its
     values such predicates as "the ground of being,"
     "the supreme goal of life," "ultimate," "holy,"
     etc., and m takes as its values concepts central
     to various doctrinal schemes (e.g., "God," "Nir-
     vana," and "Nature"). A basic proposal "gives
     the point and importance" of doctrine. (E.g.,
     "Nirvana is the supreme goal of life" partially
     explains the point and significance of "the self
     is annihilated in Nirvana.") A doctrinal scheme,

on the other hand, "elaborates the meaning of
the subject term of a basic proposal." Basic
religious proposals explicate "some paradigmatic
suggestion" (e.g., a historical event, or a
mystical experience). Most interreligious disagreements are disagreements over basic proposals.
Christian's analysis of the pattern of religious
inquiry, argument and justification is of particular interest. Among his more interesting or
controversial claims are the following: (1) "A
religious interest is an interest in something
more important than anything else in the universe."
That there is something more important (ultimate,
holy) than all other things is thus a presupposition of religious inquiry. (2) Arguments about
a basic proposal are "arguments about the consistency and coherence of the developed proposal;
arguments about its power to interpret its alternatives and thus do justice to whatever elements
of truth are contained in those alternatives;
arguments about the adequacy of the references
it permits; and arguments about the adequacy
of the support for its predication." (3) References to the subject of a basic proposal can
be made (depending upon the nature of the subject)
by ostention, by giving examples, by picking
out regularities or extraordinary events caused
by the subject, or by picking out public facts
which stand to the subject in the relation of part
to whole, appearance or manifestation to reality,
attribute to substance, etc. (4) One can support
a basic proposal by establishing the uniqueness
and primacy of its subject. (Christian examines
various ways in which this might be done.) One
of the many merits of this book (and of Ninian
Smart's book, # 955 below) is that it does not

restrict its attention to Christian discourse.

907 _____. Oppositions of Religious Doctrines,
A Study in the Logic of Dialogue among Religions.
(Philosophy of Religion Series.) London and
Basingstoke: The Macmillan Press Ltd.; New York:
Herder and Herder, 1972. ix + 129 pp.

"The major religions all present and teach patterns of life." A pattern of life includes
courses of action, aims and beliefs. Oppositions
can arise between recommendations of courses of
action, between valuations, between beliefs, and
between "heterogeneous elements," e.g., between
a belief and a valuation. Christian's book investigates the ways in which these elements can
come into conflict with one another. (The analysis
proceeds by examining test sentences which might
be employed by a Buddhist and a Jew.) Possible
oppositions are worked out carefully and in detail. As a result, Christian makes a substantial
contribution to our understanding of the logic
of religious discourse.

908 _____. "Religious Valuations of Scientific
Truths," Amer Phil Quart, 6 (April, 1969), 144-50.

If (e.g.) the object of religious attitudes is
identified with a process of nature, or with the
structure of the world, or with an agent who
acts in the world, one may be led (1) to value
statements of scientific regularity which describe that process or structure, or the effects
produced by that agent, and (2) to value knowledge of those regularities. This article is
interesting if only because it is so frequently
assumed either that there are no connections
between religion and science, or that connections

between religion and science only appear in those
places where religion and science disagree over
the natural facts.

909 Coburn, Robert Craig. "The Hiddenness of God and
     Some Barmicidal God-Substitutes," J Phil, LVII
     (October 27 and November 10, 1960), 689-712.

Coburn argues that "what is central to the concept of God is the notion of something that is
worthy of both (a) limitless praise . . . and
(b) unconditional obedience . . . in short, the
notion of something which is supremely or perfectly holy." Operating with this concept "involves being strongly inclined to conceive of"
God as both comprehensible and incomprehensible.
Coburn then considers two views which attempt
to reconcile God's "hiddenness" and "openness."
(1) According to "A-views" (which he ascribes
to Barth and Aquinas), we do not fully understand
the meaning of the theological sentences we utter.
Coburn argues that this position leads to curious
consequences. (E.g., if the A-view was correct
we would not know whether we were repeating ourselves or being inconsistent.) (2) According
to the "B-view," theological language is either
metaphorical, pictorial or quasi-ritualistic.
Each of these positions is inadequate. (a) If
God cannot be literally described, then (i) the
referent of "God" cannot be identified, and (ii)
we have no way of determining in what respects
God resembles (e.g.) a person. (b) We cannot
maintain that theological language paints pictures which express facts which elude direct
statement because facts just are the sort of
thing which true statements state. (c) According
to the third type of B-view, accepting religious

572

utterances involves (e.g.) taking the world "as a cosmic screen behind which dwells an extra-mundane person of limitless power [and] complete knowledge," much as children in play may take the couch as an ambulance. This analysis is inadequate because it empties religious belief of factual content. Coburn concludes that be-cause both "hiddenness" and "openness" are es-sential to the concept of God and because they cannot be reconciled, the concept of God is in-coherent.

910 _____. "A Neglected Use of Theological Lan-guage," *Mind*, LXXII (July, 1963), 369-85.

Theological assertions can be used to answer "limiting questions," where a limiting question is a question which (1) cannot be answered in a straightforward way ("Why does my mother suf-fer?" cannot always be satisfactorily answered by recounting her medical history), but (2) does not betray linguistic confusion and (3) is such that asking that question is a criterion of a particular "'spiritual' condition" or "state of the soul." Religious limiting questions express moral problems (e.g., conflicts between duty and interest, "conflicts between opposing moral out-looks," guilt), problems of morale "which arise out of our inability to reconcile ourselves to the various ills which flesh is heir to," and "problems concerning the ultimate significance or 'meaning' of things." Coburn argues that his theory explains such things as the close connec-tion between religious belief and religious at-titudes, the fact that religious people remain prey to doubt, and the propensity to regard God

as indescribable. A suggestive and illuminating
essay.

911 Cohen, Cynthia. "The Logic of Religious Language,"
     Relig Stud, 9 (June, 1973), 143-55.

     A critique of Ian Ramsey (#s 948-952 below).
     Cohen makes two important points. (1) Ramsey
     appears to be working with a referential theory
     of meaning. It is, e.g., because the empirical
     world only provides us with examples of limited
     wisdom that Ramsey concludes that "infinite
     wisdom" has no straightforward descriptive mean-
     ing, and it is because cosmic disclosures provide
     a referent for (e.g.) "infinite wisdom" that he
     concludes that the term is not, after all, (cog-
     nitively) meaningless. (2) Models must evoke
     disclosures and have "empirical fit." Ramsey
     never shows that those models which most effec-
     tively evoke disclosures have the best empirical
     fit, and vice versa.

912 Cox, David. "The Significance of Christianity,"
     Mind, LIX (April, 1950), 209-18.

     Cox recommends that Christians accept the Verifi-
     cation Principle but argues that the relevant
     experiences should not be restricted to sense
     experiences. Christian doctrines should be re-
     stated as statements about human religious ex-
     perience. In spite of the fact that it has re-
     ceived some attention, this is not a significant
     essay. See McPherson's reply (# 936 below).

913 Crombie, I. M. "The Possibility of Theological
Statements," Faith and Logic, Oxford Essays in
Philosophical Theology. Edited by Basil Mitchell.
London: Allen & Unwin; Boston: The Beacon Press,
1957. Pp. 31-83.

Crombie argues that theological statements are
anomalous in two respects. (1) Although "God"
stands for an individual, it is not possible
to become directly acquainted with the individual which that expression denotes. (2) While
statements which have God as their subject are
factual, they are not straightforwardly verifiable
or falsifiable. Crombie argues that even though
God cannot be "indicated," we can fix the "reference range" of "God" by referring God-statements "outside the range of possible conception
in a determinate direction." "Spirit" is an
abstract noun derived from certain processes
which we observe in human beings. Under certain
pressures (e.g., the impression that we are
strangers on earth exiled from a spiritual world
to which we really belong, or a sense of the
limitations and imperfections of our spirituality), we form the notion (but not the clear and
distinct idea) of a being or beings which are
pure spirit, thus using "spirit" as a concrete
noun. "Infinite," "Necessary," and "Non-deriva-
tive" get their sense from their opposites.
"Finite," "contingent," and "derivative" are applied to the world in order to express "an intellectual dissatisfaction with this universe as a
complete system." The conception of the divine
i.e., of "an infinite spirit") is, then, "the
notion of a complement which could fill in certain
deficiencies in our experience." Statements
about God must be understood as parables. Predicates like "love" and "anger" are to be taken

in (one of) their ordinary senses but our
(literal) conceptions of (an exalted form of)
love and anger are to be treated as images of
truth about the divine. Although Crombie's essay
is in the analytic tradition, the position which
it adumbrates is strikingly similar to traditional
theories of analogy and to theories of religious
symbolism offered by people like Tillich (see
#s 1022-1028 below). If this observation
is correct, it is significant both because
theories of that type are anathema to most analytic philosophers, and because those theories are
more fully articulated than Crombie's own theory.
Assuming that this essay is moving in the right
direction one cannot help but wonder whether
an analytic philosopher who wishes to be faithful
to the actual use of religious language will
(or should) be driven to embrace an analogy theory
or a symbol theory of the meaning of religious
sentences. (Ian Ramsey's account of religious
language [see #s 948-952 below] raises the same
question.)

914 _____. "Theology and Falsification: (ii)
Arising from the University Discussion," in #
923 below, pp. 109-30.

This influential essay contains a number of suggestive points. (1) (a) Certain distinctive
experiences (e.g., the sense of contingency,
or the impression that either moral obligation
or the order and beauty of nature is an intrusion
into nature from a different realm) provide a
meaning for "God." Without these experiences,
we would not know what "God" refers to. (b) Certain events and objects are interpreted as manifestations of the divine. "Without concrete

576

events which we feel impelled to interpret as divine we could not know that the notion of divinity had any application to reality." (c) Belief which is "begotten" in these ways is "nurtured by the practice of Christian life." (2) Religious discourse is parabolic. Words like "love," "angry," "acts," etc., are taken in their ordinary senses but the parables in which they occur are referred "out of our experience in a certain direction" by means of the word "God." (Is it possible to take "loves" in "God loves us" in its ordinary sense and yet refer the statement as a whole in the direction of the "infinite"? Can we do the latter without changing the meaning of "loves"?) We employ certain parables rather than others because of the authority of Christ. (3) Suffering counts against the claim that God is merciful, and "eternally and irredeemably pointless suffering" would count decisively against it. Crombie maintains (a) that in order to be factual an assertion about God must be verifiable in principle, and (b) that in order for me to understand it, "I must know what a test of it would be like." The second condition is assured because I know how to test similar statements in which the name of a human being replaces "God." (This is questionable given Crombie's admission that we transform the logical character of [e.g.] "Schweitzer is merciful" when we replace "Schweitzer" with "God.") The first condition is met because of the possibility of eschatological verification, and because the love and mercy displayed by Christ and the saints provide some sort of confirmation of the claim that God loves us. This essay first appeared in Socratic Digest, V (n.d.).

915 Dilman, Ilham. "Wisdom's Philosophy of Religion,
     Part I: Religion and Reason," Can J Phil, V
     (December, 1975), 473-95.

     Wisdom (#s 959, 960 and 961 below) fails to ade-
     quately distinguish between perspectives upon
     the world as a whole and perspectives upon parts
     of the world. Disputes over the rightness or
     wrongness of the latter are subject to rational
     adjudication in a way in which disputes over
     the former are not. Religious belief may arise
     from reflection upon the world and one's own
     life, and one's belief may be reasonable. It
     is, however, misleading to suggest that religious
     belief is grounded in evidence, reasons, justi-
     fication or proof. In the first place, perspec-
     tives on things as a whole are not assessments.
     They instead determine how we assess the facts
     by providing categories and measures for making
     assessments. In the second place, because re-
     ligious belief engages the will or heart, a pro-
     cess of reflection which leads one person to
     belief will not necessarily lead another to be-
     lief.

916 _____. "Wisdom's Philosophy of Religion,
     Part II: Metaphysical and Religious Transcen-
     dence," Can J Phil, V (December, 1975), 497-521.

     Wisdom only discerns two alternatives -- (1)
     to interpret God-talk on the model of talk about
     an undetectable gardener or Locke's talk about
     material substance (in which case talk about
     God is nonsense), or (2) to interpret talk about
     God as talk about patterns which can be found in
     familiar facts. Dilman argues that there is a
     third alternative, and that this alternative
     preserves God's transcendence in its religiously

significant sense. God transcends the world
of the senses in so far as He does not appear
to, or is not real for, those caught up in "a
certain mode of life and a vision of the world
internal to it," viz., the "life of the senses."
Dilman also argues that while Wisdom correctly
connects religious belief and what happens "within," he confuses psychological language and language about the soul or spirit. The latter is
not neutral, and concerns "the spirit in which
one acts," a certain comportment towards "moral
values and religious ideals," etc.

917 Durrant, Michael. The Logical Status of 'God'.
     (New Studies in the Philosophy of Religion.)
     London and Basingstoke: Macmillan; New York:
     St. Martin's Press, 1973. xiv + 117 pp.

According to Durrant, "God" is not a proper name,
it is not shorthand for a definite description,
and it is not a descriptive predicate. He concludes that we cannot "offer a coherent and consistent account of the proposition expressed by
sentences of the form 'God is F'." Durrant provides many reasons for these claims, the most
important of which appears to be the following:
There are (can be) no individuals which bear the
name "God," or which are uniquely specified by a
definite description for which "God" is shorthand,
or to which the predicate "___ is God" can be
applied. This contention is supported by arguments which purport to establish (1) that because
"spirit," "person," "transcendent being," etc.,
are not class terms but terms for categories
(terms which indicate what sorts of predicates
can be appropriately applied to an entity), they
cannot be used to specify individuals, (2) that

souls and intelligences "belong to" bodies
and cannot be independently identified, (3) that
God is not a spatial or temporal individual,
and (4) that numbers and Platonic forms fail
to provide examples of non-spatial and non-
temporal individuals. These arguments are
interesting but not fully convincing. Although
Durrant is suggestive, he is sometimes obscure
and displays an unfortunate tendency to assume
propositions whose truth is far from obvious.
See Attfield, # 897 above.

918   Evans, Donald Dwight. "Ian Ramsey on Talk About
      God," Relig Stud, 7 (June, 1971 and September,
      1971), 125-40 and 213-26.

      A valuable attempt to systematize and interpret
      ideas which Ramsey (#s 948-952 below) scat-
      tered among a number of pieces. Particular at-
      tention is paid to the analogy between the I
      (the "more" of observable behavior) and God (the
      "more" of the universe), and to the relation
      between God and the "many particular 'mores'
      of particular observables." Evans argues that
      Ramsey has failed to provide a satisfactory
      justification of the assumption that all cosmic
      disclosures are disclosures of the same thing
      and of the assumption that the "more" which is
      revealed in cosmic disclosures is best charac-
      terized as creative, beneficent, and trustworthy.

919   _____. The Logic of Self-Involvement, A Phi-
      losophical Study of Everyday Language with Special
      Reference to the Christian Use of Language about
      God as Creator. (Library of Philosophy and Theol-
      ogy.) London: SCM Press, 1963. 293 pp.

      This is one of the best attempts to combine the

insights of linguistic analysis and biblical
scholarship in order to cast light upon the nature of religious language. Evans first examines
the meaning of performatives, expressions of
feeling, and expressions of attitude (including
expressions of what Evans calls "onlooks," viz.,
looking on x as y). (Evans' discussion is heavily
indebted to the discussions of J. L. Austin but
is not merely derivative.) Evans then employs
these results in order to provide an analysis
of the biblical concept of creation. (1) It is
argued that God's creative word involves a command (to exist as God's servant), an appointment
(as God's steward), a verdict ("it is good"),
the bestowal of a gift, and a promise (to maintain the constancy of the natural order). Biblical man thus looks on God's creative act as
having various sorts of performative force. The
onlook in question is a parabolic onlook for the
likeness between God and a human agent who commands, appoints, judges, gives, and pledges can
only be specified in terms of attitudes which
are believed to be appropriate to God as well
as to a human being who stands in those relations
to us. Creation should also be viewed as an
"impressive and expressive action." "An inner
divine quality [glory and holiness] is expressed
through certain impressive observables, evoking
a correlative" response and acknowledgement (viz.,
fear, awe, worship, a commitment to a way of
life, etc.). Although glory and holiness are
objective features of God's nature, they can
only be understood in terms of the reactions
which they evoke. In short God's creative act
is a performative act with impressive and expressive significance. (2) The utterance "God is

the creator of the world" is also a performative
(God is acknowledged as Lord, Appointer, Evalua-
tor, etc.), and expresses "an attitude which includes both a feeling Response and a way of life."
(3) When human actions are performative and/or
impressive and expressive, we can abstract a
"causal 'core' and refer solely to it." (E.g.,
"He moved his arm.") This cannot be done when
the action is world creation. The nature of God
and His activity cannot be directly specified
but must instead be indirectly specified by means
of "metaphysical parabolic outlooks." These
parables (e.g., the potter) indicate that it is
appropriate to respond to God as one responds
to y but do not specify the similarity between
God and y except in terms of the appropriateness
of similar attitudes. They are accepted on authority and "may lead to experiences which seem
. . . to be confirmations of" them. (Other onlooks may, however, be quite reasonable.) This
is, perhaps, the weakest part of Evans' book,
for it can be argued that similar attitudes are
appropriate only if there is some reason to believe that God and y are similar in other respects, that (e.g.) the "imagined 'attitude' of
a pot to its maker" is not appropriate to God
unless there is some reason to believe that God's
relation to man is similar to the causal relation
between a potter and his pot. (Some remarks of
Evans suggest that "dependence-for-existence"
is -- in spite of his disclaimers -- an abstracti-
ble aspect of just such a similarity.)

920 Ewing, Alfred Cyril. "Religious Assertions in the
Light of Contemporary Philosophy," Philosophy,
XXXII (July, 1957), 206-18.

Ewing first demonstrates the implausibility of attempts to construe religious sentences as expressions of emotion, conative attitudes, etc. His criticism of Braithwaite (# 903 above) is particularly effective. Ewing then addresses himself to the claim that religious assertions are devoid of factual significance. (Most of his points are familiar.) His opponents are accused of arguing in the following way: "All instances of knowledge and rational belief have characteristic c, knowledge of or rational belief in God would not have characteristic c, therefore there can be no knowledge of or rational belief in God." Unless they independently know that propositions about God cannot be known or rationally justified, their first premiss begs the question.

921 Ferré, Frederick. Basic Modern Philosophy of Religion. New York: Charles Scribner's Sons, 1967. Pp. 335-407.

The expressive (emotive) and conative use of religious language depends upon its descriptive imagery. This imagery expresses the fundamental valuations of the religious community. Its adequacy depends upon its ability to encompass all important and relevant values, upon its ability to structure or organize these values, and (most importantly) upon its effectiveness in serving "the perceived life needs of large numbers of men over long periods of time." Although its importance is secondary, theistic imagery also has a cognitive aspect. "Theistic images in their speculative function" are metaphysical conceptual models. Conceptual models provide concrete interpretations of abstract formulae,

suggest new connections among the data within
one subject area or between different subject
areas, and open up new lines of inquiry. When
added to theories, models provide a sense of
intelligibility or "grasp." Metaphysical models
are distinguished from scientific models by their
scope. (They are associated with theories which
attempt to make sense of reality as a whole.)
In metaphysics and science, the model is subordinate to the theory which explicates and articulates it but in religion, theories are subordinate to models. Hence, the first criterion
which a religious theory must meet is "appropriateness" -- it must "fit" its model. It must
also (like any metaphysical theory) meet the tests
of coherency and adequacy. To be adequate a
theory must integrate and illuminate all "important ranges of human experience." Ferré suggests
that a theory fails to illuminate a range of experience if the people whose experiences are
being considered continue to find it unilluminat-
ing or reductive. (Would this test, then, rule
out any theory of the occult which fails to credit
the alleged occurrence of occult phenomena?)
Two other points should be noticed. (1) Religious imagery (and its associated theories) or
a metaphysical theory satisfies our desire for
understanding if it not only explains the whole
but shows that the whole is good (and, therefore,
not a brute fact). (2) While the question of
the "correspondence" or "resemblance" between
model and reality is not a critical issue in
science and metaphysics (Ferré rejects correspondence theories of truth), religious imagery is believed to somehow "resemble" or "correspond to"
reality. (Believers think that God actually

exists.) Cf. Ferré, # 1046 below.

922 _____. Language, Logic and God. New York:
Harper and Brothers, 1961. viii + 184 pp.

Although frequently cited, most of this book
possesses little interest. Ferré describes developments in "linguistic philosophy" (Flew, Hepburn, Crombie, Braithwaite, etc., etc.), inter-
spersing his own comments and observations.
While these remarks are often sound, they are
neither profound nor particularly original.
The last chapter (pp. 146-66) is of more interest.
In that chapter, Ferré argues that religious
statements are metaphysical statements, and that
metaphysics interprets reality by using models.
(Theistic models are drawn from the sphere of
personal relations.) The tests for a metaphysical system are consistency and coherence, and
the ability to provide illuminating explanations
of wide ranges of experience. Ferré's suggestions
are not worked out in any detail in this chapter
but are developed with some care in # 921 above.

923 Flew, Antony Garrard Newton and Alasdair C. Mac-
Intyre, eds. New Essays in Philosophical Theol-
ogy. (The Library of Philosophy and Theology.)
London: SCM Press; New York: The Macmillan
Co., 1955. xii + 274 pp.

"This is a collection of twenty-two papers by
sixteen different philosophers working in the
British commonwealth . . . [who] have in common
. . . a familiarity with and a great indebtedness
to the recent revolution in philosophy." The
heart of that "revolution in philosophy" was a
renewed interest in the actual uses of language.
In retrospect, many of these essays fail precisely

because they neglect the actual use of religious
language but instead approach that language with
(more or less) concealed verificationist and
naturalistic assumptions. Nevertheless, this is
a seminal book, and many of the essays contained
in it are excellent. A number of them are described elsewhere. (See #s 66, 67, 71, 75, 184,
193, 294, 464, 652, 658, 766 and 866 above and
1004 below.)

924   Gaskin, John C. A. "Disclosures," Relig Stud, 9
      (June, 1973), 131-41.

      A critique of Ian Ramsey (#s 948-952 below).
      Gaskin effectively argues that Ramsey uses "dis-
      closure" "far too widely" to cover radically
      different things, and that he is insufficiently
      sensitive to the possibility that (apparent)
      disclosures may conflict.

925   Gibson, Alexander Boyce. "Modern Philosophers
      Consider Religion," Austl J Phil, 35 (December,
      1957), 170-85.

      Well-placed criticisms of Hare (# 866 above),
      Holland (# 928 below), and others. Gibson argues
      that, because it restricts factual statements to
      empirical statements, "logical analysis is com-
      patible only with a religion far removed from
      the world and indifferent to the requirements
      of reason." (It might be argued that the works
      of Crombie [#s 913 and 914 above] and Hick [#
      810 above] provide counter-examples to this
      thesis.)

926 Hepburn, Ronald William. "Poetry and Religious
    Belief," Metaphysical Beliefs: Three Essays
    by Stephen Toulmin, Ronald Hepburn, [and] Alasdair
    MacIntyre, with a preface by Alasdair MacIntyre.
    (The Library of Philosophy and Theology.) London:
    SCM Press, 1957. Pp. 85-166.

    This essay examines a number of related questions.
    The theories of Farrer (# 801 above) and Jung
    (# 1006 below) are effectively criticized.
    Hepburn explores the connections between poetic
    inspiration, imaginative truth, and "poetic re-
    conciliation" on the one hand, and religious
    inspiration, religious truth, and "religious
    reconciliation" on the other. He attempts to
    determine whether poets succeed in giving sense
    to such notions as "eternity" or "the world as
    a whole." And so on. Hepburn's essay contains
    many valuable incidental observations and in-
    sights, but several general conclusions emerge
    from his discussion: (1) Since religious belief
    includes certain (historical and metaphysical)
    existential claims, it cannot be reduced to a
    set of images. Religious images fail to apply
    and lose their force if these beliefs are false.
    (2) The differences between religion and poetry
    are at least as significant as the similarities.
    (3) It is not clear (pace Ramsey, #s 948-
    952 below) that we can give sense to notions
    like "eternity" by the appropriate deployment
    of images.

927 High, Dallas Milton. Language, Persons, and Belief:
    Studies in Wittgenstein's "Philosophical Investi-
    gations" and Religious Uses of Language. London:
    Oxford University Press, 1967. Pp. 133-212.

    High offers an analysis of belief language which
    emphasizes both its intersubjective character

and the logical dissimilarities between first
and third person uses of "believe." "I" is said
to provide a conceptual model for "God," and
belief in other persons is said to provide a conceptual model for belief in God. The use of
first person belief language commits the speaker
to providing justification or backing for his
claims. Theological fideism is, therefore, unacceptable. High suggests that the backing for
"I believe in God" or "I believe that God exists"
is similar to the backing for "I believe in Jones"
or "I believe that Jones exists," but his discussion of the nature of this backing is too
general to be very helpful.

928 Holland, R. F. "Religious Discourse and Theological
Discourse," Austl J Phil, 34 (December, 1956),
147-63.

Holland maintains that while religious people
believe in God, worship God, pray to God, etc.,
they do not (qua religious believers) talk about
God. It follows that theological discourse is
not religious discourse. Statements which the
believer makes and which appear to be about God
are really about the believer or the believer's
relation to God. Thus, "God is my creator"
has (religious) truth if it is "uttered by one
who is grateful for his existence and finds it
good," and uttering this sentence is "like saying
'I do not owe my existence to myself'." Holland's
position appears to rest upon the assumption
that when theological discourse is regarded as
theoretical discourse, it cannot be taken seriously, upon the assumption that it is superstitious to regard God as an existent object (cf.
Tillich), and upon the assumption that the

investigation, or contemplation, or study of
God is incompatible with religious attitudes.
Holland's case is nicely presented if unconvinc-
ing. (See Gibson's response, # 925 above.)

929 Horsburgh, H. J. N. "Professor Braithwaite and
Billy Brown," Austl J Phil, 36 (December, 1958),
201-7.

A frequently cited critique of Braithwaite (#
903 above). Horsburgh's most important points
are the following: (1) Since Christian and Buddhist ethics are essentially the same, and since
one can entertain and be sustained by both Christian and Buddhist stories, it is possible upon
Braithwaite's view to be both a Christian and a
Buddhist. (2) Braithwaite is unable to accommodate the fact that some religious "stories" are
believed to be revealed. (3) Reverence is essential to (e.g.) Christianity, but one cannot revere
a figure if one regards that figure as mythical.

930 Hudson William Donald. Ludwig Wittgenstein: The
Bearing of his Philosophy Upon Religious Belief.
(Makers of Contemporary Theology.) Richmond:
John Knox Press, 1968. 74 pp.

In addition to discussions of Wittgenstein's
attitude towards religion and the bearing of
both the Tractatus and his later work upon religion and theology, this little book includes
discussions of the falsification controversy and
of the problems created by God's alleged transcendence. (The second discussion is the more interesting of the two. Hudson argues that the fact
that an agent can be distinguished from his situation, together with the fact that physical states
of that agent can be included in a description

of his situation, suggests that the concept of
a disembodied agent is coherent.) The last chapter explores the (Wittgensteinian) notion that
religious belief involves the use of certain
pictures and that theology provides the "logical
grammar" of that use. Philosophy examines the
consistency of religious discourse, investigates
its presuppositions (asks what kind of object
God is), and "maps its logical frontiers" (i.e.,
shows how religious discourse is both like and
unlike other forms of discourse). Hudson asks
whether these pictures are pictures "of anything
objectively real," and responds that questions
about real existence can only be asked from within
a conceptual framework. Religion is a form of
life, and we must (merely?) choose whether or not
to adopt that form of life. On the other hand,
Hudson concedes that legitimate questions remain
-- "How is talk about God to be differentiated
from, say, talk about Santa Claus?" "Is religious
talk unintelligible to modern man because the
form of life to which this talk belongs is ob-
solete?" "Is it rational to take this game seriously?" (Hudson discusses these questions at
greater length in # 1055 below.) He concludes
by suggesting that religion, like morality, may
be a language game or form of life which is "definitive of humanity in the sense that it is
essential to our concept of man."

931   . Wittgenstein and Religious Belief.
(New Studies in the Philosophy of Religion.)
London and Basingstoke: The Macmillan Press,
Ltd.; New York: St. Martin's Press, 1975. ix
+ 206 pp.

The first two chapters provide a general account
of Wittgenstein's life and philosophical views.

Chapter 3 is by far the most interesting. In this chapter, Hudson attempts to show that Wittgenstein was not a positivist in spite of the fact that Wittgenstein maintains in the Tractatus that anything said about "the mystical" must be nonsense. Hudson argues that Wittgenstein believed that one should keep silent about the mystical because "one does not wish to trivialize the mystical and one will be doing so, if one talks nonsense about it," and not because "one does not wish to talk nonsense and will be doing so if one talks about the mystical." Although one cannot express the mystical, the mystical shows itself in art and action. Hudson concludes by suggesting (1) that "the mystical" is suspiciously similar to the moral intuitionist's non-natural properties, and (2) that there is no more than a verbal similarity between the claim that logical form can be shown but not expressed and the claim that "the mystical" can be shown but not expressed. In chapter 4, Hudson discusses the influence of Wittgenstein upon the Vienna Circle, and provides evidence that Wittgenstein accepted Verificationism in the late 1920s and early 1930s. Most of this chapter is devoted to a rather pedestrian discussion of Verificationism with special attention to Ayer and Flew (#s 855 and 866 above). The last chapter explicates and examines Wittgenstein's Lectures and Conversations on Aesthetics, Psychology and Religious Belief (# 962 below). Hudson's interpretation of the later Wittgenstein is reasonable but, on the whole, unexciting. (Hudson is unhappy with some of the more extreme views concerning the autonomy of religious language and, in particular, with D. Z. Phillips' development of Wittgenstein's

remarks [see #s 1100-1108 below].) The author's
most interesting points are developed at more
length in # 1055 below.

932   Jeffner, Anders. The Study of Religious Language.
      (The Library of Philosophy and Theology.)   London:
      SCM Press, 1972. viii + 135 pp.

Among the more interesting features of this book
are Jeffner's consideration of religious sentences
with "fictitious localization" (these sentences
may or may not indirectly refer to the "real
world"), and his clear demonstration that analyses
of religious sentences as symbolic sentences or
performative sentences cannot succeed in avoiding
the problem created by the fact that religious
sentences are intended to be statements about the
real world but have no clear "empirical anchorage." Jeffner suggests that these sentences
should be regarded as interpretations and explanations of "ambiguous objects," where ambiguous objects are such that "different people
having an exhaustive knowledge of the same observational situation can disagree as to the
correct description of these objects." (Jeffner
points out that a religious or metaphysical
"hypothesis" cannot be true unless the experience
of the pattern or Gestalt which it explains is
somehow more adequate or correct than the experience of other patterns or Gestalts which may
be discerned in the same set of facts.)

933   Jensen, Robert W. The Knowledge of Things Hoped
      For: The Sense of Theological Discourse.   New
      York: Oxford University Press, 1969. Pp. 99-233.

This discussion is interesting primarily because

of the way in which it attempts to combine the
insights of linguistic analysis and biblical
hermeneutics. Jensen is perhaps most influenced
by the views of John Wisdom and Wolfhart Pannenberg, and by the insistence upon the necessity
of verification which pervades so much analytic
literature. Jensen maintains that "within Christian theological language the fundamental utterances . . . are all historical narratives" which
are either true or false. Coming to see their
truth is similar to coming to see the meaning of
a play. The dramas which are interpreted by
theological utterances are "the story of Jesus
Christ and the whole drama of Time." The first
story enables us to understand the second.
Jesus's life, death and resurrection provide an
anticipation of the end of history in which Jesus
will return as judge of the living and dead.
"God" must be understood in connection with this
story. On the one hand, God's attributes are
to be explained by pointing to incidents in
Jesus's history. On the other hand, by bringing
"God" into connection with this story, the story
is "referred forward" and its meaning linked
to the meaning of history as a whole. The
verification of theological utterances is eschatological. (We can anticipate the meaning of
a play while it is being performed but we must
await the denouement to find out whether our
interpretation is correct.)

934   MacIntyre, Alasdair C. "The Logical Status of Re-
      ligious Belief," Metaphysical Beliefs; Three
      Essays by Stephen Toulmin, Ronald Hepburn [and]
      Alasdair MacIntyre, with a preface by Alasdair
      MacIntyre. (The Library of Philosophy and Theol-
      ogy.) London: SCM Press, 1957. Pp. 168-211.

When judged by the Verification Principle, religious assertions are invariably found wanting. Either no evidence counts against them and they are meaningless, or (e.g.) evil counts against them and they are false. Religious beliefs when considered as a whole are best regarded as stories or myths. Since the words which are used to tell these stories are (except for the proper name "God") drawn from ordinary discourse, they can be understood in the same way in which works of fiction are understood. However, religious stories are not mere stories. They are rooted in worship and shape our attitudes and behavior, providing direction in situations in which rules fail us. Furthermore, religious stories are believed to be "in some way or other stories about a real being." Demonstrative arguments cannot be provided for religious beliefs, and would, in fact, preclude the kind of free decision which is "the essence of the Christian religion." Nor can religious belief be regarded as an explanatory hypothesis both because it is inadequate if regarded as an explanatory hypothesis, and because hypotheses are held "in a tentative and provisional way." The world may illustrate religious doctrines but it does not provide evidence for them. How, then, are religious claims justified? They justified by appealing to authority. Authority itself rests upon a decision to say, before some person, "My Lord and my God." MacIntyre's essay is fraught with a serious ambiguity. It is not clear whether he wishes to say (1) that religious claims are straightforwardly factual but are justified by authority and not by (empirical?) evidence, or (2) that religious claims are not ordinary factual claims (since

594

they are neither verifiable nor falsifiable)
but have their "own kind of logic." MacIntyre's
treatment of "Christ rose from the dead" suggests
the former. His treatment of "God loves us"
suggests the latter. (There is no clear indication that he believes the logic of these two
statements to be significantly different.) In
spite of this weakness, MacIntyre's article is
undoubtedly one of the best essays to emerge from
the verification controversy. (See Mitchell's
critique, # 941 below.)

935 McKinnon, Alastair. Falsification and Belief. The
Hague: Mouton, 1970. 106 pp.

"The world has an order" has three uses within
science. (1) When used "assertionally," "order"
has a "determinate sense." The sentence is used
to assert the existence of some particular order
or other. (Is the sentence in fact ever used
in this way?) It is, therefore, falsifiable.
(2) When used "self-instructionally," "order"
has a "heuristic use." The scientist uses the
sentence to remind himself that all events must
be treated as part of a whole, that "everything
must fit together." When used in this way the
sentence is neither true nor false and is, hence,
unfalsifiable. (3) The sentence can also be
used to make the ontological claim that the world
has some order or other. Used in this way, the
sentence is necessarily true and, therefore,
unfalsifiable. McKinnon argues that "I believe
in God" and "God is love" are used in the same
three ways. E.g., "I believe in God" may be
used to "declare belief in some particular God,"
to express a resolution to treat all events as
pointing to the real nature of God, or to affirm

595

the necessary actuality of "Ultimate Reality."
It follows that religious claims are in order
if scientific claims are in order. Ogden (# 946
below) has effectively criticized McKinnon's
analysis of religious language. It is also doubtful that McKinnon's paradigmatic scientific claim
("the world has an order") is a genuine scientific claim.

936   McPherson, Thomas. "The Existence of God," Mind,
      LIX (October, 1950), 545-50.

A reply to Cox (# 912 above). McPherson shows
that Cox is unsuccessful in his attempt to reformulate "God exists" as "Some men and women have
had, and all may have, experiences called 'meeting
God!'." If the two statements were equivalent,
God's existence would depend upon human experience
which it does not. Furthermore, the restated
doctrine is not (pace Cox) verifiable. (McPherson
implicitly assumes that "experiences called
'meeting God'" should be interpreted as "experiences which involve a real meeting with God" and
not as "experiences which are conventionally
called 'meeting God'." This assumption may be
incorrect. However, if it is incorrect, Cox's
restatement of Christian belief does not even
appear to be equivalent to its original.)

937   Matson, Wallace I. "Bliks, Prayers, and Witches,"
      Pac Phil Forum, 5 (December, 1966), 2-48, esp.
      7-16.

Matson examines Hare's concept of a "blik" (see
866 above), argues that the practice of prayer
is incoherent, speculates on the origins of religion, etc. The most valuable part of this paper

is the section in which Matson shows that Hare's
first two examples (the lunatic who believes that
all dons are out to murder him, and the man who
is obsessed with the fear that his steering mechanism will fail) are confusing and fail to exem-
plify his own definition of "blik." See Mavrodes'
reply (# 938 below).

938 Mavrodes, George Ion. "Bliks, Proofs, and Prayers,"
     Pac Phil Forum, 5 (December, 1966), 49-61.

     A reply to # 937 above. Mavrodes examines the
     claim to have refuted all arguments for the exis-
     tence of God, defends the coherence of the prac-
     tice of prayer, and addresses himself to Flew's
     challenge (see # 866 above). Flew is said to
     have made two mistakes: (1) From the fact that
     every genuine statement has a denial, Flew illic-
     itly infers that every genuine statement must
     be incompatible with some statement about events.
     (2) Flew fails to see that since "God loves his
     children" is not about events, "it cannot, by
     itself, be incompatible with any statement re-
     porting an event."

939 Miles, Thomas Richard. Religion and the Scientific
     Outlook. London: George Allen & Unwin, Ltd.,
     1959. Pp. 36-46 and 140-79.

     Miles attempts to support the claim that an asser-
     tion is factual if and only if it is verifiable,
     by arguing that we have no concept of "absolute
     existence." Consider, e.g., numbers. Although
     it makes sense to ask whether there is a number
     between 5 and 7, or to ask whether "number" is
     a thing word, it makes no sense to ask whether
     numbers exist, i.e., whether they are part of

597

the furniture of the universe. It makes no sense
to ask this question because there are no criteria
for assessing answers to it. (This is not clearly
true unless criteria are restricted to empirical
criteria and a restriction of this kind would
beg the question.) "There is a God" either ascribes absolute existence to God, in which case
it is nonsense, or places God in an "empirical
frame of reference," in which case it expresses
a straightforward (and false) empirical assertion.
Believers and unbelievers do not differ in their
factual beliefs. A believer is someone who accepts the "theistic parable," where "accepts"
means "thinks it is the right one to live by."
The theistic parable "forces us to look at the
world in a new way" and to act in a new way, but
the question of its literal truth and falsehood
does not arise. (The question "Is this parable
objectively valid?" must be "met by silence.")
At the same time, reasons can be given for one
parable and against another. (E.g., evil counts
against the theistic parable, and moral convictions may provide a reason for preferring one
parable to another.) Furthermore, some parables
may indeed be better than others. -- In spite of
disclaimers, Miles is clearly reconstructing,
and not analyzing, religious language. It is
equally clear that he has been led into this
position by his acceptance of the Verification
Principle.

940 Mitchell, Basil. "The Grace of God," Faith and
     Logic, Oxford Essays in Philosophical Theology.
     Edited by Basil Mitchell. London: Allen & Unwin;
     Boston: The Beacon Press, 1957. Pp. 149-75.

A sensitive examination of the "empirical anchorage" of the concept of grace.

941 _____. "The Justification of Religious Belief," Phil Quart, 11 (July, 1961), 213-26.

A critique of MacIntyre's contention (see # 934 above) that religious belief has nothing to do with justification and proof. Mitchell shows that reasons are relevant to religious beliefs and argues that MacIntyre fails to see this because he has made two mistakes. (1) He mistakenly supposes that if one has reasons for a belief they are either inconclusive, in which case one's belief must be held provisionally, or they are conclusive, in which case the possibility of free decision is excluded. (2) MacIntyre's understanding of justification is inadequate. By ignoring the pattern of argument in history and the humanities he has been misled into supposing that the concepts employed in a conclusion must be "translatable in terms of concepts which occur in the premisses," that conclusions must be derived from their premisses in accordance with rules, and that reasoning must proceed in a step by step manner. (In history and the humanities one typically proceeds by first offering an interpretation of the evidence and then defending that interpretation against objections rather than by drawing conclusions from premisses in accordance with clearly formulated rules.) This is an important essay, for the mistakes to which Mitchell has called our attention are pervasive. For a further development of some of these notions, see # 1065 below.

942 Muyskens, James Leroy. "Religious Belief as Hope,"
     Int J Phil Relig, V (Winter, 1974), 246-53.

     An interesting, though not entirely plausible,
     attempt to assimilate religious belief to hope.
     Both involve a similar attitude towards evidence.
     (Both will be abandoned in the face of evidence
     which shows that their object does not exist.
     Both are held in the absence of evidence which
     shows that their object does exist.) Non-cogni-
     tivist analyses are correct in so far as they
     bring out the "fact" that religious belief in-
     volves a commitment to a certain way of life but
     does not involve believing that a supernatural
     state of affairs obtains. On the other hand,
     religious belief does essentially involve hoping
     that such states of affairs obtain. Since one
     can hope that p only if one believes that p is
     possible, the non-cognitivists are mistaken in
     supposing that supernatural states of affairs
     are impossible.

943 Nielsen, Kai. "Comments on 'Empiricism and The-
     ism'," Sophia, VII (October, 1968), 12-7.

     A reply to Yandell (# 963 below). Nielsen argues
     (1) that the fact that Braithwaite's analysis of
     religious language conflicts with the orthodox
     Christian's second order beliefs about the mean-
     ing of his first order religious language is
     irrelevant, and (2) that Braithwaite's attempt
     to reconstruct religious language is justified
     because of the problematic nature of that lan-
     guage. See Yandell's reply (# 964 below).

944 _____. "On Fixing the Reference Range of
     'God'," Relig Stud, 2 (October, 1966), 13-36.

A reply to Matthews (# 876 above) and, more
especially, Crombie (#s 913 and 914 above).
Nielsen argues (1) that Crombie has failed to
give meaning to "God," (2) that because he has
failed to do so the specification of eschatological states of affairs which show that suffering
is not pointless will not provide sense to (e.g.)
"God is merciful," and (3) that because the
existence of a transcendent God cannot be directly
verified it cannot be indirectly verified. (For
a further explication of this last point, see
881 above.)

945 _____. "On Speaking of God," Theoria, XXVIII
(1962), 110-37.

God-sentences are said to be similar to ideological sentences, where an ideological sentence is
a sentence which appears to make a factual assertion but is actually a disguised normative
statement. The user of a sentence of this type
"will resist any translation of it into a non-
ideological normative sentence" since it is the
appearance of factuality which gives the sentence
its force. Nielsen's analysis of religious sentences is of some interest even though it is
predicated upon the assumption that religious
sentences are not factual because they are not
susceptible to empirical verification or falsification.

946 Ogden, Schubert Miles. "Falsification and Belief,"
Relig Stud, 10 (March, 1974), 21-43.

An effective critique of McKinnon's interpretation
of religious claims (# 935 above) which contains
a number of interesting remarks on the logical

601

dissimilarity of religion and science. Ogden
concludes by suggesting that we should distinguish between (1) religious claims (e.g., "there
is a God") which are necessarily true and, therefore, unfalsifiable, (2) religious claims (e.g.,
"Jesus was crucified") which are empirically
falsifiable, and (3) religious claims about human
existence which are not empirically falsifiable,
but can be "factually" or "existentially" falsified (or verified) by our "inner non-senuous
perception of our own existence as related to
others and to the inclusive whole of reality
as such."

947 Phillips, Dewi Zephaniah. "Infinite Approximation,"
    JAAR, XLIV (September, 1976), 477-87.

Ian Ramsey (#s 948-952 below) provides series
of models (e.g., stories about goodness or wisdom) the members of which are arranged in such
a way that later members in the series provide
more adequate models of God than earlier members.
The development of these sequences is supposed
to yield a disclosure of God. Phillips argues
(1) that the gap between model and reality cannot
be closed, and (2) that, far from these stories
leading to a disclosure of God, it is the awareness or idea of God which leads us to construct
these series. (Phillips asks us to compare the
logical gap between sense data talk and material
object talk. This gap cannot be closed by adding
still more statements about sense data. Furthermore, sense data talk depends upon material object talk, not vice versa.) Phillips' article
is suggestive and frequently on target. It is,
however, a mistake to assume that Ramsey thinks

602

that the connection between models and God is inferential.

948 Ramsey, Ian Thomas. Christian Discourse, Some Logical Explorations. (The Riddell Memorial Lectures, Thirty-Fifth Series, delivered at the University of New Castle upon Tyne on 5, 6, and 7 November 1963.) London, New York, Toronto: Oxford University Press, 1965. 92 pp.

In these lectures, Ramsey discusses (1) the language of the Bible (parables, biblical poetry, the resurrection narratives, etc.), (2) atonement theology, and (3) the language of transcendence and the ascription of personality to God. In the course of these lectures Ramsey makes a number of points which must be taken into account if one wishes to understand his position: (1) Models not only evoke disclosures, they enable us "to be articulate about what those disclosures disclose." (2) "There is only one reference for what all the models [which articulate cosmic disclosures] . . . talk about." (3) One model may dominate a set of interwoven models. (4) Cosmic disclosures lead to distinctive patterns of behavior. These distinctive patterns of behavior provide "criteria to justify our claim to a cosmic disclosure." (5) We must "check the internal connexions" of our models and "plot the external connexions with everything we want to say about the world around us," i.e., our models must have "empirical fit." (According to Ramsey, the fact that the Church "proves itself in its life and works to be an inclusive fellowship of the Spirit" shows that atonement models have empirical fit.) (6) When we develop a model (e.g., a model of the atonement)·, we may find that some of its implications are unacceptable either because they conflict with the implications of another model (e.g., a model of the Trinity) or because they conflict with our ethical notions. (7) We will be misled if we forget that our models are models and attempt to read them descriptively, or if we forget that our models are based on disclosures.

949   . Christian Empiricism. Edited by Jerry H. Gill. (Studies in Philosophy and Religion.) London: Sheldon Press, 1974. xi + 260 pp.

"A collection of Ian Ramsey's more important journal articles." Of special interest are "On Understanding Mystery" (from The Chicago Theological Seminary Register, LIII [May, 1963]), "Paradox in Religion" (Proc Aris Soc, Suppl vol. XXXIII, 1959), "Talking of God: Models, Ancient and Modern" (from Myth and Symbol, ed. by F. W. Dillistone [London: S. P. C. K., 1966]), and "Facts and Disclosures" (Proc Aris Soc, LXXII, 1971-72). This volume includes a selected bibliography of Ramsey's works.

950   . Models and Mystery. (The Whidden Lectures for 1963.) London: Oxford University Press, 1964. ix + 74 pp.

The first of these three lectures is of particular importance for understanding Ramsey's position. In this lecture Ramsey distinguishes between scale or picturing models (e.g., a wind tunnel or Bohr's model of the atom) which reproduce "selected features of the 'original'," and the more useful "analogue" or "disclosure" models which stand "somewhere between a picture and a formula." Disclosure models involve a "structural

similarity" between the model and its original.
They arise in a moment of insight "when the universe discloses itself in points where the phenomena and the model meet," and enable us to be
articulate about the phenomena. (Thus, theological models are generated by a disclosure which
"arises around" situations "of cosmic character"
that "echo, chime in with" other situations in
which we speak of [e.g.] kings or fathers and
sons, and stories about [e.g.] kings or fathers
and sons enable us to be articulate about this
disclosure.) While, on the whole, the logical
features of scientific and theological disclosure
models are similar, there is one important difference. Scientific disclosure models generate
experimentally verifiable deductions whereas
theological disclosure models do not. The latter
must, however, be able to "incorporate the most
diverse phenomena," harmonizing or fitting "whatever events are to hand." In his second lecture,
Ramsey examines the role of models in the social
sciences. The third lecture contains an important exploration of the similarity between models
and metaphors.

951 _____. "On the Possibility and Purpose of a
Metaphysical Theology," Prospect for Metaphysics,
Essays of Metaphysical Exploration. Edited by
Ian Ramsey. London: George Allen & Unwin, Ltd.,
1961. Pp. 153-77.

Ramsey argues that metaphysics is the search
for "words" (concepts) which can unify and integrate diverse languages, and that these words
"must have reference to more than observables."
"I" and "God" are examples of such words. Neither
word is descriptive although each **word** integrates
descriptive discourse (about human behavior and

about the cosmos respectively). That which is
referred to by both words is given in a disclosure
and, therefore, even though we cannot be certain
of the truth of any statement about the I or about
God, we can be certain that there is an I (the
"more" of observable behavior) and that God (the
"more" of the universe) is real.

952   . Religious Language, An Empirical Plac-
ing of Theological Phrases. (The Library of
Philosophy and Theology.) London: SCM Press,
Ltd., 1957. 191 pp.

Ramsey asks us to consider situations in which
"the light dawns" or "the penny drops," and a
set of empirical facts acquires a new dimension
or "takes on depth." He points out that in some
of these situations discernment elicits commitment. (Consider, e.g., falling in love.) The
function of religious language is to evoke the
"insight" or "discernment" which elicits religious
commitment, where religious commitment is defined
as "total commitment to the whole universe."
The function of negative attribute terms like
"immutable" and "impassible" is "to fix on mutable
and passible features of perceptual situations
and develop those features in such a way" that
one discerns that change and passibility are not
the whole story. These terms also indicate that
words for mutable and passible things are not
"exact currency" for God. Terms like "unity,"
"simplicity" and "perfection" can best be understood by considering their contrasts. Thus, we
may start with a complex fact, analyze it into
parts, analyze those parts into still further
parts, and so on, until "the penny drops" and
the meaning of "simplicity" is grasped. (This

involves a "disclosure.") The application of
these terms to God indicates that "God" is a
concept which can be used to unify and integrate
all strands of discourse. The third group of
terms includes expressions like "first cause"
and "infinitely wise." "Cause" and "wise" supply
the models and "first" and "infinitely" function
as qualifiers. Thus, the qualifier "first"
directs us to develop causal stories in a certain
direction, pressing us "backward and still backward" from cause to cause until we succeed in
evoking a sense of "something 'mysterious' which
eludes the grasp of causal language." The application of "first cause" to God also indicates
that "'God' completes causal stories." Again,
"infinitely" invites us to develop a series of
stories about wise personages in which the wisdom
depicted in the first story is surpassed by the
wisdom depicted in the second story, and so on,
until "the light dawns." The use of "infinitely
wise" also indicates that "God" stands to "all
the languages of discursive knowledge something
like a mathematical bound presides over, gathers
together, and completes a sequence." In short,
terms for divine attributes can be used both
to evoke religious disclosures and to indicate
the "logical placing" of "God." Chapters III
and IV (pp. 90-186) discuss the language of the
Bible and Christian doctrine. These chapters
are of less interest. (Ramsey attempts to show
that, in one way or another, this language tends
to evoke religious discernment.) Ramsey's theory
remains essentially the same in his later works.
In spite of its "analytic" and "empiricist" vocabulary, Ramsey's theory of religious language
is not altogether dissimilar to Paul Tillich's

theory of religious symbols (#s 1022-1028 below).
Furthermore, Ramsey's work and Tillich's work
suffer from similar defects -- repetitiousness,
imprecision, and a failure to adequately come to
terms with the question of the conditions under
which (apparent) disclosures or (apparent) "intuitions" of Being-itself are veridical. Nevertheless, Ramsey's theory, like Tillich's theory,
is influential and important. Effective but
not unsympathetic critiques of that theory are
provided by Austin, Cohen, Evans, Gaskin, and
Phillips (#s 898, 911, 918, 924 and 947 above).

953 Richmond, James. _Theology_ and _Metaphysics_. (The
     Library of Philosophy and Theology.)   London:
     SCM Press, Ltd., 1970. xii + 156 pp.

     After discussing continental and Anglo-American
     critiques of metaphysics, Richmond turns his
     attention to Wisdom's concept of "seeing as."
     (See # 959 below.) He shows that in spite of
     some misleading remarks, Wisdom interprets re-
     ligious beliefs as factual beliefs, though not
     as beliefs about future facts or facts which
     can be ascertained by mere observation. (Rich-
     mond himself clearly believes that the facts
     which are the objects of religious beliefs cannot
     be equated with patterns in the [generally acknow-
     ledged] facts which provide evidence for them.
     Whether Wisdom believed this is less clear.)
     Richmond maintains that we can enrich Wisdom's
     account of religious discourse if we attend to
     the parables of Mitchell (the Stranger [see #
     866 above]) and Hick (the Celestial City [see
     # 870 above]). A consideration of these parables
     reminds us of the existential urgency of the
     judgment (decision) which is called for, of the

fact that this decision involves trust and faith,
and of the complexity and dynamic character of
the facts which are to be fitted into the theistic
"pattern." In chapter V, Richmond examines elements in our experience which invite a theistic
interpretation. These include (1) religious
experience, (2) moral experience, (3) human existence (as interpreted by the existentialists),
(4) the history of man's spiritual life and the
history of Israel, Christ and the Church, (5)
the order, value and regularity of nature, and
(6) the conviction of the world's contingency.
Richmond argues that in order to adequately account for these things we must appeal to something
which transcends "what is spatio-temporal and
observable." In the concluding chapter he tries
to show how the concept of God can integrate
and explain these aspects of our experience.
Richmond suggests that a model for this type
of interpretation or explanation is provided by
attempts to interpret or explain human behavior
in terms of a (non-observable) mind or soul.
-- This book should be examined by anyone interested in this sort of view but it does not succeed in breaking new ground.

954 Schmidt, Paul F. Religious Knowledge. Glencoe,
     Illinois: The Free Press of Glencoe, Inc., 1961.
     Pp. 73-112.

     Schmidt maintains that religious sentences express
     and evoke attitudes which manifest themselves
     in pervasive patterns of behavior. E.g., "God
     is omniscient" expresses "the attitude of con-
     tinuous search for the solution of problems and
     of action that awards a high place to knowledge."
     Schmidt concedes that religious sentences do

perform a second function, viz., they express
empirical, ethical and metaphysical beliefs.
He argues that the attitudes expressed by religious sentences are appropriate when those beliefs are justified. However, because evidence
is irrelevant to metaphysical beliefs (they are
unfalsifiable), metaphysical beliefs are not
justified, and attitudes which depend upon them
are inappropriate. Schmidt appears to realize
that he is offering a reconstruction (and not
merely an analysis) of religious language. His
discussion is of interest because it effectively
illustrates one significant trend in the investigation of religious language. Whether it advances our understanding of religious language
is, however, a moot point.

955 Smart, Ninian. Reasons and Faiths, An Investigation
     of Religious Discourse, Christian and Non-Chris-
     tian. (International Library of Psychology,
     Philosophy and Scientific Method.) London:
     Routledge & Kegan Paul, 1958; New York: Human-
     ities Press, 1959. ix + 211 pp.

     A fruitful application of the insights of analy-
     tic philosophy. Of particular interest are (1)
     Smart's analysis of "x is holy" (modeled after
     his analysis of "x is wonderful") and the con-
     cept of divine transcendence (chapter I), (2)
     his explication of the concepts of Nirvana and
     mystical bliss (chapter II), (3) his exploration
     of the logical relations between the concepts
     of mystical religion and the techniques of mysti-
     cism (chapters II and III) and the logical rela-
     tions between theistic concepts and the practice
     of worship (chapter I), (4) his account of mysti-
     cal knowledge as a combination of knowing what
     something (viz., the experience and/or its

"object") is like, a new way of seeing the world
(as unreal or empty of value), and knowing how
to do certain things or how to live in a certain
way (chapter V), and (5) his discussion of the
relation of moral discourse to religious discourse (chapter VII). Smart's analyses are of
particular value because he is one of the few
analytically oriented philosophers who is equally
familiar with eastern and western traditions.

956   Smith, James Marvin and James William McClendon, Jr.
      "Religious Language after J. L. Austin," Relig
      Stud, 8 (March, 1972), 55-63.

      The authors provide a quasi-Austinian analysis
      of the confession "God led Israel across the
      Sea of Reeds." Their analysis successfully brings
      out the complexity of this speech act, and the
      fact that the existence and causal activity of
      God is only one of many conditions which must
      obtain if it is to be felicitous. On the other
      hand, Smith and McClendon underplay the problem-
      atic character of that condition. (This is
      unfortunate because what is primarily at issue
      in this sort of inquiry is precisely what it
      means to say "God exists and brings about such
      and such an event.")

957   Toulmin, Stephen Edelston. An Examination of the
      Place of Reason in Ethics. Cambridge: The Cam-
      bridge University Press, 1950. Pp. 202-21.

      Toulmin maintains that religion provides answers
      to limiting questions. Limiting questions (e.g.,
      "Why should I do what is right?" or "What is
      the purpose of the universe?") are questions
      "expressed in a form borrowed from a familiar
      mode of reasoning but not doing the job which

they normally do within that mode of reasoning."
Toulmin's discussion has been influential.
Nevertheless, the notion of a limiting question
is not worked out as clearly as one would like.
(Toulmin says that one can reason about these
questions even though "there is no fixed, literal
way of answering them," that limiting questions
express anxieties, desires for reassurance, etc.,
but these are only hints.)

958 Wainwright, William Judson. "Religious Statements
     and the World," Relig Stud, 2 (October, 1966),
     49-60.

     Wainwright argues that Christian statements have
     empirical implications. Type I statements (e.g.,
     "God is omnipotent, omniscient and loving") lead
     to empirical expectations. Type II statements
     (e.g., "God created the world," "God delivered
     Israel from Egypt") have historical implications
     and provide a warrant for Type I statements.
     Christian assertions are backed by authority.
     The claim that a person(s) or book possesses
     authority is rooted in the judgment that that
     person(s) or book is holy. The final section
     discusses the possibility of conflicts between
     two authoritative pronouncements, between an
     authoritative pronouncement and observation,
     etc. It is concluded that even though authori-
     tative statements take precedence over conclusions
     reached by induction, Christian belief is rational
     in the sense that it does not countenance logical
     incoherence or statements which clearly conflict
     with observation.

959 Wisdom, John. "Gods," Proc Aris Soc, XLV (New
     Series), (1944-1945), 185-206.

In this influential and important essay, Wisdom
argues (1) that disputes between believers and
non-believers are, essentially, not disputes
over what facts obtain but disputes over what
patterns can be discerned in the facts, and (2)
that these disputes are subject to rational discussion. The problem with Wisdom's approach is
that it fails to do justice to the fact that
theists not only believe that certain patterns
can be found in the facts, but also believe that
a transcendent being exists who explains, or accounts for, these patterns. For a good discussion
of Wisdom by a "Wittgensteinian Fideist," see
Dilman, #s 915 and 916 above. Also see Richmond,
953 above.

960 _____. "The Logic of God," Paradox and Discovery by John Wisdom. Oxford: Basil Blackwell;
New York: Philosophical Library, 1965. Pp. 1-22.

A further development of themes first broached
in "Gods" (# 959 above). (1) There are significant disputes, where it is important to be
right, which call for reflection, thought, reasoning and argument, but which cannot be settled
by observation, by demonstration from self-evident
premises or by any kind of mechanical decision
procedure. (2) "In Nero God was incarnate" is
absurd because it is against reason. It is,
therefore, not beyond the scope of reason. Since
"In Jesus God was incarnate" is a logically
parallel statement, it too lies within the scope
of reason. "The question is large, slippery,
subtle" but we do have some idea of how to proceed. (3) The logic of the move from the character of the order of nature to God is in some
respects similar to the logic of the move from

the behavior of a machine to the presence of
electricity, or to the logic of the move from
a host of natural incidents to the conclusion
that energy is indestructable. (None of these
moves is deductive.) In other respects, the
way in which one (allegedly) comes to know God
is similar to the "way one knows the soul or
mind of another creature." (4) It is conceded
that if there were no agreement as to what counts
for and what counts against the claim that God
exists, then the question of God's existence
would be meaningless. However, it is false that
there is no agreement as to what considerations
are relevant. Wisdom suggests that we look at
descriptions of heaven and hell, and examine
cases in which we speak of possession by "a demon
evil or good or both good and evil." ("Indeed
what makes us speak of the unconscious and the
good and evil in it . . . is closely connected
with what makes us speak of a hidden power for
good -- God -- and a hidden power for evil --
the Devil.") "The Logic of God" was written for
the BBC in 1950.

961 _____. "Religious Belief," Paradox and Discovery by John Wisdom. Oxford: Basil Blackwell;
New York: Philosophical Library, 1965. Pp.
43-56.

It is part of the "essence" of religious assertions that they "should make a claim as to what
in fact is so," that they "should express some
belief as to what the world is like." The precise force of this claim is unclear since (1)
Wisdom compares religious belief with the belief
that an action did (or did not) involve negli-
gence, and (2) admits that a "demythologized"

version of what the Greeks believed when they
"spoke of their gods, of the power of Aphrodite
and the need to remember Dionysius," (which
[merely?] puts familiar facts in a new light,
"shows us the connections in what seemed unconnected," and thus "obliges us to recognize what
is for what it is") is a genuine religious belief. This article first appeared in the Cambridge Review.

962 Wittgenstein, Ludwig. Lectures & Conversations on
Aesthetics, Psychology and Religious Belief Com-
piled from Notes taken by Yorick Smythies, Rush
Rhees and James Taylor. Edited by Cyril Barrett.
Oxford: Basil Blackwell; Berkeley and Los An-
geles: University of California Press, 1966.
Pp. 53-72.

Suggestive, influential and somewhat enigmatic
remarks on the nature of religious belief, the
religious form of life, etc. Although Wittgenstein's impact on the philosophy of religion is
now waning, it has been enormous. His influence
was due less to these brief comments than to the
views on philosophy, language and meaning expressed
in the Philosophical Investigations and The Blue
and Brown Books. Wittgenstein's (exaggerated)
emphasis on the uniqueness and independence of
the religious "language game" or "form of life"
has provided the inspiration for a new form of
fideism. (See, e.g., D. Z. Phillips, #s 1100-
1108 below.) For a balanced discussion of Wittgenstein's views on religious language, see Hudson
(#s 930 and 931 above).

963 Yandell, Keith Edward. "Empiricism and Theism,"
Sophia, VII (October, 1968), 3-11.

A critique of Braithwaite (# 903 above). Yandell

shows that Braithwaite's analysis of moral sentences (as expressions of intention) is implausible, and argues that there are religious sentences central to the Christian tradition which
neither express intentions nor (since they are
not empirically testable) belong to empirically
meaningful stories which the believer entertains
to reinforce his commitments. See Nielsen's
reply (# 943 above).

964   _____. "Reply to Nielsen," Sophia, VII (Octo-
        ber, 1968), 18-9.

A reply to Nielsen (# 943 above) which includes
a description of a non-eschatological state of
affairs which would falsify "God loves us."

965 Zuurdeeg, Willem Frederick. An Analytical Philo-
        sophy of Religion. London: George Allen & Unwin,
        Ltd.; New York: Abingdon Press, 1958. 320 pp.

Zuurdeeg provides an account of religious language with both analytic and existentialist over-
tones. Religious language is convictional language, where convictions are "all persuasions
concerning the meaning of life; concerning good
and bad; concerning representations of the ideal
man, the ideal state, the ideal society; concerning
the meaning of history, of nature, and of the
all." A "convictional situation includes a convictor" which overcomes us, witnesses who attest
to the convictor, and the "person who is overcome,
the convictus." Conviction involves decision,
commitment, an engagement of the entire personality. (Indeed, "to a certain extent we are
our convictions.") Zuurdeeg's examination of
convictional language is not without interest.

However, his treatment of the truth claims which
are involved in convictional language is inadequate. (Zuurdeeg maintains that "objective
grounds" cannot fully account for our convictions.
Although he concedes that reasoning is often
involved in arriving at a conviction and in
evaluating convictions, the nature of this reasoning [its "rules"] is not adequately explained.
Convictional language is concerned with reality
but with a reality which is [only?] real for
those who use that language. [Zuurdeeg appears
to think that something of the sort can also
be said of scientific language.] Convictional
language is said to be alogical but the examples
cited to substantiate this claim are not examples
of formal contradictions. And so on.)

The Analogy Theory

966 Anderson, James Francis. Reflections on the Analogy
of Being. The Hague: Martinus Nijhoff, 1967.
88 pp.

Anderson provides a "metaphysical analysis of
analogy." While many would accuse Anderson of
confusing the conceptual and real orders, his
study is an excellent example of its kind, and
indirectly contributes to our understanding of
the logic of analogical predication. Among his
conclusions are that: (1) All analogies of attribution are extrinsic for they rest upon relations of dependence, and relations of dependence
are extrinsic to the being of those things which
are dependent. Furthermore, because being is
prior to its relations, the analogy of proper
proportionality (which is fundamentally an analogy
of being) is prior to the analogy of attribution.

(Anderson maintains that so-called analogies of intrinsic attribution can be reduced to analogies of proper proportionality.) (2) The analogy of improper proportionality ("metaphor") is based on a similarity of effects, behavior, or operation. (E.g., Achilles is called "a lion" because his behavior is similar to that of a lion.) Since operation "is closer to being than is relation," metaphor "is more intrinsic," "strikes deeper," get us closer to the heart of things, than attribution.

967 Bocheński, Innocent Marie Joseph. "On Analogy," Thomist, XI (October, 1948), 424-47. (Reprinted in Logico-Philosophical Studies. Edited by Albert Menne. Dordrecht, Holland: D. Reidel Pub. Co., 1962. Pp. 97-117.)

In this very interesting article, Bocheński applies the tools of mathematical logic to analogy, providing (1) formal definitions of univocity, equivocity, and the analogies of attribution and proportionality, and (2) proofs that syllogisms in Barbara which employ an analogical middle term are valid. The analogy of proportionality is analyzed in two ways. The analogical term can be interpreted disjunctively, i.e., (roughly) as meaning "either P or Q." Although this interpretation of the analogy of proportionality preserves the validity of Barbara, it is inadequate because (among other things) the disjuncts need not be intrinsically connected. Bocheński suggests that analogies of proportionality involve an isomorphy of relations, and provides a proof that the validity of Barbara can be preserved if the analogy is interpreted in this way. He realizes that one may object that if the relations involved in these analogies are only formally similar, then "the meaning of our sentences about spirit, God, etc., would be extremely poor," but argues that this impression is due to the fact that "the formal properties involved in the relations used by metaphysics and theology" have not yet been exactly formulated. Compare this with Bocheński's discussion in The Logic of Religion, # 902 above.

968 Burrell, David. Analogy and Philosophical Language. New Haven and London: Yale University Press, 1973. xi + 278 pp.

This study employs insights provided by classical discussions of analogy and recent analytic philosophy. Burrell argues than any attempt to provide a formal characterization of analogy (in the manner of Cajetan, Bocheński [# 967 above] or Ross [#s 985-990 below]) is doomed to failure. In order for such an attempt to succeed we would have to be able to abstract a univocal element from the analogates whereas the whole point of analogical language rests upon the fact that certain similarities cannot be specified by isolating common features. (In fact, "any analysis of an analogous term yields analogous terms in turn.") Analogous terms are characterized "by their resistance to definition" and "by our propensity to employ them" in different fields of discourse. This propensity is linked with the activity of appraising, passing judgment and making assessments. Analogy calls for judgment because sensitivity is needed in order to discern whether a term can be appropriately employed in a new context, because analogous ·terms are explicitly or implicitly evaluative, and because

it is impossible to specify precise standards
for the application of these terms. Analogous
usage must be seen against the background of
human purposes, needs and concerns. E.g., the
irreducibly analogous transcategorical terms
("one," "being," "good," "true") would appear
to be necessary components of any usable human
language because in any human language we would
want to single out subjects of discourse (thus
implicitly employing "one"), say what things
are, make appraisals, and sort out the true from
the false. -- This study is disappointing.
Burrell provides good reasons for supposing that
the use of analogy is a legitimate and indispen-
sible feature of ordinary language, and he may
be correct when he maintains that one cannot
provide a fully adequate formal account of analogical usage. Whether his own informal and
unsystematic remarks significantly deepen our
understanding of analogy is, however, a moot
point. (E.g., Burrell maintains that even in
the absence of clearly defined standards we are
able to judge that analogies are appropriate.
He also maintains that these judgments are themselves subject to appraisal and criticism. Unfortunately, he does not tell us how to do these
things, but merely refers to the "different procedures for appraising, criticizing, and correcting analogies in different sorts of inquiry.")
Furthermore, from the fact that analogical talk
is sometimes in order, it does not follow that
analogical talk about God is ever in order.
While Burrell clearly believes that analogical
talk about God is in order, his remarks do little
to show that his belief is justified. (He maintains that if we want to talk about something

which transcends the universe we must do so analogically, and that the terms which we apply to
God [transcategorical terms and evaluative terms,
i.e., terms for "perfections"] are rooted in
human aspiration rather than in human achievement and thus transcend any descriptive meaning
which we might assign to them. Even if these
remarks are true, they are not very helpful.)

969 _____. "Religious Language and the Logic of
Analogy: Apropos of McInerny's Book and Ross's
Review," Int Phil Quart, II (December, 1962),
643-58.

A discussion of McInerny (# 977 below) and Ross
(# 988 below). Burrell argues that when terms
like "good" or "wise" are analogically predicated
of God, their "principal meaning" is the meaning
which they have in ordinary discourse. Recognizing that these terms signify perfections "ad-
mitting of indefinite perfectibility," we discern
that they are "open to use in other contexts,"
including transcendental ones. In its drive
for intelligibility (for a "reason why") the
intellect applies these terms to God in a judgment, affirming that God is the "source and final
explanation of the property that we know," and
that He "realizes it most perfectly." There
is, however, no "common notion" which applies
both to God and creatures. The intellect cannot,
therefore, understand what it is driven to affirm.
See Ross's reply (# 990 below).

970 Clarke, W. Norris. "Analogy and the Meaningfulness
of Language about God: A Reply to Kai Nielsen,"
Thomist, XL (January, 1976), 61-95.

A reply to # 982 below. Clarke objects to the

assumption that similarity entails possession
of a (univocal) common property. Most of this
essay is devoted to the exposition of a Thomistic
theory of analogy which is not open to Nielsen's
objections. Three features are of special interest: (1) Clarke's lucid account of the distinction between (a) the (analogous) property signified, (b) the different modes in which this
"common objective property . . . is . . . realized," (c) the modes of our understanding,
i.e., the "known modes of concrete realization of
the common property as ways or media" through
which we come to understand "the meaning of the
property," and (d) our mode of expressing divine
perfections (e.g., our use of tensed verbs or
subject-predicate sentences to speak of a timeless
being which transcends all distinctions). (2)
Clarke's exposition of the claim that analogical
predication presupposes that we have grounds
for affirming both that there is, "or at least
might be," a sufficient reason for all being,
and that this "cause" is similar to its "effects."
(He concedes that the movement of thought which
leads to these conclusions is itself analogical
since "cause," etc., are not univocal but analogical concepts.) (3) Clarke's insistence that
the use of analogical predication must be placed
within a certain context -- an upward movement
of the spirit in which (in longing, aspiration,
and intention) we start from the "best in us,
and then proceed to project upwards along the
line of progressive ascent . . . towards an apex
hidden from our vision at the line's end."

971 Copleston, Frederick Charles. Studies of Logical
Positivism and Existentialism. London: Burns
and Oates; Westminster, Maryland: The Newman
Press, 1956. Pp. 87-102.

Copleston argues that statements about God must
be understood analogically. In the course of
his discussion Copleston introduces a questionable
distinction between a term's "objective meaning"
(what the term actually refers to) and its "subjective meaning" ("the meaning-content which the
term has or can have for the human mind").
Copleston maintains that when I apply a term
like "intelligent" to God, I can "give no adequate positive account" of that term's objective
meaning but can only purify its subjective meaning
(a meaning which is determined primarily "by my
experience of human intelligence"). It is not
clear that this will do, for unless I have some
understanding of the term's objective meaning
I will be unable to purify its subjective meaning.
(Or does an "inadequate, negative account" of
the term's objective meaning provide enough information to enable us to effect this purification?) See Nielsen's reply (# 982 below).

972 Farrer, Austin Marsden. Finite and Infinite: A
Philosophical Essay. 2nd ed. London: Dacre
Press, 1959. Pp. 14-62.

Farrer's treatment of analogy has two distinctive
features. (1) An analogy of activity replaces
(or, more accurately, glosses) the analogy of
being. (2) Instead of employing the scale of
being (which he rightly regards as problematic),
Farrer employs the scale of conscious, voluntary
activity. ("Spiritual" acts can be more or less
conscious, rational and free.) We are directly

623

acquainted with some members of this scale and
can apply suitably modified concepts of spiritual activity to an absolute or unrestricted
activity.

973 Garrigou-Lagrange, Reginald Marie. God: His Exis-
     tence and Nature; A Thomistic Solution of Certain
     Agnostic Antinomies. Vol. II. Translated from
     the fifth French Edition by Dom Bede Rose. London
     and St. Louis: B. Herder Book Co., 1936. Pp.
     203-25 and 246-67.

     Section 56 provides a lucid account of the Tho-
     mistic doctrine of analogy as this doctrine was
     understood prior to the appearance of the cri-
     tical studies of Klubertanz (# 976 below), Mc-
     Inerny (# 977 below), Mondin (# 981 below), and
     others. (These studies reject Cajetan's inter-
     pretation of Aquinas and its stress upon the
     analogy of proper proportionality.) An interest-
     ing incidental feature of Garrigou-Lagrange's
     discussion is his explanation of the way in which
     other analogies can be reduced to the analogy
     of being. Unity, goodness and truth are conver-
     tible with being, while intellect, will and ac-
     tion (together with the perfections which pertain
     to them) are analogous precisely because they are
     essentially related to being, truth and goodness.
     Section 58 discusses Scotus and Saurez. Garrigou-
     Lagrange argues that the doctrine that "being"
     applies univocally to God and creatures blurs
     the distinction between the supernatural and
     natural orders, and leads both to monism and
     to the view that God's essence can be known by
     the created intellect.

974 Kearney, R. J. "Analogy and Inference," New Scholas,
     LI (Spring, 1977), 131-41.

A lucid examination of the problem created by
the use of such analogical terms as "will" and
"love" in argumentation. Kearney asks us to
consider the following argument: "Whatever can
will, can love; But God can will; Therefore God
can love." If we interpret "will" disjunctively
(i.e., as "will in the way God wills or will in
the way humans will"), we preserve the validity
of the argument but the analogy between the disjuncts becomes irrelevant. We can also preserve
the validity of the argument if we interpret
analogy as an isomorphy of formal properties.
(The argument then becomes: "Whatever has the
formal properties common to all willing has the
formal properties common to all loving; God has
the former; He, therefore, has the latter.")
Unfortunately, if the analogical terms are interpreted in this way, the conclusion becomes
almost vacuous. Kearney argues that we should
accept the following principle: "Except to the
extent that the contrary is stated or clearly
evident, a word is always to be understood as
having its full primary meaning." In the case
at hand, materiality and imperfection are the
only things which are clearly excluded. Hence,
the predication of "can will" entails the predication of "can love" if (as is in fact the case)
the predication of the latter is "compatible
with the total denial of any materiality or imperfection." The article contains one very questionable contention. It is sometimes said that
if "P" analogically applies to a, every predicate
entailed by "P" analogically applies to a. Kearney objects that unless there is "at least one
inference that is warranted by the predication
in the one case but not in the other;" "P" is

being used univocally. This is not clear for
it could be argued that "P" is being used analogically if either the mode in which the property
indicated by the predicate is realized or the
criteria for the application of the predicate
(neither of which are clearly included in the
entailments of the concept) vary in the two
cases.

975 Kenny, Anthony John Patrick. "Aquinas and Wittgen-
     stein," Downside Rev, LXXVII (Fall, 1959), 217-
     35, esp. 220-6.

Kenny attempts to show that there are interesting
similarities between Wittgenstein's notion of
family resemblance and Aquinas's doctrine of
analogy. Both oppose theories (e.g., those
of the Positivists or Scotus) which assume that
"there must be some element of reality, which
can be isolated at least in thought, which is
common to every occasion on which we use the
same word." The article, as a whole, attempts
to show that in spite of differences in what they
affirmed, Aquinas and Wittgenstein had the same
philosophical enemies.

976 Klubertanz, George Peter. St. Thomas Aquinas on
     Analogy: A Textual Analysis and Systematic Syn-
     thesis. (Jesuit Studies.) Chicago: Loyola
     University Press, 1960. vii + 319 pp.

Whether this historical study adds to our understanding of analogical predication is debatable.
It does, however, contribute to our understanding
of Aquinas. Klubertanz's most significant point
is that the importance of the analogy of proper
proportionality in Thomas's theory of analogy has
been greatly exaggerated, and that he in fact

abandoned it "as an apt description of the similarity between God and creatures." This book includes the Latin text of Thomas's remarks on analogy, and a useful bibliography.

977 McInerny, Ralph M. _The Logic of Analogy: An Interpretation of St. Thomas._ The Hague: Martinus Nijhoff, 1961. x + 184 pp.

According to McInerny, the doctrine of analogy is a logical doctrine, i.e., a doctrine concerned with terms and concepts and not with things. Analogies (as distinguished from the relations between things which provide the basis in reality for analogical predication) are of two types: (1) the analogy of several to one (e.g., "healthy" is applied to urine and to a proper diet because of the relation of these two things to a third thing, viz., a healthy constitution), and (2) the analogy of one to another (e.g., "healthy" is applied to a diet and to an animal's constitution because of the relation which the first bears to the second). McInerny's thesis has serveral important implications: (1) Differences in "the real order" do not entail differences in "the logical order." E.g., the fact that healthy urine is not related to a healthy constitution in the same way in which the goodness of Socrates is related to God's goodness does not entail that the _mode_ of analogical predication differs in the two cases or that the _logical_ behavior of "healthy" differs from the _logical_ behavior of "good." (2) The distinction between intrinsic and extrinsic attribution is not a formal distinction, and the analogy of proper proportionality is not a formally distinct ·type of analogy. (3) The foundation in things for analogical

627

predication is not always a causal relationship
between the things named analogously. McInerny's
study has been well received and it is not without
interest. Nevertheless, it is not clear that
it significantly adds to our understanding of the
way in which terms drawn from ordinary discourse
are predicated of God. See Ross's review (#
988 below).

978 MacIntyre, Alasdair C. "Analogy in Metaphysics,"
     Downside Rev, LXIX (Winter, 1950), 45-61.

The first half of this essay contains a rather
decent discussion of the conditions under which
one would be justified in employing analogies in
metaphysics. MacIntyre argues (1) that analogies
may legitimately be used to explicate and clarify
experience. (Thus, Farrer's resort to analogy
is in order because he believes that God is apprehended together with finite existence. [For
Farrer's position see #s 312 and 972 above]).
He also argues (2) that analogy is unavoidable
in science and metaphysics, and (3) that justified
analogies (a) are drawn from fields of experience
which are more significant or important than
others, (b) are applicable over a wide range of
experiences, (c) are fruitful in suggesting new
lines of thought, and (d) express insights which
cannot be adequately expressed in non-analogical
language. MacIntyre concludes with some very
obscure observations concerning the analogical
extension of "existence" to God.

979 Mascall, Eric Lionel. Existence and Analogy, A
     Sequel to "He Who Is." London and New York:
     Longmans, Green and Co. Ltd., 1949; Hamden,
     Connecticut: Archon Books, 1967. Pp. 92-121.

Chapter Five contains a frequently cited discussion of the Thomistic doctrine of analogy.
(Mascall's account is similar to, and should
be compared with, the accounts of Anderson,
Garrigou-Lagrange [#s 966 and 973 above], and
Phelan [# 984 below].) Mascall's essay has two
virtues. (1) It treats the doctrine of analogy
as a theory of (God-) language, and (2) it focuses
on two standard objections to that theory. These
objections are: (1) The analogy of (proper)
proportionality involves an infinite regress.
Not only are (e.g.) the life of God and the life
of man analogous, but the relation between God
and the life of God and the relation between
man and the life of man are analogous as well.
However, if this is the case, it would seem that
the relation between God and the relation between
God and the life of God must also be only analogous to the relation between man and the relation between man and the life of man, and so on
ad infinitum. (2) When analogies of (proper)
proportionality are applied to God, two terms
of the "equation" (viz., God's essence and [e.g.]
God's life) are unknown. It follows that we
cannot "solve" these "equations." Mascall's
responses to these objections are not as clear
as one would like, but appear to be as follows:
(1) The first puzzle is as specious as F. H.
Bradley's puzzle about relations. In the relevant contexts, relations are not themselves terms
which need to be joined to their terms by further
relations. In the same way, not all similarities
between analogates are themselves analogies which
need to be explicated by further analogies. (2)
In affirming God as the self-existent cause of
contingent being (an affirmation which involves

629

employing the analogy of attribution), we (partially) grasp the third term of the "equation."

980   Mavrodes, George Ion. "On Ross's Theory of Analogy," J Phil, LXVII (October 22, 1970), 747-55.

A reply to # 985 below. Mavrodes attempts to show that the same term can be univocally predicated of subjects belonging to different logical categories. He also argues that we can "abstract" a univocal core of meaning in cases in which Ross supposes that a term is being employed analogously, and that this univocal core is the meaning of the term in question.

981   Mondin, Battista. The Principle of Analogy in Protestant and Catholic Theology. The Hague: Martinus Nijhoff, 1963. x + 190 pp.

Mondin maintains that Aquinas recognizes four types of analogy: (1) Two analogies of "extrinsic denomination," viz., (a) the analogy of extrinsic attribution and (b) metaphor ("improper proportionality"). (2) Two analogies of "intrinsic denomination," viz., (a) the analogy of intrinsic attribution and (b) the analogy of proper proportionality. Analogies of intrinsic denomination are characterized by a variation in the meaning of their predicate. (E.g., "good" does not mean exactly the same thing in "Steaks are good" and "Peter is a good man"). Analogies of extrinsic denomination are characterized by a variation in the meaning of their copula. (E.g., in "Achilles is a lion," "is" means "acts like" whereas "lion" has the same meaning it has in "that beast is a lion." In "a balanced diet is healthy," "is" means "tends to produce" whereas "healthy" has the same meaning it has in "John is healthy"). Chapter III discusses the metaphysical and epistemological presuppositions of analogy. E.g., analogies of intrinsic attribution presuppose that (with suitable qualifications) effects resemble their causes, analogies of extrinsic attribution are based upon relations of material and final causality (why only these?), etc. Chapter IV discusses the theological use of analogy. Mondin argues that, for Aquinas, the most important analogy is the analogy of intrinsic attribution, and that this analogy rests upon the principle that created effects resemble their cause. He discusses that principle, the distinction between simple or unmixed perfections (perfections which entail no imperfections) and mixed perfections, the distinction between the thing signified and the mode of signification, etc. Names of simple perfections are predicated of God according to the analogy of intrinsic attribution. E.g., in calling God "good," we imply that God is intrinsically good, and that the goodness which is intrinsic to Him is the pre-eminent and transcendent cause of the intrinsic goodness of creatures. The second (and less interesting) half of this book discusses the use of analogy in classical Protestant theology, in Paul Tillich and in Karl Barth. Among the points Mondin makes are (1) that classical Protestant theology tends to interpret God-statements as either metaphors or analogies of extrinsic attribution, and (2) that Tillich's symbol theory (which denies that any God-statement [except "God is Being-itself"] is literal) should be sharply distinguished from analogy theories since, according to the latter, analogical

631

predication is itself a form of literal predication. ("A balanced diet is healthy" and "steak
is good" are literal even though both employ
analogical expressions.)

982 Nielsen, Kai. "Talk of God and the Doctrine of
     Analogy," Thomist, XL (January, 1976), 32-60.

     A critical examination of the accounts of analog-
     ical predication provided by F. C. Copleston
     (# 971 above) and James Ross (#s 985-990 below).
     Nielsen questions Copleston's distinction between
     a term's subjective meaning (the meaning it has
     for us) and its objective meaning (the thing
     referred to), and makes several astute criticisms
     of Ross's theory. His two most fundamental ob-
     jections to the analogy theory are, however:
     (1) that similarity entails the possession of
     common properties and that, therefore, wherever
     analogical predication is possible, univocal
     predication must also be possible, and (2) that
     God-statements which involve analogical predica-
     tion are neither verifiable not falsifiable in
     spite of the fact that they purport to be factual.
     See Clarke's reply (# 970 above).

983 Palmer, Humphrey. Analogy, A Study of Qualification
     and Argument in Theology. (New Studies in the
     Philosophy of Religion.) London and Basingstoke:
     The Macmillan Press, Ltd.; New York: St. Martin's
     Press, 1973. xvi + 186 pp.

     On the whole, this is a disappointing book.
     It does, however, provide a lucid statement of
     several standard objections to the analogy theory
     of meaning. Among its better chapters are V,
     VI, XIII and XVI (pp. 36-43, 47-54, 97-110, and
     131-5, respectively). (1) In chapter V, Palmer

argues that our knowledge that God is (by definition) "an infinite, eternal and self-existent
being who is responsible for everything" is insufficient to enable us to "solve" analogies of
proportionality which assert that some property
P in God is to the nature of God as (e.g.) P
in man is to the nature of man. (Palmer provides
little support for this contention. Is it obviously true?) (2) In chapter VI, Palmer argues
that the addition of the knowledge that God is
not P, Q . . . (where P, Q, etc., are kinds of
things) will not place us in a position to solve
these analogies. (Again, we are apparently supposed to just see that this is true.) (3) Chapter
XIII addresses itself to an important problem,
viz., whether the use of analogical terms spoils
arguments by introducing equivocation. (It should
be noted that classical **ad**vocates of the analogy
theory of meaning were aware of the seriousness
of this problem.) Palmer's discussion is, unfortunately, weakened by (a) the implication that
analogical terms convey as little as meaningless
terms like "wugglies," by (b) the fact that he
does not distinguish between the use of analogical
terms and the use of metaphors, and by (c) his
neglect of the notion that analogical terms are
specified by their entailments and that, therefore, if "x is P" entails "x is Q" (e.g., if
"x is wise" entails "x is living") and if "P"
analogically applies to a, then "Q" analogically
applies to a. (Whereas, if "x is P" entails
"x is Q" [e.g., if "x is a lion" entails "x has
four legs"], the fact that "P" metaphorically
applies to a does not warrant the conclusion
that "Q" metaphorically applies to a.) (4) In
chapter XVI, Palmer concedes that analogies and

metaphors play a role in science but argues that
the theologian is only entitled to appeal to
this precedent if he is prepared (a) to "regard
his own results as speculations," and (b) to
"say what possible public and private results"
will confirm or confute his theory. (One sometimes has the impression that the theory of analogy is only imperfectly understood. See, e.g.,
Palmer's remarks on the distinction between the
mode of signification and the thing signified.
While few expositions of this distinction are
models of clarity, it is clear that the distinction is not adequately described by saying that
"terms applied to God . . . may well be defective
in the meaning they convey to us, but the object
to which they refer, that which they 'really'
mean -- is not defective.")

984   Phelan, Gerald Bernard.   St. Thomas and Analogy;
      Under the Auspices of the Aristotelian Society
      of Marquette University by the Rev. Gerald B.
      Phelan.   Milwaukee: Marquette University Press,
      1941.   58 pp.

      A good brief statement of the Thomistic doctrine
      of analogy as this was understood in the first
      half of the century. Cajetan's interpretation
      of Aquinas is accepted. Analogical predication
      is said to be possible because being is intrin-
      sically analogous, and it is argued that the anal-
      ogy of proper proportionality is the only form
      of analogy which adequately expresses the analo-
      gous character of being. For a fuller statement
      of this position see Anderson, # 966 above.
      (Phelan acknowledges his debt to Anderson's
      doctoral thesis.)

985 Ross, James Francis. "Analogy and the Resolution
of Some Cognitivity Problems, J Phil, LXVII
(October 22, 1970), 725-46.

This paper should be read in conjunction with
the author's "A New Theory of Analogy" (# 989
below). Ross argues (1) that derived uses of a
term cannot be equated with non-literal uses
of that term, (2) that when a new use of a term
is derived by rules of analogy from a cognitive
use of that term, the new use is cognitive as
well, and (3) "that there is nothing about the
meaning extension of terms in religious discourse
that does not have exact . . . parallels in kinds
of discourse where meaningfulness is beyond sensible dispute." See Mavrodes' reply (# 980 a-
bove).

986 _____. "Analogy as a Rule of Meaning for
Religious Language," Int Phil Quart, I (September,
1961), 468-502.

Even though their books on religious language
frequently contain a section on analogy, analytically inclined philosophers have, on the whole,
said very little about analogy which is either
useful or interesting. (One reason for this
appears to be the conviction that analogy is a
kind of symbol of metaphor [and not a type of
literal predication] and that one cannot understand symbolic or metaphorical assertions or
know that they are true unless one understands or
knows the truth of some literal assertions about
the object which is being described in non-literal
terms. Having made this point, the discussion
typically shifts to a consideration of the possibility of literal God-predication.) Ross is

a notable exception. This article contains a
very useful analysis of the analogy of attribution and the analogy of proper proportionality.
The most questionable aspect of Ross's analysis
is his contention that analogies of proper proportionality involve a similarity of relation,
and that this similarity entails the possession
of common properties -- either common formal properties (cf. Bocheński, # 967 above) or "common
properties with respect to linguistic axioms which
are presupposed by implicit language rules governing the employment of the analogous term." This
is not very helpful. Formal similarity appears
to be insufficient. As for the latter, Ross
confesses that he is "not really sure what such
language rules would be like," although he believes that we are able to recognize the relevant
similarities when we come across them. In any
case, it is not clear that similarity entails
possession of a common property. The article
concludes with a brief characterization of religious language. Statements which describe
God's relation to the world (e.g., "God is cause
of the world") must be understood as analogies of
proper proportionality. By means of the analogy
of attribution, terms for relations (e.g., "cause
of the world") can be transformed into names of
God (e.g., "First Cause"), and by considering
the properties which God must have if these names
apply to Him still other predicates (e.g., "is
wise") can be ascribed to God by analogies of
proper proportionality. (If Ross is correct, the
analogy of proper proportionality is basic to
our talk about God and current reactions to Cajetan's interpretation of Aquinas are, therefore,
unwarranted.)

987 _____. "A Critical Analysis of the Theory
of Analogy of St. Thomas Aquinas." Doctoral
Dissertation: Brown University, 1958. 236 pp.

The theory of analogy is treated as a theory about
language and not as a theory about things. Garrigou-Lagrange, Anderson and Bocheński (#s 973,
966 and 967 above) are criticized. It is argued
that "St. Thomas' theory of analogy does not
avoid the necessity of univocal terms." And so
on. Ross's work on analogy is the most significant yet produced by an analytic philosopher.
(His dissertation should be compared with his
more recent papers on the subject.)

988 _____. Review of The Logic of Analogy by
Ralph McInerny. Int Phil Quart, II (December,
1962), 633-42.

A critical review of # 977 above. Ross makes
several telling points, perhaps the most important of which is the following: The fact that
the doctrine of analogy is a logical doctrine and
not a metaphysical doctrine does not entail that
differences in the things which are named analogously cannot provide a basis for a distinction
between types of analogical predication. Logic
includes semantics as well as syntactics, and
semantics "is not as metaphysically pure as syntactics."

989 _____. "A New Theory of Analogy," Proc Cath
Phil Ass, 44 (1970), 70-85.

Ross argues that analogy is a pervasive feature
of natural language, that analogous uses of a
term stand in ordered relations to one another,
and that natural languages contain rules which

enable us to extend the meaning of terms thus
allowing us to express "new kinds of thoughts"
and new kinds of experience. The title is somewhat misleading. Ross does not present a theory
of analogy (he only provides a few examples of
rules of analogy) but rather an account of what
such a theory would be like. He concludes by
suggesting that when analogical terms are employed
in religious or metaphysical discourse, "nothing
semantically different happens from what happens
within the discourse which is common to human life
in general."

990 _____. "Reply of Professor Ross," Int Phil
 Quart, II (December, 1962), 658-62.

This reply to Burrell (# 969 above) provides a
useful clarification of Ross's own position.
Ross also argues that in denying that "good"
in "God is good" and "good" in "Socrates is good"
have a common res significata, Burrell has un-
wittingly committed himself to the position that
the use of "good" in these sentences is totally
equivocal.

991 Sherry, Patrick J. "Analogy Today," Philosophy,
 51 (October, 1976), 431-46.

A lucid, sympathetic, but critical examination
of the Thomistic theory of analogy. The most
significant parts of this article are those in
which Sherry examines criteria for univocal predication and concludes that some putatively
analogical terms (e.g., "wise" and "morally good")
are in fact univocal, and in which he argues that
an analogical term can be employed in an argument
if certain truth conditions are necessary for

<u>any</u> statement containing that term and if it
is upon precisely those conditions that the argument depends.

992 Simon, Yves René Marie. "Order in Analogical Sets,"
     <u>New Scholas</u>, XXXIV (Winter, 1960), 1-42.

     Burrell observes that this is "among the best
     of his written works and may be taken as repre-
     senting a lifetime of critical reflection on
     this subject." Simon is concerned with analogies
     of proper proportionality in which the analogous
     property is intrinsic to each of the analogates.
     He argues that the analogates are related by
     priority and posteriority. That analogate is
     prior in which the property exists more fully
     or is freer from limitation. That analogate is
     posterior in which what is (non-univocally) common
     exists in a limited or restricted way. Whatever
     other virtues this essay may have, it does not
     succeed in deepening our understanding of the
     <u>logic</u> of analogical predication.

993 Williams, C. J. F. "Existence and the Meaning of
     the Word 'God'," <u>Downside Rev</u>, LXXVII (Winter,
     1958), 53-71.

     After observing that the application of predicates
     to God by means of the analogies of attribution
     and proper proportionality appears to presuppose
     the application of other univocal predicates to
     God ("is cause of," and a set of predicates de-
     fining the "third term" of analogies of proper
     proportionality, viz., God), Williams points out
     (1) that since, according to Aquinas, "God"
     cannot be properly applied to anything other
     than God, "God" is not itself an analogical term,

and (2) that in <u>some</u> contexts, Aquinas speaks as
though the terms which express the ways of causality, negation and eminence (ways which must be
employed to arrive at an understanding of the
meaning of "God") are univocal. However (as
Aquinas recognized) any attempt to provide a
univocal description of God must break down since
descriptive concepts apply in principle to more
that one thing and God is unique. ("Anything
that could directly apply to God cannot begin
to apply elsewhere.") Williams suggests that we
resort to analogical concepts when "we experience
something, we appreciate something, which we
cannot 'put into words'." We cannot express
what we know. Nevertheless, in attempting to
articulate these experiences we "may communicate
the compulsion, the drive, behind the attempt."
We break category rules and cannot explain what
we mean but, in <u>trying</u> to explain, we may enable
others "to recognize the compulsion, to recognize
what compels -- and we are home." In religion,
the relevant experience is the experience of the
infinite in the finite. (See Farrer, #s 312 and
972 above.) It is ultimately this experience
which gives meaning to "God." ("God" is thus,
in a sense, defined ostensively. Hence, in giving meaning to "God," we "demonstrate" His existence.) This interesting article deserves to be
more widely read.

The Symbol Theory

(See also #s 801, 926, 948,
949, 950, 951 and 952)

994 Alston, William P. "Tillich's Conception of a
     Religious Symbol," Religious Experience and Truth,
     A Symposium. Edited by Sidney Hook. New York:
     New York University Press, 1961. Pp. 12-26.

Alston makes a number of important points. (1)
He argues that those who (meaningfully) use symbols must be able to specify the symbolizandum.
in non-symbolic language. (In principle, it
would appear to be sufficient to specify the symbolizandum by some sort of pointing or ostention.)
(2) Tillich specifies the symbolizandum as Being-
itself, but this won't do. x is a symbol of y
for A only if "x tends to evoke feelings, attitudes, and behavior appropriate to y," and A can
"identify y as the symbolizandum." If Tillich
is correct, only "metaphysicians of a certain
stripe" would be able to specify that to which
religious symbols point. Furthermore, it is totally unclear what "feelings, attitudes, and
behavior" are appropriate to Being-itself. (3)
The fact that religious symbols participate in
Being-itself does not distinguish religious symbols from other things, for everything participates in Being-itself. (4) Tillich maintains
that adequate religious symbols are non-idolatrous, but his notion of an idolatrous religious
symbol is incoherent. For example, Tillich
sometimes says that an idolatrous religious
symbol is a religious symbol which has ceased to
point beyond itself. However, if an idolatrous
symbol is a symbol which has ceased to point

beyond itself then no idolatrous symbol is religious, for (by definition) religious symbols
point to Being-itself. (5) Tillich's Systematic
Theology is an attempt to do the very thing which
Tillich says cannot be done, viz., translate
symbolic language into nonsymbolic language.
(According to Alston, it would be "grotesque"
to regard Tillich's metaphysical language as
symbolic!) For Tillich's position, see #s 1022-
1028 below.

995   Altizer, Thomas J. J. "The Religious Meaning of
      Myth and Symbol," Truth, Myth and Symbol. Edited
      by Thomas J. J. Altizer, William A. Beardslee,
      and J. Harvey Young. Englewood Cliffs, N. J.:
      Prentice-Hall, Inc., 1962. Pp. 87-108.

According to Altizer, we must distinguish three
basic types of religious mythology -- the mythology of archaic religion described by Eliade (#s
1000-1002 below), the mythology of mystical religion, and the mythology of prophetic-eschato-
logical religion. The first type of mythology
can only be employed by those who live in a sacralized universe. Mythologies of the second
and third type presuppose a de-sacralized universe, and involve a devaluation of the world.
(The Sacred has become transcendent.) Myth of
any kind is inimical to the profane or secular
and its standards of truth and rationality. If
Altizer is correct, the very use of myth and
symbol (irrespective of its specific content)
rests upon questionable ontological and axio-
logical commitments.

642

996 Bevan, Edwyn Robert. Symbolism and Belief: Gifford
Lectures. London: G. Allen & Unwin, Ltd., 1938;
Port Washington, N.Y.: Kennikat Press, Inc.,
1968. Pp. 252-386.

In lecture eleven, Bevan argues that there are
two classes of symbols -- those "behind which
we can see," and those "behind which we cannot
see." Thus, when we speak of God's love "we
cannot have any discernment of the reality better and truer than the symbolical idea, and we
cannot compare the symbol with the reality as
it is more truly apprehended . . . The symbol
is the nearest we can get to the reality." When
religious people object to "symbolic interpretations" of their language, they are really ob-
jecting to attempts to replace symbols of the
second sort with symbols of the first sort.
(E.g., Instead of regarding the Resurrection as
a "symbol behind which we cannot see, the truest
statement of the reality possible in human language," one might regard it as a symbol "behind
which one sees a remarkable influence of Jesus
upon" his disciples.) Lecture twelve discusses
symbols "without conceptual meaning," i.e.,
symbols which excite (e.g.) "the feeling of the
beautiful" or "religious awe," which create the
impression of immense significance, of a reality
behind the symbolic object, but which have no
clear "intellectual content." Although adequate
religious symbols must convey the sense of the
Beyond, they must also have a definite intellectual content. In lectures thirteen and fourteen,
Bevan discusses pragmatic theories of truth,
the Thomist doctrine of analogy, and Mansel's
theory according to which we know (because we
have reason to believe that scripture is inspired)

643

that the anthropomorphic imagery of the Bible
applies to God, that (e.g.) something in God
corresponds to love in us, but do not know <u>how</u>
this imagery applies. Bevan expresses sympathy
with Mansel's position and concludes that those
symbols should be regarded as true which "when
acted upon, produce a life of a certain quality,"
and the assurance that one is "right in believing." Lectures fifteen and sixteen are concerned
with whether there are any grounds for supposing
that there is something to which these symbols
apply. Bevan argues that religious belief ultimately rests upon the human demand for "meaning"
and "purpose," i.e., for a world which is not
indifferent to value, and upon the apprehension
of the quality of the divine in human lives. (In
these two lectures Bevan is essentially arguing
that religious belief is true because it nurtures
human life. The appeal is ultimately pragmatic.)

997 Black, Max. "Metaphor," <u>Proc</u> <u>Aris</u> <u>Soc</u>, LV (New
     Series), (1954-55), 273-94.

Although it does not discuss religious language,
this essay has had an important influence upon
such diverse figures as Ian Ramsey (#s 948-952
above) and Paul Ricoeur (#s 1012-1019 below).
Many metaphors cannot be adequately analyzed
either as figurative substitutions for literal
expressions, or as disguised comparisons. An
"interaction metaphor" (e.g., "man is a wolf")
"selects, emphasizes, suppresses, and organizes
features of the principal subject [man] by im-
plying statements about it that normally apply
to the subsidiary subject [wolf]." Interaction
metaphors act as screens or filters through which
we come to see the principal subject in a new

way. They cannot be replaced by literal translations without loss of cognitive content. Some
philosophers have undoubtedly been attracted to
Black's position because it appears to justify
their inability to furnish translations of what
they believe to be cognitively significant religious symbolism. It is, therefore, important
to notice that, according to Black, interaction
metaphors demand "simultaneous awareness of both
subjects," and that an "'explication' or elabora-
tion of the metaphor's grounds" (in literal language?) "may be extremely valuable." The foot-
notes provide useful references to the literature
on metaphor. Black's essay is reprinted in his
Models and Metaphors, Studies in Language and
Philosophy. (Ithaca, New York: Cornell University Press, 1962, pp. 25-47.)

998 Bultmann, Rudolf Karl and Ernst Lohmeyer, Julius
     Schniewind, Helmut Thielicke, and Austin Farrer.
     Kerygma and Myth, A Theological Debate. Edited
     by Hans Werner Bartsch. Translated by Reginald
     H. Fuller. London: S.P.C.K., 1953. 228 pp.

     Bultmann argues that "the New Testament world
     of spirits and miracles," the Resurrection, the
     Ascension, the Descent into Hell, etc., etc.,
     neither can be nor should be accepted by modern
     man. The kerygma must, therefore, be distin-
     guished from its mythological setting. It is
     possible to make this distinction because "the
     real purpose of myth is not to present an objec-
     tive picture of the world as it is, but to express
     man's understanding of himself in the world in
     which he lives. Myth should be interpreted . . .
     anthropologically, or better still, existential-
     ly." Bultmann accordingly attempts to show that
     the New Testament expresses an understanding

of human existence which can best be explicated
by employing the categories of Heidegger. Bultmann insists, however, that attempts to "demythologize" the New Testament should not eliminate
the "event of Christ" (the human life ending in
the crucifixion), for it is this act of God which
makes "authentic being" a real possibility and
not (as it is for Heidegger) a merely theoretical
possibility. According to Bultmann, this act
of God is not a mythological event because of
"its immunity to proof." (Presumably, he means
that the claim that God has acted in Christ is
not simply bad science or bad history. Does
he also mean to imply that it is not bad philosophy?) In replying to his critics, Bultmann
argues that the expression "an act of God" is
"neither symbolical nor pictorial" but "analogical, for it assumes an analogy between the activity of God and that of man." The expression
is construed mythologically if God's activity
is regarded as an intervention in the world which
tears apart the "closed weft of cause and effect."
It is construed non-mythologically if God's activity is regarded as "something accomplished in
them [worldly happenings] in such a way that
the closed weft of history as it presents itself
to objective observation is left undisturbed,"
hidden to "every other eye than the eye of faith."
The most interesting responses are those of Farrer and Thielicke. (Thielicke argues that, in
neglecting the objective content of faith and
emphasizing the subjective experience of faith,
Bultmann continues the liberal tradition of
Schleiermacher.) See Hepburn's critique of Bultmann, # 1004 below.

999 Dilley, Frank Brown, Jr. Metaphysics and Religious Language. New York and London: Columbia University Press, 1964. Pp. 74-114.

Among the points made by Dilley are the following: (1) The adequacy of religious symbolism is partly dependent upon its conformity to an adequate metaphysics (pace Tillich). (For a description of Dilley's account of metaphysics, see # 1042 below.) (2) Whether a word is literal or analogical is often a function of the "breadth of the definition which is being used." Thus, whether "God is a person" is analogical or literal depends partly upon whether "person" is defined as a human being or as a rational agent. (3) Those who maintain that symbols express (describe) our relation to God, but not the nature of God, are mistaken. In saying that we stand in a certain relation to God, we say something about His nature.

1000 Eliade, Mircea. Myth and Reality. Translated from the French by Willard R. Trask. (World Perspectives Series, 21.) New York: Harper and Row, Publishers, 1963. Pp. 1-20.

Myths tell how something came into existence or was established, and "constitute the paradigms for all significant human acts." Myths are considered to be true because it is believed that they are concerned with realities. Those who employ myths distinguish them from what they call "false stories." (Eliade observes that the former are invariably concerned with the establishment of the fundamental facts of human existence while the latter are not.) Knowing the orgins of things is believed to confer power

647

over them. (In reciting and reenacting the primordial events, one regards oneself as participating in the creative power of those events.)

1001 _____. Patterns in Comparative Religion.
Translated by Rosemary Sheed. London, New York:
Sheed & Ward, 1958. Pp. 1-37 and 410-58.

Chapter I discusses the Sacred and the way in
which it manifests itself in ordinary objects.
Chapters XII and XIII examine the nature of myth
and symbol. Myths both disclose "a level of
reality quite beyond any empirical or rational
comprehension," and provide paradigms for human
activity. ("Every ritual and every meaningful
act that man performs repeats a mythical arche-
type.") The function of symbols "is to transform a thing or action into something other
than that thing or action appears in the eyes
of profane experience." A symbol is a substitute for a "heirophany" (a disclosure of the
Sacred in "a fragment of the universe"), or a
way of entering into a heirophany, or (sometimes)
itself a heirophany. Symbols form a system.
(Symbol systems connected with water, with the
sky, with the moon, etc., are discussed at
length in earlier chapters.) A symbol which
belongs to one of these systems can only be
fully understood when brought into connection
with the other symbols which belong to that
system. (Thus, baptism must be connected with
stories of the deluge, the waters of chaos, etc.
It is only this system as a whole which reveals
"the sacred power of water and the nature of
water.") Symbol systems do two things. They
reveal a particular modality of the sacred, and
they integrate and unify "the greatest possible

648

number of zones of human and cosmic experience"
from a particular point of view. There are a
number of problems with Eliade's account.· It
shares the epistemological difficulties which
beset most symbol theories. (Under precisely
what conditions can we assert that a symbol
or myth is true or valid?) It is also subject
to a peculiar difficulty of its own. Eliade
contends that symbols (e.g., the moon) <u>inherently</u>
convey certain meanings. Although his contention
is plausible in a number of cases and is supported by a wealth of illustrative material,
it should be treated with considerable caution.

1002   _____. The Two and the One. Translated by
           J. M. Cohen. London: Harvill Press; New York:
           Harper & Row, Publishers, Inc., 1965. Pp.
           189-211.

Symbols reveal "a modality of the real or a
condition of the World which is not evident
on the plane of immediate experience." (Thus,
water symbolism reveals "the pre-formed, the
potential, the chaotic," and the cosmic Tree
reveals the world as a "living totality" which
periodically regenerates itself.) Symbols point
to "the real . . . the powerful, the significant
. . . the sacred." Because symbols have several
meanings, they integrate "diverse realities . . .
into a 'system'." They express "paradoxical
situations . . . or patterns of ultimate reality
that can be expressed in no other way," e.g.,
that opposed or antagonistic aspects of reality
"can be fitted and integrated into a unity."
(Hasn't Eliade just expressed this particular
pattern of reality in a non-symbolic way?)
Symbols always point to something which concerns

human existence. According to Eliade, they
"preserve contact with deep sources of life,"
and confer meaning on human existence. (By
means of myth and symbol, human life is related
to other elements in the cosmos and to sacred
paradigms and is, thus, integrated into reality
as a whole, transfigured and "spiritualized.")
Another English version of this study appeared
in History of Religions: Essays in Methodology,
edited by Eliade and Joseph Kitagawa (Chicago:
The University of Chicago Press, 1959).

1003   Ford, Lewis Stanley. "The Three Strands of Til-
       lich's Theory of Religious Symbols," J Relig,
       XLVI (January, 1966), 104-30.

       Ford argues that Tillich (#s 1022-1028 below)
       has three theories concerning religious symbols.
       (1) When a concept designating a segment of
       finite reality is applied to Being-itself, it
       is simultaneously affirmed and denied thus a-
       voiding both equivocation and univocity. (This
       theory is most appropriately applied to concep-
       tual symbols.) (2) The second theory involves
       "an extended use of the metaphor of the trans-
       parency of the symbolic medium." A medium is
       transparent when it is free from "existential
       distortion" and "estrangement," negates its
       own finitude, and possesses an intrinsic affinity
       with what it symbolizes. (This theory is most
       appropriately applied to physical or historical
       symbols [e.g., Christ].) (3) The third theory
       rests upon the notion of participation. Ford
       points out that Tillich's employment of the
       concept of participation is relatively late,
       and calls our attention to the fact that he
       uses "participation" in different senses. Ford

suggests that two of these senses are "relevant
to symbolic participation," viz., "environmental participation" which "points to the individual's real relatedness to what surrounds
him," and "essential participation" which "explains the relationship between particular and
universal." Environmental participation is
involved because symbols (unlike signs) derive
their power and meaning (their connotative richness) from the fact that they are "imbedded in
particular contexts and webs of meaning." The
notion of essential participation helps to explain "any intrinsic similarity" between a symbol and that which it symbolizes (but only if
the universal is regarded as a paradigm and
the particular as its copy!). Ford concludes
that participation thus "accounts for" two features present in Tillich's earlier accounts,
viz., "connotative suggestiveness" and "intrinsic
similarity," but "does not significantly add
any new features."

1004 Hepburn, Ronald William. "Demythologizing and
      the Problem of Validity," in # 923 above, pp.
      227-42.

      Hepburn argues (1) that Bultmann (# 998 above)
      uses "myth" in different senses, (2) that he
      tends to equate "mythical" and "provable" (from
      which it follows that in demythologizing Chris-
      tianity, we render it immune to proof and dis-
      proof), (3) that from the fact that an event
      is described in mythological terms, it neither
      follows that it occurred nor that it did not
      occur, (4) that Bultmann (unlike Tillich [#s
      1022-1028 below] and Crombie [#s 913 and 914
      above]) fails to recognize that in order for

discourse about God to be intelligible at least
some statements about God must be literal, and
(5) that the existentialist concepts which Bultmann uses to translate Christian discourse are
(a) themselves symbolic, (b) more suited to a
description of faith than to a description of
its content, and (c) overly hospitable to paradox.

1005 Jaspers, Karl. _Truth and Symbol from Von der_
Wahrheit by Karl Jaspers. Translated with an
introduction by Jean T. Wilde, William Kluback
and William Kimmel. New York: Twayne Publishers, 1959. 79 pp.

Being transcends and encompasses both subject
and object. Therefore, it can only be grasped
through the "cipher" (symbol) which "is neither
subject nor object" but "objectivity which is
permeated by subjectivity." Ciphers are transparent to Transcendence. The sort of thinking
which is appropriate to empirical objects or
to subjects is incapable of grasping ciphers
and/or the Being present in them. Ciphers are
not concepts. The type of thinking appropriate
to ciphers is inconclusive, and itself transparent to, and symbolic of, Being. Jaspers'
discussion is of some interest in spite of its
obscurity. (Tillich's theory of symbols --
which is, in many respects, similar to Jaspers'
theory -- is, by comparison, a model of precision
and clarity!) _Von der Wahrheit_ was published
in Germany in 1947.

1006 Jung, Carl Gustav. _Psychology and Religion._
(The Terry Lectures.) London: H. Milford,
Oxford University Press; New Haven: Yale Uni-
versity Press, 1938. 131 pp.

Certain religious symbols force themselves upon
human consciousness. These universal archetypal
symbols appear in dreams, mythology and folk-
lore, and are the products of a collective unconscious which transcends the individual.
They "often contain a superior . . . insight
or knowledge which consciousness has not been
able to produce." The intuitive wisdom embodied
in these symbols can be used to heal and integrate the human psyche. For an effective critique of this very influential theory, see Hepburn (# 926 above).

1007   McLean, George. "Symbol and Analogy: Tillich
       and Thomas," Rev Ottowa, XXVIII (1958), 193-233.

On the whole, this essay is no more than a tedi-
ous Thomistic critique of Tillich (#s 1022-1028).
It does, however, possess the virtue of singling
out certain (apparent) features of Tillich's
theory which are often neglected, e.g., its
subjectivity and relativity. Tillich's symbols
are valid or true for certain persons at certain places and at certain times. They are
not valid or true simpliciter. Again, because
religious symbols arise from religious encounters, they are "not the means but the result of
religious knowledge." They express cognitive
encounters with God but do not provide information about God. (This is almost right. It
does seem to be the case that whereas analogical
language expresses statements about God, symbolic language [as interpreted by Tillich] does
not express statements about God but instead
presents symbols which are vehicles of, or expressions of, cognitive encounters with Being-
itself. [Symbols for Tillich are primarily

653

objects, i.e., things, events, properties --
not propositions.])

1008 Macquarrie, John. God Talk, An Examination of
the Language and Logic of Theology. New York
and Evanston: Harper and Row, Publishers, 1967.
255 pp.

Macquarrie's book contains discussions of Atha-
nasius, Barth, Bultmann and Tillich. Their
use of language and views on the nature of language are confronted with the challenge posed
by analytic approaches to language. Myth, symbol, and analogy are discussed. The sort of
view which Macquarrie wishes to defend is described below (# 1009).

1009 _____. Principles of Christian Theology.
New York: Charles Scribner's Sons, 1966.
Pp. 111-33.

Some symbols are "intrinsically connected" with
what they symbolize and can, for that reason,
illuminate their symbolizanda. (Macquarrie
concedes that in practice it is often difficult
to distinguish between those symbols [e.g.,
height] whose "inherent characteristics" have
an affinity with what they symbolize, and a
conventional symbol [e.g., the flag] which
"through historical associations had come to
'participate'" in that to which it points.)
We can speak symbolically about Being because
beings are grounded in Being, and "Being is
present and manifest in the beings it lets be."
(The foundation for symbolic language about
God is thus provided by a kind of Heideggerian
analogia entis.) Symbols "open up" Being if
they "evoke the kind of response [e.g., awe

654

or loyalty] that is aroused by Being itself,"
and/or if our relation to them (e.g., dependence)
is similar to our relation to Being. Again,
we can ascribe (e.g.) being and goodness to
God because He is "the prior enabling condition"
of all being and goodness. However, more is
involved than these relations. Being is somehow
present in, and manifest through, our symbols.
(Since Being is present in, and [potentially]
manifest through every being, any being can
function as a symbol.) The symbols which most
fully manifest Being are drawn from the sphere
of personal life both because persons unite
several dimensions of being (the material, the
organic, and the spiritual), and because human
freedom and creativity is an analogue of "Being's
letting be." Macquarrie's attempt to combine
classical analogy theory and the insights of
theorists like Tillich has two merits. It is
relatively lucid, and it exhibits some awareness
of the difficulties to which positions of this
sort are subject.

1010 Munz, Peter. Problems of Religious Knowledge.
      (The Library of Philosophy and Theology.) Lon-
      don: SCM Press, 1959. 253 pp. (See esp. 50-
      101, 118-35, 144-58, and 169-79.)

      Symbols are natural events, objects or actions
      looked at under the influence of feeling states.
      Some symbols invite interpretation of a special
      sort. They seem to indicate the presence of
      extraordinary forces of one kind or another,
      or to be revelations of a transcendent order.
      But symbols as such "stand for" nothing. They
      merely "bestow meaning upon feeling states."
      A theological interpretation of certain symbols

is natural but contemplation of "the symbol
picture" is itself intrinsically "satisfying
and illuminating." Furthermore, it is the
symbol rather than its interpretation which
is, or should be, the object of religious faith
and certainty. Although Munz's account of
(religious) symbols is of some interest, it is
inadequately supported by argument and frequently
confusing.

1011 Randall, John Herman, Jr. The Role of Knowledge
      in Western Religion. (The Mead-Swing Lectures
      given at Oberlin College, 1955-1956.) Boston:
      Starr King Press, 1958. Pp. 103-34.

Religious symbols are non-representative, and
non-cognitive. (They do not express "explanatory and verifiable" propositions which "can
be either true or false.") Religious symbols
"disclose" or "reveal" something about the world.
They make us "see" something or provide "insight"
although they "do not 'tell' us anything that
is verifiably so." (Randall compares this disclosure to the insight into a person's character
which is gained by long familiarity and cannot
"be won by any merely external observation of
his behavior.") Religious symbols "sum up"
"men's long and intimate experience of their
universe," revealing and unifying the "powers
and possibilities inherent in the nature of
things." They reveal the world "recast in the
crucible of imaginative vision," disclose an
"order of splendour" in things. Religion is
best thought of as an art, a species of knowing
how. It may (e.g.) be profitably compared with
painting. The painter imaginatively unifies
diverse elements and reveals qualities and

656

potentialities in his subject matter which would
otherwise be overlooked. In this way he enhances
its significance. The painter teaches us how
to see the world better but does not communicate
propositional truths. This is a suggestive
essay, but one might argue that the symbolic
language of religion differs from the symbolic
language of art precisely because it purports
to offer a kind of explanation and "represents"
the transcendent. By eliminating these elements
and assimilating religion to art, Randell has
reconstructed the language of religion.

1012   Ricoeur, Paul. The Conflict of Interpretations,
       Essays in Hermeneutics. Edited by Don Ihde.
       Evanston, Illinois: Northwestern University
       Press, 1974. Pp. 287-334 and 381-497.

       A number of the essays collected in this volume
       discuss religious language: "The Hermeneutics
       of Symbols and Philosophical Reflection: I"
       (see # 1016 below), "The Hermeneutics of Symbols
       and Philosophical Reflection: II," "Preface
       to Bultmann," "Freedom in the Light of Hope,"
       "Guilt, Ethics and Religion" (see # 529 above),
       "Religion, Atheism, and Faith," and "Fatherhood:
       From Phantasm to Symbol" (various translators).
       In addition to their intrinsic interest, these
       essays help us to understand the sort of reflec-
       tion which Ricoeur believes can lead to an ade-
       quate rational articulation of symbols and myths.
       For example. Traditional theodicies are said
       to distort the symbolic material which they
       interpret. Bultmann is criticized for employing
       Heidegger's analysis of human existence while
       neglecting Heidegger's reflections upon Being.
       Ricoeur suggests that some of Kant's ideas could

657

be used to provide a "philosophical approximation" or "analogon" of the kerygma of hope. (Kant's critique of transcendental illusion reminds us that the thought of the Unconditioned cannot be filled in "according to the mode of the empirical object." If we are to explicate the Unconditioned we must turn to the will with its practical demands for "the totality of conditions for a conditioned thing" and for the connection of happiness and morality, and to the practical postulates of Freedom, Immortality and God. [Immortality and God can be regarded as "hopes" or expectations of Freedom.])

1013 _____. "Creativity in Language," Phil Today, XVII (Summer, 1973), 97-111.

"This article was first presented as a lecture at the Fifth Lexington Conference on Pure and Applied Phenomenology" in 1972. (David Pellauer, translator.) Because words are "polysemic" (have several senses), discourse is ambiguous. In ordinary language, ambiguity is (partially) eliminated by context. Scientific and technical discourse stipulates precise meanings for the terms which it employs in order to ensure "identity of meaning from the beginning to the end of an argument." Metaphor is "a creative use of polysemy." Metaphors enable us to grasp "new similarities which previous categorization prevented our noticing," and are (or can be) the source of novel systems of categorization. Metaphorical discourse employs "models" or "fictions" to redescribe reality. (E.g., "Thanks to tragedy, we are prepared to look at human beings in a new way because human action is redescribed as greater, nobler than actual life

is.") Poetry discloses "the depth structure of
human life," "reaches the essence of things."
It "gives no new information," but changes "our
way of looking at things," "opens up a new way
of being for us." (Cf., Randall, # 1011 above.
How precisely do they differ? Presumably in so
far as Ricoeur, unlike Randall, does not wish
to eliminate all references to the Transcendent.)

1014 _____ . Freud and Philosophy, An Essay on
Interpretation. Translated by Denis Savage.
New Haven and London: Yale University Press,
1970. Pp. 3-56 and 494-551.

Based on the Terry Lectures given at Yale University in 1961, and lectures given in the Cardinal
Mercier Chair at the University of Louvain in
1962. Symbols have multiple meanings, desig-
nating through one meaning "another meaning
attainable only in and through the first . . ."
They must, therefore, be deciphered. Psychoanal-
ysis regards symbols as "the distortion of ele-
mentary meanings connected with wishes and desires." It is thus, like Marxism, a "hermeneutics of suspicion," "a tearing off masks."
Phenomenology regards symbols as "the manifestation in the sensible . . . of a further reality, the expression of a depth which shows itself and hides itself." Phenomenology does not,
however, raise the question of the "validity"
of symbols. The philosopher must not only
listen to symbols and allow himself to be nourished by them, he must also continue "the tradition of the rationality of philosophy." Ricoeur
realizes that the kind of reflection which he
is recommending is problematic since symbols
are not universal but rooted in particular

cultures, since "philosophy as rigorous science
seems to require univocal significations," and
since any exegesis or interpretation is inherently contestable. Nevertheless, in order to
understand itself, the self must "decipher its
own signs lost in the world of culture," and
it must decipher symbols of the sacred. Ricoeur
points out that even "the philosopher does not
speak from nowhere: every question he can pose
rises from the depth of his Greek memory," and
he suggests that hermeneutics has its own "logic
of double meaning . . . irreducible to the
linearity of symbolic logic." (But what are
the rules of this logic?) Two radically different hermeneutics must be employed -- a hermeneutics of demystification which unmasks in-
fantilism, class-interest, the archaic, etc.,
and a hermeneutics which is directed (1) towards
the "figures of the spirit" which "anticipate
our spiritual adventures . . . [and] explore
our adult life" and (2) towards "symbols of the
sacred" which "speak of the wholly Other" and
disclose a horizon which becomes distorted when
we try to reify it.

1015   _____. "From Existentialism to the Philosophy
        of Language," Phil Today, XVII (Summer, 1973),
        88-96.

        Ricoeur describes the evolution of his reflec-
        tions upon language, and the impact upon those
        reflections of psychoanalysis, structuralism,
        biblical hermeneutics, and ordinary language
        philosophy.

1016   . "The Hermeneutics of Symbols and
Philosophical Reflection," Int Phil Quart, II
(May, 1962), 191-218. (Reprinted in # 1012
above, pp. 287-314.)

Symbols possess a double intentionality. Consider, e.g., "stain," "deviation," and "burden."
Their first intentionality is their "literal
intentionality," viz., the stain, the deviation
and the weight. Their second intentionality
is "a certain situation of man in the sacred,"
"stained, sinful, guilty being" which "is like
a stain, like a deviation, like a burden." The
second intention is given in the first intention
and in no other way. Nevertheless, symbols need
to be rationally articulated. The first steps
are phenomenological and hermeneutical. The
final step is philosophical. One should not
suppose that symbols allegorize a truth which
can be stated in non-symbolic terms, and one
should not confuse symbols and concepts (as
the Gnostics did). The philosopher must instead
engage in a "creative interpretation" which
both respects the integrity of symbols and brings
out their meaning in "the full responsibility
of an autonomous systematized thought." (But
what are the criteria for this kind of thinking?
How does one assess its adequacy?)

1017   . "Metaphor and Symbol," Interpretation
Theory: Discourse and the Surplus of Meaning
by Paul Ricoeur. Fort Worth, Texas: Texas
Christian University Press, 1976. Pp. 45-69.

An expansion of a lecture given at Texas Christian University in November 1973. Ricoeur
attempts to distinguish between metaphor and
symbol. Symbol and metaphor are similar in

many respects. Nevertheless, metaphor is primarily a linguistic phenomenon, whereas symbols are rooted in the "presemantic depths" of human life and the cosmos.

1018 _____ . "Philosophy and Religious Language," J Relig, 54 (January, 1974), 71-85.

Presented as the first John Nuveen Lecture in the Divinity School of the University of Chicago (May, 1973). Linguistic analysis begins with theological statements. Hermeneutical philosophy begins with those larger units of discourse (narratives, prophecies, proverbs, hymns, etc.) which "are the ordinary expression of religious faith." It attempts to display the affinities and tensions between them, and "the space of interpretation opened up by all the forms of discourse taken together." Ricoeur introduces the notion of "the world of the text." Poetry and works of fiction present "a proposed world which I might inhabit and wherein I might project my ownmost possibilities." These worlds open up "new possibilities of being-in-the-world," and reach the "deepest essence" of reality. Religious texts are a kind of poetic text. The Bible is "revealed to the extent that the new being unfolded there is itself revelatory with respect to the world," i.e., revelation "is a trait of the biblical world." "God" must be understood in connection with these units of discourse. Even if "'God' is the religious name for being . . . 'God' says more." It coordinates the "partial discourses" of the Bible and serves as "the index of their incompleteness, the point at which something

escapes them." Ricoeur insists that religious
discourse not only claims "to be meaningful
but also to be true," although truth in this context must be understood as "manifestation"
rather than "adequation" (correspondence). The
problem of criteria is not, however, really
addressed in this essay or in Ricoeur's other
work. Are all manifestations equally valid?
If they are, then there would seem to be no reason to prefer Christian symbols to Buddhist
symbols. If they are not, then how do we distinguish those symbols or fictive worlds which
more fully disclose reality from those symbols
and fictive worlds which do so less fully?
It is worth observing that no one who has interpreted religious language symbolically has
provided an adequate resolution of this difficulty.

1019 _____. The Symbolism of Evil. Translated
from the French by Emerson Buchanan. (Religious
Perspectives Series, 17.) New York: Harper
and Row Publishers, Inc., 1967. Pp. 347-57.

Although symbols cannot be literally translated
they provide material for reflective thought.
In order to understand symbols it is not sufficient (à la Eliade) to discover the connections
which they have with other symbols and with
rites, and to grasp the way in which they unify
regions of experience. By concentrating on the
"internal coherence, the systematicity of the
world of symbols," we evade the question of
their truth. The truth of symbols is determined
by the degree to which they (or reflections
which follow their lead) illuminate human existence and reveal "the bond between man and the

sacred." When assessing these remarks it is
important to remember that the book as a whole
is intended to provide an example of the way
in which a philosophical reflection upon symbols
can deepen our understanding of our own existence and its relation to being.

1020   Rowe, William Leonard. Religious Symbols and God,
       A Philosophical Study of Tillich's Theology.
       Chicago and London: The University of Chicago
       Press, 1968. Pp. 97-242.

(1) Tillich (#s 1022-1028) has argued that symbols differ from signs in that they (a) participate in that to which they point, (b) open
up levels of reality and dimensions of the soul
which are otherwise closed to us, and (c) cannot
be produced or replaced intentionally but are
born, grow and die. Rowe argues that (a) is
never satisfactorally explained. Symbols (e.g.,
a flag) are not always similar to what they
symbolize. Tillich does assert that the attitudes which are appropriate to a symbol are similar to the attitudes which are appropriate to
that which it symbolizes, but this does not
really help for it is also true of some signs.
(E.g., a fire alarm may appropriately evoke
reactions which are similar to the reactions
evoked by the fire to which it points.) Furthermore, because Tillich believes that participation
accounts for the fact that the attitudes which
are appropriate to the symbolizandum are also
appropriate to the symbol, he cannot use that
fact to explicate the concept of participation.
Finally, Tillich uses "participation" so broadly
that (in the absence of further information)
"symbols participate in that to which they point"

tells us no more than that symbols are related
to that to which they point. (b) is not clearly
true of some symbols (e.g., the flag). Rowe
suggests that (c), when suitably qualified,
can be used to distinguish symbols from signs.
(2) Tillich appears to provide two criteria
for differentiating religious from non-religious
symbols: (a) Religious symbols point to Being-
itself and (b) are the foci of ultimate concern.
Rowe argues (against Alston, # 994 above) that
x can symbolize y for A even though A does "not
know and, hence, cannot specify" that x symbolizes y for him. (A child's doll, e.g., can
symbolize its mother even though the child is
unaware that it does so.) In practice, Tillich
uses the second criterion to pick out religious
from non-religious symbols. (That religious
symbols point to Being-itself is fundamentally
an ontological thesis introduced to explain
the fact that religious symbols are foci of
ultimate concern.) (3) Rowe maintains that even
though Tillich's ontological translations of
religious utterances are symbolic (which Tillich
recognizes), his procedure is not clearly vicious
because ontological symbols are not religious
symbols. Rowe also provides reasons for rejecting the claim that symbolic utterances are devoid
of cognitive meaning if their (alleged) cognitive
content cannot be expressed in literal terms.
(These utterances can be cognitively meaningful
if what they describe is directly accessible.)
Ontological (but symbolic) translations of religious symbols have a point if they are less
symbolic than the symbols which they translate
and/or if they are better suited to "arrive at
a conceptual grasp of the nature of ultimate

reality." (Unfortunately, Rowe does not explain how one symbol can be less symbolic than another, or better suited to theoretical purposes.) (4) False religious symbols are idolatrous religious symbols. Rowe points out that an idolatrous symbol is not a symbol which fails to manifest the holy because all religious symbols manifest the holy. A symbol becomes idolatrous when the holiness which it manifests is regarded as inherent in the symbol itself, and not as transcending the vehicle through which it discloses itself. This is by far the best treatment of Tillich's theory of symbols. It is also illuminating in its own right. (Chapter IV incorporates "Tillich's Theory of Signs and Symbols," The Monist, 50 [October, 1966], pp. 593-610.

1021   Sebba, Gregor. "Symbol and Myth in Modern Ration-
       alistic Societies," Truth, Myth, and Symbol.
       Edited by Thomas J. J. Altizer, William A. Beard-
       slee, and J. Harvey Young. Englewood Cliffs,
       N. J.: Prentice-Hall, Inc., 1962. Pp. 141-68.

An interesting study of social and political myths in modern society. This material is of value because it raises the following questions: (1) Precisely how are these myths and symbols to be distinguished from religious myths and symbols? (2) Political and social myths are non-rational and sometimes even irrational. Are religious myths also non-rational or irrational? If they are not non-rational or irrational, what accounts for the difference? (Is it perhaps the fact that the latter do not [as frequently] distort historical facts and express wrong values? Is it the fact that although there is no supra-empirical dimension to society

and its leaders, there is a supra-empirical
dimension to the world and to the saints? Or
does something else account for the difference?)

1022 Tillich, Paul Johannes Oskar. The Dynamics of
      Faith. (World Perspectives Series, 10.) New
      York: Harper and Brothers, Publishers, 1956
      [^c1957]. Pp. 41-54.

      A brief but influential statement of Tillich's
      theory of religious symbols. Most of the ma-
      terial contained in this chapter is discussed
      at more length in "Religious Symbols and Our
      Knowledge of God," # 1025 below.

1023 _____. "The Meaning and Justification of
      Religious Symbols," Religious Experience and
      Truth, A Symposium. Edited by Sidney Hook.
      New York: New York University Press, 1961.
      Pp. 3-11.

      This is Tillich's last important essay on re-
      ligious symbolism. (1) Tillich returns to the
      notion that symbols can have both an integrating
      and disintegrating effect on those who use them.
      (Tillich does not suggest that this should be
      employed as a truth criterion but his failure
      to do so is surprising in view of remarks he
      makes in other contexts [e.g., in Systematic
      Theology, vol. I, p. 105].) (2) The referent
      of religious symbols must be identified non-
      symbolically. There are two ways of doing this.
      The "phenomenological approach" identifies the
      referent of religious symbols as the Holy. The
      "ontological approach" identifies the referent
      of religious symbols as Being-itself. "Being-
      itself" acquires its meaning in the context of
      an analysis of finitude which discloses its

self-transcendence. ("Being-itself [or "the
Power of being," or "ultimate reality," or "ultimate concern"] is the name given to that to
which this analysis leads.) As a matter of
fact there appears to be another way of non-
symbolically identifying the referent although
Tillich does not appeal to it, viz., "ostension,"
for Tillich believes that each of us is immediately though non-reflectively aware of Being-
itself. (3) The criteria of religious symbols
are (a) "their adequacy to the religious experience they express" (their "authenticity"), (b)
their "self-negation and transparency to" their
referent (they must be non-idolatrous), and
(c) "the quality of their symbolic material."
(E.g., persons provide better symbols than stones
because persons include more "dimensions of
reality" than stones, and therefore, more fully
reflect or mirror that which encompasses all
aspects of reality, viz., Being-itself.)

1024 _____. "The Religious Symbol," J Liberal
Relig, II (Summer, 1940), 13-33.

Symbols are (1) "figurative," and (2) "perceptible" (either to the senses or to the imagination). (3) They possess "innate power." Signs
are conventional and can be replaced by other
signs which serve the same functions. Symbols
cannot be replaced by other symbols without a
loss of power and meaning. (4) Symbols are
"socially rooted and socially supported." Religious symbols (e.g., God or a Supreme Being)
represent the "Unconditioned," "what concerns
us ultimately." Although symbols do not provide
objective knowledge, genuine symbols do provide
"a true awareness." The criterion of the truth

of a symbol "cannot be a comparison of it with the reality to which it refers just because this reality is absolutely beyond human comprehension." (However, doesn't Tillich implicitly appeal to just such a comparison? According to Tillich, each of us is preflectively aware of the Unconditioned [see, e.g., # 297 above]. In the last analysis, it would appear to be this awareness which enables us to assess the adequacy of religious symbols.) A symbol's truth "depends on its inner necessity for the symbol-creating consciousness." Again, (and this is hardly the same thing) the only criterion of its truth is "that the Unconditioned is clearly grasped in its unconditionedness," i.e., a symbol which "elevates a conditioned thing to the dignity of the Unconditioned, even if it should not be false, is demonic." (What Tillich appears to be driving at is that religious symbols are better or truer when they more clearly express the Transcendent. What is needed are criteria for determining when a symbol clearly expresses the Transcendent.) This essay is a translation (by James Luther Adams with the assistance of Ernst Fraenkel) of a paper which first appeared in Blätter Für deutsche Philosophie, I (1928), and was reprinted in the Religiöse Verwirklichung (Berlin: Furche Verlag, 1930). It was later published in a slightly revised form in Daedalus (LXXXVII [Summer, 1958], pp. 3-21), reprinted in Symbolism in Religion and Literature, edited by Rollo May (New York: George Braziller, Inc., 1960, pp. 75-98), and published as an appendix in Religious Experience and Truth, edited by Sidney Hook (New York: New York University Press, 1961, pp. 301-21).

The publishing history of this essay attests to
the importance which Tillich attached to it.

1025 _____ . "Religious Symbols and Our Knowledge
of God," Christian Schol, XXXVIII (September,
1955), 189-97.

(1) Symbols, unlike signs, participate "in the
reality or power of that to which they point."
(Thus, because the flag participates in the
power of the nation which it symbolizes, one's
behavior towards the flag is determined by one's
attitude towards the nation.) (2) Symbols open
up levels of reality which cannot be opened up
in other ways (e.g., what a landscape of Rubens
mediates cannot be mediated except by means
of that landscape), and in opening up levels
of reality new "levels of the soul" are opened
up as well. (3) Because they possess these
characteristics, symbols cannot be replaced.
Symbols (unlike signs) are not "consciously
invented." They are born out of the womb of
what "is usually called today 'the group un-
consciousness'," and they die when the "inner
situation" of the group changes. (4) Religious
symbols unlock "the depth dimension of reality
itself," "the dimension of ultimate reality
[which] is the dimension of the Holy." (5)
Because religious symbols participate in that
to which they point (the Holy), "they always
have the tendency . . . to replace that to which
they are supposed to point, and to become ultimate in themselves," (i.e., they have the tendency to become idolatrous). (6) In discussing
the truth of religious symbols, Tillich asserts
that: (a) they are immune to empirical criticism ("the negative statement"). (b) They are

670

true in so far as they "are adequate to the
religious situation in which they are created"
("the positive statement"). Thus, the symbol
of Mary loses its power when Protestantism rejects a mediated relationship to God and "the
ascetic element . . . implied in the glorifica-
tion of virginity." (Does Tillich think that
the symbol of Mary is false because the Protestant rejection of these notions is justified,
or does he think that the symbol of Mary is
false for Protestants [whatever exactly that
means] because they reject these notions?)
(c) No symbol should "elevate itself to ultimate validity," i.e., become an idol ("the absolute statement"). This essay is reprinted
under the title "The Nature of Religious Language" in Tillich's Theology of Culture, edited
by Robert C. Kimbell (New York: Oxford University Press, 1959), pp. 53-67.

1026   _____. Systematic Theology. Vol. I. Chica-
        go: The University of Chicago Press, 1951.
        Pp. 238-41.

In the course of this brief discussion, Tillich
makes several important claims: (1) "God is
Being-itself" is the only non-symbolic statement
which can be made about God. (However, as a
matter of fact, there are other statements about
God which Tillich appears to regard as non-
symbolic, viz., "God can only be described symbolically," "God is the Unconditioned," "God is
the object of ultimate concern," and "God is the
Holy.") (2) Segments of finite reality can
symbolize Being-itself because finite reality
participates in Being-itself. (His theory of
religious language, therefore, presupposes the

671

truth of certain ontological claims.) (3) Symbols "have truth" if they adequately express
a revelation. They "are true" if they adequately
express a true revelation. (Tillich's inability
to provide fully satisfactory criteria of truth
is, perhaps, his major failing.)

1027 _____. Systematic Theology. Vol. II. Existence and the Christ. Chicago: The University
of Chicago Press, 1957. Pp. 8-10.

Tillich concedes that in order to avoid "a circle" (in order to avoid being placed in a position where one can only explain symbols by other
symbols?) one needs at least one non-symbolic
statement, and asserts that this statement is
"Everything we say about God is symbolic."

1028 _____. "Theology and Symbolism," Religious
Symbolism. Edited by F. Ernest Johnson. New
York: Institute for Religious and Social Stud-
ies, distributed by Harper and Brothers, 1955;
Port Washington, N. Y.: Kennikat Press, 1969.
Pp. 107-16.

As a whole, this essay adds little to what Tillich has said elsewhere. His remarks on p. 113
do, however, suggest three criteria for the truth
of religious symbols: (1) They are not true
if they are interpreted literally, (2) they
must be "more nearly adequate than others to
the encounter which expresses itself in" them,
and (3) they must cohere with other symbols
in "the system to which they belong." Good
critical discussions of Tillich's theory of
symbolism are provided by Ford (# 1003 above)
and (especially) Alston and Rowe (#s 994 and 1020
above). Also see McLean (# 1007 above).

1029 Urban, Wilbur Marshall. Language and Reality,
      The Philosophy of Language and the Principles
      of Symbolism. (The Muirhead Library of Philo-
      sophy.) London: George Allen and Unwin; Ltd.;
      New York: The Macmillan Company, 1939. Pp.
      401-729.

Symbols employ sensuous and intuitive material
to express "more universal and ideal relations."
Urban distinguishes between "symbolic truth"
and "the truth of a symbol." The latter can
only be determined by examining the truth of
the (relatively) non-symbolic propositions which
explicate or translate a symbol. The former
refers to the adequacy with which a symbol expresses its referent "for our type of consciousness." Religious symbols are essentially metaphysical symbols. They differ from metaphysical
symbols only in so far as they are "more concrete, richer in colour and more toned with
emotion." As in the case of other metaphysical
symbols, "perceptible" material is "distorted"
or "moulded" in order to "represent the intelligible" or "noumenal." The referent of religious symbols is the "infinitely holy" which is
"the metempirical . . . co-implicate of moral
values." Because religious symbols are implicitly metaphysical they can be "interpreted"
by a set of metaphysical statements whose import
is roughly "that values have a cosmic significance, that value and reality are inseparable."
Metaphysical statements are themselves symbolic.
The subject of a metaphysical statement is always a metempirical reality (e.g., "spirit,"
absolute, principle) and/or the whole of reality.
The predicates of metaphysical statements (e.g.,
"will," "participate," "enter into") are "taken
from various empirical domains." Since these

predicates are to be applied to the metempirical, they must be "despatialized" and "detemporalized." Since they are to be applied to the whole of reality they "must be taken from the most pervasive and fundamental [i.e., irreducible] aspects of experience." Since reality as a whole contains both being and value these predicates must be "value charged." The subjects of metaphysical discourse are not objects of experience but are given "'with' or 'within' experience." They are "implicit" in experience or "co-implicates" of experience, "suppositions . . . which must be acknowledged if communication and intelligible discourse are to be possible." The direct apprehension of these co-implicates is non-symbolic but as soon as we try to express them "symbolization begins." Metaphysical statements can only succeed in making things intelligible if they are consistent, if they cohere with one another and with experience as a whole, and if the basic symbolic predicates are drawn from domains of experience which are intrinsically intelligible. (Urban argues that this implies that these predicates must be drawn from the sphere of conscious activity.) Ultimately, that metaphysical system is true which is "intrinsically significant and meaningful," "selfauthenticatingly rational." In spite of its weaknesses, this is one of the few attempts to seriously and carefully think through the problem of symbolic language.

VIII   THE JUSTIFICATION OF RELIGIOUS BELIEF

Miscellaneous Studies

Note: All of the entries in sections II and III ("Ar-
        guments for the Existence of God" and "The
        Problem of Evil") are relevant to this question.
        Entries in section IV which discuss the validity
        of religious experience are also relevant as
        are many of the entries in section VI ("Faith
        and Revelation"), especially #s 792, 793, 794,
        810, 825 and 853. See also #s 768, 900, 902,
        906, 907, 913, 914, 921, 922, 932, 934, 941,
        953, 959, 960, 996.and 1029.

1030   Adams, Robert Merrihew. "Kierkegaard's Arguments
       Against Objective Reasoning in Religion," Monist,
       60 (April, 1977), 228-43.

       Adams finds three arguments in Kierkegaard which
       are designed to show that it is "useless or
       undesirable to reason objectively in support of"
       religious faith. (1) The "Approximation Argu-
       ment": Objective historical inquiry can never
       lead to complete certainty. Since religious
       faith is infinitely interested in its object,
       "no possibility of error is too small to be
       worth worrying about." Therefore, objective
       historical reasoning cannot justify religious
       commitment. Adams maintains that even though
       the argument may establish that (given the re-
       ligious believer's infinite interest) any possi-
       bility of error is worth worrying about, it
       does not show that it is unreasonable to base
       an infinite commitment upon objective probabili-
       ties when those probabilities are sufficiently
       high. (2) The "Postponement Argument": Since
       "objective empirical inquiry is never completely
       finished," one cannot be totally committed to
       any belief which is based upon it. Authentic

675

religious faith involves total commitment.
It cannot, therefore, be based upon objective
empirical inquiry. Adams suggests that the notion of religious commitment which is employed
in this argument is inadequate both because the
object of religious devotion is God, not a belief, and because devotion to God is conditional
(since it is "based on His goodness and love").
(3) The "Passion Argument": Religious faith
involves infinite passion. "Infinite passion
requires objective improbability." Therefore,
religious faith requires objective improbability.
The second premiss appears to rest upon the
assumption (a) that an infinite "interest in x
is an interest so strong that it leads one to
make the greatest possible sacrifices in order
to attain x, on the smallest possible chance
of success," and upon the assumption (b) that
the intensity and value of religious belief is
measured by its costliness. (Improbable beliefs
are costly because of the "anxiety and mental
suffering" which are involved in their acceptance.) Adams suggests that while "some degree
of cost and risk may add to the value of religious life," it is unreasonable to suppose that
it is desirable to increase this cost and risk
without limit. He concludes by arguing that
anyone with Kierkegaard's passionate concern
for Christianity could employ a version of Pascal's Wager to objectively justify his (practical
or prudential) choice of Christianity.

1031 Agassi, Joseph, Ian C. Jarvie and Tom Settle.
      "The Grounds of Reason," Philosophy, XLVI (Jan-
      uary, 1971), 43-50.

      Watkins (# 1083 below) has argued that Bartley's

theory of rationality (# 1037 below) is immune
to criticism since any effective criticism of
it will establish its criticizability and thus
show that it is rational by its own standards.
According to the authors, Watkins has overlooked
the fact that criticizability is a necessary
but not a sufficient condition of a belief's
being held rationally. Since criticizability
is not a sufficient condition of a belief's
being held rationally, there is no reason to
think that a refutation of Bartley's theory will
(by demonstrating its criticizability) establish
it. The authors maintain that Bartley's theory
would be refuted if any one of the critical
standards which it presupposes could be shown
to be uncriticizable (even though this refutation
would establish "the criticizability of the program as a whole"). See Watkins' reply (# 1082
below).

1032 Allen, Diogenes. "Motives, Rationales, and Reli-
      gious Beliefs," Amer Phil Quart, 3 (April, 1966),
      111-27.

Allen distinguishes biographical accounts which
describe how one came to believe and how that
belief fulfills one's needs ("motives") from
reasons which show, or tend to show, that what
one believes is true ("rationales"). It is
argued that in the absence of "specific reasons
which count decisively against the truth" of
what one believes, motives provide an adequate
rational basis for belief. "Arguments, distinctions, and counter-evidence" may be "given to
rebut challenges" to belief, thus enabling one
to continue to believe, without themselves providing the grounds or basis for one's belief.

Allen argues that only some motives can be a
ground for belief (and not merely a source of
belief). If a motive is to provide a ground
for belief there must be a relevant connection
between the satisfaction of one's needs and the
truth of what is believed. (Thus, a bird-
watcher may pronounce a picture of birds to be
good because of its subject matter, but there
is no relevant connection between his needs
and the goodness of the picture. By contrast,
there is a relevant connection between a need
for cleansing and the truth of the claim that
God is a redeemer.) Evil presents one of the
most significant challenges to theistic belief.
A theodicy provides a rebuttal to this challenge.
A successful theodicy must show that the existence of God and the existence of evil are compatible and it must also provide partial explanations of the evils that exist. These partial
explanations are sufficient if God can be shown
to exist, or if theism can be shown to have
the best explanation of evil, or if they enable
a person to maintain his religious commitment.
Possible explanations may be sufficient to enable
one to maintain a religious commitment if they
are extensions of one's religious beliefs and
are not too obviously fanciful.

1033 _____. The Reasonableness of Faith, A Philosophical Essay on the Grounds for Religious
Beliefs. Foreword by Gene Fontinell. Washington, D.C. and Cleveland, Ohio: Corpus Books,
1968. xx + 140 pp.

In Part I, Allen examines Christianity's relation
to metaphysics. According to Allen, "Christianity can be primarily regarded as a medium
of God's salvation, or one can emphasize the

678

explanatory power of Christian concepts." The
first view recommends Christianity because it
"satisfies our need to have our own personal
lives healed and saved." The second view recommends Christianity because it explains things
"in a superior fashion to other world views."
It is said to follow that "although neither of
these views denies the presence within Christianity of what the other emphasizes, the center
of gravity of each is so different that the
question concerning our ability to decide between
rival metaphysical views is highly relevant for
the latter and of no relevance whatever for the
former." Allen maintains that world views should
be judged in terms of whether they are inadequate to or distort the phenomena which they
are supposed to explain (e.g., persons), their
consistency, their comprehensiveness (they must
be applicable to "the various ranges of our
knowledge and experience"), and whether there are
any facts which they ignore. He argues that
in order to show that Christianity is superior
to other world views, one must show that Christianity takes account of a fact which rival
world views ignore, viz., deity. (To make this
out, according to Allen, one would have to establish God's existence by "a demonstration or by
an apprehension," or show that there are "cosmic
disclosures" [Ramsey] which can best be explained
by God, or show that the "question of being"
is a legitimate question which can best be answered by appealing to deity.) Part II defends
the reasonableness of faith. In chapter 4, Allen
argues that religious beliefs not only satisfy
needs which belong to man as man but also satisfy
"a distinctive range of fears, hopes, and

aspirations [e.g., fear of God's judgment or hope in His mercy] which arise only with a hearing of the gospel." (Without the latter, there would be considerable "force in the view that religious beliefs are psychological projections." However, since religious belief creates these distinctive needs, it cannot be regarded as a mere product of our needs.) These needs can be partly met by religious belief as such, but can only be fully met if these beliefs are true. In chapter 6, Allen argues that in order to awaken the desire to appreciate music in a person who is as yet unable to do so, we must appeal to wants, needs and discomforts which he now has. Once he has become the sort of person who appreciates music, he will justify his delight in music by referring to the fact that he is the kind of person who likes music and would not wish to be the sort of person he was before. Both the initial appeal and the "convert's" response to the request for justification are reasonable. They are also relevantly similar to phenomena which occur in the process of becoming a religious person. Chapters 5 and 7 incorporate the author's "Motives, Rationales and Religious Beliefs" (# 1032 above). Allen's argument is important and deserves much more attention than it has received.

1034   Alston, William P. "Psychoanalytic Theory and Theistic Belief," Faith and the Philosophers. Edited by John Hick. New York: St. Martin's Press, Inc., 1964. Pp. 63-102.

After developing and criticizing a Freudian theory of the origin of religious belief, Alston proceeds to examine the following two questions:

(1) Would an adequate account of theistic belief in terms of "reason-irrelevant natural
causes" show that theistic belief is unacceptable? (2) Would an adequate account of theistic
belief in terms of "the particular sort of natural causes specified in the psychoanalytic
explanation" show that theistic belief is unacceptable? Alston argues that there are no conclusive reasons for believing either that God
will not produce theistic beliefs by means of
natural causes, or that God will not produce
theistic beliefs by means of reason-irrelevant
natural causes. The existence of an adequate
natural explanation would, however, undermine
any argument from the idea of God to God (cf.
Descartes' third Meditation). It would also
undermine claims to be sure of God's existence
because one has directly experienced Him. (For
a fuller discussion of this point, see Alston
and Wainwright, #s 568 and 726 above.) If an
account of theistic belief cited reason-irrelevant conditions which were both sufficient and
necessary for theistic belief, then adequate
reasons for theistic belief could not be given.
(If adequate reasons could be given, "the grasp
of them by a rational man would itself be a sufficient condition of" theistic belief and, hence,
the reason-irrelevant conditions would not be
necessary after all.) However, in order to show
that a set of reason-irrelevant conditions was
necessary, one would have to show that good
reasons cannot be given for theistic belief.
The irrationality of theistic belief is, therefore, a presupposition of an account of this
type rather than a conclusion which follows
from it. If reason-irrelevant causes were

sufficient to produce theistic belief and if
most theistic beliefs were produced by them,
then it would be necessary to carefully scru-
tinize the grounds of one's own belief. Nevertheless, if, after conducting this examination,
one still found those grounds adequate, there
is no reason why one should abandon one's belief or judge it to be irrational. Alston concludes with some intelligent reflections on the
charge that religious belief is infantile or
neurotic.

1035   Austin, William Harvey. The Relevance of Natural
       Science to Theology. (Library of Philosophy
       and Theology.) London and Basingstoke: The
       Macmillan Press, Ltd., 1976. ix + 132 pp.

This book examines "the main types of argument
which might be offered in support of the proposition that science has no bearing on theology." These arguments "fall into two major
classes." (1) Science and theology are irrelevant if either an instrumentalist view of
science or an instrumentalist view of religion
is correct. (2) Science and religion are irrelevant if science and religion are concerned
with different realms or dimensions of reality.
Arguments of the first type are considered in
chapters 2 and 3. Austin attempts to show that
"the standard arguments against instrumentalism
are not conclusive against Duhem's version of
it," but that if Duhem's theory is correct,
metaphysics and theology must take account of
regularities among observed phenomena and (since
metaphysics is concerned with the real nature
of things and since the order among the mathematical signs of physics must be isomorphic with

the real order of things) physics has an indirect
bearing on metaphysics and theology. More extreme versions of instrumentalism cannot be
justified by appealing to the practice of science but instead must be justified by appealing
to rather dubious philosophical theories (e.g.,
the theory that we can only know sentences re-
porting sensations). For Austin's discussion
of Braithwaite see # 899 above. Arguments of
the second type are considered in chapters 4
and 5. If God sustains and governs all things,
then there is a prima facie objection to any
theory which distinguishes two realms (e.g.,
nature and spirit) and argues that science is
(only) concerned with one of these realms while
religion is (only) concerned with the other.
It is sometimes suggested that religion and
science deal with different dimensions or aspects of reality rather than with different
classes of things. Karl Heim is one of the
few theologians who has explored this possibility
at length. (See especially his Christian Faith
and Natural Science, London: SCM Press; New
York: Harper, 1953.) Austin maintains that
a careful examination of his work reveals that
it is unclear whether or in what way science is
supposed to be relevant to religion, and that
his doctrine of different "spaces" (dimensions)
"is so obscurely, inexplicitly, and incoherently
stated that its implications cannot be determined." Austin then considers the possibility
that the concept of different dimensions can
be explicated with the help of D. M. MacKay's
notion of complementarity. Descriptions are
complementary if they provide complete (in principle) descriptions of the same situation from

683

mutually exclusive viewpoints. A number of
problems beset any attempt to apply this notion
to theological and scientific statements. E.g.,
consider a theological and a scientific description of the Exodus events. If the two descriptions are genuinely complementary, they articulate different aspects of (patterns or relations in) a common set of components (events
or entities). If the components differ, the
situations differ. Scientific descriptions
do not take account of God. Therefore, either
God is merely an aspect or pattern or relationship (which is highly unorthodox) or (if God is
a component) the scientific description and
the theological description are not genuinely
complementary. (The scientific description
is either incomplete because it ignores a component which is part of the situation which
both statements describe, or the two descriptions
describe different sets of components and thus
different situations.) What Austin calls "linguistic arguments" attempt to show that the
logical preconditions of science and religion
differ in such a way that one can have no bearing
on the other. Austin considers the notion that
religion and science are logically independent
language games, and the notion that religious
language "can only be properly used on the basis
of personal commitment, whereas scientific language requires objectivity and detachment."
The fact that controversies between science and
religion have been a feature of religious life
for several hundred years constitutes a prima
facie objection to the first thesis. Austin
shows that self-involving utterances (cf. Evans
919 above and # 1044 below) can have factual

684

(and, therefore, presumably scientific) implications, that some religious sentences are not
self-involving while some scientific statements
are self-involving, etc. Austin concludes (chapter 6) with a brief discussion of the ways in
which science can bear upon the doctrine of providence. On the whole, this book is well-argued.
It is important because of the enormous popular-
ity of the thesis against which the author's
arguments are directed.

1036 Barbour, Ian G. Myths, Models and Paradigms, A
      Comparative Study in Science and Religion.
      Toronto: Fitzhenry & Whiteside, Ltd.; New York,
      Evanston, San Francisco, London: Harper and
      Row, Publishers, 1974. vii + 198 pp.

A theoretical model in science (e.g., the bil-
liard ball model of gases) "is an imagined
mechanism or process postulated by analogy with
familiar mechanisms or processes and used to
construct a theory to correlate a set of observations." Barbour argues that theoretical models
are neither literal pictures of reality nor mere
"useful fictions" but rather attempts to symbolically represent aspects of the world which
are not directly accessible to us. Religious
models (e.g., God as a loving father) are used
to interpret "distinctive kinds of experience
such as awe and reverence, mystical joy, moral
obligation, reorientation and reconciliation,
and key historical events." They are articulated
by more or less systematically developed sets
of religious beliefs. Like scientific models,
religious models are analogical and can be extended to interpret areas of experience which
were not envisaged when the model was originally

685

constructed. Like scientific models, religious
models are neither "useful fictions" nor literal
pictures of reality. Religious models differ
from scientific models in three respects. They
"serve non-cognitive [as well as cognitive]
functions," they "elicit more total personal
involvement," and they are more important then
the theories which articulate them. A "paradigm," or "research tradition," or "research
programme" (e.g., Newtonian physics) is a scientific tradition transmitted through historical
exemplars which initiates students into certain
methods of formulating and handling scientific
problems. Barbour argues that although it is
true that the data against which theories are
tested are theory-laden, not even the most comprehensive theories are completely incommensurable, that while "comprehensive theories are
highly resistant to falsification . . . observation does exert some control over them," that
a tenacious commitment to a research tradition is
scientifically fruitful (for it allows its possibilities to be thoroughly explored), and that
while there are no rules which can be mechani-
cally applied to decide between research pro-
grammes there are criteria of assessment (simplicity, coherence, adequacy to data, fruitfulness,
comprehensiveness) which are independent of any
particular programme. Religious traditions
(e.g., Christianity or Buddhism) are significantly similar to scientific paradigms. Interpretation exerts more influence on the data in
religion than in science. Religious paradigms
are more resistant to falsification than scientific paradigms, and the criteria for the assessment of religious paradigms are not as fully

independent of the paradigms themselves. Nevertheless, these differences are differences of
degree. -- Barbour has succeeded in showing
that, given certain rather plausible views concerning the role of theoretical models in science
(e.g., those of Mary Hesse) and the nature of
scientific paradigms (e.g., those of Thomas
Kuhn), there are interesting parallels between
religious imagery and scientific models, and
between religious traditions and scientific
paradigms. As such, this book makes a significant contribution to the epistemology of religion. Its major weakness is its failure to
explore religious models and paradigms with the
same care with which it explores scientific
models and paradigms. (What, e.g., is the precise relation between religious models and religious theory? How does one control the other?
How are criteria of assessment employed to decide between religious paradigms? A detailed
analysis of particular examples would help to
answer these questions, but Barbour does not
provide it.)

1037   Bartley, William Warren, III. The Retreat to Com-
        mitment. Toronto: Random House, Inc.; New York:
        Alfred A. Knopf, 1962. xvi + 223 + iv pp.

While the entire book is interesting, the heart
of Bartley's argument is to be found in chapters
IV and V (pp. 88-175). The appeal to commitment
is the ultimate appeal of contemporary Protestant
theologians (Barth, Brunner, Reinhold and Richard
Niebuhr, Tillich, etc.). In the last analysis
the only defense which these theologians offer
for their commitment is that commitment of some
kind is inevitable; even the rationalist who

criticizes Christian commitment is (they say)
forced to acknowledge certain principles for
which he can provide no adequate support.
(Bartley calls this the "tu quoque" argument.)
Bartley argues that there are two quite different
models of rationality. On the first model,
rationality consists in holding only those beliefs which can be proved. On the second model,
rationality consists in subjecting one's beliefs
to criticism, and in being prepared to abandon
them whenever their rejection is warranted by
criticism. Rationalists who adopt the first
model are subject to the tu quoque argument.
(Proofs cannot go on forever. One must, therefore, finally come to an unproved assumption
of some sort.) The second model excludes any
kind of unconditional commitment. Rationalists
who adopt it are not subject to the tu quoque
argument for they are even prepared to abandon
their model of rationality if it can be shown
to be inadequate. Bartley concludes this section
of his book by arguing that Protestant theology
fails to survive criticism because it tolerates
contradictions. (Although Bartley says this,
he does not seriously try to show it.) See
the critical discussion of Agassi, Jarvie and
Settle (# 1031 above), and the discussions of
Hudson, Martin and Watkins (#s 1056, 1064, 1082
and 1083 below).

1038 Broad, Charlie Dunbar. "Butler as a Theologian,"
      Hibb J, XXI (July, 1923), 637-56. (Reprinted
      in Religion, Philosophy and Psychical Research,
      Selected Essays by C. D. Broad. [International
      Library of Psychology, Philosophy and Scientific
      Method.] London: Routledge & Kegan Paul, Ltd.,
      1953. Pp. 202-19.)

An astute examination of the analogical arguments
which Butler employs in The Analogy of Religion.
Cf. Grave and Jeffner, #s 1052 and 1058 below.

1039   Butler, Ronald J. "Natural Belief and the Enigma
       of Hume," Arch Gesch Phil, 42 (1960), 73-100.

       A natural belief for Hume is a belief which is
       non-rational (cannot be supported by a priori
       or a posteriori arguments), has a certain degree
       of force, and is unavoidable. Examples of such
       beliefs are our belief in the uniformity of
       nature and our belief in an external world.
       While these beliefs cannot be supported by rea-
       son, skeptical attacks upon them fail to produce
       conviction, and one should not be faulted for
       holding them. Butler argues that Hume thinks
       that belief in a designer is a natural belief.
       Cf. Gaskin (# 1049 below).

1040   Clarke, W. Norris. "A Further Critique of Mac-
       Intyre's Thesis," Faith and the Philosophers.
       Edited by John Hick. New York: St. Martin's
       Press, Inc., 1964. Pp. 147-50.

       A reply to # 1062 below. Clarke argues that
       the fact that "a given social context may make
       it harder to believe" does not show that what
       is believed is either false or irrational, that
       MacIntyre exaggerates Christianity's dependence
       upon a particular cultural and social context,
       and that he does not adequately account for the
       fact that many contemporary Christians accept
       the canons of modern scholarship and scientific
       investigation. He concludes by pointing out
       that MacIntyre has failed to provide any "sample
       analyses of basic Christian doctrines which

are dependent for their intelligibility and
relevance upon a social context that has now
passed away." (This note is a sequel to a rather
uninteresting reply reprinted on pp. 134-47 of
the same volume.)

1041   Collingwood, Robin George. An Essay on Metaphy-
       sics. Oxford: Clarendon Press, 1940. Pp.
       3-77 and 185-227.

The aim of metaphysical analysis is to detect
absolute presuppositions, where an "absolute
presupposition is one which stands, relatively
to all questions to which it is related, as a
presupposition, never as an answer." Absolute
presuppositions are not verifiable, and "the
distinction between truth and falsehood does
not apply" to them. Since metaphysical inquiry
is an inquiry into what absolute presuppositions
are "made by this or that person or group of
persons, on this or that occasion or group of
occasions, in the course of this or that piece
of thinking," metaphysics is a historical science. E.g., God is said to be an absolute presupposition "of all thinking done by Christians,
among other kinds of thinking, that belonging
to natural science." (Collingwood explores the
connection between belief in God and the pursuit
of natural science, contending, roughly, that
Christian monotheism is a way of expressing such
things as the unity and independence of nature,
and that these are among the absolute presuppositions of natural science.)

1042   Dilley, Frank Brown, Jr. Metaphysics and Religious
       Language. New York and London: Columbia Univer-
       sity Press, 1964. 173 pp.

According to Dilley: (1) Religious language
is metaphysical language. (2) Although they
are subject to rational adjudication, metaphysical questions are neither logical questions
nor straightforward factual questions. Metaphysicians do not usually make logical mistakes
nor do they ignore "plain facts." Instead, they
differ over the proper interpretation of these
facts, and disagree as to what should count as
real facts. (3) Metaphysical systems cannot
be proved because they describe the whole of
reality from selected points of view, because
they rest upon decisions concerning what experiences provide access to the real and what concepts or symbols provide keys to the whole, and
because they partly determine what counts as
rationality and what is considered to be a fact.
(4) Tests for the adequacy of a metaphysical
system include its consistency and freedom from
logical error, "the exactness of its 'fit' in
that field" from which its root metaphor or
basic concepts are taken, and the exactness of
its "fit" in other fields to which these concepts
and metaphors are extended. Special attention
must be paid to those things which (allegedly)
the theory explains but which other theories
do not satisfactorally account for. In order
to determine the truth of a metaphysical theory
we must also determine its implications and
presuppositions and compare it with alternative
theories. Dilley is aware of the inconclusive-
ness of these tests. It should be noted that
the tests proposed by other philosophers are
similar in character and equally imprecise.
Since it is plausible to suppose that (some)
religious statements are metaphysical statements,

it is important to determine whether the tests
for determining the truth or falsity of metaphysical assertions can be stated with enough precision to enable those who employ them to decide
between conflicting metaphysical assertions or
systems. Dilley's discussion of the criteria
for metaphysical truth should be compared with
the discussions of Ferré (#s 921 and 922 above
and # 1046 below), Knox, Mitchell, Owen, Pepper,
Tillich, Walsh, and Yandell (#s 1060, 1065, 1067,
1070, 1071, 1072, 1078, 1081, 1085 and 1086
below).

1043   Durrant, Michael. "Cumulative Arguments in Theo-
       logy," _Sophia_, XV (October, 1976), 1-6.

       Basil Mitchell (# 1065 below) has argued that
       the "cumulative" arguments in theology (cf.
       Newman's _Grammar_ _of_ _Assent_) are rational because
       cumulative arguments "are actually used in re-
       spectable disciplines," viz., history and liter-
       ary criticism. Durrant replies that the fact
       that cumulative arguments are legitimate in
       certain disciplines does not imply that cumu-
       lative arguments are legitimate in all disci-
       plines (e.g., mathematics), and that although
       it does make sense to say that an instance of
       an argument of a given type is rational, it
       makes no sense to say that a mode or type of
       argument is rational since there are no criteria
       in terms of which judgments of this kind can
       be made.

1044   Evans, Donald Dwight. "Differences Between Scien-
       tific and Religious Assertions," _Science_ _and_
       Religion. Edited by I. G. Barbour. London:
       SCM Press; New York: Harper and Row, 1968.
       Pp. 101-33.

Evans argues against the currently fashionable
contention that we are unable to draw sharp
logical distinctions between scientific and theological assertions. (1) Religious assertions
are self-involving, i.e., they logically commit
the speaker to certain actions or attitudes.
Scientific assertions are not self-involving.
(2) In order to understand scientific assertions
no more is required than intelligence and scientific training. In order to understand religious
assertions one must have had "depth experiences"
(e.g., numinous experiences, I-thou encounters,
moral experiences of various sorts, etc.).
(3) Scientific assertions are testable by observation. Religious assertions are based upon
depth experiences, and not upon observation.
Depth experiences are not intersubjective in
the way in which observations are intersubjective, nor do they provide a basis for prediction
and control. These theses are hardly original.
Nevertheless, Evans' defense of these theses is
worth examining both because he firmly grasps
the reasons which have led some philosophers
to blur the distinction between religion and
science, and because he appreciates the nuances
of scientific and religious language. See Austin's critique (# 1035 above, pp. 93-108).

1045   Felder, David W.   "Disanalogies in Plantinga's
       Argument Regarding the Rationality of Theism,"
       J Scien Stud Relig, 10 (Fall, 1971), 200-7.

Plantinga has argued (# 376 above) that a belief
in God which is based upon teleological evidence
is as rational as a belief in other minds which
is based upon the analogical argument. In spite
of some infelicities (e.g., his analysis of

693

"argument A strongly resembles argument B"),
Felder does make two important points. (1)
The theist who bases his belief upon the teleological evidence must come to terms with the
existence of evil. In this respect, the position
of the theist differs from the position of a
person who bases his belief in other minds upon
the analogical argument. Unlike the former,
the latter is not confronted with evidence which
counts against his conclusion. (Plantinga denies this, however. All cases in which I observe
a connection between pain and pain behavior are
cases in which the pain is my pain. According
to Plantinga, this fact provides a reason against
the assertion that others experience pain.)
(2) The logical gap between the teleological
evidence and a belief in a unique, omnipotent,
omniscient and perfectly good designer (as distinguished from the logical gap between the teleological evidence and a belief in one or more
finite designers) is greater than the logical
gap between the analogical evidence and a belief in other minds.

1046 Ferré, Frederick. "Metaphysics, Inquiry, and
        Christian Faith," Exploring the Logic of Faith,
        A Dialogue on the Relation of Modern Philosophy
        to Christian Faith by Kent Bendall and Frederick
        Ferré. New York: Association Press, 1962.
        Pp. 163-81.

Ferré argues that an acceptable metaphysical
system must be (1) consistent, (2) coherent,
and (3) applicable "to experience of some kind."
It must also be (4) adequate, i.e., it must
"render intelligible . . . all domains of human
feeling and perception," neither ignoring nor
distorting, nor falsifying any aspect of our

experience. Finally it must be (5) effective, i.e., it must be "capable of 'coming to life' for individuals . . . becoming . . . a usable instrument for coping with the total environment," i.e., it must have a "capacity for ringing true with respect to the interests and purposes of those who use it," enabling them "to cope successfully with the challenges of life." The Christian metaphysical scheme is derived from "'the Christian model' . . . a frankly anthropomorphic master image woven from the biblical images of nature, man, and God." Ferré briefly discusses the consequences of applying the five above mentioned criteria to the Christian metaphysical system. He concludes by observing that even though we should "maintain a tentative attitude toward all our metaphysical beliefs," it is possible that we should fully commit ourselves to the Christian way of life if the evidence even slightly favors it. Cf. Ferré, #s 921 and 922 above. See also # 1042 above and #s 1060, 1065, 1067, 1070, 1071, 1072, 1078, 1081, 1085 and 1086 below.

1047   _____. "The 'Quick Way' with the Worth of Theism," Int J Phil Relig, VII (1976), 327-45.

An exploration of "the connections between origins and worth in the domain of . . . beliefs." Ferré contends that Wald's argument (see # 1080 below) fails because it ignores the fact that beliefs in the sample class may be heterogeneous. A farmer may hold erroneous opinions about astronomy, zippers, and many other things. It would, however, be unreasonable to reject his opinion on mowing on the grounds that most of his beliefs are false. Similarly, a scientifically

ignorant and barbarous people may nevertheless
be religious geniuses. Until we have excluded
this possibility it is unreasonable to reject
their religious opinions on the grounds that
their opinions on other subjects are false or
unreasonable. Ferré concludes by suggesting that
an examination of the origins of religion may
help clarify its functions.

1048   Foster, Michael Beresford. Mystery and Philosophy.
       (The Library of Philosophy and Theology.) Lon-
       don: SCM Press, Ltd., 1957. 96 pp.

Foster adopts Gabriel Marcel's distinction between a problem and a mystery. Problems have
solutions although these solutions may never be
discovered. Mysteries are irreducible. They
cannot be dispelled by the acquisition of new
information, by the application of some tech-
nique, or in any other way. In Greek thought
the mystery was being which revealed itself
to the contemplative intellect. In the Bible
the mystery is a holy being who chooses to make
himself known, and who is acknowledged in re-
pentance. The experimental method by means of
which man puts the question to nature lies at
the heart of modern science, but is an inappropriate approach to mystery. So is analytic
philosophy which assumes that all questions can
be precisely formulated, and that whatever is
intelligible can be stated clearly. Foster's
discussion is lucid, suggestive, and supported
by well chosen examples and references. This is
an able presentation of a view which many find
attractive.

1049 Gaskin, John C. A. "God, Hume and Natural Belief,"
      Philosophy, 49 (July, 1974), 281-94.

      Hume thinks that there are "natural beliefs"
      (1) which belong to naive common sense, (2)
      for which there is no rational justification,
      (3) which must be believed if we are to act,
      and (4) which are universally held. These be-
      liefs are not irrational because no evidence
      "makes it more reasonable to adopt any alterna-
      tive set of beliefs," and because we cannot
      help but act as if they were true. Natural
      beliefs include our belief in an external world
      and our belief in the uniformity of nature.
      Butler (# 1039 above) and Hick (# 1054 below)
      have argued that belief in God or an intelligent
      designer should be included in the class of
      "natural beliefs," and that, therefore, belief
      in God is justified in spite of the fact that
      God's existence cannot be proved. Gaskin points
      out that belief in God is not a "natural belief"
      because it is not necessary to act as if it
      were true, and because it is not universally
      held.

1050 Gill, Jerry Henry. The Possibility of Religious
      Knowledge. Grand Rapids, Michigan: William
      B. Eerdmans Pub. Co., 1971. 238 pp.

      In Part I, Gill argues that modern philosophy
      and theology accept an "epistemological dualism
      based on a dichotomy between fact and value."
      Part II attempts to develop "a more adequate
      theory of knowledge" based upon the insights of
      Wittgenstein, Polanyi, and others. In this sec-
      tion, Gill makes the following points: (1)
      "Rather than conceive of reality and experience

as divided into separate realms, it is more
helpful . . . to conceive of them as having
simultaneously interpenetrating dimensions,"
viz., the physical, the moral (i.e., other persons), the personal (i.e., "that aspect of
experience in which we are aware of ourselves
as persons"), and the religious. These dimensions mediate one another. Thus, self-awareness
is mediated through our awareness of our own
body and our awareness of other persons. (But
how does the religious mediate the physical?)
(2) What one knows is a function of the context
within which knowing takes place. This context
includes such things as the intentions and purposes of the knower, his previous experience,
changes and developments in the object of knowledge, etc. (3) "Focal awareness" presupposes
"subsidiary awareness." (E.g., the reader is
focally aware of the meaning of these words and
subsidiarily aware of the words themselves.)
(4) Verbal (conceptual) activity typically involves some sort of bodily activity. Bodily
activity, on the other hand, expresses judgments.
(Cf., "He misjudged the speed of that pitch.")
There is thus no hard and fast distinction between "saying" (thinking) and "doing." (5)
The interaction between focal awareness and
(primarily) conceptual activity gives rise to
explicit knowledge. The interaction between
subsidiary awareness and the subject's "more
nonverbal bodily response gives rise to tacit
knowledge." (Gill's discussion of religious
knowledge suggests that emphasis should be placed
upon "nonverbal" rather than upon "bodily.")
Explicit knowledge arises against a background
of, and depends upon, tacit knowledge. According

to Gill, our knowledge of mediated dimensions of experience is primarily tacit. (Just why this should be the case is not clear. Prima facie, it is more plausible to suppose that we are tacitly aware of the medium than to suppose that we are tacitly aware of what is mediated through it. [Cf. the relation between sensa and physical objects, or the relation between sounds or marks and their meaning.]) (6) Knowledge is personal in the sense (a) that it "is always somebody's knowledge," (b) that it requires "the personal involvement of the knower" (the knower must perform whatever tasks are necessary to obtain the kind of knowledge he is seeking), and (c) it involves a commitment both to the conceptual framework within which the inquiry is being conducted and to the results obtained by inquiry. (7) Knowledge and truth are "functional." What counts as knowledge or truth varies from context to context and the criteria of truth and knowledge are determined by complex forms of life which cannot themselves be justified. "In contexts where the physical dimension predominates," precision and explicit verifiability are "possible and necessary." In contexts where the moral and personal dimensions predominate, "criteria for truth are primarily tacit." Neither they nor the "imponderable evidence" upon which judgments in these areas are based can be made fully explicit. (How convincing is this? Compare a farmer's prediction of the weather and a jury's determination of guilt. It isn't clear that the farmer's reasoning can be made fully explicit [the meteorologist's reasoning can be made explicit but his reasoning is of a different kind] or that the reasoning

of the jury cannot be explicated with a fair
amount of precision.) (8) Tacit knowledge of
the higher dimensions must be expressed metaphorically. Since "higher" dimensions are only
mediated through "lower" dimensions, the language
which is used to articulate higher dimensions
must be derived from the language which is used
to articulate lower dimensions. (Language which
is appropriate for the latter must be extended,
distorted in order to express new meanings, etc.)
Again, since knowledge of higher dimensions is
primarily tacit, it cannot be fully expressed in
literal language. (If this knowledge could be
fully expressed in literal language, it would
not be tacit knowledge.) While this thesis may
have a certain plausibility when considered in
relation to the religious dimension and to the
discourse which expresses it, it is considerably
less plausible when considered in relation to the
personal or moral dimensions and the language
which expresses them. (Sentences like "She is
only pretending," "He ought not to speak to his
mother in that way," "I am deeply unhappy" are
typical of sentences which express our knowledge
of these dimensions and they are nor metaphorical.) In Part III, Gill applies his theory to
religious knowledge. Revelation is construed
as an awareness of a dimension of reality which
is mediated through "more familiar dimensions"
and "gives existence and meaning to them."
(How can a dimension "give existence" to another
dimension?) In response to this awareness, the
individual's life "becomes characterized by a
profound sense of commitment." One (necessarily)
articulates these disclosures by metaphors and
models. Gill is heavily indebted to Hick (# 810

above), and particularly Ramsey (#s 948-952
above). The book's originality consists in its
attempt to justify this familiar account of
religious knowledge by grounding it in a fairly
well developed account of knowledge in general.
(Thus, according to Gill, the imprecision of
Ramsey's talk about the "empirical fit" of theological models is explained by the fact that we
are dealing with a dimension which is tacitly
known and by the fact that the criteria for tacit
knowledge cannot be made fully explicit.) Gill's
account of human knowledge is not without interest and it may, in some respects, provide a
useful corrective to more standard accounts.
Whether it has been adequately explicated or
justified is, however, a moot point.

1051 _____. "Tacit Knowing and Religious Belief,"
Int J Phil Relig, VI (Summer, 1975), 73-88.

An attempt to defend the view that religious
belief is "supportable and reasonable," but
not dependent upon inductive or deductive reason. Gill begins by examining material from
Wisdom, Wittgenstein, and Polanyi. What emerges
from this discussion is the concept of "bedrock
beliefs" -- beliefs which are "all-encompassing,"
which provide bases for the human form of life,
and which are, therefore, more basic than those
beliefs which belong to particular language
games or modes of experience. These beliefs
(e.g., the belief in an external world or the
belief in other minds) "provide the structure
of experience in general," the framework within
which we reason. They can be made to "show
themselves" but cannot be established by

(inductive or deductive) arguments. Gill suggests that religious beliefs are bedrock beliefs
but admits that the fact that many people apparently reject religious belief counts against
this contention. He suggests that there may
be two ways to handle this difficulty. (1)
One might try to show that those who appear to
reject religious belief do not really reject
it (à la Tillich). (2) One might argue (à la
Hick) that the dimensions of reality (the physical, the personal, the moral, the religious)
are arranged hierarchically, and that the higher
dimensions are mediated through the lower dimensions. If the higher dimensions are mediated
through the lower dimensions, the higher dimensions will be more difficult to grasp. Metaphor,
paradox, and other kinds of evocative language
will be more useful at this point than argument,
since what is required is an apprehension or
awareness of something which discloses itself
through, but can be obscured by, a medium.
(It is not, however, clear that the second approach will solve our problem. It appears to
provide an explanation of the fact that religious
belief is not universal whereas what was to
be shown was that religious belief is universal.)

1052   Grave, Selwyn A. "Butler's Analogy," _Cambridge J_,
       I (1952-53), 169-80.

Grave's essay contributes to our understanding
of one of the more important attempts to justify
religious belief. According to Grave, we must
distinguish Butler's positive and negative uses
of analogy. "Positively: the . . . similarities
between the systems of nature and religion suggest
that the Author of nature authorizes the system

of religion. Negatively: (a) . . . our experienced incapacity to judge of the propriety of
means . . . where . . . [some] ends are known
only vaguely and others are . . . unknown, shows
analogously that we must be incompetent critics
of the perfection of divine providence. (b)
If certain features in . . . nature are . . .
admitted to be consistent" with God's perfection
"similar . . . features in . . . revealed religion cannot be held incompatible with" that
perfection. The negative analogies are more
important than the positive analogy. Butler
believes that when our happiness is at stake
and action is unavoidable, slight probabilities
must determine assent. Butler's strategy, therefore, is to remove "the grounds of disbelief"
and thus "let any positive presumption of the
truth of religion assume sufficient weight to
dictate assent."

1053 Hick, John Harwood. Arguments for the Existence
      of God. (Philosophy of Religion Series.) Lon-
      don: Macmillan, 1970; New York: Herder and
      Herder, 1971. xiii + 148 pp.

      Hick's discussion of the design, cosmological,
      moral, and ontological arguments is, on the
      whole, unexciting, his most interesting points
      having already been made in earlier publications.
      The most significant chapter is chapter 7 ("Ra-
      tional and Theistic Belief Without Proofs")
      which contains an expanded (and more accessible)
      version of "A New Form of Theistic Argument"
      (# 1054 below).

1054 _____ . "A New Form of Theistic Argument,"
Proceedings of the XIV International Congress
of Philosophy, V (1970), 336-41.

Hick argues that even though it cannot be proved
that God exists, it is rational for the religious man to believe, on the basis of his religious experience, that God does exist. In this
respect, the religious man's belief is like our
belief in an external world. The latter is one
of Hume's "natural beliefs," a belief which is
involuntary and which is such that "we can act
successfully in terms of it." Similarly, for
"the great primary religious figures," belief
in God is unavoidable, and it enables them to
live successfully. Hick realizes that many
people "avoid" religious belief without (in
any obvious way) ruining their lives but fails
to see that this fact makes it impossible to
maintain that belief in God is a natural belief
in Hume's sense. (On this point, see Gaskin,
1049 above.)

1055 Hudson, William Donald. A Philosophical Approach
to Religion. London and Basingstoke: The Macmillan Press, Ltd., 1974. xiii + 200 pp.

At the heart of Hudson's book is the following
argument: (1) A concept is constitutive for
a mode of discourse if it determines what constitutes an explanation and what constitutes
an experience within that mode of discourse.
Just as the concept of a physical object is
constitutive for scientific discourse and just
as the concept of moral obligation is constitutive for moral discourse, so the concept of
God is constitutive for religious discourse.

704

(2) The meaning of "really exists" varies radically from one mode of discourse to another. (3) It follows (from [1]) that the question "Does God really exist?" cannot arise within the universe of religious discourse, and (from [2]) that it cannot arise within a non-religious universe of discourse either. (If the question is asked within scientific discourse it can only mean "Is there some physical reality which can be identified with God?." If it is asked within moral discourse, it can only mean "Is there a moral obligation with which God can be identified?," etc.). The oddness of Hudson's conclusion might suggest that either (1) or (more likely) (2) is false. (Hudson's point, incidentally, is not that the question concerning God's existence is meaningless, for what criteria are to be used in order to determine whether something is real is ultimately a matter of decision, and we can always adopt criteria which will allow us to ask whether God [or physical objects, or moral obligations] are real.) Hudson attempts to show that religious belief is both compatible with secularization and rational. His discussion of secularization is inadequate for two reasons. (1) He assumes that its primary intellectual expression is Logical Positivism and thus ignores the importance of atheistic existentialism, Marxism, modern naturalism, etc. (2) He also appears to believe that he has met the challenge imposed by secularization because he has shown that the phenomenon of secularization does not confront the believer with good arguments against his belief. Unfortunately, this is somewhat beside the point since the primary challenge of secularization consists

in the fact that secular habits of thought make religious beliefs <u>psychologically</u> difficult. According to Hudson, religious belief can be rational in five senses of "rational": (1) A religious man can proportion his religious beliefs to the evidence. However, what counts as evidence (for, e.g., claims concerning the nature or activity of God) is determined by the relevant mode of discourse. The belief that there is a God and/or the decision to employ the religious mode of discourse cannot be proportioned to the evidence for evidence cannot be given either for or against the reality of the object of an ontological concept. In this respect, the religious man is no more irrational than the man who believes in the reality of physical objects and/or employs scientific discourse, or the man who believes in the reality of moral obligation and/or employs moral discourse. While this position deserves careful attention, Hudson's presentation suffers from two weaknesses. (a) He does not discuss the canons of evidence which are peculiar to the religious mode of discourse. (b) In an earlier chapter, Hudson offers standard criticisms of the traditional arguments for God's existence. Even if he has succeeded in showing that these arguments are unsound, it is not clear that he has shown that the sorts of considerations which are adduced in these arguments (apparent design, religious experience, the world's apparent contingency, etc.) are logically irrelevant to a consideration of the question of God's existence. (2) Religious beliefs are not inherently inconsistent. (3) Religious language can be used intelligibly. (4) Since the relevant good is

infinite, the "expected gain attached to the
adoption of a policy of religious belief outweighs the" expected gain attached to the adoption of an irreligious policy. (The notion
of expected gain presupposes that probabilities
can be assigned to the different outcomes, viz.,
a religious policy is adopted and proves to be
correct, a religious policy is adopted and proves
to be incorrect, etc. Hudson has argued that
there can be no evidence for or against God's
existence. If he is correct, how can probabilities be assigned to the relevant outcomes?)
(5) A religious man can be open minded in the
sense that within the mode of religious discourse
he is prepared to abandon any belief provided
that the evidence which is admissable within
that mode of discourse warrants his doing so.

1056   . "Professor Bartley's Theory of Ra-
    tionality and Religious Belief," Relig Stud,
    9 (September, 1973), 339-50.

Bartley (# 1037 above) appears to maintain that
the rationalist qua rationalist can choose whether to retain or reject the practice of reasoning.
Hudson argues that although a rationalist can
consistently abandon any particular theory of
rationality (e.g., Bartley's theory), it is
incoherent to suppose that the rationalist qua
rationalist can be argued out of the practice
of reasoning. (It is impossible for there to
be good reasons for the claim that there are
no good reasons.) Hudson also contends that
committed Christians need not be any less rational than scientists or moralists. In support-
ing this contention, Hudson makes two dubious
assumptions: (1) that allegiance to Christ is

707

"the logical form of Christianity" and not part
of its content, and (2) that since the nature
of the reasons (criticisms) which are in order
is a function of the appropriate context, a
religious person is rational if he holds his
religious beliefs open to criticisms which are
based upon religious reasons and is prepared
to abandon his beliefs if those criticisms become sufficiently damaging.

1057   Hughes, George E. "Plantinga on the Rationality
        of God's Existence," Phil Rev, LXXIX (April,
        1970), 246-52.

A discussion of Plantinga's contention (# 376
above) that belief in God is as rational as our
belief in other minds. Hughes argues (1) that
Plantinga never clearly articulates "the criteria of the rationality of belief," (2) that
if Plantinga is right about the defectiveness
of our evidence for the existence of other minds,
then it is not clear that our belief in other
minds is rational, and (3) that the fact that
while everyone is certain of the existence of
other minds many are uncertain of the existence
of God, suggests that "the step from observation
of the world to belief in God is greater in
degree or different in kind from the step from
observation of the bodies of others to the belief that, for example, they are in pain."

1058   Jeffner, Anders. Butler and Hume on Religion,
        A Comparative Analysis. Translated by Keith
        Bradfield, notes translated by James Stewart.
        (Studia Doctrinae Christiane Upsaliensia, 7.)
        Stockholm: Diakonistyrelsens Bokförlag, 1966.
        266 pp.

A philosophically interesting examination of
eighteenth century attempts to establish religion
by using "the experimental method" (induction
and analogy) to infer propositions about God's
existence, nature and behavior from an examination of the processes of nature. Jeffner examines the way in which Hume and Butler understood
the experimental method, Butler's attempt to show
that principles of Christian revelation are
analogous to those which govern nature, the
design argument, and the relation between Hume's
and Butler's moral views and their religious
views. Jeffner suggests (1) that Hume correctly
saw that theism is not an experimental issue,
and (2) that the disagreement between Butler
and Hume ought to be construed as a disagreement
over which patterns should be imposed upon the
facts. For Jeffner's discussion of the design
argument and miracles, see #s 364 and 756 above.

1059 Kellenberger, Bertram James. Religious Discovery,
     Faith, and Knowledge. Englewood Cliffs, New
     Jersey: Prentice-Hall, Inc., 1972. xi + 207 pp.

This book contains a number of interesting contentions. For example: (1) A distinction is
made between the way in which one comes to know
the truth of a hypothesis and the way in which
one comes to know that God exists and cares for
us. The former is a consequence of the acquisition of new facts which clearly support the
hypothesis while the latter is a consequence of
coming to see the relevance of facts which one
already knows. (2) It is suggested that the
discernment of the influence of one person on
another provides a model for the discernment
of God's influence on the world. (3) It is

709

argued that the ability to provide a justification of the statements which one believes
(as opposed to the ability to say how one knows
them) is not a necessary condition of knowledge
and that, therefore, one _may_ be entitled to
say that he knows that God cares for him because
the Bible says that God cares for him (even
though he is not able to justify his appeal
to the Bible). (4) It is maintained that faith
is compatible with knowledge. When others doubt
what one knows an element of risk enters the
picture (for the doubt of others may become one's
own). There is, therefore, room in these cases
for a commitment or faith which resists doubt.

1060 Knox, John, Jr. "A. C. Ewing -- a critical survey
      of Ewing's work," _Relig_ _Stud_, 11 (June, 1975),
      pp. 232-6.

      This section of Knox's paper contains a critical
      discussion of Ewing's criteria for metaphysical
      truth. Ewing maintains that metaphysical systems
      must not only be consistent and conform to ex-
      perience, but must also have explanatory power.
      Knox asks what the latter can amount to if it
      is not the capacity to generate predictions
      which accord with sense perception. Knox's
      discussion is valuable because of the questions
      which he raises. The claim that metaphysical
      systems explain or "illuminate" the facts es-
      pecially stands in need of clarification. (Does
      it, e.g., mean that apparently unrelated facts
      can be deduced from the system? Does it mean
      that the system provides a "model" or "picture"
      which relates diverse areas of experience?
      Does it mean that metaphysical systems provide
      answers to limiting questions [cf. Toulmin,

957 above], and, if it does, exactly what does
that amount to?) Cf. #s 921, 922, 1042 and
1046 above and #s 1065, 1067, 1070, 1071, 1072,
1078, 1081, 1085 and 1086 below.

1061 Lesher, James H. "Genetic Explanations of Reli-
      gious Belief," Phil Stud, 27 (May, 1975), 317-28.

      Lesher argues that (1) showing that "reason
      irrelevant psychological conditions" are suffi-
      cient to produce belief would not show that
      they are necessary, (2) showing that they are
      sufficient and necessary would not show that
      "reason relevant factors" are absent, (3) showing
      that such factors were absent in the adoption
      of the belief would not show that they are absent
      in the retention of the belief, and (4) showing
      that such factors are not causes of either the
      adoption or retention of the belief would not
      show that a person had no reasons for his belief.

1062 MacIntyre, Alasdair C. "Is Understanding Religion
      Compatible with Believing?" Faith and the Phi-
      losophers. Edited by John Hick. New York: St.
      Martin's Press, Inc., 1964. Pp. 115-33.

      MacIntyre agrees that in order "to make belief
      and the concepts which it embodies intelligible,"
      one must grasp "the criteria governing belief
      and behavior in the society which is the object
      of inquiry" but argues that one cannot avoid
      evoking the "established criteria" of one's
      own society. Furthermore, "what appears intel-
      ligible in one social context can appear not
      to make sense in another." The incoherence
      of a concept may not appear to those who use
      it because "certain questions are not asked

about it," or its users may be aware of difficulties but continue to use the concept because
it is "intimately bound up with forms of description which cannot be dispensed with if social
and intellectual life is to continue," or the
point of the concept may lie in "its bearing
upon behavior" in which case it will probably
be retained until "changed patterns of social
behavior deprive the concept of its point."
Medieval Christians were as clearly aware of the
internal difficulties in their beliefs as contemporary skeptics. What accounts for the fact
that these difficulties have become grounds for
disbelief and not merely incentives to further
inquiry is the "secularization of our forms of
description," and of our society as a whole.
A changed social scene has made Christian beliefs dispensable and deprived them of their
point. See Clarke's response (# 1040 above)
and Hudson's more extended discussion of Mac-
Intyre's thesis (# 1055 above).

1063   McTaggart, John McTaggart Ellis. Some Dogmas of
       Religion. London: Edward Arnold, 1906; New
       York: Kraus Reprint Co., 1969. Pp. 52-66.

       Sections 44-52 contain an effective critique
       of several related positions -- that certain
       dogmas must be true because things would be so
       bad if they were false, that it is reasonable
       to believe that our noblest desires and aspira-
       tions will be fulfilled, that no dogma can be
       true which paralyzes action, etc.

1064   Martin, Michael. "Religious Commitment and Ration-
       al Criticism," Phil Forum, II (New Series),
       (Fall, 1970), 107-21.

Martin argues that Bartley (# 1037 above) cannot
defend his definition of rationality, and that
Bartley has given no reasons for being rational
in the defined sense. (Bartley could reply
that this merely shows that his conception of
rationality is defective when judged from the
point of view of the traditional model of rationality which insists upon a justification for
every assertion and every choice.) According
to Martin, Bartley's own standards of criticism
(consistency, empirical refutability, agreement
with scientific theory, and a theory's ability
to solve the problem it was designed to solve)
are not themselves criticizable except in the
(weak) sense that they can each be assessed
by the standard of consistency. That this is
insufficient is shown by the fact that there
are sets of critical standards which Bartley
would clearly reject and which are not only
criticizable in this sense but survive critical
scrutiny. E.g., the set comprised of the standard of consistency and the standard of God's
approval can be assessed by, and meets, the
standard of consistency. Martin concludes by
arguing that religious theories are criticizable
in Bartley's sense (they can be assessed by all
four of his standards), and that they survive
this criticism.

1065 Mitchell, Basil. The Justification of Religious
Belief. (Philosophy of Religion Series.) London
and Basingstoke: The Macmillan Press, Ltd.,
1973; New York: Seabury Press, 1974. viii +
180 pp.

In Part I, Mitchell argues that God's existence
can neither be shown to be necessarily false,
nor demonstrated or "shown to be probable in

some strict sense of that word." He concludes
that either religion cannot be rationally assessed or else "it is possible to make a rational
case for and against a system of religious belief, but it is a case which relies on a set
of interrelated arguments which do not conform
to the ordinary pattern of deductive or inductive
reasoning." The remainder of the book defends
the second alternative. In Part II, Mitchell
discusses "cummulative arguments," viz., arguments to the effect that a particular "hypothesis" makes better sense of all the evidence than
any available alternative. He examines a dispute
over the correct interpretation of a poetic
text and an attempt to solve a historical problem. An investigation of this sort often begins
with a hypothesis suggested by a passage in
the text or by a few striking historical facts.
If one's interpretation of this portion of the
evidence turns out to be confirmed by or to
illuminate the rest of the evidence, then one's
initial insight is partially confirmed. The
parties to these disputes justify their positions
by attempting to show how their hypotheses can
explain all the relevant evidence and by attempting to show that alternative hypotheses either
ignore or distort some of the relevant evidence.
It can, however, be objected that rational discussion is possible in these cases because the
disputants share common assumptions. Mitchell,
therefore, turns to an examination of "disputes
in which the participants put forward" cumulative arguments, which involve "profound conceptual differences," but which are "capable of
rational solution." He believes that examples
of this sort of dispute are provided by

714

philosophical debates concerning such issues as Physicalism, and by controversies connected with "paradigm shifts" in science (T. S. Kuhn). What is at stake in these cases is a "whole conceptual web." The disputants do not share the same assumptions, nor do they fully agree about what the facts are or what problems need to be solved. However, even in these cases, disagreement over the facts is not absolute. Many relevant facts are "neutral" with respect to the theories which are in dispute. Furthermore, there are criteria which are not "conditional upon the acceptance of a particular paradigm" (e.g., elegance, consistency, coherence, explanatory power, "accuracy, scope, simplicity and fruitfulness"). What prevents people from realizing that these disputes are rational is the mistaken assumption that "a choice between theories . . . is rational if and only if it is possible to specify in advance [precise] rules acceptable to both parties in accordance with which the choice is to be made" (and which will, like the rules of logic and mathematics, unambiguously determine a solution). Mitchell concludes that disputes over metaphysical systems or world views can be rational but that the type of argument which is relevant to these disputes is a cumulative case argument. Part III defends the contention that "in its intellectual aspect, traditional Christian theism may be regarded as a world-view or metaphysical system" against the charge that Christian belief is not hypothetical. Mitchell examines cases where one is deeply committed to beliefs (e.g., in liberal democracy or indeterminism) which one recognizes to be controversial, and argues that this attitude is not necessarily irrational. Tenacity of belief is necessary to ensure that one "is not prematurely diverted from a promising course of inquiry." Again, a committed but not uncritical identification with an intellectual and moral tradition is necessary if one is to "develop any intellectual or moral depth and consistency." Furthermore, habituation "to a desirable pattern of feeling and acting" associated with a certain belief system may be a necessary condition of "coming to understand its rational basis." Nevertheless, it is true that one's commitment to a system of belief should not be unconditional. If one is rational, one must recognize the possibility that the case against the system which one has adopted could become so strong that one should abandon it. Mitchell suggests, that (although they are interconnected) belief in Christianity should be distinguished from trust in God, and that the latter can be unconditional even if the former cannot. Mitchell's case is persuasive but two things still need to be done. (1) More attention should be devoted to the articulation of the criteria (elegance, coherence, etc.) which guide these inquiries. Even if they cannot be precisely and unambiguously formulated, it is not enough to simply state them. (E.g., what exactly is meant by "explanatory power" or "make sense of the facts"?) (2) Some attention should be devoted to the charge that, because rational procedures are designed to eliminate disagreement, no set of criteria can be fully rational the fair application of which does not yield agreement. This important book contains a useful bibliography.

See Durrant's reply (# 1043 above).

1066 Ogden, Schubert Miles. "The Reality of God,"
      The Reality of God and Other Essays by Schubert
      M. Ogden. New York: Harper and Row, 1966.
      Pp. 1-70.

Faith in God is unavoidable because it is implicit in "our experience as modern, secular
men." Specifically, faith in God is implicit
in our confidence in the significance of our
scientific and moral activity and, more generally, in "the meaning and worth of life." To establish his case, Ogden needs to show (1) that
our confidence has an objective ground, and
(2) that this objective ground is God. He makes
things unduly easy for himself by asserting that
"the primary use . . . of 'God' is to refer to
the objective ground in reality of our ineradicable confidence in the final worth of existence." Having established God's reality to his
own satisfaction, Ogden proceeds to argue that
if God is to justify our confidence in life,
He must possess the characteristics ascribed
to Him by Process Theology. While Ogden's
argument is interesting, it is unconvincing.
Ogden has not shown that our confidence must
have an "objective ground" in order to be justified (why couldn't its justification simply
consist in the fact that it makes the activities
which it supports possible?), nor has he shown
that this objective ground must be identified
with the God of Process Theology. (He has at
best shown only that it is more reasonable to
identify this ground with the God of Process
Theology than to identify it with the God of
classical theology. Unfortunately, these are

not the only alternatives.) Furthermore, if
Ogden is to show that God exists (and not merely
that we cannot help but believe that God exists)
he must show that our confidence is justified.

1067 Owen, Huw Parri. The Christian Knowledge of God.
London: University of London, the Athlone Press,
1960. Pp. 168-9.

Theistic belief is reasonable (1) because it is
self-consistent, (2) because it "coheres with
and fulfils non-religious modes of experience"
(e.g., moral and scientific experience), and
(3) because it provides the most satisfactory
"explanation of those data that are intrinsically
inexplicable in terms of finite things and persons" (e.g., contingent being). Cf. #s 921,
922, 1042, 1046, 1060 and 1065 above and #s
1070, 1071, 1072, 1078, 1081, 1085 and 1086
below.

1068 Pailin, David Arthur. The Way to Faith, An Exami-
nation of Newman's "Grammar of Assent" as a
Response to the Search for Certainty in Faith.
London: Epworth Press, 1969. viii + 280 pp.

Pailin examines the historical background of the
Grammar of Assent (pp. 1-96) and provides a
critical analysis of its contents. Chapter
III discusses the "condition" of assent, viz.,
the (real or notional) apprehension of that to
which assent is given. Chapter IV examines
the "antecedent" of assent, viz., the warrants
or justifications for assent, and Chapter V
considers the act of assent. Formal reasoning
can provide a warrant for assent, but assents
are normally justified by illative reasoning.
Illative reason draws conclusions from a number

of converging factors. Its inferences are affected by our experience, by our (often half-conscious) assumptions, by our state of mind, etc. It is impossible to fully articulate either the rules for this form of reasoning or (because of the number and obscurity of the relevant considerations) the evidence from which illative reason draws its conclusions. Pailin argues that even though Newman may be overly optimistic in assuming that illative reasoning is generally sound, he is probably correct in supposing that in many areas of human life illative reasoning is the only alternative to the abandonment of reason. (Its importance is illustrated by the fact that it even determines our assessment of the force of instances of formal reasoning.) There is an interesting discussion of relation of conscience to illative reasoning. (Conscience provides us with a "real" [as opposed to notional] apprehension of God, prompts us to consider the evidence fairly, prevents us from accepting religious propositions which conflict with the dictates of morality, and -- most importantly -- under certain conditions informs us that we ought to assent.) According to Newman, there is always a logical gap between the conclusions of reasoning and our assent to these conclusions. There is normally a psychological gap as well. (Newman's language sometimes obscures this distinction, however.) Pailin argues (1) that Newman's problem of assent is primarily a problem of commitment rather than a problem of logic, i.e., that Newman is more concerned with the conditions under which personal commitment ("certitude") is possible than with the conditions which logically justify

conclusions, but (2) that, even though there
is a gap between conclusions and assents, Newman is mistaken when he assumes that assent is
a volitional act and that the gap can be bridged
by an act of will. This study is valuable both
because it deepens our understanding of Newman
and because it casts light upon the role which
reasoning and justification play in religion.

1069   Penelhum, Terence. Religion and Rationality, An
       Introduction to the Philosophy of Religion.
       New York: Random House, 1971. Pp. 203-17.

Both the theistic and secular world views are
consistent. Each can account for all the natural facts. Each, when viewed as a whole,
makes rough sense. The issue between them cannot be settled by an "appeal to any principle
that is not question begging," and each has
"seductive and plausible devices for explaining
the other's position." It follows that religious
belief and skepticism both rest upon a choice
and that neither choice is unreasonable. While
this view is rather widely held, it is seldom
articulated. There is a family resemblance between Penelhum's position and (e.g.) Wittgensteinian Fideism. However, the former rests
upon an examination of the rational case for and
against theism, while the latter purports to
be the result of conceptual analysis. Penelhum's
position is, therefore, contingently true or
contingently false. Wittgensteinian Fideism,
on the other hand, is either necessarily true
or necessarily false.

1070 Pepper, Stephen Coburn. "Metaphysical Method,"
Phil Rev, LII (May, 1943), 252-69.

A metaphysical theory is an unrestricted hypothesis to which all data are relevant. Pepper
lists "methodological items" (e.g., self-evidence, authority, induction) and "evidential
items" (e.g., space, time, consciousness, meanings) which must be handled by any unrestricted
hypothesis, and suggests that metaphysicians
select certain items from this list as the basis
of their theories. Basic items are taken more
or less at face value. Other items are then
explained in terms of these basic items. The
selection of different bases leads to the construction of different theories. Metaphysical
hypotheses are tested by "the method of corroboration which is nothing more than the method
of gathering and organizing evidence." An "adequate base is one that leads to a large amount
of corroboration in the handling of the totality
of evidence." Theories fail in scope if they
are forced not merely to reinterpret items but
to deny any reality to them. Theories fail
in precision if they are unable to "give an
unequivocal description of any item offered."

1071 _____. "The Root Metaphor Theory of Metaphysics," _J Phil_, XXXII (July 4, 1935), 365-74.

Metaphysical hypotheses are derived "through
the analysis of a selected group of facts (. . .
the root metaphor) and the expansion of that
analysis among other facts." Pepper argues
that there are a limited number of "fruitful
root metaphors," and that these root metaphors
generate different world hypotheses. The

criteria for world hypotheses are "scope and
adequacy." A hypothesis fails if it excludes
certain facts, or if "two or more descriptions,
both equally consistent with the hypothesis,
can be given" of the same fact. Pepper maintains that no world hypothesis is fully adequate.
However, since any well developed world hypothesis (e.g., mechanism or idealism) has a great
deal of explanatory power and since the rejection
of all world hypotheses has little explanatory
power, each of these hypotheses should be accepted. (Isn't this a reductio ad absurdum of Pepper's position?) Compare Pepper's account of
metaphysics and metaphysical truth with #s 921,
922, 1042, 1046, 1060, 1065 and 1067 above and
#s 1078, 1081, 1085 and 1086 below.

1072   _____. World Hypotheses, A Study in Evidence.
        Berkeley and Los Angeles: University of Cali-
        fornia Press, 1942. xiii + 348 pp.

An expanded version of "The Root Metaphor Theory
of Metaphysics" (# 1071 above). Pepper's basic
theses are presented in that essay and in "Metaphysical Method" (# 1070 above).

1073 Polanyi, Michael. "Faith and Reason," J Relig,
     XLI (October, 1961), 237-47.

Polanyi distinguishes two kinds of knowing:
(1) A knowledge which is achieved by attending
to a thing's "total appearance." In order to
arrive at this knowledge, we rely upon "clues
which cannot be clearly specified." Examples
of this sort of knowledge are provided by the
diagnosis of a disease, the identification of
an animal's species, the perception of objects,

722

the knowledge of our own bodies, and our awareness of other persons. (2) A knowledge which
is achieved by attending to a thing's parts.
In this form of knowledge, the thing as a whole
recedes into the background. Examples are provided by experimental and deductive knowledge.
The first sort of knowledge results in understanding or comprehension but the second does
not. ("All explicit forms of reasoning, whether
deductive or inductive . . . can operate only
as the intellectual tools of man's tacit powers
reaching toward the hidden meaning of things.")
Polanyi argues that religious faith is only
precluded by theories which ignore knowledge
of the whole. Just as other persons are grasped
through the particulars in which they manifest
themselves, so the "meaning of the universe as
a whole" can be glimpsed through the various
"levels of existence." Those who are excited
by Polanyi's theory of knowledge should consult
his Personal Knowledge (London: Routledge &
Kegan Paul; Chicago: The University of Chicago
Press, 1958). His views are briefly presented
in "Knowing and Being" (Mind, LXX [October,
1961], pp. 458-70) and "The Logic of Tacit Inference" (Philosophy, XLI [January, 1966], pp.
1-18). For a systematic attempt to use Polanyi's
notions to explicate religious knowledge see
Gill, # 1050 above.

1074 Powell, Jouett Lynn. Three Uses of Christian Dis-
      course in John Henry Newman: An Example of
      Nonreductive Reflection on the Christian Faith.
      (American Academy of Religion Dissertation
      Series, 10.) Missoula, Montana: Published by
      Scholars Press for the American Academy of Re-
      ligion, 1975. x + 232 pp.

Originally presented as the author's doctoral
dissertation (Yale, 1972). Powell distinguishes
between Newman's account of the process of coming
to belief, Newman's account of the exercise
of faith within the context of a Christian life,
and his account of the theological explication
of faith. Newman's discussion of the "cumula-
tion of probabilities" and the role of judgment
(the "illative sense"), and his "proof" from
conscience, belong primarily to the first account. His examination of the role played by
imagination in the religious life belongs to
the second, and his discussion of doctrine and
authority belong to the third. Powell maintains
that earlier interpretations of Newman are vitiated by their failure to distinguish between
these three accounts. Powell's dissertation
is not exciting but it does throw some new light
upon Newman and for that reason deserves our
attention. (Whatever its weaknesses, Newman's
study of the role of informal reasoning in religion continues to be of major importance.
No recent studies are superior to Newman's.
Most are markedly inferior.)

1075   Rowe, William Leonard. "God and Other Minds,"
       Nous, III (September, 1969), pp. 280-4.

Section III discusses Plantinga's contention
(# 376 above) that belief in God is as rational
as our belief in other minds. Rowe maintains
that because we "know with certainty that other
minds exist (i) there is good rational evidence
for the belief that other minds exist and (ii)
the belief that other minds exist is rational
even though we are unable to say what the

evidence for the belief is." Since, on the other hand, it is not clear that anyone knows with certainly that God exists, we are not entitled to assert that belief in God is rational until we are presented with adequate evidence for that belief.

1076 Royce, Josiah. The Sources of Religious Insight; Lectures Delivered before Lake Forest College on the Foundation of the Late William Bross, by Josiah Royce. New York: Charles Scribner's Sons, 1912. x + 297 pp.

"Insight is knowledge that makes us aware of the unity of many facts in one whole, and . . . brings us into intimate personal contact with these facts and the whole wherein they are united." Religious insight is "insight into the need and into the way of salvation." Its sources are: (1) Individual experience (the "inwardly felt . . . need of salvation," the "hunger . . . after spiritual unity and self-possession," the apparent sense of the presence of a "Deliverer"). (2) Social experience (a sense of guilt which takes the form of "a belief that one is an outcast from human sympathy," love or friendship which "seems to furnish you with a vision of a perfect life," etc.). (3) Reason (regarded as a means of viewing "many facts or principles or relations in some sort of unity or wholeness" or in "their total significance"). In claiming that one's opinion is true, one claims that it will be found to conform to an ideal synoptic vision which grasps reality as a whole. The very claim to truth thus involves an appeal to omniscience. (4) Loyalty to a cause, "which links many individual lives in one," and which is therefore essentially

superhuman, and the "spirit of chivalry" which
is "a spirit that honours loyalty" in whatever
form it may be found, i.e., which is "loyal
to the cause of all loyal people." (Loyalty
"shows you the will of the spiritual world.")
(5) The experience of good won through struggle
with sorrow and evil. (For more on this, see
536 above.) (6) Communities which "serve
the cause of loyality," providing examples of
"the unity of the Spirit," and standing "for a
reality that belongs to the superhuman world."
Royce is, as usual, suggestive and interesting.
However, a serious ambiguity infects his discussion. It is not always clear whether the
"sources" which he discusses are themselves
forms of religious knowledge, facts which can
only be adequately explained within a religious
framework, or facts which presuppose or entail
religious truths. Thus, the nature of his argument is not entirely clear.

1077 Smart, Ninian. A Dialogue of Religion. (The
      Library of Philosophy and Theology.) London:
      SCM Press Ltd., 1960. 142 pp.

      Among the criteria which can be used to deter-
      mine the rational adequacy of a religion are
      the following: (1) empirical evidence (e.g.,
      in the case of the story of the Fall literally
      interpreted or a belief in rebirth), (2) ade-
      quacy to numinous and mystical experience, (3)
      conformity with our moral insights and standards,
      (4) universality (the gods of polytheism are,
      e.g., more closely tied to a particular time
      and place than the absolutes of the higher re-
      ligions), and (5) simplicity. Smart's book is
      cast in the form of a dialogue between a

Christian, a Jew, a Muslim, a Hindu, a Ceylonese
Buddhist and a Japanese Buddhist. It furnishes
examples of the application of these criteria
and provides a model of the way in which arguments between the advocates of different religions should be conducted. Two questions ought
to be distinguished: (1) Is supranaturalism
rationally justified? (2) Are some forms of
supranaturalism rationally preferable to others?
Philosophers have tended to either address
themselves to the first question and neglect
the second, or (because, e.g., they identify
supranaturalism with theism) conflate the two
questions. (The questions are distinct. There
might be rational grounds for adopting supranaturalism but no rational grounds for preferring
one form of supranaturalism to another. Again,
some forms of supranaturalism might be rationally
superior to others even though there are no adequate rational grounds for adopting any form
of supranaturalism.) Smart's book is important
because it squarely addresses the second question. (This book was re-issued under the title
World Religions, A Dialogue [Baltimore: Penguin Books, 1966].)

1078 Tillich, Paul Johannes Oskar. Systematic Theology.
      Vol. I. Chicago: The University of Chicago
      Press, 1951. Pp. 100-5.

The test of philosophical systems is "their
efficacy in the life process of mankind. They
prove to be inexhaustable in meaning and creative in power." What Tillich appears to be
driving at is that adequate philosophical systems
"illuminate" the facts and also integrate and
heal (rather than destroy) those who use them.

Cf., #s 921, 922, 1042, 1046, 1060, 1065, 1067,
1070, 1071 and 1072 above and #s 1081, 1085 and
1086 below.

1079   Tomberlin, James Edward.   "Is Belief in God Justi-
       fied?"   J Phil, LXXVII (January 29, 1970),
       31-8.

Plantinga has argued (# 376 above) that if our
belief in other minds is justified, the theist's
belief in God is justified. Tomberlin maintains
that in order for Plantinga's argument to succeed, he must add the following premiss: "Belief
in God is basic for the theist," where a basic
belief is a belief which is "justified in the
absence of any independent adequate evidence."
If this premiss is added, Plantinga's argument
becomes superfluous, since "belief in God is
basic for the theist" entails "belief in God
is justified for the theist." Tomberlin adds
that similar considerations would show that a
belief in God's non-existence can be justified
for an atheist. This article is essentially
identical with pp. 384-90 of the author's "Plantinga's Puzzles about God and Other Minds"
(The Philosophical Forum, I [New Series],
[Spring, 1969]). In the last paragraph of his
reply to that article ("The Incompatibility
of Freedom with Determinism: A Reply," The
Philosophical Forum, II [New Series], [Fall,
1970], pp. 141-8), Plantinga points out that
he was not trying to establish the truth of
theism but only that the theist's belief in
God is rationally acceptable. Since the latter
is compatible with atheism being a rationally
acceptable position for some people, Tomberlin's
argument is beside the point.

1080 Wald, Albert W. "The Origins and the Worth of
     Theism," Int J Phil Relig, V (Spring, 1974),
     45-60.

     Wald argues that the origins or causes of a
     belief are relevant to its truth or rationality
     when it in known empirically that beliefs which
     have such beginnings or causes are usually false
     or unreasonable. See Ferré's reply, # 1047
     above.

1081 Walsh, William Henry. Metaphysics. (Hutchinson
     University Library.) London: Hutchinson & Co.
     Ltd., 1963. Pp. 154-88.

     Chapters 10 and 11 contain intelligent reflec-
     tions on the nature of metaphysics and the cri-
     teria for metaphysical truth. Metaphysics offers
     "a series of categorial principles" which can
     be used to provide "an overall reading of experi-
     ence." Walsh discusses the problems involved
     in applying the criteria of scope and adequacy,
     and suggests that metaphysics can be profitably
     compared with literary criticism. (For a fur-
     ther development of this suggestion, see Mitch-
     ell, # 1065 above.) Cf., #s 921, 922, 1042,
     1046, 1060, 1065, 1067, 1070, 1071, 1072 and 1078
     above and #s 1085 and 1086 below.

1082 Watkins, John William Nevill. "CCR: A Refuta-
     tion," Philosophy, XLVI (January, 1971), 56-61.

     In reply to Agassi, Jarvie and Settle (# 1031
     above), Watkins presents "two new results."
     The core of Bartley's theory (# 1037 above)
     contains the claim that "all non-analytic and
     rationally acceptable statements are criticiz-
     able." Call this claim C. Watkins shows (1)

729

that "C is criticizable" is analytically true,
and (2) that it is false that C is non-analytic
and rationally acceptable, from which it follows
that C is either (a) rationally unacceptable
or (b) analytic and so not "criticizable in
any serious sense."

1083 _____. "Comprehensively Critical Rational-
ism," Philosophy, XLIV (January, 1969), 57-62.

Watkins argues that Bartley's theory of rational-
ism (# 1037 above) is a "dictatorial strategy"
which permits "a player to be certain of winning
however the game may go." Bartley claims that
his theory of rationality is criticizable and,
therefore, "complies with its own conception
of rationality." In defending the claim that
his theory is criticizable, Bartley says that
he would reject his theory if it could be shown
that it was not criticizable and invites counter-
arguments. According to Watkins, this is a
bogus challenge. Any argument which tends to
show that the theory is uncriticizable is an
effective criticism of it and, therefore, shows
that it is criticizable. Thus, the theory necessarily survives any challenge. See the reply
by Agassi, Jarvie and Settle (# 1031 above).

1084 Woods, George Frederick. Theological Explanation,
A study of the meaning and means of explaining
in science, history, and theology, based upon
the Stanton Lectures delivered in the University
of Cambridge, 1953-1956. Digswell Place, Welwyn
[Eng.]: James Nisbet and Co. Ltd., 1958.
xv + 210 pp.

According to Woods, what explains must be plainer
than that which it explains. Since "our knowledge of personal being . . . is the plainest

thing we know," explanatory forms must ultimately
be derived from the sphere of personal being.
It also follows that analogy is inevitable.
Since what is plainest to me is the personal,
I will "naturally seek to explain" what is other
than myself (and is, therefore, either not personal or not personal in the way in which I am
personal) "in terms which are plain to me from
my experience as a personal being." Natural
and revealed theology simply extend this mode
of explanation to ultimate reality. This is
not an especially good book, but its attempt
to derive the nature of theological explanation
from the nature of explanation in general is
not entirely without interest.

1085   Yandell, Keith Edward. Basic Issues in the Philo-
       sophy of Religion. Boston: Allyn and Bacon
       Inc., 1971. Pp. 218-26.

       Faith is a "total interpretation" or world view.
       In deciding between total interpretations, we
       must employ formal criteria (consistency, coher-
       ence, and simplicity). We can also eliminate
       alternatives which are "self-stultifying." A
       total interpretation is self-stultifying if
       its assertion "denies its own truth conditions,"
       if its assertion implies the impossibility of
       making assertions, if its assertion implies that
       it cannot be known to be true, if the explana-
       tions which it offers adduce the same sort of
       thing which it is trying to explain, or if it
       is beset by the same type of problem which it
       purports to resolve. It is clear that self-
       stultifying world views should be rejected.
       It is not clear that the application of this

criterion will eliminate very many live alternatives.

1086 _____. "Religious Experience and Rational
Appraisal," Relig Stud, 10 (June, 1974), pp.
185-6.

Yandell lists criteria for determining the truth
of a conceptual system. In addition to those
discussed in # 1085 above, Yandell argues that
an adequate conceptual system must not (essentially) include elements "contradicted by well-
established data." It must be comparatively
free from ad hoc hypotheses which have only been
introduced in order to handle counter-evidence,
and it must explain or assimilate all phenomena
within its "relevance range," i.e., within "the
range of data for which the system provides
interpretive context and from which counter-evidence, if any, may be discovered." Yandell
admits that the application of these criteria
"will involve an evaluative skill for which
there are no formulated rules." Cf., #s 921,
922, 1042, 1046, 1060, 1065, 1067, 1070, 1071,
1072, 1078 and 1081 above.

Fideism

Note: For important presentations of Christian Fideism
see the work of Karl Barth and Emil Brunner,
#s 783, 784, 785, 786 and 787 above. See also
819.

1087 Blackstone, Richard Macartney. "Is Philosophy
of Religion Possible?" Int J Phil Relig, III
(Fall, 1972), 176-84.

Blackstone argues that if Fideism is true no
philosopher can be religious and philosophy

732

of religion is impossible. (If Fideism is true, religion involves a [deliberately and sometimes self-consciously] uncritical commitment to certain positions. Philosophy, on the other hand, maintains that any belief is in principle subject to critical reflection. It follows that one cannot [consistently] both be religious and be a philosopher. Again, if Fideism is true, a religious person cannot [as we have seen] do philosophy of religion. Since [according to Fideism] only believers can understand religion, a non-religious person cannot do philosophy of religion either. Therefore, no one can do philosophy of religion.) In fact, however, some philosophers are religious and people do philosophize about religion. Therefore, Fideism is false.

1088   Cherry, Christopher. "Understanding Understanding Religious Belief," _Relig_ _Stud_, 10 (December, 1974), 457-67.

Phillips (#s 1100-1108 below) is said to maintain both that we cannot understand religious concepts unless we place those concepts in their religious context, and that in order to understand religious concepts we must have religious beliefs. Cherry makes a rather persuasive case against the second contention, but his argument is misdirected. In spite of some misleading remarks, Phillips does not think that believers are the only ones who understand religious concepts. On the other hand, some Fideists clearly have thought that believers alone understand religious utterances.

1089 Dilley, Frank Brown, Jr. "The Status of Religious
Beliefs," <u>Amer</u> <u>Phil</u> <u>Quart</u>, 13 (January, 1976),
41-7.

Dilley argues that although Wittgensteinian
Fideism is consistent, it does not accurately
describe the way in which religious systems
actually work. Fideism pays insufficient attention to the fact that religious people provide
evidence for their views, and revise their
conceptions in the light of advances in secular
knowledge.

1090 Gill, Jerry Henry. "Saying and Showing: Radical
Themes in Wittgenstein's <u>On Certainty</u>," <u>Relig</u>
<u>Stud</u>, 10 (September, 1974), 279-90.

According to Wittgenstein, it is inappropriate
to doubt or attempt to demonstrate certain beliefs. (Consider, e.g., our belief in the reality of physical objects.) These beliefs
provide a framework or structure within which
knowing and doubting are possible. (That a
belief is "epistemological bedrock" cannot be
said but does show itself "in the way we behave
both verbally and non-verbally.") Nevertheless,
these beliefs are not beyond discussion because
it is possible to "persuade" another of (but
not "demonstrate to him") the superiority of
one's own structure. "There is a kind of 'reasoning' which characterizes persuasion," and
which sometimes leads to "conversion." Gill
compares Wittgenstein's view with Michael
Polanyi's account of "tacit knowledge," and
accuses Wittgensteinian Fideists of misrepre-
senting Wittgenstein at two points——in their
attempt to isolate religion from other language

games and forms of life, and in their insistence
that "bedrock beliefs" are not susceptible to
any sort of justification.

1091 Hick, John Harwood. "The Justification of Reli-
      gious Belief," Theology, LXXI (March, 1968),
      100-7.

      Hick contends that Phillips (#s 1100-1108 below)
      is committed to the view (1) that believing
      that God exists is the same thing as having
      the concept of God, and to the view (2) that
      the question of the truth of the affirmation
      of the reality of God cannot arise. It is not
      clear that Hick's interpretation of Phillips is
      correct although it must be admitted that some
      of the things which the latter says support it.
      Hick concludes by arguing that eschatological
      expectations can (pace Phillips) be an essential
      feature of non-superstitious religion. See
      Phillips' reply (# 1105 below).

1092 Kellenberger, Bertram James. "The Language-Game
      View of Religion and Religious Certainty," Can
      J Phil, II (December, 1972), 255-75.

      A criticism of the tenets of the "language-game
      view of religion." Kellenberger's most effective
      criticisms are addressed to the view (1) that
      God is eternal but does not exist (this view is
      said to rest upon two mistaken beliefs -- the
      belief that when we assert that God exists we
      imply that He might not exist, and the belief
      that knowledge excludes commitment), to the
      view (2) that only those who participate in
      the religious form of life can understand reli-
      gious language (D. Z. Phillips, however, does

not hold this view), and to the view (3) that there is no external evidence which can be used to determine the truth or falsity of religious belief. (Kellenberger also points out that non-believers can recognize the sorts of things which believers point to as "internal evidence" for their beliefs, and that although it is true that they cannot accept these things as [conclusive?] evidence and remain unbelievers, the same can be said of any evidence.) Kellenberger finds two views on certainty in Wittgenstein. According to the first view, there are convictions which are fundamental to a whole way of life and for that reason cannot be doubted. According to the second view, there are (quite ordinary) propositions which one cannot doubt in certain contexts although they can (sometimes) be doubted by others and although one can doubt them oneself in other contexts. Kellenberger argues that while the first view of certainty supports the language-game view of religion, the second view of certainty is more plausible.

1093   Malcolm, Norman. "Is it a Religious Belief that 'God Exists'?" Faith and the Philosophers. Edited by John Hick. New York: St. Martin's Press, Inc., 1964. Pp. 103-10.

An influential statement of one kind of Fideism. Malcolm maintains that "the supposed belief that God exists" is "a problematic concept," and that the notion that one can argue for God's existence is equally suspect. (By contrast "belief in God" is an unproblematic concept, and "within the framework of belief in God and acceptance of the testimony of the prophets, of Jesus, and of the apostles," reasons can be given "for or against various religious doctrines.") This article is a reply to Alston, # 1034 above.

1094 Nielsen, Kai. "Can Faith Validate God-Talk?" Theol Today, 20 (July, 1963), 158-73.

An effective critique of the claim that one can believe statements which one does not understand. This view has been ascribed to Karl Barth, although incorrectly. Barth's position is that believers are able to understand statements which cannot be understood by non-believers.

1095 _____. "The Coherence of Wittgensteinian Fideism," Sophia, XI (October, 1972), 4-12.

A reply to a paper by Stuart C. Brown ("Fideism, Truth and Commensurability," presented at the 46th annual meeting of the American Philosophical Association, Pacific Division, San Francisco, March 23, 1972). Brown attempted to show that Wittgensteinian Fideists cannot consistently hold that religious beliefs are incommensurable with "infidel beliefs." Since religious beliefs conflict with infidel beliefs, they must be commensurable with them. Nielsen points out that (e.g.) "The astronauts did not see God" expresses an infidel belief that conflicts with a religious belief with which it is incommensurable. ("God is in heaven" entails neither "Astronauts will see God" nor "Astronauts will not see God." The first statement is not on the same logical level with the other two statements.) The problem with Wittgensteinian Fideism is not that it is incoherent but that the concept of truth "undergoes a sea change." If the

Wittgensteinian Fideists are correct, coming to
see the truth of religious beliefs is not like
coming to see the truth of a factual statement
but is instead like coming to see the point of,
and adopting, a way of life.

1096 _____. Contemporary Critiques of Religion.
(Philosophy of Religion Series.) London and
Basingstoke: Macmillan; New York: Herder and
Herder, 1970. Pp. 94-111.

In chapter 5, Nielsen argues that Wittgensteinian
Fideists fail to see that conceptual relativism
can be turned against religion. If conceptual
relativism is true, then Christian talk is no
more and no less legitimate that "Haitian voodoo
talk" or "Dobuan talk of sacred yams." This
conflicts with the "constative force" of central
Christian utterances. These utterances "make
fundamental truth claims about the nature of
reality," and those who employ them clearly
imply that the Christian "language-game" is
superior to its competitors. Therefore, if conceptual relativism is true, Christianity is incoherent.

1097 _____. Scepticism. London and Basingstoke:
Macmillan; New York: St. Martin's Press, 1973.
Pp. 23-40.

An attack on Wittgensteinian Fideism with special
attention to Phillips (#s 1100-1108 below).
Nielsen argues that Phillips' attempt to explain
belief in God by introducing the concept of eternal love (# 1103 below) is reductionist, that
Phillips is reconstructing and not analyzing
religion, that there are "transfield" criteria
of rationality and meaning which can be used

738

to assess forms of life, and that the Fideists have not succeeded in adequately explicating the constative force ("statement-making role") of religious sentences.

1098 _____. "Wittgensteinian Fideism," _Philosophy_, XLII (July, 1967), 191-201.

This article provides a useful examination of what Nielsen was the first to call "Wittgensteinian Fideism." He observes that there is no "extended statement of this position" (D. Z. Phillips' _The Concept of Prayer_ was apparently not yet available) but that "certain remarks" made by Peter Winch, G. E. Hughes, Norman Malcolm, and others support such a position. (A useful footnote on page 191 lists the sources of these scattered remarks.) Wittgensteinian Fideism involves the belief that "forms of life taken as a whole are not amenable to criticism; each mode of discourse is in order as it is, for each has its own criteria and sets its own norms of intelligibility, reality and rationality . . . There is no Archimedean point in terms of which a philosopher . . . can relevantly criticize whole modes of discourse." Nielsen finds a number of things wrong with this position. (1) It does not come to grips with the fact that many people understand first order religious discourse but find it incoherent (whereas, e.g., no one finds first order material object talk incoherent). (2) It is true that one must place religious concepts in their proper context and see how religious people use them if one wishes to understand them. It does not, however, follow that religious concepts

are coherent. (3) In our "tribe" religion and
science are "part of the same overall conceptual
structure," and, hence, it is not clear why
considerations or modes of thought which are
at home in science should have no bearing upon
our assessment of the truth or rationality of
religious belief. (4) Religious discourse is
part of discourse as a whole, and there are logical criteria which belong to discourse as a
whole (e.g., consistency) which can be used to
appraise religious discourse. (5) Appraising
whole forms of life (e.g., witchcraft) is itself
a well established practice, i.e., that game too
is played.

1099 Palmer, Humphrey. "Understanding First," Theol,
      LXXI (March, 1968), 107-14.

      Palmer argues that one need not believe in God
      in order to understand propositions about God,
      that one need not have a religious belief in
      order to understand it, and that religious lan-
      guage is not an autonomous language game with
      its own rules. See Phillips' reply (# 1105
      below).

1100 Phillips, Dewi Zephaniah. The Concept of Prayer.
      London: Routledge and Kegan Paul, 1965; New
      York: Schocken Books, 1966. viii + 167 pp.

      Phillips is undoubtedly the most interesting
      as well as the most influential of the Wittgen-
      steinian Fideists. His position is characterized
      by its insistence upon the radical autonomy of
      religious language. Criteria of truth and real-
      ity are internal, determined by the mode of
      discourse in question. (Hence, there is no

neutral way of adjudicating the question of God's existence. The only relevant philosophical question is a question of conceptual elucidation, viz., "what kind of reality does God have?") Atheism is essentially an attitude, expressed in the sentence "Religion has no meaning for me." Two other features of Phillips' position deserve attention: (1) In spite of his attempts to dissociate himself from any form of subjectivism, Phillips' primary emphasis is upon human attitudes, stances and modes of self-understanding. (For example, when he analyzes prayers for forgiveness he emphasizes such things as self-acceptance. In analyzing prayers of thanksgiving, primary emphasis is placed upon the recognition that life has hope, etc.) In this respect, Phillips' position might be profitably compared with the position of Rudolf Bultmann (#s 789 and 998 above). (2) The influence of Simone Weil pervades the book. It is significant that Weil's attitude towards the world is almost gnostic. Her God is a God of souls, not of matter. What happens in the realm of matter is of no intrinsic importance, and to hope for its redemption is superstitious. Similarly, Phillips wishes to connect God with the fact that the world is but not with how it is. ("True" religion excludes empirical or quasi-empirical expectations and does not explain particular facts. Theodicies blasphemously treat God as a moral agent and evil must, therefore, be left unexplained. In a ["non-superstitious"] petitionary prayer for something, one is not really asking for that thing but "asking to go on living whatever happens." And so on.) The relation between Phillips'

Fideism and what might be called his "subjectivism" and "gnosticism" should be explored in
more detail. For critiques of Phillips, see
especially Cherry, Dilley, Hick, Nielsen, and
Palmer (#s 1088, 1089, 1091, 1096, 1097 and
1099 above).

1101   _____. Death and Immortality. (New Studies
        in the Philosophy of Religion.) London and
        Basingstoke: Macmillan and Co. Ltd.; New York:
        St. Martin's Press, 1970. xii + 83 pp.

Phillips distinguishes the immortality of the
soul from the survival of death and argues that
while the former is meaningful, the latter is
not. Immortality of the soul "has to do . . .
with [a person's] participation in God's life,
. . . his contemplation of divine love," and
is intimately connected with self-renunciation.
(Phillips supports this interpretation by explicating the concept of the soul in terms of
the kind of life a person is living, and his
reflection upon his life.) A concern with survival not only betrays logical confusion but
also betrays a preoccupation with self and with
compensation which is inimical to the religious
life. Phillips' account of the belief in immortality is rich and illuminating but (in spite
of his disclaimers) clearly reductionist. The
last chapter is important for understanding
Phillips' Fideism. It is misleading to speak
of pictures of the last judgment, meeting beyond
the grave, etc., as either literally or figura-
tively true. That contrast has no meaning here.
These pictures are "the expression and embodi-
ment of a reflection on, or vision of, the meaning of life and death." Believing in them "has

to do with living by them, drawing sustenance
from them, judging oneself in terms of them
. . . ." "The picture is not assessed by appeal
to evidence. On the contrary, the picture is
. . . the measure of assessment." The meaning
of the picture is bound up with its use in the
form of life to which it belongs, and the rejection of religious belief must be regarded
as the rejection of a form of life. While forms
of life die, there are no external standards
which can be used to determine the legitimacy
of a way of life, or the truth or falsity of
the pictures which are associated with them.

1102 _____. Faith and Philosophical Enquiry.
London: Routledge & Kegan Paul, 1970; New York:
Schocken Books, 1971. viii + 277 pp.

This collection of the author's papers includes
(1) "Philosophy, Theology and the Reality of
God" (see # 1104 below), (2) "Faith, Scepticism,
and Religious Understanding" (see # 1103 below),
(3) "From World to God?" (Proc Aris Soc, Suppl.
Vol. LXI, 1967), (4) "Religious Belief and Philosophical Enquiry" (see # 1105 below), (5)
"Religious Belief and Language Games" (see #
1106 below), (6) "Belief and Loss of Belief"
(Sophia, 1970), (7) "Religion and Epistemology:
Some Contemporary Confusions" (Austl J Phil,
1966), (8) "Philosophy and Religious Education"
(British Journal of Educational Studies, February, 1970), (9) "Wisdom's Gods" (see # 1108
below). (10) "Subjectivity and Religious Truth
in Kierkegaard (see # 1107 below), (11) "God
and Ought" (Christian Ethics and Contemporary
Philosophy, ed. by I. T. Ramsey, SCM Press,
1966), (12) "On the Christian Concept of Love"

(Ibid.), and (13) "Faith and Philosophy," (Universities Quarterly, March, 1967).

1103 _____. "Faith, Scepticism and Religious Understanding," Religion and Understanding. Edited by D. Z. Phillips. Oxford: Basil Blackwell; New York: Macmillan, 1967. Pp. 63-79. (Reprinted in # 1102 above, pp. 13-34.)

According to Phillips, coming to see that God exists does not involve "an extension of one's knowledge of the facts" but instead "involves seeing a new meaning in one's life, and being given a new understanding." Phillips then proceeds to show how, in a certain context, seeing that there is a God "is synonymous with seeing the possibility of eternal love," where eternal love is construed as a selfless love which is independent of circumstances. (It is independent of circumstances because it is not based upon the beloved's merits, because it can survive the destruction of any particular object, etc.) This essay may appear to support those who suspect that Phillips is reducing religious belief to certain existential attitudes. At the same time, one must insist that Phillips' remarks are (as usual) ambiguous.

1104 _____. "Philosophy, Theology and the Reality of God," Phil Quart, 13 (October, 1963), 344-50. (Reprinted in # 1102 above, pp. 1-12.)

Three important points are made in this essay. (1) The question concerning the reality of God is a question concerning the nature of a certain kind of reality. "Is God real?" is analogous to "What kind of reality is the reality of physical objects?" and not to "Is this physical

object real or not?" (It is worth observing
that Phillips refuses to distinguish between
the question "Are physical objects real?" and
the question "What kind of reality do physical
objects have?") (2) "To say that a god is not
the same as one's own God involves saying that
those who believe in him are in a radically
different religious tradition from one's own."
(Phillips appears to be saying not merely that
the criteria of identity for a god are to be
found within particular religious traditions
but that the question concerning the identity
of a god is identical with the question concerning the continuity of a particular religious
tradition.) (3) He denies that one must accept
religious belief in order to understand it.
(In this sense, then, Phillips is not a Fideist.)

1105 _____. "Religious Belief and Philosophical
        Enquiry," Theol, LXXI (March, 1968), 114-122.
        (Reprinted in # 1102 above, pp. 62-76.)

A reply to Hick and Palmer (#s 1091 and 1099
above) which essentially consists of the accusation that Hick and Palmer have misunderstood
his position, together with restatements of
that position. This exchange of papers is in-
structive, not because the remarks of Hick and
Palmer are particularly penetrating -- in fact
they are rather obvious -- but because of Phillips' contention that their remarks rest upon
misunderstanding. (It is not clear that they
have misunderstood him.) Phillips' response
to his critics is remarkably similar to the
response which (if his theory is correct) religious believers should make to unbelievers
who stand outside the religious language game.

745

1106 _____. "Religious Beliefs and Language
Games," Ratio, XII (June, 1970), 26-46. (Reprinted in # 1102 above, pp. 77-110.)

This essay is important because it clarifies
Phillips' position on several crucial points.
(1) The believer and non-believer are not contradicting one another. In order to contradict
one another both would have to play by common
rules and they don't. The rules which govern
"God" must differ from the rules which govern
other words because "God's reality is not one
of a kind; He is not a being among other beings."
(But are the rules so different that it is impossible for a believer and non-believer to
contradict one another? At this point it becomes
clear that Phillips' polemic against anthropomorphism and his insistence upon the absolute
otherness of God's reality are not incidental
to his main position.) (2) Such religious beliefs as belief in the last judgment are absolute. Since they provide ultimate criteria of
assessment they cannot themselves be assessed.
(3) Religious language is part of our common
language, and "religion has something to say
about aspects of human existence which are quite
intelligible without reference to religion:
birth, death, joy, misery . . . fortune and
misfortune." Furthermore, what religion has to
say about these things must not "violate the
facts or distort our apprehension of situations."
Again, personal tragedies can be trials for
faith. Religion is, therefore, not an "esoteric
game" isolated from the rest of life. Nevertheless, the relation between religious beliefs
and non-religious facts is not a relation between
what is justified and that which justifies it.

1107 _____. "Subjectivity and Religious Truth in Kierkegaard," Sophia, VII (July, 1968), 3-13. (Reprinted in # 1102 above, pp. 204-22.)

This essay is of interest not so much because of the light which it throws upon Kierkegaard but because of the light which it casts upon Phillips' own position. Phillips again insists that faith is not concerned with how the world goes, that it has its own internal criteria of truth and value, etc. The most revealing aspect of this essay is a set of remarks which raise the question as to the precise nature of the distinction between God and human responses to God. ("The God-given ability to give thanks in all things is the goodness of God." "The goodness of God is a given mode of [human?] response to the good and the evil in the world: it is the response of agape." "But if we forgive others, we have the spirit of God in us, and this [our forgiveness of others? the spirit of God? Are these the same?] is our forgiveness.") Phillips presumably believes that there is a distinction between God and our response to God but the nature of this distinction is never made clear.

1108 _____. "Wisdom's Gods," Phil Quart, 19 (January, 1969), 15-32. (Reprinted in # 1102 above, pp. 170-203.)

While this examination of Wisdom (#s 959, 960 and 961 above) has comparatively little intrinsic value, it is important for the following reason: Phillips criticizes Wisdom on a number of counts but not for identifying religious belief with certain responses to the (temporal) facts. His failure to do so tends to support those who accuse Phillips of reductionism.

1109 Popkin, Richard Henry. "Theological and Religious Scepticism," Christian Schol, XXXIX (1956), 150-6.

Popkin examines a number of cases in which theological scepticism has been combined with a Fideist posture, and asks how we are to distinguish cases in which scepticism is used to protect or make room for faith (Pascal, Kierkegaard, etc.) from cases in which a fideist posture is no more than a mask for complete religious scepticism (e.g., Bayle). An interesting historical essay.

1110 Shepherd, John J. "Religion and the Contextualization of Criteria," Sophia, XV (March and July, 1976), 1-10 and 1-9.

An attack upon Wittgensteinian Fideism. In the article's first installment, Shepherd attempts to show that without shared concepts of rationality, members of one culture could not understand members of another culture and anthropology would be impossible. Among the points made in the second installment are the following: (1) The very fact that our criteria of truth are criteria of truth implies that we must be prepared to assess the truth claims made by those in other cultures, for truth is inherently universal. (2) Winch (#s 1115 and 1116 below) confuses what is taken to count as a good reason with what does count as a good reason. From the fact that the former is (to a certain extent) culture dependent it does not follow that the latter

is culture dependent. (3) All people share in
a common form of life (they are "explorers-of-
the-world's-contents"), and exhibit "a basic
human drive for intelligibility." It is not
merely an accident that most people who are initiated into both Western science and (e.g.)
Azande magic reject the latter in favor of the
former. Again, there are criteria (e.g., Ockham's razor) employed both by those who accept
a religious form of life and by those who reject
it, which can be used to assess religious
beliefs.

1111 Sherry, Patrick J. "Is Religion a 'Form of Life'?"
      Amer Phil Quart, 9 (April, 1972), 159-67.

      Sherry argues that by "form of life" Wittgenstein
      meant "basic human responses like hoping, feeling
      certain, measuring, giving orders," etc., and
      that, therefore, religion is not a form of life
      although it "includes several forms of life."
      Furthermore, the alleged fact that these forms
      of life cannot and need not be justified is
      irrelevant. There may be no point in asking for
      a justification of hoping but there is a point
      in asking for a justification of (e.g.) "hopes
      for the forgiveness of . . . sins and for the
      resurrection of the dead." In fact, however,
      some forms of life (rejoicing at good things,
      being resigned to suffering, showing pity or
      affection, etc.) can be appraised as wholes and
      it would seem that praying and worshiping fall
      in this category. Sherry points out that Witt-
      genstein appears to provide two incompatible
      "answers to the question of why we have the lan-
      guage-games and forms of life which we do:

sometimes he just says 'this is what we do,
sometimes he says we must connect what we do
with facts about the world and about human nature." The first answer has been adopted by the
Wittgensteinian Fideists, but the second answer
suggests the possibility of a more fruitful approach to religion, viz., "seeking to show how
religious 'forms of life' are to be connected
with facts about the world, mankind and its
history, and with human culture, interests and
purposes."

1112 _____. "Truth and the 'Religious Language-
Game'," Philosophy, XLVII (January, 1972), 18-37.

Sherry argues that one cannot evade the issue
of the truth of the religious language-game or
form of life since "(i) language-games may pass
away because people's interests and customs
change, or because they reject certain beliefs,
e.g., in magic, and because (ii) religious belief differs from most other language-games in
being a minority interest at present and in
having phenomena like conversion, scepticism
and loss of faith associated with it." Sherry
criticizes Wittgensteinian Fideists on a number
of counts. His most important criticism is,
perhaps, the following: The truth claims which
are made by different religions conflict with
one another. (Cf., e.g., Islam and Christianity
on the doctrine of the Incarnation.) If there
are no criteria which transcend particular religious traditions and which can be used to settle disputes of this kind, then "the whole status of religious 'truth' or 'knowledge' is called
into question."

1113   Tomberlin, James Edward. "The Autonomy of Religion," _Sophia_, XI (July, 1972), 20-5.

>Tomberlin provides persuasive counter examples to the thesis that no religious statement is entailed by any set of non-religious statements, and to the thesis that no contingent religious statement is entailed by any consistent set of non-religious statements.

1114   Watt, John. "Winch and Rationality in Religion," _Sophia_, XIII (July, 1974), 19-29.

>A reply to Winch (#s 1115 and 1116 below). Watt argues that we must distinguish between the rationality of beliefs and the rationality of actions. If our beliefs are to be rational, we must respect the basic laws of logic and check factual beliefs against the facts. An action is rational if it effectively secures our ends. Winch blurs this distinction, arguing (e.g.) that the magical beliefs of the Azande are not irrational because they enable the Azande to come to terms with the inevitable contingencies of human existence. Watt argues (1) that while this consideration may show that it is rational (second sense) for the Azande to adhere to their beliefs, it does not show that the Azande's system of beliefs is rational, and (2) that the criterion to which Winch appeals in order to show that their policy of belief is rational (viz., that it is reasonable to do what is necessary in order to secure such important goods as peace and resignation in the face of life's contingencies) is not a criterion peculiar to the Azande culture, but is instead "a general norm of rational action."

1115   Winch, Peter. The Idea of a Social Science and
       its Relation to Philosophy. (Studies in Philo-
       sophical Psychology.) London and Henley: Rout-
       ledge & Kegan Paul; New York: Humanities Press,
       1958. Pp. 100-3.

       Winch maintains that even "criteria of logic
       . . . arise out of, and are only intelligible
       in the context of, ways of living or modes of
       social life. It follows that one cannot apply
       criteria of logic to modes of social life as such
       . . . within science or religion actions can
       be logical or illogical . . . . But we cannot
       sensibly say that either the practice of science
       itself or that of religion is either illogical
       or logical; both are non-logical."

1116   _____ . "Understanding a Primitive Society,"
       Amer Phil Quart, 1 (October, 1964), 307-24.

       This interesting article has had an important
       influence upon Fideism. Appealing to Wittgen-
       stein and anthropological evidence, Winch argues
       that criteria of intelligibility, truth, and ra-
       tionality are embedded in particular forms of
       life, and that there are no neutral standards
       to which one can appeal in order to adjudicate
       between these ways of life. Winch's position
       has evoked a number of replies. See, e.g., Shep-
       herd and Watt (#s 1110 and 1114 above).

Note: For other discussions of William James' "The Will
to Believe," see #s 779, 806, 817, 818 and 851.

1117 Beard, Robert William. "'The Will to Believe'
      Revisited," Ratio, VIII (December, 1966), 169-79.

      Following a suggestion of Gail Kennedy ("Prag-
      matism, Pragmaticism, and the Will to Believe --
      A Reconsideration," J Phil, LV [1958], pp. 578-
      88), Beard argues that James distinguishes be-
      tween a right to believe and the will to believe.
      The former applies when one must make a decision
      and the decision cannot be made on intellectual
      grounds alone. In those circumstances, we have
      a right to decide on "passional grounds." (Beard
      points out that it is odd to speak of a right
      to believe "as if one could have chosen not to
      adopt any belief at all.") The will to believe
      doctrine is concerned with "belief policy."
      According to that doctrine "belief beyond evi-
      dence is permissable only when belief itself is
      a necessary condition for obtaining evidence."
      The article concludes with a critique of James'
      concept of "a genuine option." Beard suggests
      that, properly understood, James' restrictions
      are so stringent that one "wonders whether moral
      and religious hypotheses could satisfy" them.
      (E.g., is the adoption or rejection of the re-
      ligious hypothesis really irreversible?)

1118 Cargile, James. "Pascal's Wager," Philosophy,
      XLI (July, 1966), 250-7.

      Cargile defends the Wager against the charge
      of immorality but maintains that it will not

convince the skeptic to whom it is addressed,
since it assumes the truth of certain statements
about the nature of God which the skeptic qua
skeptic will refuse to accept.

1119 Comstock, William Richard. "William James and the
      Logic of Religious Belief," J Relig, 47 (July,
      1967), 187-209.

James argues that, under certain conditions,
we are entitled to adopt beliefs which satisfy
our needs. The need in question, however, is
not the "desire for a state of subjective happiness" but "a basic, human . . . need for constructive and value-oriented action." Again,
we must distinguish between what James calls
"piece-meal" beliefs (e.g., a belief in Allah,
or a belief in the finite God which James discusses at the end of The Varieties of Religious
Experience), and what James calls "generic and
broad beliefs" (e.g., the belief in fatalism,
or meliorism, in pessimism or optimism, in blind
mechanism or teleology). "James applies his
logic of belief" to both but "is more convincing
when the 'total reaction' variety is considered."
Nevertheless (according to Comstock), James has
failed to show either that religious beliefs
best satisfy our need for constructive action,
or that this need is more fundamental than (e.g.)
the need for contemplation and "moral holidays."
The article includes a decent discussion of what
James means by the "truth" of religious belief.

1120 Dalton, Peter C. "Pascal's Wager: The First Ar-
      gument," Int J Phil Relig, VII (1976), 346-68.

Pascal's "first argument" does not presuppose

the assignment of a specific probability to Christian claims. It is enough that the Christian alternative is possible. However, given Pascal's insistence upon the incomprehensibility of God, the prudent skeptic should protest that he cannot wager since he does not understand what he is supposed to wager on. Again, the prize is infinite not only in duration but also in quality. Hence, it too is incomprehensible. Since prudence "calls for knowledge of the alternatives, . . . of each alternative's likelihood . . . and for caution," no prudent man would accept the wager. A very interesting essay.

1121 _____. "Pascal's Wager: The Second Argument," S J Phil, XIII (Spring, 1975), 31-46.

Dalton contends that Pascal's "second argument" is unsound because it contains a false premiss, viz., that the probability of God's existence is 1/2. It may be replied that at one point Pascal asserts that since the gain is infinite happiness and the loss is finite happiness, it is reasonable to wager on God's existence if there is "one chance of gain against a finite number of chances of loss." Dalton offers reasons for doubting that a prudent man would make the Wager even if the relevant odds and values are just what Pascal believes them to be.

1122 Flew, Antony Garrard Newton. "Is Pascal's Wager the Only Safe Bet?" The Rationalist Annual, 1960, 21-5.

"There is . . . an unlimited range of pairs of . . . [possible] religious systems encouraging and threatening every conceivable way of life

. . . with exactly the same inordinate rewards
and punishments." Because Pascal denies that
transcendent matters are accessible to reason,
he has no grounds on the basis of which he can
assign a higher probability to one of these alternatives than to another. It follows that
he can give no reason for preferring one to
another.

1123 Hacking, Ian. "The Logic of Pascal's Wager," <u>Amer</u>
      <u>Phil</u> <u>Quart</u>, 9 (April, 1972), 186-92.

      Hacking analyzes Pascal's argument, examines its
      historical setting, and considers some early
      reactions to it. He maintains that Pascal suc-
      cessively presents three distinct arguments.
      (1) According to the "argument from dominance,"
      a theistic course of action is best upon one of
      the alternatives (God exists, and will save those
      who believe in Him and damn those who do not),
      and no worse than a non-theistic course of action
      upon the other alternative (God does not exist).
      One should, therefore, adopt a Christian course
      of action. This argument rests upon the dubious
      assumption that if God does not exist, the utili-
      ty of the libertine's life is no greater than
      the utility of the Christian's life. (2) The
      second argument discards this assumption. Ac-
      cording to the "argument from expectation," the
      alternatives are equally probable. The optimal
      payoff for the Christian is much greater than
      the optimal payoff for the libertine. Hence,
      it is reasonable to adopt a Christian course
      of action. This argument rests upon the dubious
      assumption that the alternatives are equiprob-
      able. (3) The third argument discards this

assumption. According to the "argument from dominating expectation," there is some finite probability that God exists. Because salvation is infinitely preferable to temporal joys, it is reasonable to adopt a Christian course of action. -- All of these arguments are valid. Nevertheless, they are unpersuasive both because they depend upon the false assumption that the alternatives are exhaustive and because they depend upon a dubious assignment of utilities.

1124 King-Farlow, John and William Niels Christiansen. Faith and the Life of Reason. Dordrecht, Holland: D. Reidel Pub. Co., 1973. Pp. 184-226.

The "Principle of Maximizing Expected Utility" can be rationally employed by those who are concerned with truth provided that the "right utilities" (e.g., "discovering more truth," "coming closer to certainty," "growth now in wisdom," and "realization of one's human best now") are included, and provided that there has been a rational analysis of the alternatives and a reasonable assignment of probabilities and utilities. Theistic belief and belief in other minds can both be rationally based upon a consideration of their probability and utility. (It should be noted that the standard reasons for and against theism and other minds are not ignored since they are taken into account in making one's probability assignments.) This section of the authors' book incorporates material from "Rational Commitment and 'The Will to Believe'" by King-Farlow (Sophia, VIII [April, 1969], pp. 3-14), "Über Formal Entscheidbare Sätzenkonjunktionen der Principia Theologica und Verwandter Systeme" by King-Farlow and K. G. Gotkürdel

(Analysis, 30 [New Series 136], [March, 1970],
pp. 140-4), and "Gambling on Other Minds --
Human and Divine" by King-Farlow and Christiansen
(Sophia, X [April, 1971], pp. 1-6). It includes
replies to Lawrence Resnick ("Evidence, Utility
and God," Analysis, 31 [New Series 140], [Janu-
ary, 1971], pp. 87-90) and Joel Rudinow ("Gambling on Other Minds and God," Sophia, X [July,
1971], pp. 27-9).

1125 Lachelier, Jules. "Notes on Pascal's Wager," The
      Philosophy of Jules Lachelier: "Du Fondement
      de l'Induction," "Psychologie et Métaphysique,"
      "Notes sur le pari de Pascal," together with
      Contributions to "Vocabulaire Technique et Cri-
      tique de la Philosophie," and a Selection from
      his Letters. Translated and introduced by Edward
      G. Ballard. The Hague: Martinus Nijhoff, 1960.
      Pp. 97-111.

      Among the points made by Lachelier in this in-
      teresting essay are the following: (1) God is
      the object of a bet because reason is unable
      to determine anything about a transcendent and
      infinite object. (2) Pascal believed that eter-
      nal life is infinite in intensity as well as in
      duration. At one point, Pascal argues that if
      there were only one in an infinite number of
      chances in favor of the Christian hypothesis,
      and if eternal life were infinite in only one
      dimension, then it would be equally reasonable
      to wager or not wager. If, on the other hand,
      eternal life is "doubly infinite" then one ought
      to wager upon the Christian hypothesis even if
      "the number of chances is infinite and only one
      of them is in our favor." (In fact, Pascal be-
      lieved that there are only a "finite number of
      chances of losing.") (3) God, eternal life and
      the renunciation of the world (i.e., of

self-love) are interconnected in Pascal's mind because he regards eternal life as a participation in God's life and believes that it requires self-renunciation. Lachelier argues that the wager is only reasonable if eternal life is really possible and not just logically possible. Pascal has no basis for asserting that it is really possible since he believes that eternal life is transcendent and has disavowed the possibility of any rational knowledge of the transcendent. Lachelier concludes by asking whether the fact that reason and liberty transcend the sensible conditions under which they exist, establishes the real possibility of eternal life. This essay first appeared in Revue Philosophique (June, 1901).

1126 Landsberg, P. T. "Gambling on God," Mind, LXXX (January, 1971), 100-4.

Landsberg provides a "quantitative formulation" of Pascal's Wager. Among the points he makes are the following: (1) The reasonableness of betting on theism is a function of the degree of God's revengefulness. (If, e.g., God is all-forgiving, it would be prudent to reject theism and thus secure both eternal life and the joys which this world affords.) (2) The reasonableness of betting on theism is partly a function of whether one wants to maximize expected value, avoid the worst outcome, or go for the greatest gain.

1127 Martin, Michael. "On Four Critiques of Pascal's Wager," Sophia, XIV (March, 1975), 1-11.

Martin attempts to refute four objections:

(1) That we do not know that the probability
of God's existence is 1/2, (2) that the argument
fails because it overlooks the fact that there
are several versions of theism and thus many
possible gods in whom one might believe, (3)
that the argument wrongly assumes that God will
reward those who believe in Him for selfish reasons, and (4) that the argument wrongly assumes
that there are a finite number of supernatural
beings and therefore a finite number of betting
options.

1128   Mavrodes, George Ion.   "James and Clifford on 'The
        Will to Believe'," Personalist, XLIV (Spring,
        1963), 191-8.

        James correctly observes that the maxims "Seek
        truth" and "Avoid error" are not equivalent.
        In those circumstances in which we can avoid
        commitment, adherence to the second maxim will
        prevent us from betting on the truth of a prop-
        osition for which there is insufficient evidence
        (by leading us to suspend our judgment) while
        adherence to the first maxim may lead us to bet
        on its truth.   James also believes that the re-
        ligious option is forced (presumably because of
        his pragmatic theory of belief together with
        the fact that the practical consequences of athe-
        ism and agnosticism are identical).   It is only
        because the religious option is forced that the
        "will to believe" applies to it.   However, if
        the religious option is forced and one must com-
        mit oneself, the distinction between the two
        maxims loses its point since that distinction
        rested upon the possibility of avoiding commit-
        ment.   Furthermore, in those cases in which the
        option is not forced and the distinction has

a point, James recommends that we suspend judgment, thus following Clifford's maxim (viz.,
"Avoid error"). In short, the distinction is
irrelevant to forced options where the "will
to believe" applies, and in those cases in which
it is relevant James sides with Clifford. There
is another curious point. Clifford advises us
to suspend judgment where the evidence is insufficient. Thus, given that the evidence for
and against God's existence is inconclusive (and
it must be inconclusive if the "will to believe"
applies), Clifford should advise us not to believe that there is no God. However, if the op-
tion is forced, this injunction is equivalent
to "Believe that God exists." This paper was
first presented to the Western Division of the
American Philosophical Association in May of
1960.

1129   Mesnard, Jean. Pascal. Translated by Claude and
       Marcia Abraham. University, Alabama: University
       of Alabama Press, 1969. Pp. 33-55.

Mesnard's discussion of Pascal's Wager is valuable for two reasons. (1) It places the Wager
in the context of Pascal's views concerning the
impossibility of reaching rational judgments as
to the truth or falsity of Christian belief.
(2) Mesnard persuasively argues that the Wager
is addressed to the will and that, in Pascal's
own opinion, what it elicits is (since it is
based on self interest) neither an act of faith
nor conversion. The Wager is only designed to
remove obstacles, to bring the libertine "around
to a sort of rudimentary penitence in the name
of only that reason to which the libertine claims
adherance," to make the libertine uneasy by

convincing him that, in spite of his attempt
to base his actions upon self interest, he has
in fact miscalculated.

1130   Newman, Jay Alan. "The Faith of Pragmatists,"
       Sophia, XIII (April, 1974), 1-15.

A critical study of F. C. S. Schiller's volun-
tarism. (See #s 1132 and 1133 below.) Schiller
neither comes to grips with the fact that reality
is to a certain extent ready made nor with the
fact that many beliefs are good because they are
true and not true because they are good. Schiller's position is, however, less voluntaristic
than it seems. According to Schiller, theism
should be postulated because it satisfies a fundamental and universal demand for intelligibility
and not simply because we wish theism to be true,
or because we find belief in theism agreeable.

1131   Penelhum, Terence. "Pascal's Wager," J Relig,
       XLIV (July, 1964), 201-9.

Pascal presupposes that if God exists, He justly
condemns those who do not believe in Him. Penelhum argues that this policy is immoral and that
if (as Pascal believes) religious belief involves
the approval of this policy then religious belief is also immoral. It follows that even
though it may be prudent to induce in oneself
a state of religious belief, it is morally wrong
to do so. This essay is reprinted with minor
alterations in the author's Religion and Rationality (New York: Random House, 1971, pp. 211-
20).

1132   Schiller, Ferdinand Canning Scott. "The Ethical
        Basis of Metaphysics," Humanism: Philosophical
        Essays by F. C. S. Schiller. 2d ed. London:
        Macmillan, 1912; Westport, Conn.: Greenwood
        Press, 1970. Pp. 1-17.

        A slightly altered version of an essay which
        appeared in the International Journal of Ethics
        (July, 1903). "Pure reason" is a myth. Actual
        reason is "essentially pragmatical, and permeated
        through and through with acts of faith, desires
        to know and wills to believe, to disbelieve and
        to make believe . . . ." Furthermore, "what
        works best in practice is what in actual knowing
        we accept as 'true'." The conception of the
        Good should be awarded supreme authority over
        the concept of the True and the Real, for the
        real is the knowable, and thought is (and should
        be) oriented to the ends of practical life.
        For religious implications of this view, see
        the author's "Faith, Reason, and Religion,"
        # 1133 below.

1133   _____ . "Faith, Reason and Religion," Studies
        in Humanism. London: Macmillan and Co., Ltd.;
        New York; The Macmillan Co., 1907. Pp. 349-69.

        This is a slightly retouched version of an essay
        which appeared in The Hibbert Journal (January,
        1906). All thinking is permeated by emotion,
        volition, and personal interest. The distinction
        between "reasons of the head" and "reasons of
        the heart" is, therefore, a distinction without
        a difference. Even principles like the principle
        of identity, and the principle of causation are
        "postulates" which are necessary for certain
        purposes and not self-evident axioms. They are
        only "established ex post facto" by the

763

experience of their "practical success." Accepting them involves faith, i.e., "a belief in a 'verification' yet to come." Faith is "willing to take upon trust valuable and desirable beliefs before they have been proved 'true'." It is an "affair of the whole personality," but preeminently of the will, and is evoked by what is regarded as valuable. Faith involves risks, and can only be verified by "the results of its practical working," by presuming truth and acting upon this presumption. Faith, passion and interest are essential features of life and thought in general and not only of religious life and thought. It is, therefore, unfair to charge religion with irrationality. (For an exposition of Schiller's notions of reality, fact and the pragmatic criteria of truth, see "The Making of Truth" in the same volume [pp. 179-203]. See also his "Axioms as Postulates," in Personal Idealism, edited by Henry Sturt [London and New York: Macmillan, 1902, pp. 47-133].) Schiller's version of pragmatism and the will to believe has been unduly neglected. For a useful critical exposition of Schiller's position, see Newman, # 1130 above.

1134 Swinburne, Richard G. "The Christian Wager," Relig Stud, 4 (April, 1969), 217-28.

(1) Pascal's method of determining "whether the man concerned with his long term interests should become a Christian" (essentially the method of calculating the expected value of the alternatives) is "perfectly workable, but it does not necessarily yield Pascal's results." Whether it does so will depend upon what alternatives are

considered, and upon the values and probabilities
which are assigned to the various outcomes.
(2) When Christians preach to the unconverted,
they often contrast the joys of heaven and the
pains of hell, and sometimes argue that, even
in this life, the Christian is happier than the
non-Christian. Such preaching is not irrational
for it is implicitly an attempt to show that a
Christian policy will maximize expected value.
The nature of the appeal explains why traditional
Christian apologetics has been more concerned to
show that other religions are less likely to be
true than to show that non-religious systems
are less likely to be true. If a non-religious
system is true, then the gains and losses associated with Christian and non-Christian policies
are relatively small. Hence, even if it is highly probable that a non-religious system is true,
it may still be reasonable (given that the gains
and losses are great enough) to bet on the Christian alternative. Other religious systems are,
however, associated with gains and losses com-
parable to those associated with Christianity.
It is, therefore, crucial that they be less probable than Christianity. (3) Application of the
calculus need not exclude moral considerations.
Moral as well as prudential considerations can
be taken into account in assigning values to the
different outcomes. (4) Swinburne concludes with
a discussion of the morality of choosing to believe on the basis of the calculus when the probability of what one chooses to believe is low.

1135 Yarvin, Herb. "The Will to Come Out All Right,"
      Relig Stud, 12 (September, 1976), 303-9.

Yarvin argues that Pascal's Wager rests upon
certain assumptions about the nature of God,
true religion, etc. It follows that appeal to
the Wager will only be effective where those
assumptions are shared and that employment
of the Wager will only be rational if those
assumptions are rational.

Abelson, Raziel, 778
Adams, Marilyn McCord,
 111, 112, 432
Adams, Robert Merrihew,
 63, 204, 205, 433
 434, 435, 436, 1030
Agassi, Joseph, 1031
Ahern, Dennis Michael,
 742, 743
Ahern, M. B., 437,
 438, 439
Aiken, Henry David, 440
Allen, Diogenes, 1032,
 1033
Alston, William P.,
 206, 355, 568, 569,
 570, 896, 994, 1034
Altizer, Thomas J. J.,
 995
Ammerman, Robert Ray,
 779
Anderson, James Francis,
 966
Arberry, Arthur John,
 780
Atkins, Anselm, 441
Attfield, Robin, 897
Austin, William Harvey,
 854, 898, 899, 1035
Ayer, Alfred Jules,
 855, 856

Baillie, Donald Mac-
 Pherson, 389
Baillie, John, 390,
 571, 781, 782
Bambrough, Renford, 900
Barbour, Ian G., 1036
Barnes, Jonathan, 207
Barth, Karl, 1, 208,
 783, 784, 785, 786
Bartley, William
 Warren, III, 1037
Basham, Ronald Robert,
 Jr., 209
Bastow, David, 572
Bean, William, 857

Beard, Robert William,
 1117
Beatie, William J.,
 573
Bendall, Kent, 901
Benditt, Theodore,
 442
Bennett, Charles
 Andrew Armstrong,
 574, 575
Bennett, Daniel Clark,
 31, 64
Bergson, Henri, 576
Berthold, Fred, Jr.,
 858
Bertocci, Peter An-
 thony, 2, 3, 356,
 443, 577
Bevan, Edwyn Robert,
 996
Bishop, Donald H., 578
Black, Max, 997
Blackstone, Richard
 Macartney, 1087
Blackstone, William
 Thomas, 859
Blumenfeld, David,
 32, 210, 444
Bobik, Joseph, 391
Bocheński, Innocent
 Marie Joseph, 902,
 967
Boden, Margaret A.,
 744
Bonifacio, Armando F.,
 76
Botterill, George, 445
Bouquet, Alan Coates,
 579
Bowker, John, 446
Bowler, Peter John,
 357
Braithwaite, Richard
 Bevan, 903
Bramann, Jorn Karl
 Roy, 904
Brecher, R., 211
Brenner, William, 580

Bridges, Leonard Hal, 581
Brightman, Edgar Sheffield, 447
Broad, Charlie Dunbar, 212, 302, 392, 582, 745, 1038
Brown, T. Patterson, 213, 303, 304, 448, 449, 450
Browne, Henry, 583
Brunner, Heinrich Emil, 787
Buber, Martin, 584, 585, 788
Bucke, Richard Maurice, 586
Bultmann, Rudolf Karl, 789, 790, 998
Burr, Ronald, 587
Burrell, David, 968, 969
Butler, Edward Cuthbert, 588
Butler, Ronald J., 1039

Cahn, Steven Mark, 113
Calvert, Brian, 451
Campbell, Keith, 452
Campbell, Richard, 214
Capitan, William Henry, 453
Caputo, John David, 305
Cargile, James, 77, 215, 1118
Carman, John Braisted, 4
Castañeda, Hector-Neri, 114
Charlesworth, Maxwell John, 216, 217
Cherry, Christopher, 746, 1088
Chisholm, Roderick Milton, 454, 791
Christian, William Armistead, Jr., 5, 905, 906, 907, 908
Christiansen, William Niels, 1124
Church, Alonzo, 860
Clark, Walter Houston, 589

Clarke, Bowman Lafayette, 65, 218, 358
Clarke, W. Norris, 33, 306, 307, 590, 970, 1040
Cobb, John B., Jr., 6, 159, 591
Coburn, Robert Craig, 219, 220, 909, 910
Cock, Albert A., 221
Coe, George Albert, 592
Cohen, Cynthia, 911
Collingwood, Robin George, 222, 1041
Comstock, William Richard, 1119
Conway, David Alton, 308, 593
Copleston, Frederick Charles, 309, 594, 856, 971
Corr, Charles A., 223
Cosgrove, Matthew R., 224
Coval, Samuel Charles, 192
Cowan, Joseph Lloyd, 78, 79
Cox, David, 912
Crittendon, Charles, 225
Crocker, Sylvia Fleming, 226
Crombie, I. M., 913

Daher, Adel, 7
Dalton, Peter C., 1120, 1121
Danto, Arthur Coleman, 595, 596, 597
Davis, Stephen Thane, 227, 228, 229, 455, 792, 861
De Boer, Jesse, 598
Deikman, Arthur J., 599
De Martino, Richard, 607
Demos, Raphael, 793, 862
Deutsch, Eliot, 8

Devine, Philip Edwards,
230, 231, 232
Dhavamony, Mariasusai,
600
Diamond, Malcolm Luria,
863
Dietl, Paul, 747
Dilley, Frank Brown,
Jr., 999, 1042, 1089
Dilman, Ilham, 915, 916
Dodd, Charles Harold,
794
Donceel, Joseph, 34,
233
Dore, Clement Joseph,
Jr., 234, 456, 457,
458, 459, 460
Downing, F. Gerald,
461
Dubs, Homer H., 748
Duff-Forbes, Donald R.,
310, 795, 864
Dulles, A., 796
Dupré, Louis, 235
Durrant, Michael, 917,
1043
Dyck, Grace M., 160

Edwards, Paul, 311
Edwards, Rem B., 236,
359
Eliade, Mircea, 601,
1000, 1001, 1002
Englebretsen, George,
35
Evans, Donald Dwight,
797, 918, 919, 1044
Ewing, Alfred Cyril,
393, 602, 920

Fabro, Cornelio, 798
Fakhry, Majid, 603
Farges, Albert, 604
Farmer, Herbert Henry,
749, 799
Farrer, Austin Marsden,
312, 394, 462, 800,
801, 972, 998
Feigl, Herbert, 605
Felder, David W., 1045
Ferré, Frederick, 921,
922, 1046, 1047

Fethe, Charles B., 750
Findley, John Nie-
meyer, 66, 67, 193
Fitch, Frederic B.,
80, 237
Fitzgerald, Paul, 115
Flew, Antony Garrard
Newton, 463, 464,
465, 606, 751, 865,
866, 923, 1122
Ford, Lewis Stanley,
9, 36, 116, 161,
466, 1003
Forest, Aimé, 238
Forgie, James William,
239, 240
Foss, Martin, 194
Foster, Michael
Beresford, 1048
Frankfurt, Harry G.,
81
Franklin, Richard
Langdon, 68
Fromm, Erich, 607

Gale, Richard, 608
Garrigou-Lagrange,
Reginald Marie, 10,
37, 117, 313, 973
Garside, Bruce, 609
Gaskin, John C. A.,
360, 752, 924, 1049
Geach, Peter Thomas,
38, 82, 83, 162,
163, 314, 467
Gellman, Jerome, 84,
85
Gibbs, Benjamin, 86
Gibson, Alexander
Boyce, 802, 925
Gill, Jerry Henry,
1050, 1051, 1090
Gilson, Etienne, 11,
610, 803
Gingell, John, 180
Gordon, Ruth M., 611
Govier, Trudy, 804
Grant, C. K., 241, 805
Grant, Robert McQueen,
12, 753
Grave, Selwyn A., 468,
1052

Griffen, David Ray, 164, 469
Gurr, John Edwin, 315

Haack, Susan, 118, 119
Hacking, Ian, 1123
Hardon, John A., 754
Hare, Peter Hewitt, 470, 471, 806
Hare, Richard Mervyn, 866
Harris, Errol E., 242, 243
Harrison, Jonathan, 87, 88
Hartshorne, Charles, 13, 39, 120, 195, 244, 245, 395, 396, 418, 472
Harvey, Van Austin, 807
Heimbeck, Raeburne Seeley, 867
Helm, Paul, 121, 122, 123, 124, 165
Hempel, Carl Gustav, 868
Hendel, Charles William, 361
Henle, Paul, 246, 612
Henze, Donald F., 808
Hepburn, Ronald William, 316, 397, 613, 614, 615, 616, 926, 1004
Herman, Arthur Ludwig, 473
Hick, John Harwood, 69, 70, 247, 248, 317, 419, 474, 475, 476, 809, 810, 811, 812, 813, 869, 870, 871, 1053, 1054, 1091
High, Dallas Milton, 927
Hinton, R. T., 362
Hocking, William Ernest, 617
Hoitenga, Dewey James, Jr., 477
Holland, R. F., 755, 928
Hook, Sidney, 814
Hopkins, Jasper, 249

Horsburgh, H. J. N., 929
Hospers, John, 618
Houston, Jean, 660
Howe, Leroy Thomas, 250, 251, 478
Hudson, William Donald, 479, 930, 931, 1055, 1056
Hügel, Frederich von, Baron, 40, 619
Hughes, George E., 71, 181, 1057
Hughes, Martin, 182
Hurlbutt, Robert H., III, 363
Hutchings, P. Ae., 125
Huxley, Aldous Leonard, 620, 621, 622, 623, 624, 625
Hyers, Conrad M., 626

Iseminger, Gary, 126, 420

James, Edwin Oliver, 14
James, William, 627, 628
Jarvie, Ian C., 1031
Jaspers, Karl, 815, 1005
Jefferson, Howard Bonar, 480
Jeffner, Anders, 364, 756, 932, 1058
Jensen, Robert W., 933
Joad, Edwin Mitchinson, 481
Johnson, Clark B., 252
Johnston, William, 629, 630
Jones, Owen Roger, 166, 183
Jones, Rufus Matthew, 631, 632
Jordan, G. Ray., Jr., 633
Journet, Charles, 482

770

Joyce, George Hayward,
15, 89, 127, 318,
365, 398, 483, 816
Jung, Carl Gustav, 1006

Kane, Gordon Stanley,
484, 485, 486, 487
Kapitan, Tomis, 253
Kauber, Peter, 806,
817, 818
Kaufman, Gordon D.,
167, 819
Kavka, Gregory Stephen,
872
Kearney, R. J., 974
Keene, G. B., 90, 91
Kellenberger, Bertram
James, 634, 820,
821, 873, 1059, 1092
Keller, Ernst, 757
Keller, Marie-Luise,
757
Kellner, Menachen Marc,
488
Kennedy, Gail, 822
Kennick, William E.,
319, 421, 635
Kenny, Anthony John
Patrick, 72, 73, 128,
254, 320, 975
Khamara, Edward J.,
129
Khatchadourian, Haig,
489
Kielkopf, Charles
Francis, 490
King-Farlow, John,
321, 1124
Klein, Kenneth, 874
Klocker, Harry R., 399
Klubertanz, George
Peter, 976
Kneale, Martha, 41
Kneale, William C.,
42
Knox, John, Jr., 1060
Knox, Ronald Arbuth-
nott, 636
Knudson, Albert
Cornelius, 491
Koestler, Arthur, 637
Kolb, David Alan, 43

Kondoleon, Theodore
J., 492
Kordig, Carl R., 638
Kretzmann, Norman,
44, 112, 130
Krimerman, Leonard
Isaiah, 639
Kuntz, Paul Grimley,
92, 93
Kvastad, Nils Bjorn,
640, 641

Lachelier, Jules, 1125
Lachs, John, 131, 168
Lackey, Douglas Paul,
132
La Croix, Richard Ray,
45, 133, 255, 493
Lacy, William Larry,
134
Laird, John, 366
Landrum, George, 758
Landsberg, P. T.,
1126
Langerak, Edward, 135
Langtry, Bruce, 759,
760
LaPara, Nicholas, 494
Laver, Rosemary, 322
Leahy, Louis, 323
Lee, Jung Young, 46
Léonard, Augustin,
642, 643
Lesher, James H., 1061
Leuba, James Henry,
644
Lewis, Clive Staples,
169, 481, 495, 761
Lewis, David, 256
Lewis, Hywel David,
645, 646, 647
Litzenburg, Thomas
Vernon, Jr., 863
Livingston, James
Craig, 823
Lochhead, David Mor-
gan, 257
Lohmeyer, Ernst, 998
Lomasky, Loren E.,
258
Londis, James J., 648
Lonergan, Bernard
Joseph Francis, 400

771

Lucas, John Randolph,
136
Ludovic de Besse,
father, 649
Lunn, Arnold, 762
Lycan, William G.,
259

McClendon, James
William, Jr., 956
McCloskey, Henry John,
196, 496, 497, 498,
499
McCready, William
Charles, 650
McCullough, H. B.,
500
McGill, Arthur C., 248
McInerny, Ralph M., 977
MacIntosh, J. J., 824
MacIntyre, Alasdair C.,
651, 652, 923, 934,
978, 1062
Mackie, John Leslie,
94, 95, 501, 502
McKinnon, Alastair,
763, 935
Maclagen, William
Gauld, 401
McLean, George, 1007
Macleod, Alistair, M.,
16
McPherson, Thomas,
367, 653, 936
Macquarrie, John,
96, 764, 825, 1008,
1009
McTaggart, John Mc-
Taggart Ellis, 97,
324, 368, 503, 654,
826, 1063
Madden, Edward H., 470,
471
Malcolm, Norman, 254,
260, 261, 1093
Mann, William Edward,
197, 262
Maréchal, Joseph, 655
Maritain, Jacques, 325,
402, 504, 505, 656,
657
Martin, Charles Burton,
184, 658

Martin, Michael, 1064,
1127
Mascall, Eric Lionel,
17, 326, 327, 328,
875, 979
Maslow, Abraham
Harold, 659
Mason, David R., 170,
198, 199
Masters, Robert E.
L., 660
Matson, Wallace I.,
138, 329, 369, 661,
937
Matthews, Gareth
Blanc, 263, 876
Matthysse, Steven,
827
Mautner, Thomas, 330
Mavrodes, George Ion,
98, 137, 171, 264,
265, 422, 423,
506, 507, 662, 663,
877, 938, 980, 1128
Mayberry, Thomas, 185
Mayo, Bernard, 99
Mellor, D. Hugh, 370
Merton, Thomas, 664,
665
Mesnard, Jean, 1129
Miethe, T. L., 266
Miles, Thomas Richard,
939
Miller, John Franklin,
III, 878
Minas, Anne C., 186
Mitchell, Basil, 866,
940, 941, 1065
Mondin, Battista, 981
Moore, John Morrison,
666
Moore, Peter G., 667
Moraczewski, Albert
S., 668
Morillo, Carolyn R.,
331
Moulder, James, 200
Moule, Charles Fran-
cis Digbey, 765
Mozley, John Kenneth,
47
Munitz, Milton Karl,
332
Munz, Peter, 1010

Murty, K. Satchidananda,
828
Muyskens, James Leroy,
403, 942

Nakhnikian, George, 267
Nasser, Alan George,
268
Newman, Jay Alan, 404,
829, 1130
Nidditch, Peter, 879
Niebuhr, Helmut Richard,
830, 831
Niebuhr, Reinhold, 832
Nielsen, Kai, 18, 833,
880, 881, 882, 883,
884, 885, 943, 944,
945, 982, 1094, 1095,
1096, 1097, 1098
Nowell-Smith, Patrick,
766
Nygren, Anders, 187

Oakes, Robert Aaron,
269, 270, 271, 424,
508, 509, 510, 669,
670, 671, 672, 673,
674, 675
O'Briant, Walter Her-
bert, 371
Ogden, Schubert Miles,
172, 946, 1066
Olding, A., 372, 373,
511
Osborn, Catherine B.,
676
Otto, Rudolf, 677, 678,
679, 680, 681
Owen, Huw Parri, 19,
405, 682, 834, 886,
1067
Owens, Claire Myers,
683
Ozment, Steven E., 684

Pahnke, Walter Norman,
685, 686, 687, 688
Pailin, David Arthur,
20, 272, 1068
Palmer, Humphrey, 983,
1099

Passmore, John Arthur,
887
Paton, Herbert James,
406
Pearl, Leon, 374
Penelhum, Terence, 21,
48, 273, 333, 334,
425, 512, 513, 689,
835, 836, 888, 1069,
1131
Pensa, Corrado, 690
Pepler, Conrad, 691
Pepper, Stephen Coburn,
1070, 1071, 1072
Persson, Per Erik, 837
Peters, Eugene Herbert,
173
Phelan, Gerald Ber-
nard, 984
Phillips, Dewi Zapha-
niah, 947, 1100,
1101, 1102, 1103,
1104, 1105, 1106,
1107, 1108
Phillips, Richard
Percival, 139, 174,
335
Pieper, Josef, 838
Pike, Nelson Craft,
49, 100, 140, 141,
142, 143, 201, 375,
514, 515, 516, 710
Plantinga, Alvin Carl,
50, 74, 101, 144,
188, 274, 275, 276,
277, 278, 279, 280,
336, 376, 517, 518,
519, 520, 521, 522,
889
Pletcher, Galen Ken-
neth, 692, 693, 694
Polanyi, Michael, 1073
Pollard, T. Evan, 51
Pontifex, Mark, 523
Popkin, Richard Henry,
1109
Poteat, William H.,
145, 175
Potter, Vincent G.,
281
Poulain, Auguste, 695
Powell, Jouett Lynn,
1074

Pratt, James Bissett, 696
Prestige, George Leonard, 22
Price, Henry Habberly, 839, 840
Prince, Raymond, 697
Prior, Arthur Norman, 146, 147, 148
Proudfoot, Wayne, 698
Puccetti, Roland, 149, 524
Purtill, Richard L., 150, 282, 283, 841

Quinn, Michael Sean, 525

Rainer, A. C., 75
Raju, Poolla Tirupati, 699
Ramsey, Ian Thomas, 948, 949, 950, 951, 952
Randall, John Herman, Jr., 1011
Rashdall, Hastings, 407, 408
Regis, Edward, Jr., 700
Reichenbach, Bruce Robert, 337, 526
Reid, Louis Arnaud, 842
Resnick, Lawrence, 527
Richards, William A., 687
Richman, Robert J., 284, 377, 528
Richmond, James, 953
Ricoeur, Paul, 529, 530, 1012, 1013, 1014, 1015, 1016, 1017, 1018, 1019
Robbins, J. Wesley, 189, 701, 702
Robinson, Guy, 767
Robinson, Henry Wheeler, 52
Rosenberg, Jay Frank, 531
Rosenthal, David Michael, 151

Ross, James Francis, 53, 102, 176, 285, 286, 338, 426, 532, 843, 844, 985, 986, 987, 988, 989, 990
Rowe, William Leonard, 23, 24, 152, 190, 287, 288, 289, 290, 339, 340, 341, 342, 343, 427, 533, 534, 1020, 1075
Royce, Josiah, 535, 536, 537, 1076
Ruse, Michael, 378
Ryle, Gilbert, 291, 292

Salmon, Wesley C., 379, 890
Saudreau, Auguste, 703
Saunders, John Turk, 153, 154
Savage, Charles, 697
Savage, Clarence Wade, 103
Scharfstein, Ben-Ami, 704
Schiller, Ferdinand Canning Scott, 1132, 1133
Schlesinger, George, 380, 538, 539, 540, 768
Schmidt, Paul F., 705, 710, 954
Schniewind, Julius, 998
Scriven, Michael, 428, 541
Sebba, Gregor, 1021
Settle, Tom, 1031
Shaffer, Jerome, 293
Shaver, Phillip, 698
Shea, Winslow, 542
Shepherd, John J., 1110
Sherry, Patrick J., 409, 991, 1111, 1112
Shiner, Roger A., 706
Silber, John Robert, 410

Simon, Yves René Marie, 992
Singer, Irving, 191
Smart, John Jamieson Carswell, 294
Smart, Ninian, 177, 202, 344, 543, 544, 545, 707, 708, 709, 710, 711, 769, 955, 1077
Smith, George Duncan, 845
Smith, Huston, 712
Smith, James Marvin, 956
Smith, John Edwin, 713, 714
Smith, Norman Kemp, 381
Sommers, Fred, 54, 295
Sontag, Frederick, 296, 546
Sorley, William Ritchie, 411
Sosa, Ernest, 254
Spade, Paul Vincent, 429
Srzednicki, Jan, 203
Staal, Frits, 715
Stace, Walter Terence, 716, 717
Stahl, Roland, 547
Stainsby, Harold V., 412
Steuer, Axel D., 548
Stokes, Walter Elliott, 178
Streveler, Paul Andrew, 155
Sturch, Richard Lyman, 55, 382
Suzuki, Daisetz Teitaro, 607, 718, 719
Sweeney, Leo, 56, 57, 58
Swinburne, Richard G., 104, 105, 345, 383, 384, 770, 771, 1134

Taylor, Alfred Edward, 385, 386, 413, 414, 772, 773, 846
Taylor, Richard, 346, 387
Temple, William, 847
Tennant, Frederick Robert, 25, 388, 549, 720, 774, 848
Thielicke, Helmut, 998
Thompson, Samuel Martin, 347
Tillich, Paul Johannes Oskar, 26, 27, 28, 297, 430, 775, 849, 850, 1022, 1023, 1024, 1025, 1026, 1027, 1028, 1078
Tomberlin, James Edward, 59, 60, 298, 550, 1079, 1113
Tooley, Michael, 348, 891, 892
Toulmin, Stephen Edelston, 957
Trethowan, Illtyd, 551

Underhill, Evelyn, 721, 722, 723
Unger, Peter, 156
Urban, Wilbur Marshall, 1029

Van Wyk, Robert Nicholas, 415

Wainwright, William Judson, 106, 179, 431, 552, 553, 554, 724, 725, 726, 727, 728, 893, 958
Wald, Albert W., 299, 1080
Wallace, Gerald, 555
Wallace, William A., 349
Walsh, William Henry, 1081

775

Walter, Edward, 556
Walton, Douglas Niel,
  107, 557
Watkin, Edward Ingram,
  558, 729, 730
Watkins, John William
  Nevill, 1082, 1083
Watt, John, 1114
Weber, Stephen Lewis,
  350
Wengert, Robert G.,
  351
Werner, Louis, 108
Wernham, James C. S.,
  851
Westphal, Merold, 61
White, John, 731
Whitehead, Alfred
  North, 29, 30
Wiebe, D., 732
Wilbanks, Jan Joseph,
  300
Wilcox, John Thomas,
  157
Williams, Bernard,
  254
Williams, C. J. F.,
  352, 852, 993
Wilson, John, 894, 895
Wilson, John Cook,
  733
Winch, Peter, 1115,
  1116
Windt, Peter Yale, 559
Wisdom, John, 560,
  959, 960, 961
Wittgenstein, Ludwig,
  962
Wolfe, Julian, 109,
  353
Wood, Allen William,
  416
Woods, George Frederick,
  1084
Woolcombe, Kenneth J.,
  62

Yandell, Keith Edward,
  301, 354, 417, 561,
  562, 563, 564, 565,
  566, 734, 735, 776,
  963, 964, 1085, 1086
Yarvin, Herb, 1135

Young, Robert, 110,
  158, 567, 777

Zaehner, Robert
  Charles, 736, 737,
  738, 739, 740, 741
Zimmerman, Marvin,
  853
Zuurdeeg, Willem
  Frederick, 965